Bavaria

Andrea Schulte-Peevers

LONELY PLANET PUBLICATIONS
Melbourne • Oakland • London • Paris

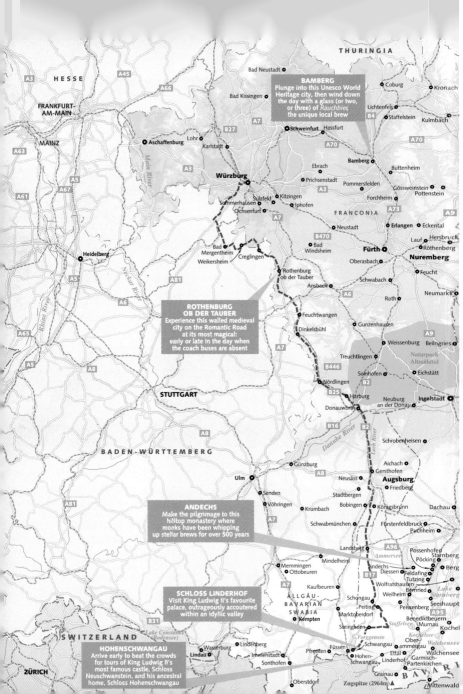

THURINGIA

HESSE

FRANKFURT-
AM-MAIN

MAINZ

BAMBERG
Plunge into this Unesco World
Heritage city, then wind down
the day with a glass (or two,
or three) of *Rauchbier*,
the unique local brew

Heidelberg

FRANCONIA

Würzburg

Nuremberg

Fürth

**ROTHENBURG
OB DER TAUBER**
Experience this walled medieval
city on the Romantic Road
at its most magical:
early or late in the day when
the coach buses are absent

STUTTGART

Naturpark
Altmühtal

BADEN-WÜRTTEMBERG

Ulm

Augsburg

ANDECHS
Make the pilgrimage to this
hilltop monastery where
monks have been whipping
up stellar brews for over 500 years

SCHLOSS LINDERHOF
Visit King Ludwig II's favourite
palace, outrageously accoutered
within an idyllic valley

ALLGÄU·
BAVARIAN
SWABIA

SWITZERLAND

HOHENSCHWANGAU
Arrive early to beat the crowds
for tours of King Ludwig II's
most famous castle, Schloss
Neuschwanstein, and his ancestral
home, Schloss Hohenschwangau

ZÜRICH

BAVARIA

Zugspitze (2964m)

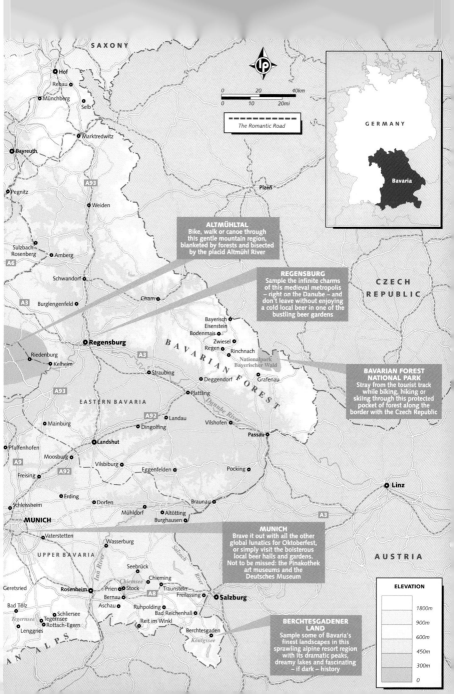

SAXONY

Hof
Rehau
Münchberg
Selb
Marktredwitz
Bayreuth
Pegnitz
A93
Weiden

Sulzbach-Rosenberg
Amberg
A6
Schwandorf
A3
Burglengenfeld
Cham

ALTMÜHLTAL
Bike, walk or canoe through this gentle mountain region, blanketed by forests and bisected by the placid Altmühl River

REGENSBURG
Sample the infinite charms of this medieval metropolis – right on the Danube – and don't leave without enjoying a cold local beer in one of the bustling beer gardens

CZECH REPUBLIC

Plzeň

GERMANY

Bavaria

Riedenburg
Kelheim
Regensburg
A3
Straubing
A93
EASTERN BAVARIA
Mainburg
A92 Landau
Dingolfing
Vilshofen
Pfaffenhofen
Landshut
A9
Moosburg
Vilsbiburg
Eggenfelden
Freising
A92
Erding
Dorfen
Schleissheim
Braunau
MUNICH
Mühldorf
Altötting
Burghausen
A3

Bayerisch Eisenstein
Bodenmais
Zwiesel
Regen
Rinchnach
Nationalpark Bayerischer Wald
Deggendorf
Grafenau
Plattling
Danube River
Passau

B A V A R I A N   F O R E S T

BAVARIAN FOREST NATIONAL PARK
Stray from the tourist track while biking, hiking or skiing through this protected pocket of forest along the border with the Czech Republic

Linz

MUNICH
Brave it out with all the other global lunatics for Oktoberfest, or simply visit the boisterous local beer halls and gardens. Not to be missed: the Pinakothek art museums and the Deutsches Museum

AUSTRIA

Vaterstetten
UPPER BAVARIA
Wasserburg
Inn River
Seebruck
Chiemsee
Chieming
Prien Stock
Traunstein
Rosenheim
Bernau
A8
Freilassing
Salzburg
Geretsried
Aschau
Ruhpolding
Bad Reichenhall
Bad Tölz
Schliersee
Reit im Winkl
Berchtesgaden
Tegernsee
Rottach-Egern
Lenggries
N   A L P S
Königssee
Saalach River

ELEVATION

1800m
900m
600m
450m
300m
0

BERCHTESGADENER LAND
Sample some of Bavaria's finest landscapes in this sprawling alpine resort region with its dramatic peaks, dreamy lakes and fascinating – if dark – history

The Romantic Road

0   20   40km
0 10 20mi

Bavaria
1st edition – July 2002

Published by
Lonely Planet Publications Pty Ltd ABN 36 005 607 983
90 Maribyrnong St, Footscray, Victoria 3011, Australia

Lonely Planet offices
Australia Locked Bag 1, Footscray, Victoria 3011
USA 150 Linden St, Oakland, CA 94607
UK 10a Spring Place, London NW5 3BH
France 1 rue du Dahomey, 75011 Paris

Photographs
Many of the images in this guide are available for licensing from
Lonely Planet Images.
w www.lonelyplanetimages.com

Front cover photograph
Neuschwanstein Castle, near Füssen, Allgäu-Bavarian Swabia (Harald
Sund, Getty Images)

ISBN 1 74059 013 9

text & maps © Lonely Planet Publications Pty Ltd 2002
photos © photographers as indicated 2002

Printed by Craft Print International Ltd, Singapore

**Although the authors
and Lonely Planet try
to make the informa-
tion as accurate as
possible, we accept
no responsibility for
any loss, injury or
inconvenience sus-
tained by anyone
using this book.**

Contents – Text

2 Contents – Text

Contents – Maps

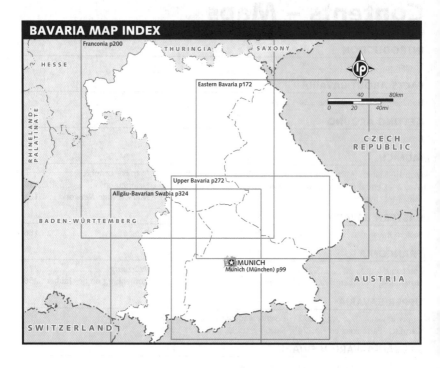

BAVARIA MAP INDEX

Franconia p200

THURINGIA

SAXONY

HESSE

Eastern Bavaria p172

RHINELAND-PALATINATE

CZECH REPUBLIC

Upper Bavaria p272

Allgäu-Bavarian Swabia p324

BADEN-WÜRTTEMBERG

MUNICH
Munich (München) p99

AUSTRIA

SWITZERLAND

0   40   80km
0   20   40mi

The Author

Andrea Schulte-Peevers

Andrea is a writer, editor and translator who caught the travel bug early in life, hitting all continents but Antarctica by the time she turned 18. After high school in Germany, Andrea decided the world was too big to stay in one place. Armed with a degree from UCLA, she turned her wanderlust into a career as a travel writer and may still chase penguins around the South Pole. Aside from *Bavaria*, Andrea has also coordinated, authored or updated many other Lonely Planet titles, including *Germany*, *Berlin*, *Los Angeles*, *Baja California*, *San Diego & Tijuana*, *California & Nevada* and *Spain* since joining the LP team in 1995.

From the Author

Although I'm German-born, Bavaria (the country's 'deep south') was largely terra incognita for me when I first landed in Munich many months ago to research this book. But thanks to a warm welcome from a small army of dedicated and competent friends, locals and officials, I was able to quite quickly develop a sense for this intriguing region and to get to know it in all its complexities. Alfred Helbrich deserves major kudos for making all the right introductions and for showing me around Regensburg. Heaps of gratitude also go to Olaf Seifert and Carin Dennerlohr in Franconia, Rolf Dehner in Allgäu-Bayerisch Schwaben, Angelika Mehnert-Nuscheler and Birgit Schmidt in Upper Bavaria, and Ulrike Eberl-Walter in Eastern Bavaria. Dozens of local tourist officials, whose insights and tips are invaluable in the creation of such a book, also helped me on my journey. The following deserve special mention (in no particular order): Georg Overs, Götz Beck, Regina Thieme, Sigrid Pronizius, Susanne Müller, Bettina Bessinger, Michael Schönemann, Susanne Reuter, Eva Rossberger, Frank Nicklas, Klaus Götzl, Martina Benkel and Vera Golücke.

Much praise also goes to those people who helped with the logistics of travel to and within Bavaria, including Johannes Fuchs, Beth Purdue, Nanci Sullivan and Barbara Hearn. Your assistance was truly invaluable and much appreciated.

Herzlichen Dank to my colleagues Jeremy Gray and Mark Honan, whose work on the Munich and Austria guides, respectively, formed the basis of this book's Munich chapter and Salzburg section.

A standing ovation for the production team in Melbourne, in particular lead editor Darren O'Connell and cartography/design maven Birgit Jordan. Chris Wyness and Mary Neighbour deserve big hugs for giving me this assignment and for all their support throughout the years.

Last but not least, to the home front: A great big kiss to David, my wonderful husband, for sticking with me through all of life's trials and tribulations – large and small, real and imagined – including Lonely Planet deadlines. A bouquet of thanks to you.

This Book

FROM THE PUBLISHER

This 1st edition of *Bavaria* was edited in Lonely Planet's Melbourne office. Production of this book was coordinated by Birgit Jordan (mapping and design) and Darren O'Connell (editorial). Valuable editing and proofing assistance was provided by Elizabeth Swan, Melanie Dankel and Shelley Muir. Mapping assistance was provided by Csanad Csutoros and Jacqueline Nguyen. Chris Wyness and Kieran Grogan saw the book through from start to finish, with proofing help from Tony Davidson, Mark Griffiths and Rachel Imeson. Thanks go to Emma Koch for the Language chapter, Margie Jung who designed the cover and Mick Weldon (MW) who provided the illustrations. Photographs were provided by Lonely Planet Images, with special thanks to Gerard Walker.

ACKNOWLEDGMENTS

Thanks to Münchner Verkehrs- und Tarifverbund GmbH (MVV) for permission to use their material.

Foreword

ABOUT LONELY PLANET GUIDEBOOKS

The story begins with a classic travel adventure: Tony and Maureen Wheeler's 1972 journey across Europe and Asia to Australia. There was no useful information about the overland trail then, so Tony and Maureen published the first Lonely Planet guidebook to meet a growing need.

From a kitchen table, Lonely Planet has grown to become the largest independent travel publisher in the world, with offices in Melbourne (Australia), Oakland (USA), London (UK) and Paris (France).

Today Lonely Planet guidebooks cover the globe. There is an ever-growing list of books and information in a variety of media. Some things haven't changed. The main aim is still to make it possible for adventurous travellers to get out there – to explore and better understand the world.

At Lonely Planet we believe travellers can make a positive contribution to the countries they visit – if they respect their host communities and spend their money wisely. Since 1986 a percentage of the income from each book has been donated to aid projects and human rights campaigns, and, more recently, to wildlife conservation.

Although inclusion in a guidebook usually implies a recommendation we cannot list every good place. Exclusion does not necessarily imply criticism. In fact there are a number of reasons why we might exclude a place – sometimes it is simply inappropriate to encourage an influx of travellers.

UPDATES & READER FEEDBACK

Things change – prices go up, schedules change, good places go bad and bad places go bankrupt. Nothing stays the same. So, if you find things better or worse, recently opened or long-since closed, please tell us and help make the next edition even more accurate and useful.

Lonely Planet thoroughly updates each guidebook as often as possible – usually every two years, although for some destinations the gap can be longer. Between editions, up-to-date information is available in our free, quarterly *Planet Talk* newsletter and monthly email bulletin *Comet*. The *Upgrades* section of our website (W www.lonelyplanet.com) is also regularly updated by Lonely Planet authors, and the site's *Scoop* section covers news and current affairs relevant to travellers. Lastly, the *Thorn Tree* bulletin board and *Postcards* section carry unverified, but fascinating, reports from travellers.

Tell us about it! We genuinely value your feedback. A well-travelled team at Lonely Planet reads and acknowledges every email and letter we receive and ensures that every morsel of information finds its way to the relevant authors, editors and cartographers.

Everyone who writes to us will find their name listed in the next edition of the appropriate guidebook, and will receive the latest issue of *Comet* or *Planet Talk*. The very best contributions will be rewarded with a free guidebook.

We may edit, reproduce and incorporate your comments in Lonely Planet products such as guidebooks, websites and digital products, so let us know if you don't want your comments reproduced or your name acknowledged.

How to contact Lonely Planet:
Online: e talk2us@lonelyplanet.com.au, W www.lonelyplanet.com
Australia: Locked Bag 1, Footscray, Victoria 3011
UK: 10a Spring Place, London NW5 3BH
USA: 150 Linden St, Oakland, CA 94607

Introduction

Planning a trip to Bavaria can be as baffling as facing a buffet of delicacies prepared by the world's finest chefs. Where do you start? How much do you take? Should you try a bit of everything or concentrate on some specialities? Well, no matter how you fill your 'vacation plate', you're sure to be rewarded with experiences, images and sights that will linger sweetly in your memory long after you've unpacked your bags back home.

Bavaria, Germany's southernmost federal state, harbours a bonanza of delights in one very visitor-friendly package. If you're here for the 'olde-worlde' stereotypes of *lederhosen*, beer halls and oompah bands, you'll find them in abundance. But if clichés alone don't do it for you, you'll soon discover a land of amazing complexity and rich history.

Munich, of course, is a must. A big city with a charming village character, it offers great art, architecture and cultural institutions on par with the best in the world. South of here, lake-studded foothills lead up to Europe's great mountain range, the Alps. This is where majestic panoramas unfold against a backdrop of craggy peaks draped in snow. You'll see pintsize churches serenely anchoring velvety meadows, their onion-domed spires reaching for the heavens. You can hike through deep valleys carved by spirited creeks or gently glide across emerald lakes fringed with muscular forests. It's an enchanting setting whose infinite charms were certainly not lost on 'Fairy-Tale' King Ludwig II. His turreted fantasy castle, Schloss Neuschwanstein near Füssen in the Allgäu Alps, has long ranked among Europe's main tourist attractions.

Venturing east of Munich brings you to another great outdoor playground, the Bavarian Forest, part of which enjoys extra protection as a national park. Eastern Bavaria's main city is delightful Regensburg, whose appearance has changed little since the Middle Ages. Then there's Franconia, the northernmost of the Bavarian regions and its most diverse. Historic cities – Nuremberg, Bamberg and Bayreuth among them – exert their magical pull. The famous Romantic Road begins in Würzburg, which is also the capital of the Franconian Wine Country. And fully half of Bavaria's nature parks are here, including the one enveloping the placid Altmühl Valley.

One thing you'll notice no matter where you travel is that Bavarians are fiercely proud of their heritage and traditions. Their history originated with three ancient tribes – the Bajuwaren (Bavarians), the Franken (Franconians) and the Schwaben (Swabians). These tribes lived in a patchwork of duchies and fiefdoms until the early 19th century when Napoleon united them all under the umbrella of the Kingdom of Bavaria. Nevertheless many locals still identify strongly with their respective roots, differentiating themselves through their dress, music, dances and other cultural trappings.

While such 'tribalism' may seem quaint to outsiders, it's important to remember that

BAVARIA

Bavaria also has a distinctly modern dimension. Powerful international companies such as BMW, Audi and Siemens have their headquarters here. And Bavaria is also Germany's most fertile breeding ground for new technologies.

It's this juggling of ancient customs and modern challenges that heightens the Bavarians' sense of otherness. Many feel like citizens of a separate country, only tenuously linked to the rest of Germany. Even Bavaria's own prime minister, Edmund Stoiber, hilariously echoed this sentiment in a recent speech in which he stated that '...more than 55,000 highly educated people moved from Germany to Bavaria in the last years' (as quoted in *Der Spiegel* magazine). Equally telling is the fact that Bavaria is the only German state to never ratify the country's constitution.

But while it's good to understand the eccentricities of the Bavarians, ultimately none of this really matters to you as a traveller. Most likely, you'll be much too busy admiring the complex artistry of a baroque church, enjoying great vistas while ambling along mountain trails, wandering in the footsteps of medieval minstrels and pompous rulers, digging into huge platters of *Schweinshaxe* and, of course, hoisting foamy mugs of superb brews. One thing's for sure: Bavaria is a pleasurable assault on the senses that will let you discover new wonders with every sunrise.

Facts about Bavaria

HISTORY

Today's territory of Bavaria unites three distinct tribes: the Bajuwaren (Bavarians), the Franken (Franconians) and the Schwaben (Swabians). Each developed quite separately until the creation of the Kingdom of Bavaria in 1806.

The earliest inhabitants were probably Celts, who were subjugated by the Romans who began pushing north of the Alps in the 1st century BC. They founded the province of Raetia, whose main settlements included Augsburg (Augusta Vindelicorum), Regensburg (Ratisbona) and Passau (Boiodurum). The *Limes*, the Roman Empire's boundary ran right through today's Altmühltal in Franconia.

The origin of the Bavarian tribe is obscure, but it's widely assumed that it coalesced from several eastern Germanic tribes and Romans left behind after the collapse of the Roman Empire in the late 5th century. The name 'Bajuwaren', which roughly translates as 'men of Baia', can be traced to a tribe hailing from Bohemia (Boiohaemum) in today's Czech Republic.

The Franconians formed from several western Germanic tribes who settled along the central and lower Rhine River, on the border with the Roman Empire, starting in the 3rd century AD. In the middle of the 5th century, as the Romans' fortune waned, they became the dominant power in Central Europe under the dynasty of the Merovingians.

The Swabians are a sub-tribe of the much larger population group of the *Alemannen*, who have roamed the south-western corner of Germany since the 2nd century AD. In the 3rd century, they expanded their territory eastward by battling the Romans. About 100 years later, they pushed even further, as far as the Lech River, which still forms today's border between Swabia and Upper Bavaria.

The Frankenreich

Of the three tribes, the Franconians were the first to become a major power player in Central Europe under the Merovingian dynasty in the later 5th century. But when fighting broke out among the aristocratic clans in the 8th century, the Merovingians were replaced by the Carolingians.

Under the Carolingian rulers, the Frankenreich (Franconian Empire) asserted its supremacy and suppressed the more or less independent duchies that had emerged in southern Germany. Their first order of business was to wrest the territories along the Main River from a duchy called Hedene, which had formed in the 7th century. They crushed Swabia in 744 and then turned their attention to Bavaria, which had been ruled by the Agilofingian dynasty since 555. Their duke, Tassilo III (ruled 748–88), tried to fight off the marauders by gaining control of Alpine passes and making an alliance with the Lombards. But, in 788, after the Franconians defeated the Lombards, he ultimately had no choice but to surrender to the Franconian king, Charlemagne, as well. All of the area that makes up today's Bavaria had thus come under the control of the Frankenreich.

On Charlemagne's death in 814, a bun fight ensued between his sons, which ended with the Treaty of Verdun (843) and the carving up of the Reich. Ludwig der Deutsche, who had controlled Bavaria since 826, now became king of *Ostfranken* (Eastern Franconia), an area that included Swabia, Bavaria, Franconia and Saxony. He ruled until 876. The other part of the Frankenreich, which included portions of today's Belgium and France, was called *Westfranken* and ruled by Karl der Kahle (Charles the Bald).

Christianisation

While the Agilofingians had adopted Christianity early on, most of the people were still pagan. This changed when a number of Irish, Anglo-Saxon and Franconian monks and bishops began spreading the gospel throughout Central European lands beginning in the early 7th century. The missionaries Emmeram in Regensburg, Rupert in

Salzburg and Korbinian in Freising were especially successful, as was Bonifatius, who concentrated on converting people in today's northern Germany as well as in Franconia. In 739, acting on the behest of Pope Gregory III, he formally made Regensburg, Salzburg, Freising and Passau episcopal sees (seats of a bishopric). The following centuries also saw the founding of monasteries, especially of the Benedictine variety, throughout the Frankenreich.

The Birth of the Holy Roman Empire

Ludwig der Deutsche, as his name suggests, promoted a distinctly Germanic cultural identity, quite separate from the Latin-speaking Westfranken. When the Ostfranken Carolingian line ended in 911 with the death of Ludwig das Kind (Ludwig the Child), the Ostfranken nobles decided to elect one of their own rather than be ruled by a distant Carolingian cousin from Westfranken. The job fell to Konrad, duke of Franconia. Simply put, this assertion of independence started the evolution of Ostfranken into Germany and Westfranken into France.

When Konrad died, the Ostfranken crown passed to Heinrich I (ruled 919–36), a Saxon. The Bavarian Duke Arnulf (ruled 907–37) tried to challenge him, but was largely rebuffed, even though he managed to maintain a certain level of independence in religious and foreign policy matters.

Konrad's son and successor, Otto I (ruled 936–973), turned out to be less tolerant of the ambitions of the Bavarian dukes and the following decades were marked by an intense and constantly changing power struggle. When Otto was crowned Kaiser (emperor) by Pope John XII in Rome in 962, it marked the formal beginning of the Holy Roman Empire, which would continue until 1806 (also see boxed text 'What was the Holy Roman Empire?').

Bavaria & the Empire

Otto's promotion did not make it any easier for the Bavarian dukes to regain their independence and Bavaria remained very much under the control of the empire, even losing some of its territory.

Things finally turned around in 1070 with Duke Welf IV (ruled 1070–1101). While the Kaiser and the pope fought over the right to control the bishoprics and their wealth in the so-called Investiture Conflict, Welf took advantage of the confusion to strengthen his own power. The Welfs would rule Bavaria for five generations, and along with the Hohenstaufen (Staufians) from Swabia, became the dominant dynasty in Germany.

Rivalry between these two families escalated into violent conflict in the early 12th

---

What was the Holy Roman Empire?

An idea, mostly, and not a very good one, it grew out of the Frankenreich, which was seen as the legitimate successor state to the defunct Roman Empire. When Charlemagne's father, Pippin, helped a beleaguered pope (Charlemagne would later do the same), he received the title *Patricius Romanorum*, or Protector of Rome, virtually making him Caesar's successor. Soon afterwards, he gave the pope a state of his own – the Vatican.

The empire was known by various names throughout its lifetime. It formally began (for historians, at least) in 962 with the crowning of Otto I, king of Ostfranken, as Kaiser, and finally collapsed in 1806, when Kaiser Franz II abdicated. Sometimes it included Italy as far south as Rome. Sometimes it didn't – the pope usually had a say in that. It variously encompassed present-day Holland, Belgium, Switzerland, Lorraine and Burgundy (in France), Sicily, Austria and an eastern swath of land which lies in the Czech Republic, Poland and Hungary.

This was the so-called 'First Reich'. The Second Reich was created by Otto von Bismarck in 1871, while the notorious Third Reich was Adolf Hitler's attempt to cash in on this dubious glory.

Anthony Haywood

century over the successor of King Heinrich V who died in 1125. Kings had always had to submit to some form of election in Germany, but relatives usually held the best cards. Under this principle, the choice for king should have fallen to the Hohenstaufen Friedrich von Schwaben, an obscure nephew of Heinrich V. Instead, the *Kurfürsten* (prince electors) – pressured by the Bavarian duke, Heinrich der Schwarze (1120–26), a Welf – decided to pass him over in favour of Lothar III (ruled 1125–37), a Saxon. Civil war ensued.

In the next generation, the tables were turned. Heinrich's son, called Heinrich der Stolze (Henry the Proud; ruled 1126–38) had married Lothar's daughter, making him duke of both Bavaria and Saxony and thus giving him a serious shot at the German crown. But upon Lothar's death, the electors ignored the Welf and made Konrad III (ruled 1138–52), a Hohenstaufen, king. In ensuing battles, Heinrich lost all his Bavarian and Saxon territories.

The Welfs remained powerless and landless until Friedrich I, also known as Barbarossa (Red Beard), succeeded Konrad as German king in 1152. As the son of a Welf mother and a Hohenstaufen father, Friedrich brought an end to the epic rivalry and also restored Saxony and most of Bavaria to the son of Heinrich der Stolze, Heinrich der Löwe (Henry the Lion; ruled 1156–80).

As double duke, Heinrich der Löwe wielded immense power and, although concentrating his efforts on Saxony, even made time to found Munich in 1158. Ultimately, however, things did not play out well for him. In 1176, Friedrich, who had become Kaiser in 1155, asked Heinrich for military assistance in fighting the Lombards. Heinrich responded that he'd be happy to help out, as long as Friedrich would make it worth his while. But the emperor would not be blackmailed. In 1179, he called a court session and, with Heinrich not even bothering to show up, sentenced him to exile and to the complete loss of all his territories.

Friedrich then separated Styria from Bavaria, making it Austrian, and gave what was left to a distant relative, Otto von Wittelsbach, whose family would rule the duchy and later kingdom – of Bavaria until 1918.

Growth, Division & Reunion

Over the next generations, the Wittelsbachs managed to vastly expand their territory and with it their sphere of influence. Otto's son, Ludwig I (ruled 1183–1231) acquired the Rheinpfalz (Rhenish Palatinate), an area along the Rhine River north-west of today's state boundaries (it would remain a part of Bavaria in one form or another until 1945). By the early 14th century, the family had become so powerful that Otto's great grandson, Ludwig IV (also known as Ludwig the Bavarian; ruled 1294–1347) was elected German king by edging out his arch-enemy, Frederick the Handsome from the Habsburg dynasty. In 1328, despite objections by Pope John XXII, Ludwig even became Kaiser.

As the first Wittelsbach on the imperial throne, Ludwig used his exalted position wisely to bring various territories, including the March of Brandenburg (around Berlin), the Tyrol (part of today's Austria) and the Dutch provinces of Holland, Zeeland, Friesland and Hennegau under Bavarian control.

In subsequent centuries much of this land was lost again, however, as the Wittelsbach's might was undermined by repeated divisions of their territory. This was in large part due to a lack of the rule of primogeniture, under which only the first-born son inherits all land and title. In Bavaria, if there was more than one son, they either had to rule the entire territory together or it had to be carved up. In the 14th century, four partial duchies emerged: Bavaria-Straubing, Bavaria-Landshut, Bavaria-Ingolstadt and Bavaria-Munich.

Bavaria wasn't reunited until well into the reign of Duke Albrecht IV, known as 'the Wise' (ruled 1460–1508), the head of the Munich branch. Georg der Reiche (George the Rich), the duke of the Landhut and Ingolstadt branches, died in 1503 without a male heir and instead appointed his daughter Elisabeth as his heir. Albrecht did not recognise her as a legitimate successor and thus began the Landshut War of Succession. It ended with a judicial order by Kaiser Maximilian, which gave Albrecht Landshut, but also carved out a new territory called the *Junge Pfalz* (Young Palatinate) for Elisabeth's sons. Its capital was Neuburg an der Donau.

The Straubing line had died out in 1425, thereby allowing Albrecht to consolidate all four Bavarian branches under his rule. One of his first acts was to pass the law of primogeniture (seems like he wasn't called 'wise' for nothing).

The Reformation

On 31 October, 1517, the monk and theology professor Martin Luther posted 95 Theses condemning the sale of 'indulgences' onto the church door in Wittenberg in northern Germany. Playing upon fears of divine punishment, indulgences were sold by the Church to assure their buyers of absolution for sins, past and future. In reality, they were nothing more than clever fundraisers to finance the church rulers' lavish – and often rather worldly – lifestyles. Although in Latin and intended only for theologians, the theses quickly spread by word of mouth across Germany, gaining popular support. The church, of course, labelled Luther a heretic and ordered him to recant his views.

In 1518, Luther was ordered to Augsburg to appear before the papal legate, Cardinal Kajetan. Kajetan demanded that he disavow his writings but Luther, remaining true to his conscience, refused at this time and also after the pope threatened him with excommunication in 1520. As a consequence, he was banned from the Reich, went into hiding for a while but ultimately continued to preach in Wittenberg, where he enjoyed the protection of a reformist ruler.

In Bavaria, the Reformation was ultimately a flop. Albrecht the Wise's son, Wilhelm IV (ruled 1508–50), was a conservative reactionary. Although initially sympathetic to Luther's cause, he feared that a reformed faith would undermine his authority and, rejecting any doctrinal innovations, began to clamp down on anyone embracing Protestantism. (As a footnote, it was under this ruler that the world's first 'consumer protection act' came to be passed in 1516: the so-called

Reinheitsgebot, under which beer may only be made from hops, malt and water. It's still in force today throughout Germany.)

In Franconia and Swabia, by contrast, Protestantism took hold rather quickly. In Franconia, Margrave Georg von Ansbach-Kulmbach was a strong supporter and many imperial cities converted as well. In Swabia, Augsburg was a Protestant stronghold.

Kaiser Karl V tried to force the Lutherans back into the Catholic Church but eventually had to succumb to the princes' demands in the Peace of Augsburg (1555). This gave each prince the right to decide the religion of their principality and put the Catholic and Lutheran churches on a more or less equal footing.

Peasant Wars

There had been regional peasant revolts as early as the 14th and 15th centuries but nothing on the scale of the Peasant Wars of 1524/25, which engulfed most of Germany, including Franconia and Swabia, although not Bavaria. Encouraged by the revolutionary spirit of the Reformation, the peasants demanded social emancipation and more rights over the use of forests, rivers and land.

As outlined in their manifesto, the '12 Articles of the Peasantry in Swabia', drafted in Memmingen, they saw divine justification in their demands, likening their liberation from serfdom to Jesus' salvation. Luther, by the way, while sympathetic to their plight, did not accept this argument. The ensuing uprising was brutally quashed by the rulers and cruel punishment meted out upon those few who had survived the fighting. The peasants would remain silenced for centuries.

Counter-Reformation & Thirty Years' War

The period between the Peace of Augsburg (1555) and the end of the Thirty Years' War (1648) is commonly known as the Counter-Reformation. Under Duke Albrecht V (ruled 1550–79) and Wilhelm the Pious (ruled 1579–97), Bavaria took on a leading role within the movement. This was also the age of the inquisition and of witch trials. In Franconia, Würzburg's prince-bishop Julius

Echter von Mespelbrunn (ruled 1573–1617) was one of the most ruthless Counter-Reformers. And in Ingolstadt, Luther nemesis Johannes Eck taught at the university.

Ultimately, the conflict between Protestants and Catholics escalated into one of Europe's most bloody dynastic wars, the Thirty Years' War (actually several wars). Bavaria, of course, fought firmly on the side of Catholic Kaiser Ferdinand II, with whom Duke Maximiliam I (ruled 1598–1651) had made an alliance in 1616. After helping the Kaiser to an early victory, Maximilian was rewarded with the title of Kurfürst (prince elector) in 1623 and given the Upper Palatinate territories in 1628.

As the war continued, other European countries such as Sweden and France were drawn into the quagmire. Devastation and death were widespread. By the time calm was restored with the Peace of Westphalia, the Reich was ravaged and splintered into over 300 states and about 1000 smaller territories. The Holy Roman Empire had turned into a nominal, impotent entity, its population depleted by war.

The Age of Absolutism

After the Thirty Years' War, Bavaria was a financial shambles. Things didn't improve much under Maximilian's successor, Kurfürst Ferdinand Maria (ruled 1651–79), a *bon vivant* who modelled the Bavarian court on its French counterpart. Lavish parties took place on palatial barges on Lake Starnberg and the Nymphenburg Canal, and operas and ballets became fixed events at the Munich Residenz.

Elector Max Emanuel (ruled 1679–1726) carried on the high lifestyle of his predecessors, which led to the construction of the baroque Schloss Schleissheim. A dabbler in foreign intrigues, Max's five-year support of the Austrian war against the Turks cost more than 30,000 Bavarians their lives.

In gratitude for Max's support, the Habsburg emperor rewarded the Bavarian ruler with the hand of his daughter, the Polish princess Therese Kunigunde. Their son was the chosen heir to the Spanish throne, but died at the age of six. A protracted and bloody dispute over the successor began,

which came to be known as the Spanish War of Succession (1704–14).

Bavaria sided with France against England and Austria, and Austrian troops occupied Bavaria from 1705 to 1714. A terrible massacre occurred in the first year of occupation when Bavarian peasants rose up against the Habsburg army at Sendlingen (now a southern suburb of Munich). As if the odds weren't already bad enough, the peasants were betrayed before they could attack, and were obliterated by Austrian soldiers.

Bavaria was finally liberated from the Austrians with the help of the French, but the land was left morally and economically drained. However, the confusion brought on by the Austrian War of Succession gave Kurfürst Karl Albrecht (ruled 1726–45) an opening to become emperor, with Prussian and French support. In 1742, he was crowned Kaiser Karl VII. Upon his death, however, the Austrian Empress Maria Theresa managed to re-establish Habsburg supremacy and get her husband, Franz Stephan von Lothringen, elected as the new emperor.

The Enlightenment

Back in Bavaria, Max III Joseph (ruled 1745–77) followed Karl Albrecht as Kurfürst and worked towards retrieving the state from beneath a mountain of debt. One of Max's key decrees allowed businesses to be set up outside the traditional trade guilds, with the aim of boosting tax revenue through economic growth. It didn't work: like many state-run enterprises today, these cloth-making, tapestry and cotton manufacturing factories ran at a loss.

The Enlightenment came late to Bavaria. The first, rather amateurish, newspaper was published in 1702, followed by more mainstream publications in 1750. National laws were reformed in 1751 (but somehow failed to outlaw torture). The Bavarian Academy of Sciences, which had leanings away from Catholicism, was founded in 1759. Max himself reformed the school system in 1771, making education compulsory for all children up to the age of 16.

Since Max III Joseph didn't have any male heirs, his succession passed to his distant cousin, Karl Theodor, the Elector of the Rheinpfalz. Kaiser Joseph II did not recognise Karl Theodor as the rightful successor and tried to take the duchy away from the Wittelsbachs. Prussia's Friedrich II, however, came to the Bavarians' rescue. Ultimately, the emperor accepted Karl Theodor in exchange for territories along the Inn River.

Karl Theodor (ruled 1777–99) was a conservative throwback who was exceedingly unpopular. He tried to remain neutral during the French Revolution, only to see the Palatinate occupied by France, putting him in political isolation. When he died, pubs filled with throngs of jubilant subjects who partied for days. Childless, he was succeeded by Maximilian IV Joseph (ruled 1799–1825), who was from a distant Palatinate line.

The Kingdom of Bavaria

The early 19th century finally brought much needed reform and renewal, courtesy of Napoleon. Max IV Joseph allied himself with France in its war against Austria and, as a reward, Bavaria was elevated to the rank of kingdom in 1806. Elector Max IV Joseph now became King Max I Joseph. Napoleon also doubled the size of the Bavarian territories, giving it Franconia and Swabia in return for the loss of the Palatinate, which France held until 1815/16.

Under Minister Maximilian von Montgelas, a number of reforms in the spirit of the Enlightenment were implemented in Bavaria. These included political as well as societal changes, such as the dissolution of privileges for the nobility, the end of serfdom for the peasants, the emancipation of the Jews and equal rights for all three main religions (Catholicism, Protestantism, Judaism), and reformed educational and legal systems.

Another major reform was secularisation, which involved the dissolution of monasteries, nationalisation of church property and even the removal of the monk from Munich's coat of arms in 1808 (it reappeared in 1835, as did many of the monasteries).

In 1806, Bavaria joined France in the *Rheinbund* (Rhine Confederation), a loose alliance of sovereign states, a move that sounded the final death knell to the Holy Roman Empire. Its last emperor, Franz II (ruled 1792–1806) packed his bags and went home to Austria, where he renamed himself Franz I of Austria.

The alliance with France finally fell apart in 1813 when Napoleon's empire started to unravel. Always the opportunist, Bavaria promptly realigned with Austria and Prussia. In 1818, Bavaria became the first German state to draft a constitution, which was largely based on the French model.

Ludwig I & the Revolution of 1848

Max's son, Ludwig I (ruled 1825–48), was determined to transform Bavaria into a cultural and artistic centre. In 1826, he moved the university from Landshut to the capital, Munich, and staffed it with respected teachers including philosopher Friedrich von Schelling, architect Friedrich von Gärtner and historian Joseph Görres. The king was also a fanatic for new technology, and promoted the development of the first German railway. The bang-up party after Ludwig's wedding came to be celebrated every year as Oktoberfest (see the special section 'The Munich Oktoberfest' in the Munich chapter).

Ludwig's reign was marked by reactionary ideas. His initial emphasis on Bavaria's constitution gave way to the leanings of an absolutist monarch. An arch-Catholic, the king backed the restoration of monasteries in Bavaria during the 1830s. In 1832, press censorship was introduced, and two years later Ludwig authorised arrests of students, journalists and university professors whom he judged to be dangerously liberal. Bavaria was turning restrictive, even as French and American democratic ideas were catching on elsewhere in Germany.

The biggest threat to Ludwig, however, turned out to be his own weakness for beautiful women. The king commissioned portraits of stunning females from all walks of life, and had them hung in a special Schönheitengalerie (Gallery of Beauties) in Schloss Nymphenburg. Details of the king's many flings were kept out of the public eye, with one notable exception: his infatuation with dancer Lola Montez, which triggered his downfall (see the boxed text 'Lola Montez, Femme Fatale').

The Lola Montez affair coincided with the democratic revolutions, which swept Europe in 1848. In March of that year, 10,000 Müncheners (or nearly 10% of the town's population) signed a petition demanding freedom of the press, and a mob of them stormed the royal arsenal. On March

22, the 60-year-old Ludwig finally stepped down. Under his son, Max II (ruled 1848–64), Bavaria enjoyed a period of liberalist expansion and relative tranquillity. Reforms included new election rules, abolition of censorship and introduction of the right of assembly. Thus freed from restrictions, new publications, parties and organisations flourished. Max was also a staunch supporter of the arts and sciences.

Lola Montez, Femme Fatale

A whip-toting dominatrix and seductress of royalty, Lola Montez (1818–61) showed the prim Victorians what sex scandals were all about. Born as Eliza Gilbert in Limerick, Ireland, to a young British army officer and a 13-year-old Creole chorus girl, Lola claimed to be the illegitimate daughter of poet Lord Byron (or, depending on her mood, of a matador). When her father died of cholera in India, her mother remarried and shipped the seven-year-old Eliza home to Scotland, where she occasionally ran stark naked through the streets. She finished school in Paris and after an unsuccessful stab at acting, reinvented herself as the Spanish dancer, Lola Montez.

She couldn't dance either and, after gigging around Europe for several years, danced just as badly as before. But her beauty fascinated men, who fell at her feet – sometimes under the lash of her ever-present riding crop. One time she fired her pistol at a lover who'd performed poorly, but he managed to escape with his trousers about his knees.

Those succumbing to her charms included the Czar of Russia, who paid her 1000 rubles for a 'private audience', novelist Alexandre Dumas and composer Franz Liszt. Eventually Liszt tired of Lola's incendiary temper, locked his sleeping mistress in their hotel room, and fled – leaving a deposit for the furniture Lola would demolish when she awoke.

When fired by a Munich theatre manager, Lola took her appeal to the court of Ludwig I himself. As the tale goes, Ludwig asked casually whether her lovely figure was a work of nature or art. The direct gal she was, Lola seized a pair of scissors and slit open the front of her dress, leaving the ageing monarch to judge for himself. Predictably, she was rehired (and the manager sacked).

The king fell head over heels for Lola, giving her a huge allowance, a lavish palace and even the doubtful title of Countess of Landsfeld. Her ladyship virtually began running the country, too, and when Munich students rioted during the 1848 revolution, Lola had Ludwig shut down the university. This was too much for the townsfolk, who joined the students in revolt. Ludwig was forced to abdicate and soon Lola was chased out of town.

Lola can-canned her way around the world; her increasingly lurid show was very popular with Californian gold miners. Next came a book of 'beauty secrets' and a lecture tour (sample topic: 'Heroines of History and Strong-Minded Women'). She shed her Spanish identity, but in doing so Lola – who had long publicly denied any link to her alter ego, Eliza – became a schizophrenic wreck. She spent her final two years as a pauper in New York, shuffling through the streets muttering to herself, before dying of pneumonia and a stroke at age 43.

Jeremy Gray

King Ludwig II

Ludwig II took the reins after his father, Max II, died in 1864 and, to everyone's surprise, seized upon his new role with the enthusiasm and idealism of youth. Initially, he worked hard to increase his people's well-being, passing a wealth of progressive measures. These included public care for the poor, a liberalised marriage law and the facilitation of free trade. Unfortunately for the young king, lasting peace would be harder to come by.

Bavaria had been part of the German Federation, an uneasy union of 39 sovereign German states, since its inception in 1815. In 1866, the rivalry between its two most powerful members – Austria and Prussia – exploded into war. Ludwig desperately tried to keep his troops out of the conflict. Bound by his alliances and pressured by his cabinet, however, he had no choice but to mobilise Bavarian soldiers against Prussia, even though defeat was inevitable. Indeed, after only three weeks, the Austrian coalition was trounced in the Battle of Königsgrätz in Bohemia.

The consequences of defeat, for Bavaria and the king, were grave. As one of the concessions, Prussia demanded that Ludwig give up supreme command over the Bavarian troops in wartime. He had no choice but to acquiesce and, despondent, even considered abdicating. Perhaps he already knew that this concession was only the first step towards Bavaria's loss of independence.

Ludwig's worst fears came true only four years later when Prussia commanded Bavarian soldiers in the war against France in 1870/71. Prussia and its allies won, and it became clear that Bavaria's absorption into the newly forming German Reich was inevitable.

Bowing to the public mood, his ministers' advice, and pressure from Berlin, Ludwig officially expressed support of the Prussian king to become German Kaiser. But he was also painfully aware that this step would reduce his sovereignty once more. Although he managed to negotiate for regular payments from Berlin into his private coffers, his pride was nonetheless stung. When the German nobility flocked to Wilhelm I's proclamation in Versailles, Ludwig II of Bavaria was conspicuously absent.

The political realities that had so diminished the status of his office and the sovereignty of Bavaria also eroded Ludwig's enthusiasm for his royal responsibilities. The exalted, almost sacred, view he held of the office of king was out of place in a society increasingly ruled by industry and the bourgeoisie. Ludwig had become a misfit, an anachronism. The Zeitgeist of the late 19th century had overtaken him.

Disillusioned, the king retreated to the Bavarian Alps, gradually withdrawing from the business of governing. Instead, he now obsessively directed his energies to building his versions of paradise on earth: the castles of Neuschwanstein, Linderhof, and Herrenchiemsee. Declared mentally unfit after a dubious psychological exam in 1886, Ludwig was dethroned and taken to Schloss Berg on Lake Starnberg. Here, he mysteriously drowned a few days later (see the boxed text 'The Mystery of King Ludwig II' in the Allgäu-Bavarian Swabia chapter).

His brother Otto, a certified nut case, was unable to take the throne, so his uncle Luitpold – then already 65 years of age – took charge as prince regent. He became one of Bavaria's most popular rulers. His motto 'the people's will is the highest law' revealed a refreshing lack of absolutist ambition. During Luitpold's reign, Bavaria shared in Germany's overall growth and progress. Around the turn of the 20th century, a very active arts scene flourished in Munich.

World War I & Aftermath

Bavaria's last king, Ludwig III (ruled 1913–18) ascended the throne on the eve of WWI. In November 1918, more than 100,000 people gathered on the Theresienwiese in Munich to protest for peace. Erhard Auer of the Social Democratic Party (SPD) and Kurt Eisner of the German Independent Socialist Party (USPD) held fiery orations, calling for revolution and a democratic constitution. Under Eisner's direction, the masses marched through town, won over what was left of the army and proclaimed a republic. The monarchy capitulated without a fight, and Ludwig III fled the Residenz with his family in the middle of the night. Five days later the king was tracked down in Bamberg, where Eisner's officials forced him to sign his abdication.

The factions behind Eisner were badly divided, and what began as a peaceful revolution deteriorated into violence. Left and right-wing Social Democrats, anarchists and communists quarrelled over the shape of the new government. In early 1919 several people died in street battles. The new prime minister also failed to win over the common people to his cause: farmers refused to provide Munich with food, and state elections two months after the revolution produced a crushing defeat for the USPD.

In February 1919, Eisner decided to yield to growing demands from all parties for him to step down. He would never get the chance. On the way to parliament to announce his resignation, Eisner was shot dead.

Dramatic events followed. In March 1919, the parties' central council elected Social Democrat Johannes Hoffmann as prime minister, but it soon became clear that his democratic ideas weren't radical enough to please the workers. A few weeks later, writers Gustav Landauer, Erich Mühsam and Ernst Toller proclaimed a Räterepublik (Republic of Councils) along Russian lines, and Hoffmann and his officials fled to Bamberg.

The Räterepublik was too fragmented to last, however. The Communists seized power in April 1919, only to be overthrown a few weeks later by the German Army and the Volunteer Corps, who were both loyal to Hoffmann. Council leaders were imprisoned or executed, and Hoffman was reinstalled – but he didn't stay in power long.

The 1920s

In the early 1920s Munich remained a political tinder-box. In March of 1920, the Hoffmann government was replaced by the reactionary regime of Gustav von Kahr. Many right-wing splinter groups set up their headquarters in Munich, meeting in beer halls and pubs. Among them was the Thulegesellschaft, an anti-Semitic association that gathered in the back rooms of the Hotel Vier Jahreszeiten. A related organisation, the Deutsche Arbeiter Partei (DAP; German Workers' Party), had been founded in 1919 by toolmaker Anton Drexler and met in the Hofbräuhaus. By the time the party was later renamed the National Socialist Workers' Party (NSDAP), its members included a failed Austrian artist – Adolf Hitler.

On 8 November 1923, he and about 600 SA troops stormed Munich's Bürgerbräukeller, proclaimed a 'National Socialist revolution' and wheeled in a machine gun to show they meant business. The mayor of Munich and officials of the Bavarian provincial government were kidnapped, and the daring move seemed successful. This event went down in history as the 'beer hall putsch'.

The next day, Hitler, SA General Erich Ludendorff and armed comrades marched victoriously through Munich to the Feldherrnhalle – where they were stopped by Bavarian police. Shots were fired, and when it was all over 19 Nazis and several policemen lay dead or dying. Hitler fled, but was apprehended several days later and sentenced to five years' prison in Landsberg, west of Munich. Here he began work on *Mein Kampf* (My Struggle), dictated in extended ramblings to his secretary Rudolf Hess. Incredibly, Hitler was released just a year later, in 1924, on grounds of 'good behaviour'.

Meanwhile, Germany was close to economic collapse, exacerbated by crushing repayments to the victorious WWI powers under the Treaty of Versailles. Inflation spiralled ever higher and, by early 1924, a wheelbarrow full of Reichsmarks was needed to buy a single loaf of bread.

Germany's monetary system was reformed in late 1924 and bit by bit, the economy began to stabilise. There were few signs of the 'Roaring Twenties' in Munich, which sank into a cultural stupor. Experimental or racy works were banned, and artists and musicians left town in droves for Berlin. Thomas Mann, one of the few leading writers who remained in Munich until 1933, condemned the city, in a 1926 speech, as 'notorious', 'anti-Semitic' and a 'stronghold of reaction'.

Capital of the Nazi 'Movement'

After Hitler took power of Germany in January 1933, Bavaria too lost its political independence but was also assigned a special status. Munich was declared the 'Capital of the Movement' and Nuremberg became the site of the Nazi party's mass rallies. In 1935, the party brass met in the latter city to pass the Nuremberg Laws, which signalled the systematic repression of the Jews. In Dachau, north of Munich, Germany's first concentration camp was built in 1933. In addition, many Nazi honchos hailed from Bavaria, including SA chief Ernst Röhm (later killed by Hitler), Heinrich Himmler, Hermann Göring and Franconia's *Gauleiter* (regional chief), Julius Streicher. Hitler himself was born just across the border, in Austria's Braunau. The Alpine resort of Berchtesgaden became the southern party headquarters.

The reign of terror against the Jews began even before 1933 and synagogues in Munich and Nuremberg were destroyed months before Reichskristallnacht (Night of Broken Glass), when Jewish businesses and houses of worship were burned to the ground throughout Germany. As has been well documented, those who didn't manage to flee or emigrate, later perished in the extermination camps.

WWII & Reconstruction

German invasion of Poland on 1 September 1939 kicked off the bloody nightmare of World War II. Few people dared to speak out against the Nazis; one of the few exceptions was the White Rose, a resistance group led by Munich university students Hans and Sophie Scholl (see boxed text 'The White Rose' in the Munich chapter).

Many Bavarian cities were obliterated by Allied bombing. After WWII, Bavaria was occupied by American troops whose military command regulated all aspects of public life, appointed officials and dismissed hundreds of former NSDAP members from public service. Fritz Schäffler, who had been head of the Bayerische Volkspartei (Bavarian People's Party) before it was outlawed under the Nazis, was installed as Bavaria's first governor on 25 May 1945. But the military command felt that he was not pursuing the de-Nazification process with sufficient resolve and, only a few months later, replaced him with the Social Democrat Wilhelm Hoegner.

In 1946, US commander General Clay allowed for a series of elections to take place, first on a village level, and later also in cities and districts. In December 1946, the people of Bavaria voted in favour of adopting a new Bavarian constitution, drawn up under the guidance of the occupational forces. In the first elections for state parliament, the Christlich-Soziale Union (CSU; Christian Social Union) won an absolute majority.

By its own choice, Bavaria has always played a special role in German postwar history. In 1949, it was the only one among the German states that did not ratify the German constitution because, in the opinion of the state government, it did not give enough independent powers to the individual states. Bavaria did, however, agree to abide by it and has done so to this day.

Bavaria's economic postwar recovery has been impressive, as it transformed itself from an essentially agrarian society into a progressive and modern state. Although thoroughly integrated within the German political construct, it nevertheless takes great pride in its 'otherness'. Its history, traditions, attitudes, political priorities and culture are, in many ways, quite different from the rest of Germany. They are uniquely Bavarian.

GEOGRAPHY

Bavaria sprawls over 70,548 sq km, making it bigger than Ireland, Portugal or Denmark. It is the largest and southernmost of Germany's 16 federal states and shares international borders with Austria in the south and the Czech Republic in the east; inner-German borders are the state of Baden-Württemberg to the west, Hesse to the north-west and Thuringia and Saxony north.

Bavaria is crammed with an immense variety of landforms, with elevations ranging from 200m above sea level in the north-west to almost 3000m in the Bavarian Alps in the south. These consist of several ranges including, west to east, the Allgäuer Alps, the Wetterstein/Karwendel Alps (with Germany's highest mountain, the Zugspitze at 2962m) and the Chiemgauer Alps.

North of here, the Alpine Foothills, a wedge between the Danube and the Alps, are typified by moorland, low rolling hills, pine forests and subalpine plateaus. The region is dappled with large glacier-carved lakes, including the Chiemsee and Lake Starnberg, plus dozens of smaller ones.

The Bavarian Forest along the Czech border in eastern Bavaria is a classic *Mittelgebirge*, a medium-altitude mountain range. Its highest mountain is the Grosse Arber (1456m). Much of Franconia is part of the Central Uplands, a complex patchwork of ranges, rifts and steep valleys that makes for a varied landscape. There are large stretches of forest in the Frankenwald and Fichtelgebirge north of Bayreuth; the latter is also part of the European watershed. South of here, the Franconian Alp is a Jurassic limestone range, with especially bizarre rock formations in the Franconian Switzerland region north of Nuremberg. The Franconian basin stretches east of Würzburg along the Main and Regnitz Rivers.

Bavaria is traversed by numerous rivers, of which the Danube (387km in Bavaria) and the Main (407km in Bavaria) are the longest. The Inn (218km in Bavaria) and the Isar (263km in Bavaria) originate in the Alps and flow into the Danube, the former at Passau, the latter near Deggendorf on the edge of the Bavarian Forest.

CLIMATE

To paraphrase a saying from a famous movie, 'the weather in Bavaria is kinda like a box of chocolates, you never know what you're gonna get'. On any given day it could be cold or warm, sunny or rainy, windy or tranquil – or any combination thereof.

Meteorologists blame the state's changeable weather conditions on alternating maritime and continental weather masses. Other factors include topography, altitude and even whether you're in an urban or a rural area.

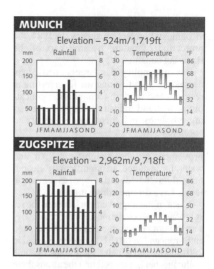

There are lots of microclimates. Take Aschaffenburg, for example, where the weather is mild enough for figs and lemons to grow. Oberstdorf in the Allgäu is drenched by an average of 1800mm of rain each year, while Nuremberg gets only 700mm.

Generally speaking, weather patterns are more stable in the northern part of Bavaria and increasingly fluctuate the further south you get. The Alps are subject to snowfall from late October to May, while there has not been snow in the Main and Danube Valleys in years. The south gets both more sunshine and more rain than the north.

Winds are stronger in the north than in the south, which is subject to the *Föhn*, a warm, dry, static-charged wind that comes down from the Alps. It provides both exquisite views of the mountains and an area of dense pressure, giving people an excuse to feel cranky and lethargic.

In other words, be prepared for anything and pack accordingly.

ECOLOGY & ENVIRONMENT

Bavarian politicians recognised early that a healthy environment was good for business, especially the tourism industry. In 1972, some 14 years before the first federal environmental minister took office, Germany's southernmost state created Europe's first environmental protection agency. In 1984, the protection of nature became part of the Bavarian constitution.

Bavarian policy has largely focused on decreasing pollution and waste, investing in research and modern technologies, educating people and industry, cleaning up existing problems and encouraging industry to regulate itself.

Officials proudly tout the fact that improvement has been significant. Air and water, for instance, are significantly cleaner now than two decades ago as emission levels have dropped dramatically.

Much of the improvement has been the result of federal regulations. Advanced catalysers are now required on most vehicles, and an European Union (EU)-wide law passed in 2001 has helped to halve the amount of some pollutants being pumped into the atmosphere by vehicles. Germans also pay an 'ecological tax' on petrol, an unpopular initiative of the Bündnis 90/Die Grünen party to promote the use of public transport.

Another reason for Bavaria's impressive environmental statistics is its heavy reliance on nuclear energy, which accounts for around 80% of its energy production (versus 35% nationwide). While nuclear power plants generate less pollution at the source than conventional plants (Bavaria's carbon dioxide is 25% below national levels), there are, of course, incalculable potential risks as well as the yet to be solved problem of nuclear waste storage.

Bavaria's energy policy is also at odds with the agreement reached by the government coalition of SPD and Bündnis 90/Die Grünen in 2000, under which all of Germany's 19 nuclear plants (four of them in Bavaria) will be phased out by 2030. Bavarian politicians are opposed to such a move and contend that it would dramatically increase pollution levels.

At the same time, the state is a leader in the development and use of renewable energies, especially hydroelectric power, with minor contributions from solar and wind energy. Bavaria produces about half of all energy generated in these ways in Germany.

As elsewhere in Germany, recycling is huge in Bavaria. There is a refund system for many types of bottles and jars, and non-refundable glass is disposed of according to colour (green, clear and brown) in special containers placed throughout communities.

Another priority has been given to protecting natural spaces. Bavaria has two national parks, 16 nature parks and over 1200 protected nature areas totalling about 4.5 million hectares. On the flipside, the extension of the Rhine-Main-Danube-Canal between Bamberg and Kelheim has been severely detrimental to plant and animal habitats. Environmentalists anticipate further destruction if the canalisation of the Danube between Straubing and Vilshofen, along the edge of the Bavarian Forest, is allowed to proceed. (Also see the boxed text 'Bavaria's Tower of Babel?' in the Franconia chapter.)

The impact of humans on the environment is also felt throughout the Alpine region, where the mountains are becoming increasingly high-tech. And it's not just the ever-expanding lift systems. Another problem is the beefed-up installation of snow-making equipment, which is increasingly needed because global warming has pushed up the altitude at which there are reliable snow levels to about 2000m.

FLORA & FAUNA
Flora

Despite environmental pressures, Bavarian forests remain beautiful places to relax and get away from the crowd. Most cities and towns have their own forest (Stadtwald), which can be easily reached by public transport or on foot. The prettiest ones are planted with varieties of beech, oak, birch, chestnut, lime, maple or ash.

Many forest regions have mixed deciduous forest at lower altitudes, changing to coniferous species as you ascend. River valleys are usually the best place to find deciduous forests.

Alpine regions have a wide range of wildflowers – orchids, cyclamen, gentians, pulsatilla, alpine roses, edelweiss and buttercups, just to mention a few. Meadow species are particularly colourful in spring and summer, and great care is taken these days not to cut pastures until plants have seeded.

Fauna

Bavaria remains home to a wide variety of animals, although many have found their way onto the endangered species list. The most common large mammals in forests are game species such as deer and wild boar, or those that have adapted well to human activities, such as squirrels and foxes.

The Alpine marmot inhabits the Alps up to the tree line, although it tends to avoid the northern slopes. This sociable rodent lives in colonies and lets out a shrill whistle-like sound when disturbed.

Wild goats were almost wiped out by hunters in the 19th century; those now found in the Alps (above the tree line) were reintroduced from northern Italy. Chamois are widespread in the Alps and Alpine Foothills, with small introduced populations in parts of Swabia.

Beavers have been endangered since the Middle Ages and faced extinction in the 19th century. They were coveted not only for their fur but also cooked up in strictly Catholic households each Friday because the good people considered them to be 'fish'. Beavers were reintroduced in Bavaria starting in 1966 and the population has since stabilised at between 1000 and 1500. Most live in reservoirs of the lower Inn River as well as along the Danube between Ingolstadt and Kelheim and its tributaries.

The hare is on the list of endangered species but can be seen frequently in fields in less-populated regions, whereas the snow hare, whose fur is white in winter, is fairly common in the Alps. You may also come across martens, badgers, hamsters and otters.

Lynx died out in Germany in the 19th century. Populations were reintroduced in the Bavarian Forest in the 1970s, much to the chagrin of local hunters and farmers (lynx attack livestock and deer). By the early 1980s, their numbers had basically dropped back down to zero. Between 1982 and 1989, Czech authorities released 17 lynx in the Bohemian Forest. Since the removal of fences along the border, a small group of brave souls have tried their luck again in the Bavarian Forest. The wild cat, another indigenous feline, has also returned to forest regions after being nearly hunted to extinction in the 1930s.

If you are very lucky, you might see a golden eagle in the Alps. In the Alpine Foothills you'll often see jays (look for the flashes of blue on their wings), which imitate the calls of other species. Forests everywhere in Bavaria provide a habitat for a wide variety of songbirds as well as woodpeckers.

Endangered Species

Estimates show that, in Bavaria, about one in four plant species have disappeared, while only 25% of what once were 35,000 native animal species still exist today. Urbanisation and industrialisation are, of course, the main culprits, even though built-up areas account for only 22% of the state's territory, while about 45% is used for agriculture and 33% is covered by forest. However, intensive cultivation, tree cutting, single-species reforestation (mostly with fast-growing conifers) and destruction of biotopes are putting enormous pressure on ecosystems.

The situation for many reptile and beetle species is grim, and ant and butterfly species are also threatened with extinction. About one third of the 100 mammals studied for the 'Red List', a list of endangered species, are in danger of dying out, including shrews and field hamsters. Permanent populations of large mammals such as wolves and European moose have virtually ceased to exist. The news is not all bad, though: sea eagles, osprey, cormorants, cranes and white storks are no longer endangered, and bats and beavers are also back in numbers.

National & Nature Parks

Of Germany's 13 national parks, two are in Bavaria. The Nationalpark Bayerischer Wald (Bavarian Forest National Park), near the Czech border, covers an area of 131 sq km and consists of mountain forests (mostly beech, fir and spruce) with upland moors. Parts of the forest have been severely damaged by acid rain, but it's still a superb outdoor playground with plenty of unspoiled hiking trails.

South of here, Nationalpark Berchtesgaden covers 210 sq km near the Austrian border, rising in altitude from about 600m to 2700m. The landscape is a contrast of lakes, limestone and dolomite cliffs, meadows, mixed forests and subalpine spruce stands. Arguably Germany's most beautiful park, this is where you can best view Alpine plants and wildlife.

Bavaria also has 16 *Naturparks* (nature parks), half of them in Franconia, including the Frankenwald and Fichtelgebirge north of Bayreuth; the Odenwald and Spessart near Aschaffenburg; the Steigerwald between Würzburg and Bamberg; the Fränkische Schweiz (Franconian Switzerland) north of Nuremberg; and the Altmühltal south of Nuremberg.

GOVERNMENT & POLITICS

Bavaria is one of 16 German states. Its government consists of the Landtag (state parliament, or legislature) and Staatsregierung (state government, the executive branch).

The Landtag has 204 representatives, who are elected by constituents in statewide elections held every five years. Women account for about 22% of the seats. Starting with the next election in 2003, the number of delegates will be reduced to 180. Landtag representatives initiate most legislation, relying on recommendations made by the 12 parliamentary commissions. These include Budget & Finance; Education, Youth & Sports; Nutrition & Agriculture; and Higher Education, Research & Culture. Their meetings are open to the public.

The Staatsregierung is headed by the *Ministerpräsident* (prime minister) and includes 10 *Staatsminister* (state ministers) and 10 *Staatssekretäre* (state secretaries).

Since the end of WWII, Bavarian politics have been dominated by a single party: the conservative Christlich-Soziale Union (CSU; Christian Social Union). Although aligned with the CDU on the national level, the CSU is actually an independent party. Every single Ministerpräsident since 1946

has belonged to the party, which has received an absolute majority in all elections since 1966. In the 1998 elections, it got 52.9% of the vote, while the centre-left SPD pulled 28.7% and the Bündnis 90/Die Grünen 5.7%. A party must gain 5% of the vote to be represented. The opposition parties have very little influence on state policy. On the local level, some of the bigger cities, including Munich, occasionally have SPD majors.

Voting is not compulsory. In the last state elections, 69.8% of those eligible to vote participated.

ECONOMY

It's hard to believe today that, until WWII, Bavaria was still a predominantly agricultural state, having been more or less bypassed by the Industrial Revolution that had swept through most of Europe since the middle of the 19th century. Since the war, however, no other German state has reinvented itself more dramatically than Bavaria, which has emerged as a modern, industrialised and progressive economic powerhouse.

In 2000, its gross domestic product (GDP) clocked in at €344 billion (second only to population-rich North-Rhine Westphalia with €446 billion) and accounted for almost one sixth of the gross national product (€1,988 trillion). Bavaria's economy is larger than that of nine of the 15 EU countries, including Belgium, Finland and Austria. Its unemployment rate of 5.3% is the envy of nearly all other German states and far below the national average of 9.4% (2001 figures).

As in the rest of Germany, Bavaria's economy is rooted in a system called *Soziale Marktwirtschaft* (social market economy) anchored in the German constitution. It ensures a broad safety net of benefits for employees and the unemployed coupled with a free market guaranteeing private ownership and competition.

One third of all German farms (154,000) are still in Bavaria, yet agriculture accounts for only 1% of its GDP. The engine of the economy is still in the manufacturing sector, which accounts for about 32% of the state's GDP. Some of Germany's biggest companies are based in Bavaria, including electronics and computing giant Siemens, turbine maker MTU and car and truck manufacturers BMW, Audi and MAN.

The top five industries in Bavaria are mechanical engineering (16.2%), car manufacturing (13.4%), electrical engineering (8.9%), food production (7.7%) and metalwork industry (5.9%). Also important are the chemical industry, broadcast and print media, as well as traditional fields such as textile production, ceramics, toys and glass manufacturing. About 95% of the state's companies are small to medium sized (ie, fewer than 500 employees), which employ 52% of its workforce.

Like the rest of Germany, Bavaria is very export-oriented, with about 38% of all manufactured goods destined for other countries. More than half of the state's trade is outside the EU; overall, the top three trading partners are the USA, Italy and France. The most popular export products are, predictably, machinery and cars.

Bavaria has also been investing in high-tech, future-oriented sectors, such as biotech and genetical engineering and information, laser and medical technology. Tourism is another pillar of the economy. In 2000, about 23 million visitors came to Bavaria, including 4.6 million from abroad.

POPULATION & PEOPLE

Bavaria is Germany's second most populous state and had about 12.16 million inhabitants in 2001. This represents a net gain of about 706,000 over 1990 figures, an increase due in large part to migration from the former eastern German states following the reunification of Germany in 1989. Another minor contributor was the slight rise in the birth rate over the death rate during the same period. About 10% of the population are non-German citizens.

About two thirds of all Bavarians are between the ages of 18 and 65, with 16% older than 65 and 19.6% younger than 18. Nearly one in two people (46%) is married, while 41.4% are unmarried; only 5% is divorced and the remainder is widowed (7.4%).

The population of the modern state is a conglomeration of three rather distinct historical tribes: the *Altbayern* ('old' Bavarians), the *Franconians* and the *Swabians*, who distinguish themselves through their customs, traditions, mentality and attitudes. Refugees and expellees who settled in Bavaria after WWII are the so-called 'fourth tribe'. Although it may seem anachronistic to outsiders, members of the various 'tribes' still identify strongly with their respective heritage.

EDUCATION

Bavaria has a highly educated population, in large part because the government has long made education a priority, spending nearly 30% of its budget on schools. There are private and religious schools, but the majority of students attend excellent free public schools. School attendance is compulsory from ages six to 18.

Following an optional two or three years at kindergarten, children attend the *Grundschule* (primary school), usually at six years of age. After four years, they transfer to one of three traditional secondary high school types: *Hauptschule* (vocational emphasis, five years), *Realschule* (commercial emphasis, six years), and *Gymnasium* (academic emphasis, nine years); or to the *Gesamtschule* (comprehensive school) which integrates the three other types. The Gymnasium culminates with the *Abitur*, an extremely rigorous multiday examination, which must be passed in order to qualify for university admission. Graduates of the Hauptschule and Realschule usually take up a two- or three-year apprenticeship taught in a system called 'dual education' where students divide their time between on-the-job training and the *Berufsschule* (vocational school).

Bavaria is home to nine public universities (Augsburg, Bamberg, Bayreuth, Erlangen-Nuremberg, Munich (two), Passau, Regensburg and Würzburg) with 151,000 students. It also has 17 polytechnics with 56,000 students. About another 4000 students attend specialised universities, such as a military academy, the Catholic university in Eichstätt, three theological colleges, two art academies, one film school and one theatre academy.

ARTS
Painting & Sculpture

Early Works The two dominant art forms during the Carolingian and Romanesque periods (about 800–1200) were frescoes and manuscript illumination. The oldest frescoes in Bavaria (AD 980) are in the crypt of the Benedictine Abbey of St Mang in Füssen. Stained glass began to pop up around 1100; the 'Prophets' Windows' in Augsburg's cathedral are the earliest in Central Europe.

Gothic Portraiture and altar painting appeared in Bavaria around 1300. A number of such works were commissioned by the Wittelsbachs, but most are believed to have been lost or destroyed. Late panel works that did survive include those by Polish artist Jan Polack (died 1519) who is regarded as Munich's most important late-Gothic painter. He produced two altars in the Peterskirche as well as the altar in the Schloss Blutenburg chapel.

Another important late-Gothic artist was the multi-talented Tyrolean Michael Pacher (1445–98), who was both a painter and a sculptor. Examples of his work include the altar of the four church fathers in the Alte Pinakothek in Munich. His high altar for the Franziskanerkirche in Salzburg was destroyed, although a surviving Madonna was later integrated within the new altar.

Among dedicated sculptors of this period, two names stand out. One is Erasmus Grasser (1450–1518), whose masterpieces include the St Peter altar in the Peterskirche in Munich and the Morris Dancers in the Munich Stadtmuseum. The other is Veit Stoss (1445–1533), a Franconian who managed to imbue his sculptures with dramatic realism. The *Annunciation* in Lorenzkirche in Nuremberg is one of his finest works. In 1503, Stoss spent a stint in jail for forgery but ultimately restored his reputation with the *Bamberger Altar* in Bamberg's cathedral, his crowning achievement.

Renaissance The Renaissance saw human elements gain importance in painting: religious figures were often depicted surrounded by mere mortals. The style limped towards Germany more than 100 years after first surfacing in Italy and only made it across the Alps in the early 16th century. When it did arrive, it quickly gained a foothold in Bavaria, with Nuremberg-born Albrecht Dürer (1471–1528) as its main exponent. Dürer's influence on the Renaissance was so great, in fact, that the period is often referred to as the Dürerzeit (Age of Dürer).

Dürer was primarily a painter and graphic artist. His subject matter ranges from mythology to religion to animals, all depicted with groundbreaking anatomical detail, natural perspective and vivid colours. Dürer began as an apprentice goldsmith and travelled widely throughout Germany before spending time in Venice and Bologna. He was the first German to grapple seriously with the theory and practice of Italian Renaissance art. Some of his work is displayed in the Alte Pinakothek in Munich, including the famous Christ-like self-portrait.

Dürer greatly influenced Lucas Cranach the Elder (1472–1553), one of the main artists of the Reformation. Cranach's work is characterised by a new approach to landscape painting which grew out of the *Donauschule* (Danube School), an artistic movement based primarily in Passau and Regensburg. Members imbued landscapes with emotionalism and mood, thus making them the focal point of the painting rather than a mere backdrop for figures or scenes. The most important Danube School artist was Albrecht Altdorfer (1480–1538) whose *Battle of Alexander the Great* in the Alte Pinakothek is a masterwork.

Other Renaissance bigwigs were the Augsburg-born Hans Holbein the Elder (1465–1524) and his son Hans Holbein the Younger (1497–1543). Father Holbein specialised in altar paintings and portraits. He used a subdued colour palette and presented his objects with great physiognomic detail. The panel paintings in the cathedral of Augsburg rank among his finest accomplishments. His son, one of the last seminal Renaissance painters, built upon his father's approach. He's famous for his portraits, but spent most of his life in England as court painter to King Henry VIII.

Also working in Bavaria was Matthias Grünewald (1480–1528), whose biblical paintings derive their mysticism through use of colour and realistic depiction. One of his best works is the *Lamentation of Christ* in the Stiftskirche in Aschaffenburg.

The brightest star among the Renaissance sculptors was Tilman Riemenschneider (1460–1531). He fell foul of authorities by supporting the peasants in the *Bauernkriege* of 1525, lost his job as mayor and was tossed in jail and tortured. Riemenschneider's greatest skill was in giving stone sculpture qualities resembling wood and in composing scenes with the interplay of light and shadow in mind. Must-sees include the altars in the Herrgottskirche in Creglingen and the Jakobskirche in Rothenburg ob der Tauber, both on the Northern Romantic Road. The Mainfränkisches Museum in Würzburg has a world-class collection of Riemenschneider sculpture.

Baroque & Rococo As with architecture, baroque art pretty much defines Bavaria. It's a style obsessed with detail, but elements are both isolated works and part of a carefully orchestrated overall design. Indeed, architecture, painting, sculpture and other art forms collaborate in creating a 'theatrum sacrum' (sacred theatre), a harmonious stage for legends and biblical scenes. Illusionary effects, the tension of light and shadow, sensual and emotional intensity are all characteristic features.

Two sets of brothers dominated the baroque period in Bavaria: Johann Baptist and Dominikus Zimmermann and Cosmas Damian and Egid Quirin Asam. For more about them, see the special section 'Architecture in Bavaria' in this chapter.

Another outstanding rococo sculptor was Johann Baptist Straub (1704–84). His most important works are his altars, which sport great elegance and an integration of sculpture and painting through such decorative touches as curtains, ornaments and clouds. Great examples are in the Marienmünster in Diessen on the Ammersee, the monastery church in Andechs and the Klosterkirche St Anna in Munich. Ignaz Günther (1725–75)

was one of his students. Look for his sculptures in the Bayerisches Nationalmuseum in Munich as well as in the Basilika St Benedikt in Benediktbeuern.

19th Century The 19th century saw a proliferation of styles, beginning with Romanticism, a movement that placed great emphasis on emotion, dreaminess, spirituality and idealism. In Southern Germany, Austrian-born Moritz von Schwind (1804–1871) was a leading light of the period. A student of Peter Cornelius (1783–1867), he is noted mostly for his moody depictions of scenes from German legend and fairy-tales. Cornelius himself was a follower of the Nazarenes, a group of intensely religious painters who found inspiration in the works of the old masters. His work can be seen in the Ludwigskirche in Munich. The Schack-Galerie, also in Munich, is a great place to get a survey of Romantic art.

By the mid-19th century, Romanticism was gradually supplanted by Realism and, later on, Naturalism, whose practitioners strove to recreate environments – both natural and urban – with meticulous detail. Artists representing this genre include Cologne-born Wilhelm Leibl (1844–1900), who studied in Munich and began as a genre and portrait painter. He later moved to the Bavarian countryside where he found inspiration in the lives of simple country folk. Look for his paintings in Munich's Städtische Gallerie im Lenbachhaus, where you'll also find some early Impressionist works by Lovis Corinth (1858–1925).

The Munich Secession & Jugendstil In the last decade of the 19th century, a group of artists intent on shaking up the art establishment emerged in Munich. In 1892, about 100 of them, including Franz von Stuck (1863–1928), Max Liebermann (1847–1935) and Corinth, split from Munich's Künstlergesellschaft (Artists' Society), a traditionalist organisation led by portrait artist Franz von Lenbach (1836–1904).

Secessionists were not necessarily linked by a common artistic style but by a rejection of reactionary attitudes in the arts academies, which sought to stifle any new forms of expression. They preferred scenes from daily life to historical and religious themes. They shunned the studio in favour of painting al fresco. They strove to erase the distinction between 'high-brow' art like painting and sculpture and 'low-brow' art like pottery or graphics.

Lenbach tried to suppress the Secessionists, but ultimately failed. In 1893 they held their first international exposition. The group was later supported by Georg Hirth, publisher of the magazine *Die Jugend*, founded in 1896, which ultimately lent its name to this new kind of art: *Jugendstil* (Art Nouveau). Jugendstil was a complex new aesthetic, incorporating such applied arts as furniture design, ceramics, textiles and poster art. It was the first 'modern' style and paved the way for the revolutionary artistic developments of the 20th century.

Expressionism One of the styles to grow out of the Secession movement was expressionism. In 1911, Wassily Kandinsky (1866–1944) and Franz Marc (1880–1916) founded the artists' group Der Blaue Reiter (The Blue Rider), which also included Paul Klee (1879–1940) and Gabriele Münter (1877–1962). Members tried to find a purer, freer approach to painting through abstraction, vivid colours and expression.

The hub of the Bavarian expressionist movement was not in Munich, but just south of it in Murnau where Münter had bought a house. Kandinsky joined her for several summers and Franz Marc lived nearby in Kochel am See, where a small museum now presents some of his work. Münter donated her entire collection of expressionist paintings to the Städtische Gallerie im Lenbachhaus.

The famous collection of German expressionists of Lothar Buchheim, author of *Das Boot*, is at the brand-new Museum der Phantasie in Bernried on Lake Starnberg. Here the focus is on works by members of Die Brücke (The Bridge), another artists' group founded in 1905 in Dresden by Karl Schmidt-Rottluff, Ernst Ludwig Kirchner, Erich Heckel and Fritz Bleyl.

Nazi Art Hitler was no great fan of 20th-century painting unless done by himself. In 1937, the Nazis organised an exhibition of *Entartete Kunst* (Degenerate Art) in Munich's Deutsches Haus der Kunst (German House of Art), now simply called Haus der Kunst (see the boxed text 'Degenerate Art'). Leading works of the day were displayed, but most were banned after the exhibition; most of the artists had already fled Germany.

Post-1945 After WWII, Germany's artistic scene was fragmented and the momentum for true revival came from elsewhere. Respected figures such as Kandinsky, Karl Schmidt-Rottluff (1884–1976) and Emil Nolde (1867–1956) returned to Germany to pull the decimated cultural scene back onto its feet. Munich and the rest of Bavaria, however, were soon eclipsed by other German

'Degenerate' Art

Expressionism, surrealism, Dadaism and other modern artistic styles were definitely not Hitler's favourite movements. The Nazis created a popular offensive against such so-called 'Jewish subversion' and 'artistic bolshevism'. This peaked around 1937, when the German term *Entartung* (degeneracy) was borrowed from biology to describe virtually all modern movements. That year, paintings by Klee, Beckmann, Dix and others were exhibited at Munich's Deutsches Haus der Kunst, defaced with signatures in protest.

About 20,000 people visited the exhibition daily, most to frown upon the works. If that wasn't enough, a year later a law allowed for the forced removal of degenerate works from private collections. Many art collectors, however, managed to keep their prized works out of Nazi hands. In Murnau, Gabriele Münter hid her entire collection of her own work, as well as that by other Blue Rider artists like Kandinsky, from the Nazis. But the fate of many other artists' works was less fortunate: although a lot of works were sold abroad to rake in foreign currency, in 1939 about 4000 paintings were burned publicly in Berlin and lost forever.

Anthony Haywood

cities, including Cologne, Düsseldorf and Hamburg, as centres of artistic renewal.

One modern genre that has found major representation in Bavaria is concrete art, even if its practitioners are usually not Bavarians. Concrete art emerged in the 1950s and basically takes abstract art to its extreme, rejecting any natural form or emotional representation and using only planes and colours. The French-Hungarian, Victor Vasarely (born 1908) is a major international artist; notable Germans include Adolf Fleischmann (1892–1968), Richard Paul Lohse (1902–88) and Camille Graeser (1892–1980). The Museum für Konkrete Kunst in Ingolstadt and the Sammlung Ruppert at the Kulturspeicher in Würzburg both have excellent collections.

Music

Early Music The church was the focal point of early German music. The *Lied* (song) describes a variety of popular styles sung as marching tunes or to celebrate victory or work. These later divided into *Volkslieder* (folk songs) and *Kunstlieder* (artistic songs). Among the latter were religious songs, such as the *Marienlied*, which had a mixture of German and Latin lyrics.

From 1100–1300, the *Hof* (court) was the focus of music. *Minnesang*, as the new style was called, had Moorish origins and was imported from southern France and Spain. These love ballads praised the women of the court, and were often performed by knights. The most famous minstrel of the time was Walther von der Vogelweide (c. 1170–1230), whose work has been recorded by modern artists.

Around the 15th century the troubadour tradition was adopted by a class of burghers who earned a living from music and were often tradesmen on the side. They established schools and guilds, and created strict musical forms. Their model was the tradesmen's guild, with *Altmeister* and *Jungmeister* (old and young masters). To become a *Meistersinger*, a performer had to pass a test and bring something new to melody and lyric. One famous Meistersinger, Hans Sachs (1494–1576), was the subject of a Richard Wagner opera, *Die Meistersinger von Nürnberg*, in the 19th century.

Renaissance & Baroque Orlandi di Lasso (1532–94) was one of the most important and versatile composers of the late Renaissance. Born in Belgium, he first went to Italy, then took a job at the Munich court of Duke Albrecht V. Here, he started out as a singer before being promoted to director of the court orchestra. His impressive body of about 2000 compositions ranges from church masses to motets (polyphonic sacred songs) to madrigals (love poems set to music) and French chansons.

The pre-Bach baroque period brought Nuremberg-born composer and organist Johann Pachelbel (1653–1706), who is most renowned for his harmonious and surprisingly playful fugues, organ chorales and toccatas. From 1695 onward he worked as chief organist in the Sebalduskirche in Nuremberg.

Christoph Willibald Ritter von Gluck (1714–87) went down in music history as a reformer of baroque opera. He essentially turned upside-down the reigning concept of opera (flashy theatricality at the expense of a meaningful plot), which was then popular in Italy and France. *Iphigenia in Tauris* (1779) is considered his masterpiece. Though not too well received in his lifetime, Gluck greatly influenced later composers, including Mozart and Wagner.

Romanticism Franz Liszt (1811–86) was a Hungarian-born pianist, composer and music director, who is most noted for creating a complex approach to music for the piano by using the full scale in new and innovative ways. The father-in-law of Richard Wagner, who married his daughter Cosima, he died in Bayreuth while attending the Richard Wagner Festival.

Richard Wagner (1813–83) was the most influential German composer of the 19th century. He balanced all the components of operatic form to produce the Gesamtkunstwerk (complete work of art). Strongly influenced by Beethoven and Mozart, he's most famous for his operas, many of which deal with mythological themes (*Der Ring des Nibelungen, Lohengrin, Tristan und Isolde*, etc), which made him popular with the Nazis. Also see the boxed text 'Richard Wagner' in the Franconia chapter.

20th Century Wagner in turn influenced and inspired Munich-born Richard Strauss (1864–1949), who lived, part-time, in Garmisch-Partenkirchen during his later life and also died there. Strauss created some famous symphonies like *Don Juan* and *Macbeth*, whose expressiveness helped pave the way for modern orchestral arrangements. He later focused on operas, the most successful of which – such as *Elektra* and *Der Rosenkavalier* (The Knight of the Rose) – were collaborations with the writer Hugo von Hofmannsthal.

Carl Orff (1895–1982) is another 20th-century Bavarian composer. Born in Munich, he began his career as a reformer of music education but then jumped into the limelight as the composer of the life-embracing cantata *Carmina Burana* (see the boxed text 'Carmina Burana' in the Upper Bavaria chapter). Simple harmonies, rhythms and hypnotically repetitive tonal arrangements are some of his hallmarks.

Werner Egk (1901–83), who was born Werner Mayer near Donauwörth on the Romantic Road, was a student of Orff's. Egk's professional breakthrough came in 1935 with the opera *The Magic Violin*. He stayed in Germany during WWII, holding such positions as conductor of the Berlin State Opera and chairman of the Composers Board at the Reich Music Chamber. After the war, he wrote numerous ballets such as *Abraxas* (1948) and operas such as *Der Revisor* (1957). From 1954 to 1974, he staged his work at the Bayerische Staatsoper.

Traditional Volksmusik No other musical genre is as closely associated with Bavaria as the Volksmusik (folk music). Every village has its own proud brass band and the state government puts serious euros towards the cultivation and preservation of traditional music. In this predominantly conservative society, clinging to ancient customs has always been a means to keep

alive the spirit of 'simpler times' and the values and ideology that existed in those days. Although it's more common in the Alpine and pre-Alpine regions, Franconia and Swabia also have their own musical traditions. Folk music is often practiced by amateurs or semi-pros, but there are of course numerous professional groups and soloists as well.

Modern Volksmusik In the 1970s and 1980s, a new style of Volksmusik emerged on the small stages of Munich, such as one at the Fraunhofer pub (see Places to Eat in the Munich chapter). Performers took the traditional folklore concept to new lengths. They gave it a political edge, freed it from conservative ideology and created new interpretations by fusing it with folk music from other countries – Ireland to Ghana. Among the pioneers was a band called the Biermösl Blosn, known for its satirical and often provocative songs. Other groups are the Fraunhofer Saitenmusik, Rudi Zapf and the Guglhupfa.

More recently, the scene has gone another step further by creating bizarre crossovers of Volksmusik with pop, rock, punk, hip hop and techno in what some have termed 'New Alpine Wave'. Look for the folk rockers Hundsbuam Miserablige, avant-garde folk artist Haindling (also known as Hans-Jürgen Buchner) and the hardcore folk punk band Attwenger. Another successful Bavarian-bred band is the Banana Fishbones from Bad Tölz, which plays a unique but eminently listenable mix of country and western, alternative rock, indie, pop and folk.

Literature
The earliest form of German literature was an oral tribal tradition based on an epic deed. During Charlemagne's reign (c. 800) educated clerical figures diligently recorded what remained of the oral tradition, giving us the *Hildebrandslied* (810–20), a father-son epic with shades of the Oedipus myth, and the *Wessobrunner Gebet* (Wessobrunn Prayer; 770–90). Christian and Teutonic traditions were sometimes combined, as in the

Ludwigslied, which celebrates victory over the Normans, or *Heiland*, a story about Christ in which Jesus is recast as a tribal leader.

The latter Middle Ages generated a handful of works which, in the 19th century, would inspire several Richard Wagner operas. The most famous of these is the *Nibelungenlied*, an anonymous epic, which draws heavily on Germanic mythology. Wolfram von Eschenbach's (c. 1170–1220) *Parzival* deals with the themes of mortal beings, God and compassion, while Gottfried von Strassburg's (c. 1200) *Tristan und Isolde* tells of a rarefied illicit love that clashes with social custom, belief and the heroes' duty.

Other medieval literary forms are the Minnesang and the Meistergesang. Since both forms are set to music, they are covered in the earlier Music section.

During the baroque era, the so-called *Jesuitendrama* was a major form of 'entertainment'. These were basically religious propaganda productions in the service of the Counter-Reformation. Highly stylised dramas, they made frequent use of allegories, prologues, epilogues and choir scenes. A prominent dramatist was Jakob Bidermann (1578–1602) whose most famous work, *Cenodoxus* (1602), retells the legend of St Bruno.

During the Romantic Age, the Franconian Jean Paul (1763–1825), whose real name was Johann Paul Friedrich Richter, wrote novels which often have a whimsical, sentimental edge. Ernst Theodor Amadeus Hoffmann (1776–1822), who began his career more or less by accident in Bamberg, is best known for his bizarre tales. His *Mademoiselle de Scudérie* is considered the forerunner of the mystery genre.

Ludwig Ganghofer (1855–1920) was a master of the Bavarian *Heimatroman*, sentimental and romantic plays and novels that naively glorify the simple country life. They're still quite popular today among the older generations and some have been made into movies.

In the late 19th century, Munich became a hotbed of creativity. In parallel to the Secession of the painting world, writers now shunned the lofty Romanticism in favour of a more realistic, often politically engaged tone.

The hottest publication of the time was *Simplicissimus*, a satirical magazine with a symbol of a red bulldog. All the big Munich names contributed, including the ones mentioned later in this section. Many of the essays exposed the hypocrisy of society during the reign of Kaiser Wilhelm II, which resulted in censorship and even landed a couple of writers in jail.

One of them was Frank Wedekind (1864–1918), a dramatist, lyricist and storyteller who, besides writing for *Simplicissimus*, also acted and directed in Munich. He's best known for the coming of age tale *Spring Awakening* (1891) and for *Pandora's Box* (1904).

Jakob Wassermann (1873–1934) was one of the most popular novelists in the early 20th century. Many of his works deal with the search for a Jewish identity, although he is perhaps best known for his fairly sentimental telling of the Kaspar Hauser story (see the boxed text 'Kaspar Hauser: The Child from the Void' in the Franconia chapter). Not surprisingly the Nazis outlawed his writing.

Ludwig Thoma (1867–1921), a lawyer from Dachau, was another leading satirist whose rather harmless parodies of Bavarian village life ruffled the feathers of his countrymen. Major works include *Lausbubengeschichten*, funny stories about a lazy boy.

Thomas Mann (1875–1955) spent about 40 years of his life in Munich, where he wrote a pile of acclaimed works, including the novella *Gladius Dei* (1902), which opens with the words: 'Munich Shone', a phrase still exploited by marketing people today (see the boxed text 'Thomas Mann & the Nazis').

Karl Valentin (1882–1967) was a screenwriter, stage comedian and film maker whose visual style was similar to Charlie Chaplin's, although the written jokes tended to be heavy going.

A major important Bavarian-born writer who went on to gain international fame is Bertolt Brecht (1896–1956). For more about his career and influence, see the

Karl Valentin, Germany's Charlie Chaplin.

boxed text 'Bertolt Brecht' in the Allgäu-Bavarian Swabia chapter.

One of the few modern Bavarian writers known outside Germany is Oskar Maria Graf (1894–1967). His most famous novel *We are Prisoners* captures the sense of disillusionment (and confusion) felt by many towards the German authorities between the world wars. His books weren't banned by the Nazis in 1933, although Graf (always the wit) commented that they deserved to be.

After WWII, writers throughout Germany either went into 'inner emigration', such as Hans Carossa and Ernst Wiechert, or tried to participate in a progressive attempt at political and intellectual renewal. The latter formed the Gruppe 47, a circle of writers, whose Munich-based members included Ilse Aichinger (1921–), her husband Günter Eich (1907–72) and Wolfgang Koeppen (1906–96).

Cinema

The Bavarians played an important role in the early development of German film. Comedian Karl Valentin set up his own makeshift studio near the Hofbräuhaus in 1912 and produced the first of 50 films made during his lifetime. Although Berlin was Germany's undisputed film capital in the 1920s, talent and money flowed into Munich as well, thanks to the excellent technical facilities at the Bavarian Film Studios, founded in 1919. Its first production was *Der Ochsenkrieg* (Oxen War), a sentimental drama based on a novel by Ludwig Ganghofer.

Most directors from this period have been forgotten today, with the exception of a then unknown, young English director. Unable to raise funds for his projects in London, Alfred Hitchcock came to Munich in 1925 and quickly found local backers for his first film *The Pleasure Garden*; a year later *The Mountain Eagle* hit the big screen. But the early promise of the industry wasn't born out; Munich's artistic scene dulled at the end of the decade and many of its leading lights left for Berlin. In the 1930s, the studios (located in the southern Munich suburb of Geiselgasteig) were pressed into service for Third Reich propaganda. Its buildings were severely damaged during WWII.

Munich benefited from the isolation of the big Berlin studios during the Cold War. Refurbished in the late 1950s, Bavaria became a laboratory studio for young German writer-directors on slim budgets. It wasn't long, however, before Munich began to lure big-name international directors and actors. Richard Fleischer's sweepingly photographed epic *The Vikings* (1958) was shot here with a star-studded cast including Kirk Douglas and Tony Curtis. Billy Wilder finished his comedy epic *One, Two, Three* in Munich when the building of the Berlin Wall in 1961 fouled up on-location shooting. Dirk Bogarde, Gregory Peck, Burt Lancaster, Liz Taylor and Richard Burton were other household names immortalised on celluloid here. Sci-fi fans will fondly remember the low-budget TV series *The Adventures of Space Patrol Orion*, Germany's answer to *Star Trek*, which emerged at the Geiselgasteig.

[Continued on page 42]

COLIN JAMES MARSH

WAYNE WALTON

Top: The baroque brilliance of the Käppele near Würzburg, Franconia

Bottom: A rococo facade in Freising, north of Munich

JEREMY GRAY

JEREMY GRAY

Top: Munich's ultra-modern Hypovereinsbank building

Bottom: Olympiapark with its transparent tent-like roof and the Olympiastadium – home to the 1972 Olympic Games

Architecture in Bavaria

NOTABLE BUILDINGS IN BAVARIA

SAXONY-ANHALT

THURINGIA

HESSE

SAXONY

CZECH REPUBLIC

Kloster Banz

Kloster Ebrach

Basilika Vierzehnheiligen

Plassenberg

Schloss Johannisburg

Coburg

Hof

Neue Residenz, Dom & Altes Rathaus

Staffelstein

Lichtenfels

Kulmbach

Schweinfurt

Aschaffenburg

Bayreuth

Markgräfliches Opernhaus

Residenz, Dom St Kilian, Neumünster & Festung Marienberg

Ebrach

Bamberg

Pommersfelden

Schloss Weissenstein

Würzburg

Weiden

Frauenkirche, St Sebalduskirche & Nazi Party Rally Grounds

Erlangen

Burg Prunn

Fürth

Nuremberg

Dom St Peter, Basilika St Emmeram, Schottenkirche St Jakob & Walhalla

Residenz Ansbach

Schwabach

Ansbach

BADEN-WÜRTTEMBERG

Dinkelsbühl

Kloster Weltenburg

Münster St Georg

Regensburg

Harburg

Kelheim

Straubing

Deggendorf

St Jakobskirche & Ursulinekirche

Harburg

Residenzschloss

Neuburg

Ingolstadt

Passau

Asamkirche Maria de Victoria

Landshut

St Martinskirche & Stadtresidenz

Rathaus, St-Anna-Kirche & Fuggerei

Augsburg

Freising

Dom Sts Maria and Korbinian

Carthusian Monastery

Buxheim

Memmingen

Ottobeuren

Kaufbeuren

Dachau

Schleissheim

MUNICH

Monastery Church

Diessen

Lake Starnberg

Neues Schloss Schleissheim

AUSTRIA

Marienmünster

Kempten

Altenstadt

Bernried

Schongau

Rosenheim

Chiemsee

Torhalle & Schloss Herrenchiemsee

Basilika St Michael

Lindau

Oberammergau

Museum der Phantasie

Schwangau

Linderhof

Ettal

Garmisch-Partenkirchen

Schloss Neuschwanstein & Schloss Hohenschwanstein

Wieskirche

LIECHTENSTEIN

Schloss Linderhof

Kloster Ettal

Alte Pinakothek, Amalienburg, Asamkirche, Bavarian State Library, Feldherrnhalle, Frauenkirche, Fünf Höfe, Gasteig, Hypovereinsbank, Klosterkirche St Anna,

Königsplatz, Ludwigskirche, Michaelskirche, Müllersches Volksbad, Neues Rathaus, Odeonsplatz, Peterskirche, Residenz & Schloss Nymphenburg

AUSTRIA

SWITZERLAND

ITALY

0   25   50km
0   15   30mi

ARCHITECTURE IN BAVARIA

Visitors to Bavaria are often surprised by the number of fine buildings that survived the ravages of wartime bombing. Many damaged buildings were restored, others so painstakingly reconstructed as to defy the believability of pictures of the ruins. This section explains the many styles you'll find.

Early Styles

The Romans founded cities such as Augsburg, Passau and Regensburg, but very little of their architecture survives even in those places. There are also some ruins of a **Roman bath** in Schwangau in the Allgäu.

The Dark Ages ended with the arrival of Charlemagne. Architecture from the period of his dynasty's reign (roughly from 750 to 1024) is called Carolingian and is loosely based on styles and techniques used in Italy. In Bavaria, only the **Torhalle**, built by Ludwig der Deutsche around 860 on the Fraueninsel in the Chiemsee, survives from this age.

Romanesque

The main influences of the Romanesque era (about 1000 to 1250) were Carolingian, Roman and Byzantine. Romanesque churches are characterised by thick walls, closely spaced columns and heavy, rounded arches; they're sometimes adorned with statues and reliefs on the portals.

Many of Bavaria's houses of worship have Romanesque origins, but most have since been severely altered. The purest example of this style is the **Basilika St Michael** in Altenstadt near Schongau on the southern section of the Romantic Road. The northern portal of the **Schottenkirche St Jakob** in Regensburg is outstanding for its detailed and mysterious iconography. Also of note is the crypt of the **Dom Sts Maria and Korbinian** in Freising.

Gothic

Title page: Walhalla – a hall of fame glorifying past famous men and women of Germany, above the banks of the Danube. (photograph by Andrea Schulte-Peevers)

Inset photograph by Andrea Schulte-Peevers

In the 13th century, the Romanesque style gradually gave way to Gothic, which originated in the Île de France (near Paris) but was slow in reaching Germany. The epitome of Gothic architecture is the grand cathedral, which usually has a floor plan shaped like a cross. The central nave is flanked by one or two aisles and bisected by a transept beyond which is the choir, the holiest part of the church, with the main (high) altar.

Other typical elements include soaring ceilings supported by pillars and columns; ribbed vaults and stained-glass windows. Hall churches, where the aisles have the same height as the nave, appeared in the late Gothic period (from about 1400).

One of the most famous Gothic architects was Hans von Burghausen (1360–1432), who designed Landshut's impressive **St Martinskirche**. The largest Bavarian hall church is the **Frauenkirche** in Nuremberg, which also boasts the oldest Gothic church on Bavarian soil, the **St Sebalduskirche**. The **Münster St Georg** in Dinkelsbühl and the **Dom St Peter** in Regensburg are both wonderfully pure examples of the style. Munich's **Frauenkirche** was the last major Gothic church built in Bavaria.

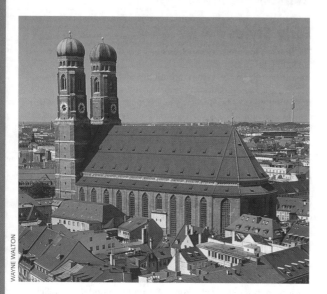

WAYNE WALTON

Renaissance

The Renaissance gradually supplanted the Gothic style starting in the mid-16th century, about 100 years after it had begun to flourish in Italy. Initially, the new style was limited to embellishing the facades of existing structures with such elements as rectangular windows, ornamented step gables and round arches. Only in the early 17th century were entire palaces, mansions and residences built in Renaissance style. One of its hallmarks was the arcaded courtyard, excellent examples of which survive in the Beautiful Courtyard of Kulmbach's **Plassenberg** and in the **Stadtresidenz** in Landshut.

Other Renaissance palaces include the formidable **Schloss Johannisburg** in Aschaffenburg and the **Residenzschloss** in Neuburg an der Donau. In Augsburg, master architect Elias Holl created the beautifully symmetrical **Rathaus** (town hall). Also in Augsburg is the **Fuggerkapelle**

Above: The landmark 99m-tall towers of Frauenkirche – the last major Gothic church built in Munich

inside the St-Anna-Kirche, which is the oldest nonsecular Renaissance structure in Germany. The most famous Renaissance church is the **Michaelskirche** in Munich, which also has a few baroque elements.

Baroque & Rococo

No style is as intimately linked with Bavaria as the baroque and its later derivative, the rococo, which flourished from about 1650 to 1750. The Counter-Reformation followed the devastation of the Thirty Years' War, and for the rejuvenated Catholic Church the baroque became somewhat of a propaganda tool, a means by which to reassert and celebrate the 'true faith'.

Baroque architecture marries structure, sculpture, stucco, ornamentation and fresco paintings into a single *Gesamtkunstwerk* (complete work of art). It had its origin in the Italy of the early 1600s; the Roman architect and sculptor, Lorenzo Bernini, is widely credited as being the 'father of the baroque'.

Compared to the simple harmony idealised in the Renaissance, the detail-oriented baroque is an exuberant and dramatic style. Meaning literally 'irregular pearl', it's dynamic, full of passion and pathos. Rigid lines are replaced by curves, bows, and arcs, as though constant breezes somehow swept the room, billowing the robes of saints and caressing the locks of cherubs. There is a sense of weightlessness and reaching towards an infinite sky.

An unprecedented construction boom began around 1680, blanketing the region – especially Upper Bavaria – with new churches and monasteries. At the same time, existing churches in older styles were painstakingly outfitted with stucco ornamentation, frescoes, paintings and other decorative, and increasingly flamboyant, flourishes.

Techniques

Fresco painting and stucco sculpture are the two hallmarks of baroque art and architecture. Both required extraordinary skill and talent, not to mention a steady hand, extensive knowledge of biblical and mythological imagery and a lively imagination.

To create a fresco, artists had to paint straight onto freshly applied lime plaster, working fast and with great precision. As the plaster dried, the water-based colours united with the base. Corrections could only be made by chiselling off the plaster, reapplying and repainting it. Imagine the pressure!

In most cases, assistants would prepare an area only big enough to be painted the same day. The artists worked straight from their paper outlines with only minimal orientation lines while lying on their backs atop a scaffold.

Stucco consists of gypsum, chalk and sand which, if mixed with water, become an easily mouldable dough that hardens quickly. It has been used for decorative purposes since antiquity but reached the zenith of its popularity during the baroque period. Any kind of shape could be fashioned from stucco: pudgy cherubs to fragile garlands to full-sized statues. Some frequently reused shapes were created from moulds and templates. But the larger pieces, such as sculptures of saints or angels, all had to be custom-made by hand. Artists usually built a frame of wood, covered it with straw and then applied several layers of stucco upon that.

The Baroque All-Stars
The leading lights of the baroque/rococo period were mostly home-grown artists and architects (presented here in order of their birth, not importance).

Dientzenhofer Brothers
The four brothers Dientzenhofer were mostly active in Bamberg and surroundings, but also in Bohemia (today's Czech Republic). They were: Georg (1643–89), Christoph (1655–1722), Leonhard (1660–1707) and Johann (1663–1726). A major patron was Bamberg's Prince-Bishop Lothar von Schönborn whom they helped to turn the city into a baroque showpiece; Leonhard was the lead architect of the biggest project here, the **Neue Residenz**. Johann designed **Schloss Weissenstein** and **Kloster Ebrach** (see Around Bamberg in the Franconia chapter), while the two collaborated on **Kloster Banz** (see Around Coburg in the Franconia chapter).

Zimmermann Brothers
Dominikus Zimmermann (1685–1766) was one of the period's most accomplished architects. His crowning achievement is the **Wieskirche** near Oberammergau, a collaboration with his brother, Johann Baptist (1680–1758), a stucco and fresco artist. Dominikus' genius lay in his ability to create perfectly proportioned halls, where each sculpture, altar, pillar or painting – created by his brother – plays its essential role in creating an effect of complete visual harmony.

The **Carthusian Monastery** in Buxheim near Memmingen is another collaboration. Johann Baptist's work can also be seen in **Schloss Nymphenburg**, the **Peterskirche** and the **Neues Schloss Schleissheim**, all in Munich, as well as in the **Kloster Ettal** near Oberammergau and the **Freising cathedral**.

Asam Family
The brothers Cosmas Damian (1686–1739) and Egid Quirin (1692–1750) Asam were arguably the finest and most prolific team of rococo artists to work in Bavaria. While Cosmas Damian was first and foremost a fresco painter and architect, Eqid Quirin earned his money as a stucco artist and sculptor. Both studied with their father, Hans Georg Asam (1649–1711), himself quite an accomplished fresco artist who, among other places, painted the Basilika St Benedikt in Tegernsee. Cosmas Damian later solidified his studies in Rome, while his brother completed an apprenticeship in Munich.

Thanks to their supreme talent and aided by their family's connections with the Benedictine order, the brothers were soon swamped with work. Both took on jobs on their own, but it's their collaborations that are the most awe-inspiring: the monastery church at **Kloster Weltenburg** at Kelheim in the Altmühltal, the **Asamkirche** in Munich, the **Asamkirche Maria de Victoria assembly hall** in Ingolstadt, the **Basilika St Emmeram** in Regensburg and the **St Jakobskirche** in Straubing.

Balthasar Neumann

Neumann (1687–1753) was the main architect of the Schönborn dynasty of prince-bishops in Würzburg for whom he designed the **Residenz**, his undisputed masterpiece and Unesco World Heritage Listed site. Neumann translated his talent and extraordinary vision into rooms of amazingly rhythmic, harmonious proportions; they're often canopied by vast vaulted ceilings that seem to float without visible support – as if suspended from heaven. The masterful pilgrimage church **Vierzehnheiligen** (see Around Coburg in the Franconia chapter) is another knockout.

JEREMY GRAY

Johann Michael Fischer

Fischer (1692–1766) trained as a mason but soon developed into one of the eminent church architects in Munich and surroundings. His body of work includes the superb **Marienmünster** in Diessen am Ammersee, the **Klosterkirche St Anna im Lehel** in Munich and the **monastery church** in Ottobeuren in the Allgäu.

François Cuvilliés

The 'vertically challenged' Frenchman Cuvilliés (1695–1768) actually began his career as a court jester to Elector Maximilian in 1707. The ruler, however, soon recognised his artistic talent and sent him to Paris to study the latest trends in art and architecture. He returned with a

Above: The baroque Residenz, in Würzburg, by architect Balthasar Neumann

distinctive rococo style and was a jester no longer. His main works are the Rich Rooms and the theatre inside the **Munich Residenz** and the **Amalienburg** in the park of that city's Schloss Nymphenburg.

Neoclassicism & Revivalism

In the late 18th century, baroque flamboyance was replaced by the strict geometry of neoclassicism. Columns, pediments, domes and restrained ornamentation became the dominant architectural features. Most structures in this style are public buildings such as museums, theatres or libraries.

In Bavaria, neoclassicism really only made major inroads in Munich, where King Ludwig I envisioned his version of Athens. For this, he pressed into service the two defining architects of the age, Leo von Klenze (1784–1865) and Friedrich von Gärtner (1791–1847).

Klenze's most impressive ensemble is the **Königsplatz**, for which he drew inspiration from Greek temples, as well as the **Alte Pinakothek museum** and the Festsaalbau sections of the **Residenz**. Klenze also designed the buildings around **Odeonsplatz** and some along the Ludwigsstrasse north of here. Here he was aided by Gärtner, who contributed the **Feldherrnhalle** as well the main university building, the **Siegestor**, the **Bavarian State Library** and the **Ludwigskirche**. Klenze's best-known work outside of Munich is the **Walhalla 'Hall of Fame'** near Regensburg, which resembles his Ruhmeshalle in Munich.

Revivalism

In the late 19th century, as society was changing and industrialisation increasingly took hold (albeit to a lesser extent in Bavaria), architectural innovation entered a vacuum. For a brief period, architects simply recycled earlier styles, sometimes even blending several together into an aesthetic hotch-potch. The most famous examples of this style are the castles of King Ludwig II, especially the neogothic **Schloss Neuschwanstein** and the neorococo **Schloss Linderhof**, as well as the neogothic **Neue Rathaus** in Munich.

The 20th Century

The first step on the road to modernism was taken by the artists and architects of the Art Nouveau movement (known as *Jugendstil* in German) around the turn of the 20th century. It's a complex, largely decorative style that overlaps with applied arts and design. The Munich Jugendstil is quite subdued, with much of it limited to facade decorations such as abstractions of natural forms and shapes as well as representations of animals and faces. Examples concentrate in the districts of Schwabing and Bogenhausen. The **Müllersches Volksbad** in Haidhausen is a wonderful Art Nouveau swimming pool; another one is the **Altes Stadtbad** in Augsburg.

GREG GAWLOWSKI

If Jugendstil was playful and frilly, Nazi architecture was the exact opposite: pompous and monumental. In Bavaria, the best examples of this style – of which hardly anything survived Allied bombing – are the **party rally grounds** in Nuremberg designed by Hitler's main architect, Albert Speer. Speer also designed the **Berchtesgaden train station**.

After Hitler, it took German architects a few years to plug back into the world scene. Postwar reconstruction demanded cheap buildings that could be erected quickly. In Bavaria, modernism never made a big splash, with a few notable exceptions.

One of the finest postwar constructions is unquestionably Günter Behnisch's expressionist modern **Olympiastadion** (Olympic Stadium) in Munich with its distinctive 'tent roof' by Frei Otto. Behnisch also designed the **Museum der Phantasie**, which opened on Lake Starnberg in 2001. Other modern and sometimes controversial buildings include the **Gasteig**, the **Hypovereinsbank** and the **Fünf Höfe shopping complex**, all in Munich.

Above: The Neuschwanstein Castle, nestled amongst trees 200m above the valley below.

[Continued from page 32]

During the 1970s, the 'New German Cinema' emerged under the leadership of Rainer Werner Fassbinder, Werner Herzog, Wim Wenders and Volker Schlöndorff, who all produced a number of acclaimed films and TV series in Munich. As a result, the city became known (within Germany at any rate) as 'Hollywood on the Isar'. Bob Fosse made his first appearance here with the Oscar-winning *Cabaret* (1972), and Monty Python also worked in Munich.

But the real breakthrough onto the international film scene came with Wolfgang Petersen's *Das Boot*, the epic submarine drama set during WWII. It was one of the most elaborate and expensive German productions ever, and much of the set has been preserved in Bavaria. Petersen's success led to other international hits such as *The Never-Ending Story* (1984), *Enemy Mine* (1985) and *Stalingrad* (1993). Many made-for-TV films and popular German soaps such as *Marienhof* and *Berliner Strasse* are also produced at the Geiselgasteig.

SOCIETY & CONDUCT
Traditional Culture

There are few places in the world where tradition plays as great a role in everyday life as in Bavaria. In 1984 the Bavarian government even added an article to its constitution 'to protect the state's natural environment and cultural heritage'. The government also spends several million euro each year on *Heimatpflege* (heritage preservation) and, since 1988, has made the teaching of Bavarian culture part of the school curriculum.

Especially in the rural areas of Upper and Eastern Bavaria, people do indeed take their traditions very seriously. Many of them belong to *Heimatverbände* (heritage associations), music or folkloric groups. Many in these regions celebrate their history in elaborate festivals, such as the Landshut Wedding or the Rothenburger Reichsstadttage. And they dress in folkloric garments called a *Tracht*; not for the tourists but because it's something they value.

The Tracht is really a total ensemble. Typical elements for men include lederhosen, worn with a shirt made of cotton or linen and combined with either a long or short jacket ('Janker' or 'Joppe').

For women there's the dirndl – usually a combination of skirt, bosom-accentuating bodice, petticoat, blouse and apron.

In the Alpine regions, the men's Tracht ensemble can be traced to the garments worn by hunters, whereas the outfits in Franconia have evolved from military uniforms. Swabians also have their own unique Tracht.

Thomas Mann & the Nazis

Born in the northern German town of Lübeck in 1875, Mann moved to Munich in 1893 and promptly fell in love with the city, writing volumes of work (including his celebrated *Death in Venice*) there before his departure 40 years later. Like countless other artists, poets and bohemians, Mann lived in Schwabing, where he also contributed to the satirical periodical *Simplicissimus* in the 1890s. By the time he won the Nobel Prize for literature in 1929, Mann was lionised as a cultural icon.

Yet Mann's attitude towards his adopted home had soured. In 1926, he decried its 'anti-Semitic nationalism' and condemned Munich as 'notorious in Germany and beyond, as a stronghold of reaction and a seat of obduracy and intractability'.

In the spring of 1933, the Third Reich banned the books of hundreds of authors, and Mann wisely stayed in Switzerland after a lecture tour. His Bogenhausen villa (which was at No 10 in the street now called Thomas-Mann-Strasse) was confiscated, and Mann and his wife sought refuge in the USA. In exile, Mann became the torchbearer for many Germans emigres, publishing numerous articles and protests against the Hitler regime. It wasn't until 1949 that he returned for the last time to Munich, briefly, for a reception held in his honour.

Jeremy Gray

The Lore & Lure of Lederhosen

Nothing sets off a great pair of legs quite like lederhosen. And with the possible exception of beer, there's very little so completely and unmistakably Bavarian.

Leather was the material of choice for the work clothes of medieval farmers because animal hides were usually in good supply. Hunters wore them also. But it wasn't until the 19th century that these workmen's clothing became socially acceptable among the higher-ups. The first to popularise them was none other than King Ludwig I who trotted them out as a fashion statement in the 1830s.

A handmade pair of lederhosen is made from 'wild' leather, preferably from deer or mountain goat. The 'fleshy' side faces the inside of the garment, while the 'hairy' outside is specially tanned so the leather can breathe. A high-quality, custom-tailored pair of deer lederhosen can cost €500 and way upwards from there; goat pants start at about half that. Mass-produced, off-the-rack versions still start at a hefty €150.

Like Scottish tartans, lederhosen have a lot to do with people's sense of identity. You can actually tell which valley someone is from by examining the embroidery. If they're from Miesbach, for instance, it's yellow. If they're from the Tegernsee, a few kilometres south, it's green. Tribalism at its most pronounced.

Do's & Don'ts

Bavarians dress quite conservatively, though not necessarily formally. In business situations or at certain social events, such as opera and theatre performances, you will probably feel more comfortable if slightly dressed up. Chic clothing is compulsory to get into Munich nightclubs.

If you're invited to someone's home, ask if there's anything you could bring. Even if the answer is no, it's still nice to arrive clutching some flowers or a bottle of wine. After a dinner party, call the next day or send a little thank you note.

At the start of a meal it is customary to say *'Guten Appetit'* (the closest equivalent in Anglo-Saxon countries is the French 'Bon Appetit') with a look around at your tablemates. Saying nothing, or digging in before everyone has been served, is considered bad manners. Before clinking glasses, the usual toast is *'prost'* (cheers) with beer or *Zum Wohl* (to your health) with wine.

Shaking hands is common among both men and women, as is a hug or a kiss on the cheek, especially among young people. When making a phone call, give your name (eg, 'Smith, Grüss Gott') at the start. Not doing so is considered impolite.

Like elsewhere in Germany, great importance is placed on the formal 'Sie' form of address, especially in business situations. Among younger people and in social settings, though, people are much more relaxed about 'Sie' and 'du'.

Academic titles (Herr or Frau Doktor) are important. If someone introduces herself as Dr Schmidt, that's what she wants to be called. If you have a title yourself, you may of course insist on it as well; this can be useful in situations where you want the extra respect.

It *is* OK to mention the war, if done with tact and relevance. After all, a lot of people you will meet will have grown up demanding explanations. What causes offence is a 'victor' mentality, which is perceived as righteous and gloating, or the concept that fascist ideas are intrinsically German.

On the whole, Bavarians are not prudish. Nude bathing and mixed saunas are commonplace. Nude bathing areas are marked FKK, or form spontaneously in certain areas on beaches or the shores of lakes.

RELIGION

Given its monastic origins, it's no surprise that Bavaria is staunchly Catholic. The Reformation didn't make great inroads, and at the last census some 67% of the state's residents were registered as Roman Catholic and 24% as Protestant. The latter are more prevalent in Franconia and, to a lesser extent, in Swabia. Upper and Eastern Bavaria are overwhelmingly Catholic.

The distinction between church and state is a bit more blurred in Bavaria than in the rest of Germany. Church representatives are members of the Broadcast Council, various advisory and planning boards on the state, regional and district levels; and social welfare commissions, among others.

Most Bavarians pay a 'church tax' amounting to 10% of their income tax. Some of the money goes towards supporting church charities and institutions such as kindergartens.

The tax isn't obligatory, but you must formally leave the church if you don't want to pay. This is still a social taboo in Bavaria, although not in other German states.

LANGUAGE

Bavarian is one of the most distinctive of the German dialects and its unique vocabulary, grammar and pronunciation are often hard to understand even for fluent German speakers. In addition, the Franconians and the Swabians each have their own dialect. What complicates matters further is that which seems to be a unified dialect to outsiders, is actually a patchwork of countless micro-dialects, which may vary from valley to valley. Fortunately for the rest of the world, practically all Bavarians speak and understand High German (and many speak some English as well).

For pronunciation details and useful phrases, see the Language chapter at the back of this book. The glossary, also at the back, contains some common German words.

Facts for the Visitor

HIGHLIGHTS
There is a wealth of wonderful places to see, explore and experience during your visit to Bavaria. Here are a few suggestions to steer you towards the highlights, although we hope that you'll also make your own personal favourite discoveries (and maybe even write to us about them).

Castles & Palaces
With castles of all periods and styles, Bavaria is a great place to indulge in fairy-tale fantasies. Places worth seeking out include Neuschwanstein and Hohenschwangau near Füssen; Schloss Linderhof near Oberammergau; Herrenchiemsee in Lake Chiemsee; the Würzburg Residenz; Rosenberg fortress in Kronach and the Plassenburg in Kulmbach, both near Bayreuth; the Residenz and Schloss Nymphenburg in Munich; the Burg in Burghausen; the Residenz Ansbach; the Kaiserburg in Nuremberg; Schloss Weissenstein near Bamberg; the fortress in Coburg; the Veste Oberhaus in Passau; and the Neues Schloss in Oberschleissheim.

Museums & Galleries
Bavaria is a museum lovers' dream. There are literally hundreds of such historical repositories displaying the entire gamut of trinkets, from the exquisite to the mundane. Fine arts aficionados won't want to leave without dropping in at the Munich trio of Pinakothek museums, not to mention the Städtische Gallerie im Lenbachhaus and many other smaller galleries. WWII buffs will be fascinated by the new Dokumentation Obersalzberg in Berchtesgaden and the Dokumentationszentrum in Nuremberg.

For an overview of German history and culture visit the Germanisches Nationalmuseum in Nuremberg, while the Bayerisches Nationalmuseum in Munich focuses on Bavaria. Also in the capital is the Deutsches Museum, which could keep science fans enthralled for days.

Often the most delightful experiences can be had in quirky one-off museums, including the Levi-Strauss-Museum in Buttenheim, the Schwabach city museum, the Cork Museum in Schloss Johannisburg in Aschaffenburg, Maisel's Brauerei-und-Büttnerei-Museum in Bayreuth, the Fuggerei (not really a museum, but anyway) in Augsburg, the Museum of the 3rd Dimension in Dinkelsbühl and the Medieval Crime Museum in Rothenburg ob der Tauber.

Historic Towns
Time stands still in many parts of Bavaria. Here are some of the villages and little towns where the spirit of yore survives: Rothenburg ob der Tauber, Dinkelsbühl and Nördlingen on the Romantic Road; Sommerhausen, Sulzfeld, Iphofen and Prichsenstadt in the Franconian Wine Country; Beilngries in the Altmühl Valley; Oberammergau; Burghausen; Neuburg an der Donau; Mittenwald; Oberstdorf; Straubing and Pottenstein. The *Altstadt* (old district) remains the heart and highlight of many large cities, with especially well-preserved examples in Bamberg and Regensburg.

Churches
Thanks to the patronage of rulers both secular and religious, Catholic Bavaria is chock-full of fantastic churches from all periods – Romanesque to Art Nouveau. Here are some of our favourites: Klosterkirche Ettal and Wieskirche near Garmisch-Partenkirchen; Asamkirche in Ingolstadt; the Benedictine Abbey in Ottobeuren; the cathedrals of Bamberg and Regensburg; St Jakobskirche in Straubing; Herrgottskirche in Creglingen; Jakobskirche in Rothenburg ob der Tauber; and the Basilika Vierzehnheiligen near Bamberg.

Outdoor Activities
Bavaria is a cornucopia for outdoor fans. There's great hiking and cycling just about anywhere you go. Hot spots for particular

sports include: the Walchensee in the Tölzer Land and the Forggensee near Füssen for windsurfing; the Alps at Mittenwald and Garmisch-Partenkirchen and for the most reliable downhill skiing; Ruhpolding, Inzell and Reit im Winkl in the Chiemgau for Nordic skiing; Lake Starnberg and the Chiemsee for sailing; and the Franconian Switzerland for rock climbing.

Beer Halls & Gardens, Nightclubs & Cafes

You will find an abundance of all these in Bavaria. As you would expect, larger cities such as Munich, Nuremberg, Augsburg, Würzburg, Regensburg and Bamberg have the most to offer. But no matter where you go, you'll always find a great inn to soak up the traditional Bavarian spirit along with some of the finest brews in the world.

SUGGESTED ITINERARIES

Depending on your interests and the length of your stay, you may want to take in the following destinations:

One week
Bavaria is packed with highlights, and we have found it impossible to recommend a single one-week itinerary that would meet everyone's interests. Instead, we've come up with three.
The West (Route A) Three days in Munich, followed by three days travelling along the Romantic Road, starting with one day in Füssen (Neuschwanstein and Hohenschwanstein castles), then north with stops in Augsburg and/or Dinkelsbühl and Rothenburg ob der Tauber, finishing with one day in Würzburg.
The South (Route B) Three days in Munich, followed by four days in the Bavarian Alps. You could base yourself in Garmisch-Partenkirchen or Füssen, then make excursions to nearby attractions (Wieskirche, Oberammergau, Zugspitze, Schloss Linderhof etc), depending on your interests. At least one day should be spent hiking or bicycling or pursuing another activity in nature.
The East (Route C) Three days in Munich, followed by one day in Regensburg, a trip through the Danube Gorge and then north through the Altmühl Valley to Nuremberg, one to two days in Nuremberg.
Two weeks
Combine Route A and Route B above (starting with Route B), which will take you as far as Würzburg; from there, travel east through the Franconian Wine Country to Bamberg and from there south to Nuremberg.
Three weeks
As for two weeks, then travel south from Nuremberg through the Altmühl Valley to the Danube Gorge and Regensburg; continue through the Bavarian Forest, ending in Passau.
One month
Bavaria is your oyster.

PLANNING
When to Go

Bavaria is a great place to visit year round, although most visitors arrive between May and September when the weather is at its most reliable. Naturally, this is also when museums and tourist attractions get the biggest crowds and cheap rooms are harder to find. But summer is also lovely because much of life moves outdoors. Beer gardens and cafes bustle at all hours; outdoor events and festivals enliven the city's streets, squares and parks; and hiking, cycling and lake swimming are among the popular outdoor pursuits – at least as long as the weather plays along. Remember that rain is a possibility in any month.

The shoulder seasons (March to May and October to early November) can bring fewer tourists and surprisingly pleasant weather. In April and May, for instance, flowers and fruit trees are in bloom, and the weather is often mild and sunny. Indian summers that stretch well into the autumn are not uncommon.

With the exception of winter sports, activities between November and early March are likely to focus more on culture and city life. In these months, skies tend to be gloomy and the mercury often drops below freezing. On the plus side, there are fewer visitors and shorter lines (except in the winter resorts). Just pack the right clothes and keep in mind that there are only six to eight hours of daylight. In December, the sun (if there is any) sets around 3.30pm.

Bavaria has plenty of ski resorts and cross-country trails in the Alps and the Bavarian Forest. Ski season usually starts in early to mid-December, moves into full swing after the New Year and closes down again with the onset of the snowmelt in March.

The Climate section and the climate charts in the Facts about Bavaria chapter further explain what to expect and when to expect it.

Maps

Most tourist offices distribute free (but often very basic) city maps, but if you're driving around Bavaria and beyond, you'll need a detailed road map or atlas. The two German auto associations, Allgemeiner Deutscher Automobil Club (ADAC) and Automobilclub von Deutschland (AvD), produce excellent road maps. Other good ones are those published by Falkplan, with a patented folding system, and the one-sheet maps by Hallwag or RV Verlag. Bookshops and tourist offices usually stock a good assortment of maps. Also look for them at the newsstands in train stations.

What to Bring

Take along as little as possible; if you forget it, you can buy it in Germany. In general, standard dress in Bavaria is casual but fairly conservative in some of the villages. Jeans are generally accepted except at certain upmarket discos, especially in Munich. Dress in layers, as weather can change drastically from region to region and from day to day.

If you plan to stay at hostels, bring your own towel and soap. Linen is usually provided (often at a fee), though you might want to take along your own sheet bag. You'll sleep easier with a padlock on one of the storage lockers which are usually provided at hostels.

Other handy items include a torch (flashlight); a 220V adaptor plug for electrical appliances; a universal bath/sink plug (a plastic film canister sometimes works); and a few clothes pegs. If you're travelling through Bavaria in July and August, a water bottle and a large cotton handkerchief that you can soak in fountains to cool off with are practical items.

Most outdoor equipment (skis, boots, windsurfing boards, water-skis etc) can be rented in places and towns where these sports are practised.

TOURIST OFFICES
Local Tourist Offices

Just about every city, town and village in Bavaria has a tourist office, which may also be called *Verkehrsverein* or *-amt*, *Fremdenverkehrsverein* or *-amt* or, in spa or resort towns, *Kurverwaltung* (resort administration). Most maintain walk-in offices where you can pick up information, maps and sometimes book a room. In remote villages, the 'tourist office' may consist of someone sitting at a desk in the Rathaus (town hall). Specific addresses are listed in the Information section of each town.

English-language pamphlets are usually available in international resorts such as Garmisch-Partenkirchen and big cities such as Munich, Nuremberg and Bamberg. With few exceptions, there's usually at least one staff member more or less fluent in English or willing to make the effort to help you.

Germany's national tourist office (GNTO; (☎ 069-97 46 40, fax 75 19 03, e info@d-z-t .com, w www.germany-tourism.de) has its headquarters at Beethovenstrasse 69, 60325 Frankfurt-am-Main.

German National Tourist Offices Abroad

If you're interested in receiving printed material about Bavaria before heading out, contact the GNTO branch in or closest to your home country:

Australia (☎ 02-9267 8148, fax 9267 9035, e gnto@germany.org.au) PO Box A980, Sydney South, NSW 1235
Austria (☎ 01-513 27 92, fax 513 27 92 22, e Deutschland.reisen@d-z-t.com) Schubertring 12, 1010 Vienna
Canada (☎ 416-968-0372, fax 968 1986, e gnto@aol.com) PO Box 65162, Toronto, Ontario M4K 3Z2
France (☎ 01-40 20 07 46, fax 01 40 20 17 00, e gntopar@d-z-t.com) 47 Avenue de l'Opéra 75002 Paris
Japan (☎ 03-3586 0380, fax 3586 5079, e gntokyo@d-z-t.com) 7-5-56 Akasaka, Minato-ku, Tokyo 107-0052
Netherlands (☎ 020-697 8066, fax 691 2972, e gntoams@d-z-t.com) Hoogoorddreef 76, 1101 BG Amsterdam ZO
Russia (☎ 095-7376 408, fax 7376 409, e dztmow@glasnet.ru) c/o Lufthansa

German Airlines, Hotel Renaissance,
Olimpiski prospekt 18/1, 129 110 Moscow
South Africa (☎ 011-643 1615, fax 484 2750) c/o
Lufthansa German Airlines, 22 Girton Rd,
Parktown (PO Box 10883), Johannesburg 2000
Switzerland (☎ 01-213 22 00, fax 212 01 75,
🇪 gntozrh@d-z-t.com) Talstrasse 62, 8001
Zürich
UK (☎ 020-7317 0908, fax 7495 6129,
🇪 gntolon@d-z-t.com) PO Box 2695, London
W1A 3TN
USA
New York: (☎ 212-661 7200, fax 661 7174,
🇪 gntonyc@d-z-t.com) 52nd floor, Chanin
Bldg, 122 East 42nd St, New York, NY
10168-0072
Los Angeles: (☎ 323-655 6085, fax 655 6086,
🇪 gntolax@aol.com) Suite 440, 8484
Wilshire Blvd, Beverly Hills, CA 90211

Additional offices are in Brussels, Budapest,
Copenhagen, Helsinki, Hong Kong, Madrid,
Mexico City, Milan, Oslo, Prague, São Paulo,
Seoul, Stockholm, Tel Aviv and Warsaw.

VISAS & DOCUMENTS
Passport
European Union (EU) nationals and those
from certain other European countries, including Switzerland and Poland, require
only a passport or their national identity
card to enter and stay in Germany. Citizens
of Australia, Canada, Israel, Japan, New
Zealand, Singapore and USA need a valid
passport (no visa) if entering as tourists for
up to three months. Make sure your passport is valid until well after your trip. If it's
just about to expire, renew it before you go.
This may not be easy to do overseas, and
some countries insist your passport remain
valid for a specified minimum period (usually three months) after your arrival.

By law, everyone, including tourists,
must carry ID on them at all times. For foreign visitors, this means a passport, national
identity card or at least a drivers' licence.

Visas
Nationals from most other countries need a
so-called Schengen Visa, named after the
Schengen Agreement that abolished passport controls between Austria, Denmark,
the Netherlands, Belgium, Luxembourg,

Germany, France, Spain, Portugal, Italy,
Greece, Finland, Iceland, Norway and Sweden. Residency status in any Schengen
country makes a visa unnecessary, regardless of your nationality.

Three-month tourist visas are issued by
German embassies or consulates. A new
fast-track visa system ensures that visas can
be issued while you wait, but this still might
not be the case everywhere. You should inquire early about how long it takes, or leave
enough time before departure to apply.
You'll need a valid passport and sufficient
funds to finance your stay. Fees vary depending on the country.

Travel Insurance
Make sure you have a travel insurance policy to cover medical problems, theft and
loss in Germany. A policy with a higher
medical-expense option is best suited.
Check the small print and know what to do
in case you need to file a claim. Some policies specifically exclude 'dangerous activities', which can include motorcycling, rock
climbing, even trekking.

You may prefer a policy that pays doctors
or hospitals directly rather than you having
to pay on the spot and file a claim later. Regardless, be sure to keep all documentation.
Some policies ask you to make a reverse-
charges call (collect call) to a centre in your
home country where an immediate assess-
ment of your problem is made. Check that
the policy covers ambulances or an emergency flight home.

Also check your medical policy at home,
since some provide worldwide coverage, in
which case you only need to protect yourself against other problems (see Health later
in this chapter).

Paying for your airline ticket with a
credit card often provides limited travel-
accident insurance, and you may be able to
reclaim the payment if the operator doesn't
deliver. Ask your credit card company what
it's prepared to cover.

Driving Licence
Drivers need a valid driving licence. You're
not legally required to carry an International

Driving Permit (IDP), but having one helps Germans make sense of your unfamiliar local licence (but make sure you take that with you, too) and simplifies the car and motorcycle rental process. IDPs are valid for one year and are issued for a small fee from your local automobile association – bring a passport photo and your regular licence.

Camping Card International

Your local automobile association can also issue the Camping Card International, which is basically a camping ground ID. Cards are also available from your local camping federation, and sometimes on the spot at camping grounds. They incorporate third-party insurance for damage you may cause, and some camping grounds offer a small discount if you sign in with one.

Hostel Cards

You must be a member of a Hostelling International-affiliated organisation in order to stay at hostels run by the Deutsches Jugendherbergswerk (DJH). Non-Germans who don't have an HI card may obtain a so-called International Guest Card (IGC) at any hostel. It costs €10/18 juniors/seniors and is valid for one year. If you don't want it, €3.10 per night will be added to your regular hostel rate; you'll be given a pass that is stamped once for each night and after six nights you automatically get the IGC. If you're German or have residency status in Germany, you can buy the DJH/HI cards at the hostel (€10/18) when checking in.

Independent (non-DJH) hostels don't require a card, but in some cases you will be charged less if you have one.

Student, Teacher & Youth Cards

These cards can get you worthwhile discounts on travel (including airfare and local transport) and travel gear, reduced admission at some museums, sights and entertainment venues. The most useful among these are the International Student Identity Card (ISIC) for full-time students, and the International Teacher Identity Card (ITIC) for full-time teachers. Both are plastic ID-style card with your photograph.

If you're under 26 but not a student, you can apply for an IYTC (International Youth Travel Card) issued by the ISTC (International Student Travel Confederation), or the Euro<26 card, which goes under different names in various countries. Both give much the same discounts and benefits as an ISIC and ITIC.

All these cards are available at student unions, hostelling organisations or youth-oriented travel agencies. They do not automatically entitle you to discounts, and some companies and institutions refuse to recognise them altogether, but you won't find out until you flash the card.

Copies

Make photocopies of all important documents (passport data page and visa page, credit cards, travel insurance policy, air/bus/train tickets, driving licence etc) before you leave home. This will help speed replacement if the documents are lost or stolen. Leave one copy with someone at home and keep another with you, separate from the originals.

EMBASSIES & CONSULATES
Your Own Embassy

It's important to realise what your own embassy – the embassy of the country of which you are a citizen – can and can't do to help you if you get into trouble. Generally speaking, it won't be much help in emergencies if the trouble you're in is remotely your own fault. Remember that you are bound by the laws of the country you are in. Your embassy will not be sympathetic if you end up in jail after committing a crime locally, even if such actions are legal in your own country.

In genuine emergencies you might get some assistance, but only if other channels have been exhausted. For example, if you need to get home urgently, a free ticket home is exceedingly unlikely – the embassy would expect you to have insurance. If you have all your money and documents stolen, it might assist with getting a new passport, but a loan for onward travel is out of the question.

German Embassies Abroad

German embassies around the world include the following:

Australia (☎ 02-6270 1911, fax 62 70 19 51)
119 Empire Circuit, Yarralumla, ACT 2600
Austria (☎ 0222-711 54, fax 713 83 66)
Metternichgasse 3, Vienna 3
Canada (☎ 613-232 1101, fax 594 93 30)
1 Waverley St, Ottawa, Ontario K2P 0T8
France (☎ 01 53 83 45 00, fax 01 43 59 74 18)
13–15 Ave Franklin Roosevelt, 75008 Paris
Ireland (☎ 01-269 3011, fax 269 39 46)
31 Trimleston Ave, Booterstown, Dublin 4
Japan (☎ 03-5791 7700, fax 34 73 42 43)
4-5-10 Minami-Azabu, Minato-ku, Tokyo 106
Netherlands (☎ 070-342 0600, fax 365 19 57)
Groot Hertoginnelaan 18–20, 2517 EG The Hague
New Zealand (☎ 04-473 6063, fax 473 60 69)
90–92 Hobson St, Wellington
Russia (☎ 095-937 95 00, fax 938 23 54)
ulitsa Mosfilmovskaya 56, 119285 Moscow
South Africa (☎ 012-427 8900, fax 343 94 01)
180 Blackwood St, Arcadia, Pretoria 0083
Switzerland (☎ 031-359 4111, fax 359 44 44)
Willadingweg 83, 3006 Bern
UK (☎ 020-7824 1300, fax 78 24 14 35)
23 Belgrave Square, London SW1X 8PZ
USA (☎ 202-298 4000, fax 298 4249) 4645
Reservoir Rd NW, Washington DC 20007-1998

Consulates in Germany

Almost all embassies are located in Berlin, but many countries maintain consular representation in Munich. Where they don't, we've listed the nearest office (either in Frankfurt or Berlin). See the Yellow Pages under Konsulate for additional countries.

Australia (☎ 069-90 55 81 24, fax 90 55 81 09)
Grüneburgweg 58–62, Frankfurt-am-Main
Austria (☎ 99 81 50, fax 981 02 25) Ismaninger Strasse 136, Bogenhausen
Canada (☎ 219 95 70, fax 21 99 57 57)
Im Tal 29, Altstadt
Czech Republic (☎ 95 83 72 32, fax 950 36 88)
Siedlerstrasse 2, Unterföhring
France (☎ 419 41 10, fax 41 94 11 23)
Möhlstrasse 5, Bogenhausen
Hungary (☎ 91 10 32, fax 910 18 53)
Vollmannstrasse 2, Bogenhausen
Ireland (☎ 20 80 59 90, 20 80 59 89) Denninger Strasse 15, Bogenhausen
Italy (☎ 418 00 30, fax 47 79 99) Möhlstrasse 3, Bogenhausen

Japan (☎ 417 60 40, fax 470 57 10) Prinz-regentenplatz 10, Bogenhausen
Netherlands (☎ 545 96 70, fax 54 59 67 67)
Nymphenburger Strasse 1, Maxvorstadt
New Zealand (☎ 030-20 62 10, fax 20 62 11 14) Friedrichstrasse 60, Berlin
Poland (☎ 418 60 80, fax 47 13 18) Ismaninger Strasse 62a, Bogenhausen
Russia (☎ 59 25 28, fax 550 38 38) Seidlstrasse 28, Maxvorstadt
Slovakia (☎ 92 33 49 00, fax 92 33 49 23)
Vollmannstrasse 25d, Bogenhausen
Slovenia (☎ 543 98 19, fax 543 94 83)
Lindwurmstrasse 14, Ludwigvorstadt
South Africa (☎ 231 16 30, fax 23 11 63 63)
Sendlinger-Tor-Platz 5, Altstadt
Spain (☎ 998 47 90, fax 981 02 06)
Oberföhringer Strasse 45, Bogenhausen
Switzerland (☎ 286 62 00, fax 28 05 79 61)
Brienner Strasse 14, Maxvorstadt
UK (☎ 21 10 90, fax 21 10 91 44; also for Australian nationals during Oktoberfest)
Bürkleinstrasse 10, Lehel
USA (☎ 288 80, fax 288 99 98) Königinstrasse 5, Lehel; Visa Information Service (in English or German): ☎ 0190-85 00 58 00 automated, 24-hour; 0190-85 00 58 live operator, 7am to 8pm Monday to Friday – services are charged at €1.80 per minute

CUSTOMS

Articles that you take to Germany for your personal use may be imported free of duty and tax with some conditions. The following allowances apply to *duty-free* goods purchased at the airport or ferries: 200 cigarettes or 100 cigarillos or 50 cigars or 250g of loose tobacco; 1L of strong liquor or 2L of less than 22% alcohol by volume *and* 2L of wine; 500g of coffee or 200g of extracts *and* 100g of tea or 40g tea extracts; 50g of perfume or scent *and* 0.25L of eau de toilette; and additional goods up to a value of €179.

You must be 17 years or over to bring in tobacco products and alcohol; the importation of duty-free coffee, oddly, is barred to those under 15. There are no currency import restrictions.

Do not confuse duty free with *duty-paid* items (including alcohol and tobacco) bought at normal shops and supermarkets in another EU country and brought into Germany, where certain goods might be more expensive. Then the allowances are more generous: 800 cigarettes or 200 cigars or 1kg of loose tobacco; 10L of spirits (more than 22% alcohol by volume), 20L of fortified wine or aperitif, 90L of wine or 110L of beer.

Note that duty-free shopping within the EU was abolished in 1999. This means that you can still take duty-free goods into an EU country, such as Germany, from a non-EU country such as USA or Australia. You can't, however, buy duty-free goods in an EU-country unless you're headed for a non-EU country.

MONEY
Currency
In January 2002, Germany introduced euro notes and coins. There are seven euro notes (five, 10, 20, 50, 100, 200 and 500 euros) and eight coins (one and two euro coins, and one, two, five, 10, 20 and 50 cent coins).

Exchange Rates

country	unit		euro
Australia	A$1	=	€0.60
Canada	C$1	=	€0.72
Denmark	Dkr1	=	€0.13
Japan	¥100	=	€0.89
New Zealand	NZ$1	=	€0.49
South Africa	R1	=	€0.10
Switzerland	Sfr1	=	€0.68
UK	UK£1	=	€1.63
USA	US$1	=	€1.14

Exchanging Money
You can exchange money at banks, post office or foreign-exchange counters at the airport and train stations (€3 to €6 transaction fee). Currency exchange machines are convenient but usually don't give good rates. Rates are quite good at Reisebank offices at large train stations as well as Postbank and Sparkasse branches.

Cash Nothing beats cash for convenience ...or risk. If you lose it, it's gone forever and few travel insurers will come to your rescue. Those that will, limit the amount to about US$300. But since Germany is still a cash-based society, you can't avoid having at least some cash, say €100 or so, in your pocket at

all times. Plan to pay in cash almost everywhere (see Credit Cards later in this section for likely exceptions). Remember that banks only exchange foreign paper money not coins.

Travellers Cheques Travellers cheques, which can be replaced if lost or stolen, are *not* commonly used in Germany. Cheques not denominated in euro must be cashed at a bank or exchange outlet (bring your passport). The Reisebank charges €3 for amounts under €50, and 1% or a minimum of €6 for higher transactions. Cheques issued by American Express and Thomas Cook are the most common and neither company charges commission for exchanges at their own offices. Keep a record of the check numbers separate from the checks themselves.

ATMs Automatic teller machines, found at most banks, are convenient for obtaining cash from a bank account back home. They're usually accessible 24 hours a day, but occasionally you may have to swipe your card through a magnetic slot to gain entry to a secure area.

Most banks are affiliated with several ATM networks, the most common being Cirrus, Plus, Star and Maestro. Check the fees and availability of services with your bank before you leave. Always keep the number handy for reporting lost or stolen cards.

Most ATMs also allow you to withdraw money using a credit card, but this can be quite expensive because, in addition to a withdrawal fee, you'll be charged interest immediately (in other words, there's no grace period as with other purchases).

Credit Cards Germany still lags behind other European countries in credit card use, but major cards (eg, MasterCard, Visa and American Express) are becoming more widely accepted, especially at petrol stations, large stores and major hotels. In Bavaria this is true more in the cities than in rural areas, where cash is definitely king. It's best not to assume that you can pay with a card – always inquire first. Some shops

Bye Bye Deutschmark, Hello Euro

By the time you're reading this, the venerable Deutschmark is history. In January 2002, Germany – along with 11 other member nations of the European Union (EU) – introduced euro notes and coins. The euro is now the common currency of Austria, Belgium, Finland, France, Germany, Greece, Ireland, Italy, Luxembourg, the Netherlands, Portugal and Spain. The value of the euro against the dollar and all other currencies – including the four EU members remaining outside the euro zone – will fluctuate according to market conditions.

Each of the euro bills represents a different epoch in European cultural history (Gothic, Renaissance, baroque etc). They feature a generic 'European' bridge on one side and a vaguely familiar but unidentifiable arch on the reverse. The coins are a bit more individualised with one side bearing the national emblem of the respective country (the other side is standard for all euro coins).

If you happen to have Deutschmarks left over from an earlier trip, you can still exchange them at the Landeszentralbank (☎ 28 89 29 38) at Leopoldstrasse 234 in Schwabing.

Research for this edition took place just before the euro big bang. Whenever possible, we obtained the euro price. Sometimes, however, a euro price was not yet available and we had to convert the DM price. You might therefore find slight differences in the price we give and the actual price in euros.

may require a minimum purchase, while others may refuse to accept a card even if the credit card companies' logo is displayed in the window.

International Transfers You will need an account at a German bank for bank-to-bank transfers. As an alternative, Western Union or MoneyGram offer ready and fast international cash transfers through agent banks such as Reisebank. Cash sent becomes available as soon as the order has been entered into the computer system, ie, instantly. Commissions are paid by the person making the transfer; the amount varies from country to country but is usually in the 10% to 15% range.

Security

Be cautious – but not paranoid – about carrying money. Use the safe at your hotel or hostel for your valuables and excess cash. Don't display large amounts of cash in public. A money belt worn under your clothes is a good place to carry excess cash when you're on the move or otherwise unable to stash it in a safe. The back pocket of your pants is a prime target for pickpockets, as are handbags and the outside pockets of daypacks and fanny packs (bum bags).

Costs

Outside major cities such as Munich and Nuremberg, Bavaria is actually not terribly expensive and there are many ways to cut costs, especially with accommodation and food. Private rooms, and rooms in simple pensions with shared bathroom, usually cost under €25 per person.

Buying passes keeps public transport costs way down. Students, seniors and children usually qualify for discounts. Prices for children often vary according to age, but the highest children's price is usually the same as, or slightly less than, the student concession price. In this book we give an adult/concession price; the cost for kids is usually a bit less than this.

Preparing your own meal or getting food from an *Imbiss* (snack bar) can save you a bundle, and many cafes and restaurants have small, inexpensive dishes or lunch time specials that are tasty and filling. At restaurants, cut down on drinks since even nonalcoholic beverages are quite expensive.

If you're very economical while travelling, you can expect to survive on €30 to €45 per day. If you can afford to spend twice that much, you can start living quite comfortably.

Tipping & Bargaining

At restaurants, the *Bedienung* (service charge) is always included in bills and tipping is not compulsory. If you're satisfied with the service, add about 5% to 10%. Rather than leaving cash on the table, tip as you're handing over the money by announcing the amount you intend to pay. For example say '30, bitte' if your bill comes to €28 and you want to give a €2 tip. If you have the exact amount, just say 'Stimmt so' (roughly 'that's fine'). Taxi drivers, too, expect a small tip, usually about 10%.

Bargaining almost never occurs in Germany, except at flea markets. At hotels, you can sometimes get a lower rate if business is slow.

Taxes & Refunds

Mehrwertsteuer (MwSt; value-added tax) of 16% is slapped on to just about everything in Germany. Non-EU residents may claim a refund on this tax (minus processing fee) for goods (not services) bought, which is definitely worth it for large purchases.

The refund only applies to purchases at shops affiliated with the system – look for the 'Tax free for tourists' sign. The shop will issue you a cheque for the VAT amount to be refunded, which you can cash in at VAT Cash Refund offices at airports when leaving the country. Before you can get your money, the Tax-Free Shopping Cheque, together with the invoices/receipts, must be stamped by German customs. You're not allowed to use the items purchased until you're outside of Germany. Look for the brochure explaining the scheme in greater detail at the affiliated shops, some tourist offices, major hotels and airports.

POST & COMMUNICATIONS

Post offices in larger cities are usually open from 8am to 6pm Monday to Friday and until noon Saturday. Occasionally, limited services are available at a late counter up to 8pm, and until 2pm on Saturday. Branch offices in the suburbs and those in small towns and villages close during lunchtime and at 5pm or 5.30pm. Main post offices are often at or near the main train station.

Stamps are sold at post offices and occasionally at souvenir and postcard shops in tourist resorts. Within Germany and the EU, normal-sized postcards cost €0.51, a 20g letter is €0.56 and a 50g letter is €1.12. Postcards to North America and Australasia cost €1.02, a 20g airmail letter is €1.53 and a 50g airmail letter is €3.07. Oversized mail is subject to a significant surcharge.

Post

Letters sent within Germany usually take only one day for delivery; those addressed to destinations within Europe or to North America take four to six days, and to Australasia five to seven days.

Poste restante mail can be sent to any post office, which will hold it for two weeks. Select one, then inquire about the address, which usually consists of the postal code only. Letters and packages should be marked clearly Postlagernd and be addressed to your name followed by the postal code. Bring your passport or other photo ID when picking up mail. This is a free service.

American Express (AmEx) offers a free client-mail service to those with an AmEx card or travellers cheques (€1 per item otherwise). The sender should include the words 'Client Mail' somewhere on the envelope. Branches will hold mail for 30 days but won't accept registered post or parcels.

Telephone

Most public pay phones accept only phonecards. Those sold by Deutsche Telecom (DT) are available for €6.14 and €25.56 at post offices, news kiosks, some tourist offices and public transport offices. Local calls cost around €0.10 per minute, while countrywide calls clock in at around €0.20 per minute. Calls made from your hotel room are charged at exorbitant rates, but incoming calls are free. You can save by relaying your hotel and room number to the person you're calling and asking them to call you back.

For international calls, ditch the standard DT phonecard in favour of a prepaid card offered by private companies such as ACC. You can buy these at large newspaper stands, kiosks and discount phonecall shops. Calls to most countries cost less than €0.40 per minute, even less to the USA and Canada. Beware of cards that charge a connecting fee of €0.50 or so; buy one that doesn't.

The cellular phone craze has spread through Germany as everywhere else. Note that calls made *to* cellular phones cost a lot more than those to a stationary number, though how much more depends on the service used by the cellular-phone provider. Most cellular phone numbers begin with 017 or 016. Numbers starting with 0800 are toll-free, 01805 numbers cost about €0.12 per minute, 0190 costs €0.62 per minute.

For directory assistance within Germany, dial ☎ 11833 (☎ 11837 for information in English). It costs €1 for the first minute and €0.49 after that. For numbers abroad, call ☎ 11834, which costs a whopping €1.48 for the first minute and €0.97 per minute after that.

To call abroad, dial ☎ 00 followed by the country and local area codes and number. The country code for Germany is 49.

Home direct services, whereby you reach the operator direct for a reverse charge call from Germany, are also only possible to some countries. To reach the operator direct, dial 0800 plus: USA 888 0013 (Sprint), 225 52 88 (AT&T) or 888 8000 (MCI); Canada 080 1014; UK 0800 044; Australia 0800 061 (Telstra).

eKno Communication Service Lonely Planet's eKno global communication service provides low-cost international calls – for local calls you're usually better off with a local phonecard. eKno also offers free messaging services, email, travel information and an online travel vault, where you can securely store all your important documents. You can join online at W www.ekno .lonelyplanet.com, where you will find the local-access numbers for the 24-hour customer-service centre. Once you have joined, always check the eKno Web site for the latest access numbers for each country and updates on new features.

Fax
Most main post offices and main train stations have public fax-phones that operate with a DT phonecard. The regular cost of the call, plus a €1.02 service charge, is deducted if the connection succeeds. Faxes can also be sent from hotels, copy shops and Internet cafes. If you carry a laptop with a fax modem, you only pay for the cost of the phonecall (keep in mind high hotel phone rates, though).

Email & Internet Access
Internet cafes, charging between €2.50 and €3.50 per half hour, exist in all major and many smaller Bavarian cities. To access your own email account, you'll need to know your incoming (POP or IMAP) mail server name, your account name and your password. Your ISP or network supervisor will be able to give you these.

Travelling with a portable computer is a great way to stay in touch with life back home, but unfortunately it's fraught with potential problems. Make sure that your AC adaptor is compatible with 220 voltage; you may also need a plug adaptor for German outlets. To be sure that your PC-card modem will work in Germany, have a reputable 'global' modem installed before leaving home. International adaptors for German telephone plugs usually accept US RJ-11 plugs, but these are not stocked by all electronics stores, so it's advisable to shop around at home first or seek out a specialist store. Some mid-range and upmarket hotels have telephone sockets that accept RJ-11.

Major Internet service providers, such as AOL or Compuserve have dial-in nodes in Germany.

For detailed information on travelling with a portable computer, see W www .teleadapt.com or W www.warrior.com.

DIGITAL RESOURCES
The World Wide Web is a rich resource for travellers. You can research your trip, hunt down bargain air fares, book hotels, check on weather conditions or chat with locals and other travellers about the best places to visit (or avoid!).

A great place to start your Web explorations is the Lonely Planet Web site (W www.lonelyplanet.com). Here you'll find succinct summaries on travelling to most places on earth, postcards from other travellers and the Thorn Tree bulletin board, where you can ask questions before you go or dispense advice when you get back. You can also find travel news and updates to many of our most popular guidebooks, and the subWWWay section links you to the most useful travel resources elsewhere on the Web.

There's a decent amount of information about Bavaria on the Internet, but as of now most sites are in German only. Unless noted, URLs mentioned in this book link you to pages in English. Please note that Web site addresses, though correct at press time, are particularly prone to change.

Bavaria.com This is an irreverent guide to all things cultural, entertaining and sports-oriented as well as to bizarre customs and traditions. The focus is on Munich.
W www.bavaria.com

Bavarian Government This is the official site of the Bavarian government, with political news and sections on history, culture, economics, education etc (in German, English and French).
W www.bayern.de

Munich Found This is a site maintained by the people of Munich Found, a monthly English-language magazine, with good insider information about Munich and beyond.
W www.munichfound.de

Munich News This site presents the latest news stories from Munich and around Bavaria as reported by BBC, Reuters, CNN, AP and other international news agencies and newspapers. It also includes lots of links to other sites of interest (in English).
W www.munichnews.com

Public Transport This site provides timetable information for public transportation within the entire state (in German and English; get there by selecting 'Elektronische Fahrplanauskunft' on the homepage).
W www.bayerninfo.de

There's also a slew of general Germany sites with information pertaining to Bavaria, including the following:

Expatica Especially useful for expats in Germany, this site is also relevant to visitors too (in English).
W www.expatica.com

German Information Run by the German Information Center in New York and the German embassy in Washington, this site is packed with useful general information and links to just about everything, be it language or exchange programs, German media, the postal-code directory, political foundations, business, law and, of course, travel (in English).
W www.germany-info.org

German National Tourist Office This site has information on travel in Germany from the German National Tourist Office (in English and German).
W www.germany-tourism.de

Inter Nationes There are interesting articles on German culture, society and politics (in English, German, Spanish and French) on this site.
W www.inter-nationes.de

Travels Through Germany Lots of information on this site is aimed at the traveller and there are useful links on many, many aspects of Germany (in English).
W www.travelsthroughgermany.com

BOOKS

Most books are published in different editions by different publishers in different countries. As a result, a book might be a hardcover rarity in one country while it's readily available in paperback in another. Fortunately, bookshops and libraries can search by title or author, so your local bookshop or library is the best place to find out about the availability of the following recommendations.

Lonely Planet

Those interested in finding out what Germany has to offer beyond the Bavarian borders, should check Lonely Planet's comprehensive *Germany*. The LP guides *Central Europe*, *Western Europe* and *Europe on a Shoestring* all include big Germany chapters for those on a grand tour, in which case the *Central Europe phrasebook* might also come in handy. Lonely Planet also publishes a *German phrasebook*. For those wanting to make an in-depth study of the Bavarian capital, the LP city guide

Munich is an invaluable source. All books are available at good bookstores or from **W** www.lonelyplanet.com.

Guidebooks

Those able to read German have a good assortment of guidebooks to pick from, although most focus on just one region or city rather than the entire state. Cultural guidebooks are very popular; *Knaurs Kulturführer* is invaluable for anyone with a special interest in architecture and the arts.

The Falk Verlag, best known for its excellent maps, also publishes a series of magazine-sized guidebooks that are most useful for getting a pictorial overview of a particular area (€7.60). The *Bildatlas* published by HB Verlag (€7.60) is similar.

History & Society

It's pretty much impossible to find a general English-language history of Bavaria. Most authors focus on relatively short periods in the state's history (the Third Reich, naturally, is a favourite) or examine Bavaria's role in the context of German history.

Popular Opinion and Political Dissent in the Third Reich, Bavaria, 1933–1945 by noted historian Ian Kershaw looks at how Bavarians reacted to Nazi policy and ideology before and after the dictator's rise to power.

Spheres of Influence by Lloyd C Gardner attempts to trace the division of Europe to British appeasement under the 1938 Munich Agreement, which traded Czechoslovakia's freedom for a brittle, short-lived period of peace.

The History Of The Eagle's Nest: A complete account of Adolf Hitler's alleged 'Mountain Fortress' by Florian M Beierl comes with hundreds of photos of the (in)famous Berchtesgaden retreat from the Nazi era and today.

The White Rose: Munich 1942–1943 by Inge Scholl chronicles the lives of her siblings, Hans and Sophie Scholl, founders of the Weisse Rose Nazi resistance group, who were executed in 1943.

Ludwig II of Bavaria: The Swan King by Christopher McIntosh tries to unravel the

mysteries surrounding the fairy-tale king without shying away from such controversial issues as his alleged homosexuality and madness.

Among more general offerings, *The Origins of Modern Germany* by Geoffrey Barraclough is an excellent introduction to the complex history of the country. *A History of Modern Germany* by Hajo Holborn is a three-volume work that begins with the 15th century and traces developments up to the division in 1945. *The Thirty Years' War* by Veronica (CV) Wedgwood, written in the 1930s, is still considered one of the seminal works on this torturous religious war which tore Europe apart in the 17th century.

Special Interest

If you enjoy a lofty, intellectual tone, Thomas Mann's carefully sculpted short stories and novellas set in Munich are a delight. *Gladius Dei* begins with the classic phrase 'Munich Shone' (which the city has adopted on numerous occasions), while *Herr und Hund* is set in and around the Englischer Garten.

Unbeatable BMW: Eighty Years of Engineering and Motorsport Success is a richly illustrated, comprehensive history of BMW from 1917 to 1997. Written by Jeremy Walton, it is an expansion of his earlier cult classic, which focuses on the years from 1959 to 1979.

In *Oberammergau: The Troubling Story of the World's Most Famous Passion Play*, Jewish scholar James Shapiro examines the inherent anti-Semitism in this famous passion play and the anxiety involved in the attempt to create a more politically correct 2000 production.

Art students and professionals will love *The Munich Secession: Art and Artists in Turn of the Century Munich* by Mara Makele, which takes a fresh look at the split between avant-gardists and traditional painters in the Bavarian capital.

Brecht: A Choice of Evils by Martin Esslin is highly recommended for anyone interested in Brecht and Germany's cultural scene in the 1920s. *Bertolt Brecht: Chaos According to Plan* by John Fuegi focuses on Brecht's methods.

For suggestions about day hikes in the Alps (though not just in Bavaria), try *100 Hikes in the Alps* by Vicky Spring.

NEWSPAPERS & MAGAZINES

You can easily find a wide selection of newspapers and magazines from around Europe and the USA at newsstands in big city train stations, and increasingly in smaller towns and tourist resorts as well. The *International Herald Tribune* (€2.05) is the most commonly available English-language daily paper.

The most widely read newspaper is the well-respected *Süddeutsche Zeitung*, which can be surprisingly liberal given the conservative fabric of Bavaria. The *Münchner Merkur* is the mouthpiece of the Bavarian conservative party, the CSU, and therefore difficult to take seriously. The *Abendzeitung* is an easy-to-digest complement to the *Süddeutsche Zeitung*, which, despite the name, appears in the morning. It teeters on the edge of the gutter but somehow manages to stay respectable.

RADIO

Bavarian radio is modelled increasingly on US stations, with oodles of pop, rock, adult contemporary and oldies. Bayern 3 is a good station for classical, opera and literature readings. Antenne Bayern is another large state-run station with very weird programming – ABBA meets the Zillertaler Schürzenjäger. Jazz fiends should check out Jazzwelle. Radio Arabella is Munich's most popular radio station at 105.2 FM, playing lots of Schlager and schmaltzy folk songs.

For quality English-language programs, the BBC World Service broadcasts on 604 MW and 90.2 FM; Britain's Radio 4 is on 198 LW. The uplifting sounds of Voice of America are beamed to Central Europe on 1197 AM, but it includes programs in other languages. Relax FM (92.4 on the band) plays light jazz and has a short CNN Radio News every hour on the half-hour. The American Forces Network (AFN) and the Armed Forces Radio & Television Service (AFRTS) are available on the AM dial and has news broadcasts read by US service people.

TV

The English-language channels BBC World, CNN, the Sky Channel and CNBC can be received in Bavaria on cable or via satellite, but not all of these in every region at all times of the day.

Germany has two national (public) channels, the ARD (Erstes Deutsches Fernsehen) and ZDF (Zweites Deutsches Fernsehen). In addition, there are the 'Dritten Programme', regional stations such as the Munich-based Bayerischer Rundfunk (BR).

Generally, public TV programming is quite high-brow, with lots of political coverage, discussion forums and foreign films. Advertising is limited to the two hours between 6pm and 8pm when it is shown in eight- to 10-minute blocks roughly every half-hour. These channels can usually be easily received with a TV antenna; no cable connection or satellite dish is necessary.

Private TV stations offer the familiar array of sitcoms and soap operas (including many dubbed US shows), chat and game shows and, of course, feature films of all kinds. DSF and EuroSport are dedicated sports channels, and MTV and its German equivalent VIVA can also be received. Commercial breaks are frequent on these stations. ARTE is a Franco-German channel with quality films, current affairs and documentaries.

VIDEO SYSTEMS

German video and TV operates on the PAL (Phase Alternative Line) system, predominant in most of Europe and Australia. It is not compatible with the American and Japanese NTSC or French SECAM standards, so pre-recorded videotapes bought in countries using those standards won't play in Germany and vice versa. Dual standard VCRs, which play back NTSC and PAL (but only record in PAL), are available in better electronics and duty-free shops; you should expect to pay somewhere around €250 for a decent one. A standard VHS tape costs about €3 to €5, depending on the brand.

PHOTOGRAPHY & VIDEO

Bavaria is a photographer's dream, with the snow-flecked Bavarian Alps, fabulous architecture, quaint mountain villages, lordly cathedrals, lively beer gardens and numerous castles, palaces and picturesque old towns.

Film & Equipment

German photographic equipment is among the best in the world, and all makes and types are readily available, as are those manufactured in other countries. Print film is sold at supermarkets and chemists, but for black-and-white and slide film you'll have to go to a photographic store. The last two types of film are sometimes hard to find (or sold at inflated prices) outside major cities.

For general-purpose shooting – for either prints or slides – 100 ASA film is just about the most useful and versatile, as it gives you good colour and enough speed to capture most situations on film. If you plan to shoot in dark areas or in brightly lit night scenes without a tripod, switch to 400 ASA.

The best and most widely available films are made by Fuji, Kodak and Agfa. Fuji Velvia and Kodak Elite are easy to process and provide good slide images. Stay away from Kodachrome: it's difficult to process and can give you lots of headaches if not handled properly. For print film you can't beat Kodak Gold, though Fuji and Agfa have just about perfected their films for print as well.

Film of any type is inexpensive in Germany, so there's no need to stock up at home. For a roll of 36-exposure standard print film, expect to pay around €3. The cost for good slide film should be around €5 to €7. The cost per roll goes down significantly if you buy in packages of five or 10 rolls, so shop around. Occasionally, processing is included with the purchase of the film, which is a great deal if you have the time to wait. With slide film, unless you specify that you want the images framed *(gerahmt)*, you will get them back unframed.

It's worth carrying a spare battery for your camera to avoid disappointment when your camera dies right after you've reached the mountaintop. If you're buying a new camera for your trip, do so several weeks before you leave and practise using it.

Chemists and supermarkets are cheap places to get your film processed, provided you don't need professional quality developing. Standard developing for print film is about €2, plus €0.20 for each 10 by 15cm print (allow about four days), and about €0.30 per print for overnight service. Processing slide film costs about €1.75 in these shops; if you want it mounted, your total comes to about €3.50. All prices quoted are for rolls of 36.

Technical Tips

When the sun is high in the sky, photographs tend to emphasise shadows and wash out highlights. It's best to take photos during the early morning or the late afternoon when light is softer. This is especially true of landscape photography.

A polarising filter is a very useful piece of gear, as it deepens the blue of the sky and water, can eliminate many reflections and makes clouds appear quite dramatic. It is best used to photograph scenes in nature. Using one at high altitudes where the sky is already deep blue can result in pictures with a nearly black and unrealistic sky. The effect of a polariser is strongest when you point your camera 90° away from the sun.

In forests, you'll find that light levels are surprisingly low, and fast film or using your camera's fill-flash function may be helpful. A monopod or lightweight tripod is an invaluable piece of gear for 'steadying up' your camera for slow exposure times or when using a telephoto lens.

Film can be damaged by excessive heat. Don't leave your camera and film in the car on a hot day, and avoid placing your camera on the dash while you are driving.

Frame-filling expanses of snow come out a bit grey unless you deliberately *overexpose* about a half to one stop. Extreme cold can play tricks with exposure, so 'bracket' your best pictures with additional shots about one stop under and overexposed.

Photographing People

Germans tend to be deferential around photographers and will make a point of not walking in front of your camera, even if you want them to. No-one seems to mind being photographed in the context of an overall scene, but if you want a close-up shot, you should ask first.

Video

American-bought video recorders can record with German-bought tapes and then play back with no problems. The size of the tapes are the same, only the method of recording and playback differs between PAL and NTSC standards.

Airport Security

In general, airport X-ray technology used to inspect carry-on baggage isn't supposed to jeopardise lower-speed film (under 1600 ASA). However, new high-powered machines designed to inspect *checked* luggage have been installed at major airports around the world. These machines are capable of conducting high-energy scans that will damage unprocessed film.

Make sure that you carry all unprocessed film and loaded cameras in your hand-luggage. If you are told that your carry-on luggage must be stowed with the checked luggage or go through a second scan, remove all unprocessed film. Ask airport security people to inspect your film manually, especially if you'll be passing through five or more check points. Pack all your film into a clear plastic bag that you can quickly whip out of your luggage. This not only saves time at the inspection points but also helps minimise confrontations with security staff. In this age of terrorism, their job is tough but they can also add to your pre-flight hell, big time.

TIME

Throughout Germany, clocks are set to Central European Time (GMT/UTC plus one hour). Daylight-saving time starts on the last Sunday in March, when clocks are put forward one hour and ends on the last Sunday in October. Without taking daylight-saving times into account, when it's noon in Berlin, it's 11am in London, 6am in New York, 3am in San Francisco, 8pm in Tokyo, 9pm in Sydney and 11pm in Auckland.

Official times (eg, shop hours, train schedules, film screenings) are usually indicated by the 24-hour clock, eg, 6.30pm is 18.30.

ELECTRICITY

Electricity is 220V, 50 Hz AC. Plugs are the European type with two round pins. Your 220V appliances may be plugged into a German outlet with an adaptor, though their 110V cousins (eg, from the USA) require a transformer. Some electric devices such as laptops or shavers work on both 110V and 220V.

WEIGHTS & MEASURES

Germany uses the metric system (see the conversion table at the back of this book). Like other Continental Europeans, Germans indicate decimals with commas and thousands with points.

LAUNDRY

Larger cities have coin-operated laundries (*Münzwäscherei*) where you can do a load of washing for around €3 to €3.50, including soap powder; the dryer is €0.50 per 10 or 15 minutes. To speed up drying, many people first put their clothes into the extractor, which costs around €0.25 per load and cuts drying time by at least half.

Some camping grounds and a few hostels have washers and dryers for guests' use. If you're staying in a family-run pension, your host might take care of your washing for a fee. Major hotels provide laundering services but rates are usually steep.

TOILETS

Finding a public toilet is not usually a problem in Bavaria, but you may have to pay anything from €0.10 to €0.75 for the convenience. Most people use the toilets in a bar, restaurant or department stores. If there's an attendant, it's nice to tip €0.25 if the toilet was clean. Overall, the standard of hygiene is high, although toilets in some pubs and nightclubs can be surprisingly grotty.

HEALTH

There are few potential health dangers in Germany. The most travellers are likely to experience is an upset stomach. In a serious emergency, call ☎ 112 for an ambulance to take you to the nearest hospital emergency room.

Predeparture Planning

No vaccinations are required to visit Germany, except if you're coming from an infected area – proof of vaccination against yellow fever is the most likely requirement. A few routine vaccinations are recommended: diphtheria and tetanus (usually combined), and tuberculosis. Some vaccinations are warned against if you're pregnant. Always carry proof of your vaccinations. If you are planning a stopover in Africa or Latin America, ask your travel agent or the German embassy about possible vaccination requirements.

Make sure you're healthy before you start travelling. If you are going on a long trip, make sure your teeth are OK. If you wear glasses, take a spare pair and your prescription. If you require a particular medication, take an adequate supply in case it's not available locally. Take part of the packaging showing the generic name rather than the brand, which will make getting replacements easier. It's a good idea to have a legible prescription or letter from your doctor to show that you legally use the medication to avoid any problems.

Health Insurance Make sure that you have adequate health insurance. The standard of health care is excellent in Germany, but is expensive unless you're a citizen from an EU country, in which case first aid and emergency health care are free with an E111 form. See Travel Insurance under Visas & Documents earlier in this chapter for details.

Medical Problems & Treatment

In case of an accident or other emergency, call ☎ 112. In any other circumstance, ask for a referral to a doctor at your hotel or check the phone book under *Ärzte*.

Except for emergencies, it is not customary to go to a hospital for treatment; instead you'd go to a doctor in private practice.

Doctor's offices are usually closed on Wednesday afternoon and on weekends.

The only place to obtain over-the-counter *(rezeptfrei)* medications for minor health concerns, such as flu or a stomach upset, is a pharmacy *(Apotheke)*. For more serious conditions, you will need to bring a prescription *(Rezept)* from a licensed physician. The names and addresses of pharmacies open after hours (it rotates) are posted in any pharmacy window.

Heat Exhaustion

Dehydration or salt deficiency can cause heat exhaustion. Take time to acclimatise and drink sufficient liquids. Salt deficiency is characterised by fatigue, lethargy, headaches, giddiness and muscle cramps; salt tablets may help, but adding extra salt to your food is better.

Hypothermia

If you are planning on hiking, mountaineering or cross-country skiing while in Bavaria, you should be prepared for sudden weather changes, especially outside the summer months.

Hypothermia occurs when the body loses heat faster than it can produce it and the core temperature of the body falls. It is surprisingly easy to progress from very cold to dangerously cold due to a combination of wind, wet clothing, fatigue and hunger, even if the air temperature is above freezing.

Dress in layers; silk, wool and some of the new artificial fibres are all good insulating materials. A hat is important, as a lot of heat is lost through the head. A strong, waterproof outer layer is essential. On multi-day hikes through the Alps, take a 'space' blanket for emergencies. Carry basic supplies, including food containing simple sugars to generate heat quickly, and fluids to drink.

Symptoms of hypothermia are exhaustion, numb skin (particularly toes and fingers), shivering, slurred speech, irrational or violent behaviour, lethargy, stumbling, dizzy spells, muscle cramps and violent bursts of energy. Irrationality may take the form of sufferers claiming they are warm and trying to take off their clothes.

Get hypothermia victims out of the wind or rain and make sure they're in warm and dry clothing. Give them hot liquids – not alcohol – and some high-calorie, easily digestible food. Do not rub victims: instead, allow them to slowly warm themselves. This should be enough to treat the early stages of hypothermia. The early recognition and treatment of hypothermia is the only way to prevent severe hypothermia, which is a critical condition.

Bites & Stings

Bee and wasp stings are usually painful rather than dangerous. However, in people who are allergic to them, severe breathing difficulties may occur and require urgent medical care. Calamine lotion or a sting relief spray will give relief and ice packs will reduce the pain and swelling.

Always check all over your body for ticks if you have been walking through a potentially tick-infested area. These tiny pests not only cause skin infections but also more serious diseases such as Lyme disease. If you find a tick attached, press down around its head with tweezers, grab the head and gently pull upwards. Avoid pulling the rear of the body as this may squeeze the tick's gut contents through the attached mouthparts into the skin, increasing the risk of infection and disease. Smearing chemicals on the tick will not make it let go. Some pharmacies carry special tweezers to extract ticks; staff can also usually tell you whether ticks exist in the area.

WOMEN TRAVELLERS

Bavaria is a very safe place for women to travel, even alone, even in the cities. Of course, this doesn't mean you can let your guard down and trust your life to every stranger. Simply use the same common sense as you would at home. Getting hassled in the streets happens infrequently and is most likely to be encountered when walking past a bunch of construction guys on a break. Simply ignore them.

In the larger Bavarian cities, younger women are quite outspoken and emancipated, but self-confidence hasn't yet translated into equality in the workplace, where they are often still kept out of senior and management positions. Sexual harassment in the workplace is more commonplace and tolerated here than in countries such as the USA, UK and Australia. Many women juggle jobs and children, but there's an extensive network of public, church-run and private kindergartens to fall back on.

In rural areas, attitudes towards women tend to be more conservative and gender roles are still more traditionally defined, even among younger generations.

If you are assaulted, call the police immediately (☎ 110). Major cities have rape crisis centres and women's shelters that provide help and support. The Frauenhaus München (☎ 089-354 83 11, 24-hour service ☎ 089-354 83 0) in Munich is a good source.

GAY & LESBIAN TRAVELLERS

Homosexuality is legal in Germany, but Bavaria does not have much of a scene. Even Munich has a relatively small community, certainly if compared to Berlin, Cologne and other larger German cities. A good first stop for information and advice is the Schwules Kommunikations- und Kulturzentrum (☎ 260 30 56), dubbed 'the Sub', at Müllerstrasse 43 in Munich. Some landlords may be reluctant to rent double rooms to gay couples, especially in the smaller, private hotels and pensions. The German word for gays is *Schwule*, lesbians are *Lesben*.

DISABLED TRAVELLERS

Overall, Germany caters well for the needs of the disabled *(Behinderte)*, especially the wheelchair-bound. You'll find access ramps and/or lifts in many public buildings, including toilets, train stations, museums, theatres and cinemas. However, other disabilities (such as blindness or deafness) are less catered for, and German organisations for disabled people continue to lobby for improvements. Most Deutsche Bahn trains and U-Bahn trains now have wheelchair access, but stepped entrances to trams and buses remain obstacles.

Organisations that specialise in the needs of disabled travellers include Access-Able Travel Source (☎ 303-232 2979, fax 239 8486) in Colorado, which has an excellent Web site at Ⓦ www.access-able.com; and Mobility International, with offices in Oregon (☎ 541-343 1284, fax 343 6812, ⓔ info@ miusa.org) and London (☎ 020-7403 5688). The latter advises disabled travellers on mobility issues and runs an educational exchange program.

SENIOR TRAVELLERS

Senior citizens are entitled to discounts on museum admission, public transport and the like. The minimum qualifying age is usually 60. In some cases, proof of age may be required. Even if no discounts are posted, it still won't hurt to ask '*Gibt es Ermässigungen für Senioren?*'.

TRAVEL WITH CHILDREN

Successful travel with young children requires planning and effort. Don't overdo things by packing too much into the time available and make sure activities include the kids as well. Include the kids in the planning of the trip, and balance that visit to the Alte Pinakothek with a trip to the planetarium or the zoo.

Children's discounts are widely available for everything from museum admissions to bus fares and hotel stays. The definition of a 'child' varies – some places consider anyone under 18 eligible for children's discounts, while others only include children under six.

Most car-rental firms in Germany have a range of children's safety seats for hire from about €4.50, but it is essential that you book them in advance. Highchairs and cots (cribs) are standard in most restaurants and hotels, but numbers are limited. The choice of baby food, infant formulas, soy and cow's milk, disposable nappies (diapers) and the like is great in German supermarkets, but the opening hours may be restricted. Run out of nappies on Saturday afternoon and you're facing a very long and messy weekend.

It's perfectly acceptable to bring your kids, even toddlers, along to casual restaurants (though you would raise eyebrows at upmarket ones, especially at dinnertime), cafes and daytime events.

DANGERS & ANNOYANCES

Bavaria is a remarkably safe place to live and travel. Along with neighbouring Baden-Württemberg, it has for years had the lowest crime rate in Germany and even this has been declining steadily since 1997. Nearly two thirds of all crimes are solved, compared to just one in two in the national average. Theft, street crime, crimes against foreigners and illegal immigration all declined in recent years, although fraud, illegal drug use, sexual abuse of children and assaults posted slight increases.

Much attention has been paid in the press to attacks on foreigners in Germany. While most of these incidents have occurred in eastern Germany, where unemployment and social dissatisfaction are generally higher than in other parts of the country, Africans, Asians and southern Europeans may on occasion encounter racial prejudice. Actual attacks on tourists are extremely uncommon. If you do find yourself in a threatening situation, leave the scene as quickly as possible and notify the police.

In the event of a real emergency, the following are the most important telephone numbers to remember:

Police	☎ 110
Fire/Ambulance	☎ 112

In the Bavarian Alps, the *Föhn* is a weather-related annoyance most common in the autumn. Static-charged wind blows from the south across the mountains, driving bad weather northward. Asthmatics, rheumatics and hypochondriacs complain of headaches, while others claim that it simply makes them cranky. But Föhn isn't all bad as it also brings exquisite views clear to the Alps.

LEGAL MATTERS

German police are well trained, fairly 'enlightened' and usually treat tourists with respect. Most can speak some English, though you may encounter communication problems in rural areas. By German law, you must carry some form of picture identification like your passport, national identity card or driving licence.

Reporting theft to the police is usually a simple, if occasionally time-consuming, matter. Remember that the first thing to do is show some form of identification.

Penalties for drinking and driving are stiff. The permissible blood-alcohol limit is 0.05%; drivers caught exceeding this amount are subject to stiff fines, a confiscated licence and even jail time.

The sensible thing is to avoid illegal drugs entirely, as penalties are generally harsh. Though treated as a minor offence, the possession of even small quantities of cannabis for personal consumption remains illegal; if you are caught, it may involve a court appearance.

If arrested, you have the right to make a phonecall. For a referral to a lawyer, contact your embassy.

BUSINESS HOURS

If you're used to lax store hours, shopping in Bavaria can be quite frustrating. Shops are legally allowed to stay open from 7am to 8pm Monday to Friday and 7am to 4pm Saturday. Except in the major cities and some tourist centres, though, most storeowners lock doors as early as 5.30pm or 6pm and also insist on observing a two- or three-hour lunch break. Petrol stations are convenient – if expensive – outlets to stock up on basic food and drink when everything else is closed.

Banks usually open from 8.30am to 1pm and from 2.30pm to 4pm Monday to Friday (many stay open until 5.30pm on Thursday). Travel agencies and other offices are usually open 9am to 6pm Monday to Friday and 9am to noon Saturday. Government offices, on the other hand, close for the weekend as early as noon on Friday. Museums are almost universally closed on Monday; some art museums are open late one evening per week.

Restaurant hours vary greatly, but many close for a few hours in the afternoon between lunch and dinner. Most stop serving food at about 9.30pm and observe a closing day *(Ruhetag)*, usually Monday or Tuesday. Shops and banks remain closed on public holidays.

PUBLIC HOLIDAYS & SPECIAL EVENTS

Public holidays observed in Bavaria are:

New Year's Day 1 January
Epiphany 6 January
Easter March/April Good Friday, Easter Sunday
   & Easter Monday
Labour Day 1 May
Ascension Day 40 days after Easter
Whit/Pentecost Sunday & Monday May/June
Corpus Christi 10 days after Pentecost
Assumption Day 15 August
Day of German Unity 3 October
All Saints Day November 1
Christmas Day December 25
Boxing/St Stephen's Day December 26

Bavaria has a very active festival schedule. Each event mentioned below is described in greater detail under the respective destination.

January & February

The year kicks off with international ski-jumping competitions in Oberstdorf and Garmisch-Partenkirchen as part of the **Vier-schanzen-Tournee**. Garmisch also hosts the **Hornschlittenrennen**, a race using historical sleds. In February, **Carnival** *(Fasching)* festivities precede the six weeks of Lent, with the biggest partying going on in Munich.

March & April

The festival season gets in high gear with the **International Klezmer Festival** in Fürth and the **Frühlingsfest**, a miniature Oktoberfest, in Munich. Rothenburg ob der Tauber kicks off its season of **Historical Shepherds' Dances**, with performances continuing through October. Munich also has the **Auer Dult**, a huge flea market. Late in the month, Burghausen holds its **Jazzwoche**, a top-rated international jazz festival.

May

Many Bavarian towns let their collective hair down over the Whitsuntide/Pentecost weekend (dates vary). Rothenburg ob der

Tauber celebrates the historical **Master Draught Festival**; Regensburg holds its big **Dult** fun fair; Erlangen's **Bergkirchweih** is a big folk and beer festival; and Nördlingen, on the Romantic Road, holds its **Pfingstmesse**, a street fair. Also this month is the **Jazz Festival** in Dinkelsbühl and Bayreuth's festival of opera and ballet, the **Fränkische Festwoche**.

June

This is another festivals-packed month. Important music festivals are the **Rococo Festival** in Ansbach, the **Würzburger Mozartfest**, the **Richard-Strauss-Tage** in Garmisch-Partenkirchen and the **Festspiele Europäische Wochen** in Passau. Car-racing aficionados may want to make the **Norisring Car Races** in Nuremberg a stop, while fans of world culture should seek out the **Africa-Festival** in Würzburg and the **Tollwood Festival** in Munich. Bamberg stages the **Calderón Festival**, an open-air theatre festival.

July

This month's highlights include two mega-festivals featuring children in re-creations of their town's history: the **Tänzlfest** in Kaufbeuren and the **Kinderzeche** in Dinkelsbühl. Landshut celebrates the **Hofmeistertertage** early music festival every two years and the **Landshut Wedding** historical festival every four years. Coburg cuts loose during its **Samba Festival**, while Kulmbach brings in the crowds for its **Bierfest**. Munich has another **Auer Dult** flea market, Ansbach a prestigious **Bach Week** (every other year) and Feuchtwangen the **Kreuzgangspiele**, an open-air theatre festival. And let's not forget **Christopher Street Day**, with the biggest parties happening in Munich.

August

Things slow down a bit this month, but there's still plenty to do. The highlight is the **Richard Wagner Festival** in Bayreuth, but more earthy delights can be had at Bavaria's second-biggest beer festival, the **Gäubodenfest** in Straubing. Bamberg's **Sandkerwa** and the **Regensburg Dult** are both big folk festivals in the Oktoberfest mould.

Nuremberg chimes in with the **Bardentreffen**, a medieval music festival.

September

Munich's **Oktoberfest** steals the show this month, but the **Michaelis-Kirchweih** street carnival in Fürth is another big party, as is the **Altstadtfest** in neighbouring Nuremberg. Rothenburg re-enacts its medieval history during the **Reichsstadt-Festtage**, while Ansbach honours the tragic **Kaspar Hauser** with a festival every other year.

October & November

As the days get shorter, the festival season slows down too. Rothenburg has a harvest festival, the **Rothenburger Herbst**, and Munich draws people to another instalment of the **Auer Dult** flea market. In early November, the **Leonardifahrt** is an important pilgrimage, with the most famous in Bad Tölz.

December

Christkindl-Markt (Christmas markets) run throughout Bavaria starting in late November and ending around December 23. The ones in Munich and Nuremberg are the best known and biggest, but those in Regensburg, Bamberg, Rothenburg ob der Tauber and countless other towns and villages are just as charming. Bamberg also has the added bonus of a beautiful **Krippenweg**, a series of large-scale nativity scenes.

ACTIVITIES

Bavaria lives up to its reputation as a splendid outdoor playground, offering a wealth of outdoor pursuits suitable for everyone from couch potatoes to adventure seekers.

Hiking & Mountaineering

There's excellent hiking just about anywhere in Bavaria. Thousands of kilometres of trails travel through all regions, from Franconian Switzerland and the Frankenwald forest in Franconia to the Bavarian Forest National Park, the Altmühltal Nature Park, the Alpine Foothills, the Allgäu, and many more. Trails are usually marked with signs or symbols, which are sometimes painted on tree trunks.

Munich has a thriving jazz scene – best exemplified at the Jazzclub Unterfahrt

Friedensengel stands sentinel over Munich

Christmas time in the streets of Munich

Hand-made Christmas angel decorations

ESBIN ANDERSON PHOTOGRAPHY

BMW's futuristic headquarters and Museum in Munich

JEREMY GRAY

Lily pond, Botanischer Garten

KIM GRANT

Schloss Nymphenburg

JEREMY GRAY

Surf's up in Munich's Englischer Garten

ESBIN ANDERSON PHOTOGRAPHY

Munich's popular meeting spot – Fischbrunnen

Nearly every tourist office has free or low-cost maps and brochures about local hiking routes. In addition, several marked long-distance trails traverse Bavaria.

The Bavarian Alps, naturally, are the centre of mountaineering in Germany. You can go out on moderate one-day hikes or plan multi-day treks from hut to hut. Some routes traverse difficult terrain along so-called *Klettersteige*, which is essentially a form of rock climbing using pre-attached cables; you'll need a special harness, kara-biners and a helmet. Always check local weather conditions before setting out and take all precautions concerning clothing and provisions. And always let someone know where you're going.

For potential problems and how to deal with hypothermia, see the Health section earlier in this chapter.

Deutscher Alpenverein The Deutscher Alpenverein (German Alpine Association, DAV; ☎ 089-14 00 30, fax 140 03 98, ✉ info@alpenverein.de, ⓦ www.alpenverein .de), Von-Kahr-Strasse 2–4, 80997 Munich, is a good resource of information on hiking and mountaineering.

The DAV also maintains numerous Alpine mountain huts, many of them open to the public, where you can spend the night and get a meal. These range from simple, remote shelters (category 1) to comfortable cabins suitable for multi-day stays (category 2) to easy-access places geared primarily towards day-trippers (cat-egory 3). Nonmember rates range from €7.50 to €20 per night. Members pay about half, get priority if space is tight, have access to cooking facilities and enjoy a number of other privileges.

To become a member, you have to join a local chapter. Annual fees vary a bit but you can expect them to be around €50 for those over age 27, €32 for ages 18 to 27 and €15.50 for ages 14 to 18; membership is free for members' children under 14. There's also a one-time €20 sign-up fee.

Local DAV chapters organise a number of courses (climbing, mountaineering etc) and guided treks, with which you can link up. The local tourist offices also often have information about DAV activities.

Cycling

Pedalling around Bavaria is extremely popu-lar both in cities and the countryside, and dozens of long-distance bicycle trails criss-cross the state. Routes are marked and are often a combination of lightly travelled back roads, forestry access roads and dedicated bike lanes. The Bavarian state government publishes an overview map called *Bayern-netz für Radler* (Bavaria's Cycling Network), which shows the course of all routes; it also includes a map of local trains on which you may transport your bicycle for free. Detailed descriptions of individual routes are avail-able on its Web site ⓦ www.bayerninfo.de, although it's unfortunately in German only. Here are some of the most popular trails:

Altmühltal (190km) Rothenburg ob der Tauber to Beilngries – along the Altmühl River and through the Altmühl Valley Nature Park

Bodensee-Königsweg (399km) Lindau to Berchtesgaden – traverses the Alpine Foothills, with magnificent views of the mountains

Donauradweg (434km) Neu-Ulm to Passau – a delightful riverside trip along one of Europe's great streams

Maintal (71km) Bamberg to Kulmbach – a short-ish trail through a lovely part of Franconia

Nationalparkradweg (88km) Zwiesel to Haidmühle – this trail explores the Bavarian Forest and even dips across the border into the Czech Republic (bring passport; check visa requirements for some nationalities)

Romantic Road (347km) Würzburg to Füssen – one of the nicest ways to explore Germany's most famous holiday route

For shorter routes, staff at the local tourist offices are usually a fount of information and also sell topographical maps. Many hotels and pensions cater specifically for bicycle tourists. The national cycling or-ganisation ADFC publishes a useful direc-tory called *Bett & Bike Bayern* (€6.50), which lists many such establishments. It is available from ADFC branches (see Bicycle in the Getting Around chapter); for a partial listing, although in German only, see its Web site at ⓦ www.bettundbike.de.

Responsible Hiking

The popularity of hiking is placing great pressure on the natural environment. Consider the following tips and help preserve the ecology and beauty of Bavaria's natural areas.

Rubbish

Carry out all your rubbish, including those easily forgotten items, such as silver paper, orange peel, cigarette butts and plastic wrappers. Make an effort to carry out rubbish left by others.

Never bury your waste: Digging disturbs soil and ground cover and encourages erosion. Buried rubbish will more than likely be dug up by animals, which may be injured or poisoned by it. It may also take years to decompose, especially at high altitudes.

Minimise the waste you must carry out by taking minimal packaging and taking no more food than you will need. If you can't buy in bulk, unpack small-portion packages and combine their contents in one container before your trip. Take reusable containers or stuff sacks.

Rather than bringing bottled water, use iodine drops or purification tablets instead. Sanitary napkins, tampons and condoms should also be carried out despite the inconvenience, as they burn and decompose poorly.

Human Waste Disposal

Contamination of water sources by human faeces can lead to the transmission of hepatitis, typhoid and intestinal parasites such as Giardia, amoebas and roundworms. It can cause severe health risks not only to members of your party, but also to local residents and wildlife.

Use toilets where available or bury your waste, including toilet paper, by digging a small hole 15cm deep and at least 100m from any body of water. Consider carrying a lightweight trowel for this purpose. Cover the waste with soil and a rock.

Washing

Don't use detergents or toothpaste in or near bodies of waters, even if they are biodegradable. Use biodegradable soap and a water container (or even a lightweight, portable basin) at least 50m away from any body of water. Wash cooking utensils 50m from bodies of waters using a scouring brush, sand or snow instead of detergent.

Erosion

Hillsides and mountain slopes, especially at high altitudes, are prone to erosion. It is important to stick to existing tracks and avoid short cuts that bypass a switchback. If you blaze a new trail straight down a slope, it will turn into a watercourse with the next heavy rainfall and eventually cause soil loss and deep scarring. If a well-used track passes through a mud patch, walk through the mud; walking around the edge will increase the size of the patch. Avoid removing the plant life that keeps topsoil in place.

Bicycles can be hired in most towns; see the Getting Around sections of the individual towns. See also the detailed discussion under Bicycle in the Getting Around chapter. Always have a good lock for your bike.

Skiing

Bavaria has three major skiing areas. The Bavarian Alps are only one hour south of Munich and offer the country's best downhill skiing as well as the greatest variety of pistes and the most reliable ski conditions. The Olympic Games town of Garmisch-Partenkirchen is the most popular Alpine resort, but nearby Mittenwald is actually cheaper and, many say, more charming. Another option is Reit im Winkl in the Chiemgau, an area that also offers some of the best cross-country skiing, especially around Ruhpolding. There's also skiing in Berchtesgaden.

The Bavarian Forest has surprisingly reliable snow conditions despite its moderate elevations (up to 1456m). It's less crowded and more low-key and therefore well suited to families. The downhill action centres on the Grosser Arber mountain, while fans of Nordic skiing flock to the trails in the Bayerischer Wald Nationalpark. The main resort of the Allgäu is Oberstdorf, a picture-perfect mountain town, which is largely car-free and offers excellent downhill conditions.

The skiing season generally runs from late November/early December to March, although this of course depends on specific elevations and weather conditions. All winter resorts have equipment rental facilities. The lowest daily rate for downhill gear is about €10, less if you rent gear for longer periods. Cross-country equipment also costs slightly less. Daily ski-lift passes start at around €15.

For more information, contact the Deutscher Skiverband (German Skiing Association; ☎ 089-85 79 02 13, fax 85 79 02 63) at Hubertusstrasse 1 in 82152 München-Planegg.

Water Sports

In summer, Bavaria's lakes often teem with colourful sails, which from a distance look like a swarm of exotic butterflies. The Walchensee in the Tölzer Land is famous for its wind conditions and is a mecca for windsurfers, including the sport's elite. The Forggensee near the royal castles in the Allgäu isn't bad either. Sailors will feel more at home on Lake Starnberg and the Chiemsee, which are larger. Diving is a possibility in the Walchensee and Lake Starnberg, where water-skiing is also a popular pastime. For rafting and canoeing, the Isar River offers the best conditions.

Check with the local tourist office about equipment rental places.

Spas & Saunas

Germans love to sweat it out in the sauna, and most public baths *(Stadtbäder)* have sauna facilities, usually with fixed hours for men and women as well as mixed sessions. Prices start from around €6. Note that not a stitch of clothing is worn, so leave your modesty in the locker. Bring, or rent, a towel.

Booking in for a regimen of sauna, bath, massage and exercise in a spa resort *(Kurort)* is also popular. The local spa centre *(Kurzentrum)* or spa administration *(Kurverwaltung)* will have price lists for services. Expect to pay upwards of €20 for a full massage. Sauna/massage combinations are popular. Services can usually be booked at short notice.

COURSES

A wide variety of courses are offered in Bavaria, including hands-on sessions in pottery, sculpture or skiing which require no special language skills. The best sources of information are the local or regional tourist offices, particularly in popular resort areas. Local newspapers are another good place to look.

Language

The Goethe Institut is a government-subsidised nonprofit, cultural and language organisation that promotes German language and culture abroad. Besides offering a comprehensive course program, it's also engaged in staging some 10,000 cultural events year round, including theatre performances, symposia, lectures, film and music festivals. In Bavaria, the Goethe Institut has centres in Munich, Murnau, Prien and Rothenburg ob der Tauber.

Goethe Institut language courses cater to all age groups and stages of proficiency – from absolute beginner to professional level. The program is divided into three general levels – *Grundstufe* (basic), *Mittelstufe* (intermediate) and *Oberstufe* (advanced) – and each is further divided into sublevels.

Intensive courses cost from around €1546 to €1602 (eight weeks), €862 to €878 (four weeks) and €694 (two weeks), excluding accommodation and meals. The institute also runs three-week summer programs for children and youths aged 10 to 20 years from €1750, including accommodation and meals.

Get detailed course information from the Goethe Institut's central registration office (☎ 089-15 92 12 00, fax 15 92 14 44), Helene-Weber-Allee 1, 80637 Munich. You can also find information on the Internet at Ⓦ www.goethe.de.

WORK

It is illegal for non-EU citizens to work in Germany without a work permit and a residency permit. The former requires an application with the Arbeitsamt (Employment Office), while the latter is issued by the Ausländerbehörde (Foreigners' Office). Obtaining either is a tedious process, to say the least.

EU citizens don't need a work permit but still need to obtain an EU residency permit (EU-Aufenthaltserlaubnis), which is a mere formality in most cases.

Bavaria has one of the lowest unemployment rates among the German states (5.3% in 2001 versus 9.4% nationwide), but even here finding work is not all that easy. One complicating factor is that Germans place great importance on formal qualifications – especially German qualifications.

However, like most other European countries, Germany lacks qualified workers in the computer and software branches. It has therefore introduced a so-called temporary 'Green Card' for foreign specialists. Information on the scheme is available in English on the Web at www.arbeitsamt.de /hst/international/egcindex.html, or ask at any German embassy.

Au Pair

Work as an au pair is relatively easy to find and there are numerous approved au pair agencies you can approach. A useful guide is *The Au Pair and Nanny's Guide to Working Abroad* by Susan Griffith & Sharon Legg. *Work Your Way Around the World*, also by Susan Griffith, is another suggestion.

Teaching English

You may be able to find work teaching English at language schools or privately, but you will still need work and residency permits, as well as valid health insurance at all times. Teaching English is certainly no way to get rich, but it might help to keep your head above water or prolong a trip. The hourly rate varies dramatically – from a low of €15 per hour rising to about €40 for qualified professionals in large cities. Local papers are the best way to advertise, but other good places to start are notice boards at universities, photocopy shops or even local supermarkets.

ACCOMMODATION

Accommodation in Bavaria is generally comfortable and well organised. If you have no advance booking, head to the local tourist office. They have lists of local hotels and private rooms and can sometimes help you find a place to stay, usually for a small fee. If the office is closed, look for listings in the window or exterior display cases. Some branches have electronic reservation boards or touch terminals that connect you directly to a local establishment. When making a reservation, always tell the receptionist what time they can expect you and stick to it or ring again. Many well-meaning visitors have lost rooms by turning up late.

A wonderful feature of German hotels and pensions is that room rates almost always include breakfast, usually in the form of an all-you-can-eat buffet with cheeses and cold cuts, jams and honey, various breads and rolls, a choice of cereals and unlimited coffee or tea. Unless noted, all room rates quoted in this book include breakfast. Hotels and pensions with attached restaurants often offer half board (breakfast and dinner) or even full board (breakfast, lunch and dinner) for an extra fee.

Germany's reputation for cleanliness extends to accommodation; even budget places are usually spotlessly clean. Television, in-room phones and lifts are not standard amenities, so check ahead if this is important to you.

Some places still have rooms with varying levels of comfort. While some rooms come with full private bath (shower or tub and toilet), others may require you to share sanitary facilities with other guests. Occasionally, rooms have a private shower cubicle but no toilet. This set-up usually explains the big range in room rates.

If you're driving, note that most city hotels don't have their own parking. Street parking may be elusive, requiring you to leave your car in an expensive public garage (about €13 per night) which may even be located quite a distance from the hotel. Top-end hotels may have their own car parks or valet parking, though in either case this will still add around €13 per day to your hotel bill.

Kurtaxe

A nightly *Kurtaxe* (resort tax) is charged to overnight guests in most resorts and spas. This may be a nominal €0.25 or a hefty €3 per night and is usually not included in the quoted room rate. Paying the tax is compulsory and usually gets you a *Kurkarte* (resort card) good for small discounts to museums or concerts and other events.

Camping

Camping is a viable budget alternative and camping grounds are ubiquitous in Bavaria, especially in the rural areas. Having your own transportation is a definite advantage, as many sites are in remote locales and often not served by public transport.

The season generally runs from May to September, but many camping grounds stay open all year. The range of facilities varies greatly, from the primitive to the luxurious. Some camping grounds rent out cabins, caravans or rooms in a pension. For camping on private property, permission from the landowner is required. Nightly costs in camping grounds vary according to the standard, but €2.50 to €5 is common for tent sites. Many then charge around €3.50 per person and €1.50 for cars.

Hostels

The Deutsches Jugendherbergswerk (DJH) coordinates all affiliated Hostelling International (HI) hostels in Germany. All require DJH or HI membership cards (see Hostel Cards earlier in this chapter). Bavarian hostels are only open to people under 26, except for group leaders and parents accompanying their children under 26. Some hostels may make exceptions if business is slow. It never hurts to ask nicely.

To make reservations, contact the hostels directly by phone, fax or email or use the online booking system at [w] www.djh-ris.de.

There are 87 hostels in Bavaria, many of them in scenic locations or taking up historic buildings or even castles. Most are open year round, but some close for a few weeks and sometimes for a few months in winter during lulls in visitor activity. By contrast, most fill up quickly on weekends and throughout summer. In April/May and September/October, they're often booked out by rambunctious school groups.

DJH hostels have different levels of comfort and amenities, which is reflected in the price. Dorm beds range from about €12 to €23, including breakfast and linen. Hostels don't have cooking facilities, but rates include breakfast; lunch or supper costs between €2.60 and €5.

Check-in hours vary, but you must usually be out by 9am. You don't need to do chores at the hostels and there are few rules. Curfews are common (as early as 10pm, but often midnight or even 2am in cities) and some hostels have daytime lockouts.

Independent, ie, non-DJH hostels, are prevalent only in the bigger cities. They're often party places without curfews and staffed by hip young people in the know about their city.

Hotels & Pensions

Budget hotel rooms can be a bit hard to come by in July and August, although there is usually not much seasonal variation in price. It's increasingly rare to find single rooms with facilities for less than €20, and most are in the €25 to €45 bracket. Doubles work out substantially cheaper – you will find good quality ones in many cities for €65 or less. Prices are higher in major cities such as Munich and Nuremberg.

Mid-range hotels generally offer the best value. In-room amenities are often comparable to upscale abodes, there's usually a bar and/or restaurant and sometimes even a sauna and fitness room.

Expensive hotels offer few advantages for their upmarket prices. The best time to splurge on them is on weekends or during a lull in trade-fair and conference activity, when you can sometimes take advantage of a package deal or special discounts.

Pensions are like small budget hotels that offer the basics of hotel comfort without charging hotel prices. Many of these are private homes somewhat out of the centre of town with several rooms to rent. More often than not, sanitary facilities are shared and only breakfast is served. Most charge around €25 to €35 for singles and €35 to €45 for doubles. Gasthäuser or Gasthöfe (guest houses or inns) are similar but usually have a restaurant attached.

Many hotels and pension have 'family' rooms with three or four beds, or can place a fold-up bed in the room for a child.

Private Rooms

Especially in tourist resorts, many locals make a few extra euros by renting rooms in their private house to visitors. Not only is this a very inexpensive way to stay overnight, but it also has the advantage of allowing you to catch a glimpse of how local people live. You can expect clean and often nicely furnished rooms, but amenities are usually limited to a radio and, sometimes, a TV. Facilities are often but not always shared.

Since these places cannot afford to advertise, the easiest way to find out about them is through the local tourist office, which keeps lists of available rooms. You'll usually be expected to make your own reservations but may be able to sweet-talk the staff into helping you if your German isn't up to it.

Owners will often inquire about the length of your stay before giving room prices. Generally, the longer you stay, the cheaper the daily room price. If you intend to stay for more than one night, it is always a good idea to say so at the start. In some resort towns, owners are reluctant to let rooms for just one night. It is generally a little more difficult to find singles than doubles, and for use of a double room as a single room *(Einzelbelegung)* you might end up paying 75% of the double-room rate.

In the absence of a tourist office, look for signs saying '*Zimmer frei*' (rooms available) or '*Fremdenzimmer*' (tourist rooms) in house or shop windows.

Farm Stays

Tourist offices can help with rooms or holiday flats on farms. This may be a basic room on a fully-fledged farm where 'Junior', waving from the tractor, makes hay while the sun shines, or one holiday flat among many, nominally on a farm, where tourists are the main crop. Farm stays are quite common throughout Bavaria, especially in Upper Bavaria, and are very popular with families. Generally, you'll need your own transport to get to and away from these places.

Rental Accommodation

Renting an apartment for a week or longer is a popular form of holiday accommodation in Bavaria. Tourist offices have lists of *Ferienwohnungen* or *Ferien-Appartements* (holiday flats or apartments). Most have cooking facilities (which means breakfast isn't included) and can be rented in cities and the country for a minimum period, usually three days.

Some pensions and hotels also have a couple of apartments, and occasionally owners are willing to rent holiday flats for one night for a surcharge. This can be truly budget accommodation for groups of two to four people.

Mitwohnzentralen If you're going to stay in any one city for a month or longer, you might consider renting a room or an apartment through a *Mitwohnzentrale* (flat-sharing agency). These match up people willing to let their digs temporarily with those in need of a temporary home. Accommodation can be anything from rooms in shared student flats to furnished apartments.

In order to find a place, you first must fill out an application form, which you can pick up in person, receive in the mail or download from the Internet. Also use the agencies' Web sites (most are also in English) for a general overview of what's available.

Rates vary by agency and type of accommodation but, generally speaking, a room in a flat costs about €300 to €400 per month and a one-bedroom apartment ranges from €400 to €650. Commission (up to one month's rent) and VAT (16%) must be added to the rental rate.

The final tally almost always comes to less than what you'd pay in a hotel. In general, the longer you rent, the less expensive it gets. Even if you're not staying, say for an entire month, it may still work out cheaper to pay the monthly rent and leave early.

The Verband der Mitwohnzentralen (☎ 089-194 45, fax 27 32 29 29, **e** home company-muenchen@t-online.de), Georgenstrasse 45, 80799 Munich, is an umbrella association of over 40 such services throughout Germany. Also see the contact information for local Mitwohnzentralen in each sections of individual cities and towns.

FOOD
Bavarian food is hearty, thigh-slapping fare, which only gives a passing nod to the vegetable kingdom. Much of it is delicious, soul-sustaining and hugely satisfying, but if you're worried about your waistline or your arteries, you'll need to pick your way through a menu with great care. Many meals feature some combination of pork, potatoes, gravy and braised or boiled cabbage. The dishes meant to be extra special are billed as *Schmankerl*.

All German beef is tested for BSE, of which fewer than 100 animals were found positive since compulsory testing began. The risk is therefore minimal; organic meat offers a more expensive alternative to factory-farming products and is now available at meat counters in some supermarkets.

Sausages
Bavarians have a keen love affair with *Wurst* (sausage), which exists in a bewildering variety. It is traditionally served with sweet *(süss)* or spicy *(scharf)* mustard *(Senf)*, with either sauerkraut or potato salad, and a piece of bread or a roll.

The culinary flagship of Munich is the *Weisswurst*, a white veal sausage 'invented' by a local pub owner in 1857. This being Bavaria, strict rules apply for preparing and eating Weisswurst. The Munich Sausage Controls Board (yes, there is one) has ruled that Weisswurst must contain at least 70% veal, with the remainder made up of brains, hide, spleen and other yummy ingredients. It must be simmered but *never* boiled, peeled before eating and consumed with sweet, grainy mustard. Bavarians generally enjoy it as a mid-morning 'snack' – the traditional 'Weisswurst break' – and the only drink that can possibly do it justice is a foamy Weissbier. Unlike local beers, Weisswurst has few friends beyond the Bavarian border, and some Germans still refer to that frontier as the *Weisswurstäquator* (equator).

In Eastern Bavaria and Franconia, the *Bratwurst*, a nicely spiced sausage, rules. These come in various sizes, but Nuremberg and Regensburg make the most famous versions: finger-sized links that are eaten by the half dozen to dozen (also see boxed text 'The Nuremberg Sausage – Links to the Past' in the Franconia chapter). Sulzberg in the Franconian Wine Country is famous for its *Meterbratwurst*, a 1m-long variety that curls up on your plate.

Other sausages include *Blutwurst* (blood sausage) and the non-Bavarian *Krakauer*, a paprika-spice sausage of Polish origin.

A *Wurstteller* is a generous spread of sausage served with a couple of slices of bread and a token sprig of parsley, while a *Schlachtplatte* (literally, 'slaughter platter') includes liver and blood sausage.

Traditional Specialities
No part of the pig is safe from Bavarian chefs. The most popular dishes are *Schweinebraten* (pork roast), *Schweinshax'n* (pork knuckles), *Schweineschäuferl* (pork shoulder) and *Rippchen* (spare ribs). If you're one of those people who takes pride in eating anything, *Züngerl* (pig's tongue) and *Wammerl* (pig's belly) should present suitable challenges. *Kronfleisch* (beef diaphragm) also falls into this category.

Now that we've grossed out most of you, here are some safer choices: *Hendl* (chicken) are sold roasted in halves or whole, and *Fleischpflanzerl*, the Bavarian version of the hamburger, is good too. Another favourite is *Leberkäs* (literally, 'liver cheese'), a complete misnomer since it contains neither liver nor cheese. It's actually a smooth spicy meatloaf, served in thick, juicy slabs and generally delicious. *Tellerfleisch* is slices of lean boiled beef served with horseradish or spicy mustard.

The main vegetable is the potato, which comes prepared in umpteen ways, most commonly boiled, fried, as salad or shaped into dumplings *(Knödel)*. Dumplings can also be made of bread *(Semmelknödel)* or liver *(Leberknödel)*. Cabbage is another common culinary companion, usually in the form of *Sauerkraut* (white cabbage marinated in vinegar) or boiled red cabbage.

Nonmeaty specialities are few but delicious. A popular food, especially at festivals and in beer gardens, is *Steckerlfisch*, skewers of small mackerel which are grilled over a charcoal fire. Carp and trout are delicious and usually available during all months containing an 'r' (ie, January, February, but not June). The month of May is peak season for *Spargel* (white asparagus), which is classically paired with boiled potatoes and hollandaise sauce. Also in spring, look for *Bärlauch*, a wild forest herb with a faint garlic aroma that is usually turned into a pesto sauce.

As for dessert, *Dampfnudeln* (steamed dumplings) are doughy sweet dumplings sprinkled with cinnamon or poppy seeds and drowned in custard sauce. Apple strudel is a tasty alternative.

Vegetarian

In the land of meat and potatoes, vegetarianism hasn't exactly made huge inroads. Most restaurant menus feature a few token 'vegetarian' options, but some chefs don't see anything wrong with using chicken or beef stock in the preparation. Fish is also often considered a 'meatless' dish and salads may have eggs and ham mixed in with the lettuce and tomatoes. Indian, Thai, Vietnamese and other Asian eateries often have tofu or vegetable-based mains.

Fast Food

German fast-food places are called *Imbiss* or *Schnellimbiss* and they're ubiquitous. In addition to the international burger chains (Burger King and McDonald's are the most common), a few home-grown places exist as well.

Nordsee is a fish Imbiss where you can pick up a quick sandwich or sit down for an inexpensive and usually quite good hot meal. An outfit specific to Bavaria is Vinzenzmurr, a butcher-deli, which has a variety of hot meals, from burgers to Leberkäs to pork roast with dumplings. Some branches also have a salad bar where you buy by weight. Kochlöffel is a so-so German burger chain with good prices.

Turkish food is another good option, at least in the cities. The most popular dish is the doner kebab – a sandwich made from slivers of roasted meat (traditionally a veal and lamb combination) stuffed into lightly toasted bread along with fresh salad and a garlicky yoghurt sauce. It's a filling meal usually costing no more than €2.50. A delicious vegetarian alternative is Turkish 'pizza' called *lahmacun*, made by putting lots of salad vegetables onto a pancake-shaped bread that's been topped with a spicy red sauce, drizzling it all with tzatziki and rolling it up like a burrito.

Other takeaway offerings include individual slices of pizza, sausages and simple sandwiches.

Meal times

German breakfasts *(Frühstück)* are veritable feasts, usually consisting of white and wholegrain rolls; different types of sliced bread, jam, cold cuts and cheese; eggs (usually boiled), plus coffee, tea or hot chocolate. At hotels and pensions, the all-you-can-eat breakfast buffet is now pretty much commonplace and usually included in your room rate – a great way to tank up on energy before a day of rigorous sightseeing. Among young people, going to a cafe for Sunday brunch is becoming increasingly popular.

Lunch *(Mittagessen)* is traditionally the biggest meal and in Bavaria many businesses and shops actually close for a couple of hours around noon. Old-style restaurants often offer a *Stammgericht*, which is a daily changing main dish served at lunchtime only. Chinese and other Asian eateries sometimes have set lunch menus consisting of a soup or salad followed by a hot main dish.

Dinner *(Abendessen* or *Abendbrot)* in restaurants is served from 5pm or 6pm until about 9pm or 10pm. Eating out in Germany is a social event and most restaurants figure on only one or two seatings per night, so you don't need to feel rushed after you've finished your meal. You may stay on for another hour or so just nursing a drink, chatting and enjoying the atmosphere. The bill will only be presented to you when you request it.

Bavaria also has a fourth meal time, the *Brotzeit*. Literally meaning 'bread time', Brotzeit is actually a snack break between the main meals. Typical 'snacks' include sausages, Leberkäs, bread with *Schmalz* (lard), pretzels, sausage salad and Fleischpfanzerl. In restaurants, a special Brotzeit menu is offered only in the afternoon. Some people indulge in a Weisswürste Brotzeit around 11am to tide them over between breakfast and lunch. In the Alps, many *Almen* (rustic mountain restaurants) offer Brotzeit to hikers all day.

DRINKS
Nonalcoholic

Tap water is fine to drink but asking for a glass at a restaurant will raise brows at best and may be refused altogether because they want to sell you an expensive bottle of mineral water *(Mineralwasser)*. This almost always has bubbles, although still water is becoming more popular. If you're picky, be sure to specify what you want when ordering. Soft drinks are widely available, although the diet versions are not. If familiar brands such as Pepsi or Coca-Cola taste slightly different from what you're used to, it's because they've been reformulated to meet German tastes. A refreshing drink is *Apfelschorle*, which is apple juice mixed with sparkling mineral water.

Nonalcoholic beer *(alkoholfreies Bier)* is very good and has become quite popular. Clausthaler is a popular brand, and Löwenbräu is also a tasty nonalcoholic beer that is frequently served on tap.

Coffee is usually fresh and strong. It comes in cups *(Tasse)* or pots *(Kännchen)* and you should specify what you want when ordering. Condensed milk and sugar will usually be served alongside. In trendy cafes you'll often see people nursing huge cups of coffee, called *Milchkaffee* (milk coffee) and containing a large amount of hot milk. One warning: the bottomless cup is *not* a concept here, and a single cup can cost as much as €2.50. If you just want a quick cuppa, grab it at a Stehcafé or the counters of the Eduscho or Tschibo coffee stores where it'll cost around €1.30.

A very annoying custom, especially prevalent in tourist resorts, is the refusal to serve you just a cup of coffee if you are sitting on the outdoor terrace of a cafe or restaurant. There's nothing less endearing than the sound of a server snarling a '*Draussen nur Kännchen*' (Pots only outside) at you.

If you're ordering tea, and don't want a pot, ask for *ein Glass Tee* (glass of tea). It'll usually be served in the form of a teabag with sugar and maybe a slice of lemon. If you want milk, ask for *Tee mit Milch*.

Alcoholic

Beer Bavaria is the most productive beer region in the world, and the locals have made a science out of brewing. All beers adhere to the Reinheitsgebot (Purity Law) passed in 1516. You'll have a stunning choice, including *Pils* (pilsener), which is a good standby even if occasionally bitter. More common is the pale ale called *Helles*, its darker counterpart known as a *Dunkles*, and *Schwarzbier*, a stout similar to Guinness (but without the creamy foam). *Starkbier* and *Bockbier* are strong varieties brewed mostly in springtime.

A popular Bavarian brew is *Weissbier*, also known as *Weizenbier*. It's made with wheat instead of barley malt and served in tall, half-litre glasses. Weissbier comes pale or dark and also as a cloudy variety called

Hefeweizen, with a layer of still-fermenting yeast on the bottom of the bottle.

If you want to go easy on the brew, order a sweetish *Radler* which comes in half or full litres and mixes pale ale and lemonade. A *Russe* ('Russian') is generally a litre-sized concoction of Weissbier and lemonade.

Wines
Bavaria's only wine-growing region is the Franconian Wine Country in and around Würzburg. Despite what you may have heard – or tasted – back home, German wines are remarkably good. Their reputation as being sweet and headache-inducing is largely undeserved. The 'problem' is that Germany doesn't produce a great amount of wine and most of the good stuff is consumed within its borders, leaving only the swill for export. Riesling, Müller-Thurgau and Silvaner are the three most celebrated German varietals. A *Weinschorle* is white wine mixed with sparkling mineral water. Wine is drunk as an aperitif or with meals.

ENTERTAINMENT
While Bavaria offers much in the way of *Hochkultur* (high culture), it also has lots of wonderful beer halls, beer gardens, and discos and clubs where you can mix it with a thronging crowd.

Pubs & Bars
The variety of *Kneipen* (pubs) in Bavaria is enormous, ranging from vaulted-cellar bars through to theme pubs, Irish pubs and historic student pubs. Some are absolute dives packed with drunks slugging down rotgut, others are stylish affairs with good food and drink. You'll usually be able to tell rather quickly which one you're in. There are also American-style stand-up bars in larger cities. While beers are relatively inexpensive, mixed cocktails can cost as much as €7.50 or €10. Wine is also rather expensive. A few words on procedure. In most cases, it's customary not to pay for your drinks upon ordering or when they are served. A tab is kept and you pay when leaving.

In many traditional pubs (and beer halls, see next), you'll often see a brass plaque, a flag or some other symbol atop a table. This means that it's a *Stammtisch*, a table reserved for regulars, usually groups of elderly men. You'll often see them gesticulating wildly in heated debates about *Gott und die Welt* (God and the world) while hoisting big mugs of beer and occasionally taking a dip from their snuff box. Even in touristy places, sitting down at such tables invites trouble – even if you're spared an angry tirade, you won't be served unless you're part of the group.

Beer Halls & Beer Gardens
Beer halls are large pubs with rustic and plain decor and usually affiliated with a particular brewery. Although food is served, they really are dedicated drinking places. The world's most famous beer hall is the Hofbräuhaus in Munich. There's often live entertainment, usually in the form of oompah bands, which creates a jolly, sometimes raucous atmosphere.

As soon as the last winter storms have blown away, pallid Bavarians re-acquaint themselves with the sun as the action moves outdoors into the beer gardens where you sit at long wooden tables beneath ancient chestnut trees. Usually you'll be required to pay a *Pfand* (deposit) on the glass (about €2.50). Periodic attempts to curb opening times for beer gardens have caused uproars throughout Bavaria, and locals scornfully tag them 'Prussian' measures.

Discos & Clubs
Discos are popular throughout Bavaria and exist even in the rural areas. Most play different music on different nights, depending on the DJ and the targeted crowd – techno freaks, *Schlager* (schmaltzy German pop) fans, gays, or aficionados of Latin salsa, country and western or disco. Getting into clubs is fairly easy everywhere except Munich, where the Gucci and Armani crowd rules many of the trendiest venues. Discos in the countryside are generally low-key, but you may need to organise your own transport to get there and back.

Generally, admission to clubs is between €2.50 and €5, though it can be as little as

And There's Food, Too!

Many Bavarian beer gardens, especially those in Munich, allow you to bring your own food as long as you consume their drinks and don't sit at tables featuring tablecloths and utensils (these are reserved for people ordering food from the restaurant). In many cases, drinks are self-service at these tables.

If you do decide to order food, you'll find very similar menus at all beer gardens. Typical dishes include roast chicken, spare ribs, huge pretzels and Bavarian specialities such as *Schweinebraten* (roast pork) and roast chicken.

Radi is a huge, mild radish that's eaten with beer; it's cut with a *Radimesser*, which sticks down in the centre – you twist the handle round and round, creating a radish spiral. Buy a Radimesser at any department store and buy the radish at a market, or buy prepared radish for about €4. If you do it yourself, smother the cut end of the radish with salt until it 'cries' to reduce bitterness (and increase your thirst!).

Obazda (**oh**-batsdah) is Bavarian for 'mixed up' – this cream-cheese-like speciality is made of butter, Camembert and paprika. Spread it on *Brez'n* (a pretzel) or bread. If you hate it while sober, you may like it after a few drinks.

nothing or as much as €10. Check if there's a minimum drink purchase in addition to the admission; sometimes the price already includes a drink or two.

Opera & Classical Music

Fans of classical music have plenty to enjoy throughout Bavaria. Opera aficionados will get their fill with the world-class Bayerische Staatsoper, which performs at the Nationaltheater in Munich; Nuremberg and Regensburg also have operas. One of the world's most famous opera festivals is the Richard Wagner Festival in Bayreuth, which also hosts the Fränkische Festwoche, a concert and opera series at the Margravial Operahouse. Other highlights on the festival calendar are the Richard-Strauss-Tage in Garmisch-Partenkirchen, the Mozart Festival in Würzburg and Bach Week in Ansbach.

Munich has the most famous orchestras, including the Münchener Philharmonie and the Symphonieorchester des Bayerischen Rundfunks, but a concert by the Bamberger Symphoniker in Bamberg is also a special treat for lovers of classical music.

The Regensburger Domspatzen and the Tölzer Knabenchor are famous boys' choirs.

Concerts often take place in historical venues, including the Festival Hall at Schloss Dachau, the Schaetzlerpalais in Augsburg, the Sängersaal in Neuschwanstein, the Spiegelsaal in Herrenchiemsee and the Schöner Hof courtyard on the Plassenburg in Kulmbach.

Bavaria's grand churches are often settings for organ recitals; the cathedrals of Bamberg and Passau and the Benedictine Abbey in Ottobeuren are just a few notable examples.

Theatre

Munich has the greatest variety of theatres, including a few English-language troupes, but other cities, including Nuremberg and Regensburg, also maintain their own ensembles. Bamberg has the ETA Hoffmann Theatre. Ludwig II's life story forms the fodder of a melodramatic musical staged in a custom-built theatre in Füssen.

In the Alpine resort towns, you'll often find *Bauerntheater* (literally, 'peasant theatre'), which are usually silly and rustic tales performed in dialect by amateur or semi-pro actors dressed in folkloric outfits. Even if you're unable to understand the language (and trust us, most non-Bavarians are), you'll probably be able to follow the plot anyway and definitely get a good dose of local colour.

Another popular theatrical form is the *Kabarett*, which is political and satirical entertainment featuring clever monologues and short skits. The Comödie Fürth and the Münchner Lach- und Schiessgesellschaft are two popular troupes.

Cinemas

Films are popular but tickets are pricey, with Saturday night tickets at a fancy multiplex costing as much as €9. Seeing a show on *Kinotag* (film day, usually Tuesday or Wednesday) or before 5pm usually saves a couple of euro.

Most mainstream Hollywood movies are dubbed into German. Movies shown in their original language without subtitles are denoted by the acronym 'OF' *(Originalfassung)*; those shown *with* subtitles are denoted 'OmU' *(Original mit Untertiteln)*. These types of screenings are more commonly found in cities.

SPECTATOR SPORTS
Football
Football *(Fussball)*, or soccer, is by far the most popular sport. For the last two decades, Munich's FC Bayern has been the dominant team in the German premier national league, the *Bundesliga*. It's been national champion 11 times (the last time in 2001) and has also won several other major German competitions. Even top teams have their ups-and-downs, though, and the 2001/2 season, while still underway at the time of writing, was not shaping up so well.

Munich's secondary team, the TSV 1860 München has also played in the premier league for many seasons. In the 1999/2000 season, the two were joined by an upstart team from the Munich suburb of Unterhaching. It reached a surprising 10th place that season, but has since dropped back to second league.

The only other Bavarian team playing in the premier league is the 1 FC Nürnberg, but at the time of writing it hovered near the bottom of the division.

Football season runs from September to June, with a winter break from Christmas to mid-February.

Skiing
Skiing is another major spectator sport with World Cup races held annually in several resorts, including Oberstdorf, Reit im Winkl and Berchtesgaden. Around New Year's, Oberstdorf and Garmisch-Partenkirchen are the first two stops on the *Vierschanzentournee* World Cup ski-jumping competition (the other two are in Innsbruck and in Bischofshofen).

SHOPPING
Products made in Germany are of high quality but rarely cheap.

If you're in the market for traditional Bavarian dress, expect to spend at least €200 for a quality adult leather jacket or a dirndl (women's dress). Bavaria is also the place to buy hunting gear, especially if you have a penchant for traditional hunting hats.

Anyone seeking quality toys should visit Nuremberg, where a tradition of toy manufacture dates back to the 16th century. The city was famous for its wooden dolls with movable limbs, and later for toys made out of tin. It remains a centre for toys, traditional as well as modern plastic, many of which can be found at its Christmas market.

The Bavarian Forest is famous for its crystal glassware and Franconia for its wine. Beer steins are best bought from breweries or beer halls.

Germany excels in optical goods such as binoculars and lenses, and its Leica and Zeiss brands have an excellent reputation worldwide. Therapeutic footwear, such as the sandals and shoes made by Birkenstock and orthopaedic inlays by Scholl, is another niche market.

Art reproductions, books and posters are sold in some museums and speciality shops. Also of high quality are illustrated calendars and coffee-table books. Collectors of antiquarian books will find a large selection in *Antiquariat* bookshops in the major centres or university towns. English-language books, except for those used in schools, tend to be overpriced; if you need to stock up on reading material, go to larger second-hand bookshops or shop around before you buy.

The annual Christmas markets are good places to pick up presents. Wax candles and ceramic goods are always well represented. Wooden toys and wooden boards (used by Germans for breakfast and the evening meal) are other options.

It is difficult to find real bargains at flea markets where 1970s junk dominates. But collectors of kitsch will be in their element; records and cassettes can usually be picked up for a euro or two and second-hand souvenirs sometimes for even less.

Getting There & Away

If you live outside Europe, chances are you'll be flying into Bavaria. Even if you're already in Europe, a flight may still be the fastest and cheapest option, especially from faraway places like Greece, Spain or Finland. Otherwise, train travel is the most efficient and comfortable method of travel, though buses are a viable – and usually cheaper – alternative. Bear in mind that seats fill up quickly and prices often surge during summer school holidays.

AIR
Airports & Airlines

Many European and international airlines compete with Germany's flagship airline, Lufthansa, which has a huge network of both domestic and international flights. Its Web site is at [W] www.lufthansa.com; it is a member of the Star Alliance of 15 airlines and its subsidiary Condor has charter flights mainly to holiday destinations in southern Europe.

Bavaria's central location within Europe makes it easily accessible from several airports, including those in other countries and German states. In addition to the main gateways described below, Nuremberg and Augsburg also have small airports with mostly domestic departures.

Munich Bavaria's main hub is Munich's Franz-Josef-Strauss airport. Completed in 1992, it is a showpiece of German engineering and the country's second-busiest airport after Frankfurt-am-Main. It embraces a huge shopping centre, an underground car park and bus and S-Bahn stations. Check-in, departures and arrivals are on Level 4, where you'll also find snack bars, restaurants, the lost and found office and airport information desks. Banks with ATMs, a pharmacy, a post office, car-rental outlets and lots of shops are on Level 3, where there's also an information desk that fields simple tourist queries.

Frankfurt-am-Main If you're headed for destinations in northern Bavaria, such as

Würzburg or the Romantic Road, the Frankfurt airport is actually more convenient than Munich's. An added advantage is that flights here are often cheaper than to any other German airport. There are two terminals linked by an elevated railway called the Sky Line. Departure and arrival halls A, B, and C are in the old Terminal 1, the western half of which handles Lufthansa flights. Halls D and E are in Terminal 2.

Salzburg Salzburg's airport is an alternative to Munich if you're headed to destinations in Eastern Bavaria or the Bavarian Alps. It's about 4km west of the city centre and has regular scheduled flights to/from Amsterdam, Brussels, London Stansted, Paris and Zürich.

Buying Tickets

If you're flying to Bavaria from outside Europe, your plane ticket is likely to be the

Air Travel Glossary

Alliances Many of the world's leading airlines are now intimately involved with each other, sharing everything from reservations systems and check-in to aircraft and frequent-flyer schemes. Opponents say that alliances restrict competition. Whatever the arguments, there is no doubt that big alliances are the way of the future.

Courier Fares Businesses often need to send urgent documents or freight securely and quickly. Courier companies hire people to accompany the package through customs and, in return, offer a discount ticket which is sometimes a bargain. However, you may have to surrender all your baggage allowance and take only carry-on luggage.

Fares Airlines traditionally offer 1st class (coded F), business class (coded J) and economy class (coded Y) tickets. These days there are so many promotional and discounted fares available that few passengers pay full fare.

Lost Tickets If you lose your airline ticket, an airline will usually treat it like a travellers cheque and, after inquiries, issue you with another one. Legally, however, an airline is entitled to treat it like cash and if you lose it then it's gone forever. Take very good care of your tickets.

Onward Tickets An entry requirement for many countries is that you have a ticket out of the country. If you're unsure of your next move, the easiest solution is to buy the cheapest onward ticket to a neighbouring country or a ticket from a reliable airline which can later be refunded if you do not use it.

Open-Jaw Tickets These are return tickets where you fly out to one place but return from another. If available, this can save you backtracking to your arrival point.

Overbooking Since every flight has some passengers who fail to show up, airlines often book more passengers than they have seats. Usually excess passengers make up for the no-shows, but occasionally somebody gets 'bumped' onto the next available flight. Guess who it is most likely to be? The passengers who check in late. If you do get 'bumped', you are normally offered some form of compensation.

Reconfirmation Some airlines require you to reconfirm your flight at least 72 hours prior to departure. Check your travel documents to see if this is the case

Restrictions Discounted tickets often have various restrictions on them – such as needing to be paid for in advance and incurring a penalty to be altered or cancelled. Others are restrictions on the minimum and maximum period you must be away.

Round-the-World Tickets RTW tickets give you a limited period (usually a year) in which to circumnavigate the globe. You can go anywhere the carrying airlines go, as long as you don't backtrack. The number of stopovers or total number of separate flights is decided before you set off and they usually cost a bit more than a basic return flight.

Ticketless Travel Airlines are gradually waking up to the realisation that paper tickets are unnecessary encumbrances. On simple one-way or return trips, reservations details can be held on computer and the passenger merely shows ID to claim their seat.

Transferred Tickets Airline tickets cannot be transferred from one person to another. Travellers sometimes try to sell the return half of their ticket, but officials can ask you to prove that you are the person named on the ticket. On an international flight, tickets are compared with passports.

biggest expense in your budget. The Internet is a useful resource and most travel agencies and airlines have their own Web sites. But you have to research the options carefully to make sure you get the best deal.

As a general rule, get your ticket as early as possible, because some of the cheapest fares must be bought weeks or months in advance, and popular flights sell out early. Full-time students and people under 26 years (under 30 in some countries) usually qualify for better deals than other travellers.

For long-term travel there are plenty of discount tickets, which are valid for 12 months, allowing multiple stopovers with open dates. For short-term travel within Europe, cheaper fares are available by travelling mid-week, staying away at least one Saturday night or taking advantage of short-lived promotional offers.

When you're looking for bargain air fares, there is almost never an advantage to buying a ticket direct from the airline. Discounted tickets are released to selected travel agents and specialist discount agencies, and these are usually the cheapest deals going.

One exception to this rule is the expanding number of 'no-frills' carriers, which mostly sell directly to travellers. Unlike the 'full service' airlines, no-frills carriers often make one-way tickets available at half the return fare, making it easy to put together a return ticket when you fly to one place but leave from another.

The other exception is booking on the Internet. Some online airlines sell seats by auction or simply cut prices to reflect the reduced cost of electronic selling. Airlines such as buzz or Ryanair offer very competitive fares to Web surfers.

The days when some travel agents routinely fleeced travellers by running off with their money are, happily, almost over. Paying by credit card generally offers protection, as most card issuers provide refunds if you can prove you didn't get what you paid for. You may decide to pay slightly more than the rock-bottom fare by opting for the safety of an established travel agent. Firms such as STA Travel and Council Travel with

offices worldwide, Travel CUTS in Canada and Flight Centre in Australia are not going to disappear overnight, and they do offer good prices to most destinations, especially to students and those under 26.

Always make a photocopy of your ticket and keep it somewhere separate. This will simplify getting a replacement in case of loss or theft.

Travellers with Special Needs

If they're warned early enough, airlines can often make special arrangements for travellers such as wheelchair assistance at airports or vegetarian meals on the flight. Children under two years travel for 10% of the standard fare (or free on some airlines) as long as they don't occupy a seat. They don't get a baggage allowance. 'Skycots', baby food and nappies should be provided by the airline if requested in advance. Children aged between two and 12 can usually occupy a seat for half to two-thirds of the full fare, and do get a baggage allowance.

The disability-friendly Web site, **W** www .everybody.co.uk, has an airline directory that provides information on the facilities offered by various airlines.

Departure Tax

A departure tax of around €4 to €5 per person and airport security fees are included in the price of an airline ticket purchased in Germany. However, in the wake of the terrorist attacks in the US on 11 September 2001, some airlines have begun charging additional security fees.

Other Parts of Germany

Travelling by plane within Germany is quite expensive and not always faster than using the train. There are domestic flights connecting Munich and Frankfurt to all major German airports and vice versa. Domestic flights also depart from smaller airports in Augsburg, the main hub for the Lufthansa affiliate Augsburg Air, as well as from Nuremberg. Lufthansa has by far the largest network of flight routes but flights are also offered by Eurowings, Deutsche BA and LTU.

The UK & Ireland

Discount air travel is big business in London. For the latest fares, check out the travel page ads of the Sunday newspapers, *Time Out* and the freebie *TNT*.

In recent years, the main airlines serving Munich and Frankfurt – Lufthansa and British Airways – have been getting major competition from some of the smaller low-frills airlines. Expect to pay £125 on Lufthansa or British Airways year-round.

Nonstop flights to Munich from London Stansted from around £70 are offered by the British Airways' low-budget subsidiary, Go (☎ 0870 60 76543 in the UK, W www .go-fly.com). The Irish airline Ryanair (☎ 0870 1569 569 in the UK, 01-6097800 in Dublin, W www.ryanair.com) has direct flights from London Stansted, Shannon and Glasgow to Frankfurt-Hahn, a former military airport about 100km north-west of Frankfurt proper.

Buses connect Hahn with the Frankfurt Hauptbahnhof five times daily (1¾ hours), with a stop at the Frankfurt Airport. Ryanair also operates nonstops from Stansted to Salzburg.

Buzz (☎ 0870 240 7070 in the UK, ☎ 01803 10 20 40 in Germany, W www .buzzaway.com) flies from London Stansted directly to Frankfurt-am-Main. Eurowings (☎ 0345 22 21 11 in the UK, 01805 359 322 in Germany) has nonstop flights from London's City Airport to Nuremberg.

For students or travellers under 26, popular travel agencies in the UK include STA Travel (☎ 020-7361 6144), which has an office at 86 Old Brompton Rd, London SW7 3LQ, and other offices in London and Manchester. Visit its Web site at W www.sta travel.co.uk. It sells tickets to all travellers but caters especially for students. Other recommended travel agencies include:

Bridge the World (Long Haul ☎ 020-7734 7447, Transatlantic ☎ 020 7916 0990) 4 Regent Place, London W1.
W www.b-t-w.co.uk
Flightbookers (☎ 020-7757 2000) 177–178 Tottenham Court Rd, London W1
W www.ebookers.com

Trailfinders (Europe line ☎ 020 7937 1234, Long-haul line ☎ 020-7938 3939, Transatlantic 020 7937 5400) 194 Kensington High St, London W8.
W www.trailfinders.co.uk

Continental Europe

Discount flights to Munich or Frankfurt are available from many major cities in continental Europe. Salzburg airport has nonstop flights to/from Zurich, Paris, London Stansted, Brussels and Amsterdam. Lufthansa connects all major cities directly with both Frankfurt and Munich. Eurowings flies to Nuremberg from Paris, Milan and Breslau (Poland).

Recommended travel agencies in France include:

Nouvelles Frontières (nationwide number ☎ 08 25 00 08 25, Paris ☎ 01 45 68 70 00) 87 blvd de Grenelle, 75015 Paris. With branches across the country.
W www.nouvelles-frontieres.fr
OTU Voyages (☎ 01 44 41 38 50) 39 ave Georges-Bernanos, 75005 Paris. With branches across the country, this is a student and young person specialist agency.
W www.otu.fr
Voyageurs du Monde (☎ 01 42 86 16 00) 55 rue Ste-Anne, 75002 Paris.

In Belgium recommended agencies include:

Air Stop (☎ 02 223 22 32) 28 rue Fossé-aux-Loups, 1000.
Connections (☎ 02550 01 00) 19–21 rue du Midi, 1000 Brussels. With branches in other Belgian cities. Specialist in student travel.
W www.connections.be
Nouvelles Frontières (☎ 02 547 44 44) 2 blvd Maurice Lemmonier, 1000 Brussels. Plus branches in Anvers, Bruges, Liège and Gand.
W www.nouvelles-frontieres.be

The USA

Flights to Germany from major cities in the USA abound. Lufthansa flies nonstop to Frankfurt and Munich from Atlanta, Chicago, New York (JFK), Philadelphia and Washington, DC.

In addition, Frankfurt is served by direct flights from Boston, Detroit and Los Angeles.

American carriers serving both cities include Delta, United Airlines and USAirways; American Airlines only goes to Frankfurt.

Airfares rise and fall in a cyclical pattern. The lowest fares are available from early November to mid-December and then again from mid-January to Easter, gradually rising in the following months. Peak months are July and August, after which prices start dropping again. Expect to pay US$850/500 return in high/low season from New York City, US$930/600 from Chicago and US$970/700 from Los Angeles.

To scour the Web for cheap fares, try W www.orbitz.com, W www.expedia.com, W www.travelocity.com or W www.ticketplanet.com.

Council Travel (☎ 800-226 8624) and STA Travel (☎ 800-777 0112) are reliable budget travel agencies with offices throughout the USA. Call or check their Web sites for the branch nearest you. Council Travel's Web address is W www.counciltravel.com while STA's is W www.sta-travel.com.

Stand-by Fares Flying stand-by can be a cheap way to reach Europe from the US if you are flexible.

Airtech (☎ 212-219 7000), Suite 204, 588 Broadway, New York, NY 10012, provides stand-bys from New York to Frankfurt, also from US$169. Flights offered may not get you exactly where you want to go, but the savings are so huge that you might opt for an onward train or bus. Check out the Web site at W www.airtech.com. Another outfit offering much the same is Airhitch with offices in New York (☎ 800-326 2009 or ☎ 212-864 2000), Los Angeles (☎ 800-397 1098 or ☎ 310-726 5000) and San Francisco (☎ 800-834 9192 or ☎ 415-834 9192). Its Web address is W www.airhitch.org.

Canada

Lufthansa and Air Canada fly to Frankfurt from all major Canadian airports, with prices starting at C$1400/1200 in high/low season. Travel CUTS (☎ 800-667-2887) is Canada's national student travel agency and has offices in all major cities. Its Web address is W www.travelcuts.com. Also check the travel sections of the *Globe & Mail*, *Montreal Gazette*, *Toronto Star* and *Vancouver Sun* for travel agents' ads.

Australia

Cheap flights from Australia to Europe generally go via South-East Asian cities, such as Kuala Lumpur, Bangkok or Singapore. Lufthansa and other major international airlines offer a range of flights and fares to Frankfurt, with onward travel to Munich. Some travel agents, particularly smaller ones, advertise cheap airfares in the travel sections of weekend newspapers. Prices start at A$2000 in high season and A$1680 in low season for a flight from Sydney to Munich.

Two well-known agents for cheap fares are STA Travel and Flight Centre. STA Travel (☎ 03-9349 2411) has its main office at 224 Faraday St, Carlton, in Melbourne, with offices in all major cities and on many university campuses. Call ☎ 131 776 Australia-wide for the location of your nearest branch or visit its Web site at W www.statravel.com.au. Flight Centre (☎ 131 600 Australia-wide) has a central office at 82 Elizabeth St, Sydney, and there are dozens of offices throughout Australia. Its Web address is W www.flightcentre.com.au.

New Zealand

Depending on which airline you choose, you may fly across Asia, with possible stopovers in India, Bangkok or Singapore, or across the USA, with stops in Honolulu or Los Angeles. Prices start at NZ$2600/2200 in high/low season.

The *New Zealand Herald* has a travel section in which travel agents advertise fares. Flight Centre (☎ 09-309 6171) has a large central office in Auckland at National Bank Towers (corner of Queen and Darby Sts) and many branches throughout the country. STA Travel (☎ 09-309 0458) has its main office at 10 High St, Auckland, and has other offices in Auckland as well as in Hamilton, Palmerston North, Wellington, Christchurch and Dunedin. The Web address is W www.statravel.co.nz.

LAND
Train

The train is a good way to get to Germany if you're already in Europe, and it's more comfortable than the bus. It's not worth spending the extra money on a 1st-class ticket, since travelling 2nd class on German trains is perfectly comfortable. If you are *in* Germany and want to travel internationally, the Deutsche Bahn has lots of deals (mostly on return trips) to cut costs. Tell the person at the counter where you want to go, the length of stay, and ask for the cheapest deal. The Web site W www.bahn.de is a good place to start looking (for English, link to 'International Guests').

Long-distance trains between major German cities and other countries are called EC (EuroCity) trains. The most comfortable travel option is to take an overnight train. Supplements vary a bit. If it's calculated as a supplement to the standard ticket price, expect to pay from €14 to €20 per person for a bunk in a six-person couchette, €21 to €27 in a four-person couchette, and €42 to €62 in two-person compartments.

If you have a sleeper or sleeping berth, the train conductor will usually collect your ticket before you go to sleep and hand it back to you in the morning. If you're in a regular seat, however, expect to be woken up by conductors coming aboard in each country to check your ticket.

Be sure to make a seat reservation on EC trains, especially during the peak summer season and around major holidays. Trains can get extremely crowded, and you may find yourself stuck in a narrow corridor for hours. Reservations cost €2.50 and can be made as late as a few minutes before departure.

Also see the Getting Around chapter for additional information about the German railway system.

Eurail Passes Eurail Passes are convenient and excellent value if you're covering lots of territory in a very limited time. Available to non-residents of Europe only, they should be bought before arriving in Europe. A limited number of outlets also sell them within Europe, but your passport must show that you've been there for less than six months.

Eurail Passes are valid for unlimited travel on national railways (and some private lines) in 17 European countries. They also cover many ferries, eg, from Sweden to Germany, as well as steamer services in various countries. A variety of passes is available.

If you're under 26, a Eurailpass Youth gives unlimited 2nd-class travel for periods of 15 or 21 consecutive days (US$401/518) or one/two/three months (US$644/910/1120). The Eurailpass Youth Flexi, also for 2nd class, is valid for travel on freely chosen days within a two-month period: 10 days of travel cost US$473, 15 days are US$622.

For those aged over 26, the equivalent passes cost more but provide 1st-class travel. The standard Eurailpass costs US$572/740 for unlimited travel on 15 or 21 consecutive days and US$918/1298/1606 for one/two/three months. The Eurailpass Flexi costs US$657/888 and gives you unlimited travel on 10 or 15 days of your choice within a two month period. Children ages four to 11 get 50% off on any of these passes.

In 2002, various other passes were introduced as well, including the Eurail Selectpass, good for travel in three adjacent European countries, and the Eurail Saver and Eurailpass Saver Flexi geared towards small groups from two to five persons.

In North America, travel agencies specialising in all types of European rail passes, including the German Rail Pass (see the Getting Around chapter), are Rail Europe (☎ 888-382-7245 in the US; ☎ 800-361-7246 in Canada, W www.raileurope.com) and DER Travel Services (☎ 800-782-2424, fax 800-282-7474, W www.dertravel.com). If you're from another country, contact your travel agent.

InterRail & Euro Domino Passes If you have lived in a European or North African country for at least six months, you qualify for the InterRail Pass. It divides Europe into eight zones (Germany shares one with Denmark, Austria and Switzerland) and is good for one month of travel within one, two, three or all zones. Prices for those under/over 25 are €198/282 for one zone, €264/370 for two zones, €299/420 for three zones and €351/496 for all zones. Tickets should be available at all major railway stations.

The EuroDomino Pass is good for three to eight days of travel within one month in 27 European countries. It costs €132/260 for those under/over 25 for three days, with each additional day priced at €12/23. Prices vary slightly by country where you buy this pass.

Bus

In some cases, bus travel is a good alternative to the train if you're already in Europe and on your way to Bavaria. Especially for shorter distances, it's usually, though not always, cheaper than taking the train. The downside is, of course, that it's slower. Most coaches are quite comfortable, with toilet, air-conditioning and snack bar. Advance reservations may be necessary at peak travel times. In general, return fares are markedly cheaper than two one-way fares.

Eurolines Eurolines (W www.eurolines .com) is the umbrella organisation of numerous European coach operators with 500 routes in 25 countries across Europe. The main company operating in Germany is Deutsche Touring, which has an office at Arnulfstrasse 3 on the north side of the Munich Hauptbahnhof (☎ 089-545 87 00, fax 54 58 70 21, e muenchen@deutsche-touring .com). Note that tickets must be purchased in person either here or at select travel agencies (including DER affiliates) or at the Deutsche Bahn travel agencies inside the Reisezentrum ticket offices at major train stations. In Munich, most buses leave from the Park + Ride car park in the northern suburb of Fröttmaning (a stop on the U6).

Eurolines offices in other countries include the following (check the Web site for a full list):

Austria (☎ 01-7120 4530) Invalidenstrasse 5–7, 1030 Vienna
Czech Republic (☎ 02-2481 4450) Coach Station Florenc, Krizikova 4–6, Prague 8
France (☎ 08366 95 252) Gare Routière International, 28 Ave du Général de Gaulle, Bagnolet Paris
Italy (☎ 055 357 110) Via Mercadente n 2b, 50144 Florence
Netherlands (☎ 020-560 87 88) Amstel Busstation, Julianaplein 5, 1097 DN Amsterdam
UK (☎ 01582 404 511) 52 Grosvenor Gardens, London SW1W OAU

Buses connect Munich with numerous European cities, including:

destination	fare (one way/ return)	duration (hours)	frequency (weekly)
Florence	€79/142	9½	2
London	€75/120	20	3
Paris	€56/101	13	4
Prague	€27/48	6	5
Vienna	€36/64	6¼	4

The Eurolines Pass allows for unlimited travel between 48 cities within a 15-/30-/60-day period. From June to mid-September, passes cost €200/296/324 (ages 4-25 and seniors over 60) or €240/370/430 (ages 26-59). The rest of the year, rates drop to €150/215/270 and €180/270/340 respectively. Passes may be purchased online if the start date is 21 days ahead of the booking day. Otherwise, they must be bought at a Eurolines office.

BerlinLinienBus Berlin-based BerlinLinienBus (☎ 030-861 93 31 in Berlin, e info@ berlinlinienbus.de) runs daily buses between Berlin and Munich for €68/79 one way/return. Seniors and those under 28 pay €41/73. In Munich, buses depart from Arnulfstrasse on the north side of the Hauptbahnhof. In Berlin, the terminus is the ZOB (central bus station) at the Funkturm.

Busabout Busabout (UK ☎ 0207-950 1661, fax 950 1662, e info@busabout.com) is a UK-based budget alternative aimed at backpackers, which runs coaches along interlocking European circuits. There is no upper age limit, but those aged 26 and under, students and teachers qualify for lower rates. Its FlexiPass allows you to travel during a limited number of days within a specified period. For instance, six days of travel within one month cost €289, 15 days of travel within two months are €619. With the ConsecutivePass, you can travel as much as you want within a limited number of days, eg, two/three weeks of travel cost €299/419.

At the time of writing, the only Busabout route passing through Bavaria was Munich-Paris (via Frankfurt). From Salzburg, a route goes to Venice. For the complete low-down, check the company's Web site at W www.busabout.com.

Car & Motorcycle

Driving in Bavaria can be a lot of fun, as the overall quality of the roads is very high and having your own vehicle provides you with the most flexibility to get off the beaten track. The disadvantage is that traffic in urban areas can be horrendous, and parking in the cities is usually restricted to expensive car parks. See the Getting Around chapter for more detailed coverage (roads, road rules, motoring organisations etc) of driving in Germany.

If you're taking your own vehicle, you should always carry proof of ownership. Driving licences from most countries are valid in Germany for one year. You must also have third-party insurance to enter the country. It is compulsory to carry a warning (hazard) triangle and first-aid kit in your car at all times.

If you're coming from the UK, the quickest option (apart from the Channel Tunnel) is to take the car ferry or Hovercraft from Dover, Folkestone or Ramsgate to Calais in France; you can be in Germany in three hours from there. The main gateways to southern Germany are Munich, Freiburg and Passau. Heading for Poland and to the Czech Republic, you may encounter long border delays.

For information about car rental and purchase while in Bavaria, see the Getting Around chapter.

Bicycle

Cycling is a cheap, convenient, healthy, environmentally sound and, above all, fun way of travelling. If you are bringing your bicycle to Germany, check for wear and tear before you leave and fill your repair kit with every imaginable spare. As with cars and motorcycles, you won't necessarily be able to buy that crucial gizmo for your machine when it breaks down somewhere in the back of beyond.

Bicycles can travel by air, which can be surprisingly inexpensive. You *can* take them to pieces and put them in a bike bag or box, but it's much easier simply to wheel your bike to the check-in desk, where it should be treated as a piece of baggage. You may have to remove the pedals and turn the handlebars sideways so that your bike will take up less space in the aircraft's hold; check all of this with the airline well in advance, preferably before you pay for your ticket.

For information about transporting your bicycle by train in Germany, see the Bicycle section in the Getting Around chapter.

Hitching & Ride Services

Lonely Planet does not recommend hitching, but travellers intending to hitch should not have too many problems getting to and from Bavaria via the main autobahns and highways. See the Hitching section in the Getting Around chapter for a discussion of the potential risks.

Aside from hitching, the cheapest way to get to or away from Bavaria is as a paying passenger in a private car. Such rides are arranged by *Mitfahrzentralen* (ride-share agencies) found in all major cities and many smaller ones as well. Most belong to umbrella networks like ADM (☎ 194 40) or Citynetz (☎ 194 44). For local listings of Mitfahrzentralen see the Getting There & Away section in the individual cities and towns.

Fares comprise a commission to the agency and a per-kilometre charge to the driver. Sample fares (including commission) from Munich are: Vienna €22, Berlin €35, €39, Paris €39, Prague €35 and Warsaw €45.

The people answering the phone at Mitfahrzentrale offices usually speak English well. If you arrange a ride a few days in advance, it's a good idea to call the driver the night before and again on the departure morning to make sure they're definitely going.

LAKE

Coming from Switzerland, one possibility for travel to Bavaria is by taking the Friedrichshafen-Romanshorn ferry across Lake Constance. It operates year round (hourly in daylight), takes 45 minutes and costs Sfr8 (students Sfr4.80). Bikes are Sfr6 and cars, including two passengers, are Sfr18 to Sfr46 depending on the size. Friedrichshafen is just 21km east of the Bavarian lakeside town of Lindau via the B31 (see the Allgäu-Bavarian Swabia chapter). Trains leave at least hourly (€4, 35 minutes).

ORGANISED TOURS

There are many options for organised travel to Bavaria. The German National Tourist Office in your country is the single best source for a list of tour operators (see Tourist Offices in the Facts for the Visitor chapter). It is always worth shopping around for value, but such tours rarely come cheap. While they can save you hassles, they also rob you of independence.

Among the options available, DER Travel Service is one of the most experienced Germany specialists with a huge selection of holidays in Munich and Bavaria, including independent and escorted package holidays as well as balloon rides and river cruises. In the UK contact ☎ 0207-290 11 11, fax 629 74 42 or check out **W** www .dertravel.co.uk; in the US call ☎ 800-549-3737 or look up the Web site at **W** www .dertravel.com.

Two other good UK-based Germany specialists are Moswin Tours (☎ 0116-271 99 22, fax 271 6016, **e** sales@moswin.com), 21 Church Street, Oadby, Leicester LE2 5DB and the German Travel Centre (☎ 020-8429 2900, fax 8429 4896, **e** sales@german-travel-uk.com), 403–409 Rayner's Lane, Pinner, Middlesex HA5 5ER.

US-based operators include Viking River Cruises (☎ 800-707-1287, **e** info@ vikingrivers.com), which runs multi-day trips aboard luxury cruise boats on major German rivers, including the Danube. Its 12-day Romantic Danube tour (from US$2800, air inclusive) starts in Budapest and takes in Vienna, Passau, Regensburg and the Rhine-Main-Danube-Canal in conjunction with a three-day stay in Prague. Others include Adventures on Skis (☎ 800-628-9655, fax 413-562-3621, **e** tours@ ad-vonskis.com), which sells winter ski packages to Garmisch-Partenkirchen and summer bicycle tours along the Romantic Road. Austro Tours/Ski Europe (☎ 800-333-5533, fax 713-960-8966, **e** travel@ ski-europe.com) specialises in custom-designed group tours to various German destinations, including Munich and the Romantic Road and themed tours like Christmas Markets.

Timberwalks (☎ 803-366-1502, fax 366-1625, **e** greatvacations@timberwalks.com) does guided hiking trips in Europe, including the Bavarian Alps. Rebel Tours (☎ 800-227-3235, fax 661-294-0981) runs escorted RV tours along itineraries that include popular sights such as the Romantic Road and the Bavarian Alps.

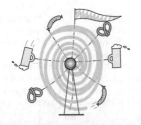

Getting Around

The Germans are whizzes at moving people around, and the public transport network is among the best in Europe. Though not cheap, it's usually good value. The two best ways of getting around are by car and by train. Regional bus services are crucial in the few places not adequately served by the rail network.

AIR

Lufthansa (☎ 01803-80 38 03, Ⓦ www .lufthansa.de) and Eurowings (☎ 01805-35 93 22, Ⓦ www.eurowings.de) have flights within Bavaria (ie, Munich-Nuremberg), but they're expensive and actually slower compared to the train or car.

TRAIN

Operated almost entirely by the Deutsche Bahn (DB), the German rail system is justifiably known as the most efficient in Europe. A wide range of services and ticket options is available, making travelling by train the most attractive way to get around, sometimes even better than car. With 41,000km of track, the network is Europe's most extensive, serving over 7000 cities and towns. All trains have 1st- and 2nd-class compartments; long-distance trains have a restaurant car.

All large (and many small) train stations in Germany have coin-operated left-luggage lockers (€1/2 for small/large lockers per 24 hours). *Gepäckaufbewahrung* (left-luggage offices) are sometimes more convenient than lockers and charge similar rates.

For information on how to transport your bicycle by train, see the Bicycle section later in this chapter.

Note that at the time of writing, DB was planning to introduce a new fare structure in (probably) late 2002. This should favour travellers who book early, are not travelling alone, and those who travel frequently. Ask at the DB counter for the latest deals, or check the Web site (Ⓦ www.bahn.de), which has a link to International Guests for English.

Train Passes & Special Tickets

German Rail Passes If your permanent residence is outside of Europe, you qualify for the German Rail pass, which may be especially worthwhile if your itinerary includes non-Bavarian cities. It entitles you to unlimited 1st- or 2nd-class travel for four to 10 days within a one-month period. Sample prices are US$180/248/316 for four/seven/10 days of travel in 2nd class and US$260/ 359/458 in 1st class. The pass is valid on all trains within Germany and some river services operated by the KD Line.

In the USA and Canada, agencies specialising in selling the German Rail and other passes, as well as regular DB train tickets, are Rail Europe (USA ☎ 888-382-7245, Canada ☎ 800-361-7246, Ⓦ www.raileu rope.com) and DER Travel Services (☎ 800-782-2424, fax 800-282-7474, Ⓦ www.der travel.com). If you live in another country, contact your travel agent. If you're already in Germany, five- and 10-day passes are available at the EurAide office in Munich (see Information in the Facts for the Visitor chapter).

If you're aged between 12 and 25, you qualify for the German Rail Youth Pass which costs US$142/180/216 and is only good for 2nd-class travel. Two adults travelling together should check out the German Rail Twin Pass for US$270/372/474 in 2nd class and US$390/537/687 in 1st class. Children aged between five and 11 pay half the adult fare.

If Prague is on your itinerary, consider buying the Prague Excursion Pass. It covers round-trip travel (and all supplements) to Prague from the Czech border and back within seven days. The 2nd-class pass costs €31 (€23 if you're under 26) and is available from DB offices or EurAide in Munich.

Bayernticket The Bayernticket (Bavaria Ticket) costs €21 and is an excellent deal. It allows you and up to four accompanying passengers (or one or both parents plus all their children under 18 years) unlimited travel on one weekday (Monday to Friday) from 9am until 3am of the following day within Bavaria. It's good for 2nd-class travel on all RE, RB and S-Bahn trains (see Train Types later in this section), as well as all public transportation in greater Munich and Nuremberg. For travel in IR or D trains, a supplement of €13 applies. The ticket is not valid in IC, EC, ICE or any other trains.

Naturally, travel can be quite time-consuming but the savings with the Bayernticket are enormous, especially if you're travelling as a group. Simply consider the price of a regular ticket from the far north-western corner of Bavaria to its far south-eastern corner – Aschaffenburg to Berchtesgaden, say – which is €71.40 per person, then do the maths. Sure, it takes eight hours and requires three changes of train, but if cost cutting is your aim, this is the way to go.

Schönes-Wochenende-Ticket There is also the Happy Weekend Ticket which costs €28 and works in a similar way to the Bayernticket, except that it's good for one day of travel from midnight Saturday or Sunday until 3am the next day. The good news is that you can travel anywhere within Germany, not just Bavaria. IR and D train supplements are not available for this ticket, but all the other conditions are the same as for the Bayernticket.

Guten-Abend-Ticket The Good Evening Ticket is valid for unlimited train travel from 7pm until 3am the following day (from 2pm Saturday) and costs €30 in 2nd class, or €36 in 2nd class on a InterCity Express (ICE) train. There are black-out periods around Easter and Christmas – check with DB for details. A surcharge of €8.10 applies for travel on Friday to Sunday.

Sparpreis The Saver Ticket, a return ticket between any two stations in Germany, costs a flat €127/191 in 2nd/1st class. If you're travelling in a group, each additional adult pays only half (€64/96) and each child one quarter (€32/48). The maximum group size is 4½ passengers (children count as 'half').

You can travel on any day of the week, but your stay must include a Friday night, or one of the travel days has to be a Saturday or Sunday.

If you want to use the InterCity Express (ICE) trains, the Sparpreis is €152 and €76/38 for accompanying adult/child in 2nd class and €228/114/57 in 1st class.

Cheaper still is the Super-Sparpreis Ticket (Super Saver Ticket), which allows you to travel any day but Friday and Sunday. Your stay must include a Friday night or the travel day has to be a Saturday. It costs €99 for the first person, €50 for each additional adult and €25 for children in 2nd class and €149/75/38 in 1st class. With ICE trains, the cost is €127/64/32 for 2nd class and €191/96/48 in 1st class.

Twen Ticket Passengers aged between 12 and 25 automatically qualify for 20% to 50% off standard fares on most European railways, as well as Morocco and Turkey. Within Germany, the deduction is 20%.

Train Services

The most straightforward way of obtaining train schedules is at the station, where large yellow posters show all trains departing each hour (but not fares). In some of the larger stations, you'll also find interactive terminals where you can create itineraries and get fares.

For ticket and timetable information (in English) by telephone, call ☎ 01805-99 66 33 from anywhere in Germany for €0.12 per minute. Timetable and/or fare information is also available from DB's Web site at Ⓦ www.bahn.de. Some routes can already be booked at steeply discounted prices on this site by clicking on the Surf&Rail link (in German only) and DB has ambitious plans to extend this option.

One-way tickets for distances of less than 100km are valid for the day of travel. Tickets for distances of over 100km are valid for up to four days, with as many breaks in the journey as you wish; note that each leg of the journey is valid for four days. It's always a good idea to let conductors know if you intend to break your journey.

Return tickets cost exactly double and are valid for one month (two months for international return tickets). Long-distance train tickets and passes are also valid on the SchnellBahn (S-Bahn).

Buying Tickets At many train stations passengers must buy tickets from vending machines for distances under 100km – it's generally more convenient, anyway. If you're travelling further than anywhere indicated on the machine, press button 'X' for the maximum fare and contact the conductor on board. Ticket machines for long-distance services (including ICE) accept major credit cards. The touch screens can be a bit unresponsive sometimes (in that case, press firmly on the screen), and the process is often tedious, but once you get the hang of it, it's fast and you can avoid the queues at the counter.

If you don't want to deal with a machine, buy your tickets from the ticket counter or the *Reisezentrum* (travel centre) in most larger train stations. Staff here can also help you plan an itinerary, although English is sometimes a problem.

Supplements & Surcharges DB builds into its ticket prices a standard supplement for EC/IC (€3.50, or €4.50 from the conductor), and for IR and the few remaining D trains (€1.50, or €2.50 from the conductor). ICEs, Thalys and night trains have their own fare structure.

If you buy your ticket from the conductor on the train, you must pay a surcharge of about €1.50 for a ticket priced up to around €15, €3 from around €15 to €50, and €4.50 for longer distances or 2nd class in ICEs (1st class is €7.50). An increasing number of services (generally slower, regional ones) operate without a conductor. For these trains, passengers are required to buy a ticket *before* boarding, so ask if you are in doubt. Anyone caught without a valid ticket is liable for a fine of €31.

Costs The average per-kilometre price of 2nd-class train travel is currently €0.138; for 1st class the average is €0.209 per kilometre.

In this book we give the 2nd-class fares. Children aged three and younger travel free, children from four to 11 pay half-price.

Though train travel in Germany does offer good value, without a rail pass or a ticket bought through a special offer, it can be expensive: it costs about €62 for a Munich-Frankfurt ticket on a non-ICE service and €75 on an ICE train.

Reservations We highly recommend that you make reservations for long-distance travel, especially if you're taking an ICE and InterCity (IC) train, or you are travelling on a Friday or Sunday afternoon, during holiday periods or in summer. The fee is a flat €2.50, regardless of the number of seats booked, and reservations can be made as late as a few minutes before departure. Most *night* trains are equipped with 1st-class (two-berth) and 2nd-class (four- or six-berth) sleeping compartments, which must be booked at least one day in advance; otherwise turn up on the platform and ask the conductor.

Train Types

InterCity Express Travelling at speeds of up to 280km/h, ultra-rapid, modern InterCity Express (ICE) trains dominate some long-distance routes between large cities, such as Frankfurt-am-Main–Munich (€61.80, 3¾ hours) and Hamburg-Munich (€137.80, six hours).

ICEs have restaurants and bistros, telephones, audio programs (and video in some carriages), huge picture windows and generally great service. Most toilets and compartments are wheelchair accessible. Smoking is permitted only in the first 1st-class and last 2nd-class carriages of the trains, and in restaurant cars. At least one carriage per train allows uninterrupted mobile phone transmission.

InterCity & EuroCity InterCity (IC) trains go between German cities, while EuroCity (EC) trains travel between German cities and cities outside Germany. They're still comfortable and relatively fast, but ICE trains they ain't.

InterRegio InterRegio (IR) trains cover regional and a growing number of cross-country routes at two-hour intervals. Many people find the seating, the ventilation and the travel atmosphere much more pleasant in IRs than in ICEs (and they walk all over shoddy ICs). For trips longer than two hours, you can usually get to your destination faster by using a high-speed train.

Regional & Local Services The RegionalBahn (RB) is the slowest DB train, not missing a single one-horse town or junction of roads – so sit back and enjoy. Regional Express (RE) trains are local trains that make limited stops and link the rural areas to the national and commuter networks.

SchnellBahn (S-Bahn) services are suburban-metropolitan shuttle lines. These originate in a Hauptbahnhof and reach far-flung suburbs; in the case of Munich, Nuremberg and Frankfurt, the S-Bahn also serves as the main city-to-airport train link.

BUS

Wherever there is a train, you should probably take it, but in remote rural areas, buses are often the only way to get around without your own set of wheels. This is especially true of pockets of Eastern Bavaria, such as the Bavarian Forest, sections of the Alpine foothills and the Alpine region. In this book, we only list bus services if they're a viable and sensible option.

Separate bus companies operate in the different regions. In cities, buses converge at the central bus station *(Busbahnhof* or *Zentraler Omnibus Bahnhof/ZOB)*, which is usually close or adjacent to the Hauptbahnhof. Tickets are available directly from the bus companies, which often have offices or kiosks at the bus station, or from the driver on board. Ask about special fare deals, such as day passes, weekly passes or special tourist tickets.

Frequency of service varies dramatically depending on the destination and can be as little as three buses daily, sometimes even fewer on weekends. Routes geared to commuters suspend operation on weekends altogether. If you depend on buses to get around, always keep this in mind or risk finding yourself stuck in a remote place on the weekend.

Europabus

The Europabus operates within Germany as Deutsche Touring, a subsidiary of DB. In Bavaria, it offers daily coach service along the Romantic Road (Romantische Strasse), Germany's most popular holiday route (see boxed text in the Franconia chapter for details). The main booking office (☎ 069-790 30) is at Römerhof 17 in Frankfurt-am-Main but tickets can also be bought at many travel agencies and railway stations. Its Web site (W www.deutsche-touring.com) has detailed fare and timetable information, but it's in German only.

CAR & MOTORCYCLE

Most German roads are excellent, and as a result, motoring can be a great way to tour Bavaria. Major *Autobahnen* (motorways) running throughout Bavaria include the A3 (Passau-Düsseldorf), the A7 (Allgäu-Hamburg), the A8 (Munich-Stuttgart), the A9 (Munich-Berlin, via Nuremberg), the A8 (Munich-Salzburg), the A95 (Munich-Garmisch-Partenkirchen), and the A96 (Munich-Lindau). Road signs (and most motoring maps) indicate national autobahn routes in blue with an 'A' preceding the number while international routes have green signs with an 'E' and a number.

Though very efficient, the autobahns are often busy, and literally 'life in the fast lane'. While border signs proudly indicate that there's no speed limit, there are actually many restricted segments (not that many German drivers take much notice). Tourists often have trouble coping with the very high speeds and the dangers involved in overtaking – don't underestimate the time it takes for a car in the rear-view mirror to close in at 200km/h.

Secondary, or 'B' roads, are usually two-lane highways meandering through the countryside. They still present a fairly fast way of getting from place to place and are usually the best option in Bavaria's rural areas. Speeds here are slower but you'll have to pay close attention to the road, especially when passing slower vehicles.

Parking

Parking in garages is expensive (about €1.50 per hour, up to €12 per day), but in cities and towns it will often be your only option. Automated car parks with signs indicating available space are now fairly ubiquitous.

Parking meters are becoming rare but the 'pay and display' system is quite widespread. This requires you to buy a parking voucher for the time you intend to park from a *Parkscheinautomat* (ticket-vending machine) as soon as you've parked your car (it should be kerbside just a few metres away). Then display the voucher visibly on the dashboard inside the car. Hourly rates are around €1. Check the machine or signposts for enforcement hours.

Hotels don't always have their own garages or car parks, meaning that you will either have to find street parking or put the car into a garage, which will add about €12 to your overnight costs.

In many villages, free street parking is easier to find, but watch for signs indicating parking restrictions or risk a ticket or tow. In some of the busier tourist resorts, including Oberstdorf and Rothenburg ob der Tauber, you are not allowed to drive into the town centre (unless you have a hotel reservation), requiring you to leave your car in a designated car park.

Road Rules

Driving is on the right-hand side of the road. Road rules are easy to understand and standard international signs are in use. Pedestrians at crossings have absolute right of way over all motor vehicles. Similarly, you must give right of way to cyclists in bicycle lanes when you're turning – many won't even look so you'd better be prepared.

The usual speed limits are 50km/h in built-up areas (in effect as soon as you see the yellow town sign as you enter, to the same sign with a red line through it as you leave) and 100km/h on non-autobahn highways. Technically, there is no speed limit on autobahns but, in an effort to increase safety and curb noise pollution, many segments have limits ranging from 100km/h to 130km/h.

The highest permissible blood-alcohol level for drivers is 0.05% (also see Legal Matters in the Facts for the Visitor chapter). Obey the road rules carefully: the German police are very efficient and issue stiff on-the-spot fines; speed and red-light cameras are common, and notices are sent to the car's registration address wherever that may be.

There are emergency phones every kilometre or so along most autobahns to be used in the event of breakdown. Lift the metal flap, follow the (pictorial) instructions and help will arrive.

Motoring Organisations

Germany's main motoring organisation, the Allgemeiner Deutscher Automobil Club (ADAC) has offices in all major cities and many smaller ones. It's headquartered in Munich (☎ 089-767 60, fax 089-76 76 28 01) at Am Westpark 8.

The ADAC provides some of the best on-road and off-road services of any motoring club in the world. Members (€38 annually domestic, €70 worldwide) can get help planning trips, free road maps, discounts on auto insurance and even international health insurance from any ADAC office in the country, as well as roadside breakdown assistance *(Pannenhilfe)* 24 hours a day.

ADAC's services, including its roadside assistance program, are available to members of participating motoring organisations around the world – including American or Australian AAA, Canadian CAA and British AA. Call the ADAC road patrol (☎ 0180-222 22 22) if your car breaks down. Technicians probably won't speak English, but gestures work very well – impersonate the sound your heap was making before it died, and the mechanic will probably figure it out directly. ADAC mechanics also carry a multilingual auto-part dictionary, so they can tell you if it's your brake lining or fuel pump.

Petrol

Fuel prices in Germany are quite stiff, even by European standards, costing a little more than in the UK and a bit less than in

Road Distances (km)

	Aschaffenburg	Augsburg	Bamberg	Bayreuth	Lindau	Munich (München)	Nuremberg (Nürnberg)	Passau	Regensburg	Rothenburg ob der Tauber	Würzburg
Aschaffenburg	---										
Augsburg	320	---									
Bamberg	174	235	---								
Bayreuth	238	238	71	---							
Lindau	376	157	367	371	---						
Munich (München)	354	70	230	233	178	---					
Nuremberg (Nürnberg)	185	170	62	84	296	166	---				
Passau	400	244	276	278	369	192	222	---			
Regensburg	284	177	162	162	300	123	104	120	---		
Rothenburg ob der Tauber	143	183	150	180	238	243	106	311	196	---	
Würzburg	80	251	96	160	301	279	110	324	209	67	---

Scandinavia. They fluctuate considerably, and in 2001 climbed to over €1.06 for unleaded super, €1.09 for unleaded super plus, and €0.85 for diesel, about 20% higher than a year earlier (by the way, taxes account for 80% of the bill). Autobahn filling stations are slightly more expensive than main-street ones and can be found every 40km or so throughout the country. Most stations in Germany are open late; the major players – Aral, BP, Elf and Agip – usually run 24-hour operations complete with mini-markets.

Rental

In general, in order to rent a car in Germany you'll need to be at least 21 years old and hold a valid driving licence (an international licence is not necessary) and a major credit card. American Express, Diners Club, Visa and Euro Card/MasterCard are almost always accepted; JCB (Japan Credit Bank) is good only sometimes at airports, and they'll almost never take a Discover Card unless you've prepaid in the USA. There may be a supplement for additional driver(s). Safety seats for children under four are not required by law but are highly recommended. Baby seats cost from €4.50 per day. The cost of ski or luggage racks is a bit more variable (€4.50 is common, though); these are not always available, so inquire first and order early. Some companies require a €75 deposit on both.

Generally speaking, you're allowed to drive cars rented in Germany pretty much anywhere in Western Europe, and pretty much nowhere in Eastern Europe. If you enter these places with a rental car, your insurance is revoked, the rental agreement rendered void and the rental company could even report the car as stolen. An exception is Auto Europe, which lets you go into Poland and the Czech Republic if you tell them in advance and pay an extra charge.

Insurance

You could seriously screw yourself by driving uninsured or even under-insured. Germans are very fussy about their cars, and even nudging another car at a red light could lead to months of harassing phone calls until you pay for an entire new rear bumper.

Liability insurance covers you for legal action filed against you when you crash your car against anyone or their property. This might be calculated separately from the rental price. Always confirm on rental that you have this insurance.

Collision damage waiver (CDW) is protection for the car if you cause an accident. It reduces the amount you'll have to reimburse the rental company. Although it pushes up the rental price considerably, never drive without this either. The cost varies from company to company and their driver-age conditions and cars. Weekend deals sometimes include CDW, making them good value.

If you have an American Express or a Gold or Platinum Visa or EuroCard/MasterCard, you may be covered for CDW if you use the card to pay for the rental and decline the policy on offer from the rental company. Be sure to check with your credit card issuer to see what coverage they offer in Germany before assuming it will cover you, and note that CDW is *not* liability coverage.

Personal accident insurance (PAI) covers you and your passenger(s) for medical costs incurred as the result of an accident. If your health insurance from home does this as well, save yourself the €5 to €10 per day.

Rental Companies

The main international companies operating in Bavaria are Avis (☎ 0180-555 77), Europcar (☎ 0180-580 00), Hertz (☎ 0180-533 35 35) and Sixt-Budget (☎ 0180-526 02 50), but there are a number of smaller local ones too, often with deals on limited kilometres. These hotline reservation numbers cost €0.12 per minute, and Hertz doesn't rent to anyone under 25. Alamo (☎ 0800-462 52 66) might be worth checking as it can be a bit cheaper. For weekend deals, expect to pay from €100 to €130 including CDW and

other insurance (see Insurance earlier in this section). The outfits listed have offices in so many Bavarian cities that printing them here is folly. Suffice to say that wherever you are – from Aschaffenburg to Zwiesel – there's a rental office nearby.

It's generally more economical to make reservations ahead of time with the central reservation office in your country, preferably with fly-drive. Otherwise, shop around. Check the smaller agencies, though the larger firms, feeling the crunch, often have some exceptional deals.

A company that usually offers great deals (although these fluctuate with the exchange rate) is the US-based AutoEurope, which negotiates low rates and excellent conditions with all the major companies. Credit-card reservations can be made 24 hours via a toll-free number with an English-speaking operator. Cars are available in all sizes and categories, and there's no surcharge for one-way rentals or airport drop-offs. There's also no charge for cancellations or changes, and the minimum rental age is usually 19. The major downside is the three-day minimum rental (but no penalty for turning it in early). An economy car will cost you around US$143 for the three-day minimum, including unlimited kilometres, VAT and CDW and other insurance.

If you need a car and you're already in Germany, dial ☎ 800-822 19 80. Other toll-free numbers include: ☎ 800-223-5555 in the US; ☎ 800-12 64 09 in Australia; ☎ 0800-44 07 22 in New Zealand; ☎ 0800-90 17 70 in France; ☎ 0800-899 893 in the UK. For additional countries and further details, check its Web site at W www.autoeurope.com.

Fly-drive deals can be excellent value for money; Lufthansa offers deals for around €75 for a VW Golf for three days, including CDW and other insurance. You can book it either when you buy your ticket or else in Germany at Lufthansa when you arrive.

Purchase

Unless you're staying put in Germany for a while, buying a car here is more hassle than it's worth due to the costs and paperwork involved. EU nationals must register the car with the Ordnungs- und Strassenverkehrsamt (Public Order & Traffic Office) in most larger towns. You will need proof of ownership, proof of insurance and a passport or ID. You're also subject to a motor vehicle tax. The vehicle also has to pass a safety inspection by the Technical Supervision Agency (TÜV) every two years in order to be kept legally on the road. Don't buy any vehicle without making sure it has its *current* TÜV certificate.

Non-EU nationals quickly find themselves in a Catch 22 situation. While allowed to *buy* a car, they may *not* register it, since you have to be a German or EU resident to do so.

BICYCLE

Bicycle touring *(Radwandern)* is very popular in Bavaria, which has an extensive network of secondary and tertiary roads as well as designated bike paths. In urban areas, the pavement is often divided into separate sections for pedestrians and cyclists. Cycling is strictly *verboten* on the autobahns.

Numerous long-distance bike trails crisscross Bavaria. For details see Activities in the Facts for the Visitor chapter. There are well-equipped cycling shops in almost every town, and a fairly active market for second-hand touring bikes.

Transporting a Bicycle

You can take a bicycle with you on most trains, though you'll have to buy a separate ticket *(Fahrradkarte)* for it. On all long-distance trains, including IC, D, IR and some ICE trains, these cost €8 and advance bookings are necessary. The cost on RE, RB and S-Bahn is €3 per trip, but on certain lines it is free. If bought in combination with one of the saver tickets, such as the Bayernticket or the Schönes-Wochenende-Ticket, the €3 fee is good for multiple trips within one day. For information, check the DB Radfahrer-Hotline (☎ 01805-15 14 15, €0.12 per minute). DB also publishes the useful free brochure *Bahn & Bike* (in German), which lists the free lines (*Kostenfreie Fahrradmitnahme*) and all stations where you can rent bikes.

With three-day advance notice, you can take bicycles on the Europabus travelling along the Romantic Road (see boxed text in the Franconia chapter). Many regional companies use buses with special bike racks. Bicycles are also allowed on practically all boat services on Bavaria's lakes and rivers.

Cycling Organisations

Germany's main cyclist organisation, Allgemeiner Deutscher Fahrrad Club (ADFC) operates *Infoläden* (information centres) in several Bavarian cities, including:

Augsburg (☎ 0821-371 21, **e** info@
   adfc-augsburg.de) Heilig-Kreuz-Strasse 30
Ingolstadt (☎ 08450-92 37 57, **e** adfc_I@
   yahoo.de) Weicheringer Strasse 101
Memmingen (☎ 08331-96 31 05, **e** info@
   adfc-memmingen.de) Kalchstrasse 1
Munich (☎ 089-77 34 29, **e** zentrale@
   adfc-muenchen.de) Platenstrasse 4
Nuremberg (☎ 0911-39 61 32, **e** adfc-nbg@
   t-online.de) Rohledererstrasse 13

Rental & Purchase

The cost of renting bikes varies from €3 to €13 per day, depending on the type of bike and where you rent it; holders of rail passes or train tickets sometimes get a small discount. You might also be able to get weekly prices at some stations. For lists of stations offering this service, see DB's free *Fahrrad am Bahnhof* or *Bahn & Bike* brochures. If you plan to spend several weeks or longer in the saddle, buying a second-hand bike works out cheaper than renting a bike or bringing your own; good reconditioned models go for €150 to €200. If you are flying to Frankfurt-am-Main and wish to purchase a bike there, try Per Pedale (☎ 069-707 691 10, fax 707 691 13, **e** info@perpedale.de, **w** www .perpedale.de), Leipziger Strasse 4, in Bockenheim; or Uni Bikes (☎ 069-77 79 90, fax 77 75 50), Homburger Strasse 26.

HITCHING

Hitching *(Trampen)* is never entirely safe in any country in the world and, as a rule, we don't recommend it. However, in some of the rural areas in southern Bavaria it is not uncommon to see people thumbing for a ride. If you do decide to hitch, understand that you are taking a small but potentially serious risk. Remember that it's safer to travel in pairs and be sure to let someone know where you are planning to go.

It's illegal to hitch on autobahns or their entry/exit ramps, but service stations can be very good places to pick up a ride. Prepare a sign clearly showing your intended destination in German. You can save yourself a lot of trouble by arranging a lift through a *Mitfahrzentrale* (ride-share agencies; see Hitching & Ride Services in the Getting There & Away chapter).

BOAT

Though arguably geared towards tourists, boats are a pleasant and leisurely way to get around. Bayerische Seenschifffahrt operates ferries on all of Bavaria's major lakes: the Chiemsee, Königssee, Starnberger See and Ammersee. In Lindau on Lake Constance, Bodensee Schiffsbetriebe runs trips to practically all lake communities on the German and Austrian shore. Regular boat service is also offered on several rivers, including the Main, the Danube and the Altmühl, as well as the Rhine-Main-Danube-Canal.

LOCAL TRANSPORT

Local transport includes buses, trams, S-Bahn and/or U-Bahn (underground train system). Most public transport systems integrate buses, trams and trains; fares are determined by the zones or the time travelled, or sometimes both. Multi-ticket strips or day passes are generally available and offer far better value than single-ride tickets. For details, see Getting Around in the appropriate city and town sections.

Bus & Tram

Cities and towns operate their own local bus and/or tram services. In most places, you must have a ticket before boarding and validate it aboard (or risk paying a fine of around €30). Tickets are sold mainly from vending machines at train stations and tram or bus stops. Bus drivers usually sell single-trip tickets, but these are more expensive than tickets bought in advance.

Train

Metropolitan areas such as Nuremberg and Munich have a system of suburban train lines called the S-Bahn. These cover a wider area than buses or trams, but tend to be less frequent. S-Bahn lines are often linked to the national rail network, and often interconnect urban centres. Train passes and conventional train tickets between cities are generally valid on these services.

Taxi

Taxis are expensive and, given the excellent public transport systems, not recommended unless you're in a real hurry. (They can actually be slower than trains or shuttle buses if you're going to/from the airport.) Look up *Taxi Ruf* in the phone directory to find the nearest taxi rank. Taxis are metered and cost up to €2.30 at flag fall and €1.30 per kilometre; in some places higher night tariffs apply. For more information on taxis, see the Getting Around sections in the appropriate city sections.

ORGANISED TOURS

Most local tourist offices offer free or low-cost guided walking tours to the main sights, which usually last an hour or two. They can be a good idea if you're pressed for time or just want to get a quick overview before starting your own explorations. Sometimes, tours will give you access to locations otherwise restricted to the public.

Scheduled English-language tours for individual travellers are rare, except in tourist resorts popular with Anglo-American travellers such as Rothenburg ob der Tauber and Munich. If you're travelling as a group, most tourist offices can arrange for a private tour in English.

Tourist offices also offer longer tour options, including day or multi-day adventures, spa and wine-tasting packages.

Many of the larger museums offer guided tours of their collections at specific hours, often at no additional cost to the admission price.

For organised tours to Bavaria, see the Getting There & Away chapter.

Munich

☎ 089 • pop 1.3 million • elevation 530m

Munich (München) is the Bavarian mother lode. It's home to world-class museums, a lively cultural scene, splendid architecture and a boisterous nightlife scene. It is also one of Germany's most prosperous cities. Only since reunification has it become the nation's second most popular destination, after Berlin.

Munich became Bavaria's capital in 1504 but really didn't achieve prominence until the guiding hand of Ludwig I in the 19th century. It has seen many turbulent times, but the 20th century has been particularly rough. WWI practically starved the city to death, and WWII (which in many ways began here with the infamous Munich Agreement) brought bombing and more than 200,000 deaths.

Whether you visit the city during the tourist-packed summer, the madness of Oktoberfest or the cold stillness of a February afternoon, Munich offers the chance to see Bavarians and the values and attitudes that so dominate the exported image of 'Germany'.

HISTORY

There's evidence of settlement here as early as AD 525 , but it's generally agreed that the most important settlers were Benedictine monks around the 8th century; the city's name derives from *Ze den Munichen*, or 'with the monks'.

The history of Munich as a town begins in 1158. It was founded by Heinrich der Löwe, a duke of Saxony who had been given the Duchy of Bavaria by his cousin, Emperor Frederick Barbarossa. Heinrich's control over the city, tenuous at the best of times, was repealed just three decades later when Barbarossa handed it over to the House of Wittelsbach, which would run the city (as well as Bavaria) until the 20th century.

Munich became a ducal residence in 1255 under Ludwig the Bavarian. He dramatically changed Munich's infrastructure by rebuilding areas destroyed by the Great

Highlights

- Peruse the fabulous art collections of the trio of Pinakothek museums
- Spend a warm and sunny day at Schloss Nymphenburg and its folly-filled gardens
- Quaff a cool *Mass* in one of Munich's many lively beer gardens or beer halls
- Go bar-hopping in the lively Gärtnerplatzviertel or in Haidhausen
- Treat your ears to the sounds of the Münchener Philharmoniker at the Gasteig, or the Bavarian State Opera at the Nationaltheater in the Residenz
- Linger over a buffet brunch at one of the city's cafes and watch the world on parade
- Do it at least once in your life, and do it right: the Munich Oktoberfest

AUSTRIA

Fire of 1328 and erecting fortifications. He also ensured Munich's regional power by granting it a salt-trading monopoly.

This established a wealthy trading city, and over the next 200 years Munich continued to prosper. By 1504 the city had 13,500 residents and had become the capital of the Duchy of Bavaria.

Dozens of outbreaks of the plague began in 1349 and continued for the next 150 years, despite frantic efforts to cordon off the city. Reinforcements were constructed and sewage and sanitation improved, but the city's population was ravaged. As the plague passed, the *Schäffler* (coopers) began a ritualistic dance in 1517, which they vowed to perform every seven years as long as the city was spared further outbreaks. Now the tradition – the *Schäfflertanz* – is re-enacted daily by the little figures on the city's *Glockenspiel* (carillon) on Marienplatz.

The Reformation hit Munich particularly hard. Under Duke Wilhelm IV, Protestants were persecuted and by the outbreak of the Thirty Years' War local residents were resolutely Catholic. During the war, the city was invaded with little fanfare. General Tilly, realising his Catholic forces were hopelessly outnumbered, wisely surrendered it to Swedish King Gustav Adolphus in 1632.

The city then fell under Habsburg rule from 1705 to 1714, and Munich was rejuvenated in the 18th century, with an explosion of spectacular baroque and Italianate architecture throughout the city.

In the 19th century, Napoleon's conquest of the territories and his rejigging of the German royal hierarchy elevated Bavaria to the rank of kingdom, and made Max Joseph the first king. The marriage in 1810 of Max Joseph's son, Crown Prince Ludwig, later to become King Ludwig I, to the Saxon-Hildburghausen Princess Therese marked what would become the Oktoberfest.

Munich saw runaway expansion under King Ludwig I, who was determined to transform his capital into a cultural and artistic centre. He hired architects including Leo von Klenze and Friedrich von Gärtner, and commissioned landmarks such as Königsplatz, the Alte Pinakothek and Ludwigstrasse. After Ludwig was forced to abdicate in 1848, (intrigued? see the boxed text 'Lola Montez, Femme Fatale' in the Facts about Bavaria chapter) his son, Maximilian II, continued many of the buildings and infrastructural improvements his father had envisioned.

Upon Max II's death in 1864 his son, Ludwig II, took the royal reins. The new king took little interest in building in Munich, especially after the city prevented him from financing an opera house for Richard Wagner. (The composer had made himself unpopular with Müncheners, whom he described as 'devoid of artistic sense'.) Instead, he channelled his fortune into other projects, particularly the castles of Neuschwanstein, Linderhof and Herrenchiemsee.

Arrested after being declared mentally unfit, Ludwig was found drowned (with his doctor) in highly mysterious circumstances in Lake Starnberg (see the boxed text 'The Mystery & Mystique of Ludwig II' in the Allgäu-Bavarian Swabia chapter). His brother Otto, a certified nutcase, was unable to take the throne, so his uncle, Prince Luitpold, took over as regent.

Under the relaxed hand of Luitpold, Munich enjoyed a golden age of sorts and he became one of Bavaria's most popular rulers. Between 1886 and Luitpold's death in 1912, Munich's population more than doubled to almost 600,000, making it Germany's third-largest city after Berlin and Hamburg. Munich gradually assumed the character of a modern metropolis; by 1893, it had the best electrical lighting in Europe.

The artistic scene flourished as never before. In 1873, portraitist Franz von Lenbach founded the *Künstlergesellschaft* (Artists' Society), and 13 years later, the Academy of Arts opened. Among its students at the turn of the 20th century were Wassily Kandinsky, Franz Marc, Paul Klee and Max Liebermann. The painters' presence also acted as a magnet for other famous artists, including composer Richard Strauss, writer Thomas Mann and playwright Henrik Ibsen. From about 1890 until WWI, the bohemian district of Schwabing was the focal point of artistic life.

During WWI Munich was spared collateral damage – only three bombs fell in the first and only air raid in 1916 – but the city was soon gripped by hunger and unemployment. Moreover, what began as a patriotic diversion led to the death of 13,000 Müncheners on the battlefields.

After the war, political turmoil and infighting – along with runaway inflation and economic collapse – created fertile ground for Adolf Hitler's National Socialist movement. It was here, in the Hofbräuhaus in 1920, that the failed artist addressed the party's first large meeting.

The budding dictator spent the next several years consolidating power and raising money, with great success. On 8 November 1923, he and about 600 troops stormed Munich's Bürgerbräukeller and kidnapped officials of the Bavaria provincial government. The caper was a fiasco. Nazi troops fled the next day, and Hitler was arrested and jailed. While serving his sentence, he began work on *Mein Kampf*.

Munich was severely damaged by Allied bombing during WWII, and on 30 April 1945 the city was occupied by US forces. Reconstruction was largely finished when the city was awarded the 1972 Olympic Games, a celebration of West Germany's rebuilding that ended in tragedy when 10 people were killed in a terrorist hostage-taking incident (see the boxed text 'Munich's Olympic Tragedy' later in this chapter).

Today, Munich wears a rich, self-assured reputation as, according to national opinion polls, the German city with the highest quality of life. Its large student population gives it a young feel and there's a vibrant theatre and arts scene as well. Yet its cultural sophistication is tempered by conservative traditions. Müncheners will be the first to admit that their 'metropolis' is little more than a 'Weltdorf' – a world village.

ORIENTATION

Munich is the capital of Bavaria, located on a vast plain in the southern part of the state. The Isar River rushes down from the Alps some 60km to the south and up through Munich, just east of the Altstadt. Munich is officially divided into numerous neighbourhoods. Formerly separate villages, they have been absorbed into the greater metropolitan area.

Altstadt

The Altstadt is Munich's historic centre, located within the old town walls which in modern times were replaced with a ring road. The heart of the Altstadt is Marienplatz, about 1km east of the Hauptbahnhof via the pedestrianised Neuhauser Strasse and its continuation, Kaufinger Strasse, Munich's main shopping streets.

North of Marienplatz is the Residenz (the former royal palace), packed with museums and theatres, and Odeonsplatz with the landmark Theatinerkirche. To the east of Marienplatz is the Platzl quarter with its traditional pubs and restaurants including the Hofbräuhaus, while south of the square is the Viktualienmarkt.

Gärtnerplatzviertel

The Gärtnerplatzviertel, the former Jewish quarter, is due south of the Altstadt proper and is one of the liveliest districts with plenty of fun bars and venues. Along with the Glockenbachviertel west of here, it is also the centre of Munich's gay and lesbian scene.

Ludwigsvorstadt

Ludwigsvorstadt is immediately west of the Altstadt and anchored by the Hauptbahnhof. The area immediately north and south of the station teems with budget and mid-range hotels, and there are also plenty of cheap computer and electronics shops, as well as Turkish grocer and doner stands. Some streets can be a bit seedy, but there's not really any danger here.

Westend

West of the Hauptbahnhof, the Westend – also sometimes called Schwanthaler Höhe – was once a slum area, but now bristles with renovated houses, hip cafes and wine bars and some nicer hotels. It's just west of the Theresienwiese, the former trade fairgrounds where the Oktoberfest is held.

Schwabing

Bustling Schwabing, Munich's former artist and bohemian quarter, is home to the university (although the 'Latin' quarter spills over into the eastern sections of Maxvorstadt). The main stretch of chichi cafes is along Leopoldstrasse, while the more down-to-earth establishments, as well as some nice Art Nouveau architecture, are west of this main artery. To the east, Schwabing is bounded by the Englischer Garten, a huge city park.

Maxvorstadt
North-west of the Altstadt, Maxvorstadt was Munich's first planned city expansion in the early 19th century. It's filled with world-class museums and, along with western Schwabing, is also Munich's 'Latin' (university) quarter.

Neuhausen
West of the Hauptbahnhof is cosmopolitan Neuhausen, a mostly residential (not terribly pretty) district with Rotkreuzplatz as its hub. One of the city's most popular hostels is here and there are plenty of good restaurants and pubs to keep you fed and lubricated.

Nymphenburg
Although a neighbourhood unto its own, the main reason for coming here is to tour the wonderful Schloss and its gardens. If the season's right, cap off the day with a cold *Mass* (1l mug) at one of the delightful beer gardens here.

Olympiapark
North of Neuhausen, Olympiapark is the site of the 1972 Olympic Games. One of Germany's most celebrated soccer clubs, the FC Bayern München, and its less successful local rival, Müchnen 1860, play in the Olympiastadion. The Olympiahalle is a vast entertainment centre and hosts big-ticket performers like the Rolling Stones or Janet Jackson. The BMW Museum is north-east of the park.

Bogenhausen
East of the Englischer Garten, Bogenhausen has long been the address of choice for Munich's rich and beautiful. The main thoroughfare is Prinzregentenstrasse. Streets around here are lined with immaculate villas and mansions, many sporting Art Nouveau design. The northern section, called Arabellapark, offers quite a contrast with its futuristic look.

Lehel
Lehel is a quiet and peaceful neighbourhood east of the Altstadt and west of the Isar River, filled with great 19th-century architecture and home to a string of museums along Prinzregentenstrasse, its northern boundary.

Haidhausen
Haidhausen is a youthful, multicultural neighbourhood with a creative flair. East of Lehel, it's packed with pubs, restaurants serving food from around the world and top-notch entertainment at the Gasteig cultural centre. Further east, near the Ostbahnhof, is Kunstpark Ost, an enormous nightlife complex containing discos, restaurants, bars and cinemas. On an island in the Isar, is Museumsinsel, with the Deutsches Museum and the Forum der Technik.

INFORMATION
Tourist Offices
The Munich Tourist Office has two convenient branches. One is in the Neues Rathaus on Marienplatz (☎ 23 32 82 42 or 22 23 24, fax 23 33 02 33, e tourismus@ muenchen.btl.de), which is open 10am to 8pm Monday to Friday and until 4pm Saturday. The other (☎ 23 33 02 57/58), outside the Hauptbahnhof at Bahnhofsplatz 2, is open 9am to 8pm Monday to Saturday and 10am to 6pm Sunday. Expect to queue during summer when stress levels among staff and travellers run high.

The room-finding service at the tourist office is free. You can book in person or by calling ☎ 233 30 236/237 with a credit card.

Both offices sell the Munich Welcome Card for €6.50/15.50 for one/three days; a three-day card good for up to five adults costs €22.50. The card gives you unlimited public transport and up to 50% discount on some 30 museums and attractions during its validity period.

EurAide (☎ 59 38 89, W www.euraide.de), in Room 3 next to Track 11 in the Hauptbahnhof, is a great place to head first thing if arriving by train. Its staff speak fluent English and can help you find rooms (€4 fee), buy train tickets or plan routes, book you on tours and provide a variety of other services. From

June to October, it's open 7.45am to noon and 1pm to 6pm daily. Otherwise, it closes at 4.45pm Monday to Friday and is not open on weekends. EurAide's free newsletter, *The Inside Track*, brims with practical information about the city and its surroundings, and gives discounts on money-changing (see Money later in this section).

The Jugend-Informations-Zentrum (Youth Information Centre; ☎ 51 41 06 60), just south-west of the Hauptbahnhof at Paul-Heyse-Strasse 22, is open noon to 6pm Monday to Friday (until 8pm Thursday). It has a wide range of printed information for young visitors to Munich and Germany.

The German motoring organisation Allgemeiner Deutscher Automobil Club (ADAC) has several offices in town. The biggest one (☎ 54 91 72 34) is on Sendlinger-Tor-Platz.

Money

Reisebank has two branches at the Hauptbahnhof. Travellers who present a copy of EurAide's newsletter *The Inside Track* pay only half the regular commission. Sparkasse branches are all over town, including a central one at Sparkassenstrasse 2, near Marienplatz. On Marienplatz itself, Hypovereinsbank has a hip outlet with ATMs and an Internet cafe with free Net surfing.

Deutsche Bank and Citibank both have offices on Rotkreuzplatz, close to the DJH hostel. The Postbank, which usually offers good exchange rates, is in the post office opposite the Hauptbahnhof. You'll find American Express (☎ 29 09 01 45) at Promenadeplatz 6 in the Altstadt and Thomas Cook (☎ 383 88 30) at Kaiserstrasse 45 in Schwabing.

Post & Communications

Munich's main post office is at Bahnhofplatz 1, just opposite the Hauptbahnhof, with telephone and fax services. It's open 7am to 8pm Monday to Friday, 8am to 4pm Saturday and 9am to 3pm Sunday. The poste restante address is Postlagernd, Bahnhofplatz 1, 80074 Munich.

Email & Internet Access

The post office shares a building with Germany's first branch of easyEverything, a new chain of Internet emporia which is bound to kill the competition. This one has around 550 terminals, is open 24 hours and charges €2.50 per hour.

The Internet Café (☎ 260 78 15), Altheimer Eck 12 near Marienplatz, has about a dozen cyber-terminals and is open from 11am to 1am daily. Access is free if you order one of its pizza or pasta dishes, or else pay €2.50 per half hour. There's a second branch (☎ 129 11 20) at Nymphenburger Strasse 145 in Neuhausen, just east of Rotkreuzplatz near the hostel, which is open 11am to 4pm daily.

South of the Hauptbahnhof, on Bayerstrasse 10a, is the Times Square Online Bistro (☎ 550 88 00), open from 6.30am to 1am daily, where you can surf for a stiff €2.25 per 15 minutes. There are also phone and video-conferencing facilities.

In Schwabing there is Cyberice-C@fe (☎ 34 07 69 55), Feilitzschstrasse 15, where you can sweeten your session with ice cream. It's open 10am to 1am daily and rates are €3/5 per 30/60 minutes.

Internet Resources

Munich's official Web site (W www.muenchen-tourist.de) is voluminous and user friendly, with good English-language sections. The expat magazine *Munich Found* also has an excellent Internet presence at W www.munichfound.de.

Travel Agencies

EurAide (see Tourist Offices) is the best place to go with complicated rail pass inquiries or to book train travel within Germany or elsewhere in Europe.

Munich is a great city for bucket shops and cheap airfares. Try Council Travel (☎ 39 50 22) at Adalbertstrasse 32 in Schwabing, or Travel Overland (☎ 27 27 61 00) at Barer Strasse 73 in Maxvorstadt. Studiosus Reisen (☎ 50 06 00) at Riesstrasse 25 near Olympiapark specialises in educational trips. Full-service mainstream agencies include Atlas Reisen (☎ 26 90 72), with outlets in the Kaufhof department stores, including the one at Kaufinger Strasse 1–5.

Bookshops

To stock up on major English-language newspapers and magazines, try Sussmann Presse + Buch in the Hauptbahnhof, which also has a decent range of books.

You might also try EurAide, which sells second-hand paperbacks. There's no shortage of great bookshops in Munich, including the following:

Geobuch (☎ 26 50 30, Rosental 6, Altstadt) Opposite Viktualienmarkt, this is the most comprehensive travel bookshop in town.

Hugendubel (☎ 01803-48 44 84) This national chain has an excellent general range as well as plenty of Lonely Planet titles and English-language novels. There are branches on Marienplatz and on Karlsplatz. You can sit on sofas and read before you buy.

Anglia English Bookshop (☎ 28 36 42, Schellingstrasse 3, Schwabing) This place is wacky but well stocked – if you can find anything.

Words' Worth Books (☎ 280 91 41, Schellingstrasse 21a, Schwabing) Down the street in the courtyard is this place with a similar assortment of books.

Max&Milian (☎ 260 33 20, Ickstattstrasse 2, Glockenbachviertel) South-east of Sendlinger Tor, this is easily the best-established gay bookshop.

Libraries

Each Munich district has a *Stadtbücherei* (city library), which usually has some English-language books. Branches include those at Rosenheimer Strasse 5 (☎ 48 09 83 16) in the Gasteig in Haidhausen; at Schrenkstrasse 8 (☎ 50 71 09) in Westend; and at Hohenzollernstrasse 16 (☎ 33 60 13) in Schwabing. The Bavarian State Library (☎ 286 22 93), Ludwigstrasse 16, also in Schwabing, has several reading rooms, including one stocked with hundreds of international newspapers and magazines. It's open 9am to 7.30 Monday to Friday and 9am to 4.30pm Saturday.

Munich's two main universities both have large academic libraries. The British Council and Amerika Haus (see Cultural Centres) also maintain libraries which specialise in books about culture and business in those countries.

Universities

Munich is home to some 100,000 students. About 44,000 of them attend the Ludwig-Maximilians-Universität München (☎ 218 00), at Geschwister-Scholl-Platz 1 in Schwabing. The top three faculties are medicine, economics and law.

The Technische Universität München (☎ 289 01), Arcisstrasse 21 in Maxvorstadt, has about 22,000 students studying mainly mathematics, physics, chemistry, biology and earth sciences.

Cultural Centres

Cultural organisations abound; the *München im...* publication (see the Entertainment section) has the complete list. There are active branches of Amerika Haus (☎ 552 53 70), Karolinenplatz 3 in Maxvorstadt; the British Council (☎ 290 08 60), Rumfordstrasse 7 in the Gärtnerplatzviertel; and the Institut Français (☎ 286 62 80), Kaulbachstrasse 13 in Schwabing. Cultural events sponsored by the Goethe-Institut (☎ 15 92 10) take place at the Goethe-Forum at Dachauer Strasse 122 in Neuhausen.

Laundry

The best laundry close to the city centre is Der Wunderbare Waschsalon, Theresienstrasse 134 in Maxvorstadt, open from 6am to midnight daily. It's spotless, has cafe-style tables, drinkable coffee and a pleasant atmosphere.

Close to the Hauptbahnhof, but swarming with layabouts, is City-SB Waschcenter (☎ 601 40 03) at Paul-Heyse-Strasse 21, open 7am to 10pm daily. There's also Schnell + Sauber at Klenzestrasse 18 in the Gärtnerplatzviertel, and a 24-hour Waschsalon at Landshuter Strasse 77, at the corner of Volkartstrasse, in Neuhausen, about 10 minutes from the DJH hostel.

Medical & Emergency Services

The US and British consulates can provide lists of English-speaking doctors on request.

Help in medical emergencies is available through the Kassenärztlicher Notfalldienst (☎ 55 17 71); for an ambulance, call ☎ 192 22. Staff at most pharmacies speak some

English. Designated 'international' ones include a branch at the airport (☎ 97 59 29 50); the Bahnhof-Apotheke (☎ 59 41 19), Bahnhofplatz 2; and the Ludwigs-Apotheke (☎ 18 94 01 00) at Neuhauser Strasse 11 in the Altstadt. For an emergency dentist, call ☎ 723 30 93.

There's a police station on Arnulfstrasse right by the Hauptbahnhof.

Dangers & Annoyances

Crime and staggering drunks leaving the beer halls and tents are major problems during Oktoberfest, especially at the southern end of the Hauptbahnhof. It's no joke: drunk people in a crowd trying to get home can get violent, and there are about 100 cases of assault every year. Leave early or stay cautious, if not sober, yourself.

ALTSTADT (MAP 2)

The Altstadt is Munich's historic heart and the place where you're likely to spend most of your time. Many of the major sights are located here and simply wandering the web of narrow lanes, making your own special discoveries, is a true delight. The action centres on Marienplatz, Munich's main square.

Marienplatz

Marienplatz, the famous square and Munich's heart and soul, marks the beginning of our Walking Tour. Framed by a series of

Altstadt Walking Tour

The attractions described in the sections from Marienplatz to the Viktualienmarkt are linked as a walking tour, though you can also treat each entry as a separate sight and pick and choose what you would like to visit.

This extensive circuit covers the main sights within the bounds of Munich's historic centre. Starting at Marienplatz, moving north to the Residenz and arching anticlockwise back to the starting point, the tour takes about two to 2½ hours if you're walking at a leisurely pace. Include visits to all the museums and churches and you've got (at least) a two-day itinerary on your hands.

landmark buildings, it's a popular meeting place and lively outdoor stage for street musicians, artists and colourful characters. In December, dozens of fancifully decorated stalls create a magical atmosphere during one of Germany's most beloved Christmas markets.

The golden figure of the Virgin Mary, carved in 1590 and originally located in the Frauenkirche, peers down from the glowing **Mariensäule** (St Mary's Column), erected in 1638 to celebrate the removal of Swedish forces during the Thirty Years' War.

Neues Rathaus The neogothic New Town Hall (1867–1908) wraps around six courtyards, including the **Prunkhof**, which come alive during festivals and events several times a year. Grimacing gargoyles and stately statues jut out from the captivating facade; see if you can spot the dragon climbing the turrets at the corner.

Just before 11am (November to April only), noon and 5pm (both year round), hordes of tourists stream onto the square to see the incessantly photographed **Glockenspiel** (carillon) spring into action. Its mechanical figures depict two festivities that took place on the square: the Ritterturnier, a knights' tournament held in 1568 in honour of the marriage of Duke Wilhelm V to Renata von Lothringen, and the Schäfflertanz, a dance celebrating the end of the plague. The night scene – featuring the Münchner Kindl and Nachtwächter (night watchman) characters – runs at 9pm.

You can take a lift to the top of the 85m-tall tower *(adult/concession €1.50/0.75; open 9am-4pm Mon-Thur, 9am-1pm Fri, 10am-7pm Sat-Sun & holidays)*. The cashier is on the 4th floor. Fitness fiends who take the staircase will be rewarded with close-ups of the decorated corridors and inner courtyard.

St Peterskirche In the south-eastern corner of Marienplatz, the Church of St Peter *(☎ 260 48 28, Rindermarkt 1; open 7.30am-7pm daily)* is Gothic in its core but now boasts a flamboyant baroque interior. The high altar with sculptures of St Peter (1517) by Erasmus Grasser and of the four church fathers (1732) by Egid Quirin Asam is a top eye-catcher. The ceiling frescoes by Johann Baptist Zimmermann were recently restored to their graceful splendour.

The bell tower – colloquially known as 'Alter Peter' – is 92m high and you can climb its 297 steps for some of the finest views of the central city *(adult/concession €1.25/0.75; open 9am-6pm Mon-Sat, 10.15am-7pm Sun & holidays)*.

Fischbrunnen The Fish Fountain's original purpose was to keep river fish alive during the medieval markets. Later it served as the ceremonial dunking spot for butchers upon completion of their apprenticeships, a tradition only abandoned in 1954. Today, it's simply a good meeting place. Local legend suggests that dipping an empty purse into the water here on Ash Wednesday guarantees that it will always be full.

Altes Rathaus The Gothic Old Town Hall (1474), by Jörg von Halspach (who also built the Frauenkirche), punctuates the eastern end of Marienplatz. Destroyed by lightning and bombs, it was rebuilt in a plainer style after WWII. Inside, the main interest is the former council chamber, canopied by a barrel-vaulted, carved ceiling and lined by a frieze of coats of arms and medallions. It's often used for official and private functions, but otherwise not accessible to the public.

The town hall's southern tower lodges the **Spielzeugmuseum** *(Toy Museum; ☎ 29 40 01, Marienplatz 15; adult/concession €2.50/0.50; open 10am-5.30pm daily)*. It celebrates a time of greater innocence with its endearing collection of pre-Nintendo era toys, mostly from Europe and North America. Right outside is a wind-powered sculpture that releases pent-up energy every few minutes by clanging and banging. The bronze statue on the tower's southern side depicts Julia (as in Romeo and Juliet) and was a gift from Munich's sister city, Verona.

Heiliggeistkirche
A short stroll east on Im Tal will soon get you to the Church of the Holy Spirit *(1392;*

☎ *22 44 02, Im Tal 77; open 7am-6pm daily)*. Munich's oldest Gothic hall church at first appears almost economical in design until you look up to see the frescoes by Cosmas Damian Asam. These were added around 1730, when the interior received a rococo make-over. The high altar, festooned with a gaggle of sprightly angels, dates from the same period, while the Marienaltar (1450) is a leftover from the original Gothic church.

Hofbräuhaus
Continue north on Maderbräustrasse to Orlandostrasse and the celebrated, if infamous, Hofbräuhaus *(☎ 22 16 76, Am Platzl 9)*, crawling with tourists all day from opening time at 10am. The ballroom upstairs was the site of the first large meeting of the National Socialist Party on 20 February 1920; you can visit if the rooms aren't being used for a function. Back downstairs, after guzzling a *Mass* (1L mug) or two of beer (€5.50 to €6.50 apiece), drivers can check their alcohol level in the coin-op breathalysers by the toilets.

Alter Hof & Münzhof
From the Hofbräuhaus, head west on Münzstrasse, turn left into Sparkassenstrasse, then duck into the Ledererstrasse alleyway which leads to Burgstrasse. Turn right (north) to get to the central courtyard of the Alter Hof (Old Court), the Wittelsbach residence from 1273 until the court outgrew it and moved to the Residenz (which you'll see later on this tour), in 1474. Its most prominent resident was Emperor Ludwig the Bavarian, who lived here until 1347; later, various administrative offices moved into the complex.

Note the ornate late-Gothic oriel on the southern facade, which is nicknamed 'Monkey Tower'. A nice story tells how the oriel was supposedly home to a monkey that played in the bedroom of the infant Ludwig the Stern. One day, a market pig attacked Ludwig's cradle and the monkey grabbed the young royal and brought him to safety on the pinnacle of the oriel. Unfortunately, this is a tale as cute as it is tall: the oriel wasn't built until many years later.

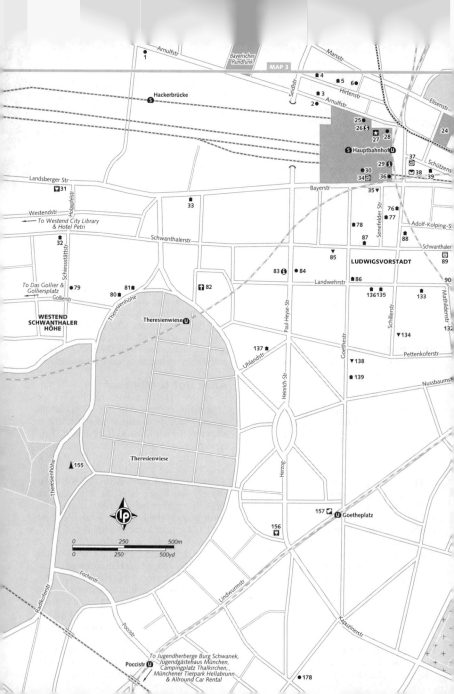

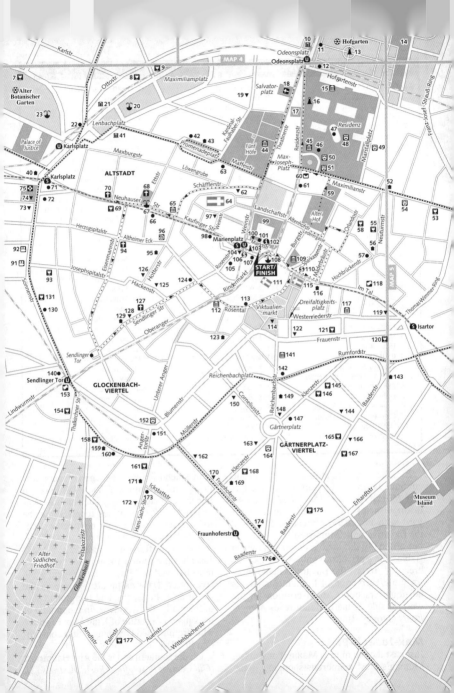

MAP 2 – CENTRAL MUNICH

PLACES TO STAY

3 Hotel Amba
4 Hotel Alfa
5 4 You München
32 Kurpfalz Hotel
33 Hotel Jedermann
39 Hotel Excelsior; Vinothek Geisel
40 Hotel Königshof
43 Bayerischer Hof; Night Club
52 Kempinski Vier Jahreszeiten München
56 Hotel Mandarin Oriental Munich
76 Hotel Helvetia
77 Euro Youth Hotel
78 In Via Marienherberge
80 Hotel Seibel
81 Hotel Krone
86 Hotel Mirabell
87 Hotel Cristal München
88 Hotel Monaco
95 Hotel Arosa
116 Hotel Schlicker
123 Hotel Blauer Bock
129 Hotel Atlanta
133 CVJM-YMCA Jugendgästehaus
135 Andi München City Center
136 Pension Marie-Luise
137 Hotel Uhland
139 Hotel-Pension Mariandl; Café am Beethovenplatz
143 Hotel Advokat
149 Deutsche Eiche
159 Pension Eulenspiegel
169 Pension Am Gärtnerplatztheater
171 Hotel Olympic

PLACES TO EAT

19 Dukatz im Literaturhaus
35 Pizzeria Ca' doro
62 Münchner Suppenküche
73 Vinzenzmurr
74 Müller Bakery; Nordsee & Grillpfanne
85 Kebab Antep
90 Kandil Restaurant
97 Andechser am Dom
100 Ratskeller
104 Café Glockenspiel
114 Bratwurstherzl
119 Riva
122 Buxs
125 Prinz Myschkin
126 Hundskugel
128 Vinzenzmurr
132 La Vecchia Masseria
134 Mensa
138 La Fiorentina
144 Joe Peña's
148 Interview
150 Forum
162 Fraunhofer
163 Shida
166 Ganga
170 Kleinschmidtz
172 Maitoi
174 Der Kleine Chinese

GALLERIES & MUSEUMS

15 Staatliches Museum Ägyptischer Kunst
44 Kunsthalle der Hypo-Kulturstiftung
45 Residenzmuseum
65 Deutsches Jagd- und Fischereimuseum
109 Altes Rathaus & Spielzeugmuseum
112 Münchener Stadtmuseum; Filmmuseum & Stadtcafe
117 Centre for Unusual Museums
141 Jüdisches Museum München

PUBS & BARS

7 Parkcafé
8 Soul City; Nachtcafé
9 Fortuna Musikbar
31 Augustiner Bräustub'n & Brewery
53 Schumann's
55 Atomic Café
58 Hofbräuhaus
69 Augustiner-Grossgaststätte
93 Iwan
120 Braunauer Hof
121 Master's Home
131 New York
145 Klenze 17
146 Bei Carla
154 The Stud
156 Mister B's
158 Ochsengarten
161 Ksar
165 Pacific Times

Exit the courtyard at its northern end and continue north on Hofgraben, past the former **Münzhof** *(Mint; 1567; Hofgraben 4)*, distinguished by a nice Renaissance courtyard with three-storey arcades. It housed the Bavarian State Mint from 1809 to 1983, but originally did double duty as the ducal stables and a private art gallery of Duke Albrecht V. Today, the Bavarian State Office for the Preservation of Monuments has its headquarters here. An inscription on the western side of the building reads *Moneta Regis* (Money Rules).

Max-Joseph-Platz

Just past the old mint is **Maximilianstrasse**, Munich's most glamorous shopping street, with splendiferously expensive shops and the grand Kempinski Vier Jahreszeiten Hotel (see Places to Stay later in this chapter) at No 17. Sculptures representing the four seasons and the four continents decorate its facade.

Turning left, you'll soon reach Max-Joseph-Platz, home to some of Munich's most beloved buildings. Among them is the five-tiered **Nationaltheater**, home to the Bavarian State Opera, and the granddaddy of them all – the Residenz. In the middle of the square is a **statue** of King Max I Joseph, who promulgated Germany's first constitution in 1818.

On the southern end is the **Alte Hauptpost** *(Old Central Post Office, Residenzstrasse 2)*, originally the town mansion of a local count. The frescoed arcades, added by Leo von Klenze in 1830, give the building a touch of Tuscany. The place still dispatches mail; enter at the western side.

Residenz

Generations of Bavarian rulers lived, loved and governed in the sprawling Munich Residence from 1385 to 1918. The vast complex you see today actually had its origin in a small moated palace but grew over time along with the self-representational needs of the Wittelsbachs.

Important additions included the construction of northern wings to create several interior courtyards, such as the Emperor,

Apothecary and Fountain courtyards and two smaller ones, Chapel and King's Tract, in the late 16th century.

The palace got its current look under the rule of King Ludwig I who commissioned star architect Leo von Klenze to build the *Königsbau* (King's Building) facing Max-Joseph-Platz and the *Festsaalbau* (Festival Hall) near the court gardens to the north. Klenze looked south to Florence (Italy) for inspiration, and found a way to imbue the mega-compound with a light-hearted style. WWII took a heavy toll, leaving only the ground floor rooms standing. Reconstruction, which is more or less wrapped up today, cost around €50 million. Most sections are now open as museums and theatres.

MUNICH

Culture at a Discount

If you're planning on visiting all or most of Munich's major palaces and their museums, consider getting the *Verbundkarte* for €15, which gives you 14 days to visit the following: the Residence Museum, the Residence Treasury, the Old Residence Theatre, the Ruhmeshalle and Bavaria, Schloss Nymphenburg, Amalienburg, Marstallmuseum and Badenburg. It's available at any of these places.

There are three entrances to the various attractions inside the Residenz: Max-Joseph-Platz (south), Residenzstrasse (west) and Hofgartenstrasse (north). To continue the walking tour, head north on Residenzstrasse.

As you walk north on Residenzstrasse, note the two lions guarding the gates to the palace. Rubbing one of the lions' shields is said to bring you wealth (look for the one that's been buffed to a gleaming shine).

Residenzmuseum The Residenzmuseum *(Residence Museum; ☎ 29 06 71, enter from Max-Joseph-Platz 3; adult/concession €4/3, combination ticket with Residence Treasury €7/5.50; open 9am-6pm Fri-Wed, 9am-8pm Thur Apr–mid-Oct, 10am-4pm daily mid-Oct–Mar)* is a treasure-filled maze of roughly 130 rooms. It reflects not only the enormous wealth and power of the Wittelsbachs but also their passion for art and architecture.

The museum is so large that it's divided into two sections, which take about two hours each to see; one is open in the morning, one in the afternoon. You can see it all during guided tours or on your own with a copy of the excellent English-language guide *Residence Munich* (€3, available at the cash desk), which has room-by-room tours with photographs and commentary.

The enclosed **Grottenhof** (Grotto Court), one of the first places you'll see after entering, is home to a fountain featuring a statue of Perseus and a rather dilapidated statue of Mercury. At the request of museum curators, Germans on beach holidays in the 1950s brought back many of the shells covering the walls.

Top billing goes to the famous **Antiquarium** (1571), an intensely decorated, tunnel-shaped Renaissance hall built to house Duke Albrecht V's huge antique collection and later used for banquets and festivals.

The **Kurfürstenzimmer** (Elector's Rooms) contain some stunning Italian portraits. Also here is a long passageway lined by two dozen views of Italy painted by Carl Rottmann, a leading local romantic painter.

Other highlights include the **Ahnengalerie** (Ancestors' Gallery), with 121 portraits of the rulers of Bavaria (note the larger paintings of Charlemagne and Ludwig the Bavarian); the **Nibelungensäle** designed by Leo von Klenze and smothered in scenes from the medieval Nibelungen epic; and François Cuvilliés' **Reiche Zimmer** (Rich Rooms) in exuberant rococo style.

The **Porzellankammern** (Porcelain Chambers) contain 19th-century porcelain services from factories in Berlin, Meissen and Nymphenburg, while the **Asian Collections** feature Chinese and Japanese lacquerware, tapestries, carpets, furniture and jewellery.

Schatzkammer der Residenz The Residenzmuseum entrance also leads to the Residence Treasury *(☎ 29 06 71, enter from Max-Joseph-Platz 3; adult/concession €4/3, combination ticket with Residenzmuseum €7/5.50; open 9am-6pm Fri-Wed, 9am-8pm Thur Apr–mid-Oct, 10am-4pm daily mid-Oct–Mar).* It's an Aladdin's Cave worth of jewels, ornate goldwork and other precious objects. Some of the more intriguing treasures are portable altars, the ruby jewellery of Queen Theresa, amazing pocket watches, and 'exotic handicrafts' from Turkey, Iran, Mexico and India. It's definitely worth the admission price. The English-language guide to the collection, *Treasury in the Munich Residence*, is another €3.

Altes Residenztheater The Residenz also harbours one of Europe's finest rococo theatres, the Old Residence Theatre *(1753; ☎ 29 06 71, enter from Residenzstrasse 1; adult/concession €2/1.50; open 9am-6pm*

Fri–Wed, 9am-8pm Thur Apr–mid-Oct, 10am-4pm daily mid-Oct–Mar, closed during rehearsals). Also known as Cuvilliés Theatre for its architect, the elegant and lavish interior is considered a rococo masterpiece.

Staatliches Museum Ägyptischer Kunst

At the Egyptian Art Museum *(☎ 29 85 46, enter from Hofgartenstrasse; adult/ concession €2.50/1.50; open 9am-9pm Tues, 9am-4pm Wed-Fri, 10am-5pm Sat-Sun)* you can take a journey through 4000 years of Egyptian art and culture from the Old, Middle and New Kingdoms (2670–1075 BC). Also on view is sculpture from ancient Nubia (present-day Sudan) and examples of Coptic art. The collection was started by Duke Albrecht V in the 16th century and expanded by King Ludwig I in the 19th.

Odeonsplatz & Around

Residenzstrasse culminates in Odeonsplatz, built by Klenze as a transition between the Altstadt and Schwabing to the north. The wide and impressive Ludwigstrasse, one of Europe's classic promenades, emanates north from the square, which is ringed by further Klenze creations. These include the namesake **Odeon**, originally a music and dance hall and now a government office. Just north of here is the **Leuchtenberg-Palais** (1821; Map 3), a stately town palace modelled after the Palazzo Farnese in Rome and today home of the Bavarian Finance Ministry.

Hofgarten East of Odeonsplatz, the neoclassical **Hofgartentor** (1816) leads to the former Royal Gardens, crisscrossed by lovely paths. To the left (north) of the entrance is the **Café Tambosi**, an expensive street cafe usually chock-a-block with cashed-up tourists. The entrance itself consists of **Klenze's Arcades**, bearing frescoes of Bavarian historical scenes and of the Wittelsbachs.

The Royal Gardens have humble origins as a vegetable garden for the court until the 18th century. Paths culminate in the centre at the **Hofgartentempel**, a striking octagonal pavilion honouring the Greek goddess Diana. In summer, it's a favourite spot for impromptu classical recitals.

North of the gardens is the **Deutsches Theatermuseum** *(German Theatre Museum; Map 3; ☎ 210 69 10, Galeriestrasse 4a/6; admission free; open 10am-4pm Tues-Sun).* Its vast collection of stage sets, props, costumes, masks and theatre programs thoroughly documents the history of the theatre in German-speaking countries. At the time of writing, a permanent exhibit was in the works, but meanwhile three to five special exhibits, along with readings and other events, are organised each year.

East of the Hofgarten is the modern **Bayerische Staatskanzlei** (Bavarian State Chancellory), which houses the offices of the Bavarian governor. It was the last big architectural order placed by the CSU's powerful former party chief, Franz-Josef Strauss, before his death in 1988. The old-style cupola is in fact the only remaining section of the ruined Army Museum that was left here as a war memorial. Known in its entirety as the 'glass palace', the combination with the modern wings caused quite a fuss when the blueprint was unveiled.

Feldherrnhalle The Field Marshals' Hall, built in honour of the military leaders under the Wittelsbachs, squats on the southern end of Odeonsplatz. Klenze competitor Friedrich von Gärtner created this neoclassical confection in 1844 with the Loggia dei Lanzi in Florence serving as a model.

Among its statues is that of General Tilly, who surrendered Munich to the Swedes during the Thirty Years' War. On November 9, 1923, police stopped Hitler's attempt to bring down the Weimar Republic – the so-called Beer Hall Putsch – right outside the Feldherrnhalle in a fierce skirmish that left 20 people, including 16 Nazis, dead.

Hitler was tried and sentenced to five years in jail, but ended up serving a mere nine months which he used to pen *Mein Kampf.* After his rise to power in 1933, he had a memorial plaque honouring the victims of the putsch installed on the building's facade and required passers-by to give the Hitler salute.

Theatinerkirche The ensemble of twin towers and giant copper dome of this mustard-yellow **Stiftskirche St Kajetan** *(1663–90; Theatinerstrasse 22)*, in the south-western corner of Odeonsplatz, forms a distinctive landmark in Munich's skyline. Built to commemorate the birth of Prince Max Emanuel, it is the creation of Italian architect Agostino Barelli and the city's first baroque church. François Cuvilliés added the snail-like flourishes to the facade about a century later.

Inside, the intensely stuccoed high dome stands above the **Fürstengruft** (royal crypt), containing the remains of Wittelsbach family members, including Max Emanuel himself, his parents Ferdinand and Henriette, King Max Joseph I and Crown Prince Rupprecht of Bavaria.

Until at least late 2003, the full visual impact of the interior is likely to be marred by scaffolding while a thorough restoration continues.

Fünf Höfe

Heading south on Theatinerstrasse will soon get you to the eastern entrance of the new Fünf Höfe, an exclusive shopping mall built around five courtyards. The complex, which recycles several existing buildings, is the work of the Swiss architectural team of Jacques Herzog and Pierre de Meuron, winners of the prestigious Pritzker Architecture Prize in 2001. Fans of minimalist architecture (lots of metal and glass) will have plenty to admire. Well-heeled shoppers can stock up on designer duds at dozens of top international and local speciality boutiques. Those with less cash on hand can still watch the human parade while sipping a cappuccino in one of the several cafes.

Kunsthalle der Hypo-Kulturstiftung

This privately sponsored museum is a veritable delicacy on the Munich arts 'banquet'. Part of the Fünf Höfe complex, the Kunsthalle *(☎ 22 44 12, Theatinerstrasse 8; adult/senior/student €7/6/4, half-price on nonholiday Mon; open 10am-8pm daily)* regularly hosts temporary exhibitions of international calibre ranging from antiquities to modern classics such as Monet, Chagall and Picasso.

Frauenkirche

Continue south on Theatinerstrasse, then turn right on Schäfflerstrasse which leads to Frauenplatz. This plaza is dominated by Munich's most famous landmark, the late-Gothic Church of Our Lady (1468–88), since 1821 the seat of the Munich archbishop. Its twin copper onion domes punctuate the skyline, but otherwise, the red-brick edifice is a vast but remarkably unadorned church, both inside and out. The whitewashed interior consists of a central nave flanked by two side aisles – as is typical of the Gothic period – with 22 octagonal pillars supporting the lofty ceiling. Aside from the 'devil's footprint' (see boxed text 'The Devil's Footprint'), focus on the original stained-glass windows and the tomb of Ludwig the Bavarian and other Wittelsbach rulers in the choir. On a clear day, it's worth riding up the 98m-tall southern tower *(adult/concession €2/1; open 10am-5pm Mon-Sat Apr-Oct)*.

Deutsches Jagd- und Fischereimuseum

Walk south on Liebfrauenstrasse to Kaufinger Strasse, the main shopping drag, turn

---

The Devil's Footprint

Local legend has it that Jörg von Halspach, builder of the Frauenkirche, struck a deal with Satan. Halspach needed money to complete the church, and the devil agreed to provide it on the condition that Halspach build the church without a single visible window.

When Satan came to inspect the Frauenkirche, he saw the tall Gothic windows from a distance and rejoiced, because he thought he'd won the architect's soul. But Halspach led the devil to a spot in the foyer, from where not a single window could be seen. Furious, Satan stamped his foot and stormed off, leaving a hoofed footprint in the pavement of the entrance hall.

Restoration work after WWII means the illusion no longer works, but the outline (which looks more like that of a modern loafer) remains.

Jeremy Gray

right and you'll find the German Hunting & Fishing Museum *(☎ 22 05 22, Neuhauser Strasse 2; adult/concession €3/2; open 9am-5pm Tues, Wed, Fri-Sun, 9.30am-9pm Mon & Thur)*. Although it contains room after room of stuffed animals and antlers, this place is not just for rod-and-rifle freaks. Among the more intriguing exhibits are rococo hunting sleighs, Stone-Age fishing tackle and Chinese scroll paintings. The museum is in the former Augustinerkirche (1290) and boasts lavish interior decoration.

Michaelskirche & Around
Further west, Kaufinger Strasse turns into Neuhauser Strasse where, at the corner of Ettstrasse, is the **Church of St Michael** *(1590; ☎ 231 70 60, Neuhauser Strasse 52; open 8am-7pm daily)*. Although considered to be the most famous Renaissance church in southern Germany, it also sports a few baroque touches. Its most distinctive feature, though, is the 20m-wide barrel-vaulted ceiling which seemingly floats – without any supporting pillars – above the lavish white stucco interior (only St Peter's in Rome has a larger one).

The church was commissioned by Duke Wilhelm V, a fervent supporter of the Counter-Reformation. The main facade's rich sculptural iconography reflects the triumph of Catholicism over Protestantism: up above is Christ holding up a golden globe – the earth – while the bronze statue between the two entrance portals shows the archangel Michael in combat with the devil. The church crypt contains several Wittelsbach tombs, including those of Wilhelm V and 'Fairy-Tale' King Ludwig II.

Outside the church is the **Richard Strauss Brunnen** (1962), a modern fountain with streams of water that recall the *Dance of the Seven Veils* in Strauss' opera *Salomé*. A little further on, at Neuhauser Strasse 48, is the **Bürgersaalkirche** (1710), its inconspicuous facade belying the fact that it's actually a church. Built in the early 18th century, it serves as the gathering place for a Marian congregation and contains the tomb of Rupert Mayer, a Jesuit priest and noted Nazi opponent, who was beatified in 1987.

Asamkirche & Asamhaus
Backtrack a few steps on Neuhauser Strasse then turn south on Eisenmannstrasse, pass by the ornate **Damenstiftskirche** to your left, then continue south to **Sendlinger Tor**, the 14th-century southern city gate. From there, bear north-east on Sendlinger Strasse, a relaxed shopping street with one-of-a-kind boutiques. About 200m further on your left at No 62 is the small St Johann Nepomuk church, better known as the Asamkirche (1733–46).

In 1729, Egid Quirin Asam bought an ensemble of four houses on Sendlinger Strasse, one to live in, two to convert into his private church and one to serve as the home for the resident priest. Working jointly with his brother, Cosmas Damian, Asam had the luxury of designing the church exactly to his own specifications, unencumbered by the visions of a patron. One neat trick was that the main altar could be seen through a window from his house next door.

In the end, the brothers concocted a jaw-dropping interior that is certainly a rococo masterpiece, but whose overwhelming opulence can be a tad suffocating. It's a visual extravaganza of silver, gold, marble, carved wood and stucco with lots and lots of sculptural and ornamental decoration. Nary a square centimetre remained unembellished in this space, which – measuring a mere 9m by 28m – is of rather intimate proportions.

Münchener Stadtmuseum
Carry on along Sendlinger Strasse, then turn right on Rosental which leads to the Munich City Museum *(☎ 23 32 23 70, St-Jakobs-Platz 1; adult/concession €2.50/1.50, free on Sun, special exhibits €4/2; open 10am-6pm Tues-Sun)*. The permanent exhibit traces the evolution of the city from royal residence to modern metropolis. Worth seeking out is the large-scale model of Munich in 1572 and the delightful *Moriskentänzer* (Morris Dancers; 1480), an ensemble of 10 half-metre-tall wooden figurines by Erasmus Grasser.

The upper floors house several speciality collections: the **Musical Instruments Museum** features around 2000 instruments from all periods and many countries; the **Fashion Museum** has changing exhibits displaying clothing from the 18th century to today; the **Puppet Theatre Museum** has an astonishing collection of dolls and marionettes; and the **Photography Department**, which was undergoing an overhaul at the time of writing, will soon focus again on the early years of the medium beginning around 1840.

Also part of the premises is the **Filmmuseum**, which owns a huge archive of German silent movies and is otherwise engaged in preserving, restoring and supporting German film. Its cinema presents two or three movies nightly (€4 each).

Viktualienmarkt & Around

Carry on east along Rosental to emerge at the bustling Viktualienmarkt, one of Europe's great food markets. In summer, the entire place becomes one of the finest and most expensive beer gardens around, while in winter people huddle for warmth and schnapps in the small pubs surrounding the market. The merchandise and food are of the finest quality, but bargains don't exactly abound (see Self-Catering in Places to Eat for suggestions).

A short walk east of Viktualienmarkt is the bizarre Zentrum für Aussergewöhnliche Museen *(Centre for Unusual Museums; ☎ 290 41 21, Westenriederstrasse 41; adult/concession €4/2.50; open 10am-6pm daily)*. Inside is a most peculiar gathering of collections, including chamber pots, perfume bottles, Easter bunnies and locks. There's also a collection of items associated with 'Sisi' (that's Empress Elisabeth of Austria to you). We could make lots of jokes about this place, but to paraphrase Groucho Marx, it doesn't need our help.

This is where the tour ends. To get back to Marienplatz, backtrack to Viktualienmarkt, then north to Im Tal and a few steps west and the square will be right there.

GÄRTNERPLATZVIERTEL (MAP 2)

The Gärtnerplatz district is a fun and lively quarter with lots of alternative bars, pubs and restaurants. It's also the hub of Munich's gay and lesbian scene. Also referred to on maps as Isarvorstadt, it stretches south of Viktualienmarkt between Sendlinger Tor and Isartor.

The centre of the neighbourhood is, of course, the circular Gärtnerplatz, anchored by the **Staatstheater am Gärtnerplatz**. Founded by citizens in 1865, the theatre was taken over by Ludwig I after the owners went bankrupt. It opened with Jacques Offenbach's *Salon Pitzelberger* and light opera has been the main fare here ever since.

The area has sprung up from the former Jewish quarter, a reminder of which is the small **Jüdisches Museum München** *(Jewish Museum; ☎ 20 00 96 93, Reichenbachstrasse 27; admission free, donations encouraged; open 9am-noon Wed & 2pm-6pm Tues-Thur)*. It presents temporary exhibits chronicling the fate of the Jews in Munich and Bavaria. A synagogue and community house are in the same building.

Glockenbachviertel

The westernmost section of the Gärtnerplatzviertel is also known as the Glockenbachviertel. The name, which means 'bell brook quarter', derives from a bell foundry once located on one of the little streams nearby. Many of the city's carvers and woodworkers lived here, giving rise to street names such as Baumstrasse (Tree Street) and Holzstrasse (Wood Street).

The loveliest spot is undoubtedly the path along the babbling brook, the **Glockenbach**, which runs south along Pestalozzistrasse. It's the only survivor of a network of creeks that once crisscrossed Munich; the rest have been re-routed or paved over. It parallels the **Alter Südlicher Friedhof**, a cemetery with a host of celebrity corpses (look for a plaque with names and grave locations near the entrance).

Nowadays, the Glockenbachviertel is increasingly becoming an extension of the gay scene of the Gärtnerplatzviertel. Müllerstrasse, which connects the two neighbourhoods, is chock-full of cafes and bars flying the rainbow flag. The area also has plenty of cool boutiques and secondhand shops catering for a mixed crowd. Other good streets to explore are Fraunhoferstrasse and Hans-Sachs-Strasse.

LUDWIGSVORSTADT (MAP 2)

West of the Altstadt, and anchored by the Hauptbahnhof, Ludwigsvorstadt is home to many downmarket hotels but poorly endowed with actual sights. What there is, clusters in the area north and west of the Karlsplatz.

Karlsplatz

The Karlsplatz is the western gateway to the Altstadt and is anchored by the medieval **Karlstor** (originally known as Neuhauser Tor) and an enormous modern **fountain**, a favourite meeting point. It marks the western terminus of the pedestrianised shopping streets, Neuhauser Strasse and Kaufinger Strasse, and is also a major tram, bus, U-Bahn and S-Bahn connection point.

In 1791, Elector Karl Theodor ordered the destruction of the city wall, sparing only the Karlstor and ordering the building of the square to be named for him. Locals, to this day, however, refer to the square as **Stachus**, which is most likely derived from a beer garden called Wirtshaus zum Stachus operated by a certain Eustachius Föderl near the gate since 1755.

Justizpalast

The dignified edifice rising up just west of Karlsplatz is the Palace of Justice *(Elisenstrasse 1a)*, built from 1891 to 1898 according to a design by Friedrich von Thiersch in neo-Renaissance and neobaroque style. It was here that Hans and Sophie Scholl were tried for 'civil disobedience' and condemned to death in 1943 (see the boxed text 'The White Rose' in this chapter). Behind it, the **Neuer Justizpalast** (New Palace of Justice), with its red-brick facade and stepped gables, is more of a neogothic confection.

Alter Botanischer Garten

Behind the courthouses, the Old Botanical Garden is a great place for a respite after a shopping spree through the Altstadt. Created under King Maximilian in 1814, it was Munich's pride and joy until thick, polluted air put the survival of the tender exotic plants in serious jeopardy. After WWI, the whole thing moved to more salubrious grounds north of Schloss Nymphenburg. All remaining 'foreign' plants were removed under the Nazis in 1935, who turned it into a pleasant, if rather generic, park. The **Neptunbrunnen** by Joseph Wackerle dates back to the same year. The neoclassical entrance gate is called the 'Kleine Propyläen' and a leftover from the original gardens.

Lenbachplatz

A short walk north-east of Karlsplatz, Lenbachplatz is fringed by a number of ornate neoclassical buildings. The edifice at No 2 is home to both the Deutsche Bank and the Bavarian Stock Exchange (Börse).

Next door at No 6 is the impressive **Palais am Lenbachplatz**, designed by Friedrich von Thiersch in the late 19th century for the textile merchant Lehmann Bernheimer as one of the first dual-purpose residential and office buildings. In the 1980s, one-time property speculator Jürgen Schneider bought the palais; it is now owned by the Deutsche Bank after Schneider landed in jail for large-scale embezzlement. Today, its main tenant is the trendy restaurant and bar, **Lenbach**, which has a back entrance (in Ottostrasse) illuminated by two Olympic-style torches. British design maven, Terence Conran, created the interior.

On the opposite (eastern) side of the square stands the neo-Renaissance **Künstlerhaus am Lenbachplatz** *(Lenbachplatz 8)*, built by Gabriel von Seidl in 1900. The front has been invaded by the Mövenpick restaurant chain, but the interiors are stunning, especially the Venetian Room, a sweeping ballroom styled like an Italian palazzo (and decorated by Franz von Lenbach). The exterior is brilliantly lit at night.

In the middle of the square is the splendid **Wittelsbacher Brunnen**, a lovely fountain whose two groups of figures illustrate the beneficial and destructive power of water.

WESTEND (MAP 2)

West of the Hauptbahnhof, the Westend would be unremarkable except for the fact that this is where the Oktoberfest grounds are located. The district, which became part of Munich in 1890, is roughly bounded by

Theresienwiese in the east and by Barth-strasse in the west; north-south borders are Landsbergerstrasse and the Ganghofer Bridge.

As early as 1830, the area was a slum for foreign workers and retired people, and day labourers slept under the open sky. With the arrival of the railway, halfway through the 20th century, parts of the area gradually turned into 'respectable' middle-class communities.

The most venerable part of the neighbourhood is around Holzapfelstrasse, West-endstrassse and Schwanthalerstrasse. Here, you'll find several breweries, including **Hacker-Pschorr** and **Augustiner**. Augustiner Bräustub'n is a charming beer hall in front of its brewery at Landsbergerstrasse 19.

Near the western edge of the Westend is **Golliersplatz**, a leafy oasis where the neighbourhood children play. It's the site of a lively flea market in summer.

Theresienwiese

The Theresienwiese (Theresa Meadow, better known as 'Wies'n') is the site of the annual Oktoberfest (see Special Events in this chapter). During the rest of the year, it's really just a vast empty space used for parking and occasional flea markets.

Overlooking the grounds from her perch on the meadow's western edge is **Bavaria** *(adult/concession €2/1.50, includes Ruhmeshalle; open 9am-6pm Fri-Wed, 9am-8pm Thur Apr–mid-Oct, 9am-8pm daily during Oktoberfest, closed mid-Oct–Mar)*, designed by Leo von Klenze for Maximilian II. The 19m-tall buxom statue, which was cast in 1850 by foundry artist Ferdinand von Miller, was the biggest thing to be made in bronze at the time. Miller poured it in three parts, finishing just before his workshop burned to the ground. It has a cunning design that makes it seem as if the thing is solid. It isn't – and you can climb to the head to get a so-so view of the city or a great view of the Oktoberfest.

Behind the Bavaria rises Klenze's sweeping neoclassical **Ruhmeshalle** *(Hall of Fame; 1843–53; admission see Bavaria statue)*, commissioned by Ludwig I and containing busts of 70-odd Bavarian rulers

and other historical figures. Its 11m-high base has 60 steps, and it's another 121 steps to the top for a view of the Wies'n. Restoration work, begun in early 2002, was scheduled to be completed by September 2002.

The best views, however, are from the tower of the **St Paulskirche**, a neogothic basilica just north of the grounds.

SCHWABING (MAP 3)

Until 1890 Schwabing was its own little peaceful village north of Munich, where the bourgeoisie built marvellous villas for their weekend retreats from the bustle of the city. In the late 19th century, the founding of the Academy of Arts launched Schwabing's ascent as one of Germany's most thriving creative colonies, a period that lasted until 1914.

Painters such as Klee, Kandinsky and Corinth would wander along the tree-lined boulevards, easels in hand. Writers such as Thomas Mann, Brecht and Rainer Maria Rilke would sip coffee in the so-called *Künstlerlokale* (artists' pubs and bars), while future revolutionaries like Lenin were cranking out underground pamphlets down the street. A vibrant, creative atmosphere reigned in those heady days, when Munich clearly eclipsed Berlin as Germany's 'centre of hip'.

In 1896 the red bulldog became the symbol for *Simplicissimus*, a bitingly – so to speak – satirical periodical. Another avant-garde magazine, *Die Jugend* (The Youth), also printed withering caricatures of leading political figures and later lent its name to the emerging German Art Nouveau movement, here called *Jugendstil*.

Today, Schwabing still has some of the finest examples of Art Nouveau architecture in Munich but, sadly, much of the creative flair has disappeared. To be sure, and thanks to the university, the district bristles with pubs and bars, even if many have a *schicki-micki* (Munich slang for 'trendy') rather than a bohemian bent. The more interesting places cluster in the area west of Leopold-strasse and its southern continuation, Ludwigstrasse, where they rub shoulders with second-hand bookshops, unique boutiques and good restaurants. The liveliest streets

MAP 3 – SCHWABING

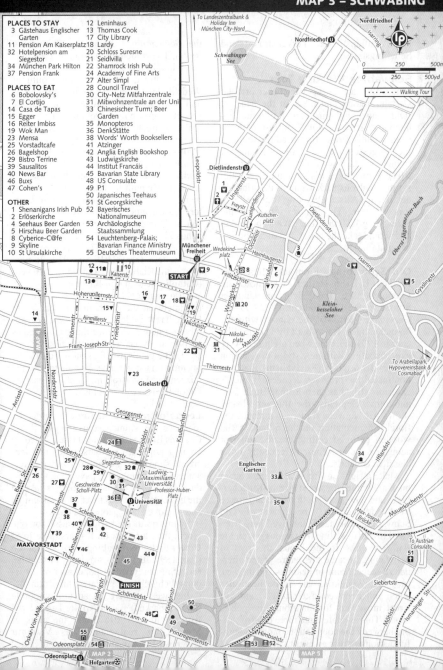

PLACES TO STAY
- 3 Gästehaus Englischer Garten
- 11 Pension Am Kaiserplatz
- 32 Hotelpension am Siegestor
- 34 München Park Hilton
- 37 Pension Frank

PLACES TO EAT
- 6 Bobolovsky's
- 7 El Cortijo
- 14 Casa de Tapas
- 15 Egger
- 16 Reiter Imbiss
- 19 Wok Man
- 23 Mensa
- 25 Vorstadtcafe
- 26 Bagelshop
- 29 Bistro Terrine
- 39 Sausalitos
- 40 News Bar
- 46 Buxs
- 47 Cohen's

OTHER
- 1 Shenanigans Irish Pub
- 2 Erlöserkirche
- 4 Seehaus Beer Garden
- 5 Hirschau Beer Garden
- 8 Cyberice-C@fe
- 9 Skyline
- 10 St Ursulakirche
- 12 Leninhaus
- 13 Thomas Cook
- 17 City Library
- 18 Lardy
- 20 Schloss Suresne
- 21 Seidlvilla
- 22 Shamrock Irish Pub
- 24 Academy of Fine Arts
- 27 Alter Simpl
- 28 Council Travel
- 30 City-Netz Mitfahrzentrale
- 31 Mitwohnzentrale an der Uni
- 33 Chinesischer Turm; Beer Garden
- 35 Monopteros
- 36 DenkStätte
- 38 Words' Worth Booksellers
- 41 Atzinger
- 42 Anglia English Bookshop
- 43 Institut Francáis
- 44 Ludwigskirche
- 45 Bavarian State Library
- 48 US Consulate
- 49 P1
- 50 Japanisches Teehaus
- 51 St Georgskirche
- 52 Bayerisches Nationalmuseum
- 53 Archäologische Staatssammlung
- 54 Leuchtenberg-Palais; Bavarian Finance Ministry
- 55 Deutsches Theatermuseum

are Amalienstrasse, Türkenstrasse and Schellingstrasse.

Schwabing Walking Tour

This walk starts at the Münchener Freiheit U-Bahn station and takes in the heart of 'Old Schwabing' – meaning the former bohemian district – and its beautiful Art Nouveau architecture before heading south to the Siegestor and the university quarter (which overlaps with the Maxvorstadt district). From here, it's just another 300m south to Odeonsplatz, which is described in detail in the Altstadt Walking Tour earlier in this chapter. The entire route of the Schwabing Walking Tour covers about 5km and should take the better part of a morning or an afternoon.

Old Schwabing From the Münchener Freiheit U-Bahn station, head north on Leopoldstrasse, then right on Ungerer Strasse to the **Erlöserkirche** (☎ 39 71 95, Germaniastrasse 4), the church with the bold clockface. It was built by Thomas Fischer in 1901 at a time when architects were experimenting with new styles in rejection of the Historicism (Revivalism) that had dominated the previous decades. While its exterior still has neo-Romanesque and neogothic elements, the interior clearly shows Art Nouveau traits; for instance the floral ornamentation on the pillars. A flat wooden coffered ceiling creates superior acoustics and the church frequently hosts classical concerts.

Make a right on Freystrasse, right again on Kunigundenstrasse to Arthur-Kutscher-Platz and then head south on Occamstrasse to **Wedekindplatz**, the heart of Old Schwabing. Thomas Mann lived here from 1899 to 1901, writing his famous novel, the *Buddenbrooks*. In the 1960s, this part of Schwabing became the centre of the alternative scene; home of beatniks and hippies. In 1962, Wedekindplatz made headlines when police moved in to arrest a gaggle of street musicians for disturbing the public peace. This escalated into three days of rioting between the cops and the mostly youthful demonstrators; an event known since as the *Schwabinger Krawalle* (Schwabing Riots). The student revolution of 1968 also had a hub in this area.

By contrast, the streets just south of Wedekindplatz – lined with beautiful villas and town houses – exude a much more peaceful atmosphere. From the eastern end of the square, head south on Werneckstrasse where you'll pass the baroque garden of **Schloss Suresne** *(also known as Werneck-Schlösschen; 1718; Werneckstrasse 1, entrance on Mandlstrasse, one block east)*, a small palace built for Franz Xaver von Wilhelm, a leading government official of Elector Max Emanuel. His impoverished widow sold off the estate in 1756 and it changed hands 27 more times until purchased by the Catholic Church in 1937. Paul Klee had a studio here from 1919 to 1922. It now houses the Katholische Akademie in Bayern (Catholic Academy in Bavaria).

Turn right on Nikolaistrasse where immediately on the southern side stands the **Seidlvilla** *(☎ 34 26 87, Nikolaiplatz 1B)*, another gorgeous residence that has served as a community centre and art gallery since 1991. The gate's usually shut but check the opening times; you may be able to ring the buzzer and just stroll in. Continue east on Nikolaistrasse to Leopoldstrasse.

Leopoldstrasse & Around Regarded by many as the Munich equivalent of Paris' Champs Èlysées, Leopoldstrasse is lined by arching poplars, chic bars, cafes and ice-cream shops. In the summer, art markets sometimes set up on the pavement. On Sunday afternoons, locals and tourists take to the broad promenades to stroll, drink coffee and – above all – 'people watch'.

Swing north on Leopoldstrasse for one block, then turn left on Kaiserstrasse to St **Ursulakirche**, Schwabing's parish church since 1897. Its style is strikingly Florentine, reflecting a revival of popularity of cross-domed churches in the late 19th century.

Just west of here, in an unremarkable (and unmarked) flat at No 46, **Lenin** lived from 1900 to 1901. Under the alias of Meyer (his real name was Vladimir Ulyanov), the Soviet leader-to-be published two periodicals: the influential underground *Der Funke* (The Spark) as well as *Die Morgenröte* (The Dawn). He also wrote some essays and articles under the name Lenin for the first time, including *What is to be done?*, which laid down principles for the October Revolution of 1917.

Art Nouveau Quarter The roads south of St Ursulakirche are heaven for fans of Art Nouveau architecture. A suggested route through the neighbourhood is to head south on Friedrichstrasse, turn right on Hohenzollernstrasse, left on Römerstrasse and left again on Ainmillerstrasse.

Ainmillerstrasse was home to some of the founding members of the artists' group, Der Blaue Reiter (The Blue Rider): Paul Klee lived at No 32, and Gabriele Münter and Wassily Kandinsky at No 36; poet Rainer Maria Rilke made his home at No 34. The crowning glory of the street is the vintage facade at No 22 with wonderful blue-and-gold arches topped with the helmeted heads of Roman soldiers, and Adam and Eve reclining under the Tree of Knowledge. The flowery cream-and-grey edifice next door is also spectacular.

Make a right on Friedrichstrasse and continue for three blocks or so to see Munich's first Art Nouveau block of tenements, at No 3, and its gilded artwork.

Continue left on Georgenstrasse, which runs parallel to the **Akademie der Bildenden Künste** (Academy of Fine Arts; 1886), a three-storey neo-Renaissance building. Founded in 1808 by Maximilian I, it advanced to become one of Europe's leading arts schools in the second half of the 19th century. Famous students included Max Slevogt, Franz von Lenbach and Wilhelm Leibl and, in the early 20th century, Lovis Corinth, Klee, Kandinsky, Franz Marc and others who went on to become modern art pioneers. All this changed after WWI as Berlin took the spotlight and Munich, increasingly under the influence of nationalist tendencies, was relegated to provincial backwater status.

Now you're back on Leopoldstrasse and face to face with its landmark Siegestor.

Siegestor The monumental Siegestor (Victory Gate; 1852) is a triumphal arch by Friedrich von Gärtner and modelled on the Arch of Constantine in Rome. Crowned by a triumphant *Bavaria* riding in a lion-drawn chariot, it originally honoured the prowess of the Bavarian army during the Napoleonic Wars of Liberation (1813–15).

After WWII, during which it was badly damaged, the arch was stripped of its martial meaning and turned into a peace memorial. The inscription on the upper section reads: *Dem Sieg geweiht, vom Kriege zerstört, zum Frieden mahnend* (Dedicated to victory, destroyed by war, calling for peace).

Ludwigstrasse South of the Siegestor begins the wide and impressive Ludwigstrasse, one of Europe's classic promenades. Ludwig I commissioned it in 1816 when he was still crown prince in an attempt to turn Munich into an 'Athens of the North'. It culminates 1km south at the Feldherrnhalle on Odeonsplatz and sports a remarkable uniformity of neoclassical style and proportions courtesy of court architects Leo von Klenze and Friedrich von Gärtner.

Ludwig-Maximilian-Universität (LMU) Around 44,000 students pursue about 120 fields of study at the Ludwig-Maximilian-Universität, which was actually founded in 1472 in Ingolstadt under Duke Ludwig der Reiche (Ludwig the Rich). In 1800, it moved to Landshut under Elector Max IV Joseph, who later became King Max II. (It's these two rulers who gave the university its name.) Finally, in 1826, Ludwig I transferred it to Munich – and Landshut, once bigger and more powerful than Munich, sank into relative obscurity. Some two decades later, the students 'thanked' the king by playing an instrumental role in forcing his abdication in 1848.

Over the years, LMU has attracted numerous academic heavyweights, including philosopher Friedrich von Schelling; Justus von Liebig, the father of scientific agriculture; and Wilhelm Röntgen, the discoverer of the X-ray.

MUNICH

The heart of the university beats on Geschwister-Scholl-Platz, anchored by two huge, bowl-shaped fountains and dominated by the main university building designed by Gärtner (1835–40). Inside, its most striking features are the large vaulted **Aula** (assembly hall) and the light and airy **Lichthof** (atrium).

The square itself, which links the university with the priests' seminary opposite, was named – following WWII – for Hans and Sophie Scholl, students and founding members of the Weisse Rose (White Rose) resistance group (see boxed text). A memorial exhibit called **Denk Stätte** (☎ 21 80 30 53, Geschwister-Scholl-Platz 1; admission free; open 10am-4pm Mon-Fri, 10am-9pm Thur) is in the lower mezzanine behind the foyer. It includes a library dedicated to the WWII resistance movements, along with photos and documents about the activities of the various groups.

Ludwigskirche Just south of the university stands the Church of St Ludwig (1829–44; ☎ 28 83 34, Ludwigstrasse 20; open 8am-8pm daily), also by Gärtner. It's distinguished by alabaster towers in Florentine campanile style. A solemn ambience reigns inside, which makes the huge Last Judgment fresco in the choir pop out all the more. Painted by Peter Cornelius, a member of the Nazarene School, it is one of the world's largest frescoes, intended to rival Michelangelo's.

Bayerische Staatsbibiliothek The next major building south of the church is the Bavarian State Library (1832–43) at Ludwigstrasse 16, also by Gärtner. The four sculptures atop the stairway are the philosophers Aristotle, Hippocrates, Homer and Thucydides. With around 7.2 million volumes, this library holds the most extensive scientific collection in Germany, not to mention 250,000 maps, 800 atlases and over 42,000 periodicals. Also on view are 16th-century globes of the earth and cosmos made for Duke Albrecht V.

This is the end of the Schwabing Walking Tour.

The White Rose

Public demonstrations against the Nazis were rare during the Third Reich: after 1933, intimidation and the instant 'justice' of the Gestapo and SS served as powerful disincentives. One of the few groups to rebel was the ill-fated Weisse Rose, led by Munich University students Hans and Sophie Scholl.

Robert Scholl had warned his children against the Nazis, but Hans joined the Hitler Youth, and another sister, the older Inge, became a group leader of its female counterpart, the Bund Deutsche Mädel. Hans soon became disillusioned with the Nazis and attempted to build his own, liberal group within the Hitler Youth. This triggered a Gestapo raid on the Scholl home in Ulm in 1937, and from then on the family was marked as enemies of the state.

In 1942 Hans and Sophie met a group of like-minded medical students and formed the White Rose, which aimed to encourage Germans to resist Hitler. At first its members acted cautiously, creeping through the streets of Munich at night and smearing slogans such as 'Freedom!' or 'Down With Hitler!' on walls. Growing bolder, they printed and distributed anti-Nazi leaflets, leaving them in telephone boxes and sending them to other German cities. The leaflets reported on the mass extermination of the Jews and other Nazi atrocities. One read: 'We shall not be silent – we are your guilty conscience. The White Rose will not leave you in peace.'

In February 1943 Hans and Sophie took a suitcase of leaflets to the university and placed stacks outside each lecture hall. Then, from a top landing, Sophie dumped the remaining brochures into the atrium. A janitor saw her and had both of them arrested and charged with treason along with their best friend, Christoph Probst. After a four-hour trial, the three were condemned to death and beheaded the same afternoon. Sophie hoped that their self-sacrifice would stir thousands to action, but there was to be no more resistance at Munich University – in fact, some fellow students applauded the executions.

Jeremy Gray

Englischer Garten

So what's the skinny on all the nudies in the English Garden? Come on, surely you've heard about this. Nude sunbathing in a public park? Can this be legal? Well, it is, and on balmy summer days, you're bound to see hundreds of people letting it all hang out, so to speak, in pursuit of the seamless tan. There are formal FKK (nude bathing) zones, especially along the Eisbach, the little creek that runs north from just behind the Haus der Kunst, but no-one (not even the police) seems to take much notice. So there.

Now that we've got that out of the way, maybe you'll be impressed to know that the Englischer Garten is actually one of the world's largest metropolitan parks (yes, bigger than London's Hyde Park or New York's Central Park). Starting just north of Prinzregentenstrasse in the Lehel district, it stretches all the way north for about 5km and essentially forms Schwabing's eastern boundary. On the other side, the Isar River separates it from residential areas like Bogenhausen.

A favourite playground for Müncheners and visitors alike, it's a great oasis for relaxing and outdoor fun and, yes, you can keep your clothes on.

The Englischer Garten was conceived in 1789 – perhaps, not coincidentally, the year of the French Revolution – as a 'garden for the people' by Elector Karl Theodor. He assigned the design job to his Minister of War, Benjamin Thompson (the later Count Rumford, an American lieutenant-general who had emigrated to Munich) who in turn called in help from accomplished court gardener Friedrich von Sckell. Karl Theodor had at first thought he would name the park after himself, but then wisely settled on the more generic 'Englischer Garten', a suitable choice, really, given that it was designed in English landscape style.

Today, you'll see walkers, bicyclists and joggers roaming the network of leafy paths. Crowds cheer on street musicians and other entertainers. Children squeal with delight while flying their kites. Groups of students feverishly discuss the last lecture. Teens play an impromptu game of soccer. Grandmas feed the ducks with their grandkids.

Sooner or later, you'll find your way to the **Kleinhesseloher See**, a lovely lake which is pretty much the heart of the park. Rent a paddleboat and treat your sweetheart to close-ups of the three little islands. Then cap off a day of sightseeing with a foamy one at the Seehaus beer garden on the eastern shore (see Entertainment later in this chapter).

An even more famous beer garden is at the **Chinesischer Turm** (1790) south of the lake. Tables sprawl in the shadow of a Chinese pagoda built during the 18th-century fad for anything 'oriental'. There's been a restaurant here since the early 19th century. Just south of the Chinesischer Turm is the heavily photographed monument **Monopteros** (1838), a Greek-style tower by Leo von Klenze, from the top of which you can enjoy good views but which, alas, needs to be regularly cleared of graffiti and junkies.

Another hint of Asia awaits further south, near the Haus der Kunst, where Mitsuo Normura built a **Japanisches Teehaus** (Japanese Teahouse) during the 1972 Olympics in the middle of a lovely duck and geese pond. Authentic tea ceremonies take place here every second and fourth weekend between April and October at 3pm, 4pm and 5pm. Reservations are not necessary. Call ☎ 22 43 19 for details.

Alas, the Englischer Garten is not really a safe place to spend the night. Police patrol frequently and muggers, drug fiends, proselytisers and other colourful characters are everywhere. In other words, forget it.

MAXVORSTADT (MAP 4)

North-east of the Altstadt, Maxvorstadt was the first planned city expansion begun by King Maximilian I in 1808 and continued under his successors, most notably King Ludwig I. Ludwig conceived the Ludwigstrasse, a broad and flashy boulevard lined by neoclassical edifices, which runs from Odeonsplatz to the Siegestor.

With no fewer than nine museums, Maxvorstadt is 'nirvana' for culture vultures. There are two main clusters of museums: one around Königsplatz and the other – the trio of Pinakothek art museums – just north of here.

MAP 4 – WESTERN M

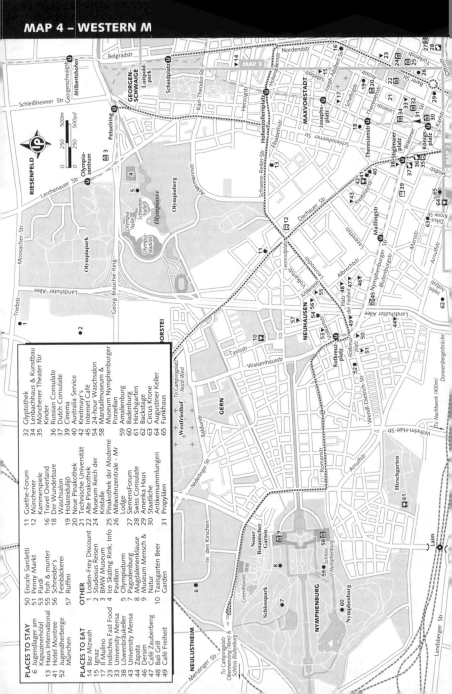

RIESENFELD

GEORGEN-SCHWAIGE

MAXVORSTADT

Olympiapark

Olympiaberg

Olympiasee

Olympia-Stadion

Schwimm-Halle

NEUHAUSEN

GERN

NEULUSTHEIM

NYMPHENBURG

Schlosspark

Neuer Botanischer Garten

Hirschgarten

Laim

Westfriedhof

PLACES TO STAY
6 Jugendlager am Kapuzinerhölzl
13 Haus International
41 Hotel Montree
52 Jugendherberge München

PLACES TO EAT
14 Bar Mizwah
15 Ignaz
17 Il Mulino
23 Indisches Fast Food
33 University Mensa
38 Löwenbräukeller
43 University Mensa
44 Zapata
46 Dersim
47 Café Zauberberg
48 Bali Grill
49 Café Freiheit
50 Eiscafe Sarcletti
51 Penny Markt
53 Pardi
55 froh & munter
56 Schneider's Feinbäckerei
57 Ruffini

OTHER
1 Loden-Frey Discount
2 Studiosus Reisen
3 BMW Museum
4 Ice Skating Rink; Info Pavillion
5 Olympiaturm
7 Pagodenburg
8 Magdalenenklause
9 Museum Mensch & Natur
10 Taxisgarten Beer Garden
11 Goethe-Forum
12 Münchener Kammerspiele
16 Travel Overland
18 Der Wunderbare Waschsalon
19 Holareidulijö
20 Neue Pinakothek
21 Technische Universität
22 Alte Pinakothek
24 Museum Reich der Kristalle
25 Pinakothek der Moderne
26 Mitwohnzentrale - Mr Lodge
27 Siemens-Forum
28 Swiss Consulate
29 Amerika Haus
30 Staatliche Antikensammlungen
31 Propyläen
32 Glyptothek
34 Lenbachhaus & Kunstbau
35 Münchener Theater für Kinder
36 Russian Consulate
37 Dutch Consulate
39 Cinema
40 Australia Service Kreitmayr's
42 Internet Café
45 24-hour Waschsalon
54 Marstallmuseum & Museum Nymphenburger Porzellan
58 Amalienburg
59 Badenburg
60 Hirschgarten
61 Backstage
62 Circus Krone
63 Augustiner Keller
64 Funkhaus

To Campingplatz Obermenzing (4km) & Schloss Blütenburg

To Campingplatz Nord-West

To Nachtwerk (400m)

The northern Maxvorstadt, where it spills into Schwabing (see later this chapter) is also Munich's 'Latin quarter', home to the city's three largest universities, the Technische Universität, the Ludwig-Maximilian-Universität (LMU) and the Fachhochschule München (Munich Polytechnic). Since many students also live in the neighbourhood, the streets are filled with cafes, restaurants, pubs, quirky boutiques and bookshops.

Note that for organisational reasons the sights lining Ludwigstrasse are covered in the Schwabing Walking Tour section earlier in this chapter.

Königsplatz

Königsplatz is a Greek-revivalist square created by Klenze for Ludwig I. Hitler had it turned into parade grounds, and it wasn't until 1988 that the slabs were removed and the square grassed over. It is anchored by the Doric-columned **Propyläen** gateway and orbited by three museums.

Glyptothek The Glyptothek *(☎ 28 61 00, Königsplatz 3; adult/concession €3/1.75, free Sun, combined with Antikensammlungen €5/3; open 10am-5pm Fri-Mon & Wed, 10am-8pm Tues & Thur)*, Munich's oldest museum, presents an exquisite survey of Greek and Roman sculpture from 560 BC to AD 400. Among the most precious exhibits are sculptures from the Greek Aphaia Temple in Aegina, excavated by German and English archaeologists in the early 19th century. Not to be missed either is the **Barberini Faun**, a marble statue of a sexy sleeping satyr with astonishing anatomical detail. Rooms X to XII contain superb busts, including one of a youthful Alexander the Great and several of Emperor Augustus. Also of note are the **tomb reliefs** of Mnesarete.

The inner courtyard has a calm and pleasant **cafe** where, in summer, classical theatre takes place under the stars.

Staatliche Antikensammlungen One of Germany's finest antiquities collections *(☎ 59 83 59, Königsplatz 1)* is housed in a building on the southern side of Königsplatz.

It features an extraordinarily rich assembly of vases, gold and silver jewellery and ornaments, bronzework, and Greek, Roman and Etruscan sculptures and statues. Its reopening (following renovations) was scheduled for mid-2002.

Lenbachhaus & Kunstbau Franz von Lenbach (1836-1904), a leading late-19th-century portraitist, used his considerable fortune to construct a residence in Munich between 1887 and 1891. Lenbach's widow sold it to the city in 1924 and threw in a bunch of his works as part of the deal. Today, this fabulous villa is open as the **Städtische Gallerie im Lenbachhaus** *(☎ 23 33 20 00, Luisenstrasse 33; adult/concession €4/2 or 6/3 during special exhibits, tickets also good for Kunstbau; open 10am-6pm Tues-Sun)*.

The museum collection's particular strength lies in paintings by members of Der Blaue Reiter (The Blue Rider), a movement begun in 1911 by Franz Marc and Wassily Kandinsky. The group, which also included Paul Klee, Alexej Jawlenski, August Macke and Gabriele Münter, is acknowledged as the high point of German expressionism. The irony here is that Lenbach himself vigorously opposed the Secessionist painters who paved the way for the innovations of the Blue Rider group.

Also look for paintings by Lenbach himself as well as other 19th-century masters, including Lovis Corinth and Wilhelm Leibl.

Another focal point is on **contemporary art**, especially by such avant-gardists as Joseph Beuys, Anselm Kiefer, Dan Flavin and Andy Warhol. Works by these and other practitioners are shown on a rotating basis in the **Kunstbau**, a 120m-long underground room above the U-Bahn station Königsplatz completed in 1994 as an adjunct to the Lenbachhaus.

Pinakothek Museums

A short walk north of Königsplatz is the Technical University and Munich's two major art museums, with a third one set to open in 2002. A mineral museum is also here.

Alte Pinakothek A treasure trove of European Masters awaits visitors to the Alte Pinakothek *(☎ 23 80 52 16, Barer Strasse 27, enter from Theresienstrasse; adult/concession €4.50/3, free Sun; open 10am-5pm Fri-Wed, 10am-10pm Thur; closed Mon)*. Housed in a neoclassical temple commissioned by Ludwig I and designed by Leo von Klenze, it is one of the most important such collections in the world and a delicacy that not only art connoisseurs will appreciate.

Nearly all the paintings were collected or commissioned by various Wittelsbach rulers, starting with Duke Wilhelm IV in 1528, and mirror their rather eclectic tastes.

The collection ranges from the 14th to the 18th century, although it's especially strong with regard to **Old German Masters**. The oldest works, many of them by anonymous artists, are altar paintings, of which the one depicting the four church fathers (1475) by Michael Pacher stands out. From the next generation, Lucas Cranach the Elder's *Klage unter dem Kreuz* (Crucifixion; 1503) is an emotional rendition of the suffering Jesus.

Perhaps the single most important room in the entire museum is the so-called **Dürersaal** (Room II) upstairs. Here hangs Albrecht Dürer's famous Christ-like *Selbstbildnis im Pelzrock* (Self-portrait in fur coat; about 1500), a seminal work that shows the artist gazing self-confidently straight at the viewer.

Also here is his final major work, *Die vier Apostel* (The Four Apostles; 1529). It shows John, Peter, Paul and Mark as rather humble men, a reflection of the more sober interpretation of Christianity introduced by the Reformation (Dürer had embraced Protestantism early on). Compare this to Matthias Grünewald's *Die Heiligen Erasmus und Mauritius* (Sts Erasmus and Maurice, early 16th century), which shows the saints dressed in rich robes like kings.

For a nonreligious theme, inspect Albrecht Altdorfer's *Alexanderschlacht* (Battle of Alexander the Great; 1529) which freeze-frames in dizzying detail a scene from a 6th-century war pitting Greeks against Persians.

The museum also owns a world-class collection of **Old Dutch Masters**, including an altarpiece by Rogier van der Weyden called *The Adoration of the Magi* (about 1460), *The Seven Joys of Mary* (1480) by Hans Memling, *Danae* (1527) by Jan Gossaert and *The Land of Cockayne* (1567) by Pieter Bruegel the Elder.

Rubens fans will rejoice at the breadth and depth of the collection here. One of the most memorable portraits is that of *Hélène Fourment* (1631), a youthful beauty who was the aging Rubens' second wife. Other Flemish 17th-century artists represented here include Rubens' one-time assistant, Anthonis van Dyck and, of course, Rembrandt with his intensely emotional *Passion Cycle*.

Although it's not the Alte Pinakothek's strength, there are also outstanding examples of art from southern European artists, including such Italian heavyweights as Botticelli, Rafael, Leonardo da Vinci and Titian. Spanish crowd-pleasers include El Greco, Murillo and Velàzquez, while the French have fielded Nicolas Poussin, Claude Lorrain, François Boucher.

Free audio-guides with taped commentary about 90 works in four languages, including English, are available in the lobby. The audio-guides cost €4 on 'admission-free' Sundays.

Neue Pinakothek Just north of the Alte Pinakothek is the Neue Pinakothek *(☎ 23 80 51 95, Barer Strasse 29, enter from Theresienstrasse; adult/concession €4.50/3, free Sun; open 10am-5pm Fri-Wed, 10am-10pm Thur; closed Tues)*. The focus here is on paintings and sculpture by European masters working between the second half of the 18th century and the early 20th century. The core of the exhibit, though, is 19th-century German art from the collection of Ludwig I.

Styles represented range from neoclassicism to Romanticism and Realism to Art Nouveau. Among the most memorable canvasses are those by the Romantic painter Caspar David Friedrich who manages to imbue landscapes with emotionalism and ominous moodiness.

An entire room is dedicated to Hans Marées (1837–87), who specialised in realistic country scenes injected with a touch of sentimentality, as well as portraits. French Impressionists such as Edgar Degas always draw sizable crowds, as do postimpressionists such as van Gogh who is represented with the famous *Sunflowers* (1888). There are also several works by Gauguin, including *Birth of Christ* (1896) and *Breton Peasant Women* (1894), and Manet, eg, *Breakfast in the Studio* (1869).

Pinakothek der Moderne Picking up where the Neue Pinakothek leaves off, this museum will present a thorough survey of 20th-century art. It is set to open in 2002 in a new structure immediately south-east of the Alte Pinakothek. For its exhibits, it taps into various existing collections: the State Modern Art Gallery will contribute paintings, sculpture, installations and new media works; from the State Museum of Applied Arts will come design and arts & crafts pieces; the Architecture Museum of the Technical University is the source of drawings, photographs and models; and the State Graphics Collection contributes lithographs and etchings. Check with the tourist office about updates.

Other Museums
Museum Reich der Kristalle Just north of the Pinakothek der Moderne is the dazzling collection of crystals of the Museum of the Crystal Realm (☎ 23 94 43 12, *Theresienstrasse 41, enter from Barer Strasse; adult/concession €2/1; open 1pm-5pm Tues-Fri, 1pm-6pm Sat & Sun*). Exhibits demystify the formation of crystals and their underlying molecular structures. A large Russian emerald and numerous diamonds are among the most prized possessions.

SiemensForum About 350m east of the Pinakothek der Moderne is the Siemens Forum (☎ 63 63 26 60, *Oskar-von-Miller-Ring 20; admission free; open 10am-5pm Sun-Fri*). The huge modern complex contains fascinating exhibits covering 140 years of company history: electronics and

microelectronics from the telegraph to the multimedia personal computer. It's a fun, hands-on kind of place – and it's free, so why not?

NEUHAUSEN (MAP 4)
North-west of the Hauptbahnhof, Neuhausen is one of Munich's oldest neighbourhoods dating back to the 12th century in municipal records, although there's evidence that it's even two centuries older. Perhaps it's this long history and association with the royal family that gives Neuhausen an air of relaxed confidence, although there isn't too much here worth exploring.

Neuhausen's development took a giant leap forward in the 17th century, when it became the 'servants' quarter' of the newly built Schloss Nymphenburg (see later in this chapter). Fire consumed the original village in 1794, an event that prompted Maximilian I to have a planned neighbourhood laid out in the early 19th century. From then on Neuhausen became a residential pad for the well-heeled, with the villas along Nymphenburg Canal resembling second-string royal residences.

Nymphenburger Strasse was actually one of the first commuter roads into Munich, laid down to ease transport of the royals into town. The city's first tram – a horse-drawn vehicle – served the boulevard from 1876. Neuhausen was already a part of Munich, in spirit, by the time the neighbourhood was absorbed in 1890.

WWII swept away many of Neuhausen's old buildings, and as was the case elsewhere in Munich, their modern successors were less than tasteful. Landshuter Allee, with its huge amount of traffic, roars right through the district.

Modern, bustling **Rotkreuzplatz** is the aesthetically challenged centre of Neuhausen. Its only redeeming value is the large number of good restaurants, cafes and bars around here. Ice-cream fans should indulge their cravings at **Eiscafe Sarcletti** (☎ 15 53 14, *Nymphenburger Strasse 155*), a local institution. The Jugendherberge München (see Places to Stay later in this chapter) is a short walk west of the square.

In southern Neuhausen, at the corner of Marsstrasse and Wredestrasse, is the hugely popular **Circus Krone**, a Munich fixture for decades. Performances run from December to March, and then, when it's all over, the circus leaves in a grand procession, with elephants and camels driven along Arnulfstrasse towards the Hauptbahnhof. The hall is left to host rock concerts and other events during the rest of the year. See also Children's Theatre in the Entertainment section.

NYMPHENBURG (MAP 4)

If the Residenz hasn't satisfied your passion for palaces, visit the amazing Schloss Nymphenburg *(☎ 179 80/00; combined ticket to everything except Marstallmuseum adult/concession €7.50/6 Apr–mid-Oct, €6.50/5.50 mid-Oct–Mar; Tram: No 17, Bus: No 41)*. Begun in 1664 as a villa for Henriette Adelaide, wife of Elector Ferdinand Maria, the palace and gardens were continually expanded and built upon over the next century to create the royal family's summer residence.

Today, the palace, outbuildings and grounds (the surrounding park is worth a long stroll) are open to the public. North of the palace is Munich's lovely Neuer Botanischer Garten (New Botanical Garden), which replaced the old one near the Hauptbahnhof in the early 20th century. Schloss Blutenburg, east of the palace and technically already in the suburb of Obermenzing, is another attraction.

Schloss Nymphenburg

The main palace building *(☎ 179 08; adult/concession €3.50/2.50; open 9am-6pm Fri-Wed, 9am-8pm Thur Apr–mid-Oct, 10am-4pm daily mid-Oct–Mar)* consists of a main villa and two wings with sumptuously decorated rooms.

The circuit begins upstairs in the **Steinerner Saal** (Stone Hall), a two-storey dining hall with fantastic stucco and frescoes by Johann Baptist Zimmermann. The **Gobelinzimmer**, with its stunningly detailed tapestries, is almost as good. The tour also takes in the **Wappenzimmer** (Heraldic Room) and the **Chinesisches Lackkabinett**

(Chinese Lacquer Room), but take time out to see the cute **chapel** in the western wing.

Our favourite is Ludwig's **Schönheitengalerie** (Gallery of Beauties), in the southern wing, formerly the apartments of Queen Caroline. It's now the repository of 38 portraits of women whom Ludwig I considered beautiful. The most famous of these is the *Schöne Münchnerin*, the portrait of Helene Sedlmayr, daughter of a shoemaker, but you'll also find a smouldering one of court dancer Lola Montez, who cost Ludwig his crown (see the boxed text 'Lola Montez, Femme Fatale' in the Facts about Bavaria chapter).

Guided palace tours are available to groups only; pick up a copy of the unintentionally hilarious English-language translation of the guide *Nymphenburg* (€2.50) at the cash desk.

Museum Nymphenburger Porzellan & Marstallmuseum In the palace's southern wing, the coaches and riding gear of the royal families are suitably displayed in the former royal stables, now called the Marstallmuseum *(☎ 17 90 80; adult/concession €2.50/2; open 9am-6pm Fri-Wed, 9am-8pm Thur Apr–mid-Oct, 10am-4pm daily mid-Oct–Mar)*. This includes the wedding coach of Ludwig II that was never used after his engagement to Princess Sophie fell apart.

On the 1st floor is a collection of porcelain made by the world-famous Nymphenburger Manufaktur. Known as the Sammlung Bäuml, it presents the entire product palette from the company's founding in 1747 to 1930.

Museum Mensch & Natur The palace's northern wing is occupied by the Museum of Humankind & Nature *(☎ 17 13 82)*. This is a natural science museum with three thematic focal points: the history of the earth and life on it; the great variety of organic life; humans as part of and creators of nature. On 1 January 2002, the museum closed for a major renovation expected to last at least one year. Call, or check with the tourist office for updates.

Amalienburg

A highlight west of the palace is the frilly Amalienburg *(1734–39;* ☎ *179 08; adult/concession €1.50/1; open 9am-6pm Fri-Wed, 9am-8pm Thur Apr–mid-Oct, 10am-4pm daily mid-Oct–Mar)*, a small hunting lodge with a large domed central room, built for Electress Amalia by François Cuvilliés. The place drips crystal and gilt decoration; don't miss the amazing Spiegelsaal (Mirror Hall).

Gardens & Outbuildings

The royal gardens are a magnificently sculpted English park. In front (east) of the palace is a long canal, on which locals can be seen curling and ice-skating in winter. At the eastern end of the canal is the **Hubertus Fountain**, a huge braying stag that spouts water behind the elaborate trellis. Behind (west of) the castle, the royal gardens ramble on around the continuation of the Nymphenburg Canal.

The whole park is enchanting and contains a number of intriguing buildings and follies. Landscape architect Friedrich Ludwig von Sckell, who also designed the Englischer Garten, laid out the broad design of today's gardens. He softened the originally rather harsh lines of the French layout and modelled the grounds more after a landscape garden, English-style, of course.

Elector Max Emanuel provided the impetus and cash for three of the outbuildings constructed between 1716 and 1728. The two-storey **Pagodenburg** *(1717-19; adult/ concession €1/0.50; open 9am-6pm Fri-Wed, 9am-8pm Thur Apr–mid-Oct, closed mid-Oct–Mar)* was built as a Chinese teahouse and is a good example of the 18th-century vogue for oriental architecture (the Chinesischer Turm in the Englischer Garten is another). More than 2000 ceramic tiles painted with landscapes, figures and ornamentation cover its walls. It's been undergoing a lengthy renovation but should have reopened by the time you're reading this.

Opposite, by the lake of the same name, is the **Badenburg** *(☎ 179 08; adult/concession €1.50/1; open 9am-6pm Fri-Wed, 9am-8pm Thur Apr–mid-Oct, closed mid-Oct–Mar)*, a sauna and bathing house of which the original heating system survives.

Elsewhere in the park, there's the **Magdalenenklause** (see Pagodenburg for hours and admission), built as an artificial hermitage in a deliberately 'ruined' style.

Neuer Botanischer Garten

If you're into plants and flowers, don't leave Nymphenburg without wandering the extensive grounds and greenhouses of the New Botanical Garden *(☎ 17 86 13 50, Menzinger Strasse 65; adult/concession €2/1, children under 12 free; open 9am-7pm daily May-Aug, 9am-6pm daily Apr & Sept, 9am-4.30pm daily Nov-Jan, 9am-5pm daily Feb-Mar & Oct; Tram: No 17 from Hauptbahnhof to Neuer Botanischer Garten)*. Built between 1909 and 1914 just north of Schloss Nymphenburg, it sprawls over 22 hectares dappled with about 15,000 plant species, including a famous collection of tropical and subtropical plants in the **Palmenhaus**. Throughout the gardens, you'll come across some lovely **porcelain statues** from the palace's own factory.

Schloss Blutenburg

About 4km west of Schloss Nymphenburg, in the suburb of Obermenzing, lies the picturesque Schloss Blutenburg *(☎ 891 21 10, cnr Pippinger Strasse/Verdistrasse)*. It's idyllically encircled by the little Würm River, creating the illusion of a moated castle. First mentioned in 1425, there's evidence that it's older still. Duke Albrecht III enlarged the complex and his son Sigismund added the beautiful **chapel** (1488), considered a prime example of late-Gothic architecture. Inside, the altar paintings by Jan Polack and the stained-glass windows are worth a closer look.

In 1676, Freiherr von Berchem acquired the palace, which was already in bad shape. He tried to fix it up as much as possible, but eventually money ran out and his heirs sold it back to Elector Max Emanuel in the early 18th century. Now state-owned, it underwent a sweeping restoration from 1980 to 1983 and today houses the **Internationale Jugendbibliothek** *(International Youth Library;*

☎ 891 21 10; open 10am-4pm Mon-Fri), a rather unique research and lending library with about half a million children's books in 130 languages.

Also in the library is the tiny **Michael-Ende-Museum** (☎ 891 21 10; adult/concession €2/1; open 2pm-5pm Tues-Sun), with books, photos and personal effects of the author of The Never-Ending Story. (You really need to be a Michael Ende fan to enjoy it.) Concerts are held in the inner courtyard several times a year, and there's a pleasant little restaurant and beer garden as well. Take S-Bahn S1 or S2 to Obermenzing, then bus Nos 73, 75 or 76 to Pippinger Strasse.

OLYMPIAPARK & AROUND (MAP 4)

About 30 years after the Olympic Games for which it was built, Olympic Park remains an integral part of life in the city. The complex stands on historic grounds: in the 19th century this was a practice field for royal riders, in 1909 the first Zeppelin airship landed here, and in 1929 it became the site of Munich's first civil airport.

The centrepieces today are the 290m Olympiaturm (Olympic Tower), the 75,000-sq-m transparent 'tented' roof canopying the Olympiastadion (Olympic Stadium), the Olympiahalle (Olympic Hall), the Olympia-Schwimmhalle (swimming centre) and the Olympia-Eisstadion (ice-skating rink).

The park is open as a collection of public facilities, and the grounds are the site of celebrations, concerts, fireworks displays and professional sporting matches year round. There's an Info Pavillion (☎ 30 67 24 14) near the ice-skating rink at the eastern end of the complex.

Wandering around the grounds is free, but to get inside the **Olympiastadion** isn't (admission €1.50; open 9am-4.30pm daily Oct–mid-Apr, 8.30am-6pm daily mid-Apr–Sept, closed on events days).

You can also see the whole complex on a guided tour. Two types of tours run daily from April to October (meet at the Info Pavillion): a one-hour Soccer Tour at 11am, which visits the Olympia Stadion, VIP area and locker rooms (€4.60/3.10); and a 90-minute Adventure Tour that covers the entire Olympiapark on foot and in a little train (€6.65/4.60).

If you like heights, zoom to the top of the **Olympiaturm** (adult/concession €2.30/1.50; open 9am-midnight daily, last trip 11.30pm). You'll have great bird's-eye views of the grounds and, if the weather's good, also of the city. If you're feeling cashed up and hungry, you can have a meal at the revolving **restaurant** (☎ 308 10 39).

BMW Museum

Just north-east of Olympiapark is the popular BMW Museum (☎ 38 22 33 07, Petuelring 130; adult/concession €3/2; open 9am-5pm daily, last entry 4pm; U-Bahn: U3 to Olympiazentrum). Just look for the striking silver cylinders – an architectural attraction in their own right – which also house the BMW (Bayerische Motoren Werke) headquarters. Museum exhibits include not just BMW cars, but also motorcycles, planes, concept cars and, near the top, simulators and interactive displays.

The BMW factory, adjacent to the headquarters and museum, offers free tours in German and English; call ☎ 38 22 33 06 for information.

BOGENHAUSEN

Since the late 19th century, Bogenhausen has been an exclusive residential quarter for Munich's well-to-do. Elegant villas with elaborate facades sprang up from the 1870s onwards, and the rise of Art Nouveau later that century reverberated throughout the area.

Good streets to soak up the refined ambience include Möhlstrasse, branching north-east from the Europa-Platz near the Friedensengel. Exclusive villas built for Munich's super-rich line this chic street; many are now occupied by foreign consulates and law offices. East of here (via Siebertstrasse and Ismaninger Strasse) is Holbeinstrasse, which has some of Munich's finest Art Nouveau houses, all of them listed monuments. The one at No 7 is a particularly fine example.

[Continued on page 133]

The Munich Oktoberfest

Rio has its Carnival, Indianapolis its 500, Cannes its film festival. But they all take a back seat to the world's biggest party: Munich's Oktoberfest – an unapologetic assault on the senses and sensibility. Incomparable Bavarian brew, the smell of oxen roasting on a spit, and the roar of more than six million people combine to put an entire city on sensory overload. For 16 wild days in late September, Munich is ruled by lovers of beer and pretzels, food and foolishness, rides, parties, music and almost every other indulgence under the sun.

Oktoberfest actually is a small temporary city with its own infrastructure. It employs about 12,000 people and has its own police force, lost and found, childcare centre, fire brigade, consumer protection unit, baggage checkroom, post office and first-aid station. It installs its own sewage system, power stations, and U-Bahn terminal. And to channel beer in the appropriate manner, there are 1440 Portacabins, although even these cannot stop large numbers of visitors from heading off into the darkness when nature calls to indulge in what the Bavarians call '*wildes Bieseln*' ('wild peeing').

Other revellers contain their rollicking excursions to the bright lights of the midway with its roller coaster, Ferris wheel and all sorts of low-key and high-tech rides. Wide-eyed five-year-olds clutch giant gingerbread hearts like prized possessions. The sweet aroma of roasted almonds wafts through the air. Nights become a mesmerising mosaic of smoke, boisterous song, and ruddy faces illuminated by strobes and enough dazzling lights to put Las Vegas to shame.

In the giant beer tents, an endless stream of foaming amber-coloured beer cascades into the famous gargantuan steins in a futile effort to parch the thirst of the crowds. Oompah music, provided by the some of the best brass bands in Bavaria, has crowds roaring and swaying. Locals in dirndls and lederhosen hoist, guzzle and toast with a United Nations of visitors. It's a sight to behold, at least once in a lifetime.

History

Gazing around at all the mayhem and merriment, it's hard to believe the festival had its origins in a simple horse race. The year was 1810, and the marriage of Bavarian Crown Prince Ludwig (later to become King Ludwig I) to Princess Therese of Saxe-Hildburghausen was set for October 12. Two officers of the Bavarian National Guard persuaded King Maximilian to cap off his son's wedding festivities with horse races on a meadow outside town. The event was such a smashing success that it became an annual bash. In honour of the princess, the meadow was named Theresienwiese (Theresia Meadow).

Horses charged down the Wies'n for over a century until the races were dropped in 1938. Since then, Oktoberfest has evolved into a mega-amusement park that blends new technology with tradition in a slow, thoughtful way.

Title page: Souvenir cards good enough to drink (photograph by Martin Moos)

Inset: Smiley face, Oktoberfest version (photograph by Martin Moos)

Top: Oktoberfest by night

Middle: Partying in the Schützen-Festhalle

Bottom: A quiet night at one of Oktoberfest's beer halls

JEREMY GRAY

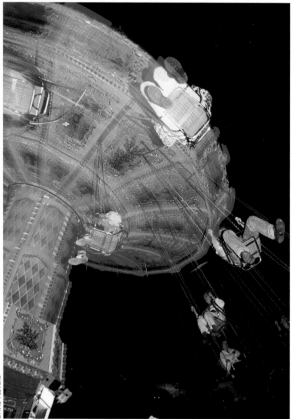

DAVID PEEVERS

Top: Lederhosen is still the 'in thing' at the Oktoberfest International Folklore Parade

Bottom: The nightly scientific experiment: mixing steins and steins of beer, Bratwurst and stomach-churning rides

Facts & Figures

Gluttony is big business at the Oktoberfest. In a typical year, more than seven million people put about €225 million into the coffers of brewers, tent landlords, carousel owners, shop owners and other concessionaires. Counting money spent outside the Wies'n on hotels, transportation and shopping, the figure rises to a whopping €800 million.

Here's the breakdown:

Beer 6.5 million litres
Wine 27,000 litres
Sparkling wine 18,800 bottles
Coffee, tea 246,000 cups
Water, lemonade 639,500 bottles
Chicken 681,250 birds
Pork sausage 235,474 pairs
Pork knuckles 62,490 servings
Oxen 94 animals

Highlights

Brewer's Parade

The parade through the city centre, from Sonnenstrasse to the fairgrounds via Schwanthalerstrasse, begins at 11am on the first day of the festival. At noon, the lord mayor stands before the thirsty crowds at Theresienwiese. With due pomp, he slams home a wooden tap with a mallet. When the tap breaks through the cask's surface and beer gushes forth, the mayor exclaims, *'Ozapft ist's!'* (It's tapped!).

Right: Lots of smiling aboard a float during the Brewer's Parade

JEREMY GRAY

Costume Procession

On the second day, starting at 10am, a young girl dressed as the *Münchener Kindl* on horseback leads 7000 performers from all over Europe (wearing pretzel bras and other traditional drunkenwear) through the streets of the city centre.

Folklore International

About 500 performers from the costume procession stage musical, dance and folklore performances in the Circus Krone building on Arnulfstrasse at 8pm on the first evening of Oktoberfest.

MW

Gay Meeting

There's a big gay meeting on the first Sunday of Oktoberfest at the Bräurosl tent, with legions of butch-looking guys in leather pants. It is timed to coincide with a gay leather convention; it's huge fun and open to all.

Schicht'l Tent

On the midway, amid the high-tech roar, a few nostalgic favourites have survived. Among these are the magic shows at Schicht'l Tent where 'beheadings' are a speciality. Generations have gasped at this bloody spectacle, and even master illusionist David Copperfield lost his head here a few years ago.

Flea Circus

Oktoberfest also boasts Germany's last remaining flea circus – a fixture since the 19th century – where trained pests provide fleapower for miniature chariots that outweigh them a thousandfold. Gotta see it to believe it!

The Lowdown

The Oktoberfest runs for 16 days from mid-September to the first Sunday in October and is held at the Theresienwiese, a 15-minute walk south-west of the Hauptbahnhof (or one stop on the U4 or U5 to 'Theresienwiese').

There are 16 tents, which open between 10am and 10.30am (as early as 9am on Sunday) and close at 11.30pm. Only Käfers Wiesnschenke and the Wein- und Sektzelt are licensed until 1am. Regardless, it's a good idea to leave around 9pm or 10pm as crowds can get a bit unruly when the beer supplies are turned off. Rides operate from 10.30am to 11.30pm Monday to Thursday and to midnight Friday to Sunday.

Beer tents are most crowded all day on Saturday and Sunday and least crowded on Monday and before 5pm Tuesday to Friday. During the first week, weekday evenings are not overly swamped either. Admission to the tents is free. In 2001, a *Mass* (1L beer) cost between €5.85 and €6.40.

There's no central reservation system for tables. With a lot of advance planning, you can apply for a table with the tent owners

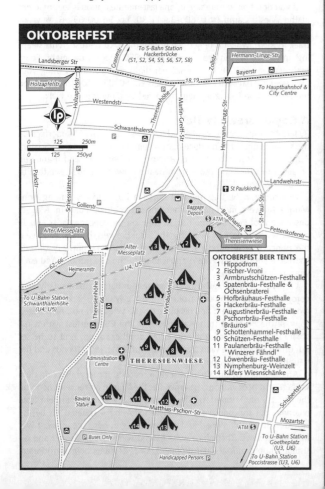

OKTOBERFEST BEER TENTS
1 Hippodrom
2 Fischer-Vroni
3 Armbrustschützen-Festhalle
4 Spatenbräu-Festhalle & Ochsenbraterei
5 Hofbräuhaus-Festhalle
6 Hackerbräu-Festhalle
7 Augustinerbräu-Festhalle
8 Pschorrbräu-Festhalle "Bräurosi"
9 Schottenhammel-Festhalle
10 Schützen-Festhalle
11 Paulanerbräu-Festhalle "Winzerer Fähndl"
12 Löwenbräu-Festhalle
13 Nymphenburg-Weinzelt
14 Käfers Wiesnschänke

directly. For addresses, see the Munich tourist office Web site (W www.munich-tourist.de).

Oktoberfest food is not cheap. If cutting costs is your aim, eat before you arrive, as the reluctance to part with €10 and up for a beer and a chicken leg tends to fade after a litre or two of amber liquid. The streets around, especially off the eastern edge, are filled with *Imbiss* making inexpensive doner kebabs, pizzas and filled pastries.

Reserve accommodation as early as you can (like a year in advance). Hotels book out very quickly and prices skyrocket during the fair. If you show up during Oktoberfest, expect to find only extremely pricey rooms – if any at all – in Munich.

If you don't mind roughing it, one last-minute option is to rent a tent at the Wies'n Camp (☎ 01805-33 11 30, fax 94 00 69 96, W www .munich-oktoberfest.com), a makeshift camping ground at the horse-track in Riem, which is only open during the Oktoberfest. Tents sleeping up to four persons go for €40 (plus €50 deposit) per night. Foam mattresses are €8 (€50 deposit) per night, but you must bring your own sleeping bag and pillow. Parking is €7.50. It's a 10-minute ride on the S6 direction Erding to Riem, followed by a five-minute walk.

A Royal 'Brew-Ha-Ha'

By law, the only breweries allowed to serve beer at the Oktoberfest are the six large ones that produce right within the city boundaries: Spaten, Augustiner, Hofbräu, Hacker-Pschorr, Löwenbrau and Paulaner. Smaller breweries and those from nearby towns are not permitted to sell on the grounds.

Not surprisingly, this rule has raised a hue and cry among non-Munich brewers, most notably one Prinz Luitpold von Bayern. A direct descendant of Ludwig I, he has, for the last two decades or so, made a semi-serious sport of tweaking the local brewery barons. Each year the prince – who happens to own the Kaltenberg brewery outside Munich – submits his Wies'n application to the city fathers. And each year he is shot down.

One year, though, His Royal Highness initiated a particularly rancorous incident. He made a bet with a big Munich brewer that this would be the year he'd find his place on the Wies'n. If not, he pledged to walk the 30 miles from Kaltenberg to the Oktoberfest with a full stein in his hand. Well, the prince lost another round. And so he set out on his pilgrimage with an entourage of some 1500 friends and the national media in hot pursuit.

Accompanied by brass bands, several coaches, the local shooting club, sausage and beer wagons, he arrived at the Wies'n entrance at noon on the last day of Oktoberfest. City officials initially tried to bar them from entering, but the prince and his loyal following – cheered on by the crowds – finally triumphed and crashed the grounds. The incident was front-page news. The prince was charged with duress, slander and resisting a public official (later dropped). Sales of Kaltenberg skyrocketed.

[Continued from page 126]

Prinzregentenstrasse, the main artery, divides Bogenhausen from the lively former workers' quarter of Haidhausen to the south (see later in this chapter). Aside from the sights mentioned below, a worthwhile stop along here is at **Feinkost Käfer** *(☎ 416 80, Prinzregentenstrasse 73)*, a fancy gourmet emporium for the fat-wallet set.

Prinzregentenstrasse (Map 5)

Friedensengel Just east of the Isar River, the Friedensengel (Angel of Peace) statue stands sentinel over the city from its windy perch atop a 20m-high column. The graceful, gilded female is a replica of the Nike figure on the Greek mountain of Olympia. It commemorates the 1871 Treaty of Versailles, which ended the Franco-Prussian War. The base contains some lovely golden frescoes and is party central on New Year's Eve.

Museum Villa Stuck Franz von Stuck (1863–1928) was a leading Jugendstil painter with a rebellious streak whose former *fin-de-siècle* home has been reincarnated as the Museum Villa Stuck *(1897; ☎ 455 55 10, Prinzregentenstrasse 60; admission €1; open 10am-6pm Tues-Sun)*. Stuck's villa, luxuriously furnished with wainscoting, tapestries and handmade furniture, forms the perfect backdrop for the exhibits, including some of Stuck's own works.

Of note here is the painting *Die Sünde* (The Sin; 1912), with unabashed eroticism that caused quite a stir back in the old days. Changing exhibits focus on art by Stuck's contemporaries as well as later 20th-century avant-gardists and contemporary artists. The villa has undergone gradual renovation in recent years, but this should all be wrapped up by the time you're reading this.

Munich's Olympic Tragedy

Munich's bid for the 1972 Olympic Games came after official recognition of the GDR by the UN in 1965. The philosophy behind the move was that, through the Olympics, West Germany would put itself forward as a rebuilt nation, a model of international cooperation and the proud parent of Munich, which had undeniably become a world-class city.

The Games got off to an auspicious start: these were the heady days of the Cold War, and much of the action was dominated by contests between East and West, such as the basketball duel between the USA and the Soviet Union.

However, on 6 September, Palestinian terrorists from a group calling itself Black September raided the Israeli athletes' dormitory in the Olympic Village, kidnapping nine team members and coaches and killing two immediately.

Black September demanded the release of prisoners from Israeli jails and threatened to kill the remaining hostages if their demands weren't met immediately. German authorities frantically negotiated for the release of the athletes. They offered money, even a swap of the Israelis for 'substitute' hostages, including federal interior minister Hans-Dietrich Genscher and former Munich mayor Hans-Jochen Vogel – all to no avail.

After hours of failed negotiations, and with every indication that the terrorists were about to start killing the hostages, the German government decided to take military action. It arranged for three helicopters to fly the terrorists and hostages to a military airfield at Fürstenfeldbruck, west of Munich, where they were promised a plane that would fly them all to Cairo.

When the choppers arrived at Fürstenfeldbruck, police sharpshooters opened fire on the terrorists, who immediately began shooting hostages. One terrorist detonated a hand grenade inside a helicopter. The nine Israelis, as well as five of the terrorists and a Munich police officer, were killed in the shoot-out.

Jeremy Gray

MAP 5 – LEHEL & HAIDHAUSEN

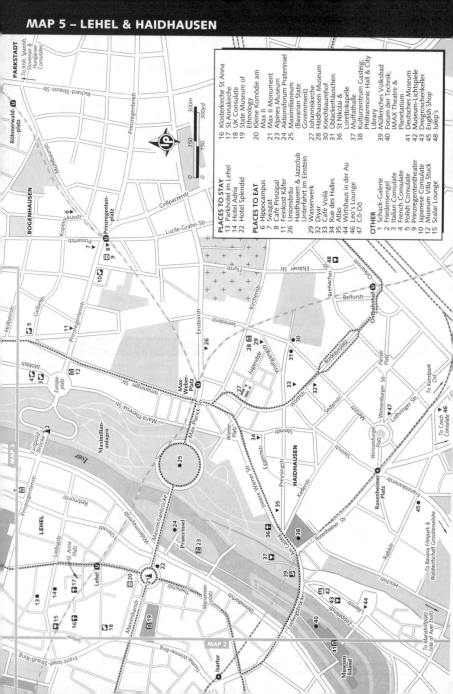

Prinzregententheater Bogenhausen's other main landmark is the Prinzregententheater (☎ 21 85 29 59, Prinzregentenplatz 12). It is a combination of Art Nouveau and neoclassical styles built by Max Littman for Prince-Regent Luitpold as a festival house for Richard Wagner operas. After WWII, it housed the Bavarian State Opera while the Nationaltheater was being restored. By the time that project had been completed, in 1963, the Prinzregententheater itself was in such bad shape that it was closed. Restoration took more than 30 years and it wasn't until 1996 that the theatre reopened to the strains of Wagner's Tristan und Isolde. The Bavarian Theatre Academy also has its home here; students often perform in the small on-site Akademietheater.

Northern Bogenhausen (Map 3)

Near Max-Joseph-Brücke stands the charming little rococo St Georgskirche (Bogenhauser Kirchplatz 1). In its churchyard lie buried some of Munich's key cultural figures, including writers Erich Kästner, Annette Kolb, Oskar Maria Graf and film director Rainer Werner Fassbinder, and it's fascinating to read the inscriptions.

Kirchplatz was the centre of the original village of Bogenhausen, and harkens back to a world much simpler than that ruled by Mercedes-Benzes and shampooed poodles.

East of here, **Arabellapark** is a modern business, industrial and residential district. There's not much to lure you out here, except perhaps some rather daring postmodern architecture. The building that definitely takes the cake is the headquarters of the **Hypovereinsbank** (1981; Arabellastrasse 12; U-Bahn: U4 to Richard-Strauss Platz). One of Munich's few skyscrapers, the eye-popping design consists of a quartet of cylindrical towers whose silvery aluminium shell gives it a distinctly space-age feel.

Another Arabellapark attraction is the **Cosimabad** (☎ 23 61 79 21, Cosimastrasse 5; pool admission €3, sauna €9; open 7.30am-11pm daily, waves from 2pm & all day Sat & Sun), Munich's most modern indoor swimming complex with a great wave-motion pool.

LEHEL (MAP 5)

Lehel (pronounced 'Lechl') is a relaxed neighbourhood just east of the Altstadt proper, roughly bounded by the Englischer Garten to the north, the Isar to the east, the Isartor to the south and the Altstadt ring road to the west. Throughout the Middle Ages, it was the quarter of the poor craftspeople and artisans not allowed to settle within city boundaries. Times have certainly changed. Today, the district's quiet streets are lined with lovely residential buildings from the Gründerzeit period (late 19th century) and only the well-to-do can afford to live here.

St-Anna-Platz

Author Lion Feuchtwanger grew up in the house at No 2 of this leafy square and, in the 1920s, wrote the novels Erfolg (Success), a critique of early-20th-century Munich, as well as the classic Jud Süss.

Today, St-Anna-Platz, flanked by two pretty churches, is the spiritual centre of the Lehel. The **Klosterkirche St Anna** (☎ 21 12 60, St-Anna-Platz 21; open 6am-7pm daily), built between 1723 and 1733, launched the rococo style in Munich and indeed Upper Bavaria. It's an early collaboration by some of the biggest names in church construction at the time. Architect Johann Michael Fischer came up with the basic oval shape, Cosmas Damian Asam added the ceiling fresco, and his brother Egid Quirin as well as Johann Baptist Straub signed for the stucco decoration and sculpture. Alas, the original was wasted in WWII, but it's all been successfully restored.

On the square's eastern side looms **St Annakirche** (☎ 2121820, St-Anna-Platz 5; open 8am-6pm daily), which came into the picture in the late 19th century after the Klosterkirche became too small for its growing congregation. A neo-Romanesque pile by Gabriel von Seidl, it is considered a supreme example of revival architecture and worth a look for its huge altar and impressive nave paintings.

Prinzregentenstrasse

Prinzregentenstrasse was laid out from 1891 to 1912 in a gesture of self-promotion by Prince-Regent Luitpold. Today, it serves as a main traffic artery, lined by several fine museums and foreign consulates.

For Prinzregentenstrasse sights east of the Isar, see the Bogenhausen section in this chapter.

Bayerisches Nationalmuseum (Map 3)

Near the southern boundary of the Englischer Garten awaits a highlight of Munich's museum scene: the Bavarian National Museum (☎ 211 24 01, Prinzregentenstrasse 3; adult/concession €3/2, Sun free; open 10am-5pm Tues-Sun, 10am-8pm Thur). It is chock-full of exhibits illustrating the art, folklore and cultural history of southern Germany, Bavaria in particular, from antiquity to the early 20th century.

Founded by King Maximilian II in 1855, the museum soon outgrew its original space in what now houses the Völkerkundemuseum on Maximilianstrasse (see later in this section). In the late 19th century, it fell to architect Gabriel von Seidl to create this vast purpose-built museum. He came up with an oddly engaging architectural blend of various styles, from the Romanesque to Gothic and Renaissance, baroque and rococo.

The ground floor has paintings, sculpture, tapestries, furniture and weapons from the early Middle Ages to the rococo period. Carved wood sculptures by Erasmus Grasser and Tilman Riemenschneider, two of the greatest of the genre, stand out from the crowd, although the works by Johann Baptist Straub and Ignaz Günther are nothing to sneeze at either. Upstairs, collections in the eastern wing focus on the 19th century. Here you can admire Nymphenburg porcelain, precious glass and exquisite Jugendstil (Art Nouveau) items by Lalique, Tiffany and others.

The western wing has specialised collections of musical instruments, games and silverware, including a ridiculously ostentatious silver table setting once owned by the Hildesheim prince-bishop. By contrast, the basement shows the ways of life of the simple peasant folk through a series of period rooms. Also here is a celebrated collection of creches from the 17th to the 19th centuries.

Archäologische Staatssammlung (Map 3)

Behind the Nationalmuseum, the Archaeological Collection (☎ 211 24 02, Lerchenfeldstrasse 2; adult/concession €2.50/1.50, Sun free; open 9am-4.30pm Tues-Sun) traces the settlement of Bavaria from the Stone Age to the early Middle Ages. Treasures and items from everyday life illustrate how the various cultures and civilisations which – at one time or another – settled in Bavarian territory lived their lives. Findings include Celtic coins, sculptures, weapons, precious objects found in burial sites and lots more.

Schack-Galerie

Count Adolf Friedrich von Schack (1815–94) was a great fan of 19th-century Romantic painters such as Böcklin, Feuerbach and Moritz von Schwind. His collection is now housed in the former Prussian embassy, the Schack-Galerie (☎ 23 80 52 24, Prinzregentenstrasse 9; adult/concession €2.50/1.75; open 10am-5pm Wed-Mon). A tour of this intimate space is like an escape into the idealised fantasy worlds created by these artists.

Maximilianstrasse

Maximilianstrasse, which connects the Altstadt with Haidhausen, is one of Munich's grandest royal boulevards. Starting at the Residenz, it travels east for about 1.2km to the Maximilianeum, the seat of the Bayerischer Landtag (Bavarian State Government). It makes for an interesting stroll that will take you past posh hotels and elegant fashion boutiques, as well as a mish-mash of architectural styles ranging from Bavarian rustic to Italian and English Gothic.

Built between 1852 and 1875, the avenue was essentially an ego trip of King Max II. He harnessed the skills of architect Friedrich von Bürklein to create this unique hotch-potch that, perhaps not surprisingly, became known as the 'Maximilianic Style'.

Maximilianstrasse is also home to several of Munich's finest theatrical venues, including the Residenztheater, the Nationaltheater, the Kammerspiele and the Kleine Komödie am Max II. For details, see the Entertainment section in this chapter.

Staatliches Museum für Völkerkunde
After crossing Thomas-Wimmer-Ring, a
roaring road that's an undisputed postwar
eyesore, you'll soon reach the State Museum of Ethnology (☎ 210 13 60, Maximilianstrasse 42; adult/concession €3/1.75;
open 9.30am-4.30pm Tues-Sun). Inside is a
bonanza of non-European art and objects
that allows for an eye-opening journey
through exotic cultures and civilisations.
The museum's collection, one of the oldest
and most comprehensive in Germany, is
particularly strong in sculpture from West
and Central Africa; Peruvian ceramics, jewellery and even mummy parts; and artefacts
from Micronesia and the South Pacific.

Max II Denkmal Next up, in the middle of
a traffic circle, is a bronze statue of a balding
King Max II gazing down upon 'his' boulevard. Clinging to the base are four rather
stern-looking 'children' holding the coats of
arms of the Bavarian tribes of Bavaria, Franconia, Swabia as well as the Palatinate.

Maximilianbrücke & Praterinsel Carrying on, you'll soon cross the Isar on Maxi-
miliansbrücke (1905), designed by Friedrich
von Thiersch and adorned with photogenic
sculptures. Resist the temptation to snap pictures of the nude bathers relaxing on the Praterinsel below. Or maybe not...

Also on the island, in a former schnapps
distillery, is the **Aktionsforum Praterinsel**,
an art and cultural centre with studios for
around 20 artists and an active events
schedule including exhibits, open-air performances and parties.

On the island's southern tip, in a beautiful white building, is the **Alpines Museum** (☎ 211 22 40, Praterinsel 5; adult/
concession/children to age 14 €3/2/1;
open 1pm-6pm Tues-Fri, 11am-6pm Sat &
Sun). Maintained by the Deutscher Alpenverein (German Alpine Association), it
has loads of mountain paintings, graphics,
scientific instruments and a detailed history of the organisation.

Maximilianeum Just past the bridge, and
technically already in Haidhausen, is the

crowning glory of Maximilianstrasse: the
Maximilianeum, completed in 1874, 10
years after the king's sudden death. It's an
imposing structure, perched on a sprawling
pedestal, festooned with mosaics and generously decked out with paintings and other
artistic objects. There's a free exhibit about
the Bavarian parliament, which moved here
in 1949.

Since 1876, the building has also been
the seat of a study foundation for Bavarian
scholars and home to an art gallery. Until
1918, the Royal Servant School was here as
well. North and south of the structure is an
undulating park called the **Maximiliananla-
gen**, which is a haven for cyclists in summer and tobogganists in winter.

HAIDHAUSEN (MAP 5)
Like all the outerlying boroughs, Haidhausen is actually much older than Munich
and only became absorbed into the big city
in the 19th century. During the Industrial
Revolution, its population grew exponentially from about 5000 in 1850 to 45,000 by
the turn of the 20th century. Most of the
residents were factory workers, artisans,
masons and tradesmen of all sorts.

Haidhausen's transformation from workers' quarter to trendy district began in the late
1960s when students, artists and those in
search of an alternative lifestyle moved into
the dilapidated tenement buildings. Gentrifi-
cation got another shot in the arm with the
opening of the Kulturzentrum Gasteig, a
mega-sized cultural complex, in 1985.

These days, Haidhausen is one of the
most happening districts in Munich, with a
youthful and artsy ambience and a lively
pub and restaurant scene. By some measures, it outranks Schwabing as the city's
best entertainment quarter.

Kulturzentrum Gasteig &
Around
Haidhausen is home to one of Munich's
finest cultural venues, the Gasteig Culture
Centre, a postmodern boxy glass-and-brick
complex with a design that caused quite a
controversy during construction back in the
70s and 80s. Things have, of course, settled

down since and today more than two million people stream into the centre each year.

There are four concert halls, including the 2500-seat Philharmonie, the permanent home of the Münchener Philharmoniker, which also hosts renowned international orchestras. More intimate venues are the Carl-Orff-Saal (590 seats), the Kleiner Konzertsaal (Small Concert Hall; 190 seats) and the Black Box (250 seats), which presents mostly experimental theatre and dance. Also here is the Richard Strauss Conservatory, a huge municipal library branch and an adult school.

The name 'Gasteig', by the way, is derived from the Bavarian term 'gaacher Steig', meaning 'steep trail'.

Right on the Isar, west of the Gasteig, is the lovely **Müllersches Volksbad**, Munich's first public swimming pool and an awesome Art Nouveau structure from 1901 (see Swimming later in this chapter). Nearby is the giant **Muffathalle** culture centre, converted from an old power plant.

The prim church ensemble north of here is the **St Nikolai & Lorettokapelle**. St Nikolai was first built in Gothic style in 1315 only to go baroque in 1660. The design of the little Loretto Chapel, added in 1678, emulates the *Gnadenkapelle* in Altötting (see the Upper Bavaria chapter). It's surrounded by a covered walkway protecting the remarkable Stations of the Cross reliefs made of Nymphenburg porcelain.

Wiener Platz & Around Walking north from the Gasteig on Innere Wienerstrasse will take you to Wiener Platz with a daily produce market.

East of the square stands the slender red pinnacle of the huge **St-Johann-Baptist-Kirche**. Dubbed 'Haidhausen's Cathedral' after being built from 1852 to 1863, the church boasts 21 neogothic windows decorated with a wonderful cycle of religious paintings. The surrounding square is pleasant, with its leafy park and town houses, and is well shielded from the traffic noise of busy Max-Weber-Platz just to the north.

One architectural gem nearby is the incongruous, timber-framed **Kriechbaumhof** at Preysingstrasse 71. Restored to its original

17th-century form, it's home today to a youth centre; the impression is one of a cottage plucked from an Alpine meadow. Directly opposite, at No 58, is the **Üblacker House**, a WWI-era labourer's flat which has been turned into a standing exhibit.

To learn more about Haidhausen's intriguing history, visit the **Haidhausen Museum** (☎ 448 52 92, Kirchenstrasse 24; free; open 4pm-6pm Mon-Wed, 2pm-6pm Sun).

Deutsches Museum

If science and technology warm the cockles of your heart, then this museum is a must. But even if you've slept through physics class, the exhibits at the vast German Museum (☎ 217 91 or 217 94 33 (recording), Museumsinsel 1; adult/concession/family €6/4/12.50, children under 6 free; open 9am-5pm daily) are likely to unlock previously unknown interests in you.

To be sure, it can all be a bit overwhelming at first. Squatting on Museum Island, south-east of the Isartor, this behemoth has no fewer than eight floors dedicated to the entire gamut of scientific discovery through the ages. You could easily spend days here and not see it all, so it's wise to limit yourself to those areas that interest you most.

The basement is devoted to mining and automobiles, and the ground floor to tunnel construction, railways and aeronautics. The 1st floor has a flimsy and dated section on physics and chemistry, but also lots of wonderful musical instruments. The 2nd floor has the Altamira cave exhibit (don't miss this one!). The 3rd floor is a mixed bag of geodesy, weights and measures, microelectronics and telecommunications. The 4th to 6th floors are dedicated to astronomy and amateur radio.

Forum der Technik

In the north-eastern corner of Museumsinsel, near Rosenheimer Strasse, is the Deutsches Museum-affiliated Forum of Technology (☎ 21 12 51 83, Museumsinsel 1). It's comprised of two attractions: an **IMAX Theatre** (incidentally Germany's first) with a changing roster of big-screen movies, and a state-of-the-art **planetarium** with educational programming as well as a Pink Floyd laser show. IMAX 2D or regular planetarium shows are €6.75/5.25 (adult/concession) each; two shows on one day are €11. IMAX 3D and planetarium laser shows are €8.25/7 each, with two shows costing €14. The Pink Floyd laser show is €9.50/7.50. On Monday the concession price applies to everyone.

OTHER ATTRACTIONS
Münchener Tierpark Hellabrunn
The Hellabrunn Zoo (☎ 62 50 80, *Tierparkstrasse 30, Thalkirchen; adult/concession €6/3; U-Bahn: Thalkirchen, Bus: No 52*) was the first 'geo-zoo' (one with distinct sections dividing animals by continents). Today, it has about 5000 animals representing 460 species, including rhinos, elephants, deer, bucks and gazelles. It's absolutely worth the admission if only to gain access to the petting zoo, crawling with sheep, deer and lambs that you can feed. Perhaps the best exhibit, though, is the tropical bird that shouts, loudly, '*Arschloch!*' (Asshole!) at giggling tourists.

Bavaria Filmpark München
An often-missed treasure is the Bavaria Filmpark München (☎ 64 99 23 04, *Bavariafilmplatz 7; adult/concession €8.50/6; tours 9am-5pm; U-Bahn: Silberhornstrasse, then tram No 25 to Bavariafilmplatz*) in the southern suburb of Geiselgasteig. You'll see sets of *Enemy Mine, Das Boot, Cabaret* and *The Never-Ending Story*, all of which were filmed here. Numerous German TV series and films are still shot here as well.

WHAT'S FREE
Munich is not a cheap city and very few things come free. Museums that have free admission at all times are the Deutsches Theatermuseum, the SiemensForum, the Jüdisches Museum, the DenkStätte – White Rose exhibit and the Haidhausen Museum. Crowdpleasers such as the Alte Pinakothek, the Neue Pinakothek, the Glyptothek, the Münchener Stadtmuseum, the Bayerisches Nationalmuseum and the Archäologische Sammlung have free admission on Sundays,

and BMW runs complimentary factory tours. Everything is described in greater detail in this chapter.

HIKING & CLIMBING
If you're planning on venturing into the Alpine foothills or the Bavarian Alps for some hiking and mountain climbing, Munich is a good place to stock up on information and gear. The Deutscher Alpenverein (German Alpine Association) has an information centre (☎ 29 49 40) at Praterinsel 5, the same location as its Alpines Museum (see earlier).

For gear and equipment, Sport Schuster, Rosenstrasse 1–5, and the better Sport Scheck (☎ 216 60), nearby at Sendlinger Strasse 6, both have multiple floors of everything imaginable for the adventurer, from simple camping equipment to expedition wear, plus excellent bookshops. There's also a discount Sport Scheck at the Ostbahnhof selling discontinued merchandise.

SWIMMING
Bathing in the Isar River isn't advisable because of pollution. The two best public swimming pools are the Olympia-Schwimmhalle (☎ 30 67 22 90) at Olympiapark and the spectacular Müllersches Volksbad (☎ 23 61 34 34), Rosenheimer Strasse 1 in Haidhausen.

The latter, in splendid Art Nouveau style, is worth visiting even without getting wet. Pool access is €3, or €4.50 with private cabin (in which to take a hot bath). Four-hour sauna sessions are €11 (women only Tuesday and Friday). Hours are 7.30am to 11pm for the pool, and from 9am for the sauna.

The pool at Olympiapark is usually open 7am to 11pm daily, though this may vary throughout the year. Admission is €2.80/2.30; add a sauna and the price is €10.25/7.70. Tanning beds (€3) are available as well.

BOATING
The most popular spot in town to take a little tootle on a boat is the Englischer Garten's Kleinhesseloher See, where rowing/pedal boats cost around €6 per half

hour for up to four people. Olympiapark is another place to rent boats.

ORGANISED TOURS
Walking Tours
For a fun and fact-filled introduction to Munich, take a tour with Munich Walks (mobile ☎ 0177 227 59 01). These English-language walking tours run daily, last two to 2½ hours and cost €9/7.50 for people over/under 26 (children under 14 are free with an adult).

All tours leave from the EurAide office, at track 11 of the Hauptbahnhof. Discount coupons of €1 may be printed from its Web site at ⓦ www.berlinwalks.com.

Munich Walks' Discover Munich tour covers the heart of the city and gives good historical background and architectural information. It ends at the Hofbräuhaus. Tours leave at 10.15am daily from April through November, with an additional tour at 2.15pm daily except Sunday from May to August.

The same company also runs the Infamous Third Reich Sites tour, which covers exactly that. It runs at 2.30pm Saturday in April, at 10.15am Monday, Thursday and Saturday from May to August and at 2.15pm Monday and Saturday in September and October. Check with EurAide or call Munich Walks to confirm hours.

Bicycle Tours
Mike's Bike Tours (☎ 25 54 39 87/88, mobile ☎ 0172 852 06 60, ⓔ mike@bavaria .com) offers guided walking tours of Munich, although its speciality really is bike tours of the city. The standard tour covers about four miles in four hours (with a 45-minute beer-garden break) and costs €20. The extended tour goes for six hours, covers 10 miles and costs €25. Tours operate at least once daily from April to mid-November from outside the Toy Museum on Marienplatz. You don't have to be in shape, because the guide stops about every 400m to explain a point of interest.

Bus Tours
If you prefer to sit back in a bus and be shown around town, take a tour with Panorama Tours (☎ 55 02 89 95). Its one-hour Munich

Highlights tours run up to 10 times daily year round (€9.70/5.10 adult/child). Longer themed tours are offered on a regular schedule as well (most are under €20), as are day trips to the surrounding countryside (mostly around €40). They're OK, but the commentary is given in two languages, which can get tedious. Buses leave from outside the Hertie department store opposite the Hauptbahnhof.

SPECIAL EVENTS
Munich has a busy festival calendar. In February, Carnival marks the beginning of Lent (the six weeks preceding Easter) and is celebrated with street parades, balls, stage shows and other well-lubricated events. During Lent, the **Starkbierzeit**, held the third and fourth week before Easter, dates back to the old days when the monks drank strong beer to make up for all that fasting.

In late April, the **Frühlingsfest**, a miniature Oktoberfest, also takes place on the Theresienwiese. The **Auer Dult**, which runs for eight days starting on the last Saturday in April, is a great flea market which is repeated in July and October.

June's highlight is the **Tollwood Festival**, a world culture festival held at Olympiapark, with food, clothes and merchandise and nightly concerts, weather permitting. Admission is free but the concerts cost something (anywhere from €3 to €20). Call ☎ 383 85 00 for information.

Christopher Street Day takes place in July, as does the **Opera Festival**, featuring works by the Bayerische Staatsoper; it always concludes on 31 July with Wagner's *Die Meistersinger von Nürnberg*. Call ☎ 21 85 01 for information.

For details on the Oktoberfest, see the special section 'The Munich Oktoberfest'.

The festival season wraps up in December with the **Christkindlmarkt**. The biggest one is on Marienplatz, but other districts, notably Schwabing, hold their own less touristy versions.

PLACES TO STAY
Munich crawls with visitors from May to October, so at times it can get a little squeezy. It's a good idea to make reservations during

these peak months and especially around the time of the Oktoberfest. The flow thins considerably between November and March when rates may drop and special deals abound. Prices skyrocket again around the Christmas and New Year's holidays.

Munich offers the entire gamut of lodging options – hostels to luxury abodes – but room rates, overall, tend to be high. Even if you book through EurAide or the tourist offices (see Information), you're unlikely to find anything under €30/45 for a single/double with shared facilities. The DJH and independent hostels offer the cheapest accommodation. Otherwise, you will find a slew of budget pensions and hotels – some a bit seedy and cramped, others quite OK – clustered around the Hauptbahnhof.

'Mid-range' in Munich can mean paying over €100 per double, but you may do far better by joining a package tour or booking through a travel agency. Hotels at the top of the heap are what you'd expect: clean, luxurious and very, very expensive.

PLACES TO STAY – BUDGET
Camping
Campingplatz Nord-West (☎ 150 69 36, fax 15 82 04 63, ⓔ office@campingplatz-nord-west.de, Auf den Schrederwiesen 3) Tent/car/person €3-5/2.50/3. Open year round. This pleasant camping ground is about 2km from Olympiapark and within walking distance of three swimming lakes. There's a store and a snack bar as well.

Campingplatz Thalkirchen (☎ 723 17 07, fax 724 31 77, Zentralländstrasse 49) U-Bahn: U3 to Thalkirchen, then bus No 57 to Thalkirchen or 15-minute walk along river. Tent/car/person €2.80-3.60/4.30/4.40 (€8 per person during Oktoberfest). Open mid-Mar–Oct. This central camping ground is about 4km south-west of the city centre and can get incredibly crowded, although it always seem to squeeze in one more tent. It's a full-service camping ground, scenically located on the Isar River. If you don't have your own tent, they also rent bunks in caravans for €10.50, including floor mat, heat, light and cleaning.

Campingplatz Obermenzing (☎ 811 22 35, fax 814 48 07, Lochhausener Strasse 59) Tent/car/person €3.75/3/4.25. Open mid-Mar–Oct. This camping ground, on the outskirts of an upmarket neighbourhood in western Munich, is in a park-like setting and counts a coin-op laundry and small store among its facilities.

DJH Hostels
Jugendlager am Kapuzinerhölzl (☎ 141 43 00, fax 17 50 90, In den Kirschen 30) Tram: No 17 from Hauptbahnhof to Neuer Botanischer Garten, then 2-minute walk. Bed & breakfast €6.50-8.50. Open mid-June–early Sept. Nicknamed 'The Tent', Munich's summer budget favourite is a mass camp north of Schloss Nymphenburg. There's no curfew but the usual 26-year age limit applies (with priority given to people under 23). The cheapest 'beds' (a thermal mattress and blanket in the big tent) cost €7.50, including shower and breakfast. Bunk-style beds in smaller tents are €9.50.

Jugendherberge München (☎ 13 11 56, fax 16 45 45, ⓔ jhmuenchen@djh-bayern .de, Wendl-Dietrich-Strasse 20, Neuhausen) U-Bahn: Rotkreuzplatz. Beds €17. Closed Dec. This sparkling hostel is north-west of the Altstadt. Although it's relatively loud and busy, it's also popular and friendly without curfew or day-time lockouts. There is a restaurant and garden on the premises.

Jugendgästehaus München (☎ 723 65 50/60, fax 724 25 67, ⓔ jghmuenchen@djh -bayern.de, Miesingstrasse 4) U-Bahn: Thalkirchen, then follow the signs. Bed & breakfast €18, including linen. This more modern hostel is in the south-western suburb of Thalkirchen, but good public transportation connections make it feel less remote. There's no curfew.

Jugendherberge Burg Schwaneck (☎ 793 06 43/44, fax 793 79 22, Burgweg 4–6) S-Bahn: Pullach, plus 10-minute walk. Dorm beds €13.30, singles/doubles €19/36. Closed mid-Dec–mid-Jan. This hostel is in a grand old castle in the southern suburbs. All rooms have shower and toilet.

Independent Hostels

Munich has quite a few non-DJH hostels or hotels that offer cheap dorm accommodation as well as simple rooms.

Euro Youth Hotel (☎ 59 90 88 11, fax 59 90 88 77, ⓔ info@euro-youth-hotel.de, Senefelderstrasse 5, Ludwigsvorstadt) Bunk in 24-bed dorm €16, 3- to 5-bed dorms €20, singles/doubles €40/45 (shared bath), doubles €65 (private bath). This 24-hour hostel still wears the faded grandeur of the illustrious Hotel Astoria it was until WWI. On-tap half litres of Augustiner cost just €1.90 (the brewery owns the place), and optional breakfast is €4.25 (included in singles/doubles rates).

Two more Euro Youth Hotels, located in Schillerstrasse and near the airport, were scheduled to open in 2002. Call ☎ 59 90 88 71 for updates.

CVJM-YMCA Jugendgästehaus (☎ 552 14 10, fax 550 42 82, ⓔ info@cvjm-muenchen .org, Landwehrstrasse 13, Ludwigsvorstadt) Dorms/singles/doubles €21/27/46. This is a bit of a pernickety place. Smoking and alcohol are forbidden except in the restaurant, and it's closed from 12.30am to 7am.

IN VIA Marienherberge (☎ 55 58 05, fax 55 02 82 60, ⓔ invia.muenchen.marienher berge@t-online.de, Goethestrasse 9, Ludwigsvorstadt) Dorms/singles/doubles €15/20/36. Women under 26 can try this Catholic hostel behind an innocuous door (look for the tiny buzzer). There's a midnight curfew.

4 you münchen (☎ 552 16 60, fax 55 21 66 66, ⓔ info@the4you.de, Hirtenstrasse 18, Ludwigsvorstadt) Dorm beds €13-31, singles €40-76, doubles €33-51. Just north of the Hauptbahnhof, this place bills itself as an 'ecologically correct' hostel. It offers childcare and 75% of the rooms are accessible by wheelchair. Guests over 26 pay 16% more. The pricier rooms have private baths.

Haus International (☎ 12 00 60, fax 12 00 66 30, ⓔ info@haus-international.de, Elisabethstrasse 87, Neuhausen) U-Bahn: Hohenzollernplatz, Tram: No 12 to Barbarastrasse. Singles €28-43, doubles €42-50. A bit worn on the edges, but still OK, this vast 564-bed place has a pool, disco,

beer garden and cafeteria. The pricier rooms are larger and have more amenities.

Hotels & Pensions

Altstadt (Map 2) There are many budget options close to town.

Hotel Atlanta (☎ 26 36 05, fax 260 90 27, ⓔ info@hotel-atlanta.de, Sendlinger Strasse 58) Singles/doubles from €31/60 (shared bath), from €50/71 (private bath). The somewhat run-down but friendly Hotel Atlanta is nicely located between Sendlinger Tor and the Asamkirche. Go through the creepy door and up the creepy stairs to clean but rather threadbare rooms.

Hotel Arosa (☎ 26 70 87, fax 26 31 04, Hotterstrasse 2) Singles/doubles from €39/52 (shared bath), from €52/73 (private bath). A couple of blocks west of Marienplatz, this hotel has a range of rooms with varying levels of comfort. Amenities are few but at these prices, who's to complain?

Hotel Blauer Bock (☎ 23 17 80, fax 23 17 82 00, Sebastiansplatz 9) Singles/doubles from €41/61 (shared bath), from €56/82 (private bath). Not far from the Stadtmuseum, this hotel has clean, comfortable, central and reasonably spacious rooms.

Ludwigsvorstadt (Map 2) Budget places abound in the area close to the Hauptbahnhof.

Hotel Helvetia (☎ 590 68 50, fax 59 06 85 70, ⓔ info@hotel-helvetia.de, Schillerstrasse 6) Singles/doubles from €28/41 (shared bath), doubles €51-66 (shower), triples/quads/quintuples from €54/72/89. This hotel is popular with backpackers and comes with IKEA-type furniture, soundproofed windows, phones and laundry service.

Hotel Jedermann (☎ 54 32 40, fax 54 32 41 11, ⓔ info@hotel-jedermann.de, Bayerstrasse 95) Singles/doubles from €33/49 (shared bath), from €49/66 (private bath). A recent renovation has propelled this pleasant hotel into a new league where creature comforts are taken more seriously than in the past. Rooms are attractive, staff speak English and there's free Web surfing. Recommended.

Pension Marie-Luise (☎ 55 25 56 60, fax 55 25 56 66, Landwehrstrasse 35) Singles/

doubles from €28/41 (shared bath), doubles €59-82 (private bath). A good option for the monetarily challenged is this cramped but reasonably clean pension. Reception is next door at the Andi München City Center (see Hotels – Mid-Range)

Hotel-Pension Mariandl (☎ 53 41 08, fax 54 40 43 96, e *hotel.mariandl@t-online .de, Goethestrasse 51)* Singles €36-51, doubles €51-100. At this congenial place, rooms are outfitted in the 'olde-worlde' mould and many overlook Beethovenplatz. All rooms have shared bath. Early risers should request a quiet room to avoid the sounds wafting up from the popular downstairs restaurant (mains €4 to €9), which has live jazz or classical music nightly at 8pm (also see Entertainment later in this chapter).

Hotel Monaco (☎ 545 99 40, fax 550 37 09, e *info@hotel-monaco.de, Schiller-strasse 9)* Singles/doubles from €31/56 (shared bath), from €56/65 (private bath). In a morass of sex shops, this place rises above it all with floral elegance. Take the lift to the 5th floor, where you'll find artful paper roses in the halls and rooms. Book ahead.

Schwabing (Map 3) The area around the University provides many budget options.

Pension Frank (☎ 28 14 51, fax 280 09 10, e *pension.frank@ gmx.net, Schelling-strasse 24)* U-Bahn: Universität. Singles €33-38, doubles €43-56. This 16-room place has lovely wrought-iron beds, a small collection of English novels and a communal kitchen; all rooms have shared facilities. It's a great choice but often overrun by Anglo-Saxons.

Pension Am Kaiserplatz (☎ 34 91 90, Kaiserplatz 12)* Singles €30-46, doubles €46-54. This eclectic pension has interiors ranging from down-home Bavarian country to bordello velvet. It's run by an engaging old lady and is in a great location. Rooms have shared facilities.

Hotelpension am Siegestor (☎ 39 95 50/51, fax 34 30 50, e *siegestor@t-online .de, Akademiestrasse 5)* Singles €33-43, doubles €49-56 (shared bath). This delightful pension sprawls over the three upper floors of an old villa right by the Siegestor. Many rooms overlook the pretty Academy

of Fine Arts across the street. The lift is a delightful old Art Nouveau contraption.

PLACES TO STAY – MID-RANGE
Altstadt (Map 2)
Hotel Schlicker (☎ 22 79 41, fax 29 60 59, e *schlicker-munich@t-online.de, Im Tal 8)* Singles €74-100, doubles €97-199. Handy to the Viktualienmarkt and other Altstadt attractions, the 400-year-old Schlicker offers a pretty good deal for its spacious, modern and recently renovated rooms. Prices *don't* go up in the summer or at Oktoberfest, but the place is very popular and reservations are advisable.

Pension Am Gärtnerplatztheater (☎ 202 51 70, fax 20 25 17 22, e *PensionGaert nerplatztheater@t-online.de, Klenzestrasse 45, Gärtnerplatzviertel)* Singles €46-51 (shared bath), singles/doubles from €61/77 (private bath). Escape the tourist rabble by checking in at this fine establishment with antique-filled rooms in the cool Gärtnerplatz quarter.

Ludwigsvorstadt (Map 2)
Hotel Alfa (☎ 545 95 30, fax 545 95 32 99, Hirtenstrasse 20)* Singles/doubles from €46/61 (shared bath), €72/97 (private bath). The Alfa offers cramped but clean quarters, a bar and courtyard parking (€7.50 per night).

Hotel Amba (☎ 54 51 40, fax 54 51 45 55, e *info@hotel-amba.de, Arnulfstrasse 20)* Singles/doubles from €49/66 (shared bath), from €77/97 (private bath). Just north of the Hauptbahnhof, this place has simple rooms but is clean, well run and perfect for catching an early train.

Andi München City Center (☎ 55 25 56 60, fax 55 25 56 66, Landwehrstrasse 33)* Singles/doubles from €59/77 (shared bath), from €74/89 (private bath). South of the Hauptbahnhof, this hotel has quiet and nicely equipped rooms; prices include breakfast and pleasant banter at the reception desk.

Hotel Mirabell (☎ 549 17 40, fax 550 37 01, e *info@hotelmirabell.de, Landwehr-strasse 42)* Singles/doubles €66/82. A few doors west, behind the ghastly purple facade, the Mirabell has attractive rooms of a high standard, with soundproofed windows, light wood panelling and pleasant wall prints.

Schwabing (Map 3) & Maxvorstadt (Map 4)

Gästehaus Englischer Garten (☎ 383 94 10, fax 38394133, Liebergesellstrasse 8, Schwabing) Singles/doubles €72/77 (shared bath), €94/107 (private bath). This snug pension occupies a graceful old mill with a private garden where you can enjoy breakfast on sunny summer days. Most of the antique-filled rooms have private bath and TV. It's steps away from the Englischer Garten and Kleinhesselhoher See. Reserve rooms as far ahead as possible.

Hotel Montree (☎ 542 71 90, fax 54 27 19 60, e info@hotel-montree.de, Dachauer Strasse 91, Maxvorstadt) Singles/doubles €61/81. This hotel won't win any style awards, but for those wanting a good range of modern amenities at good prices, it's an excellent choice. It's on a busy street, but rooms have soundproof windows and most face towards the garden side. Assets include an underground garage (€5).

Lehel (Map 5)

Hotel Adria (☎ 29 30 81, fax 22 70 15, Liebigstrasse 8a) Singles €82-102, doubles €102-148. This is a pleasant hotel run which is run with efficiency and has a welcoming ambience. Rooms are of a decent size and outfitted with all major accoutrements, including direct-dial phones. If you feel so inclined, you can kick off the day with a champagne breakfast.

Parkhotel im Lehel (☎ 21 10 50, fax 21 10 51 29, e pil@golden-leaf-hotel.de, Unsöldstrasse 10) Singles/doubles from €55/75. Recently taken over by the Golden Leaf chain, this lovely hotel offers a high standard at affordable prices. Rooms are smallish but equipped with top-quality mattresses, cable and pay-TV, direct-dial phone and data port. Special deals are available all the time – just ask.

Hotel Splendid (☎ 29 66 06, fax 291 31 76, e splendid-muc@t-online.de, Maximilianstrasse 54) Singles/doubles from €64/97

(shared bath), from €97/128 (private bath). Relive old-world grandeur at this traditional Bavarian hotel, although the frilly decor of the rooms may not be to everyone's taste. Antiques, heavy rugs and chandeliers complete the look.

Westend (Map 1)

Right near the Theresienwiese, several places offer good value outside the Oktoberfest season.

Hotel Krone (☎ 508 08 00, fax 50 80 80 70, e hotel-krone@gmx.de, Theresienhöhe 8) Singles €76-169, doubles €97-210. An oldie but goodie, the Krone has worn English-style interiors, but is otherwise OK, though perhaps a tad too pricey for what you get.

Hotel Seibel (☎ 540 14 20, fax 54 01 42 99, Theresienhöhe 9) Singles €61-122, doubles €76-184. Next door to the Krone, this one has a pleasant atmosphere, very friendly staff, lovely wrought-iron beds and hardwood furniture. Rooms at the back are quieter, away from the busy thoroughfare out front.

Hotel Petri (☎ 58 10 99, fax 580 86 30, Aindorferstrasse 82) U-Bahn: Laimer Platz. Singles €51-89, doubles €87-112. This is perhaps the best deal in the Westend. Rooms have distinctive antique wooden furniture and a TV, and there's also a garden and a small indoor swimming pool.

Kurpfalz Hotel (☎ 540 98 60, fax 54 09 88 11, Schwanthalerstrasse 121) Tram: No 18 or 19 to Holzapfelstrasse, then 5-minute walk. Singles €46-107, doubles €61-148. Come here for pleasant Bavarian-style rooms, satellite TV, and an Internet terminal for guests.

Hotel Uhland (☎ 54 33 50, fax 54 33 52 50, e Hotel_Uhland@compuserve.com, Uhlandstrasse 1) Singles €64-112, doubles €77-158. One of our enduring favourites is in a lovely late-19th-century villa just east of the Theresienwiese. The rooms reflect the English-speaking owners' attention to detail and are very comfortable (some have a tiny balcony). Assets include an Internet terminal for guests.

Reflecting on the shores of the Hintersee, Upper Bavaria

Gentian on an Alpine meadow

Bavarian hare

The Zugspitzbahn chugs its way to the top of Germany

Rothenburg door

The enchanting grounds of Schloss Linderhof near Oberammergau

Stalls lit up for Nuremberg's world-famous Christkindlesmarkt

Painted dwarf face in Ettal

Distinctive gable of building in Nördlingen, a popular stop along the Romantic Road

A Nördlingen old town gate

Candles burning in Berchtesgaden's cemetery for All Saints Day

PLACES TO STAY – TOP END

If you feel the urge to splurge – or are simply accustomed to the full range of creature comforts – you'll find no shortage of fine hotels in stylish Munich.

Altstadt (Map 2)

Hotel Advokat (☎ *21 63 10, fax 216 31 90,* e *advokathot@aol.com, Baaderstrasse 1, Gärtnerplatzviertel)* Singles €97-148, doubles €118-169. This is Munich's first designer hotel, ensconced in a renovated 1930s apartment block steps away from bars, restaurants and theatres. Wake up for a day of sightseeing in rooms featuring simple but tasteful lighting and furniture designed by owner Kevin Voigt himself.

Bayerischer Hof (☎ *212 00, fax 212 09 06,* e *hbh@compuserve.com, Promenadeplatz 2-6)* Singles €192-228, doubles €261-376. The Bayerischer Hof is one of the grande dames among Munich *caravanserais* and oozes old-world elegance. The lobby bursts with antique furniture and makes for some stellar people-watching (lots of celebrities). It's right behind Marienplatz, has a pool and a snazzy jazz club downstairs (see Entertainment).

Hotel Königshof (☎ *55 13 60, fax 55 13 61 33,* e *koenigshof-muenchen@t-online .de, Karlsplatz 25)* Singles €204-227, doubles €239-342. Luxury is taken very seriously at this classy abode on the edge of the Altstadt, overlooking Karlsplatz. A thorough makeover a few years ago resulted in larger rooms sheathed in appealing hues and furnished in a modern, elegant style. Downstairs is a piano bar and a renowned restaurant with an award-winning chef.

Hotel Mandarin Oriental Munich (☎ *20 09 80, fax 22 25 39,* e *info-momuc@mohg .com, Neuturmstrasse 1)* Singles €280-382, doubles €351-1266. Munich's most expensive hotel was already a favourite with celebrities and the in-crowd before being taken over by the Hong Kong-based Mandarin chain. A boutique hotel in a gorgeously restored neo-Renaissance villa, it's just around the corner from the Hofbräuhaus. Service is polite almost to a fault, with liveried servants wherever you look. Be sure to

check out the rooftop swimming pool. Garage parking and breakfast add €18 and €19, respectively, to your final tally.

Hotel Olympic (☎ *23 18 90, fax 23 18 91 99, Hans-Sachs-Strasse 4, Glockenbachviertel)* Singles €97-133, doubles €118-143. This one is just south of the Altstadt in one of Munich's prettier streets. It has quiet, well-furnished rooms around a picturesque little courtyard. Rates sometimes drop if business is slow.

Kempinski Vier Jahreszeiten München (☎ *212 50, fax 21 25 20 00,* e *reservation .hvj@kempinski.com, Maximilianstrasse 17)* Singles €251-404, doubles €312-465. This illustrious hotel is just east of the Residenz and couples old-world charm with a full range of amenities. Its grand facade features statues of the managers, the four seasons, and the four continents. The rooms don't have as many amenities as you might expect.

Ludwigsvorstadt (Map 2)

Hotel Cristal München (☎ *55 11 10, fax 55 11 19 92, Schwanthalerstrasse 36)* Singles €120-182, doubles €141-189. A bit south of the Hauptbahnhof are two options operating under the Best Western umbrella. We recommend only this one with nice, clean rooms and friendly staff. Prices often drop dramatically at weekends.

Hotel Excelsior (☎ *55 13 70, fax 55 13 71 21,* e *excelsior-muenchen@geisel-hotels .de, Schützenstrasse 11)* Singles €155-168, doubles €193-232. This chic establishment is just a few hundred metres from the Hauptbahnhof, but inside it's a world away: hushed voices, fancy lighting, antique furniture and an atmosphere reminiscent of pre-WWII. It's especially popular with the expense-account crowd, but also draws locals to its exquisite wine bar, the Vinothek Geisel.

Schwabing (Map 3)

Holiday Inn München City-Nord (☎ *38 17 90, fax 38 17 97 61,* e *info@muenchen .holidayinn-queens.de, Leopoldstrasse 194)* Singles €97-332, doubles €112-358. This is a tower hotel built for the 1972 Olympic Games. It has a chic lobby and rooms, and the service is as nice as you'd expect from a high-class hotel chain.

München Park Hilton (☎ *384 50, fax 38 45 25 88, Am Tucherpark 7)* Singles/doubles €233/297. This is a modern 15-storey tower where every room has picture windows overlooking the Englischer Garten. Facilities include a heated outdoor pool, sauna, and a lovely view of the Isar from its terrace restaurant.

Long-Term Rentals

Renting a room in a flat or an entire apartment through a *Mitwohnzentrale* (flat-sharing agency) is an economical option if you intend to stay in Munich for one month or longer. Agencies to try include:

City Mitwohnzentrale (☎ 194 30, fax 59 45 64, **e** muenchen@mwz-muenchen.de, **w** www.mitwohnzentrale.de) Lämmerstrasse 4, Ludwigsvorstadt

Mitwohnzentrale an der Uni (☎ 286 60 60, fax 28 66 06 24, **e** mwz@mwz-munich.de, **w** www.mwz-munich.de) Adalbertstrasse 6, Schwabing

Mitwohnzentrale – Mr. Lodge (☎ 340 82 30, fax 34 08 23 23, **e** mrlodge@mrlodge.de, **w** www.mrlodge.de) Barer Strasse 32, Maxvorstadt

PLACES TO EAT

Munich has a fine selection of restaurants in all price ranges, including some excellent top-end places. Although lunch is usually the main meal in Bavaria, dinner takes on a more prominent role in Munich. One in four residents is a foreigner, which guarantees a large number of ethnic eateries. Most neighbourhoods have a spate of restaurants, so chances are you won't have to go far.

Eateries come and go. This, along with the screaming popularity of many places, means you should try to call ahead to book a table. Otherwise, you may find yourself stuck at the house bar (if there is one) to await a free table.

Unless noted, restaurants listed below serve lunch and dinner daily.

Asian

Ganga (☎ *201 64 65, Baaderstrasse 11, Gärtnerplatzviertel)* Mains €9-16.50, lunches €6. Lunch Mon-Fri, dinner nightly. At this friendly Indian restaurant the curries, Tandoor and vegie dishes are a feast for eyes and palate, while the decor registers a mere '2' on the 'kitsch-o-meter'. Nibble on free papadums while waiting for your food.

Der Kleine Chinese (☎ *202 11 32, Fraunhoferstrasse 35, Gärtnerplatzviertel)* Mains from €6. A good-value option is this place with cheap sit-down meals served in snug quarters lit by surreal egg-shaped lanterns.

Shida (☎ *26 93 36, Klenzestrasse 32, Gärtnerplatzviertel)* Mains €10-15. This intimate Thai place is the size of a shoebox, so be sure to make reservations. The mostly coconut-based curries are aromatic flavour bombs savoured by a stylish but pretty low-key clientele. An interactive alternative: preparing your own dinner on tiny table-top grills.

Gay & Lesbian Accommodation

By law, no hotel may turn away gay couples, though some may pretend to be full, or frown upon homosexual guests. Hotels catering exclusively for gays and lesbians are still very rare in Munich. Both places here are in the Gärtnerplatzviertel.

Deutsche Eiche (☎ *231 16 60, fax 23 11 66 98, Reichenbachstrasse 13)* Singles €64-74, doubles €89-100. This has been a Munich institution for nearly 150 years, and once saved from the wrecking ball by German film director Rainer Fassbinder. Its modern rooms are fully equipped and there's a big sauna and roof terrace.

Pension Eulenspiegel (☎/*fax 26 66 78, Müllerstrasse 43a)* This is a small and cosy guesthouse in a quiet back courtyard close to some of the best nightlife.

Maitoi (☎ *260 52 68, Hans-Sachs-Strasse 10, Glockenbachviertel*) Mains €15-20. This is a very slick, unfussy Japanese restaurant serving respectable sushi as well as cooked dishes. It's pricey but there's usually some promotion or special going on (such as three-course early-bird dinners for €20).

Swagat (☎ *47 08 48 44, Prinzregentenplatz 13, Bogenhausen*) Mains €6.50-15. This Indian contender is ensconced in a former wine cellar. In fine weather, the breezy outdoor terrace is the preferred setting to enjoy the flavour-packed mains streaming from the kitchen.

Cô-Dô (☎ *448 57 97, Lothringer Strasse 7, Haidhausen*) Mains €10-15. Dinner nightly. The decor of this Vietnamese eatery is Zen minimalism at its finest: black-and-white photos on bare walls. More imagination is definitely going into the food, which is first-rate with delicious fragrances and mysterious spices. Service is excellent too, only the portions could be a bit bigger.

Bali Grill (☎ *18 16 66, Albrechtstrasse 39, Neuhausen*) Mains €6-12. Closed Mon. This pan-Asian restaurant was already pulling in customers when the Beatles topped the charts for the first time. Dishes are mostly of Chinese, Vietnamese and Indonesian heritage, making it likely that you'll find your favourite on the extensive menu.

Bavarian & German

Andechser am Dom (☎ *29 84 81, Weinstrasse 7a, Altstadt*) Mains €5-14. A mostly middle-aged, bourgeois crowd hangs out at this traditional restaurant in the shadow of the Frauenkirche, where the kitchen produces all the standards and the bar staff pours lovely monastery beer. The heated, arcaded terrace is a cool spot even in the rain.

Augustiner-Grossgaststätte (☎ *55 19 92 57, Neuhauser Strasse 27, Altstadt*) This place has a less raucous atmosphere than the Hofbräuhaus (not to mention decent food), yet it's a more authentic example of an old-style Munich beer hall.

Bratwurstherzl (☎ *29 51 13, Dreifaltigkeitsplatz 1, Altstadt*) Mains €5-10. Lunch Mon-Sat, dinner Mon-Fri. Cosy panelling and a vaulted brick ceiling form the backdrop of this traditional chow house, where dishes have a Franconian twist. A plate of six Nuremberg sausages is €5, or €7.50 with sauerkraut.

Hundskugel (☎ *26 42 72, Hotterstrasse 18, Altstadt*) Mains €10-17.50. Munich's oldest restaurant, founded in 1440, feels a bit like an old-fashioned doll's house. But it's famous and the food's quite good.

Ratskeller (☎ *219 98 90, Marienplatz 8, Altstadt*) Mains €10-18. No animal is safe from the menu of this vast, cavernous restaurant beneath the historic Rathaus. The quality is dependably high, and service is efficient, if not personable.

Löwenbräukeller (☎ *52 60 21, Nymphenburger Strasse 2, Maxvorstadt*) U-Bahn: U1 to Stiglmaierplatz. Mains €6-11. The less calorically conscious could also try this place, which is usually uncrowded, serves huge portions, and has good service and prices (also see Beer Halls & Gardens in the Entertainment section). Although its name suggests that it's a cellar, you actually have to walk *up* the stairs to get there. The place burnt to a cinder in 1986 but has been so well rebuilt, you won't be able to tell the difference.

Fraunhofer (☎ *26 64 60, Fraunhoferstrasse 9, Gärtnerplatzviertel*) Mains €5-11. Open dinner only. This bustling restaurant is as comfortable as a hug from an old friend. The 'old Bavaria' look (mounted animal heads, portrait of Ludwig II, stucco ceiling) contrasts with the menu, which is loaded with interesting variations of German staples, and the hip, inter-generational crowd.

Wirtshaus in der Au (☎ *448 14 00, Lilienstrasse 51, Haidhausen*) Mains €8-15. Open lunch Sat-Sun, dinner nightly. Night after night, tables fill with youthful patrons hungry for the fresh takes on Bavarian classics served at this unpretentious place. In summer, the action moves to the sidewalk canopied by chestnut trees. It's a short walk east of the Deutsches Museum.

Unionsbräu Haidhausen (☎ *47 76 77, Einsteinstrasse 42, Haidhausen*) Mains €5.50-14. Dried hops dangle from the ceiling of this sophisticated brewery-pub which caters to business types at lunchtime and a more rollicking crew after dark. There's a jazz club in the basement (see Entertainment later in this chapter).

French

Kleinschmidtz (☎ 60 85 18, Fraunhoferstrasse 13, Gärtnerplatzviertel) Mains €15-20, 3-course meal €25-35. Open dinner nightly. Serious foodies flock to this snug eatery where the chef whips up interesting concoctions using choice seasonal ingredients.

Bistro Terrine (☎ 28 17 80, Amalienstrasse 89, Maxvorstadt) Mains €16-26. Open lunch Tues-Fri, dinner Mon-Sat. Fans of classic French cooking will get their fill at this elegant Art Deco bistro. Large mirrors, crisp linens and warm lighting create a soothing ambience. If only the tight table layout allowed for a little more privacy...

Rue des Halles (☎ 48 56 75, Steinstrasse 18, Haidhausen) Mains €18-25. Open dinner only. Attracting a 'Rolls-Royce crowd' is this excellent but expensive French restaurant near the Gasteig. It has a light, modern interior and fairly attentive service. Count on spending about €75 for a three-course meal, including one glass of wine.

International

Münchner Suppenküche (☎ 22 67 82, Schäfflerstrasse 7, Altstadt) Dishes €2.65-5. Open 9am-7pm Mon-Sat, closed Sun. This nicely tiled self-service soupery north of the Frauenkirche also serves chicken casseroles, chilli con carne and other filling snacks.

Atlas (☎ 480 29 97, Innere-Wiener-Strasse 2, Haidhausen) Mains €5-15. Postmodern simplicity creates a no-nonsense backdrop for the global cuisine at this eatery owned by German actress Iris Berben. Munch on Thai curry, lasagne, tuna melt sandwiches and other satisfying concoctions.

Wasserwerk (☎ 48 90 00 20, Wolfgangstrasse 19, Haidhausen) Mains €6.50-14. Open dinner only. Dine on quality international cuisine while seated in a quirky room strewn with ducts, pipes and wheels reflecting the 'waterworks' theme of the restaurant's name.

Café Zauberberg (☎ 18 99 91 78, Hedwigstrasse 14, Neuhausen) Mains €10-16,

lunch special €7. Open lunch Tues-Fri, dinner Tues-Sat. A 10-minute walk east of Rotkreuzplatz, this is an upscale cafe and bar popular for its low-key, tasteful decor, friendly service and consistently splendid global cuisine. Slimmed down German classics, Italian stalwarts and clever Eurasian fusion food are all at home on the inventive menu. The lunch special is a steal.

Italian

Munich's proximity to Italy means that good and relatively inexpensive Italian options abound throughout the city.

Riva (☎ 22 02 40, Im Tal 44, Altstadt) Mains €7-15. The thin-crust pizza is to die for, as they say, and generously laden with tried-and-true toppings like mushrooms and pepperoni or creative variations such as the shrimp-leak-ginger combo. Make reservations, or come before dinner-time to get your fill.

Il Mulino (☎ 523 33 35, Görresstrasse 1, Maxvorstadt) Mains €5-10. In business for more than two decades, this classy little restaurant continually woos back a loyal clientele with delicious pizzas and pasta sauces that pack a punch. In summer, the leafy beer garden fills up quickly. Service is snappy.

La Vecchia Masseria (☎ 550 90 90, Mathildenstrasse 3, Ludwigsvorstadt) Pizzas €4.50-5.50, pastas €4.50-7, 3-course meals from €20. This is one of the best-value places in town and perfect for a romantic evening. The beautiful atmosphere comes with great service and nice touches such as fresh aniseed bread. The beer garden in the courtyard is lovely too.

La Fiorentina (☎ 53 41 85, Goethestrasse 41, Ludwigsvorstadt) Mains €7-10. Closed Sun. This small local hang-out has good pizzas and specials, which change daily, with an emphasis on Tuscan country cooking.

Hippocampus (☎ 47 58 55, Mühlbaurstrasse 5, Haidhausen) Mains €15-25, set menus €30-40. One of Munich's top restaurants, this trendy, upmarket place right near the Prinzregententheater has stylish interior, romantic ambience, celebrity clientele and great food.

Jewish

Jewish cuisine is slowly entering Munich's culinary landscape – at least around the universities – although there's no official kosher restaurant yet. Contact the Jewish community house (☎ 202 40 00) at Reichenbachstrasse 27, if you'd like to know where to find kosher food.

Bagelshop (☎ 271 21 86, Barer Strasse 72, Maxvorstadt) Bagels €1.50-5. The classic lox with cream cheese tops the charts, but other fillings are also available for eating in or takeaway at this little coffeeshop. They also bake respectable muffins, brownies and other US-style goodies.

Bar Mizwah (☎ 30 72 54 25, Fallmerayerstrasse 28, Schwabing) Mains €8-15. This place is a relative newcomer and serves lox on toast, salads, gefilte fish, latkes and other staples of both Eastern European and Middle Eastern Jewish cuisine.

Cohen's (☎ 280 95 45, Theresienstrasse 31, Schwabing) Mains €8.50-12.50. Tucked away in a back courtyard, this brightly lit, modern place serves up big portions of German/Eastern European dishes, such as Königsberger Klopse (veal dumplings in caper sauce) or gefilte fish. The menu changes with the seasons, but the mixed appetiser platter (€9) is always a good choice for the undecided.

Mexican

Tex-Mex has taken Munich by storm, with 'cantinas' popping up all over town. If you know the real thing, you may find the food a bit wimpy in the spice department, but that's just how most Germans like it.

Joe Peña's (☎ 22 64 63, Buttermelcherstrasse 17, Gärtnerplatzviertel) Mains €10-16. Open dinner nightly. This festively decorated restaurant is regarded as Munich's best Tex-Mex place and is often packed to the gills. The food's tasty but prices are overblown. Happy hour runs from 5pm to 8pm (drinks €3.75).

Sausalitos (☎ 28 15 94, Türkenstrasse 50, Schwabing) Mains €9-12. Close to the university, this is the 'in' Mexican place for students. After 8pm, it's full of fashion victims and usually has standing room only.

The menu is stocked with all the standards from burritos to fajitas to nachos, and you can watch it all being prepared in the open kitchen. The margaritas are killer.

Zapata (☎ 166 58 22, Schulstrasse 44, Neuhausen) Mains €8-16. Open dinner nightly. This rustic restaurant pioneered Tex-Mex in Munich and is still packed night after night. It's definitely a bit on the pricey side, but the lively ambience and respectable food compensate for the stretched wallet.

Spanish

El Cortijo (☎ 33 11 16, Feilitzschstrasse 32, Schwabing) Mains €8.50-17.50. Open dinner only. At this classic Spanish restaurant, the cooking is with an accent on seafood and heavy meat dishes. The paella for two costs €22.

Casa de Tapas (☎ 27 31 22 88, Bauerstrasse 2, Schwabing) Tapas from €3, mains €6.50-12. Open lunch Mon-Sat, dinner nightly. The painted ceiling and rustic decor of this convivial tapas bar help to mentally transport you to the Iberian peninsula. The food is solid if not terribly inspired. Cocktails are a mere €3.50 during happy hour from 4pm to 8pm. It's pretty small, so reserve ahead, come early or forget about a table.

Turkish

There's more to Turkish food than the ubiquitous doner kebab and these restaurants are here to prove it.

Diyar (☎ 48 95 04 97, Wörthstrasse 10, Haidhausen) Appetisers €4.50-8, mains €7-16. When the belly dancers arrive, this place turns into party central. But even on less eventful evenings, this unassuming restaurant offers good value and a fun ambience. Try the grilled meats or make a meal of the hot and cold appetisers; there's also a few meatless mains.

Dersim (☎ 123 54 54, Jutastrasse 5, Neuhausen) Mains €7-14. Open dinner only. This place is light years away from the doner stands near the Hauptbahnhof but still affordable. The chef's forte is lamb and the aromas are wonderful as almost everything's bought fresh from the markets.

Pardi (☎ *131850, Volkartstrasse 24, Neuhausen*) Mains €10-19. If you've never had 'real' Turkish food, this is the place to lose your 'virginity'. Complexion-friendly candlelight, a stylish bar and friendly service immediately put you at ease. Lamb is the star of the show here, although the extensive menu has plenty of other options in store.

Vegetarian

As might be expected, your choices among vegetarian eateries are greater in Munich than the rest of Bavaria.

Buxs (☎ *291 95 50, Frauenstrasse 9, Altstadt;* ☎ *28 02 99 40, Amalienstrasse 38, Schwabing*) Dishes €1.75 per 100g. Open 11am-8.30pm Mon-Fri, 11am-3.30pm Sat. Freedom of choice reigns at this self-service buffet serving some 45 different kinds of soups, salads and antipasti. 'Weigh' your appetite carefully, as the final bill adds up quickly.

Prinz Myschkin (☎ *26 55 96, Hackenstrasse 2, Altstadt*) Mains €13-16.50. Closed Sun. Considered by many to be Munich's best vegetarian restaurant, this fancy haunt has an impressive antipasti selection, although the food occasionally gets too creative for its own good. It's also a smart hang-out for wine or coffee.

Ignaz (☎ *271 60 93, Georgenstrasse 67, Maxvorstadt*) Mains under €6. Open 8am-10pm Mon-Sat, 9am-10pm Sun. This is a nonsmoking eatery with vegetable quiches, pastas, soups and salads, plus a few meaty selections, which come in handy in case you're dining with a carnivore. The breakfast buffet for €5.50 is good value but only served from Monday to Friday until 10.30am.

Das Gollier (☎ *50 16 73, Gollierstrasse 83, Westend*) Mains around €9. Open lunch Sun-Fri, dinner nightly. The look is traditional Bavarian, but the food is 20th-century meatless modern. Casseroles, pizzas, crepes and grain dishes all make an appearance on the menu. There's a separate section for nonsmokers and a children's corner as well. The cash-strapped set crowds the place for brunch when you can fill up for a flat €6, and during happy hour between 5pm and 8pm when all dishes cost just €4.50.

Cafes & Bistros

Munich cafes are enticing places for a chat, writing postcards, reading a magazine or simply watching the world on parade. Most are casual eateries attracting people of all ages and lifestyles. The culinary repertoire may be limited to simple hot and cold snacks, although many now also serve more substantial meals. The afternoon *Kaffee und Kuchen* (coffee and cake) is a classic German cafe tradition and a nice way to give your feet a rest from sightseeing.

Cafes usually change identity in a chameleon-like way over the course of a day, starting out as a breakfast place, then offering a small lunch menu and cakes in the afternoon before turning into a restaurant-bar or just a bar at night. In fact, many places listed here would fit just as well into the earlier Restaurant section or the Bars & Pubs section of the Entertainment chapter.

Altstadt & Around (Map 2) There are plenty of cafes in the city centre.

Dukatz im Literaturhaus (☎ *291 96 00, Salvatorplatz 1, Altstadt*) Cafe mains €4.50-12. A stomping ground for the chic and the intellectual – the Dukatz serves up designer sandwiches and latte macchiato in its cafe section (with a nice terrace) and stratospherically priced mains in its restaurant.

Café Glockenspiel (☎ *26 42 56, Marienplatz 28, Altstadt*) Dishes €5-15. On sunny days or tepid nights, the tables on the terrace overlooking Marienplatz are as coveted as tickets to a Madonna concert. The food is Mediterranean and the cocktails excellent. It's the best place to watch the Glockenspiel at eye level.

Stadtcafé (☎ *26 69 49, Stadtmuseum, St-Jakobs-Platz 1, Altstadt*) Meals €5-12. This culture haunt inside the city museum has panorama windows with views of the square and attracts a chatty crowd of students, creative types and museum-goers. The lovely courtyard is a treat in summer.

Forum (☎ *26 88 18, Corneliusstrasse 2, Gärtnerplatzviertel*) Mains €5-11. This is a great place any time of day with good breakfasts, inventive lunches and dinners, and a lively bar scene. The desserts are extra good.

Interview (☎ 202 16 49, *Gärtnerplatz 1, Gärtnerplatzviertel*) Mains €5-14, set lunches €8-12.50. Closed Sun night. This is a pleasant street-side cafe with front-row views of the Theater am Gärtnerplatz. Specialities include grilled fish and creative pasta using seasonal ingredients. Breakfast is served until 5pm.

Schwabing (Map 3) Students equals cafes in Scwabing.

Bobolovsky's (☎ 29 73 63, *Ursulastrasse 10*) This place takes the happy hour concept to new lengths. From Monday to Friday, the Happy Breakfast gets you any breakfast for €5, including hot beverage, from 9am to 4pm. On Happy Monday after 8pm, you can fill up at the all-you-can-eat American buffet for €8.50. During Happy Cocktails (Sunday to Thursday 9pm to 10.30pm) all mixed drinks cost €4.25.

Egger (☎ 39 85 26, *Friedrichstrasse 27*) Mains €6.50-11. Egger is a relaxed place with leafy plants and candles. Portions are generous and two-course lunch specials are just €6 to €8.

News Bar (☎ 28 17 87, *Amalienstrasse 55*) Breakfast €2.50-8, dishes €4.50-9. This trendy cafe has a huge selection of magazines and newspapers for sale.

Vorstadtcafé (☎ 272 06 99, *Türkenstrasse 83*) Mains €8.50-12.50. This is one of many lively student hang-outs where breakfast is served until 4pm and there's an interesting array of moderately priced daily specials.

Bogenhausen & Haidhausen (Map 5) There are a few options east of the city.

Leo's Lounge (☎ 48 95 30 50, *Rosenheimer Strasse 98, Haidhausen*) This is a clone of Bobolovsky's (see Schwabing in the Cafes & Bistros section) with similar specials and friendly ambience.

Cafe Prinzipal (☎ 455 06 50, *Prinzregentenplatz 12, Bogenhausen*) Mains €7.50-17.50. Painted walls (including a wonderful kitsch rendition of Ludwig II in a swan boat) give the place a theatrical feel – appropriate given its location next to the Prinzregententheater. The small menu is heavy on Italian classics.

Café Voilá (☎ 489 16 54, *Wörthstrasse 5, Haidhausen*) Mains €4-9, 2-course lunch under €7.50. The high stucco ceilings, giant mirrors and picture windows make this a great place to watch the world go by. Baguettes, burgers and vegetarian options are all priced fairly. It's also popular for breakfast.

Neuhausen (Map 4) There are some good trendy cafes around Neuhausen.

Café Freiheit (☎ 13 46 86, *Leonrodstrasse 20*) Mains €4-10. This painfully trendy cafe has very good *Milchcafé* (café au lait), served steaming hot in giant bowls, and three eggs with ham for €4.50, but service is terrible.

froh & munter (☎ 18 79 97, *Artilleriestrasse 5*) Dishes €3-8. Near Rotkreuzplatz, this is a welcoming and totally untouristed place to sit and chat. You can munch on snacks, soups and great Spanish-style tapas and wash it down with organically prepared Unertl beer (€3), an excellent Weissbier. The menu changes nightly. Food is served until 11pm and the service is friendly.

Ruffini (☎ 16 11 60, *Orffstrasse 22*) Meals €7-10. In fine weather, consider yourself lucky to snag a seat on this cafe's great rooftop terrace. You'll be joining a casual crowd tucking into substantial breakfasts or delicious Italian salads and pastas made with mostly organic ingredients. There's no table service on the terrace, so you'll have to balance your own tray up a steep staircase.

Student Cafeterias

Student-card holders can fill up for around €2.50 in any of the university *Mensas* (food service 11am to 2pm only). The best one is on Schillerstrasse just north of Pettenkoferstrasse in Ludwigsvorstadt, and there are others at Leopoldstrasse 13a in Schwabing, another at Arcisstrasse 17 in Maxvorstadt, and also at Lothstrasse 13d in Neuhausen.

Snacks & Fast Food

Eating cheaply in Munich is much like anywhere else in Germany: sausages, pizza, burgers and Turkish fast-food are the leaders of the snack pack.

Any *Müller* bakery Stehcafé offers coffee (around €1) and pretzels or bread rolls covered with melted cheese (about €1.50) or with bacon or ham (€1.50 to €2).

Throughout the city, branches of *Vinzenzmurr* have hot buffets and prepared meals; a big lunch – like *Schweinebraten mit Knödel* (roast pork with dumplings) and gravy – can be as low as €4, and hamburgers cost about €2. Some branches even have salad bars.

Ludwigsvorstadt (Map 2) The streets south of the Hauptbahnhof are alive with the smells and sounds of a Turkish bazaar, which explains the area's nickname 'Little Istanbul'.

Kebab Antep (☎ 53 22 36, Schwanthalerstrasse 45, enter from Goethestrasse) Kebabs €2.75. This tiny place makes great kebabs and serves spinach pie and other vegetarian offerings.

Kandil Restaurant (☎ 54 82 82 52, Landwehrstrasse 8) Mains €1.75-7.50. Kandil has a wide selection of full cafeteria-style eats and also does breakfast (from €2.75).

Bayerstrasse has lots of tourist traps, but you can grab a quick bite at the street window of *Pizzeria Ca'doro* at the corner of Senefelder Strasse, where large slices are €1.75 to €4.

Cheap eating is also available in various department stores. Opposite Karlsplatz, on the Kaufhof's ground floor are three good options: a *Müller* bakery, *Nordsee* seafood and *Grillpfanne* for sausages.

Schwabing (Map 4) There are plenty of chances to grab a quick snack in Schwabing.

Reiter Imbiss (Hohenzollernstrasse 24) Meals around €3. This butcher/Imbiss combination is a good source for budget-priced heaps of meaty stuff; there's also a salad bar (€0.90 per 100g).

Wok Man (☎ 39 03 43, Leopoldstrasse 68) Mains €4.25-5.75, buffet €6.50/9.50 small/large plate. It's probably not the best Chinese food you'll ever have, but the selection at this self-service restaurant is impressive and the prices modest. A la carte dishes are prepared in the open kitchen.

Indisches Fast Food (☎ 28 75 51 11, Barer Strasse 46) Mains €5.50-7.50.

Heaped spoonsful of fragrant Basmati rice accompany the tasty Indian standards at this simple eatery near the Neue Pinakothek. Knock €1 off all dishes for takeaway.

Self-Catering

Schneider's Feinbäckerei (☎ 26 47 44, Volkartstrasse 48, Neuhausen) Close to the hostel Jugendherberge München, this tiny place is one of Munich's best bakeries, making scrumptious rolls, loaves and cakes.

Supermarkets large and small abound throughout the city (the Turkish ones often have some of the best prices for fruit and vegetables). *Norma* and *Aldi* supermarkets are the cheapest chains and good for buying staples. For a last-minute stock-up before your train leaves, hit *Tengelmann* at Bayerstrasse 5, just opposite the Hauptbahnhof.

The *supermarket* in the basement of the Kaufhof department store opposite Karlsplatz has a far more upmarket selection, plus goodies like fresh mozzarella, superb sliced meats and cheeses, and a good bakery.

Several stores cater for Munich's large expat population, including *Australia Service* (☎ 18 60 51, Dachauer Strasse 103, Neuhausen), which has everything from Vegemite to Fosters to Akubra hats and Lonely Planet *Australia* guides. For British stuff, head to *English Shop (☎ 48 84 00, Franziskanerstrasse 14, Haidhausen)*, while homesick Americans can stock up on things such as Aunt Jemima syrup, baking soda and cooking spray at *G&A Grocery Store (☎ 201 70 31, Baaderstrasse 65, Gärtnerplatzviertel)*.

Viktualienmarkt At Viktualienmarkt, just south of Marienplatz, deep-pocketed travellers can put together a gourmet picnic of breads, cheeses and salad to take off to a beer garden or the Englischer Garten. Prices are high, so choose carefully. Make sure you figure out the price before buying, and don't be afraid to move on to another stall.

Nordsee has good, well-priced seafood. *Thoma* is a wonderful cheese-and-wine shop. Behind it you'll find the *Juice Bar*, with great fruity concoctions from €1.50 to €3.50. Right next to the maypole, look for the *Oliven & Essiggurken* stand, with olives and pickles plus marinated garlic and loads more. More prosperous picnickers might prefer the legendary *Alois Dallmayr*, one of the world's greatest (and priciest) delicatessens, with an amazing range of exotic foods imported from every corner of the earth.

ENTERTAINMENT

Munich's nightlife is not as raucous as Hamburg's or as cutting-edge as Berlin's, but there's enough going on to keep you busy. Fans of highbrow pursuits have numerous theatres, renowned opera and ballet companies, four major orchestras and several jazz bars to steer towards after dark.

Those bent on more earthy entertainment can look forward to pubs and bars of all sorts and, of course, beer halls and, in summer, beer gardens. Most of these are casual and convivial places, although some of the more chichi bars may frown upon jeans and tennis shoes. Definitely dress to kill to get into nightclubs. Most employ dim doorstaff who are notoriously rude and 'discerning' and intent on keeping out everyone not sufficiently rich, beautiful or *schicki-micki*.

Listings

If you have even rudimentary German, one of the best sources of information is the free *in München*, available at bars, restaurants, ticket outlets and other venues. The yellow, city-published monthly *München im...* (€1.55) is an excellent A-to-Z listing of almost everything the city has to offer – museum exhibitions, festivals, theatre and other events.

A new guide (sold at newsstands) is the monthly *Go* (€1), which includes listings of bars, discos, clubs, concerts and other nightlife. Bigger newsstands and shops sell *Munich Found* (€2.25), an English-language city magazine with somewhat useful listings.

Tickets

Tickets to entertainment and sports events are available at official ticket outlets *(Kartenvorverkauf)* throughout the city. Try the kiosks in the U-Bahn stations Karlsplatz (☎ 54 50 60 60) or Marienplatz (☎ 26 46 40) or München Ticket (☎ 54 81 81 81) in the Neues Rathaus next to the tourist office.

Beer Halls & Gardens

Many people go to beer halls and gardens to drink rather than to eat – food, given the usually low quality, tends to be a secondary consideration.

Most of the places listed here are gardens or gardens-cum-restaurants; almost all open from 10am to at least 10pm daily in the warmer months.

Unless noted, beer gardens listed here allow you to bring your own food, although you'll have to buy their drinks (see Self-Catering in the Places to Eat section for suggestions on where to stock up). A few have live music (from oompah to Dixieland) but the main thing is being outside with the beer.

Beer costs €5 to €6.50 per litre. For a primer on food options at beer halls and gardens, see the boxed text 'And There's Food, Too' in the Facts for the Visitor chapter.

Altstadt (Map 2) Beer halls are all the go in the Altstadt.

Hofbräuhaus (☎ 22 16 76, Am Platzl 9) This is certainly the best known and most celebrated beer hall, and a *de rigeur* pilgrimage for beer lovers from Tokyo to Texas to Timbuktu. A live band plays Bavarian folk music much of the day, but the sideshow of tipsy tourists making complete fools of themselves may prove even more entertaining. To get away from the madness, head for the secluded beer garden.

Viktualienmarkt (☎ 29 75 45, Viktualienmarkt 6) A Munich institution since 1807, this is a wonderful place right in the centre.

Braunauer Hof (☎ 22 36 13, Frauenstrasse 42) Near the Isartor, this traditional Bavarian inn also has a little-known beer garden tucked away in a snug courtyard. The decor seems to be somebody's vision of 'paradise on earth': picture a hedge maze, gurgling fountains, plaster statues and a preposterous mural of Moses possibly inspired by Cecil B DeMille's *Ten Commandments*. Truly a campy classic.

Schwabing (Map 3) The Englischer Garten provides a perfect setting for beer gardens.

Chinesischer Turm (☎ *383 87 30, Englischer Garten 3)* This is one of Munich's oldest (since 1791) and most popular beer gardens and – with 7000 seats – also one of the largest. A motley mix of students, businessfolk, tourists, families and junkies clump around the Chinese pagoda, entertained by what has to be the world's drunkest oompah band. All varieties of Löwenbräu are on tap.

Hirschau (☎ *36 99 42, Gysslingstrasse 15)* U-Bahn: U6 to Dietlindenstrasse, then 15-minute walk. This beer garden with 1400 seats is less crowded, though a smugger crowd abounds. Spaten and Franziskaner are on tap.

Seehaus (☎ *381 61 30, Kleinhesselohe 3)* Be prepared for a competitive jostle with the schicki-micki crowd and tourists for space in this hugely popular beer garden. It's right on the Kleinhesseloher See with dreamy views of the lake and the park. Paulaner is the featured libation.

Elsewhere around Town Beer halls get bigger and bigger outside the city centre.

Löwenbräukeller (☎ *52 60 21, Nymphenburger Strasse 2, Maxvorstadt)* U-Bahn: U1 to Stiglmaierplatz. This place deserves another mention here (also see Places to Eat) for its earthy locals, a relative dearth of tourists and a grand main hall (which seats 2000), with regular Bavarian music and heel-slapping dances on stage. The beer garden is a playground for 1800 quaffing the great variety of Löwenbräu beers available.

Augustiner Keller (☎ *59 43 93, Arnulfstrasse 52, Ludwigsvorstadt)* This large and shady beer garden, about 500m west of the Hauptbahnhof, has a laid-back atmosphere ideal for recreational drinking. It's one of the oldest and most popular beer gardens in Munich with space for 5000 and a playground for children. The food's not great and service can be on the rude side, but the beer is some of the best and there's no oompah music.

Taxisgarten (☎ *15 68 27, Taxisstrasse 12, Neuhausen)* Bus: No 177 from Rotkreuzplatz to Klugstrasse. North of Rotkreuzplatz, this is another peaceful place mainly frequented by local families. Freshly baked pretzels, homemade Obatzda and other beer garden goodies go down especially well with mugs of Franziskaner and Spaten.

Hirschgarten (☎ *17 25 91, Hirschgartenallee 1, Nymphenburg)* S-Bahn: Laim. We absolutely love the Hirschgarten, just south of Schloss Nymphenburg, which is packed with locals. The shady garden is the largest in town with space for up to 8000 revellers. Watch for the deer that wander in just on the other side of the chain-link fence.

Pubs & Bars

Nachtcafé (☎ *59 59 00, Maximiliansplatz 5, Altstadt)* Open until 6am daily. This is a classic Munich mainstay with bouncers that won't let you in unless you're *très chic*, female and dressed in a tight black dress, or throwing euros around. Once inside, you'll be able to toast the sunrise with a perfectly mixed caipirinha.

Master's Home (☎ *22 99 09, Frauenstrasse 11, Altstadt)* This is a wonderfully quirky cellar just east of the Viktualienmarkt. The off-centre decor timewarps you back to the colonial era – antique furnishings, plenty of knick-knacks and oddities such as a room built around a bathtub.

Schumann's (☎ *22 90 60, Maximilianstrasse 35, Altstadt)* The high celebrity quotient certainly helps, but it's really the consistently honest drinks that have kept this American-style bar hopping all these years. Sure, the 'kissie-kissie' crowd can be annoying, but proprietor Charles Schumann makes sure that even 'nobodies' don't have to feel left out.

Atzinger (☎ *28 28 80, Schellingstrasse 9, Maxvorstadt)* Generations of students have downed beer and chowed on simple but satisfying fare at this classic haunt with its wood panelling and framed poster art.

Scalar Lounge (☎ *21 57 96 36, Seitzstrasse 12, Lehel)* Chrome and wood combine with vibrant aquariums in this retro lounge. Drinks are pretty good and the stylish crowd provides a serious serving of eye candy.

Baader Café (☎ *201 06 38, Baaderstrasse 47, Gärtnerplatzviertel)* This is something of a literary think-and-drink place with a big crowd of regulars and even the occasional celebrity. The Sunday brunch is among the best in town.

Klenze 17 *(☎ 228 57 95, Klenzestrasse 17, Gärtnerplatzviertel)* Whiskey fans, listen up: some three dozen varieties of malted madness (€4 to €11) are on the menu at this lively neighbourhood bastion. Nice touch: the free candy bowl by the door.

Ksar *(☎ 26 40 38, Müllerstrasse 31, Glockenbachviertel)* This is a bar with perfect pitch: a hip and happening crowd, bartenders with generous elbows and cool music. Definitely a keeper.

Pacific Times *(☎ 20 23 94 70, Baaderstrasse 28, Gärtnerplatzviertel)* You'd need stamina, time and deep pockets to drink yourself through the 64-page cocktail and whiskey menu. Named 'Best Bar of 1999' by that arbiter of taste, *Playboy* magazine, it often crawls with people who are either way too thin or way too rich.

Alter Simpl *(☎ 272 30 83, Türkenstrasse 57, Schwabing)* Good jazz and a reasonable menu (€4 to €12.50) distinguish this watering hole from the rest. Thomas Mann and Hermann Hesse used to hang out here, and the place retains an alternative feel.

Lardy *(☎ 34 49 49, Leopoldstrasse 49, Schwabing)* If you get past the goon patrol at the door, you'll find a snooty cellar bar where it's all about sipping cocktails and checking out the scene (and being checked out). The Spanish food is surprisingly good, though.

Shamrock *(☎ 33 10 81, Trautenwolfstrasse 6, Schwabing)* This place celebrates Irish-German friendship by serving delectable brews from both countries. There's usually live music after 9pm, otherwise you could make new friends playing darts or monitoring the soccer matches.

Julep's *(☎ 448 00 44, Breisacherstrasse 18, Haidhausen)* A scene favourite, this place comes with a cocktail menu as long and confusing as a Dostoyevsky novel. Happy hour is from 5pm to 8pm and all night Sunday.

Dreigroschenkeller *(☎ 489 02 90, Lilienstrasse 2, Haidhausen)* At this cosy and labyrinthine cellar pub all rooms are themed after Bertolt Brecht's *The Threepenny Opera*, ranging from a prison cell to a red

satiny salon. Besides great beer and wine, there's an extensive food menu (mostly hearty German stuff).

Kreitmayr's *(☎ 448 91 40, Kreittmayrstrasse, Neuhausen)* Just east of Erzgiessereistrasse, this is a real barcrawler's bar, with pub grub, strong drinks, a pool table, darts and pinball, and live music on Thursday (from Irish folk to jazz). It also has a beer garden in summer.

Dance Clubs

Cover charges for discos depend on the day but average between €2.50 and €10.

Atomic Cafe *(☎ 228 30 52, Neuturmstrasse 5, Altstadt)* Lava lamps and sofas recall the 1960s but the legions of twisting and gyrating twenty-somethings are definitely 'New Millennium'.

Parkcafé *(☎ 59 86 79, Sophienstrasse 7, Ludwigsvorstadt)* Under new ownership, this place is once again in favour among Munich trendoids. Beautiful scenesters draped upon comfy sofas sip potent martinis or check out the action on the dance floor. DJs keep the crowd hopping with everything from Europop to house to acid.

P1 *(☎ 29 42 52, Prinzregentenstrasse 1, Schwabing)* P1 is still *the* place where the 'scene' comes to be 'seen', the kind of place that boils Munich down to its most superficial elements. Expect extremely choosy and effective bouncers, snooty staff and the occasional celebrity. Dress to the nines and you may stand a chance to party with the in-crowd.

Skyline *(☎ 33 31 31, Leopoldstrasse 82, Schwabing)* Party with soul and hip hop on the rooftop of the Hertie department store. It's right next to the Münchener Freiheit U-Bahn station.

Kunstpark Ost *(☎ 49 00 27 30, Grafinger Strasse 6, Haidhausen)* Officially set to close in 2003, the Kunstpark Ost for now remains a driving force in Munich's nightlife. It's a multiple disco-restaurant-bar-cinema complex behind the Ostbahnhof in a former potato-processing factory. The look is pure grungeville but it's swarmingly popular. Watch your valuables in the side alleys, where some very unsavoury characters hang out. Discos at Kunstpark Ost often host live and sometimes very large concerts. Places include **Bongo Bar** (☎ *49 00 12 60*), in an over-the-top 1920s mirrored hall with go-go dancers and kitsch extraordinaire; **Milch + Bar Faltenbacher** (☎ *49 00 35 17*), a cruising ground for a leathery twenty-something crowd; and the enormous and more mainstream **Babylon** (☎ *450 69 20*), attracting big-name concerts and 'parties with thousands' on weekends. Friday night is 'Fruit of the Room', with 1970s and 1980s stuff and *Schlager* (romantic German pop songs).

Muffathalle (☎ *45 87 50 75, Zellstrasse 4, Haidhausen*) This is another large complex which hosts concerts and, in summer, an open-air disco on Friday with drum 'n' bass, acid jazz and hip hop. It's always crowded, so expect long queues.

Backstage (☎ *18 33 30, Helmholzstrasse 18, Neuhausen*) Less pretentious, this concert venue and disco offers crossover, psychedelic, hip hop, trash and other freaky music.

Nachtwerk (☎ *578 38 00, Landsberger Strasse 185, Laim*) West of the Westend in the district of Laim is this place with middle-of-the-road house and dance-chart music for a predominantly teenaged crowd.

Gay & Lesbian Munich

It is estimated that about 100,000 gays and lesbians call Munich home. Much of the nightlife is located in the so-called 'Bermuda Triangle' formed by Sendlinger Tor, Gärtnerplatz and the Isartor.

Listings & Information Information and support for gay men and lesbians is available through Schwules Kommunikations-und Kulturzentrum, dubbed 'the Sub' (information ☎ 260 30 56, counselling ☎ 194 46), at Müllerstrasse 43. It's open 7pm to 11pm daily (counselling 7pm to 10pm Monday to Friday). LeTra/Lesbentelefon (☎ 725 42 72), Angertorstrasse 3, caters specifically for lesbians and is open 2.30pm to 5pm Monday & Wednesday, 10.30am to 1pm Tuesday, 6pm to 2pm Thursday. Both places are in the Glockenbachviertel.

An excellent free guide to the city's gay and lesbian scene is the handy bilingual *Our Munich*, published monthly. *Sergej* is a magazine-sized German-only freebie.

Bars & Cafes Unless noted, all places listed below are in the 'Bermuda Triangle'.

Morizz (☎ *201 67 76, Klenzestrasse 43*) There's great service, good food and cocktails at the mirror-heavy Morizz, which looks a lot like an Art Deco Paris bar. It's very quiet early in the night with lots of theatre types from Gärtnerplatz, but gets rowdier as the night wears on.

Deutsche Eiche (☎ *231 16 60, Reichenbachstrasse 13*) Once film-maker Rainer Werner Fassbinder's favourite hang-out, this place still packs in a mixed crowd with its comfort food and fast service.

Iwan (☎ *55 49 33, Josephspitalstrasse 15, Altstadt*) Iwan began as an *über-chic* place but has since 'democratised' its clientele. The two floors host a motley mix of lesbigays and heteros of all ages. In summer, the action moves to the nice outside terrace.

Bei Carla (☎ *22 79 01, Buttermel herstrasse 9*) Though mostly lesbian, this bar gets a good mixed crowd, both in terms of gender and age, including lots of regulars. If you get the munchies, a small menu of snack foods should tide you over.

Inge's Karotte (☎ *201 06 69, Baaderstrasse 13*) This is Munich's oldest lesbian pub, although they've been trying to get more (gay) men through the door as well. It's similar to Carla, and also has some snacks.

Ochsengarten (☎ *26 64 46, Müllerstrasse 47*) Munich's first leather bar has a forbidding entrance, rustic interior, lots of boots hanging from the ceiling and a 30- to 40-year-old crowd.

Cafe Glück (☎ *201 16 73, Palmstrasse 4*) Hosts Adrian and Alex have created a living-room ambience that makes everyone feel welcome. The food ain't bad either.

Dance Clubs There are plenty of options for the dancers.

New York (☎ *59 10 56, Sonnenstrasse 25, Altstadt*) Open from 11pm daily. It's 'raining men' at this posing, preening and cruising club where nonstop high-energy dance music with laser shows creates an electric party atmosphere. There's a bar on the ground floor.

Soul City (☎ *59 52 72, Maximiliansplatz 5, Altstadt*) Open from 6pm Tues-Wed, from 10pm Thur-Sat. There's a bar and cafe on the 1st floor, while the second level has a disco and dancefloor with a young and mixed crowd. Friday and Saturday, though, men rule.

Fortuna Musikbar (☎ *55 40 70, Maximiliansplatz 5, Altstadt*) Open from 10pm Thur-Sat. This place is a popular lesbian disco and live music venue. Gay men are welcome as well.

The Stud (☎ *260 84 03, Thalkirchner Strasse 2*) Open Thur-Sun. This is a Levi's and leather place with a dark, coal-mine-like interior and lots of butch guys with no hair. The clientele is gay and lesbian (in fact, they're always looking for more lesbians, so if that fits, head on over). On Sunday it's men only.

Live Music

Rock Large rock concerts are staged at Olympiapark. Most other rock venues are also listed in Discos & Clubs, including the **Muffathalle**, which does jazz, salsa, world music and other concerts as well; **Nachtwerk Club** and **Babylon** at Kunstpark Ost.

Schlachthof (☎ *76 54 48, Zenettistrasse 9*) U-Bahn: Poccistrasse. There are concerts held regularly at this vast venue, right in front of a huge abattoir complex. It also hosts a regular TV show called 'Live aus dem Schlachthof' with Marc Owen, and comedy nights. It attracts a thirty-something crowd.

Jazz Munich has a very hot jazz scene with plenty of possibilities.

Night Club (☎ *212 09 94, Promenadeplatz 2-6, Altstadt*) You can go a bit more upmarket with this club at the Hotel Bayerischer Hof, which has regular jazz as well as reggae, blues and gospel.

Brunnenhof der Residenz (☎ *93 60 93, Residenzstrasse 1, Altstadt*) This snazzy spot for open-air concerts hosts a broad range of concerts, including rock, jazz, swing, classical and opera.

Mister B's (☎ *53 49 01, Herzog-Heinrich-Strasse 38, Ludwigsvorstadt*) This is Munich's smallest jazz club, just west of Goetheplatz, with performances from Thursday to Saturday.

Café am Beethovenplatz (☎ *54 40 43 48, Goethestrasse 51, Ludwigsvorstadt*) This cafe has jazz or classical music nightly at 8pm and a jazz brunch on Sunday.

Jazzclub Unterfahrt im Einstein (☎ *448 27 94, Einsteinstrasse 42, Haidhausen*) This is perhaps the best-known jazz place in town with live music from 9pm and open jam sessions on Sunday night.

Waldwirtschaft Grosshesselohe (☎ *79 50 88, Georg-Kalb-Strasse 3, Grosshesselohe*) In a southern suburb, this is a popular beer garden known for some mean Dixieland and other jazz played daily to the consternation of local residents.

Classical Music & Opera Several major venues stage classical concerts.

Nationaltheater (*box office* ☎ *21 85 19 20,* e *tickets@st-oper.bayern.de, Max-Joseph-Platz 2, Altstadt*) Box office open 10am-6pm Mon-Fri, 10am-1pm Sat. The Bayerische Staatsoper (Bavarian State Opera) performs at this historic place, which is also the site of many cultural events, including the opera festival in July. You can buy tickets at regular outlets or at the box office.

Staatstheater am Gärtnerplatz (*box office* ☎ *21 85 19 60,* e *tickets@st-gaertner .bayern.de, Gärtnerplatz 3, Gärtnerplatzviertel*) This theatre occasionally has classical concerts, but opera, operetta, jazz, ballet and musicals are also mainstays of its entertainment menu.

Philharmonie im Gasteig (☎ *48 09 80, Rosenheimer Strasse 5, Haidhausen*) Munich's premier venue for classical concerts has one large and three smaller stages. The renowned Münchener Philharmoniker play here.

Funkhaus (☎ *55 80 80, Rundfunkplatz 1, Ludwigsvorstadt*) The Bayerischer Rundfunk maintains its own symphony orchestra, whose repertoire concentrates on works by Mozart, Tchaikovsky, Gershwin and other more easy-going and accessible composers.

Concerts also take place in the Prinzregententheater (see Theatres, later), in the Circus Krone building (see Children's Theatre) when the circus is on tour, in the Herkulessaal in the Residenz and at various churches around town.

Cinemas

Check any listings publication for show information. *Amerika Haus* and the *British Council* (see Cultural Centres in the Information section) both show undubbed films, as do the following movie theatres:

Filmmuseum (☎ 23 32 23 48) St-Jakobs-Platz 1, Altstadt

Atelier (☎ 59 19 18) Sonnenstrasse 12, Ludwigsvorstadt

Atlantis (☎ 55 51 52) Schwanthalerstrasse 2, Ludwigsvorstadt

Museum-Lichtspiele (☎ 48 24 03) Lilienstrasse 2, Haidhausen

Cinema (☎ 55 52 55) Nymphenburger Strasse 31, Neuhausen

Theatre

Munich has a lively theatre scene, including several subsidised state and municipal companies. Tickets usually go on sale two weeks before the performance and often sell out.

Bayerisches Staatsschauspiel (tickets ☎ 21 85 19 40) Bavaria's leading ensemble is known for its classical repertoire from Shakespeare to Ibsen. It performs at three venues: the Residenztheater at Max-Joseph-Platz 1; the intimate rococo Cuvilliés Theater, also within the Residenz; and the Theater im Marstall on Marstallplatz just east of the Residenz.

Münchener Kammerspiele (☎ 23 33 70 00, Leonrodplatz, Dachauer Strasse 114, Neuhausen) This theatre stages serious drama by German playwrights or works translated into German. The theatre's *Werkraum* (workshop) stage specialises in experimental and offbeat works. The box office is at Maximilianstrasse 26–28, Altstadt.

Kleine Komödie am Max II (☎ 22 18 59, Maximilianstrasse 47, Lehel) Light-hearted comedy is the main theatrical fare in this theatre. Good German skills (better yet, Bavarian skills) are definitely required.

Deutsches Theater (☎ 55 23 44 44, Schwanthalerstrasse 13, Ludwigsvorstadt) This is Munich's answer to London's West End or New York's Broadway: touring roadshows (usually popular musicals such as *Beauty and the Beast*) are performed here.

Prinzregententheater (☎ 21 85 29 59, Prinzregentenplatz 12, Bogenhausen) This historic theatre is a large multi-use venue, where the program ranges from opera and ballet to flamenco and classical concerts.

*Kulturzentrum Gasteig (☎ 48 09 80, *e* zentral@gasteig.de, Rosenheimer Strasse 5, Haidhausen)* This is a major cultural centre with theatre, classical music and other special events in its several halls. Theatre performances take place either in the Carl-Orff-Saal or the intimate Black Box.

English-Language Theatre Munich has several English-language troupes performing at various venues, including the *Amerika Haus* (see Cultural Centres earlier in this chapter). The *American Drama Group Europe* does mostly traditional fare like *Pygmalion*, while *The International Outcast Theatre Group* is known for its unconventional and often provocative productions with a cross-cultural bent. The newest kid on the block is the *Entity Theatre Workshop* with an offbeat, improvisational edge. Check the listings magazines for upcoming performances.

Children's Theatre The *Münchner Marionettentheater (☎ 26 57 12, Blumenstrasse 32, Glockenbachviertel)* is the main venue for puppet theatre.

Circus Krone (☎ 545 80 00, Zirkus-Krone-Strasse 1–6, Neuhausen) Performances Christmas-Apr. This famous circus with classic clown acts, wild animals like elephants and tigers, and trapeze artists is a big hit – and not just with children.

Münchner Theater für Kinder (☎ 59 38 58, Dachauer Strasse 46, Maxvorstadt) Performances (including puppet shows) are staged here year round.

Soccer Munich's two premier national league teams, the FC Bayern and the TSV

1860 München, both play at the Olympia-stadion. For FC Bayern tickets (€23 to €40), call ☎ 69 93 13 33 or order on the Net at www.fcbayern.de. Tickets for 1860 games (€8 to €40) may be ordered by calling ☎ 01805-60 18 60 or online at W www.tsv1860.de.

SHOPPING
The first stop for most shoppers is the central pedestrian zone in Munich's Altstadt, comprised of Kaufinger Strasse, Neuhauser Strasse and the area around Marienplatz. Here the mainstream department, clothing and shoe stores are located. International designer and jewellery boutiques – Cartier, Gucci, Jil Sander, Armani, Kenzo etc – cluster on Maximilianstrasse and Brienner Strasse. Im Tal and other streets around Viktualienmarkt are packed with intriguing antique, decorating and speciality shops.

Outside the Altstadt, especially in Schwabing and Haidhausen, you'll find that the shops (and clientele) are decidedly more offbeat, with some very good deals. In Schwabing, Schellingstrasse, Türkenstrasse and Hohenzollernstrasse have quirky boutiques, galleries, bookstores and import shops; in Haidhausen, the area between Wiener Platz and Rosenheimer Strasse has some marvellous boutiques and hole-in-the-wall shops that make for great browsing.

Munich shopping hours are 9am to 8pm Monday to Friday and from 10am to 4pm Saturday.

Flea Markets
Munich has several excellent flea markets, where you can find unique treasure without robbing your bank account. Show up early and be willing to haggle.

Containerbahnhof Open 7am-6pm Fri-Sat. Just west of the Hauptbahnhof at the corner of Arnulfstrasse and Hackerbrücke in an old freight depot and has plenty of electronics, clothes and fresh produce.

Kunstpark Ost Open 9am-6pm Fri, 7am-6pm Sat. Set in the nightlife complex at Grafingerstrasse 6 in Haidhausen, this market has lots of cool retro stuff from the 1950s and 1960s.

Alter Flughafen Riem Open 6am-4pm Sat; S-Bahn: S6 to Riem, then bus No 91 to Flohmarkt Riem. You'll have to travel to the 'burbs to browse the tables here, but you'll be rewarded with good prices as most vendors are just regular private folks cleaning out their closets.

The ***Auer Dult***, a huge flea market on Mariahilfplatz in Haidhausen, has great buys and takes place during the last weeks of April, July and October.

Bavarian Stuff
Bavarian dress is the most distinctive of traditional German clothing.

Loden-Frey (☎ 21 03 90, Maffeistrasse 5–7, Altstadt) This is a specialist department store which stocks a wide range of Bavarian wear. Expect to pay at least €200 for a good leather jacket, lederhosen or a women's *dirndl* dress.

The outlet store, ***Loden-Frey Discount*** (☎ 149 00 80, Triebstrasse 36–38), knocks up to 40% off the normal price, but it's inconveniently located north of Olympiapark (U3 to Olympiazentrum, then bus No 41 to Triebstrasse).

Wallach (☎ 22 08 71, Residenzstrasse 3, Altstadt) Come here for traditional dress (especially nice women's stuff with embroidery) as well as porcelain mugs, bedclothes and other household goods.

Holareidulijö (☎ 271 77 45, Schellingstrasse 81, Maxvorstadt) The quirky name is a phonetic yodel, appropriate for this store, which carries pre-loved lederhosen and other folkwear in good condition.

Beer steins and *Mass* glasses are available at all the department stores, as well as from the beer halls themselves.

GETTING THERE & AWAY
Air
Munich's Franz-Josef Strauss airport (general ☎ 975 00, flight inquiries ☎ 97 52 13 13) is second in importance only to Frankfurt for international and domestic flights. The main carrier is Lufthansa (☎ 01803-80 38 03), which has an in-town office at Lenbachplatz 1 near Karlsplatz. Also see the Getting There & Away chapter.

International airlines serving Munich's airport include:

Air France ☎ 97 59 11 00
Alitalia ☎ 97 59 11 50
British Airways/Deutsche BA ☎ 97 59 13 20
Delta Air Lines ☎ 97 59 16 20
Eurowings ☎ 97 59 23 50
Finnair ☎ 01803-34 66 24
Sabena ☎ 97 59 25 20
Scandinavian Airlines (SAS) ☎ 01803-80 38 03
United Airlines ☎ 01803-80 38 03
Virgin Express ☎ 97 59 21 03

Train

Munich is a major train hub with rapid connections at least every two hours to all major cities in Bavaria and other parts of Germany, as well as frequent but usually nondirect services to European cities such as Vienna (5½ hours); Prague (seven hours) and Zürich (six hours).

There are direct InterCity Express (ICE) train connections to Nuremberg (€38, 1¾ hours) and Frankfurt (€75.60, 3½ hours) and regional trains to Regensburg (€19.20, 1½ hours).

Prague extension passes to your rail pass are sold in the Reisezentrum at the Hauptbahnhof, or through EurAide (see Information earlier in this chapter).

Bus

For more details about bus services, see the Getting There & Away chapter.

Munich doesn't really have a big central bus station. Eurolines buses serving many European cities leave from the huge Park & Ride car park in the northern suburb of Fröttmaning, a ride on the U6 away.

Other buses leave from Arnulfstrasse on the northern side of the Hauptbahnhof. These include the Munich-Berlin service offered by BerlinLinienBus (☎ 030-861 93 31 in Berlin, ℮ info@berlinlinienbus.de), which runs daily via Ingolstadt, Nuremberg, Bayreuth and Leipzig (nine hours).

Munich is also a stop for Busabout, a UK-based bus company geared towards backpackers. Buses pick up from the Euro Youth Hostel or Camping Thalkirchen (see Places to Stay).

Munich is also linked to the Europabus travelling along the Romantic Road to Würzburg from April to October. Northbound buses leave from Munich at 9am daily from Arnulfstrasse. Tickets are sold through Deutsche Touring (☎ 545 87 00) near platform No 26 off Arnulfstrasse on the northern side of the Hauptbahnhof. For full details, see the boxed text 'The Romantische Strasse' in the Franconia chapter.

Car & Motorcycle

Munich has autobahns radiating on all sides. Take the A9 to Nuremberg, the A92/A3 to Passau, the A8 to Salzburg, the A95 to Garmisch-Partenkirchen and the A8 to Ulm or Stuttgart.

All major car-rental companies have offices at the airport. Sixt (Budget), Hertz, Avis and Europcar have counters on the second level of the Hauptbahnhof. An independent car-rental company with good rates is Allround (☎ 723 83 83, ℮ info@allround rent.de), Boschetsriederstrasse 12, whose smallest car rents for €33 per day, including 300km, 16% VAT and insurance. It's located near the Jugendgästehaus in southern Munich (U3 to Obersendling, left on Tölzer Strasse, then a right on Boschetsriederstrasse).

Ride Services

For shared rides, contact the ADM-Mitfahrzentrale (☎ 194 40), near the Hauptbahnhof at Lämmerstrasse 4. Sample fares (including commission) are: Vienna €22, Berlin €35, €39, Paris €39, Prague €35 and Warsaw €45. The CityNetz Mitfahr-Zentrale Känguruh (☎ 194 44), at Adalbertstrasse 10–12 in Schwabing, arranges lifts for women with female drivers.

GETTING AROUND

Central Munich is compact enough for exploring on foot. In order to get to the outer districts, make use of the efficient public transportation system.

To/From the Airport

Munich's Flughafen Franz-Josef Strauss, about 45km north-east of the city, is connected to the Hauptbahnhof by the S1

Schnellbahn-Netzplan

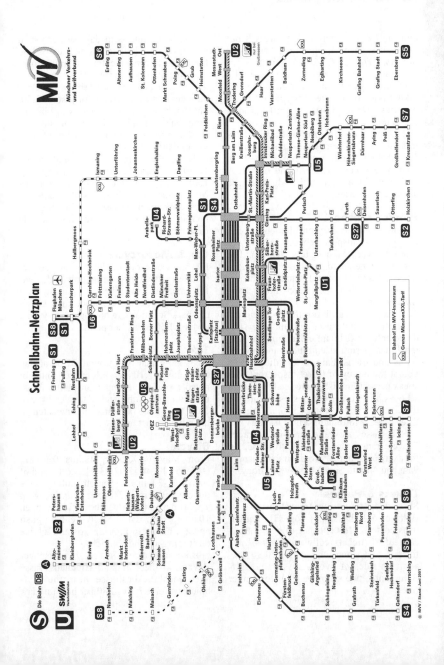

© MVV / Stand: Juni 2001

and the S8. One-way tickets are €8 but you can save by using eight strips of a *Streifenkarte* for €7.20. A day pass for €9 might also come in handy (see Public Transport later in this section). The trip takes about 40 minutes and runs every 20 minutes from 3.30am until around 12.30am.

The Lufthansa Airport Bus travels at 20-minute intervals from Arnulfstrasse near the Hauptbahnhof (one way/return €9/14.50, 45 minutes) between 5.10am and 7.50pm. A taxi from the airport to the Altstadt costs about €45 to €50.

Public Transport

Getting around is easy on Munich's excellent public-transport network (MVV; see Train Network Map in this chapter). The system is zone-based, and most places of interest to visitors (except Dachau and the airport) are within the 'blue' inner zone *(Innenraum)*.

Tickets are valid for the S-Bahn, U-Bahn, trams and buses but must be validated before use by time-stamping them in machines at station entrances and aboard buses and trams. Failure to validate puts you at the mercy of ticket inspectors who speak perfect English, have seen and heard all possible excuses and possess admirable efficiency when it comes to handing out fines of €30 for unauthorised travel.

Rail passes are valid on S-Bahn trains. Bicycle transport costs €2 per trip or €2.50 for a day pass, but is forbidden from 6am to 9am and 4pm to 6pm Monday to Friday.

Tickets & Passes

Short rides (four bus or tram stops; two U-Bahn or S-Bahn stops) cost €1, regular trips cost €2. It's cheaper to buy a strip-card of 10 tickets called a *Streifenkarte* for €9, and stamp one strip (€0.90) per adult on rides of two or less tram or U-Bahn stops, two strips (€1.80) for longer rides.

The best value is in day passes, which cost €4.50 for individuals and just €7.50 for up to five people for the inner zone; three-day passes cost €11/17.50.

You can also buy a weekly *Isarcard* pass covering four zones for just €12.50, but the catch is that it's only valid beginning on a Monday (ie, if you buy on Wednesday, the Isarcard is still only good to Sunday).

The U-Bahn ceases operation at around 12.30am from Monday to Friday and 1.30am on weekends, but a network of *Nachtbusse* (night buses) still operates – very convenient for disco- and club-goers. Pick up the latest route and time schedule from any tourist office.

Car & Motorcycle

It's not worth driving in the city centre; many streets are pedestrian-only, ticket enforcement is Orwellian and parking is a nightmare. The tourist office map shows car-park locations, which generally cost about €1.50 to €2 per hour.

Taxi

Taxis are expensive (around €2.50 at flag fall, plus €1.10 per kilometre) and not much more convenient than public transport. For a radio-dispatched taxi, call ☎ 216 10 or ☎ 194 10. Taxi ranks are indicated on the city's tourist map.

Bicycle

From May to October, Radius Touristik (☎ 59 61 13, ☎ 55 02 93 74), at the end of tracks 31-33 in the Hauptbahnhof, rents out city bikes for €3/14 per hour/day, with a €50 deposit or ID. The office is open 10am to 6pm daily. Staff speak English and are happy to provide tips and advice on touring around Munich.

Bikes are also for rent by Discover Bavaria at the corner of Brauhausstrasse and Hochbrückenstrasse near the Hofbräuhaus for €7.70/12.80 per half/full day.

Around Munich

One of the great delights of Munich is that it's just an S-Bahn ride away from a quite varied menu of destinations ranging from the enlightening to the exciting to the horrifying.

DACHAU

☎ 08131 • pop 38,000 • elevation 508

Mention 'Dachau' and the instant association is with the Nazi concentration camp, visited by more than 800,000 people each year. Few of them realise that there was a Dachau some 1100 years before the camp was built. Fewer still ever make it to the town's little Altstadt with its historic buildings and pretty Renaissance palace and garden.

First mentioned in 805, Dachau became the residence of the local counts in the early 12th century. About 400 years later, their castle formed the basis of the summer palace built by the Wittelsbach dukes. In the 19th century, Dachau had a thriving artists' colony which included Lovis Corinth and Max Liebermann. Their work can be seen in the **Dachauer Gemäldegalerie** next to the tourist office. Even today, about 100 artists live in Dachau.

Orientation & Information

Dachau's Bahnhof is about 1km south-east of the Altstadt and about 3.5km south-west of the concentration camp memorial.

The tourist office (☎ 845 66, fax 845 29, e kulturamt@dachau.de), at Konrad-Adenauer-Strasse 1, is open from 9am to 1pm and 2.30pm to 5pm Monday to Friday and 9am to noon Saturday.

Schloss Dachau

Schloss Dachau (☎ 879 23, Schlossstraße 7; adult/concession €1.50/1; open 9am-6pm Tues-Sun Apr-Sept, 10am-4pm Tues-Sun Oct-Mar) was built by 16th-century dukes Wilhelm IV and Albrecht V as a vast four-winged summer residence in Renaissance style. In 1715, Prince-elector Max Emanuel had the south-western wing cloaked in a baroque mantle. It is the only

section to survive the wrecking ball, which demolished the rest of the complex in the 19th century because of its dilapidated state. Behind its cream-and-honey-coloured facade is an exquisite festival hall with a famous ceiling that is a timbered glorification of the Wittelsbach rulers, especially Albrecht V. Today, it is the setting of the Dachauer Schlosskonzerte, a classical concert series (tickets €15 to €31).

Behind the Schloss, the smallish **Hofgarten** (admission free; open 7am-dusk, 8pm max) blends an orchard, a rose garden and paths sheltered by a leafy canopy. It's a quiet oasis and perfect for relaxing when the sun's out. The garden is overlooked by the terrace of the Schlosscafe.

Dachau Concentration Camp Memorial

The Dachau concentration camp was the Nazi's first and it was built by Heinrich Himmler in March 1933. It 'processed' more than 200,000 prisoners, killing nearly 32,000, and is now a haunting memorial. Note that children under 12 may find the experience too disturbing. Expect to spend two to three hours at the memorial, sections of which are undergoing renovation at the time of writing.

Information The memorial (☎ 17 41, Alte Römerstrasse 75; admission free; open

9am-5pm Tues-Sun) is in the north-eastern corner of Dachau. Free map-pamphlets in about a dozen languages are available on your left as you enter the Documentary Exhibit near the entrance to the camp. For more in-depth descriptions, pick up the brochure *Concentration Camp Dachau* (€1.50) or the detailed catalogue (€13). Proceeds go directly to the Survivors Association of Dachau.

A 22-minute English-language documentary runs at 11.30am and 3.30pm. Dachauer Forum and Action Reconciliation runs free two-hour tours in English on Saturday and Sunday at 12.30pm (Tuesday to Sunday from June to August). The tours are excellent and informative; the bigger the group, the longer the tour.

From April to October, Munich-based Radius Touristik (☎ 089-55 02 93 74) offers in-depth English-language tours to the memorial camp at 10am and 1pm from Tuesday to Sunday, with additional tours at noon in June and July. Tours run daily at noon from November to March. The four- to five-hour excursions cost €18, including public transportation, and leave from its offices in the Munich Hauptbahnhof opposite the end of tracks 31-33. Reservations are advised.

The Memorial Your first stop at the memorial should be the **Documentary Exhibit** housed in the former utility building, where the kitchen, laundry and storage rooms were located. In the foyer, a wall-sized map shows camp locations throughout Germany and Central Europe, with special symbols for the extermination camps.

The exhibit consists of photographs and models of the camp, its officers and prisoners, and of horrifying 'scientific experiments' carried out by Nazi doctors. Other exhibits include a whipping block, a chart showing the system for prisoner identification by category (Jews, homosexuals, Jehovah's Witnesses, Poles, Roma and other 'asocial' types) and documents relating to the camp and the persecution of 'degenerate' authors banned by the party. There's also exhibits on the rise of the Nazi party and the establishment of the camp system.

Outside this building, in the former roll call square, is the **International Memorial** (1968), inscribed in English, French, Yiddish, German and Russian, which reads 'Never Again'. Nearby are large stakes on which prisoners were hanged, sometimes for days, with their hands shackled behind their backs.

Behind the exhibit building, the **Bunker** was the notorious camp prison where inmates were tortured; some of the cells are too tiny for prisoners to sit, let alone lie down. Executions took place in the prison yard.

Normally, inmates were housed in large barracks lining the Lagerstrasse, the main road, which stretched out north of the roll call square. The **crematorium** is in the camp's far north-western corner. Also here is a gas chamber, disguised as a shower room, which was never used. Instead, prisoners marked for gassing were sent to other camps. Outside the crematorium is a statue to 'honour the dead and warn the living' and a Russian Orthodox chapel. Nearby are churches and a Jewish memorial.

Getting There & Away

Dachau is about 20km north of central Munich and best reached by the S2 (direction: Laim), which leaves from the Hauptbahnhof every 20 minutes (€4, 22 minutes). From here, Bus Nos 724 or 726 heads to the concentration camp and Bus No 722 to the Altstadt. Tickets are good all the way to the camp.

To get into town from the camp, take Bus No 726 to John-F-Kennedy-Platz, then change to No 722 to Rathaus. By car, take Dachauer Strasse out to Dachau, then follow the KZ-Gedenkstätte signs.

OBERSCHLEISSHEIM

☎ 089 • pop 5700 • elevation 486m

Palace lovers, listen up. The northern Munich suburb of Oberschleissheim has not one, not two but – count 'em – three dashing palatial edifices that compete with anything in the heart of the city. They're surrounded by the impressive and picnic-friendly **Hofgarten** (free), a baroque garden bisected by a canal and enlivened by a cascading waterfall.

The crown jewel of the trio is the **Neues Schloss** (☎ *315 87 20, Max-Emanuel-Platz 1; adult/concession €3/2, combination ticket with Schloss Lustheim €4.50/3.50; open 9am-6pm Tues-Sun Apr-Sept, 10am-4pm Tues-Sun Oct-Mar*). A rather pompous palace modelled after Versailles, it was dreamed up in 1701 by the ambitious – some might say, deluded – prince-elector Max Emanuel (1679–1726) in anticipation of being promoted to emperor. Unfortunately for him, things didn't go all that well in the War of the Spanish Succession, which forced him into exile and suspended construction.

Upon his return in 1715, Max Emanuel lassoed local architect Joseph Effner to pick up where the Italian Enrico Zucalli had left off. Effner created a 330m-long white facade with yellow trim, while Ignaz Günther contributed the eastern portal. Inside, a vaulted ceiling drenched in frescoes by the prolific Cosmas Damian Asam, and a dining hall with stucco by Johann Baptist Zimmermann, are among the more extravagant design touches.

The rooms provide a fitting setting for the **Gemäldegalerie**, a selection of European baroque art drawn from the Bavarian State Collection. While the ground floor focuses on works by Italian, German and Spanish artists, the upstairs has top works by Flemish painters, including Jan Brueghel the Elder and Anthonis van Dyck.

West of the Neues Schloss is the considerably less ostentatious **Altes Schloss** (☎ *315 52 72, Maximilianshof 1*). Duke Wilhelm V originally had the idea to build a retreat here in 1597, a plan continued by his son Maximilian I. Badly damaged in WWII, the palace today houses the **Sammlung Weinhold** (*adult/concession €2.50/2; open 9am-6pm Tues-Sun Apr-Sept, 10am-4pm Tues-Sun Oct-Mar*). This exhibit documents the various customs and traditions that developed around the world in celebrating the major religious festivals, such as Easter and Christmas.

In the southern wing, you'll find a museum chronicling the history and culture of Prussia (*adult/concession €1.50/0.75; open 10am-5pm Tues-Sun*). You can safely skip this one.

Finally, on a little island at the eastern end of the Schlosspark stands **Schloss Lustheim** (☎ *315 87 20*). Closed for renovation at the time of writing, it normally houses a famous collection of Meissen porcelain.

Flugwerft Schleissheim

South of the palaces, on what is Germany's oldest air field (1912), is the aviation branch of the **Deutsches Museum** (☎ *315 71 40, Effnerstrasse 18; adult/concession €3/2, combination ticket with Deutsches Museum €7; open 9am-5pm daily*). Displays sprawl over 7800 sq metres within three historical buildings – the command centre, tower and construction hall – as well as a new hall. Feast your eyes on an international cast of around 60 planes and helicopters (mostly of the military kind), plus hang-gliders, engines and flight simulators. Highlights include the MiG-21 (1973), a Soviet-era supersonic fighter plane, and the F-4E Phantom (1968), which saw much action during the Vietnam War. Also on view is a reconstructed glider first built by Otto Lilienthal in 1894.

Getting There & Away

Take the S1 (direction: Freising) to Oberschleissheim, then walk about 15 minutes along Mittenheimer Strasse towards the palaces or the Flugwerft. By car, take Leopoldstrasse north until it becomes Ingolstädter Strasse or travel north on the A99 to the Neuherberg exit. Enter from the southern end of the airfield.

FREISING
☎ 08161 • pop 36,000 • elevation 446m

Freising, a few more stops north on the S1, entered the history books around the 8th century as a residence of the Agilolfingian Duke Theodo. Wanting to do his part in Christianising the heathens, Theodo managed to talk an itinerant Franconian monk named Korbinian into laying the foundation for a bishopric here in 720, which was formally founded by Bonifatius in 739. For more than 1000 years, until secularisation in 1803, Freising's cathedral quarter remained the spiritual and cultural centre of southern Bavaria. After the archdiocese was restored in 1821, the bishop moved his chair to Munich, relegating Freising to secondary status.

Freising is built on three hills, nicknamed the Lehrberg (Teaching Hill) with the Dom and religious education centres; the Wehrberg (Army Hill) with an army barracks; and the Nährberg (Nourishing Hill), home to a brewery and a university.

Freising's tourist office (☎ 541 22, fax 542 31, e touristinfo@freising.de), at Marienplatz 7, is open 9am to 4.30pm Monday to Friday and, from April to September only, also 9am to noon Saturday.

Things to See

Freising is a remarkably lively town with a charming **Altstadt** crisscrossed by a tangle of lanes lined by neatly kept townhouses from the Renaissance and baroque eras. The baroque tower of the **Stadtpfarrkirche St Georg** stands sentinel over the ensemble; it can be climbed from 2pm to 5pm on Saturday between May and October, weather permitting.

The Altstadt is dominated by the Domberg, with the twin-towered **Dom St Maria and St Korbinian** *(☎ 18 10; open 8am-noon & 2pm-5pm daily, until 6pm May-Oct)* as its focal point. Although originally a 12th-century Romanesque basilica, much of its interior has been cloaked in decorations from later periods.

To experience the solemn elegance of Romanesque architecture, you'll have to descend into the **crypt**, a veritable forest of pillars, where Korbinian's mortal remains are kept. Note that none of the pillars look the same and pay particular attention to the famous **Bestiensäule** (Beast Pillar). Its delicate carvings allegorise the fight of Christianity against evil represented by crocodile-like monsters.

The main church received its rococo makeover in 1723/24 to celebrate the 1000th anniversary of the arrival of St Korbinian in Freising. It is a splendid work by the Asam brothers, with stucco by Egid

Quirin and frescoes by Cosmas Damian. Remnants from the Gothic era include the choir stalls and a *Lamentation of Christ* group in the left aisle. The main altar painting is by Peter Paul Rubens (it's a copy, the original is in Munich's Alte Pinakothek).

Also worth a look are the **cloisters**, emanating east of the Dom, with stucco by Johann Baptist Zimmermann, and the **cathedral library** *(open 2pm-3pm Mon-Fri mid-May–Oct)*, with baroque decorations by François Cuvilliés.

In a former seminary at the western end of the Domberg is the **Diözesanmuseum** *(☎ 487 90, Domberg 21; adult/concession €3/1.50; open 10am-5pm Tues-Sun)*. It is the largest ecclesiastical museum in Germany and brims with treasures from Bavaria, Salzburg and Tirol. The nativity scenes in the basement are worth a gander, while on the ground floor you can admire richly bejewelled silver and gold monstrances, reliquaries and other ceremonial items. The highlight here is the **Lukasbild**, a 12th-century Byzantine icon sheltered by a baroque silver altar. Upstairs is plenty of medieval and baroque art, including some by such heavy hitters as Rubens, Tiepolo and Zimmermann.

On the 'Nährberg', south-west of the Domberg, a former Benedictine monastery now contains the well-respected University of Agriculture with specialised schools for brewing, food technology and dairy science. Also here is the **Staatsbrauerei Weihenstephan**, a state brewery with a tradition going back to 1040. You can sample its output right in the beer garden or in the redbrick vaulted cellar of the **Bräustüberl** *(☎ 130 04, Weihenstephan 1)*.

Getting There & Away

Freising is about 35km north-west of Munich at the northern terminus of the S1 (25 minutes). The Domberg and Altstadt are a 10-minute walk from the train station.

STARNBERGER FÜNF-SEEN-LAND

• pop 80,000 • elevation 584m

The Starnberg Five-Lakes-District is a fast and easy getaway from the urban bustle of

Munich for locals and visitors alike. The namesake lake, Starnberger See, is just 30 minutes by S6 from Munich (two zones or four strips of a Streifenkarte). Besides Starnberger See (21km long, 3km to 5km wide and up to 127m deep), the district also comprises the Ammersee and the much smaller Pilsensee, Wörthsee and Wesslinger See. Swimming, sailing, windsurfing and water-skiing are popular activities, especially on the two larger lakes.

The area has long been a favourite with Bavarian nobility. 'Fairy-tale' King Ludwig II (1845–86) had a soft spot for the Starnberger See, at least until he tragically drowned in it near his palace in Berg on the eastern shore. The present head of the Wittelsbach family, Duke Franz, still uses Ludwig's former palace as one of his own residences. Ludwig's bosom-buddy, Empress Sisi of Austria (1837–98), spent many a summer in Possenhofen on the western shore. Her descendent, Otto von Habsburg, head of the Austrian royal family, has been living in nearby Pöcking since 1954. Princess Gloria von Thurn und Taxis (see Regensburg in the Eastern Bavaria chapter) owns Schloss Garatshausen just south of here.

Since WWII, the old guard has been joined by the 'new aristocracy', including politicians, actors, musicians, soccer stars, industrialists and other moneyed folk.

Information

The district tourist office (☎ 08151-906 00, fax 90 60 90, e tourist-info@starnberger -fuenf-seen-land.de) is at Wittelsbacher Strasse 2c in Starnberg, a short walk north of Bahnhofsplatz. It is open 8am to 6pm Monday to Friday, and also 9am to 1pm Saturday from June to October. Its staff operate a free room-finding service and can help you plan public transport between here and other lake towns.

Starnberg

The town of Starnberg, at the northern end of the lake, is the gateway to the lake district and is its commercial hub. Unfortunately, construction sins from the 1960s and 1970s are still in evidence and most people prefer

heading on to the other communities. Getting off at the train station puts you steps away from the cruise-boat landing docks, pedal boat rentals and the district tourist office.

Just west of the Bahnhof is the **Heimatmuseum** (☎ 08151-77 21 32, Possenhofener Strasse 5, enter from Bahnhofsplatz; adult/ concession €1.50/0.75; open 10am-noon & 2pm-5pm Tues-Sun, closed Feb). In a nicely restored wooden 17th-century farmhouse, this extensive local history museum illuminates numerous aspects of life in the lake region. The collection of art includes a prized sculpture by Ignaz Günther (1755).

Berg

On the eastern shore of the Starnberger See, is this exclusive enclave sprouted around **Schloss Berg**, a one-time summer residence of King Ludwig II and also where he spent his final days. The palace and its lovely gardens are still owned and inhabited by the Wittelsbach family and are not open to the public.

You are free, however, to walk through its forest-like park to the **Votivkapelle** (☎ 52 76; admission free; open 9am-5pm daily Apr-Oct), which was built in honour of Ludwig. Shrouded by mature trees, it's a rather pompous Romanesque-style chapel, which overlooks the spot in the lake – marked by a simple cross – where Ludwig's dead body was supposedly found. For more about the king and his mysterious death, read the boxed text 'The Mystery & Mystique of Ludwig II' in the Allgäu-Bavarian Swabia chapter.

Bus No 961 travels from Starnberg to Berg throughout the day (less on weekends).

Possenhofen & Feldafing

Austrian empress Sisi, cousin and confidante of Ludwig II, spent her childhood summers at **Schloss Possenhofen**, a well-proportioned cream-coloured palace with crenelated towers. Still sitting pretty on the western lakeshore, the complex has been converted into fancy condominiums and is closed to the public. It is surrounded by a lush park designed by famous garden architect, Peter Joseph Lenné. Dappled with mature leafy trees, it's great for picnicking, lounging, sun bathing and lake swimming. Access is free, but it's often suffocatingly crowded on sunny summer weekends.

Sisi was so taken with the area that she returned here as an adult to spend summers in what is now the **Kaiserin Elisabeth Hotel** (☎ 08157-930 90, Tutzinger Strasse 2–6) in Feldafing, a couple of kilometres south. A larger-than-life sculpture in the garden shows her with a book in a relaxed repose, gazing back at the hotel. You can eat in the *Sisi Stüberl* (see Places to Eat) or the stuffy restaurant where aproned waiters serve the 'Sisi Menu', featuring dishes Sisi allegedly had the day Ludwig died.

Sisi and Ludwig frequently rendezvoused on the romantic offshore **Roseninsel** (Rose Island), where Ludwig also received other illustrious guests, Richard Wagner among them. After the king's death, the island fell into a deep slumber, the roses withered and the villa decayed. Restoration began a few years ago, to be completed in time for the 150th anniversary of this royal refuge in 2003.

In fine weather from Easter to October, ferryman Norbert Pohlus can take you to the island aboard his historical rowboat called *Plette* (☎ 0171-722 22 66; adult/child under 15 €3.50/2, 2 passenger minimum).

Fans of Art Nouveau villas should take a spin around Feldafing, which also has a popular swimming beach, the **Strandbad Feldafing** (☎ 08157-82 00; adult/child €1.50/1 Mon-Fri, €2/1.25 Sat & Sun; open 9am-8pm daily).

Possenhofen and Feldafing are both stops on the S6 from Munich.

Museum der Phantasie

Right on Starnberger See, about 1km north of Bernried, a placid village with ancient wooden homes, is the Museum der Phantasie (☎ 08158-99 70 60, Am Hirschgarten 1; adult/concession €7.80/3.50; open 10am-6pm Mon-Fri, 10am-8pm Sat-Sun Apr-Oct, 10am-5pm Mon-Fri, 10am-6pm Sat-Sun Nov-Mar). Opened in May 2001, it features the private collection of Lothar-Günther Buchheim, best known as author of

the novel *Das Boot*, the basis for Wolfgang Petersen's Oscar-nominated U-boat epic.

The museum's heart and soul is Buchheim's famous collection of expressionist paintings by members of the artists' group Die Brücke (The Bridge; 1905–13). Founders Karl Schmidt-Rottluff, Erich Heckel and Ernst Ludwig Kirchner were later joined by other heavyweights of the genre, including Emil Nolde, Max Pechstein and Otto Müller. Their artistic goal was to break with the conventions of traditional art academies. Shapes and figures that teeter on the abstract (without ever quite getting there), bright, emotional colours and unusual perspective characterise their paintings. The Nazis, predictably, called this work subversive and had much of it destroyed.

Arts and crafts from around the world supplement the modern art, allowing visitors to observe parallels between so-called 'primitive' and Western art. Other rooms are dedicated to Buchheim's own artistic efforts.

The museum itself is a streamlined postmodern building purpose-designed by Stuttgart architect, Günter Behnisch, whose firm also built the Munich Olympiastadion. Combining glass, wood and white stucco, it vaguely resembles a ship, an effect further enhanced by a 12m-long footbridge on stilts leading from the main structure out over the lake.

RegionalBahn (RB) trains make the trip from Munich to Bernried in 40 minutes, with a change in Tutzing (€6.60). From the station, it's a 15-minute walk north to the museum.

Andechs

The district's most popular tourist attraction is the Benedictine monastery of Andechs (☎ 08152-37 60, Bergstrasse 2; church admission free, monastery tours adult/concession €2.50/1.50, brewery tours adult/concession €2.50/1.50; monastery tours 3pm Mon-Fri, brewery tours Mon & Tues 1.30pm), where the resident monks have been whipping up their famous brews since 1455.

For centuries, people have clambered up the **Heiliger Berg** (Sacred Mountain), as

Andechs is known, to worship both in the lovely rococo church as well as in its beer hall and garden (see Places to Eat).

The monastery was founded in the 10th century and has been an important place of pilgrimage for nearly as long. The objects of veneration are several relics, including branches from Christ's crown of thorns, the victory cross of Charlemagne and three sacred hosts. These are all locked up in the Holy Chapel along with hundreds of offertory candles, some more than 1m tall. In the Middle Ages, the relics were 'lost' for nearly 200 years until, so legend has it, a little mouse tipped off worshippers to their whereabouts in 1388.

The church itself is of Gothic design but got its festive rococo mantle in the mid-18th century. It boasts frescoes by Johann Baptist Zimmermann, sculptures by Johann Baptist Straub and an altar by Franz Schmädl. The building has been under restoration for years and may still be partly closed during your visit.

Hardly anyone who's made it up here leaves without having enjoyed a mug of beer at the **Braustüberl**. Six varieties are on offer, from the rich and velvety Doppelbock Dunkel to the fresh, unfiltered Weissbier. If you can't decide, sample each during the Andechser Bierprobe (beer tasting €6, with snack €8.50).

The beer is truly excellent, but unfortunately the place is often so overrun with people, it's easy to forget that you're in a religious institution, pious though as your love for the brew may be. Summer weekends are especially busy.

Andechs is served three times daily (twice on Sunday) by Bus No 751 from the S-Bahn station in Starnberg (S6; 35 minutes) and the one in Herrsching (S5; 10 minutes). The last bus from Andechs to Herrsching leaves at 6pm, to Starnberg at 4.46pm (always doublecheck these times).

Diessen

About 11km west of Andechs, in the southwestern corner of the Ammersee, the small town of Diessen is home to the **Marienmünster** (☎ 08807-94 89 40; open 8am-noon & 2pm-6pm daily), one of the area's most magnificent baroque churches. Part of a monastery complex (1739), this festive symphony in white stucco, red marble and gold leaf is a collaboration of some of the most accomplished artists of the 18th century. Master architect Johann Michael Fischer put considerable energy into the rhythmic and harmonious design, while François Cuvilliés dreamed up the stunning high altar. The painting above the altar, showing Mary ascending into heaven, is by Giovanni Battista Tiepolo. A peculiarity are the four matching pairs of side altars, designed by four different artists, including Johann Baptist Straub.

Boat Cruises

From Easter to mid-October, Bayerische Seenschifffahrt (☎ 08151-120 23) runs scheduled boat service between the communities on the Starnberger See and the Ammersee, a leisurely way to explore the region. In Starnberg, boats leave from the landing docks just south of the Bahnhof. The company also offers narrated tours of both lakes. These vary in duration from one to four hours and cost from €7 to €13.50. Bicycles are €2.50. Tours on the Starnberger See pass by five castles as well as the Ludwig II cross.

Activities

If cruises are too tame for you, consider taking a spin around the lake under your own steam. **Boat rentals** are available on the Starnberger See, the Ammersee and the Wörthsee. In Starnberg, Paul Dechant (☎ 08151-722 86), Bootshaus 2 near the train station, has rowing, pedal and electric-powered boats for a steep €11 per hour. In Herrsching, near Andechs on the Ammersee, Alfred Schlamp (☎ 08152-96 95 38), Summerstrasse 30, charges €6 per hour for his pedal and rowing boats.

The **bicycle** is an excellent way to explore the area. The tour around Starnberger See, for instance, is 50km and partly travels along dedicated bike paths with no car traffic. For guided bike tours (from €25), contact **Bike It** (☎ 08151-73 93 83, Perchastrasse 8e,

Starnberg). It also rents bikes from €20 to €40 per day. There's a famous **inline skating** stretch on the eastern shore between Berg and Ambach. There are 10 marked **hiking** trails in the district. A delightful, moderate half-day trip starts in Tutzing and goes up to the Ilkahöhe, a 730m-high 'mountain' with panoramic views of the lake and the surrounding countryside.

Places to Stay
The Starnberg Five-Lakes-District has six *camping grounds*, one in Herrsching on the Ammersee (☎ 08152-12 06), one on the Wörthsee (☎ 08152-764 45), one on the Pilsensee (☎ 08152-72 32) and three on Starnberger See, including one in Münsing-Ambach on the eastern shore (☎ 08177-546). For details, call or check with the tourist office.

DJH hostel Possenhofen (☎ 0911-22 38 10, Kurt-Strieber-Strasse 18, Pöcking-Possenhofen) Bed & breakfast €16.40-17.20. This hostel was still under construction at the time of writing, with the opening scheduled for mid-2002.

Hotel Garni Kefer (☎ 08157-931 70, fax 93 17 37, Hindenburgstrasse 12, Pöcking-Possenhofen) Singles/doubles from €35/50. Staff is stingy with smiles and the breakfast buffet is a bit anaemic, but otherwise this old-fashioned hotel in a pretty villa will do in a snap.

Landgasthof zur Linde (☎ 08157-93 31 80, Wieling 5, Feldafing) Singles €50-65, doubles €65-125. Flowerboxes spilling over with geraniums offer a cheerful welcome to this 34-room inn, about 2km south of the Feldafing train station. Rooms are furnished in modern country-style and there's a good restaurant with a beer garden as well.

Places to Eat
Sisi's Stüberl (☎ 08157-930 90, Tutzinger Strasse 2–6, Feldafing) Brotzeit €6.50-8.50, mains €10-20. Dinner only, closed Tues. On cold nights, it's a treat to sit near the fireplace in this cosy tavern, digging into a soulful menu ranging from salads to roast beef. Reservations are recommended. It's part of the Kaiserin Elisabeth Hotel; don't confuse this place with the stuffy hotel restaurant.

Forsthaus Ilkahöhe (☎ 08158-82 42, Auf der Ilkahöhe, Tutzing) Mains €18-24. Open Wed-Sun, beer garden daily in good weather. It's hard to tell what's more appealing about this place: the gourmet regional cuisine or the spectacular views of the Starnberger See and the Alps. Come for a full meal or just a foamy *Mass* in the beer garden.

Braustüberl (☎ 08152-37 62 61, Bergstrasse 2, Andechs) Open 10am-8.45pm daily. Crispy grilled pork knuckles and steaming pretzels are the things to get at this beer hall/garden right on the 'Sacred Mountain'. A self-service deli sells most items by weight (eg, 100g pork knuckle for €1.75). To avoid standing in line for 30 minutes or more, you can also bring your own picnic as long as you eat it at the designated tables in the beer garden.

Klostergasthof Andechs (☎ 08152-930 90, Bergstrasse 9, Andechs) Mains €9-18. For a more formal atmosphere and service, grab a table in one of several dining rooms, some anchored by tiled fireplaces.

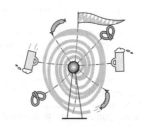

Eastern Bavaria

Eastern Bavaria (Ostbayern) combines the administrative districts of Niederbayern (Lower Bavaria) and Oberpfalz (Upper Palatinate). Along with Upper Bavaria, Eastern Bavaria more or less constitutes Altbayern, the original Bavarian territory before the incorporation of Franconia and Swabia in the early 19th century.

Eastern Bavaria is the home of one of the loveliest cities in all of Germany: romantic Regensburg and Passau, on the border with Austria, were founded by the Romans and derive their relaxed air from the presence of the Danube, which traverses the entire region. Landshut, only 70km north-east of Munich, completes the fabulous trio of cities. Incidentally, both Regensburg and Landshut were capitals of the Duchy of Bavaria long before Munich made its mark on the map of history.

Eastern Bavaria is also home to the Bavarian Forest, which wraps around Germany's first national park, the Nationalpark Bayerischer Wald, and hugs the Czech border where it blends into the Bohemian Forest. This is a superbly scenic part of the state and as of yet mercifully undiscovered by mass tourism. Prices here are considerably lower and trails less crowded than in the famous Alpine resorts to the south. There's skiing here in winter – the Grosser Arber, the highest mountain, rises to 1456m – and all sorts of other outdoor pursuits year round. The Bavarian Forest is also a major glass-producing centre and there are many opportunities to see the artists at work and to stock up on souvenirs.

REGENSBURG
☎ 0941 • pop 142,000 • elevation 330m
When it comes to finding a snappy quote, no-one proves a more reliable source than that rock of German culture, Johann Wolfgang von Goethe. 'Regensburg liegt so schön, diese Gegend musste eine Stadt herlocken' (Regensburg is so beautifully situated, the surroundings were bound to attract a city), he rhapsodised in 1786.

Highlights

• Sample the infinite charms of Regensburg, the medieval metropolis right on the Danube, then finish the day with a cold local brew in a lively beer garden

• Also while in Regensburg, board a boat for Walhalla, a monumental temple perched high above the Danube, which honours Germany's greatest minds

• Get away from the crowds while roaming the trails of the Bavarian Forest National Park

• Let your hair down at Straubing's Gäubodenfest, one of Bavaria's largest drinking festivals

• Come to know the work of the Asam brothers in the Basilika St Emmeram in Regensburg or Straubing's Ursulinenkirche and St Jakobskirche.

• Stand at the confluence of the Danube, Inn and Ilz Rivers in Passau, whose pedigree goes back to Roman times

More than 200 years later, the master's favourable impressions still ring true.

Simply ponder the city panorama while standing on the northern bank of the Danube.

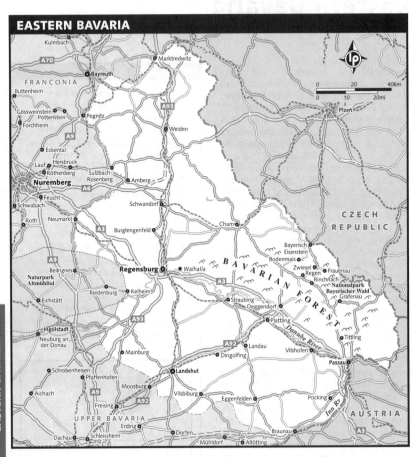

EASTERN BAVARIA

Unfolding before you is a magnificent silhouette crowned by the filigree spires of the Dom St Peter dancing above a harmonious hotch-potch of red-tiled rooftops and the sturdy towers of patrician mansions. It's a skyline that has largely been undisturbed since the Middle Ages when Regensburg was one of Europe's leading commercial, political and cultural centres. The fact that it has survived with such purity and completeness is the city's greatest touristic asset.

But this is not to say that Regensburg feels like it's been frozen in time. Bavaria's fourth largest city is the hub of the Oberpfalz (Upper Palatinate) region with a thriving university whose students do their part in livening up the atmosphere. As to the historical buildings, very few of them are indeed museums. Since they are so ubiquitous, people prefer to inhabit and use them rather than simply enshrine them. Go to a bookstore and you'll find a former medieval kitchen integrated within the children's section. The ribbed vaulted ceiling of the boutique isn't a newfangled design idea; it's the remnant of a Gothic chapel. And the wall you're leaning against at the bus stop may have been put there by the Romans.

The Altstadt's liveliness is as arresting as the populace is friendly and unspoiled – even by the large hordes of tourists they see each year. Oskar Schindler lived in Regensburg for years, and now one of his houses bears a plaque to his achievements commemorated in the Spielberg epic *Schindler's List*.

Regensburg is easily worth a couple of days on any Bavarian itinerary and is also an excellent base from which to explore the surrounding countryside. Beer lovers can look forward to investigating the local product made by three breweries, the Bischofshofbrauerei, the Spitalbrauerei and Kneitinger.

History

It's the Romans who deserve credit for putting Regensburg on the map, even though the area has been peopled since the Stone Age and Celtic tribes founded a settlement here about 500 BC. But by AD 80/90, Roman troops erected a military camp here, enlarged under Emperor Marcus Aurelius in AD 179 and named Castra Regina. This endured for about 200 years and, after the Romans, Bavarian tribes took over. Under the Agilolfingian dynasty, Regensburg became a flourishing duchy capital and, by 788, posed such a threat to the Frankish king – and later emperor – Charlemagne that he promptly removed the incumbent duke from power and made Bavaria part of his Frankish empire.

Ironically, Regensburg benefited greatly from the ambitious usurper. Charlemagne built a palace, a bridge, cathedral and city wall. By the 10th century, it was a medieval metropolis with as many as 10,000 inhabitants. From here on, Regensburg's prominence rose steadily, culminating in 1245 when it became a Free Imperial City, accountable only to the Holy Roman Emperor and not to the Wittelsbach dukes who had taken possession of Bavaria in 1180. Many of the buildings you see today date back to this time when Regensburg was one of Europe's most prosperous trading hubs.

By the 16th century, however, things had turned around as competition from other trading centres such as Augsburg and Nuremberg plunged the city into bankruptcy, which triggered the expulsion of the Jews in 1519. Regensburg regained some of its stature when, in 1663, it became the seat of the Perpetual Imperial Diet, a sort of permanent parliament, which convened here until 1803.

After Regensburg was absorbed into Bavaria in 1810, it was demoted to a provincial backwater. In the 19th century, industrialisation completely bypassed the city and things didn't really turn around until after WWII when various industries – electronics, automotive and high-tech among them – began settling here. The founding of the university in 1967 provided further stimulus. In hindsight, however, the earlier neglect may have been a godsend for Regensburg, allowing it to preserve the medieval character that makes it so fascinating today.

Orientation

Regensburg is divided by the east-flowing Danube, separating the *Altstadt* (old district), where all the main sights are located, from the northern banks. Islands in the middle of the river, mainly Oberer Wöhrd and Unterer Wöhrd, are populated as well. The Regen River joins the Danube north of town.

The Hauptbahnhof is at the southern end of the Altstadt. From here, it's about 700m north on Maximilianstrasse to Kornmarkt, just east of the cathedral and the historic centre. The university is south of the train station.

Much of the Altstadt is closed to private vehicles but open to buses and taxis.

Information

Tourist Offices The tourist office (☎ 507 44 10, fax 507 44 19, e tourismus@regensburg .de), in the Altes Rathaus (Old Town Hall), is open 8.30am to 6pm Monday to Friday, 9am to 4pm Saturday and 9.30am to 2.30pm Sunday and holidays (until 4pm April to October). Ask about the *Verbundkarte* (€10/5/2.50 for a family/adult/concession ticket), which is good for entry to four of the city's main museums.

The local ADAC branch (☎ 55 16 65) is at Luitpoldstrasse 2.

EASTERN BAVARIA

REGENSBURG

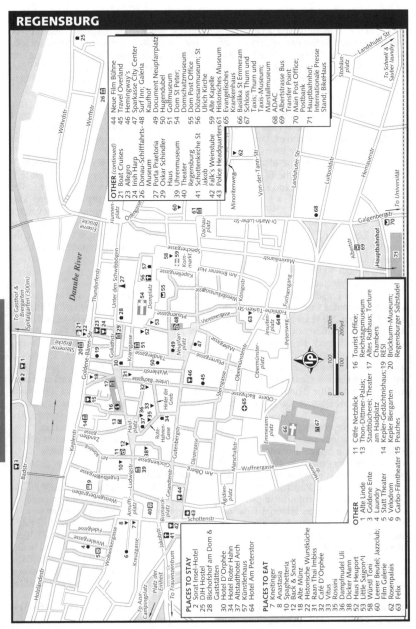

OTHER (continued)
21 Boat Cruises
22 Travel Overland
23 Allegro
24 Irish Harp
26 Donau-Schifffahrts-Museum
27 Porta Praetoria
29 Oskar Schindler Haus
39 Uhrenmuseum
40 Theater Regensburg
41 Schottenkirche St Jakob
42 Falk's Weinstube
43 Police Headquarters
44 Neue Film Bühne
45 Travel Overland
46 Hemingway's
47 Sparkasse City Center
48 Surf Inn; Galeria Kaufhof
49 Document Neupfarrplatz
50 Hugendubel
51 Golfmuseum
54 Dom St Peter; Domschatzmuseum
55 Dom Post Office
56 Diözesanmuseum; St Ulrich Kirche
59 Alte Kapelle
61 Historisches Museum
65 Evangelisches Krankenhaus
66 Basilika St Emmeram
67 Schloss Thurn und Taxis; Thurn und Taxis-Museum; Marstallmuseum
68 ADAC
69 Albertstrasse Bus Transfer Point
70 Main Post Office; Postbank
71 Hauptbahnhof; Internationale Presse Stand; BikeHaus

PLACES TO STAY
2 Sorat Insel-Hotel
25 DJH Hostel
28 Bischofshof am Dom & Gaststätten
30 Hotel D'Orphée
34 Hotel Roter Hahn
37 Altstadthotel Arch
57 Künstlerhaus
64 Hotel Am Peterstor

PLACES TO EAT
7 Kneitinger
8 Anastasia
10 Spaghetteria
12 Back & Snack
18 Alte Münz
22 Historische Wurstküche
31 Raan Thai Imbiss
32 Café D'Orphée
33 Vitus
35 Rossini
36 Dampfnudel Uli
38 Dicker Mann
52 Haus Heuport
53 Little Saigon^l
58 Würst Toni
60 Leerer Beutel; Jazzclub; Film Galerie
62 Rosenpalais
63 Felix

OTHER
1 Alte Linde
3 Goldene Ente
4 Laundry
5 Statt Theater
6 Velodrom
9 Garbo-Filmtheater
11 C@fe Netzblick
13 Thon-Dittmer-Palais; Stadtbücherei; Theater am Haidplatz
14 Kepler-Gedächtnishaus; Chambers
15 Peaches
16 Tourist Office; Reichstagsmuseum
17 Altes Rathaus; Torture Chambers
19 RESI
20 Brückturm-Museum; Regensburger Salzstadel

Money Change money at the Postbank next to the Hauptbahnhof or at the Sparkasse City Center on Neupfarrplatz. More banks are along Maximilianstrasse.

Post & Communications The main post office is adjacent to the Hauptbahnhof, but the one on Domplatz is more central.

C@fe Netzblick (☎ 599 97 00), Am Römling 9, is a fun Internet cafe in vaulted medieval chambers; surf or mail for €2.50/4 per 30/60 minutes. It's open from 6pm to 1am daily. In the daytime, try Surf Inn inside the Galeria Kaufhof department store at Neupfarrplatz 8, which charges €1/1.50 per 15/30 minutes.

Internet Resources Regensburg has a useful Web site at W www.regensburg.de, with sections in English.

Travel Agencies Travel Overland (☎ 59 30 10) at Obere Bachgasse 9 is a good place for well-priced plane and train tickets as well as package tours.

Bookshops & Libraries Get English books and magazines at the Hauptbahnhof's Internationale Presse Stand. Hugendubel (☎ 58 53 20), Wahlenstrasse 17 (with another entrance on Tändlergasse), has the usual good collection of English-language and travel books and a reading area. The Stadtbücherei (city library; ☎ 507 14 77) is at Haidplatz 8 in the Thon-Dittmer-Palais and has a decent selection of English-language newspapers and magazines.

University The main campus of the Universität Regensburg (☎ 94 31) is in the south of the city. Its 20,000 students study mostly theology, economics, medicine, philosophy and mathematics. Take Bus No 6 or 11 to the Universität stop.

Laundry The most central laundry to be found in Regensburg is at Winklergasse 4, although the Schnell & Sauber coin laundry at Hermann-Geib-Strasse 5, on the corner of Landshuter Strasse south of the Hauptbahnhof, is larger.

Medical Services & Emergency The largest hospital close to the centre is the Evangelisches Krankenhaus (☎ 504 00) on Emmeramsplatz. Call ☎ 192 22 for an ambulance. Police headquarters are on the southern side of Bismarckplatz in the Altstadt.

Steinerne Brücke

Regensburg's 16-arched Stone Bridge, built in only 11 years (1135–46), was a veritable miracle of engineering at the time. According to legend, its crafty builder promised the devil the first soul to cross the bridge – if he let him beat the cathedral builder who had bet on completing his church first. The bridge builder won and hoodwinked Satan too, for the first to cross the bridge was a donkey.

For the local merchants, the bridge was not only a symbol of their already substantial wealth but it also greatly facilitated their trading activities, thus making them richer still. For more than 800 years, the Stone Bridge was the city's only permanent Danube crossing.

Ensconced in its southern tower is the **Brückturm-Museum** (☎ 567 60 15, Weisse-Lamm-Gasse 1; adult/concession €2/1.50; open 10am-5pm daily Apr-Oct). It has a small historical exhibit about the unique bridge, but most people come for the bird's-eye view of the town, the river and the ancient crossing. The building abutting the tower is the **Regensburger Salzstadel** (1620), once a giant salt warehouse and now partly a restaurant.

Altes Rathaus

From 1663 to 1803, the Perpetual Imperial Diet met in the small but richly decorated **Reichssaal** (Imperial Hall) upstairs in the Altes Rathaus. Today, the complex houses the tourist office and the **Reichstagsmuseum** (Imperial Diet Museum; ☎ 507 44 11, Altes Rathaus; adult/concession €2.50/1.25; tours 9.30am-11.30am, 2pm-4pm Mon-Sat, 10am-noon Sun; English-language tours 3.15pm Mon-Sat). Tours take in not only the Reichssaal but also the stomach-turning original **torture chamber** in the basement. Walk into the old holding cell and look down to the dungeon before entering the interrogation room, which bristles with tools such as the rack, the Spanish Donkey (a tall wooden wedge on which naked men were made to sit with weights shackled on their ankles), spiked chairs and other charming objects.

The Rathaus itself was progressively extended from medieval to baroque times. Today, Regensburg's three mayors govern from here.

East of Altes Rathaus

Dom St Peter The Dom St Peter ranks among Bavaria's grandest Gothic cathedrals (☎ 597 10 02, Domplatz; admission free; tours (in German) €2.50/1.50; tours (in English) 10am, 11am & 2pm Mon-Sat, noon & 2pm Sun & holidays May-Oct, 11am Mon-Sat & noon Sun Nov-Apr). Construction began in the late 13th century, mostly as an ambitious vanity project to show off the city's prosperity. Very soon, however, it became painfully clear that the bishop and the burghers had overestimated not only the architects' ability but also their cash flow. In the end, it took 300 years – until 1525 – to complete the building. The spires weren't added until the 19th century. Made of green sandstone, which erodes quickly, their renewal still keeps a fleet of stonemasons in business.

Inside the dark, cavernous cathedral, its most prized assets immediately leap into view: the kaleidoscopic original 13th- and 14th-century **stained-glass windows** above the choir and in the south transept.

A charming highlight is a pair of sculptures (1280), attached to pillars just west of the altar. One shows the **Angel of the Annunciation**, his smiling mug beaming at the **Virgin** on the opposite pillar as he delivers the news that she's pregnant.

At the western entrance, note the statuettes known as **Satan and his grandmother**, which serve as reminders that outside these walls bad things await. Especially if you don't make a donation.

If you happen to be in town on Sunday, try to catch the 9am service accompanied by the angelic voices of the Regensburger Domspatzen (Cathedral Sparrows), the cathedral's famous boys' choir.

The **Domschatzmuseum** (Cathedral Treasury; ☎ 576 45; adult/concession €1.50/0.75; open 10am-5pm Tues-Sat, noon-5pm Sun Apr-Nov, less in winter) has the usual assortment of vestments, monstrances, tapestries and other church treasures.

Alte Kapelle After a thorough face-lift, the graceful Alte Kapelle (Alter Kornmarkt 8) once again makes first-time visitors gasp in awe at its rich and harmonious rococo decorations. The core of the church, however, is Romanesque, while the Gothic choir was added in the 15th century. The ceiling frescoes show allegories of the four continents and scenes from the life of Emperor Heinrich II and his wife Kunigunde. Since the church is only open during services, peering through the wrought-iron gate will only give you partial views.

Roman Wall The Roman wall, with its seriously impressive **Porta Praetoria** arch, dates to AD 179. It follows Unter den Schwibbögen onto Dr-Martin-Luther-Strasse and is the most tangible reminder of the ancient Castra Regina.

Golfmuseum You'd have to be a serious golf fan to shell out the steep admission to the small Golfmuseum (☎ 510 74, Am Neupfarrplatz cnr Tändlergasse 11; adult/concession €7.50/3.75; open 10am-7pm Mon-Fri, 10am-4pm Sat). It's in the 14th-century vaulted cellar underneath the antique store Insam, owned by the same man who also assembled the golf collection (with items for sale as well, at the right price, you understand). The tiny rooms are laden with everything from antique golf clubs to golf shoes to golf balls (the oldest being from 1830), plus an assortment of trophies, paintings and sculpture. Among the most prized items is a dinner menu from the club at St Andrews (Scotland) signed by Eisenhower.

Historisches Museum The city's historical museum (☎ 507 24 48, Dachauplatz 2–4; adult/concession €2/1; open 10am-4pm Tues-Sun) features exhibits from the Stone Age to the Middle Ages, and an art collection focusing on 14th- and 15th-century handicrafts, painting and sculpture. There's also a large collection of Bavarian folklore.

Donau-Schifffahrts-Museum The town's Donau-Schifffahrts-Museum *(Danube Navigation Museum; ☎ 525 10, Werftstrasse on Unterer Wöhrd; adult/concession €2/1.50; open 10am-5pm daily Apr-Oct)*, near the hostel, is a historic paddle-wheel steam tugboat moored on the Danube, with exhibits on the history of navigation on the river.

South of Altes Rathaus
Neupfarrplatz In the Middle Ages, the heart of the Jewish community was on today's Neupfarrplatz. In the early 16th century, with Regensburg on the brink of bankruptcy, came one of the darkest chapters in the city's history: the expulsion of the Jews in 1519. That year, their great protector, Emperor Maximilian I, had died.

Since Jews were the city's main moneylenders, throwing them out was one convenient way for the cash-strapped merchants to wipe out their debts. The Jewish quarter was razed along with the synagogue, which was later replaced with the Neupfarrkirche, Regensburg's first Protestant church after the city introduced the Reformation in 1542.

Remains of the Jewish quarter, as well as of Roman buildings, were found during excavations in the mid-1990s. Since late 2001, a subterranean multimedia exhibit called **Document Neupfarrplatz** *(☎ 507 14 52; tours €2.50/1.25; tours 2.30pm Thur-Sat)* provides insight into the square's 2000-year history. Access is only on guided tours.

There's also a memorial plaque to Regensburg's Jews in the pavement west of the Neupfarrkirche and a memorial to concentration-camp victims on the northern side of the Steinerne Brücke.

Diözesanmuseum The painted medieval Church of St Ulrich *(☎ 516 68, Domplatz 2; adult/concession €1.50/0.75, €2.50 including cathedral treasury; open 10am-5pm Tues-Sun Apr-Oct)* houses a collection of religious art.

Schloss Thurn und Taxis & Museums
In the 15th century, a certain Franz von Taxis (1459–1517) scratched out his place in history by establishing the first European postal system, which remained a family monopoly until the 19th century. In 1748, one of his descendants, Prince Alexander Ferdinand, became the emperor's representative at the diet meetings. He and his family took up residence in the former Benedictine monastery of St Emmeram. Pretty soon, the old monastic quarters had been converted into one of the most modern palaces in Europe *(☎ 504 81 33, Emmeramsplatz 6; tours adult/concession €6/5, combined ticket to all Schloss attractions €8.50/6; tours 11am-5pm Mon-Fri, 10am-5pm Sat & Sun)*. Running water and central heating matched a lavish interior of exquisite furniture, silver chandeliers, Gobelins, thick carpets and other items indispensable to the lifestyle of a noble family. It's still owned by the Thurn und Taxis today.

All this can only be seen on tours, which also include a look at the cloister of the **Basilika St Emmeram** *(☎ 510 30, Emmeramsplatz 3; church free, cloister €3/2.50; closed Fri & Sun morning)*, which is a masterpiece by the Asam brothers. Sheltered in its crypt are the remains of Sts Emmeram, Wolfgang and Ramwold, as well as those of several Carolingian rulers.

The complex also contains two museums. The **Thurn und Taxis-Museum** *(adult/concession €3/2)* presents porcelain, glass, furniture and other items from the family's private collection. The **Marstallmuseum** *(tours €3.50/3)* has historic carriages and sleighs as well as the opulent festival rooms.

North & West of Altes Rathaus
Schottenkirche St Jakob The monastery of St James was founded in 1090 by Benedictine monks. The church *(Jakobstrasse 3)* was built in 1183 and is a rather simple three-nave construction with a coffered ceiling. 'Simple', however, is not the word to describe the amazing north portal, a supreme example of Romanesque architecture in Germany. Its numerous reliefs and sculptures (which were originally painted

and covered in gold-leaf) form an incredibly complicated iconography whose meaning continues to baffle even the experts.

Uhrenmuseum The breezy little privately owned Uhrenmuseum *(Watch Museum; ☎ 599 95 95, Ludwigstrasse 3; adult/concession €2/1; open 10am-4pm Wed-Mon)* has a fabulous collection of valuable and notable watches by such companies as Jaeger-LeCouitre, Patek Phillippe and…ahem …Swatch. Also here is what is billed as the world's most 'complicated and expensive' watch, the Blancpain 1735, and the first digital watch, the 1972 Pulsar. Admission is worth it, if you're a watch nut.

Kepler-Gedächtnishaus The astronomer and mathematician Johannes Kepler lived and died in this house, now the Kepler Memorial House *(☎ 507 34 42, Keplerstrasse 5; tours adult/concession €2/1; tours 10am, 11am, 2pm & 3pm Tues-Sun Apr-Oct, no tours Sun afternoon Nov-Mar)*.

Organised Tours

Guided English-language 1½-hour walking tours (€5/2.50 adult/concession) start at the tourist office at 1.30pm Wednesday and Saturday from May to September. German tours depart year round at 2.45pm Monday to Saturday (Saturday also at 10.15am), and at 10.45am and 2pm Sunday and holidays. From April to October there's an extra tour at 10.15am Monday to Friday.

The Schifffahrtsunternehmen Klinger (☎ 521 04) operates 50-minute Danube cruises from the landing just east of the Steinerne Brücke from late March to October hourly from 10am to 4pm (€6.50). It also runs boat tours to Walhalla (see Around Regensburg later in this chapter).

Special Events

Every spring around Whitsuntide/Pentecost and at the end of August, Regensburg parties at the **Dult**, a big fun fair with carousel rides, beer tents and stalls selling everything from magical household cleaners to exotic spices and teas. It's held on Dultplatz at the Oberpfalzbrücke north of the Altstadt.

All December long, the Alter Kornmarkt square fills with the smells, sights and sounds of Christmas during the **Christkindl-Markt**.

Places to Stay – Budget

Azur-Campingplatz (☎ 27 00 25, fax 29 94 32, ⓔ info@azur-camping.de, Weinweg 40) Bus: No 6 from Hauptbahnhof. Person/site €4/3.50-7.25. This camping ground is about 2km west of the Altstadt on the southern Danube bank. The bus goes right to the entrance.

DJH hostel (☎ 574 02, fax 524 11, ⓔ jhregensburg@djh-bayern.de, Wöhrdstrasse 60) Bus: No 3 from Albertstrasse to Eisstadion. Bed & breakfast €15.85. Regensburg's modernised hostel is on Unterer Wöhrd island in a great location north of the Danube and about a 10-minute walk east of the Altstadt.

The tourist office has a list of *private rooms* from about €15 per person.

Gasthof Spitalgarten (☎ 847 74, fax 890 31 68, ⓔ Spitalgarten@t-online.de, St-Katharinen-Platz 1) Singles/doubles €20/40. North of the Steinerne Brücke in a 13th-century hospice, this inn has basic rooms but is not a bad bet for the price.

Places to Stay – Mid-Range

Hotel D'Orphée (☎ 59 60 20, fax 59 60 22 22, ⓔ info@hotel-orphee.de, Wahlenstrasse 1) Singles/doubles from €30/60 (shared bath), €64/72 (private bath). This hotel is a pleasure to recommend. Each room has a unique theme and offers great value, especially the stunningly romantic No 7. Downstairs rooms have baths (No 5's bathroom entrance is hidden in a secret door). There's also a nice common room with a large terrace; breakfast is at the nearby Café D'Orphée (see Places to Eat).

Hotel Am Peterstor (☎ 545 45, fax 545 42, Fröhliche-Türken-Strasse 12) Singles/doubles €40/50. This central hotel offers great value for money in the Altstadt. The decor won't win design awards, but rooms are functional, modern and clean.

Künstlerhaus (☎ 571 34, fax 599 84 11, ⓔ künstlerhaus-regensburg@t-online.de, Alter Kornmarkt 3) Singles/doubles from

€56/66. Let your fantasies go wild in any of the five themed rooms in what is the Altstadt's narrowest house. Choices include the Space Room (calling all Trekkies), the Asian-style Wind and Water Room and, our personal favourite, the mysterious Oriental Room.

Hotel Roter Hahn (☎ 59 50 90, fax 595 09 40, e hotel@roter-hahn.com, Rote-Hahnen-Gasse 10) Singles €51-61, doubles €66-112. Old on the outside, but modern within, this family-run hotel is a winner with quirky rooms, some with trompe l'oeil murals, and a good restaurant.

Places to Stay – Top End

Altstadthotel Arch (☎ 586 60, fax 586 61 68, e arch@onlinehome.de, Haidplatz 4) Singles €65-87, doubles €81-107. This is another city landmark in a stately patrician building. Some rooms are set aside for non-smokers, while the beamed *Ratsherrenzimmer* are the most romantic.

Bischofshof am Dom (☎ 584 60, fax 58 41 46, Krauterermarkt 3) Singles €63-94, doubles €115-166. This upmarket hotel occupies the former bishops' residence. Rooms, decked out in country-style, wrap around a flower-filled courtyard (with beer garden in summer). Some are within the Roman walls – nice touch, eh? The restaurant (☎ 594 10 10; lunch mains €6.40 to €12, dinner €10 to €20) consists of a series of fancifully decorated historic rooms; there's a classic cafe as well.

Sorat Insel-Hotel (☎ 810 40, fax 810 44 44, e regensburg@sorat-hotels.com, Müllerstrasse 7) Singles €102-132, doubles €122-153. The modern and shining Sorat on Oberer Wöhrd has an awesome location at the island's tip and great views of the town's skyline. The generously sized rooms and public areas all sport Art Deco touches. Service is impeccable.

Places to Eat

Restaurants There is a huge range of restaurants in Regensburg.

Alte Münz (☎ 548 86, Fischmarkt 7) Mains €9.50-14.70. This well-respected restaurant offers seasonal regional fare using choice ingredients and traditional recipes. Anything featuring game is good and the chef always whisks together a couple of vegetarian selections as well. The name, which means 'old mint', comes from Roman coins discovered underneath the medieval building.

Anastasia (☎ 584 15 79, Arnulfsplatz 4) Mains €6.50-14.50. Sample fin-de-siècle elegance in a former Russian consulate, with fine meat and vegetarian dishes on offer. Specialities include the *Hussar's Spiess*, an enormous, tender pork and beef kebab with trimmings for €13.50.

Dicker Mann (☎ 573 70, Krebsgasse 6) Dishes €9-12. One of the oldest restaurants in town, this one has dependably good local Bavarian food, usually swift service and a little beer garden.

Kneitinger (☎ 524 55, Arnulfsplatz 3) Meals €5-11. If you want to see Regenburgers of all ages let their hair down, this earthy brewery-pub is the place. The smallish menu features hearty home cooking for big appetites, best washed down with the house brew.

Leerer Beutel (☎ 589 97, Bertoldstrasse 9) Mains €7.50-15. This stylish restaurant inside a cultural centre serves creative, light cuisine, including lots of salads. Black-and-white photographs of jazz greats form the backdrop. The two-course weekday lunch menu for €5.50 is the best deal.

Rosenpalais (☎ 599 75 79, Minoritenweg 20) Bistro mains €10-18, restaurant mains €22-27, gourmet meals from €65. Closed Sun. The silver service restaurant upstairs was awarded a Michelin star in early 2002. It's the perfect place for a special rendezvous with multi-course dinners accompanied by matching wines. Gourmets on a budget can sample culinary artistry downstairs in the bistro. The weekday two-course lunch special is a mere €9.

Rossini (☎ 56 77 85, Haidplatz 3, enter from Rote-Hahnen-Gasse 2) Mains €8-15. This snug Italian restaurant does a bit more than the standard pizza and pasta. A wooden ceiling, mirrors and stencilled walls provide a suitably theatrical backdrop for the daily changing menu. The antipasti are recommended.

EASTERN BAVARIA

Spaghetteria (☎ *0130-78 57 00, Am Römling 12)* Dishes €5-8. For heavenly pastas and a spirited crowd, step into this former 17th-century chapel. You can pick fresh noodles, sauces and side dishes from the buffet and get out the door, with a glass of house wine, for under €10.

Cafes & Bistros
Cafes are also abundant.

Felix (☎ *590 59, Fröhliche-Türken-Strasse 6)* Dishes €3-13. A vibrant buzz reigns all day at this trendy cafe-bar, with the first troops descending for breakfast and the last leaving at 1am after that final martini. In fine weather, there's sidewalk seating, but otherwise you'll be surrounded by a campy castle ambience with arty chandeliers, faux torches and big framed mirrors. The food ranges from sandwiches to steaks.

Haus Heuport (☎ *599 82 97, Domplatz 7)* Breakfast €3-7, bistro mains €3.50-14, restaurant mains €15-23. In a former merchant home, this place draws a mixed clientele. The scene comes to be seen at the downstairs bistro (breakfast until 6pm), while the fat-wallet set humps it up a grand old wooden staircase to the signature restaurant with views of the Dom. The cuisine here is Mediterranean with Asian touches, while the bistro banks on sandwiches, salads, pastas and various munchies.

Café D'Orphée (☎ *529 77, Untere Bachgasse 8)* Mains €12.50-17.50. Delightful French food is on the menu at this quintessential brasserie. Red velvet, mirrors and dark wood create a Belle Epoque ambience.

Vitus (☎ *526 46, Hinter der Grieb 8)* Mains €5-15. Colourful canvasses mix with Gothic vaulted ceilings at this popular place serving country-style French food. Sit in the bistro section with wicker furniture or the more formal restaurant.

Snacks & Fast Food
There is a daily fresh *produce market* called *Viktualienmarkt* at Neupfarrplatz.

Dampfnudel Uli (☎ *532 97, Watmarkt 4)* Dishes under €5. Open 10.01am-6.01pm Tues-Fri, 10.01am-3.01pm Sat. This quirky place serves steamed doughnuts with custard (€3.90), a Regensburg speciality.

Back & Snack (*Haidplatz 5)* This take-away-only place has good baked treats for under €2.50.

Historische Wurstküche (☎ *590 99, Thundorfer Strasse 3)* Sausages €4.50/5.80/8.70 per 6/8/12. Closes at 7pm. There's been a sausage kitchen in this riverside spot since construction of the Stone Bridge began in 1135. Tourists and locals alike love the little links, served with kraut and mustard, at this congenial place. On request, they'll also make a takeaway *Bratwurstsemmel* – sausage and kraut in a bun – for €2.

Little Saigon (☎ *56 77 52, Domplatz 5)* Dishes €3-8.50. Come here for standard Asian fast food with egg rolls, salads and other vegie and meaty treats.

Raan Thai Imbiss (☎ *56 38 79, Untere Bachgasse 1)* Meals under €5. Closes at 8pm, at 4pm Sat. Raan's cooks prepare a different menu daily, but typical offerings include red curry, sweet and sour chicken, or soups and spring rolls for €1.75.

Würstl Toni (*Am Kornmarkt)* Open till the wee hours. If the Wurstküche is closed, your next best sausage bet is this simple stand with cult status among night owls. It's on Kornmarkt's eastern end; the awning reads 'Wurstbraterei Schmidl'.

Entertainment
The city-published *Regensburger Kulturkalendar* guide is available at the tourist office (free). RESI (Regensburger Schwulen-und-Lesben-Initiative; ☎ 514 41) is a central gay and lesbian group at Blaue-Lilien-Gasse 1. Lesbians can also contact the Frauenzentrum (☎ 242 59) at Prüfeninger Strasse 32, but it's a long way west of the Altstadt.

Beer Gardens
There are a number of beer gardens, mostly around the Altstadt.

Alte Linde (☎ *880 80, Müllerstrasse 1)* Alte Linde runs a large and leafy beer garden just off the Steinerne Brücke with a panoramic view of the Altstadt – lovely on summer evenings. The food's pretty good and inexpensive (meals €5 to €10).

Goldene Ente (☎ *854 44, Badstrasse 32)* Mains €5-10. This place is a student favourite and has a lovely location right on the Danube, which is just as well because service moves slower than the river.

Kepler *(☎ 56 06 35, Keplerstrasse 3)* Next to the Kepler Memorial House, this pub-cum-beer garden draws a youthful clientele with its unpretentious ambience and lovely setting.

Spitalgarten *(☎ 847 74, St-Katharinen-Platz 1)* North of the Altstadt, this is one of the oldest hospital breweries in Bavaria. The beer garden, filled with a convivial mix of young and old, locals and visitors, has grand views of the city, and friendly service.

Pubs & Bars There are plenty of chances to whet the palate in Regensburg.

Allegro *(☎ 527 14, Taubengässchen 2)* This place is open all day, even serving breakfast until 2pm, but it's really more of a night spot. It's popular with the lesbigay crowd, although there's plenty of heteros thrown into the mix.

Falk's Weinstube *(☎ 539 08, Bismarck-platz 4)* Closed Sun. This snug wine tavern near the theatre draws a more sedate clientele than Allegro, with its select Austrian vintages and snacks from that country.

Hemingway's *(☎ 56 15 06, Obere Bach-gasse 6)* Black wood, big mirrors and photos of Papa himself add to the trendy atmosphere of this Art Deco 'American' bar. The bartenders can whip up about 40 cocktails, while the chef creates local takes on Asian and Cajun dishes.

Irish Harp *(☎ 572 68, Brückstrasse 1)* This Irish pub has the usual Guinness on tap and occasional live bands (free).

Neue Film Bühne *(☎ 570 37, Bismarck-platz 9)* Theatrical decor with incongruous Asiatic touches characterises this trendy cafe-bar frequented by an eclectic crowd of students, yuppies and young families. In summer, the terrace overlooking Bismarck-platz is great for lounging.

Peaches *(☎ 534 81, Baumhackergasse 2)* This is a fun and fashionable cocktail bar with a popular happy hour (7pm to 9pm Sunday to Thursday) with all drinks for €3.75. On Monday, when any jumbo-sized pizza costs just €5, the place is busier than a three-legged dog on ice skates. Come early.

Jazz The **Jazzclub im Leeren Beutel** *(☎ 56 33 75, Bertoldstrasse 9)* has concerts two to three times weekly. It shares premises with an art gallery, cinema and stylish restaurant (see Places to Eat).

Classical Music Opera, operettas, ballet and classical-music performances are held at the **Theater Regensburg** (see Theatre later in this section). The Regensburger Domspatzen boys' choir sings during the 9am Sunday service at the Dom, and classical concerts are held in various churches, the theatre and the university's Audimax hall (check the Kulturkalender for dates).

Cinemas Catch a flick in Regensburg.

Film Galerie *(☎ 56 09 01, Bertoldstrasse 9)* Part of the Leerer Beutel cultural centre, this cinema often shows movies in the original language, including English. Look for the acronym 'OmU' *(Original mit Untertiteln)*.

Garbo-Filmtheater *(☎ 575 86, Weissger-bergraben)* This is another movie theatre showing classic Hollywood movies and modern filmic fare in English.

Theatre Regensburg's municipal theatre operates three venues. Tickets are available at the tourist office or at the Velodrom (see later).

Theater Regensburg *(Bismarckplatz)* This main stage reopened in late 2001 following a thorough renovation. For tickets, call ☎ 507 24 24.

Theater am Haidplatz *(Haidplatz 8)* This venue also presents a summer season on an open-air stage in the courtyard of the Thon-Dittmer-Palais.

Velodrom *(☎ 507 24 24, Arnulfplatz 4b)* What was once a bicycle rink, now hosts opera, theatre, musicals and ballet.

Statt Theater *(☎ 533 02, Winklergasse 16; closed Mon, Tues & July)* This privately owned venue specialises in alternative dramas, plays and cabaret.

Getting There & Away

Mainline trains run from Frankfurt through Regensburg on their way to Passau and Vienna. Several of the Munich-Leipzig and

Munich-Dresden services also pass through. Sample ticket prices are Munich (€19.20, 1½ hours), Nuremberg (€14, one hour) and Passau (€20.20, one hour).

The A3 autobahn runs north-west to Nuremberg and south-east to Passau, while the A9 runs south to Munich.

For a lift, call the local Mitfahrzentrale (☎ 194 40).

Regensburg is a key player on the Danube Bike Trail; all approaches to the city are well signposted along bike paths. There are bike lockers at the Hauptbahnhof on platform 1 (€0.50 per day). See Getting Around for bike rentals.

Getting Around

Bus The main point for city bus transfers is one block north of the Hauptbahnhof, on Albertstrasse. Other major hubs are Arnulfsplatz, Domplatz and Neupfarrplatz. Bus tickets cost €0.75/1.40 for short/long journeys in the centre; strip tickets cost €6 for six rides (two strips per ride in town). An all-day ticket is a better deal, costing just €3 for the centre. On weekdays, the Altstadtbus runs between the train station and the Altstadt every six minutes for €0.50.

Car & Motorcycle The Steinerne Brücke is closed to private vehicles. The main bridge across the river is the Nibelungenbrücke east of the Altstadt. From the south, it's accessed via Weissenburgstrasse. There is an exit from Nibelungenbrücke onto Unterer Wöhrd and the hostel.

Car parks in the centre charge from €1 per hour and are well signposted.

Taxi For a taxi, call ☎ 194 10, ☎ 570 00 or ☎ 520 52 (flag fall €2, plus €1.20 per kilometre).

Bicycle BikeHaus (☎ 599 81 93 or 24-hour hotline ☎ 0177-831 12 34) is in the western wing of the train station (closed Sunday). It rents children's/touring/trekking bikes for €5/8/9 per day and has bike storage facilities. Staff can help plan bike trips along the Danube and in other regions. Hours are 9am to 7pm (less from October to March).

AROUND REGENSBURG
Walhalla

According to German mythology, Walhalla is the home of the Gods into which warriors chosen by the Valkyries may be admitted. But did you know that it's actually located just 10km east of Regensburg? Here, lording over the banks of the Danube, is a bombastic marble temple housing the 'Hall of Fame' of the immortal giants of Germanic thought and deed. The brainchild of King Ludwig I of Bavaria, Walhalla (☎ 09403-96 16 80; adult/concession €2/1.50; open 9am-5.45pm daily Apr-Oct, 10am-11.45am & 1pm-3.45pm daily Nov-Mar) was built by Leo von Klenze and modelled on the Parthenon in Athens; it opened in 1842.

A gallery of 96 marble busts and 64 commemorative tablets – of statesmen, scientists and artists – dominates the interior, which is fitted out entirely in coloured marble. Every five to seven years, the Bavarian Council of Ministers assumes the role of the Valkyries and selects a new worthy German to be admitted to this illustrious circle. Only three busts are of women, although, in early 2002, the council approved the addition of the bust of a fourth woman, Nazi Resistance fighter Sophie Scholl (for more details see the boxed text 'The White Rose' in the Munich chapter). It will be installed in spring 2003.

The sheer weight of the august personages is perhaps a bit overwhelming, but if passing under the gaze of Beethoven, Luther and Copernicus doesn't leave you at least a little in awe, you're probably vacationing in the wrong country.

To get to the monument by car, follow the road to Donaustauf, paralleling the northern bank of the Danube. In fine weather, the most pleasant way to get here is by cruise boat, which leaves from Regensburg's Steinerne Brücke landing docks at 10.30am and 2pm daily from April to mid-October (€6.50/9.50 one way/return, two hours total, including a one hour stop at Walhalla).

STRAUBING

☎ 09421 • pop 44,000 • elevation 331m

Straubing, some 30km south-east of Regensburg on the southern Danube bank, is a small and pleasant city in the heart of the Gäuboden, one of the most fertile agricultural regions in Bavaria. The townscape is littered with an amazing array of churches, many built and decorated by top architects and artists, including the Asam brothers, Wolfgang Dientzenhofer and Hans von Burghausen. Settled since Celtic times, Straubing's 'modern' history began in 1218 with the founding of the Neustadt by Duke Ludwig the Kelheimer. During the town's heyday from 1353 to 1425 it was the seat of the duchy of Straubing-Holland, a side line of the Wittelsbach dynasty.

Orientation & Information

The historical centre, compact and easily walkable, is sandwiched between the Danube to the north and the Hauptbahnhof to the south. A short walk north on Bahnhofstrasse takes you straight to the heart of town, an elongated square consisting of Theresienplatz and Ludwigsplatz.

The tourist office (☎ 94 43 07, fax 94 41 03, e stadt@straubing.de), at Theresienplatz 20, is open from 9am to 5pm Monday to Friday and until noon on Saturday. Straubing's Web site is at w www.straubing.de.

Things to See & Do

Straubing's Altstadt is chock-a-block with attractive buildings. Dividing Theresienplatz from Ludwigsplatz is the **Stadtturm** (1316), a proud, 68m-high Gothic watchtower that doubles as the town's symbol.

Next to the tower is the **Rathaus**, with the tourist office on the ground floor. It originally consisted of two 14th-century merchants' homes but was repackaged in neogothic style in the 19th century. Just east of the tower is the gleaming golden **Dreifaltigkeitssäule** (Trinity Column), erected in 1709 as a nod to Catholic upheavals during the Spanish War of Succession.

Straubing has about half a dozen historic churches. Among the most impressive is the **St Jakobskirche** on Pfarrplatz, a few steps north of the tourist office. This late-Gothic hall church preserves its original stained-glass windows but received a partial baroque makeover in the 18th century,

courtesy of the Asam brothers. The two also designed the exuberant interior of the **Ursulinenkirche** on Burggasse, their final collaboration. Its ceiling fresco depicts the martyrdom of St Ursula surrounded by allegories of the four then-known continents.

North of the church, on Fürstenstrasse, is the **Herzogschloss**, the former ducal palace which now houses the tax office and a small religious museum.

About a 10-minute walk east of here, via Donaugasse and Petersgasse, is **Kirche St Peter** (1180), Straubing's oldest church built on the site of a Roman fortress. A pair of tympanums (the section at the top of portals), a Christ figure and a pietà survive from the Romanesque founding period. The surrounding graveyard contains the Agnes-Bernauer-Kapelle (see the boxed text 'The Woeful Tale of Agnes Bernauer') and the Seelenkapelle with a Dance of Death fresco cycle (1763).

Back in the Altstadt, wrap up your explorations with a stop at the small but exquisite **Gäubodenmuseum** (☎ 818 11, Frauenhoferstrasse 9; adult/concession €2/1.50; open 10am-4pm Tues-Sun). Besides town history, it displays items from one of the most seminal excavations (1950) of Roman treasure on German soil. Exhibits are beautifully displayed with intimate spotlighting and include imposing ceremonial armour and ornate masks worn by both soldiers and horses.

Special Events

Every August, Straubing erupts into a beery roar for 10 days during the **Gäubodenfest**, one of Bavaria's biggest collective drink-ups. Begun in 1812 as a social gathering for grain farmers, the fair now lubricates up to 1.3 million visitors. The entire town centre turns into an enormous beer garden with 23,000 seats – often it's standing room only. Finding lodging during the festival is a tall order. Plan well ahead or stay outside of town.

Places to Stay

Campingplatz (☎ 897 94, Wundermühlweg 9) Sites €7.50-20. Open May-mid-Oct. Straubing's modern camping ground is north of the Danube.

The Woeful Tale of Agnes Bernauer

Star-crossed love always makes for a good story. The year is 1432. Our tragic heroes are Albrecht III, heir to the duchy of Bavaria, and Agnes Bernauer, the daughter of Augsburg barber and bathhouse owner, Kaspar Bernauer. The two first meet at a tournament in Augsburg, fall madly in love and marry secretly shortly thereafter. Naturally, Albrecht's family is less than thrilled, feeling that a commoner is simply beneath the future duke.

Despite such adversity, the couple lives happily for a few years, mostly in Straubing, and even has a daughter. In 1435, however, Albrecht's father, Duke Ernst I (ruled 1397–1438), decides to take action. He sends his son away under some pretext and, in a cloak-and-dagger operation, has Agnes tried for witchcraft, found guilty and thrown into the Danube with her legs tied. She somehow manages to get rid of the shackles and swim ashore only to be greeted by the executioner who finishes her off by holding her head under water.

Albrecht, though heartbroken at first, quickly finds solace in another marriage, this time to a 'proper' aristocrat. His aging father, meanwhile, struck by sudden remorse, builds a memorial chapel for dear Agnes in the churchyard of Kirche St Peter. These days, Straubing honours the tragic woman with a festival held in the courtyard of the Schloss every four years (next one in 2003).

Tent camping (☎ *125 22, Kagerser Hauptstrasse 44)* Pitching a tent is usually possible on the riverside grounds of the local canoe club a short walk from town. Call for rates.

DJH hostel (☎ *804 36, fax 120 94,* e *jugendherberge@straubing.de, Friedhofstrasse 12)* Bed & breakfast €10.50-11.30. Closed Nov-Mar. Straubing's small hostel (57 beds) is in a leafy part of town about a 15-minute walk east of the Bahnhof.

The tourist office can help you find *private rooms* starting at €13 per person.

Hotel-Restaurant Röhrlbräu (☎ *990 80, fax 99 08 28, Theresienplatz 7)* Singles €40-45, doubles €60-65. Rooms won't win any design awards but most are well-sized and have private baths, TV and phones.

Hotel-Restaurant Seethaler (☎ *939 50, fax 93 95 50, Theresienplatz 25)* Singles/doubles/triples/quads €60/90/110/125. A recent face-lift has given rooms at this central hotel fresh colours, shiny wooden floors and sparkling bathrooms.

Hotel-Restaurant Wittelsbach (☎ *94 30, fax 816 41, Stadtgraben 25/26)* Singles/doubles €45/65. This is a family-run place with homey, comfortable rooms with many amenities, including air-con. In fine weather, you can relax with a beer on the tree-canopied terrace.

Places to Eat

All hotels mentioned in Places to Stay also have restaurants.

Gaststätte Unterm Rain (☎ *227 72, Unterm Rain 15)* Mains €4-9. Open dinner only. A local favourite, this congenial inn cum beer garden next to the old town wall serves sizable portions of hearty Bavarian cuisine (their schnitzels are reportedly big enough for two). Definitely try a mug of Röhrl, the local brew.

Molise (☎ *105 08, Theresienplatz 38)* Pizza & pasta €4.50-7, mains €8.50-18.50. Closed Tues. This lively place enjoys an excellent reputation locally. Pizza and pasta are good, but to really get a sense of the chef's talents, go for one of the daily specials.

Rapunzel (☎ *83 11 22, Regensburger Strasse 61F)* Mains 2.50-11. This place is popular with a younger crowd and serves simple but satisfying bistro fare.

Cafe Krönner (☎ *109 94, Theresienplatz 22)* This traditional coffeehouse will satisfy anybody's coffee and cake cravings. The Agnes-Bernauer-Torte is their speciality.

Every morning (except Sunday), a *produce market* enlivens Ludwigsplatz.

Getting There & Away

Direct RegionalBahn (RB) trains run to/from Regensburg about hourly (€6.60,

30 minutes), while InterCity (IC) trains make the trip to/from Passau every two hours (€14.30, 50 minutes). Trains to/from Munich (€19, two hours) require a change, usually in Plattling. Straubing is at the junction of the B8 and B20 highways, just south of the A3.

PASSAU
☎ 0851 • pop 50,000 • elevation 302m

A hint of Italy welcomes you as you approach Passau, located in a breathtaking setting at the confluence of the Danube, the Inn and the Ilz rivers. The town's Italian-baroque essence has not doused the medieval feel, best experienced while wandering the lanes, tunnels and archways of the Altstadt and monastic district to the Dreiflüsseeck, where the rivers meet.

Thanks to a university founded in 1978, Passau is a fairly lively city, even though, judging by the large number of churches (52 in all, 50 of them Catholic), people do take their faith pretty seriously. As they do their beer! Passau manages to support no fewer than five breweries (Innstadt, Hacklberger, Andorfer, Löwen and Peschl).

Passau is a main stop for cruise boats travelling on the Danube and is often deluged with day visitors. It is also the hub of long-distance cycling routes, eight of which converge here, and a good jumping off point for explorations into Upper Austria.

History
Originally a Celtic settlement, Passau became a Roman camp from the 1st to the 5th century AD. Some time during that same century, St Severin founded a small monastery, which, by pope's orders, morphed into a bishopric in 739. In 1217, Emperor Friedrich II promoted the local bishop to prince-bishop, thus making him – and his successors – both secular and religious rulers. This situation lasted until 1803, when Passau was absorbed into the Bavarian kingdom. In an ironic twist, the city survived the Thirty Years' War, which destroyed so many other places, unscathed only to be devastated in the Great Fire of 1662, which ruined a large number of medieval buildings.

Orientation
Passau is divided into three sections: the Ilzstadt north of the Danube, the Altstadt between Danube and Inn and the Innstadt south of the Inn.

The Altstadt is a narrow peninsula with the confluence of the three rivers at its eastern tip. The little Ilz approaches from the north, the Danube from the west and the Inn from the south. The Hauptbahnhof is about a 10-minute walk west of the central Altstadt, where most sights, hotels and restaurants are located. Exceptions include the Veste Oberhaus and the hostel in the Ilzstadt, and the Kastell Boitro in the Innstadt.

Information
Tourist Offices The tourist office has two branches. One is opposite the Hauptbahnhof at Bahnhofstrasse 36 (☎ 95 59 80, fax 572 98, e tourist-info@passau.de) and is open 9am to 5pm Monday to Friday and until 1pm Saturday and Sunday from Easter to mid-October. The other in the Altstadt at Rathausplatz 3 (☎ 95 59 80, fax 351 07), which is open 8.30am to 6pm Monday to Friday and 9.30am to 3pm Saturday and Sunday during summer. From mid-October to Easter, its hours are 8.30am to 5pm, until 4pm Friday, closed Saturday and Sunday and for one hour at lunchtime.

Money Change money at the Postbank in the main post office, the Sparkasse at Residenzplatz 9 or the Commerzbank at Ludwigstrasse 13.

Post & Communications The main post office is just east of the Hauptbahnhof on Bahnhofstrasse. CompUse is an Internet cafe at Neuburger Strasse 19 and is open 1pm to 9pm daily.

Laundry Wash your smalls at Rent-Wash, Neuburger Strasse 19, for €3 per load. Dryers cost €1.50 per 15-minute session.

Altstadt Walking Tour
This tour starts and finishes at the tourist office on Rathausplatz and covers a distance of about 1.75km.

PASSAU

PLACES TO STAY
1 Zeltplatz Ilzstadt
2 DJH Hostel
7 Pension Rössner
17 Hotel Wilder Mann;
   Passau Glasmuseum
26 Gasthof Blauer Bock
28 Hotel König
34 Rotel Inn
40 Hotel Weisser Hase
52 Hotel Spitzberg

PLACES TO EAT & DRINK
11 Weisses Kreuz
12 Chandni
18 Residenz Café
19 Zum Grünen Baum
29 O Sole Mio

30 Shamrock
32 KÖPA Schmankerlpassage
33 Peschl-Terrasse
37 Camera
38 Kochlöffel
39 Nordsee
41 Heilig-Geist-Stiftsschänke
42 Café Duft
43 Café Nyhavn
44 Goldenes Schiff
45 Zi'Teresa Pizzeria
46 Café Kowalski
47 Cantina Ensenada

OTHER
3 Veste Oberhaus;
  Oberhausmuseum
4 Veste Niederhaus

5 Dreiflüsseeck
6 Museum Moderner
  Kunst
8 Fahrrad – Klinik
9 Kloster Niedernburg
10 St-Michaels-Kirche
13 Scharfrichterkino
14 Altes Rathaus
15 Wurm + Köck –
   Rathausplatz Landing
   Docks
16 Tourist Office
   Rathausplatz
20 Wittelsbacher Brunnen
21 New Bishop's
   Residence; Cathedral
   Treasury Museum
22 Dom St Stephan

23 Stadttheater
24 Statue of Maximilian I
   Joseph
25 Sparkasse
27 Wurm + Köck Main
   Landing Docks
31 Commerzbank
35 Tourist Office –
   Bahnhofstrasse
36 Post Office; Postbank
48 Wallfahrtskirche Kloster
   Mariahilf
49 Römermuseum – Kastell
   Boitro
50 Metropolis
51 CompUse Internet Cafe;
   Rent-Wash Laundry
53 Police Station

Altes Rathaus Rathausplatz is clearly dominated by the colourful Altes Rathaus (Old Town Hall; 1399). Its tower, decorated with a large clock face, blends in very well with the rest of the building but wasn't actually built until 1891. Inside it is what purports to be Bavaria's largest **carillon**, which erupts into chimes several times daily (hours are listed on the wall, which also shows historical flood levels).

Through the entrance on Schrottgasse, you'll get to the **Grosser Rathaus Saal** (*Great Assembly Room; adult/concession €1.50/1; open 10am-4pm daily Apr-Oct),* a collaboration of two Italian artists, Carlo Lurago and Giovanni Carlone. The vivid murals were painted by local artist and crackpot Ferdinand Wagner in the late 19th century and depict scenes from Passau's history, both real and mythological. Look for Kriemhild's arrival in the city to visit her uncle Pilgrim, then bishop of Passau (971–91), as reported in the medieval *Nibelungen* epic. Another wall commemorates the wedding of Emperor Leopold I to Eleonore of Palatinate-Neuburg in 1676.

If it's not being used for a wedding or a meeting, also sneak into the adjacent **Small**

Assembly Room for a peek at the ceiling fresco showing buxom beauties and a fierce-looking man as allegories of the three rivers.

Wagner, who used to live in the huge building on the northern bank of the Danube, just to the right of where the Luitpoldbrücke is today, threatened to move out if the bridge was built. It was, he did, and after viewing the paintings, you wonder whether the city made the right choice.

Passau Glasmuseum On the other side of Schrottgasse, in the Hotel Zum Wilder Mann, is the Museum of Glass (*☎ 350 71, Am Rathausplatz; adult/concession €4/2.50; open 10am-4pm daily June-Oct, 1pm-4pm daily Nov-May*). It contains a splendid collection of over 30,000 items of Bohemian glasswork and crystal spanning 250 years. Even if you charge through the place, you'll need at least an hour to view all the glass cases filled with Art Nouveau, baroque, classical and Art Deco pieces.

Empress Elizabeth (Sisi) of Austria, a bosom friend of King Ludwig II, once stayed in the Hotel Zum Wilden Mann, still one of the city's finest (see Places to Stay), during a family reunion in 1862.

Residenzplatz Walk south on Schrottgasse, then turn right (west) on Messergasse which leads to Residenzplatz. It's a pretty square hemmed in by patrician town houses and anchored by the **Wittelsbacher Brunnen** (1903), a sprightly fountain built on the occasion of the 100th anniversary of the formation of the Kingdom of Bavaria. At the top is a figure of Mary, the patron saint of Bavaria, while the figures below are allegories of the trio of rivers. Continue west on Messergasse, which will take you to Domplatz.

Dom St Stephen The characteristic green onion domes of Passau's cathedral float serenely above the town silhouette. There's been a church in this spot since the 10th century, but the original version – a Romanesque-Gothic combination – was almost entirely destroyed during the 1662 fire, only a few decades after it had received the finishing touches.

When reconstruction began six years later, architect Carlo Lurago managed to integrate the remaining Gothic features into his design, which clearly belongs to the baroque.

The frescoes show vivid scenes of heaven inspired by a tapestry series called *Triumph of the Eucharist* by Peter Paul Rubens. There's the usual assortment of altars, some of them decorated with paintings by Michael Rottmayr. The modern high altar is a bit of a surprise. It was designed by Josef Henselmann, a Munich professor, in 1953 and shows the stoning of St Stephen by the Pharisees. Also of note is the pulpit (1725) with superb carvings.

The true pièce de résistance, though, is the **cathedral organ** (1927). With 17,774 pipes and 231 stops, it is considered the largest in the world. Half-hour organ recitals take place at noon Monday to Friday (€2/1 for adult/concession), a good time to appreciate the church's superb acoustics.

Outside the cathedral, on Domplatz, stands a statue of Maximilian I Joseph (1779–1825), who began his career as Elector Maximilian IV Joseph before Napoleon promoted him to Bavaria's first king.

Neue Bischöfliche Residenz From the right (southern) aisle of the cathedral, a spiralling staircase leads to the New Bishops' Residence (1730), home of Passau's prince-bishops until 1871. Inside is a glorious open staircase, built by Melchior Hefele, a student of Neumann. There's also fanciful stucco and a preposterous ceiling fresco entitled *The Gods of Olympus Protecting Immortal Passau*.

Most of the Residenz is occupied by the administrative offices of the Passau diocese, but one section houses the **Diözesan Museum** (*Cathedral Treasury & Museum; Residenzplatz 8; adult/concession €1/0.50; open 10am-4pm Mon-Sat May-Oct*). The amazing range of ecclesiastical finery – including monstrances, goblets, sculptures and paintings, vestments – leave little doubt about the wealth and power of the Passau archbishops. Be sure not to miss the baroque library, where frescoes by Giovanni Carlone provide the requisite flourish.

EASTERN BAVARIA

Abbey Quarter Turn right as you exit the residence, which will take you back to Residenzplatz. Continue down a small staircase called the *Hofstiege* to Innbrückgasse and follow it downhill to the riverbank and the Innbrücke. On your right will be the **Stadttheater** (1783), housed in what used to be the prince-bishops' private opera house. From here, continue east along the Innkai, a pedestrian promenade paralleling the river with nice views of the pilgrimage church Mariahilf (see later in this chapter) on the other side of the Inn. Turn north onto Schwabgasse, which leads past the **St-Michaels-Kirche** (1678), another work by Giovanni Carlone.

North of the church, turn right on Jesuitengasse which leads straight to **Kloster Niedernburg**. Starting in 1000, Benedictine nuns began running the abbey, which had been founded 260 years prior. It contains the flower-bedecked tomb of one of its first abbesses, the much revered Queen Gisela. The sister of Heinrich II, she took up the nun's habit after the death of her husband, Stephen of Hungary, in 1042. The former convent itself is now a Catholic girls' school.

Museum Moderner Kunst Jesuitengasse eventually merges with Bräugasse, home of the Museum of Modern Art (☎ 383 87 90, *Bräugasse 17; adult/concession €4/2.50, more during special exhibits; open 10am-6pm Tues-Sun*). A constantly rotating exhibition of 20th-century art passes through this building, whose Gothic architecture is sometimes more engaging than what's on display.

Dreiflüsseeck Follow Bräugasse east to the banks of the Danube for terrific views of the mouth of the Ilz River and the Niederhaus and Oberhaus fortresses. Strolling a bit further east along Donaukai will take you to the Dreiflüsseeck (Three Rivers Corner), the very tip of the Altstadt peninsula and the only point from which you can actually see all three of the rivers (except from above, of course). Heading west on Donaukai gets you back to Rathausplatz, where the Altstadt tour ends.

Ilzstadt

The Ilzstadt is dominated by the mighty fortress, the Veste Oberhaus which is connected to the river-level Veste Niederhaus.

Veste Oberhaus This 13th-century fortress, built by prince-bishops for defence purposes (and later taken over by Napoleonic troops), towers over the city with patriarchal pomp. Not surprisingly, views from up here are superb, either from the castle tower (€1) or from the **Batterie Linde**, a lookout with a great bird's-eye view of the confluence of all three rivers.

Oberhausmuseum Inside the bastion is the Oberhausmuseum (☎ 49 33 50, *Oberhaus 125; adult/concession varies slightly by exhibit, usually around €4/2.50; open 9am-5pm Mon-Fri, 10am-6pm Sat & Sun, closed Jan-late Mar*). This regional history museum does quite a bit more than display dusty artefacts. The biggest crowds flock to its high-calibre special exhibits, which are of international renown. In addition, there are permanent themed departments. 'Weisses Gold' deals with Passau's period as a centre of the medieval salt trade. Another section is dedicated to the skills and traditions of tradespeople and artisans, while a third displays locally manufactured porcelain.

The hostel is up here as well.

Innstadt

Römermuseum To study up on Passau's Roman origins, cross the Fünferlsteg Inn footbridge and head to the Roman Museum (☎ 347 69; *adult/concession €1/0.50; open 10am-noon & 2pm-4pm Tues-Sun Mar-May & Sept-Nov, 10am-noon & 1pm-4pm June-Aug*). It occupies a late medieval building that stands on the grounds of the Kastell Boiotro (Boiotro Fortress) whose ruins are still in situ. Exhibits range from a scale model of the complex to excavated objects that document both civilian and military life.

Wallfahrtskirche Kloster Mariahilf Views of the Altstadt and the Innstadt are best from the hilltop Wallfahrtskirche Kloster Mariahilf (1627), a Renaissance pilgrimage church. To get there, cross the Innbrücke, then turn left on Römerstrasse, which takes you past remnants of the old town wall to Kapuzinerplatz. From here, praying pilgrims climb up the 321 steps of the Pilgrim's Stairs whose walls are decorated with votive tablets. The object of devotion is a painting of Mary (actually a copy of the original by Lucas Cranach the Elder). It has been venerated since Emperor Leopold I (successfully) prayed here in 1683 for help in defeating the Turks who were besieging Vienna.

The church is less than 1km from the Austrian border.

Activities

From March to November, **Wurm + Köck** (☎ 92 92 92) runs short **cruises** (adult/concession €6/3, 40 minutes) to the confluence of the three rivers several times daily from the docks near Rathausplatz.

It's a pleasant, easy **hike** along the *Ilztalwanderweg* across the isthmus and through the tunnel to Gasthaus zur Triftsperre (☎ 511 62), Triftsperrstrasse 15, a very nice beer garden and restaurant on a peaceful section of the Ilz. Ask at the tourist office for hiking maps.

Special Events

The annual Festspiele Europäische Wochen is one of the few tri-national festivals in Europe, with events held in Passau as well as in Upper Austria and the Czech Republic. It brings together top international talent for opera, concerts, readings, theatre, film and art and has a different theme each year. In 2002, it will be 'Thank you, America' as a tribute to the US officers who helped found the festival in 1952, with playwright Arthur Miller as patron. Performances take place from mid-June to mid-July in various locations. Tickets (☎ 75 20 20, e kartenzentrale@ew-passau.de) often sell out months ahead.

Places to Stay – Budget

Zeltplatz Ilzstadt (☎ 414 57, Halser Strasse 34) Bus: No 1, 2, 3 or 4 to Exerzierplatz-Ilzbrücke. Sites adult/youth €5/3.50. This

camping ground is for tents only and located beyond the Ilz River bridge.

DJH hostel (☎ 49 37 80, fax 493 78 20, e jhpassau@djh-bayern.de, Veste Oberhaus 125) Bed & breakfast €13.30, including linen. This clean and newly renovated hostel is right in the fortress. To get there, see Getting Around later in this section.

Rotel Inn (☎ 951 60, fax 951 61 00, e info@rotel.de, Donaulände am Hauptbahnhof) Singles/doubles €24/38. Open May-Sept. This quirky place caters primarily to bicycle tourists but anyone is welcome. It's on the banks of the Danube just two minutes' walk from the Hauptbahnhof. Built in the profile of a reclining man, the place has tiny yet clean rooms with a reasonably private hall-shower/toilet. Optional breakfast costs an extra €4 per person.

Pension Rössner (☎ 93 13 50, fax 931 35 55, e info@pension-roessner.de, Bräugasse 19) Singles/doubles from €30/40. This pension on the eastern tip of the Altstadt peninsula is good value. Rooms are clean and have private facilities; many also have fortress views.

Gasthof Blauer Bock (☎ 346 37, fax 323 91, e blauer.bock@t-online.de, Höllgasse 20) Singles/doubles from €25/50, doubles with private bath €70. This guesthouse has very simple rooms, some with views of the Danube.

Places to Stay – Mid-Range & Top End

Hotel Spitzberg (☎ 95 54 80, fax 955 48 48, e info@hotel-spitzberg.de, Neuburger Strasse 29) Singles/doubles €45/75. This is a good mid-range option, handy to the train station. Some rooms have stucco or beamed ceilings, although it's best to get one facing away from the busy road.

Hotel König (☎ 38 50, fax 38 54 60, e hotel-koenig@t-online.de, Untere Donaulände 1) Singles €50-60, doubles €75-110. Rooms here don't win points on style, but are well appointed and clean. Right on the Danube, it's often packed with bus tourists.

Hotel Weisser Hase (☎ 921 10, fax 921 11 00, e info@weisser-hase.de, Heilig-Geist-Gasse 1) Singles €65-85, doubles €85-130.

Just off the pedestrian zone, this hotel has friendly staff and modern and comfortable rooms, plus a sauna and solarium.

Hotel Wilder Mann (☎ *350 71, fax 317 12,* e *info@rotel.de, Am Rathausplatz)* Singles €44-49, doubles €78-138. Royalty and celebrities, from Empress Sisi of Austria to Neil Armstrong, have stayed at this historical hotel. Rooms seek to recapture a lost grandeur, but some of the singles are very small. The Museum of Glass is in the same complex. The ambience-laden restaurant serves top-notch classic Bavarian fare by an award-winning chef.

Places to Eat

Restaurants Traditional and international restaurants abound in Passau.

Goldenes Schiff (☎ *344 07, Unterer Sand)* Mains €5.50-9. This is one of the most promising places for vegetarians, although the menu also features German and Austrian classics. In summer try snaring a table in the small garden out back.

Zum Grünen Baum (☎ *356 35, Höllgasse 7)* Mains €5-8.50. This is a great little restaurant tucked away in a tight alley near the Rathaus tourist office. The menu is mostly meaty German, with the occasional vegetarian offering thrown into the mix.

Heilig-Geist-Stiftsschänke (☎ *26 07, Heilig-Geist-Gasse 4)* Brotzeit €3.50-9, mains €7-16, 3-course menu €13. Traditional food, prepared with panache, is served either in the classy, walnut-panelled tangle of dining rooms or in the leafy beer garden where hedges create separate little 'outdoor rooms'.

Peschl-Terrasse (☎ *24 89, Rosstränke 4)* Mains €3.50-10. This old-style brewery-pub, with a spacious dining terrace overlooking the Danube, serves home-style German meals.

Residenz Cafe (☎ *363 50, Schrottgasse 12)* Mains €2.50-7.50. Closes at 6pm. Inside you'll eat beneath crystal chandeliers, but the sidewalk tables offer better people watching as you relax over coffee and cake or fill up on budget-priced mains.

Cantina Ensenada (☎ *93 11 46, Löwengrube 4)* Mains from €8. This is a good Spanish/Mexican restaurant, open in the evenings, with a cosy courtyard. It's across the Inn bridge, south of the Altstadt.

Chandni (☎ *26 69, Michaeligasse 4)* Mains €9-12.50. Open dinner only, closed Mon. A surprise find in tradition-bound Passau is this classy Indian restaurant.

O Sole Mio (☎ *321 35, Rosstränke 12)* Pizzas €4.50-6.50, meat dishes €10-13.50. This great Italian place has trendy decor but old-fashioned prices.

Zi'Teresa Pizzeria (☎ *21 38, Theresienstrasse 26)* Mains €4.50-8. People of all ages flock here for delicious pizzas and pastas, as well as good appetisers and salads.

Snacks & Fast Food For cheap eats, Ludwigstrasse has the Kochlöffel at No 26 and Nordsee at No 25. KÖPA Schmankerlpassage at No 6 has fruit stalls, meat and fish counters. The restaurant upstairs serves breakfast and lunch under €5.

A *farmers' market* is held on Domplatz every Tuesday and Friday.

Entertainment

Student-oriented cafes and restaurants cluster west of the Dom along Theresienstrasse and its side streets.

Café Duft (☎ *346 66, Theresienstrasse 22)* This cafe has intimate lighting, vaulted ceilings and an individualistic crowd. Tapas are €2.50 each and mains (€2.50 to €7.50) range from hearty to healthful.

Café Kowalski (☎ *24 87, Oberer Sand 1)* This place draws the local youth for breakfast (€2 to €9), snacks (€3.50 to €10) or simply a drink, all served with a view of the Inn.

Café Nyhavn (☎ *375 57, Theresienstrasse 31)* Come here for crisp Nordic decor and a small menu of light, international fare.

Shamrock (☎ *934 60 93, Rosstränke 5–7)* This is Passau's predictably boisterous Irish pub with party hours nightly from 7pm.

Weisses Kreuz (☎ *317 35, Milchgasse 15)* A huge beer selection plus inexpensive snacks make this place a winner with the cash-strapped. Chili con carne, toasted baguettes and big plates of cheesy wholemeal *Spätzle* (Swabian noodles) all feature on the menu.

Camera (☎ 342 30, *Am Ludwigsplatz*) Open nightly at 10pm. This is a happening dance club which also hosts the occasional live band.

Metropolis (☎ 75 28 15, *Dr-Hans-Kapflinger-Strasse*) West of the Altstadt is this three-screen complex which shows mostly new release Hollywood movies; shows after 10pm on Saturday are in the original language.

Scharfrichterkino (☎ 26 55, *Milchgasse 2*) The former home of Passau's executioner is now a lively cultural centre, with a stage for theatre and cabaret, a cafe and a cinema which screens nonmainstream filmic fare, often in the original language.

Getting There & Away
Train Passau is on the main rail line linking Cologne, Frankfurt, Nuremberg, Regensburg and Vienna. Trains run direct to/from Munich (€27, 2¼ hours), Regensburg (€20.20, one hour) and Nuremberg (€34.40, two hours). The trip to Zwiesel (€19, 1¾ hours) and other Bavarian Forest towns require a change in Plattling.

There are nearly a dozen direct train connections daily to/from Linz (€18, 1¼ hours) and at least 11 to/from Vienna's Westbahnhof (€37, 3½ hours).

Car & Motorcycle The A3 runs from Passau to Linz (Austria) and Vienna, or back to Regensburg. The A92 from Munich connects with it.

Boat From mid-April to early October, Wurm + Köck (☎ 92 92 92), Höllgasse 26, has a daily boat service down the Danube to Linz in Austria, leaving Passau at 9am and 1.10pm (one way/return €20/23, return by bus or train €25). Boats leave from the main landing docks near Untere Donaulände.

Getting Around
Passau is compact, so most sights are reachable on foot. The City Bus regularly connects the Bahnhof with the Altstadt (€0.25). Longer trips within Passau cost €1.25; day passes and four-trip tickets are €3.

The walk up the hill to the Veste or the hostel, via Luitpoldbrücke and Ludwigsteig path, takes about 30 minutes. From April to October, a shuttle bus operates from Rathausplatz (one way/return €1.50/2). A taxi from the train station costs about €6.

The Fahrrad-Klinik (☎ 334 11), Bräugasse 10 rents out bikes from €10 per day.

BAVARIAN FOREST
Together with the Bohemian Forest on the other side of the Czech border, the Bavarian Forest (Bayerischer Wald) forms the largest continuous woodland area in all of Europe. It's a lovely landscape of rolling hills and muscular tree-covered mountains interspersed with small and largely undisturbed valleys.

A large portion of it is protected as the **Nationalpark Bayerischer Wald** and its wild frontier nature is still the region's chief attribute. Go out of your way to do some hiking in this surprisingly rugged region. Main towns include Zwiesel, Bodenmais, Frauenau, Grafenau and Bayerisch Eisenstein.

The Bavarian Forest is also a good stopover if you're heading to Prague or other points in the Czech Republic. The border crossing is in Bayerisch Eisenstein. Note that Australian and Canadian nationals are among those required to have a valid visa for entering the Czech Republic. EU-residents and citizens of the USA and New Zealand qualify for the visa waiver program. Always double-check visa requirements.

For travel around the Bavarian Forest, see the Getting There & Away sections in the respective towns below. From mid-May to October, the best value is usually the Bayerwald-Ticket, a day pass good for unlimited travel on bus and train throughout the forest area (€5).

Nationalpark Bayerischer Wald
The Bavarian Forest National Park is a paradise for outdoor enthusiasts. Created in 1970 and expanded in 1997, it now stretches for about 24,250 hectares along the Czech border from Bayerisch Eisenstein

in the north to Finsterau in the south. Its thick forest is crisscrossed by some 320km of hiking trails, 170km of cross-country trails and 200km of biking trails. Mountain spruce dominates, but at the lower elevations you'll also find white fir, beech, sycamore and mountain elm. The three main mountains – Rachel, Lusen and Grosser Falkenstein – rise up to between 1300m and 1450m. Deer, wild boar, lynx, fox, otter and countless bird species make this protected area their habitat.

The park's superb **visitor centre** is housed in the Hans-Eisenmann-Haus (☎ 08558-961 50, fax 26 18), Böhmstrasse 35 in Neuschönau. Here you can pick up maps and leaflets (some in English) and check out quality exhibits about the park's flora, fauna and environmental issues. There's also a children's discovery room and a library. It's open 9am to 5pm daily and admission is free.

One of the most beautifully located hostels in Bavaria is the *DJH Neuschönau-Waldhäuser* (☎ 08553-60 00, fax 829, e *jhwaldhaeuser@djh-bayern.de, Herbergsweg 2)*, right in the national park and an ideal base for hiking and cycling. Bed and breakfast costs €14.30.

Getting There & Around From mid-May through October, the Igel-Bus navigates around the national park on four routes. Of these, the most useful is the Lusen-Bus, which goes from the Grafenau train station to the Hans-Eisenmann-Haus, the Neuschönau-Waldhäuser hostel and the Lusen hiking area. The Rachel-Bus provides access to the park from Spiegelau, a stop on the Waldbahn from Zwiesel to Grafenau (see Getting There & Away under Zwiesel). One-day/three-day/weekly tickets cost €4/10/15.

Hiking & Skiing

Numerous long-distance routes cut through the Bavarian Forest, including the European Distance Trail E6 (Baltic Sea to the Adriatic) and the E8 (North Sea to Carpathia). There are mountain huts throughout the forest. Another popular hiking trail is the Goldener Steig (Golden Trail) in the southern forest. Detailed maps and hiking suggestions are

available at the local tourist offices and at the Hans-Eisenmann-Haus.

Some hiking trails cross the border into the Czech Republic, so be sure to take a passport and/or visa.

The Bavarian Forest has seven ski areas, but downhill skiing is relatively low-key, even though the area's highest mountain, the Grosser Arber, occasionally hosts European and World Cup ski races. The best resorts are in the north, such as Bischofsmais near the Geisskopf (1097m), Bodenmais near the Grosser Arber and Neukirchen near the Hoher Bogen (1079m). More popular here is cross-country skiing, with 2000km of prepared routes through the ranges. The ski season generally runs from mid-December to early March.

Zwiesel

☎ 09922 • pop 10,500 • elevation 585m
Zwiesel is one of the forest's bigger towns, and a good base thanks to its good train and bus connections. The helpful tourist office (☎ 84 05 23, 13 08, fax 56 55) is in the Rathaus at Stadtplatz 27, about 800m south of the Bahnhof.

Things to See & Do Forest, local customs and glass-making are the main themes of the **Waldmuseum** *(Forest Museum; ☎ 608 88, Stadtplatz 28; adult/concession €1.50/0.50; open 9am-5pm Mon-Fri & 10am-noon Sat & Sun mid-May–mid-Oct, 10am-noon daily & 2pm-5pm Mon-Fri mid-Oct–mid-May)*. Exhibits help you discover the special flora and fauna of the forest and how they've changed over the centuries. The glass exhibit focuses on arty creations from the local Glasfachschule, a highly specialised glass making school. Of note too is the collection of ornate snuff boxes, made of glass, of course.

Another attraction in town is the **Dampfbier-Brauerei** *(☎ 846 60, Regener Strasse 9; tours €7; tours 10am Wed)*, where you can join a brewery tour and sample the peppery ales.

Large glass factories include the well-known **Schott-Zwiesel Glaswerke** *(☎ 980, Dr-Schott-Strasse 35; tours 11am Mon-Fri)*. In the Glaspark, north of town, is **Glashütte**

Theresienthal (☎ 50 60, Theresienthaler Strasse; tours 9.30am-1.30pm daily). Both have shops where you can stock up on fragile souvenirs. You'll also find lots of smaller, less commercial studios throughout town.

Places to Stay & Eat Zwiesel is crammed with budget accommodation.

Azur-Ferienpark Bayerischer Wald (☎ 80 25 95, fax 80 25 94, @ zwiesel@azur-camping.de, Waldesruhweg 34) Person/tent €4-6/3.50-4.60. Zwiesel's camping ground is 500m north of the train station, near public pools and sports facilities.

DJH Zwiesel (☎ 10 61, fax 601 91, @ jhzwiesel@djh-bayern.de, Hindenburgstrasse 26) Bed & breakfast €12.30-13.10, including linen. Closed mid-Nov–mid-Dec. This hostel has just 53 beds and is about a 30-minute walk or short bus ride south of the Bahnhof.

Pension Herta (☎ 21 35, Ahornweg 22) Singles/doubles €16/32. In a quiet location, right next to the forest, this lovely little pension has plenty of amenities and largish rooms with private bath. If you ask, they'll pick you up for free from the train station.

Pension Haus Inge (☎ 09922-10 94, fax 45 97, @ haus-inge@t-online.de, Buschweg 34) Singles/doubles from €16/32. Excellent value is this pension which stands at the edge of the forest and has comfortable rooms with private facilities.

Pension Fernblick (☎ 09922-94 09, Brücklhöhe 48) Singles €16-21, doubles €31-43. This is a quiet place in the hills at nearby Rabenstein.

Hotel Zur Waldbahn (☎ 09922-30 01, fax 85 70, @ zurwaldbahn@gmx.de, Bahnhofplatz 2) Singles/doubles from €35/70. Tradition and modern comforts combine at this friendly inn, conveniently located opposite the Bahnhof. The restaurant is top-rated (mains €7 to €16).

Hotel-Gasthof Kapfhammer (☎ 09922-843 10, fax 65 46, Holzweberstrasse 6–10) Singles/doubles from €30/60. British royalty has overnighted at this charming place, which nonetheless has a down-to-earth atmosphere and a good Bavarian restaurant (mains €7.50 to €14).

Restaurant Nepomuk (☎ 09922-605 30, Stadtplatz 30) Mains €5-12. Opposite the tourist office, this place has selections for small and big appetites and various wallet sizes. There's traditional food as well as some lighter and vegetarian choices.

Gasthof Zwieseler Hof (☎ 840 70, Regener Strasse 5) Mains €6-13. This place has a comfortable ambience despite the plastic plants. The extensive menu includes fish, lamb and Bavarian dishes.

Getting There & Away Zwiesel is reached by rail via Plattling from Munich (€27.60, 2¾ hours), Regensburg (€17.20, two hours) and Passau (€15.40, 1¾ hours); most trains continue to Bayerisch Eisenstein, with connections to Prague.

The Waldbahn regional train shuttles hourly between Zwiesel and Bodenmais (€2.50, 20 minutes) and less frequently between Zwiesel and Grafenau (€5.50, 50 minutes). From Grafenau you can catch the Igel-Bus into the National Park (see earlier in this section).

Bodenmais
☎ 09924 • pop 3500 • elevation 689m

Beautifully located Bodenmais, about 15km north-west of Zwiesel, is the most popular resort town in the Bavarian Forest with more than 850,000 overnight visitors a year. The tourist office (☎ 77 81 35, fax 77 81 50) is in the Rathaus at Bahnhofstrasse 56, right next to the train station. Bahnhofstrasse is also the main street where glass and souvenir shops rub shoulders with hotels and restaurants.

Grosser Arber Rising north above Bodenmais, the Grosser Arber is the highest mountain in the Bavarian Forest. You can get to the top by hiking along a thrilling trail parallelling the Rissbach creek and traversing a gorge with the Rissloch waterfalls. The easy alternative is a gondola ride aboard the **Arber-Bergbahn** (☎ 09925-941 40; one way/return Nov-Apr €5.50/8) which, incidentally, is owned by the royal Hohenzollern family. In winter, there's skiing here, with ski passes costing €19 per day or €14 for four hours; other tickets are also available.

Bavaria's Glass Forest

The Bavarian Forest has a centuries-old glass-blowing tradition, which is still practised today. All along the **Glasstrasse** (Glass Road), a 250km holiday route connecting Neustadt an der Waldnaab with Passau, you can visit glass-blowing studios, big factories and many many stores where you can buy the local product. Stock up on vases, goblets, bowls, glasses, pitchers, figurines and other items in famous towns including Zwiesel, Frauenau, Bodenmais and Spiegelau, where such internationally known firms as Schott, Joska, Eisch and Nachtmann have their factories and showrooms.

The **Gläserner Steig** is a 99km-long hiking trail from Arrach to Grafenau, through the heart of glass-making country. 'Hiking without Luggage' packages, with pre-booked rooms and luggage transfer between hotels, start at €200. Contact the tourist office in Bayerisch Eisenstein (☎ 09925-327, fax 478, e info@bayerisch-eisenstein.de).

Both the road and the trail pass through Frauenau, where the big attraction is the **Glasmuseum** (☎ 09926-94 00 35; adult/concession €2.50/1.50; open 9am-5pm Tues-Sun mid-May–Oct, 10am-4pm Tues-Sun mid-Dec–mid-May). It traces 2500 years of glass making – from ancient Egypt to today – explains the technology behind the process, and exhibits exquisite glass made locally and worldwide. Another excellent glass museum is the one in Passau (see that section earlier in this chapter).

The valley station is on the northern side of the mountain and is served by Bus No 8645 from Bodenmais. Buses also stop at the **Grosser Arbersee**, a pleasant lake often overrun by coach tourists.

Silberberg Another popular destination, especially with kids, is the much lower Silberberg (955m; ☎ 94 14 11, Barbarastrasse 1). It's a former mining mountain (silver, iron ore and other minerals) that was in operation from the 12th century until 1962. You can ride the gondola close to the mountain station, where there's a petting zoo, then hike to the top for views of the Grosser Arber and Bodenmais. From the middle station, you can swoosh back downhill on a **Sommerrodelbahn**, a 600m-long fibreglass track, or descend into the depths of the mountain for a tour of the former mines at the **Historisches Besucherbergwerk** (adult/concession €4/2; tours 10am-4pm Apr-June, 9am-4.45pm July & Aug, less during other months). It gets chilly down there, so bring a jacket. A children's playground and restaurant are also here.

The Silberberg is a short distance east of Bodenmais and served by Bus No 8645.

Places to Stay & Eat Bodenmais has a bewildering number of hotels, pensions and private rooms, all offering excellent value. The tourist office can help you make a selection, or try one of these places:

Ferienpension Adam (☎ 90 22 70, fax 90 22 71, e info@sportpensionadam.de, Hirtenweg 1) Doubles/triples €36/54, apartments €30-35. Run by a young family, this place offers superb value and is especially geared towards sporting types, with free mountain bikes as well as cross-country ski rentals. Rooms are cosy and have satellite-TV, direct-dial phones, private bath and balcony. There's a sauna as well.

Hotel Bayerischer Hof (☎ 90 21 18, fax 919 56, e bayerischer.hof@t-online.de, Bahnhofstrasse 29) Singles/doubles/triples €27/54/81. Near the train station, right in the heart of town, this is a comfortable and spotless hotel. All rooms have private facilities and some come with balcony. The restaurant serves Bavarian and international specialities.

Die Waidlerstub'n (☎ 822, Marktplatz) Mains €4.50-13. Bodenmais' oldest restaurant has outdoor seating on the market square in fine weather and serves an inspired menu of hearty specials, plus a good selection of salads and vegetarian choices.

Getting There & Away The Waldbahn regional train connects Zwiesel with Bodenmais (€2.50, 20 minutes) hourly. Bus No 8645 goes from Bodenmais via the Silberberg and Grosser Arber to Bayerisch Eisenstein.

Kloster Metten

The Benedictine Abbey of St Michael *(0991-910 80, Abteistrasse 3)* in Metten was founded in 766 by two priests named Gamelbert and Utto and endowed with land in 792 by Charlemagne. The emperor was for long erroneously credited for the founding, as the fresco in the foyer of the **Klosterkirche** still attests. Several churches stood in this spot until the current one was built in the 14th century. It's Gothic at its core but got its exuberant baroque guise in the 18th century, with frescoes by Cosmas Damian Asam who also painted the high altar.

The attached monastery is home to a famous **Bibliothek** *(library; adult/concession €2/1; tours 10am & 3pm daily)*, a walk-in jewel box of golf-leaf, marble, and frescoed vaults held aloft by statues of Atlas. Also of note is the **Festsaal** (Festival Hall), but it's not always open.

The monastery is still active with monks running a prestigious boarding school and day school as well as a book binding business, a nursery and small publishing house.

Kloster Metten is on the western edge of the Bavarian Forest, about 40km southwest of Zwiesel, just north of the A3 near Deggendorf.

Museumsdorf Bayerischer Wald

In Tittling on the southern edge of the Bavarian Forest, about 44km south of Zwiesel, is the Bavarian Forest Museum *(☎ 08504-84 82, Herrenstrasse 11; adult/concession €3/2; open 9am-5pm daily Apr-Oct)*.

This 20-hectare open-air museum features 150 typical Bavarian Forest buildings – farmhouses, chapels, mills, smithies etc – from the 16th to the 19th centuries.

Also on display are clothing, furniture, pottery, farming implements and tools. It's really worth the trip, but a bit difficult to reach without your own transport.

Coming from Zwiesel, you would have to take the Waldbahn to Grafenau, then switch to Bus No 8772, but connections are not very smooth.

From Passau, Bus No 8771 makes the trip to Tittling.

LANDSHUT

☎ 0871 • pop 60,000 • elevation 385m

Landshut, about 70km north-east of Munich, has been the seat of the government of Niederbayern (Lower Bavaria) since 1839. It's a political role it played once before as the capital of the duchy of Bavaria-Landshut under the so-called 'Rich Dukes' from 1393 to 1503. The beautifully preserved medieval town ensemble created in those heady centuries is still Landshut's greatest asset today. Every four years, it forms the backdrop of the Landshuter Hochzeit (Landshut Wedding), a historical festival that commemorates a royal wedding of 1475 (see the boxed text 'Landshuter Hochzeit' in this chapter).

Orientation

Landshut is bisected by the Isar River, which splits into two arms – the Kleine Isar and the Grosse Isar – in the town centre. Nearly all of Landshut's sights are concentrated along a major thoroughfare, the partly pedestrianised Altstadt, which is paralleled by another main street called Neustadt. The Hauptbahnhof is about 2km north-west of here. Several bus lines connect the train station with the Altstadt, or else it's a walk straight south on Luitpoldstrasse and across the Isar.

Information

The tourist office (☎ 92 20 50, fax 892 75, ℮ verkehrsverein@landshut.de) is in the Rathaus at Altstadt 315 and is open from 9am to noon and 1.30pm to 5pm Monday to Friday and until noon Saturday. The post office has branches in the Hauptbahnhof and next to the Heiliggeistkirche. You'll find numerous banks along the Altstadt where you can change money. For Internet access, go to the Börsencafe (☎ 974 91 11) at Altstadt 218. The town's Web site at ⓦ www.landshut.de has some English-language sections.

Altstadt

If it wasn't for the modern businesses ensconced on the ground floors of the historic gabled mansions, Landshut's Altstadt would easily time-warp you back into the

Middle Ages. Gothic townhouses, painted in a rainbow of colours and with Renaissance and baroque embellishments, fringe both sides of this beautiful street which is book-ended by two churches. The main procession of the Landshuter Hochzeit comes through here, which is especially fitting since some of the buildings have historical connections to the actual event.

Hedwig stayed at the **Grasberger Haus** (1453) at Altstadt 300 (note the lovely vaulted foyer), while Emperor Friedrich III shacked up in the **Pappenberger Haus** (1405) at No 81, right opposite the **Rathaus** at Altstadt 315, Landshut's triple-gabled town hall. Here, in the **Prunksaal** *(state hall; admission free; open 2pm-3pm Mon-Fri)*, the royal couple took their first spin on the dance floor. In the late 19th century, the city magistrates – with financial backing from none other than King Ludwig II himself – decided to redecorate the room as a tribute to the event. It ended up swathed in murals retelling the story of the wedding, capped with a heavy carved oak ceiling and illuminated by crown-like chandeliers. Today, it's a baronial setting for concerts and official functions.

A few steps south is the magnificent **Stadtresidenz** *(☎ 92 41 10, Altstadt 79; adult/concession €2/1.50; 45-minute tours 9am-5pm Apr-Sept, 10am-3pm Nov-Mar, closed Mon)*. Built between 1536 and 1543, it's considered the first Renaissance palace north of the Alps. The arcaded inner courtyard provides access to the richly decorated rooms, including the **Italienischer Saal** (Italian Great Hall), with festive stucco and mythological frescoes by Hans Bocksberger the Elder.

Towards the southern end of the Altstadt, one more mansion is worth a closer look: the **Alte Post** at Altstadt 28 whose ornate painted facade is a who's who of Wittelsbach rulers.

St Martinskirche

Nearby is Landshut's Gothic Church of St Martin *(open 7am-6.30pm Apr-Sept, 7am-5pm Oct-Mar)*, a superb architectural specimen of exquisite proportions and brimming with top art treasures. Built by Hans von

Burghausen, its size and dignified appearance are an expression of the citizenry's enormous pride and wealth during the town's medieval heyday. Legend has it that the plan was to build the church so high as to be able to peer right into the dinnerpot of the duke residing in the hilltop Burg Trausnitz. To this end, presumably, the steeple soars 130m above the town, making it the world's tallest brick tower.

The three nave interior is characterised by a surprising lightness and harmony, accentuated by the high lancet windows and slender pillars whose tops blend into elegantly net-vaulted ceilings. High above the choir dangles a **Triumphal Cross** (1495), hewn from a single tree trunk and with a Jesus figure four times life-size. At the end of the right aisle is a precious **Madonna**, carved around 1518 by Hans Leinberger. Also note the oak **choir stalls** (1500) with their expressive detail, and the sculpture-festooned **stone altar** (1424).

The most bizarre sight, though, is from last century. Walk over to the left aisle and stop before the second stained-glass window. The sequence ostensibly depicts the life and martyrdom of St Castulus, but if you look closely you'll notice that the artist has assigned the likenesses of real world 'bad guys' to some of the saint's tormentors: Hitler, Goebbels and Göring, which is why the window is nicknamed 'Nazifenster'.

Burg Trausnitz

Burg Trausnitz *(☎ 92 41 10; adult/concession €2.50/2; 45-minute tours 9am-5pm, to 7pm Thur Apr-Sept, 10am-3pm Oct-Mar)* imperiously overlooks Landshut from its hilltop throne. Begun in 1204, the castle served as residence of the local dukes until 1503. Each fiddled with its appearance and size to bring it into line with the style of the day. From the Romanesque period stems the **Georgskapelle**, a two-storey chapel decorated with exquisite Gothic sculpture. The Renaissance brought the **Narrentreppe** (Fools' Stairs) decked out with cheeky murals depicting commedia dell'arte scenes.

The castle is reached via a set of stairs nicknamed 'Ochsenklavier' (oxen piano)

which veers off Alte Bergstrasse. Views of the town are excellent from up here. Behind the castle, the **Hofgarten** makes for a nice stroll.

Other Sights

The northern end of the Altstadt is punctuated by the 15th-century **Heiliggeistkirche**, which today functions both as a house of worship and as a museum of sacred art. The modern altar is by internationally renowned Landshut sculptor Fritz Koenig, who also founded the **Skulpturenmuseum** (☎ 890 21, Hofberg; adult/child €3/2; open 10.30am-1pm & 2pm-5pm Tues-Sun), which opened in 1998. Exhibits are set up in former malt storage rooms hewn into the Hofberg mountain and so far have featured Koenig's own work and examples from his private collections.

Special Events

Aside from the famous Landshuter Hochzeit, the town also hosts the biannual **Landshuter Hofmeistertage**, a European festival of medieval, Renaissance and baroque music held over two weeks in July (next one in 2004).

Places to Stay

Campingplatz Landshut (☎/fax 533 66, Breslauer Strasse 122) Open Apr-Sept. Site/tent/person €5/2.50/4. Pitch your tent in this riverside camping ground north-east of the Altstadt.

DJH hostel (☎ 234 49, fax 27 49 47, e stadt.landshut.jh@landshut.org, Richard-Schirrmann-Weg 6) Bus: No 1, 3 and 6, direction Altstadt. Bed & breakfast €12.30-17.70. Closed Christmas-7 Jan. In a cleverly modernised medieval building, this hostel is halfway between the Altstadt and Burg Trausnitz and has 100 beds in two- to eight-person dorms.

Bergterrasse Hotel Garni (☎ 891 90, fax 276 40 19, Gerhart-Hauptmann-Strasse 1a) Singles/doubles €35/60. Staying at this snug place feels a bit like being invited into a private home. Rooms are modern and comfortable, and it's near a park, about a 10-minute walk south-east of the Altstadt.

Landshuter Hochzeit

Every four years, the people of Landshut really do it up during the Landshuter Hochzeit, one of the largest historical festivals in Europe. About 2300 locals dress up in medieval costume to re-enact the 1475 marriage of Georg, son of Duke Ludwig the Rich, to Hedwig, daughter of the king of Poland. There's jousting tournaments, dances, medieval music, fun and games around a bonfire, markets and merriment all around. Held over four weekends in July, it can bring as many as 80,000 visitors into town on a single day.

By all accounts, the original event was a grandiose spectacle indeed. The wedding ceremony took place at St Martinskirche, presided over by the archbishop of Salzburg and attended by the crème de la crème of European royalty, including Emperor Friedrich III and his son Maximilian. This was followed by a bridal procession through the Altstadt with the townspeople waving and cheering from the windows of their mansions. In the town hall, the couple enjoyed their first dance, thus kicking off one full week of a raucous free-for-all courtesy of the duke's coffers. The final gustatorial tally included around 320 oxen, 200,000 eggs, 2300 sheep and 11,500 geese, not to mention entire rivers of beer and wine.

Today's festival isn't quite as lavish, but it's a good party nonetheless. The next one is scheduled for 2005.

Hotel-Gasthof Zum Ochsenwirt (☎ 234 39, fax 43 01 80, Kalcherstrasse 30) Bus: No 7 to Kalcherstrasse. Singles/doubles €56/86. Thanks to a recent overhaul, this cosy inn near the Burg now has individually decorated rooms with all main amenities. The restaurant serves simple Bavarian food, and there is also a beer garden in summer.

Hotel Goldene Sonne (☎ 925 30, fax 925 33 50, e info@goldenesonne.de, Neustadt 250) Singles €61-84, doubles €92-102. One of the nicest hotels in town couples modern amenities with a long tradition. Service is a bit perfunctory but the restaurant is excellent, and there's a lovely beer garden out back.

EASTERN BAVARIA

Places to Eat

Zum Ainmiller *(☎ 211 63, Altstadt 195)*
Mains €4.50-10. Stepping into this charming restaurant feels a bit like entering a large wooden box with ceiling, floors and walls sheathed in polished timber. The food is honest-to-goodness Bavarian; try the excellent pork roast paired with dark beer sauce. The salads are creative and may feature sprouts, sunflower seeds and sweet corn.

Fürstenhof *(☎ 925 50, Stethaimerstrasse 3)* Mains €16-25, set menus €33-66. Closed Sun. This is the town's silver service restaurant whose chef Andre Greul has one Michelin star to his credit. It's formal, so make reservations and leave those tennis shoes at the hotel.

Cafe Ganymed *(☎ 235 85, Altstadt 216)* Mains €6-11. Tucked into a quiet courtyard, this is a popular student haunt with an English-pub feel. The salads are excellent, but bigger appetites could go for the *Grillteller* with meats and scampi. On Sunday, it does a popular brunch (€10, served 9.30am-2pm).

Gasthof zur Insel *(☎ 92 31 60, Badstrasse 16)* Mains €4-10. When the sun's out, the beer garden tables right on the Grosse Isar are the most coveted (after sunset, mosquitos move in). The menu is mostly hearty Bavarian with a few meatless selections and salads.

Martinsklause *(☎ 238 64, Kirchgasse 229)* Lunch €5-8, dinner €6.50-15. Closed Mon. The menu is a culinary journey around the world from Thai to Italian to French to German. In fine weather, the courtyard garden where hedges separate the tables is a perfect setting for a leisurely lunch or romantic dinner.

Woch'nblatt *(☎ 257 76, Altstadt 362)* Mains €5-10. This is a fun cafe with an arty flair expressed in framed posters, a big central bar with a ceiling mural and various Art Nouveau touches. The menu offers few surprises from typical bistro fare: toasted sandwiches, pizza, pasta, salads etc.

Getting There & Around

Landshut is directly connected by regional trains to Munich every 30 minutes (€10.70, 50 minutes), to Passau every two hours (€16.20, 1¼ hours) and to Regensburg every hour (€9, 40 minutes). The A92 runs right past the town, which is also at the crossroads of the B11, B15 and B299.

The centre is eminently walkable, but buses (single trips €1.25, day passes €1.50) cover all corners of the town. You can rent bicycles at Zweirad Eckert (☎ 222 86) at Zweibrückenstrasse 677, just north of the Altstadt.

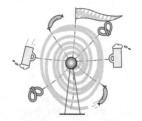

Franconia

Franconia occupies the northern part of Bavaria and is the largest of its holiday regions. It's also the most diverse: a veritable mother lode of German culture, art and architecture, with lovely rolling hills, thick forests and sophisticated cities. Other assets include a lush wine region along the Main River, lots of medieval castles and palaces, nine nature parks and countless romantic, half-timbered villages.

Franconia consists of three administrative regions: Oberfranken (Upper Franconia) Mittelfranken (Central Franconia) and Unterfranken (Lower Franconia). The region only became part of Bavaria under Napoleon in the early 19th century and many of its people still don't consider themselves fully 'Bavarian'. To be sure, their dialect, dress, food and traditions are distinctly different. This is not lederhosen and dirndl country and the staunch conservatism, so prevalent in areas farther south, is often tempered with more liberal tendencies. Franconia also has a large proportion of Protestants, whereas the rest of the state is predominantly Catholic.

Franconia is densely packed with historical cities, especially the famous trio of Nuremberg, (home of Albrecht Dürer but also of Hitler's Nazi Party rallies); Bamberg, the Unesco World Heritage city; and Würzburg, capital of the Franconian Wine Country. Numerous smaller cities and towns also warrant a stay, Aschaffenburg, Coburg, Ansbach and Eichstätt among them. The northern half of the famous Romantic Road also travels through Franconia; this is where you'll find the medieval towns of Rothenburg ob der Tauber and Dinkelsbühl.

Franconia produces some exceptional wines, most of them white. These are bottled in the distinctive *Bocksbeutel*, a flattened teardrop-shaped flagon that is only used for these wines and for those from the Württemberg region west of here. The oldest variety of wine in Franconia is Bocksbeutel Silvaner.

Highlights

- Bike, bus or drive along the Romantic Road, one of Bavaria's most scenic routes
- Experience walled Rothenburg ob der Tauber at its most magical: early or late in the day when the coach buses are absent
- Pack a picnic, rent a canoe and glide down the willow-fringed Altmühl River to find your own little private beach
- Admire the genius of Balthasar Neumann in the Würzburg Residenz and the Basilika Vierzehnheiligen near Coburg
- Bundle up, then hit Nuremberg's Christkindlsmarkt for browsing, guzzling steamy cups of mulled wine and devouring the city's famous finger-sized sausages
- Plunge into Bamberg, a Unesco World Heritage city, then wind down the day with a glass (or two, or three) of *Rauchbier*, the unique local brew

Bamberg p220

Bayreuth p230

Würzburg p238

Rothenburg ob der Tauber p256

Nuremberg (Nürnberg) p202

NUREMBERG

☎ 0911 • pop 500,000 • elevation 289m

Nuremberg (Nürnberg) is Bavaria's second-largest city and a major tourist magnet. It woos visitors with a wonderfully restored medieval Altstadt, a proud castle, major

FRANCONIA

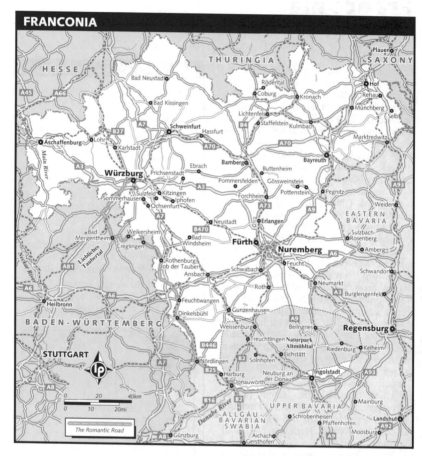

museums and the world-famous Christmas market. Other assets are of the culinary variety: the Nürnberger Bratwürste (sausages), are an irresistible speciality, as are the Lebkuchen – large and soft gingerbread cookies, normally eaten at Christmas time but available here year round.

History

During its medieval heyday, Nuremberg was, for centuries, the unofficial capital of the Holy Roman Empire and the preferred residence of German kings. Numerous imperial diets took place here, thanks to the 'Golden Bull', a law passed in 1356 by Emperor Karl IV. Among other things, it required every newly elected king or emperor to hold his first gathering of parliament in Nuremberg. From 1424 to 1800, the city was also the empire's 'treasure chest', acting as guardian to the crown jewels and many of the priceless artworks we see today.

A progressive and tolerant city, Nuremberg's artistic climate also flourished, especially in the 15th century. Numerous masters, local boy Albrecht Dürer foremost among them, lived and worked here, leaving their legacy throughout the city.

With the Thirty Years' War, both Nuremberg's population and its prestige began to decline. It reached its nadir in 1806 under Napoleon, when the former Free Imperial City – now weakened and bankrupt – was absorbed into the Kingdom of Bavaria. Nuremberg made a comeback later that century with the onset of industrialisation and the founding of several important manufacturing businesses, including the Faber company, makers of lead pencils to this day. A major milestone came in 1835 when Germany's first railway began operating between Nuremberg and Fürth.

In the 20th century, Nuremberg became linked with, and heavily burdened by, the legacy of the National Socialists. After seizing power in 1933, Hitler selected Nuremberg as the site for his mass party rallies. His main architect, Albert Speer, designed the bombastic grounds, still partially there today. In 1935, the infamous *Nürnberger Gesetze* (Nuremberg Laws), which stripped Jews of German citizenship in addition to other repressive measures, were also enacted in the city. The sadistic brutality of Hitler's local henchman, Gauleiter Julius Streicher – who also published the rabidly anti-Semitic weekly *Der Stürmer* – prompted more than 5000 of Nuremberg's Jews to emigrate. Of those who stayed, few survived the war.

Allied bombing raids killed about 6000 people and destroyed about 90% of the Altstadt. After WWII, numerous top Nazis, including Streicher, Göring and Speer, were tried by an international military tribunal at the so-called Nuremberg Trials. The Marshall Plan and local dedication spurred the painstaking reconstruction – using the original stone – of almost all main buildings, including the castle and the three medieval Altstadt churches. These days, Nuremberg is once again a thriving metropolis. Together with Fürth, its neighbour to the north, it forms an important industrial region focused on engineering, printing and plastics, toys and food. It also hosts the International Toy Fair (trade only) in late January, early February.

The best time to visit is in summer and during the Christkindlesmarkt in December, although crowds are largest then.

Orientation

Nuremberg's landmark Kaiserburg (Imperial Castle) lords it over the Altstadt, home to most of the major sights and neatly enclosed by a reconstructed town wall. The placid Pegnitz River separates the quiet and statelier Sebalder Altstadt in the north from the southern Lorenzer Altstadt, which is a partly pedestrianised shopping precinct.

The Hauptbahnhof is just outside the walls south-west of the Altstadt. From here, Königstrasse, the main artery, runs north to Hauptmarkt, the main square.

The Reichsparteitagsgelände (Nazi rally grounds) is about 4km south-east of the Altstadt in the suburb of Luitpoldhain, while the Nuremberg Trials courthouse is just west of the Altstadt.

Information

Tourist Offices Nuremberg's tourist office has two branches: one in the Künstlerhaus (☎ 233 61 31/32, fax 233 61 66, e tourismus@nuernberg.de) at Königstrasse 93, near the Hauptbahnhof, and another at Hauptmarkt 18 (☎ 233 61 35, fax 233 61 66) in the Altstadt. The former is open 9am to 7pm Monday to Saturday year round; the latter closes at 6pm but keeps Sunday hours from 10am to 4pm from May to September. During Christkindlesmarkt, the Hauptmarkt office is also open until 7pm (from 10am Sunday).

Staff sell the Nürnberg KulTour Ticket (€15), available to overnight visitors only and good for two days of unlimited public transport and admission to most museums and attractions. It's also available at many hotels, the hostel and the camping ground.

The ADAC (☎ 01805-10 11 12) has a service hotline and the municipal Lost & Found (☎ 431 76 24) is at Siebenkeesstrasse 6.

Money Banks include a Reisebank in the Hauptbahnhof, a Commerzbank at Königstrasse 21 and a Hypovereinsbank at Königstrasse 3. American Express (☎ 23 23 97) is at Adlerstrasse 2, just off Königstrasse.

Post & Communications The main post office is at Bahnhofplatz 1 by the station.

FRANCONIA

NUREMBERG (NÜRNBERG)

Rieterstr
Kirchenweg
Archivstr
Meuschelstr
Sandrartstr
Bucherstr
Pirckheimer Str
Kreilstr
Rollnerstr
Friedrichstr
Maxfeldstr
Lindenaststr
To ADFC &
Ride on
a Rainbow
Pirckheimer Str
To L'Osteria (90m)
& Jugend-Hotel
Nürnberg
1
Veldottstr
Maxtorgraben
Johannisstr
Burgschmietstr
Neutorgraben
Vestnertorgraben
Vestnertorgraben
Maxtormauer
Lange Gasse
Trebelstr
Maxtormauer
Laufertor
Äusserer
Laufer
Platz
Lauffertormauer

6
Tiergärtnerplatz
4
Obere Söldnersgasse
Weberplatz
Hirschelgasse
Äusserer Laufer Gasse-Platz

Neutor
Neutormauer
7
Am Olberg
8 9
10
11
12
A-Dürer-Platz
Schildgasse
3
Tetzelgasse
Egidienplatz
Am Laufer
Schlagturm
Aussere Laufer Gasse

2
Beckschlagergasse

Neutor
A-Dürer-Str
13
Agnesgasse
Füll
14
15
Theresienstr
16
Bindergasse
Judengasse
Grübelstr
Rosental

Pegnitz
Hallertor
Lammsgasse
Innerstr
Hensgergergass
Weinmarkt
19
17
18
Rathaus-platz
26
27
Tuchergasse
Schmausengasse
To Poliklinik
Hospital (250m)

Kettensteg
Brücke
21
Maxplatz
20
23
24
25
Hauptmarkt
28
Neue Gasse

Kontumazgarten
22
River
Henkerstee
Weintrau-bengasse
August-inerstr
29
30
Spitalgasse
31
Insel Schütt
Kasematten-tor
Wespennest

Westtor
40
39
Fleisch-brücke
Museums-brücke
Wöhrder
Wiese

41
Unschlitt-platz
Karlbrücke
38
34
Findelgasse
Bankgasse
Pfaingsse
Katharinengasse
Marientorgraben
Blumenstr

Spittlertormauer
Schlottegegasse
44
42
43
K-Grillenberger-Str
Hintere Mühlgasse
Ledergasse
Josephsplatz
Adlerstr
Kasernstr
37
36
35
Peter-Vischer-Str
Theatergasse
33
32

Weisser
Turm
46
45
47
48
49
Vordere Ledergasse
Karolinenstr
Brunnengasse
Lorenzkirche
50
51
52
Lorenzer Platz
53
Lorenzer Str

Jakobsplatz
Ludwig-platz
Breite Gasse
57
Frauen-Gasse
58
59
56
55
54
Bauhof
Marientor
72
73

Spittlertor
Ottostr
Am
Jakobsmarkt
Schotten-gasse
Jakobstr
Kornmarkt
Klaragasse
Peungasse
69
70
71
König-str
Königstor
Bahnhofstr

To Nuremberg
Trials Courthouse
& Fürth
60
Kolpinggasse
64
65
Luitpoldstr
67
68
66
74
To Reichsparteitagsgelände
(Luitpoldhain) &
Knaus-Campingpark
'Am Dutzendteich'

To Fahrradkiste
Frauentormauer
61
Karthäusertor
Sterntor
Frauentorgraben
Hauptbahnhof
76
75

Opernhaus
62
63
Richard-Wagner-Platz
Eilgutstr
Hauptbahnhof
Köhnstr

Kohlenhofstr
77
Hinterm Bahnhof
Galgenhofstr
80

To Hirsch &
Twilight
78
79
Aufess-platz
To Roxy

NUREMBERG (NÜRNBERG)

PLACES TO STAY		
1	Haus Vosteen	
3	Burg-Hotel Stammhaus	
4	DJH Jugendgästehaus	
13	Agneshof	
20	Hotel Elch	
42	Pension Altstadt	
43	Hotel Avenue	
45	Am Jakobsmarkt	
54	Pension Sonne	
61	Lette'm sleep	
66	Gasthof zum Schwänlein	
67	Probst-Garni Hotel	
69	Hotel Drei Raben	
73	Bayerischer Hof	
77	InterCity Hotel	
78	Pension Vater Jahn	

PLACES TO EAT	
5	Burgwächter
17	Goldenes Posthorn
19	Alte Küch'n
21	Kettensteg
24	Bratwursthäusle
27	Bratwurst-Röslein
28	Enchilada
31	Heilig-Geist-Spital
39	Café am Trödelmarkt
41	Naturkostladen Lotus
48	Nordsee
55	Barfüsser Kleines Brauhaus
57	Wok Man
64	Restaurant Mendel
70	Doneria

OTHER	
2	Meisengeige
6	Kaiserburg; Kaiserburg Museum
7	Tiergärtnertor
8	Der Hase (The Hare)
9	Pilatushaus
10	Historischer Kunstbunker
11	Albrecht-Dürer-Haus
12	Hausbrauerei Altstadthof
14	Dürer Monument; Felsengänge
15	Stadtmuseum Fembohaus
16	Altes Rathaus & Lochgefängnisse
18	St Sebalduskirche
22	Unfallklinik Dr Erler
23	Spielzeugmuseum
25	Schöner Brunnen
26	Tourist Office – Hauptmarkt
29	Pfarrkirche Unsere Liebe Frau
30	Lebkuchen Schmidt
32	Stadtbiblikothek
33	O'Shea's
34	Hypovereinsbank
35	Käthe Wohlfahrt
36	Mach 1
37	American Express
38	Café Lucas
40	Weinstadel
44	Treibhaus
46	Weisser Turm & Ehekarussell Brunnen
47	Hugendubel
49	Peter-Henlein-Brunnen
50	Naussauer Haus
51	Tugendbrunnen
52	Lorenzkirche
53	Commerzbank
56	Police Station
58	Buchhandlung Edelmann
59	Internet Café Max; Spielwaren Schweiger
60	Plärrer Reisen
62	Verkehrsmuseum
63	Städtische Bühnen
65	Germanisches Nationalmuseum
68	Neues Museum
71	Tourist Office – Künstlerhaus
72	Amerika Haus; Dai Cinema
74	Main Post Office
75	Reisebank
76	Handwerkerhof & Bratwurstglöcklein
79	Lost & Found
80	ADM Mitfahrzentrale

The Internet Cafe Max (☎ 23 23 84), Färberstrasse 11, charges €2.50 per hour until 3pm, €4.50 thereafter; it's open till midnight (till 1am Friday and Saturday).

Internet Resources Nuremberg has a comprehensive Web site in German and English at W www.nuernberg.de.

Travel Agencies Plärrer Reisen (☎ 92 97 60) at Gostenhofer Hauptstrasse 27 is a good general travel agency that also has a last-minute ticket desk at the airport.

Bookshops & Libraries Hugendubel (☎ 236 20), Ludwigplatz 1, has English-language books and a good selection of travel literature, including Lonely Planet titles. Buchhandlung Edelmann (☎ 99 20 60), Kornmarkt 8, has a travel section upstairs and some English-language novels

downstairs. The Stadtbibliothek (central city library; ☎ 231 26 72) is at Gewerbemuseumsplatz 4. The research library at the Germanisches Nationalmuseum (see that entry later in this section) has 500,000 volumes and 1500 periodicals.

Cultural Centres Amerika Haus (☎ 23 06 90), at Gleissbühlstrasse 13 near the Hauptbahnhof, runs an impressive range of cultural and artistic programs each month. There's an English-language discussion group and a resource library.

Laundry Schnell und Sauber (☎ 180 94 00) has four coin laundries. All are outside the Altstadt and open 6am to midnight: Sulzbacher Strasse 86 in the north (tram No 8 to Deichslerstrasse), Allersberger Strasse 89 in the south (tram Nos 4, 7 and 9 to Schweiggerstrasse), Schwabacher Strasse 86 in the west (U2 to St Leonhard) and Schweppermannstrasse 27 (tram No 9 to Krelingstrasse). A load costs €3.50, while drying is €0.50 per 12 minutes.

Medical Services For an ambulance, call the Bayerisches Rotes Kreuz (Bavarian Red Cross; ☎ 192 22). The most central clinics are the Poliklinik (☎ 192 92) at Kesslerplatz 5 and the Unfallklinik Dr Erler (☎ 272 80) at Kontumazgarten 4–18.

Altstadt Walking Tour

This circuit starts at the Hauptmarkt, goes north to the castle and loops anticlockwise back to the market square. It covers the main sights of the historic city centre over a leisurely two-hour walk. With stops, though, it could take the better part of two days.

The bustling **Hauptmarkt** is the site of daily markets and the famous Christkindlesmarkt (see Special Events). At the square's eastern end is the ornate Gothic **Pfarrkirche Unsere Liebe Frau** (1350–58), or simply the Frauenkirche. The work of Prague cathedral builder Peter Parler, it is the oldest Gothic hall church in Bavaria and stands on the ground of Nuremberg's first synagogue. It has a beautifully ornamented western facade where, every day at noon, crowds crane their necks to witness a spectacle called *Männleinlaufen*. It features seven figures, representing electoral princes, parading clockwise three times around Emperor Karl IV to chimed accompaniment. The scene commemorates the passage of the Golden Bull in 1356.

Near the tourist office the 19m-tall **Schöner Brunnen** (Beautiful Fountain), a replica of the 14th-century original, rises from the square like a Gothic spire. Look for the seamless **golden ring** in the ornate wrought-iron gate. Local superstition has it that if you turn it three times, your wish will come true.

Altes Rathaus & St Sebalduskirche

Walk north of Hauptmarkt to Rathausplatz and the Altes Rathaus (1616–22), a hulk of a building with lovely Renaissance interiors and the basement **Lochgefängnisse**

(medieval dungeons; ☎ 231 26 90, Rathausplatz; tours adult/concession €2/1; tours half-hourly 10am-4.30pm Tues-Sun Apr-Oct, 10am-4.30pm Tues-Fri Nov-Mar, 10am-4.30pm daily during Christkindlesmarkt). The dungeons, which consist of 12 small cells and a torture chamber, must be seen on a 20-minute guided tour and might easily put you off lunch.

Opposite the Altes Rathaus is the 13th-century **St Sebalduskirche**, Nuremberg's oldest church, whose exterior is replete with religious sculptures and symbols. Note the ornate carvings over the Bridal Doorway to the north, showing the Wise and Foolish Virgins. Inside, the highlight is unquestionably the bronze **shrine of St Sebald**, a Gothic and Renaissance masterpiece that took its maker, Peter Vischer the Elder, and his two sons more than 11 years to complete. (Vischer's in it too, sporting a skullcap.)

Stadtmuseum Fembohaus North of here, Rathausplatz gives way to Burgstrasse whose main attraction is the municipal museum, the Stadtmuseum Fembohaus *(☎ 231 25 95, Burgstrasse 15; adult/concession € 4/2 for either Noricama or general exhibit, €6/3 for both; open 10am-5pm Tues & Wed, Fri-Sun, 10am-8pm Thur Mar-Oct, 1pm-5pm Tues-Fri, 10am-5pm Sat & Sun Nov-Feb).* Recently revamped, the museum provides an entertaining overview of 950 years of city history. Highlights include the restored historic rooms of this 16th-century merchant house and a flashy multimedia show, called Noricama, which journeys through Nuremberg history using video, sound and other technologies.

Felsengänge Backtrack south on Burgstrasse, then turn right (west) on Halbwachsengässchen to get to Albrecht-Dürer-Platz, appropriately moored by the **Albrecht Dürer Monument**. Directly beneath it are the chilly Felsengänge *(☎ 22 70 66; tours adult/concession €3.50/2.50; tours 11am, 1pm, 3pm & 5pm, 3-person minimum).* Tours, departing from Dürer Monument, take you down into this four-storey subterranean warren from the 14th century, which once housed a brewery and a beer cellar. During WWII, it served as an air-raid shelter. Take a jacket against the chill.

Tiergärtnerplatz Continue north on Bergstrasse to get to this square, which is framed by lovely half-timbered houses and lorded over by the Gothic **Tiergärtnertor**. On the square's eastern edge stands the beautiful **Pilatushaus** fronted by Jürgen Goertz's 1984 bronze sculpture **Der Hase – Hommage á Dürer** (The Hare – A Tribute to Dürer). This nod to Dürer's water-colour original called *Junger Feldhase* (1502) shows the dire results of tampering with nature.

A few steps further east is the **Historischer Kunstbunker** *(Historical Art Shelter; ☎ 22 70 66, Obere Schmiedgasse 52; tours €3.50/2.50; tours 3pm daily Apr-Oct & Dec, 3pm Sat & Sun Jan-Mar & Nov)*. During WWII, some prescient officials moved key artworks to this network of caves underneath the Kaiserburg (see next) as early as 1940. This was technically a form of resistance, since Hitler forbade such 'defeatist' thinking. Guided tours go down there today, but there isn't all that much to see.

Kaiserburg Tiergärtnertor leads on to the humongous Kaiserburg *(Imperial Castle; ☎ 22 57 26, Burg; adult/concession €5/4 including museum, €2/1.50 well & tower only; open 9am-6pm Fri-Wed, 9am-8pm Thur Apr-Sept, 10am-4pm daily Oct-Mar)*. Construction began during the reign of Hohenstaufen King Konrad III in the 12th century and dragged on for about 400 years. The complex, which served for centuries as the 'treasure chest' of the Holy Roman Empire, consists of three parts: the Kaiserburg and Stadtburg (the emperor's palace and city fortress), as well as the Burggrafenburg, which was largely destroyed in 1420. Wedged between its surviving towers is the Kaiserstallung (Royal Stables), which today houses the DJH hostel.

The whole thing is roomier than the exterior lets on. Sections open to visitors include the royal living quarters, the Imperial and Knights' Halls and the Romanesque

Doppelkapelle (twin chapel). The latter poignantly illustrates medieval hierarchy: common folk sat in the dimly lit lower section, with the royals looking down from above, having entered the church directly from the palace.

Enjoy panoramic city views from atop the **Sinwellturm** (Sinwell Tower; 113 steps) or peer into the depth of the amazing 48m-deep **Tiefer Brunnen** (Deep Well) – they lower a platter of candles so you can see how deep it is), which still yields drinking water.

Also here is the **Kaiserburg Museum** *(☎ 200 95 40, Burg; adult/concession €4.50/3.50; open 9am-5pm daily Apr-Sept, 9.30am-4pm daily Oct-Mar)*. It chronicles the history of the castle and provides a survey of medieval defence techniques.

Behind the castle is a pleasing **garden** (open seasonally). The grassy knoll at the south-east corner is Am Ölberg, a favourite spot to sit and gaze out over the city's rooftops. One fine place to do that is in the Burgwächter restaurant (see Places to Eat).

Albrecht-Dürer-Haus Backtrack to Tiergärtnerplatz where the major attraction is the Albrecht-Dürer-House *(☎ 231 25 68, Albrecht-Dürer-Strasse 39; adult/concession €4/2; open 10am-5pm Fri-Wed, 10am-8pm Thur)*. Dürer, Germany's famous Renaissance draughtsman, lived and worked here from 1509 until his death in 1528. After learning a bit about the man, his accomplishments and times during a multimedia show, visitors embark on a self-guided audio-tour of the four-storey house. This is available in five languages, including English, and is narrated by 'Agnes', Dürer's wife. On the two lower floors, you'll learn what daily life was like during the Renaissance, while hands-on demonstrations in the re-created studio and print shop on the 3rd floor acquaint you with art techniques practiced during that period. Finally, in the attic, a gallery features copies and originals of Dürer's work along with temporary exhibitions.

Special tours led by an actress dressed as Dürer's wife take place at 6pm Thursday, 3pm Saturday and 11am Sunday; an English-language tour is at 2pm Saturday.

Spielzeugmuseum Continue south on Albrecht-Dürer-Strasse, then turn left (east) on Füllstrasse and wind around the back of the Sebalduskirche to Karlsstrasse. Here, a stately Renaissance building houses Nuremberg's Toy Museum (☎ 231 31 64, Karlstrasse 13–15; adult/concession €4/2; open 10am-5pm Tues & Thur-Sun, 10am-9pm Wed). Nuremberg has long been a centre of toy manufacturing, and this collection presents them in their infinite variety – from historical wooden and paper toys to toy trains, books and computer games.

From the Toy Museum carry on south, then cross Karlsbrücke to reach a tiny island surrounded by a particularly scenic stretch of the Pegnitz River. On the north bank is the impressive half-timbered **Weinstadel** (1448), an old wine depot festooned with geraniums in summer. It is now a student dormitory. Also here is the covered wooden **Henkersteg** (Hangman's Bridge).

Ludwigsplatz to Lorenzplatz South of Henkersteg, continue along Hutergasse to Vordere Ledergasse, turn right (west), then south on Schlüsselstrasse to get to the fortified **Weisser Turm** (White Tower). At its foot stands the amazing **Ehekarussell Brunnen**, a large metallic fountain with six interpretations of marriage (some of them quite harrowing) based on a verse by Hans Sachs, the medieval cobbler-poet. Head east on Ludwigsplatz to get to another modern fountain, the **Peter-Henlein-Brunnen** on Hefnerplatz, dedicated to the 16th-century tinkerer credited with making the first pocket watch.

Continue east on Karolinenstrasse to reach the city's oldest house, **Nassauer Haus** at No 2. Karolinenstrasse eventually culminates in Lorenzplatz.

Lorenzkirche Lorenzplatz is dominated by the Gothic Church of St Lawrence, which is chockfull with artistic highlights. Spend some time studying the 15th-century tabernacle in the left aisle whose delicate carved strands wind up to the vaulted ceiling. Remarkable also are the stained glass (including a rose window 9m in diameter)

and Veit Stoss' *Engelsgruss* (Annunciation), a wooden carving with life-size figures, suspended above the high altar.

North of the church, the **Tugendbrunnen** (1589) is a fountain featuring the seven Virtues proudly spouting water from their breasts with a figure of Justice looking on. Continuing north on Königstrasse will return you to the Hauptmarkt, where this tour started.

Germanisches Nationalmuseum

The German National Museum (☎ 133 10, Kartäusergasse 1; adult/concession €4/2, free 6pm-9pm Wed; open 10am-5pm Tues & Thur-Sun, 10am-9pm Wed) is the country's most important general museum of German culture, spanning from prehistory to the early 20th century. It features works by German painters and sculptors, an archaeological collection, arms and armour, musical and scientific instruments and toys. Among its many highlights are Dürer's *Hercules Slaying the Stymphalian Birds*, confirming the artist's superb grasp of anatomical detail. Free guided tours in English take place on the first and third Sunday of each month at 2pm (normal admission still applies).

In Kartäusergasse at the museum's entrance is the **Way of Human Rights**, a symbolic row of 29 white concrete pillars (and one oak tree) bearing the 30 articles of the Universal Declaration of Human Rights. Each pillar is inscribed in German and, in succession, the language of peoples whose rights have been violated. The oak, a sturdy specimen with generous foliage, represents the languages not explicitly mentioned.

Verkehrsmuseum

Nuremberg's Transportation Museum (Lessingstrasse 6; adult/concession €3/2; open 9am-5pm Tues-Sun) combines two major exhibits under one roof: the **Deutsche Bahn Museum** (German Railway Museum; ☎ 219 24 24) and the **Museum für Kommunikation** (Museum of Telecommunications; ☎ 23 08 80). The former explores the origins and history of Germany's legendary railway system. The main crowd-pleaser is a replica of the *Adler*, Germany's first steam train that chugged between Nuremberg and Fürth in 1835. At the Museum of Telecommunications, pride of place goes to postal vehicles from several centuries, as well as historic telephones dating back almost 100 years. Some displays, such as a Morse code machine, are interactive.

Neues Museum

The latest addition to Nuremberg's already impressive museum landscape is the Neues Museum *(New Museum;* ☎ *240 20 20, Luitpoldstrasse 5, enter from Klarissenplatz; adult/concession €3.50/2.50, Sun free; open 10am-8pm Tues-Fri, 10am-6pm Sat & Sun)*. It presents a unique juxtaposition of international contemporary art and design, thus allowing visitors to observe parallel developments in the two genres.

The collection, which includes paintings, sculpture, photography, video art and installations, is housed in a spectacular building designed by Berlin architect Volker Saab. Its unifying element is a 100m long glass facade, through which you can sneak a free preview of the artworks.

A spiralling staircase connects the two spacious exhibition floors. An excellent bookstore on the ground floor stocks primarily art and architecture-related works. Next door is Proun, the museum-operated restaurant, whose cutting-edge design is more convincing than the food (mains €8-12.50, closed Mon).

Reichsparteitagsgelände

Nuremberg's role during the Third Reich is emblazoned in minds around the world: the black-and-white images of ecstatic Nazi supporters thronging the city's flag-lined streets as goose-stepping troops salute their Führer.

The rallies at the Nazi Party Rally Grounds were part of an orchestrated propaganda campaign that began as early as 1927 to garner support for the NSDAP. In 1933, Hitler decided that a purpose-built venue would be a better backdrop than the Altstadt, so the party planned a ridiculously outsized complex in the Luitpoldhain suburb to the south-east. Nazi leaders hoped to bridge a metaphorical link between Nuremberg's illustrious past as *Reichstagstadt* (where parliament met during the Holy Roman Empire) and the Third Reich's new rally centre (the *Reichsparteitag*).

Much of the Reichsparteitagsgelände, which was never finished, was destroyed during 1945 bombing raids, but enough is left to get a sense of the dimension and scale of this gigantic complex. At the area's north-western edge once stood the **Luitpoldarena**; designed for mass SS and SA parades, it's now a park. South of here, the half-built **Kongresshalle** (Congress Hall), meant to outdo Rome's Colosseum in both scale and style, is the largest remaining Nazi building.

Further east, across the artificial Dutzendteich, is the **Zeppelinfeld**, fronted by a 350m-long grandstand – the **Zeppelintribüne** – where most of the parades, rallies and events took place. The grounds are bisected by the bombastic 60m-wide **Grosse Strasse** (Great Road) which culminates, 2km south, at the **Märzfeld** (March Field), planned as a military exercise grounds. West of the Grosse Strasse was to have been the **Deutsches Stadion**, with a seating capacity of 400,000. Its construction never progressed beyond the initial excavation; the hole later filled with groundwater to become today's Silbersee.

In 1906, long before the Nazis pressed it into party service, the area was originally laid out for the Bavarian Jubilee Exhibition. Nowadays the Zeppelintribune hosts sporting events (including the Norisring car races in June) and rock concerts.

Dokumentationszentrum In autumn 2001 a permanent Documentation Centre *(☎ 231 56 66, Bayernstrasse 110; adult/ concession €5/2.50, includes audio-guide; open 9am-6pm Mon-Fri, 10am-5pm Sat & Sun; Tram: No 4 to Dutzendteich, or No 9 to Luitpoldhain)* opened in the north wing of the Kongresshalle. Its goal: to put the Nazi party rally grounds into a historical context and to create a place of learning and dialogue.

Austrian architect Günther Domenig has created a futuristic exhibition space whose most stunning visual element is a walkway of glass. It diagonally cuts through the complex, ending in a terrace with a view of the interior of the congress hall.

Inside, an exhibition called 'Fascination and Terror' examines the causes, relationships and consequences of the Nazi terror regime. Besides chronicling the rise of the NSDAP, it examines the cult around Hitler, the propaganda and reality of the party rallies, the Nuremberg Trials and more.

Also here is the Education Forum, where lectures and seminars provide additional background information to school and adult groups.

Nuremberg Trials Courthouse

Schwurgerichtssaal 600 (court room 600) of what is today the Landgericht Nürnberg-Fürth was where the captured Nazis were tried in 1945–46 for crimes against peace and humanity (☎ 231 54 21, *Fürther Strasse 110, enter from Bärenschanzstrasse; adult/concession €2/1; tours Sat & Sun 1pm-4pm on the hour; U-Bahn: U1 to Bärenschanze)*. The Allies decided to hold the trials in Nuremberg for obvious symbolic reasons. They chose this courthouse because it was easily accessible and one of the few such large structures to survive the war intact.

The trials resulted in the conviction and sentencing of 22 Nazi leaders and 150 underlings, and the execution of dozens. Among those condemned to death early on were Joachim von Ribbentrop, Alfred Rosenberg, Wilhelm Frick and Julius Streicher. Hermann Göring, the Reich's portly field marshal, cheated the hangman by taking a cyanide capsule in his cell hours before his scheduled execution.

Organised Tours

The tourist office runs English-language walking tours (2½ hours, €7, plus admission to Kaiserburg, free if under 14) at 1pm daily from May to October and in December from the Hauptmarkt branch. History For All (☎ 33 27 35), a nonprofit association, conducts various tours, including two-hour explorations of the Nazi rally grounds weekends at 2pm

(Sunday only from December to March) for €5/3.50. Meet at Luitpoldhain, the terminus of tram No 9.

Nürnberger Altstadtrundfahrten (☎ 42 19 19) is a tourist choo-choo that loops through the Altstadt for half-hour guided tours in German (also in English with minimum of five people). The cost is €3.50; from April to October, tours depart daily every 45 minutes starting at 10am from Hauptmarkt (weekends only in November and March, special schedule in December).

Special Events

Nuremberg's famous **Christkindlesmarkt** draws millions of visitors to the Hauptmarkt every year from late November to Christmas Eve. Browse the colourful stalls, warm up with a mug of mulled wine, gorge on some roast sausages and be merry all around.

The Altstadt also comes to life during several summer festivals. The **Bardentreffen** in early August is an open-air medieval music festival, but the highlight is the 12-day **Altstadtfest** in September when the entire old town is taken over by music and theatre, stalls selling specialty foods, crafts stands and lots more. Auto racing fans should check out the **Norisring Races**, a formula 3 race around the Zeppelintribüne in late June, early July.

Places to Stay

Accommodation gets tight during the Christkindlesmarkt and the toy fair. That said, cheap rooms can be found at other times, especially if you book ahead.

Places to Stay – Budget

Knaus-Campingpark 'Am Dutzendteich' (☎/fax 981 27 17, Hans-Kalb-Strasse 56) U-Bahn: U1 to Messezentrum. Tent/person €1.75/4.50. This camping ground is near the lakes in the Volkspark, south-east of the city.

DJH Jugendgästehaus (☎ 230 93 60, fax 23 09 36 11, ℮ jhnuernberg@djh-bayern .de, Burg 2) Bed & breakfast €17, including linen. This excellent hostel within the castle grounds is about 20 to 30 minutes' walk north of the Hauptbahnhof.

Lette 'm sleep (☎ 992 81 28, ℮ seeyou@ backpackers.de, Frauentormauer 42) Dorm beds €13-15, doubles per person €22-26. Open to people of all ages, this relatively new independent hostel is in an excellent location right within the old town wall and only five minutes from the train station. It has 59 beds, including five double rooms, a guest kitchen and TV lounge as well as Internet access. There's also a bar in the basement.

Jugend-Hotel Nürnberg (☎ 521 60 92, fax 521 69 54, Rathsbergstrasse 300) U-Bahn: U2 to Herrnhütte, then bus No 21 north to Felsenkeller. Singles €24-27, doubles €38-47. This hotel north of the city centre is another budget option for those aged over 26, but it's a long way out of town, near the regional airport. Rooms at this hotel have private bath but breakfast is an extra €2.

Probst-Garni Hotel (☎ 20 34 33, fax 205 93 36, Luitpoldstrasse 9) Singles/doubles €28/40 (shared bath), €48-56 (private bath). The most reasonably priced pension is this friendly place on the 3rd floor in a creaky building near the Neues Museum. Some singles are tiny, but other rooms are perfectly adequate and some of the staff are quick with a smile.

Pension Altstadt (☎ 22 61 02, fax 22 18 06, Hintere Ledergasse 4) Singles/doubles from €25/46. For those wanting little more than a roof over their head, this little pension is a good and central option.

Gasthof zum Schwänlein (☎ 22 51 62, fax 241 90 08, Hintere Sterngasse 11) Singles/doubles €25/40 (shared bath), €36/51 (private bath). Those rolling into town late in the day could try this inn with basic rooms near the train station.

Pension Sonne (☎ 22 71 66, Königstrasse 45, entrance from Theatergasse) Singles/doubles €29/48. This is one of the city's best budget places (rooms with shared bath) and is near the theatre.

Pension Vater Jahn (☎ 44 45 07, fax 431 52 36, Jahnstrasse 13) Singles/doubles from €20/30 (shared bath), €32/48 (private bath). This simple and friendly pension is south-west of the Hauptbahnhof and has rooms with TV.

Haus Vosteen (☎ 53 33 25, Lindenaststrasse 12) Singles €20-28, doubles €41-48. This low-frills place just north-east of the Altstadt has bathless rooms and caters for nonsmokers only.

Places to Stay – Mid-Range

Unless noted, hotels in this category all have rooms with private facilities.

Hotel Avenue (☎ 24 40 00, fax 24 36 00, e avenue-hotel@t-online.de, Josephsplatz 10) Singles/doubles €74/107. South of the Pegnitz River, the Avenue has modern, comfortable rooms with very good facilities for the price. Ask about their special weekend deals.

Bayerischer Hof (☎ 232 10, fax 232 15 11, e hotelbayerischerhof-nbg.de, Gleissbühlstrasse 15) Singles €69-80, doubles €99-112. Expect friendly staff, comfortable rooms with old-fashioned elegance and a most memorable breakfast buffet at this central hotel.

Burg-Hotel Stammhaus (☎ 20 30 40, fax 22 65 03, e nuernberg@burghotel-stamm .de, Schildgasse 14–16) Singles €50-65, doubles €80-100. Near the Kaiserburg, this welcoming hotel offers good value. Rooms come with such extra amenities as a mini-bar and hair dryer, and there's a small indoor pool as well.

Hotel Elch (☎ 2492980, fax 24 92 98 44, Irrerstrasse 9) Singles €56-99, doubles €71-130. A 15th-century, half-timbered house has morphed into this snug hotel with a nice ambience and its own parking garage. Rooms have telephone and TV; nonsmoking rooms are available.

Places to Stay – Top End

Agneshof (☎ 21 44 40, fax 21 44 41 44, Agnesgasse 10) Singles €84-135, doubles €101-177. Entering the Agneshof is a pleasure. Public areas have an upbeat, artsy touch. Polite staff and first-rate rooms and facilities make it worth the money.

Am Jakobsmarkt (☎ 200 70, fax 200 72 00, Schottengasse 5) Singles €77-97, doubles €94-117. Choose from contemporary or traditional rooms at this well-run place, reached via a tiny courtyard near the Spittlertor. Sauna, solarium and fitness room are on the premises.

FRANCONIA

Hotel Drei Raben (☎ 20 45 83, fax 23 26 11, **e** *hotel-drei-raben@t-online.de, König-strasse 63)* Standard rooms €80-120, 'mythology' rooms €125-170. Nuremberg's most original hotel is this charmer right in the heart of town. The design builds upon the legend of the three ravens perched on the building's chimneystack, which tell each other stories from Nuremberg lore. Each of the 'mythology' rooms uses decor and art to reflect a particular tale, which may include anything from the life of Albrecht Dürer to the history of the local soccer club. The popular junior suites have claw-foot tubs. Standard rooms do not have a theme.

InterCity Hotel (☎ 247 80, fax 247 89 99, *Eilgutstrasse 8)* Singles €131-200, doubles €105-153. The InterCity at the Hauptbahnhof offers functionality and modern amenities but nothing in the way of memorable ambience. Weekend rates may be available.

Places to Eat

Restaurants – Traditional Traditional Bavarian cooking is big in Nuremberg.

Alte Küch'n (☎ 20 38 26, Albrecht-Dürer-Strasse 3) Dishes €5-8.50. Blue-and-white tiles, snug banquettes, plenty of bric-a-brac and an open kitchen transport you back to a long ago time. The menu focuses on regional specialities with international and vegetarian excursions. Try the *Backers,* a kind of potato pancake served with various side dishes.

The owners also run a rustic, medieval-themed restaurant called *Im Keller,* downstairs in the same building. Reservations are recommended for either place.

Barfüsser Kleines Brauhaus (☎ 20 42 42, Königstrasse 60) Brotzeit €3.30-6.50, mains €5-11. Munch on hearty Franconian food or seasonal specials in this atmospheric brewery-pub. A wooden staircase descends to a vaulted cellar where you'll be surrounded by copper vats, framed old advertisements and bundles of knick-knacks.

Burgwächter (☎ 22 21 26, Am Ölberg 10) Mains €5-12. In the shadow of the castle, this is a great place with a terraced beer garden and terrific city views. The menu will please carnivores with their prime steaks and grilled cuts.

Heilig-Geist-Spital (☎ 22 17 61, Spital-gasse 12) Mains €10-15. This classic Nuremberg restaurant has a large dining hall spanning the river. There's an extensive local wine list and regional goodies, including roast pork. Tour groups occasionally invade, but the quality doesn't suffer.

Kettensteg (☎ 22 10 81, Maxplatz 35) Mains €6-14. This leafy, centuries-old restaurant is Nuremberg's best open-air option with a prime view of the Pegnitz away from the crowds. It has updated (read: slimmed-down) Franconian fare, a few meat-free selections and a pretty interior as well.

Goldenes Posthorn (☎ 22 51 53, Glöck-leinsgasse 2) Mains from €11-30, 4-course menu €38. Closed Sun. Light, seasonal cuisine is the hallmark at this regional gourmet emporium. The charming restaurant has been in business since 1498 and brims with historic art and trinkets, including Albrecht Dürer's drinking cup and Hans Sachs' playing cards.

Restaurants – International From Mexico to Italy, there are a world of options in Nuremberg.

Enchilada (☎ 244 84 98, Obstmarkt 5) Mains €7.50-13. This trendy Mexican place behind the market serves decent taco platters, burritos and nachos in a candlelit setting. Wind down after a day of sightseeing during their kick-ass Happy Hour with half-price cocktails (5pm to 8pm daily).

Restaurant Mendel (☎ 244 97 74, Kartäusergasse 1) Mains € 6-16. Closed Mon. This trendy bistro-style spot next to the German National Museum caters for appetites large and small with a classy menu that includes many vegetarian options. Individual portions are rather small and allow you to taste several dishes without punishing your waistline.

L'Osteria (☎ 55 82 83, Pirckheimer Strasse 116) Mains €5.50-12. This place makes the best pizza in town and has oodles of atmosphere. Picture rustic tables with large bottles of wine to which you just help yourself. People-wise it's a wild mix from students to elderly couples.

The Nuremberg Sausage – Links to the Past

The sausage belongs to Nuremberg like froth belongs on cappuccino and it's been that way since the early 14th century. The city's famous links are tiny – by law – to emphasise that 'bigger' is not necessarily 'better'.

Strict regulations require the classic Nürnberger Bratwurst to weigh between 20g to 25g and to be 7cm to 9cm long. It may only contain ground pork meat (no innards), which is blended with toothsome spices (mostly marjoram) and lovingly packed into sheep intestines. The finished product is then grilled slowly over a glowing wood fire and typically served with potato salad, sauerkraut or horseradish.

Locals will tell you, with a wink, the reason for the sausages' petiteness. It harkens back to the 15th century when clever innkeepers came up with a way to continue feeding hungry customers after official closing hours: they simply passed the little devils through large keyholes!

Another apocryphal story involves a medieval jailbird who was granted one final wish before being locked up for life. He asked to be served two Nuremberg sausages every day in prison and in the end consumed more than 27,000 during his 38 years behind bars. The current record for most sausages in a single sitting, by the way, stands at 121 in two hours: without doubt an enduring testament to 'intestinal fortitude'.

Whatever you do, don't leave Nuremberg without 'hitting the links'. Each local has their favourite place, of course, and you too are likely to find yours among these atmospheric sausage kitchens:

Bratwursthäusle (☎ 22 76 95, Rathausplatz 2) Sausages €5/6/7.50/8.80 for 6/8/10/12. Closed Sun. This rustic place cooks 'em right in the middle of the dining room. The sausages are served on heart-shaped pewter platters and taste even better when washed down with a local Patrizier or Tucher brew.

Bratwurstglöcklein im Handwerkerhof (☎ 22 76 25, Handwerkerhof) Sausages €5/6/7.50/8.80 for 6/8/10/12. Closed Sun. We found this one to be just as good with identical prices – only the plates here are bell-shaped. It's part of the Handwerkerhof, a tourist-oriented re-creation of a medieval crafts quarter near the Königstor.

Bratwurst-Röslein (☎ 21 48 60, Rathausplatz 6) No dish over €6. This is one of the best and cheapest Altstadt restaurants. Besides sausages, they also serve such delicacies as roast duck or Franconian Sauerbraten (marinated beef) with Lebkuchen sauce and dumplings. Eat in the huge dining hall, individually decorated smaller rooms or the beer garden. There's also frequent live music and other events.

Cafes & Fast Food The ubiquitous **Nordsee** fish Imbiss chain has an outlet at Hefnersplatz 12 (sandwiches €1.50-3, mains €6-9). Königstrasse has several fast food outlets, including **Doneria** at No 69 which has doners and rice dishes for around €2.50.

Café am Trödelmarkt (☎ 20 88 77, Trödelmarkt) Breakfasts from €3.50, lunch €5-10. A lovely place on a sunny day, this cafe overlooks the covered Henkersteg bridge and the Weinstadel. It offers continental breakfasts, sandwiches and salads.

Naturkostladen Lotus (☎ 25 36 78 96, Untere Kreuzgasse) Dishes €1.75-7.50.

Closed Sun. Help unclog your arteries with organic, wholesome fare from the small kitchen integrated into this health-food shop. Order pizza, salads or a variety of other daily changing main courses and wolf it down at the stand-up tables. The fresh bread and cheese counter available at this cafe is worth a look for picnic supplies, although it's all rather pricey.

The self-service **Wok Man** (☎ 20 43 11, Breite Gasse 48) is a decent Chinese fast-food place in the pedestrian zone in Nuremberg with spring rolls for €1.75 and large platters of chow mein also available for around €7.

FRANCONIA

Entertainment

The excellent *Plärrer* (€2), available at newsstands throughout the city, is the best source for events around town and also has information for gays and lesbians. The tourist office's *Das Aktuelle Monats-magazin* also has cultural events listings.

Pubs & Bars Many of the best bars are in the pedestrian zone south of the Pegnitz.

Treibhaus (☎ 22 30 41, Karl-Grillen-berger-Strasse 28) This bustling and smoky cafe is a Nuremberg institution and popular with students, shoppers and anyone else in search of an unpretentious and convivial ambience. Breakfast is served until the evening, but the hot and cold snacks (€2.50-4.50) are also worth a try.

O'Shea's (☎ 23 28 95, Wespennest 6–8) O'Shea's is a peach of a place just south of Schütt island in the middle of town, with cavernous vaulted rooms, Guinness and Kilkenny beers, and Irish dishes such as cottage pie and trimmings (€7.50).

Café Lucas (☎ 22 78 45, Kaiserstrasse 22) This two-storey cafe in the pedestrian zone draws the designer set for convincing cocktails and snacks; there's a nifty outside section with a platform overlooking the river.

Meisengeige (☎ 20 82 83, Am Laufer Schlagturm 3) In the north-east Altstadt, Meisengeige is a comfortable hole-in-the-wall cafe-bar that's been around since the late 60s and looks it. Students and bon vivants make up most of the clientele, which comes for cappuccino and snacks. A small cinema is attached.

Live Music & Discos Catch a band at one of Nuremberg's live venues.

Hausbrauerei Altstadthof (☎ 20 39 82, Bergstrasse 19) Closed Sun. Near the castle, this is a brewery-pub with a basement cellar which often resonates with live music – mostly of the folk, blues and rock variety – by local and English bands.

Hirsch (☎ 42 94 14, Vogelweiherstrasse 66) U-Bahn: U1 to Frankenstrasse. A converted factory south of the centre, the Hirsch has live alternative music concerts almost daily, as well as theme nights and a

good beer garden. On Friday and Saturday nights, a DJ spins everything from drum 'n bass to acid jazz and 70s disco.

Mach 1 (☎ 20 30 30, Kaiserstrasse 1–9) Cover €4-6. Open from 10pm Thur-Sat. This legendary dance temple is party central right in the heart of town. It's a labyrinthine venue with imaginative decor, which attracts top international DJs and occasionally hosts after-work lounges and gay parties. A youthful crowd invades most nights, but the door policy is pretty strict.

Twilight (☎ 941 46 66, Nimrodstrasse 9) This dimly lit high-tech club caters exclusively for gays and lesbians. The music ranges from Top 40 to techno, and there's a quiet bar upstairs.

Cinemas Movie houses in town include:

Roxy (☎ 488 40, Julius-Lossmann-Strasse 116) Tram: No 8 to Am Rangier-bahnhof. This cinema in the Südstadt district specialises in English- and French-language first-run films, but it's a bit hard to get to by public transport.

DAI Cinema (☎ 23 06 90, Gleiss-bühlstrasse 13) The Deutsch-Amerikanisches Institut (DAI) near the Hauptbahnhof regularly screens first-run and classic US and UK films.

Theatre & Classical Music Opera and theatre get a good run in Nuremberg.

Altstadthof (☎ 22 43 27, Bergstrasse 19) Tickets €8-12. This small, independent theatre is tucked away in a complex that also includes a brewery-pub (see Live Music & Discos in this section) and small boutiques. It presents mostly entertaining comedies and other light fare; in summer, the action moves into the courtyard.

Städtische Bühnen (Municipal Theatres; box office ☎ 231 39 08, Richard-Wagner-Platz 2-10) Tickets €5-75. Nuremberg's theatre complex consists of the *Opernhaus*, the *Schauspielhaus* and the *Kammerspiele*. The renovated Art Nouveau opera house presents opera, ballet and readings, while the latter two offer a varied program of both classical and contemporary plays. The Nürnberger Philharmoniker also perform here.

Shopping

Lebkuchen Schmidt (☎ 89 66 31, Haupt-markt) Lebkuchen are a Nuremberg speciality and some of the best are made by Schmidt, which has a branch in the southeast corner of Hauptmarkt.

Spielwaren Schweiger (☎ 20 38 88, 241 89 89, Färberstrasse 11) One of the largest toy stores in Germany, Schweiger, in business for more than a century, stocks everything from board games and doll houses to Nintendo, beanie babies and Pokemón.

Käthe Wohlfahrt (☎ 240 56 75, Königstrasse 8) This is the Nuremberg branch of the Rothenburg-based Christmas ornament emporium.

Getting There & Away

Nuremberg airport (☎ 937 00), 7km north of the centre, is served by regional and international carriers including Lufthansa (☎ 01803-80 38 03), Air Berlin (☎ 01801-73 78 00), Air France (☎ 0180-583 08 30).

ICE or IC trains run hourly to/from Frankfurt (€41, 2¼ hours) and Munich (€38, 1¾ hours). Regional trains travel hourly to Bamberg (€9, one hour) and Würzburg (€14.40, 1¼ hour) and every other hour to Regensburg (€14, one hour).

Several autobahns converge on Nuremberg, but only the north-south A73 joins B4, the ring road. There's an ADM Mitfahrzentrale (☎ 194 40) at Strauchstrasse 1, about 500m south-east of the train station.

Getting Around

To/From the Airport The U-Bahn No 2 runs every few minutes from the Hauptbahnhof to the airport in 12 minutes between 5am and 12.30am. A taxi to/from the airport costs about €12.50.

Public Transport Walking's the ticket in the Altstadt. Tickets on the bus, tram and U-Bahn/S-Bahn network cost €1.35/1.75 per short/long ride. A day pass costs €3.50/5.55 for one/two adults.

Taxi Dial ☎ 194 10 to call a taxi. Flag fall in local is €2.50, and it's €1.25 per kilometre after that.

Bicycle Allgemeiner Deutscher Fahrrad Club (ADFC; ☎ 39 61 32), with an office at Rohledererstrasse 13, organises group rides throughout the year.

Nearby, at Adam-Kraft-Strasse 55, Ride on a Rainbow (☎ 39 73 37) rents mountain bikes for €7 and trekking bikes for €9. Its main rival, and closer to town, is Fahrradkiste (☎ 287 90 64) at Knauerstrasse 9, which has kids' bikes, trekking & mountain bikes and tandems for €4.50/7.50/15 per day.

The tourist office sells the ADFC's *Fahrrad Stadtplan* (€4.50), a detailed map of the city and surrounding area. It also hands out a list of 'bicycle friendly' hotels in town that are willing to store bicycles for travellers.

AROUND NUREMBERG
Fürth

☎ 0911 • pop 110,000 • elevation 297m

Some call it a 'suburb' of Nuremberg; others Nuremberg's 'twin city'. But Fürth is really much more than an appendage to its big city neighbour 9km to the south. It's a spirited town with its own identity and a 1000-year history. For centuries, Fürth was fought over by a trio of political entities: the bishop of Bamberg, the margrave of Ansbach and the Free Imperial City of Nuremberg. This bizarre tug of war inspired the town's unusual nickname *Kleeblattstadt* (Cloverleaf City). It ended only in 1806 when Fürth was absorbed into the Bavarian kingdom.

Traditionally of a liberal and tolerant bent, Fürth once had the largest Jewish community in southern Germany. Jews began settling here in 1528 and thrived until the Third Reich regime forced about 1500 of them into emigration; those who stayed – about 900 – perished in the camps. Among the emigrants was the later US Secretary of State, Henry Kissinger, who was born here in 1923. In recent years, the community has grown to 350 members.

Fürth's tourist office (☎ 40 66 15, fax 40 66 17, e tourist-info@fuerth.de) is at Maxstrasse 42, just north-west of the Hauptbahnhof, and is open from 9am to 6pm Monday to Friday and to 1pm Saturday. The city's Web page at w www.fuerth .de has English sections.

Jüdisches Museum Franken For an engaging and informative overview of the region's Jewish history from the Middle Ages to today, visit the Jewish Museum of Franconia *(☎ 77 05 77, Königstrasse 89; adult/concession €3/1.50; open 10am-5pm Sun, Mon & Wed-Fri, 10am-8pm Tues)*.

The exhibit, which highlights both religious and everyday aspects, is housed in a handsomely restored 17th-century former Jewish home. Stucco ceilings, a room for celebrating the Feast of Tabernacles and a ritual Mikwe bath in the basement are tangible reminders of the building's heritage. Modern amenities include a cafeteria and a superb bookstore.

Admission here is also good at the branch museum in the village of Schnaittach *(☎ 09153-74 34, Museumsgasse 12–16; open 11am-5pm Wed-Sun May-Oct, 11am-5pm Sun Nov-Apr)*. Here you can tour the former synagogue, a Mikwe and the cantor's and rabbi's quarters. Schnaittach is about 50km north-east of Nuremberg, off the A9. From Nuremberg Hauptbahnhof, trains make the 40-minute trip to Schnaittach hourly (every two hours on weekends; €3.90 each way).

Rundfunkmuseum A journey through 80 years of German radio and television history awaits visitors to the newly revamped Rundfunkmuseum *(Radio Broadcasting Museum; ☎ 756 81 10, Kurgartenstrasse 37; adult/concession €3/2; open noon-5pm Tues-Fri, 10am-5pm Sat & Sun; U-Bahn: U1 to Stadtgrenze, then 200m walk)*.

The 12 exhibit rooms in the former headquarters of the Grundig electronics corporation chronicle events and milestones, from the first radio broadcast in Berlin in 1923 to propaganda radio in WWII to the latest digital technology.

Special Events Yiddish culture is celebrated during the **International Klezmer Festival** in March. Another major event is the 11-day **Michaelis-Kirchweih**, a huge street carnival with rides, food and merriment, in late September.

Places to Stay Fürth is a good overnight alternative to Nuremberg.

Hotel Prima Vera (☎ 74 01 50, fax 740 15 60, e info@hotel-primavera.de, Mathildenstrasse 26) Singles €38-72, doubles €51-87. This central place has old-fashioned charm paired with modern amenities, including rooms with TV, direct-dial phones and data ports.

Werners Hotel (☎ 74 05 60, fax 740 56 30, Friedrichstrasse 22) Singles €51-60, doubles €77-87. The cheerful aesthetics of southern France come to Fürth at this charming hotel close to the train station, tourist office and shopping. Rooms in the new wing have upscale country-style furnishings, sparkling baths and all amenities. For sustenance, choose from the gourmet bistro or the atmospheric tapas bar (see Places to Eat).

Hotel am Europakanal (☎ 97 37 20, 9737215, e europakanal@t-online.de, Unterfarnbacher Strasse 222) Singles €49-95, doubles €64-128. Romantics should check out the themed rooms at this unusual hotel north of the city centre. Choices include the 'Starlight Room' and the 'Tuscany Room'. The standard rooms are cheaper. Buses to the centre leave every 10 minutes.

Places to Eat Fürth has an excellent choice of restaurants.

Berolzheimer (☎ 74 92 99 47, Theresienstrasse 1) Mains €3-10, 2-course weekday lunch €7.50. In the same historic building as the Comödie Fürth (see Entertainment), this stylish and hip bistro serves global favourites.

Die Kartoffel (☎ 77 05 54, Gustavstrasse 34) Dishes €5-17. The chef at this rustic eatery has infinite imagination when it comes to turning the lowly potato into an interesting meal. Even if nothing strikes your fancy, there are several more restaurants and cafes along this street, which is the main drag of Fürth's pintsize Altstadt.

La Tasca (☎ 74 05 60, Friedrichstrasse 20–22) Tapas €4.50-9.50, mains €10-20. Dark wood, Mediterranean tiles and candlelight contribute to a fun fiesta atmosphere at this restaurant, part of Werner's Hotel (see Places to Stay). The large fish platter is a real treat.

Entertainment Comedy and jazz lead the bill in Fürth.

Comödie Fürth (☎ 74 93 40, Theresienstrasse 1) Tickets €10-25. German-speakers will enjoy the biting humour of comedians Volker Heissmann and Martin Rassau. They perform in the Berolzheimerianum, a gorgeous Art Nouveau mansion from 1906.

Cafe Fenstergucker (☎ 97 79 79 00, Schwabacher Strasse 66) Time-travel back to the 1950s in this sleek coffeehouse. Besides good breakfast and cakes, there's live jazz on Thursday nights.

Getting There & Away The U1 makes the trip from Nuremberg's Hauptbahnhof to Fürth several times hourly (€1.75, 15 minutes). Regional trains are faster but less frequent.

Erlangen
☎ 09131 • pop 101,000 • elevation 279m

About 24km north of Nuremberg, Erlangen is a pleasant university and Siemens company town. It languished in relative obscurity until the Huguenots, expelled from France by the 1683 Edict of Nantes, settled here and established the town as a pre-industrial and trading centre. Quaint streets, ivy-covered buildings and a lovely Schloss make Erlangen worth a quick stop. If you happen to visit around Whitsuntide/Pentecost, you'll probably enjoy the **Erlanger Bergkirchweih**, an immensely popular 12-day folk and beer festival on the Burgberg, with the city as backdrop.

Orientation & Information A short walk east of Bahnhofplatz is Hugenottenplatz, from where the pedestrianised Hauptstrasse leads north to Schlossplatz and the Altstadt with lots of student-oriented bars and restaurants.

The tourist office (☎ 895 10, fax 89 51 51, e tourist@stadt.erlangen.de, w www.erlangen.de) is inconveniently located at Rathausplatz 1, about 1km south of the train station. It's open 8am to 6pm Monday, to 4.30pm Tuesday to Thursday and to 12.30pm Friday.

Things to See & Do Erlangen has several interesting churches, including the **Hugenottenkirche** and **Universitätskirche**, both on Hugenottenplatz, but unfortunately these are usually closed except for services.

The **Schloss** houses the university administration. Stock up on goodies at the farmers' market on Schlossplatz (daily except Wednesday and Sunday), then stroll over to the picnic-friendly **Schlossgarten**, right behind the Schloss, with its eye-catching fountain, the Hugenottenbrunnen. Concerts occasionally take place in the park or in the adjacent **Botanical Garden** *(☎ 852 26 69; admission free; open 8am-6pm daily, greenhouses shorter hours)*.

Local history starting with the Huguenot settlement is chronicled at the **Stadtmuseum Erlangen** *(☎ 86 24 00, Martin-Luther-Platz 9; adult/concession €2.50/1.50; open 9am-1pm Tues-Fri, 2pm-5pm Tues & Wed, 11am-5pm Sat & Sun)*. It's in the beautiful, baroque Altstädter Rathaus, about 400m north of Schlossplatz.

Places to Stay Erlangen has accommodation options from camping grounds to four-star hotels.

Naturfreunde Erlangen (☎ 284 99, Wöhrmühle 6) Tent/person/car €2/4.50/3.50. This camping ground is right on the Regnitz River about a five-minute walk from the Hauptbahnhof. Enter the tunnel on Bahnhofplatz, carry on two blocks and follow the signs.

DJH Hostel (☎ 86 25 55, fax 86 21 19, Südliche Stadtmauerstrasse 35) Bed & breakfast €12.25, including linen. This hostel is attached to a leisure centre with a public pool and occasionally admits people over 26 on a space-available basis.

Hotel Central (☎ 788 50, fax 78 85 55, Westliche Stadtmauer 12) Singles €38-48, doubles €56. This newly renovated hotel by the train station has comfortable and pleasantly furnished rooms. The ones in the back are pricier (and quieter). There are specials on the weekend.

Hotel Luise (☎ 12 20, fax 12 21 00, Sophienstrasse 10) Singles/doubles from €65/76. This is a four-star hotel with a 'green' conscience, sporting furnishings and amenities good for body...and rainforests.

Places to Eat Look for fast-food options as you exit the train station. *Nordsee* has an outlet at Hauptstrasse 30.

Alter Simpl (☎ 256 26, Bohlenplatz 2) Mains €6-12. On a square just off Friedrichstrasse awaits this warren of a restaurant with hearty (read: meaty) hot and cold dishes. Meat grilled over beech wood is a speciality.

Grüner Markt (☎ 20 77 51, Einhornstrasse 9) Mains €3-10. The €5 weekday lunch fills this place to capacity, but at other times too, locals and visitors alike chow down on delicious, seasonal fare.

Pleitegeier (☎ 20 73 24, Hauptstrasse 100) Meals €1.50-6.50. This is a popular student hangout in the Altstadt. The menu features filling international fare, including sandwiches, pizza, gyros and tzaziki, and vegetarian options.

Getting There & Around Regional trains to Nuremberg leave several times hourly (€3.05, 15 minutes). Erlangen is on the A73 autobahn, just north of the A3.

Single local bus tickets are €1.35, day passes are €2.70.

Schwabach
☎ 09122 • pop 39,000 • elevation 339m

About 16km south-east of Nuremberg, Schwabach has a lovely Altstadt, a richly decorated parish church and an intriguing local history museum. Originally part of a Cistercian monastery, the town grew in importance after coming under the rule of the margrave of Brandenburg-Ansbach in 1415. Over time, it rose to prominence and prosperity as a centre for brewing and for the quaint craft of gold beating (making handmade gold leaf).

Today, all the breweries have closed but the gold beating tradition lives on. At its zenith before WWI, the town had 125 workshops with 1500 employees; nine are still in existence. Schwabach's gold leaf graces numerous buildings in town, but most of it is exported, especially to Russia, Italy, the Ukraine and Arab countries. One of the biggest jobs in recent history was the delivery of 450,000 leaves for the restoration of the Dôme des Invalides in Paris.

To celebrate this unique heritage, the town was planning to open a **Goldschlägermuseum** (Gold Beaters' Museum) with hands-on demonstrations in a former workshop on Mauerstrasse in 2002. Check with the tourist office (☎ 86 02 41) at Ludwigstrasse 16, 3rd floor, about its status.

Altstadt The lovely Königsplatz is the heart and soul of Schwabach's old town. It's framed by an ensemble of historical houses, including the **Fürstenherberge**, where Emperor Karl V had Elector Johann Friedrich of Saxony imprisoned in 1547, and the inn **Zum Weissen Lamm** where Goethe sojourned in 1797. Two fountains anchor the square, the baroque **Schöne Brunnen** (Beautiful Fountain; 1717) and the neoclassical **Pferdebrunnen** (Horse Fountain; 1823). Also here is the arcaded **Rathaus** (Town Hall), a nice edifice from 1528, enlarged in 1799.

Behind it, the 72m-high tower of the **Stadtkirche** (Parish Church; 1495) stands guard over the Altstadt. Its exterior is rather modest, but as soon as you pass through the heavy doors, you'll find yourself in a Gothic hall church of elegant, harmonious proportions and filled with art treasures. Dotted around the aisles are nine precious 15th- and 16th-century altars, including the exquisitely carved and painted wooden **high altar**. It's a masterstroke from the workshop of Michael Wolgemut, the teacher of Albrecht Dürer, with possible assistance from Veit Stoss.

Stadtmuseum Local history museums tend to be dusty exhibits that rarely get rave reviews. Not so the Stadtmuseum Schwabach (☎ 83 39 35, Museumsstrasse; admission free, donation suggested; open 2pm-5pm Wed, Thur, Sun & holidays; Bus: No 661 from Bahnhof to Ansbacher Strasse).

Museum curator Jürgen Söllner reigns over an eclectic bunch of collections presented in the no-nonsense setting of a former US barracks north of the Altstadt.

The focus of the **History Section** is on events and daily life in Schwabach in the

20th century. Exhibits are especially strong in chronicling the Third Reich era and don't shy away from such subjects as Nazi atrocities and the fate of the local Jews.

Other rooms deal with the changing role of women in society, the history of the US barracks, and postwar recovery.

The museum also contains several quirky speciality exhibits of which the **Eiersammlung** (Egg Collection) is the most famous. It features more than 2600 natural eggs – from the 5mm-long humming bird egg to 70 million-year-old dinosaur eggshells – plus an even greater number of decorative eggs.

The undisputed star exhibit is the priceless 'Gorbachev Egg', designed by Fabergé for the former Soviet prime minister. Only five such eggs exist and this is the only one on public display. Another part of the museum deals with soap production and the history of the Schwabach-based company Ribot, one-time purveyors of suds to the royal court. A new exhibition of model trains was planned to open in mid-2002.

Getting There & Around Schwabach is right on the A6 autobahn and connected to Nuremberg every 20 minutes by S-Bahn (€2.50, 18 minutes) and less frequently by RE train (€2.50, 10 minutes). The train station is south-east of the Altstadt, right next to the brand-new central bus station. Take bus Nos 667 or 668 into town.

Ansbach

☎ 0981 • pop 40,000 • elevation 409m

About 50km south-west of Nuremberg, Ansbach still preserves the graceful charm of the margravial residence it was for nearly 500 years. Founded as a Benedictine monastery by St Gumbertus in 748, the settlement came under the rule of the Hohenzollern clan in 1331, who made it their residence in 1456. Ansbach reached its cultural heyday in the early 18th century. The magnificent baroque palace and many of the statuesque town mansions lining the Altstadt's largely car-free lanes date back to this era. Ansbach is also associated with one of the most enduring crime stories revolving around the life and death of Kaspar Hauser

(see boxed text 'Kaspar Hauser: The Child from the Void'). Today, it is the capital of the administrative district of Central Franconia.

Orientation & Information The train and bus stations are about a 10-minute walk south of the Altstadt, near the south-western edge of the Hofgarten (Palace Garden). Walking north on Bischof-Meiser-Strasse will take you straight to the Residenz and the Altstadt just west of here.

The tourist office (☎ 512 43, fax 513 65) is at Johann-Sebastian-Bach-Platz 1, next to the Gumbertuskirche. The town's Web site at W www.ansbach.de has English sections.

Residenz Ansbach The maxim of the local margraves may well have been, 'living well is the best revenge.' This may help explain the opulence of their palace, the Residenz Ansbach *(☎ 953 83 90, Promenade 27; adult/concession/under 18 €3/2/free; guided tours daily on the hr 9am-5pm Apr-Sept, 10am-3pm Oct-Mar)*. Starting out in the 14th century as a moated castle, the palace went through a Renaissance makeover before getting its baroque looks in the first half of the 18th century. At the helm was Italian architect Gabriel de Gabrieli, who also gave Eichstätt in the Altmühl Valley its Italianate flair; Karl Friedrich von Zocha and Leopold Retti had supporting roles.

Buy your tickets in the net-vaulted **Gothic Hall**, where you can peruse glass-encased porcelain and faiences while waiting for the compulsory tour to begin (in German only, but ask for an English-language pamphlet). Over the next 50 minutes, you'll see 27 magnificently furnished rooms, including the **Festsaal** (banquet hall) with a ceiling fresco by Carlo Carlone; the **Kachelsaal** (tile hall) smothered in 2800 hand-painted tiles; and the dizzying **Spiegelkabinett** (mirror cabinet) decked out with precious Meissen porcelain. The less splendiferous sections of the palace, by the way, now house the regional government of Central Franconia.

East of the palace, across Promenade, is the sprawling **Hofgarten** whose architectural focus is the **Orangerie**.

FRANCONIA

Kaspar Hauser: The Child from the Void

Imagine a human intelligence thrust rudely into light and life, overwhelmed by frightening things beyond its comprehension and loathed and tormented by all because of its strangeness. This was the fate of the sixteen-year-old Kaspar Hauser who first surfaced – barely able to stand and in dire physical condition – in a Nuremberg square on Whit Monday in 1828.

The boy's feet were as soft as those of a newborn and – like an infant – his eyes could not see in direct sunlight. Repeatedly uttering the phrase 'I want to be a rider like my father', he was thought to be retarded and held in a jail cell for two months, becoming a local freak show where his torments brought him near collapse. But at this point a local teacher – one Professor Daumer – came to his rescue and some of Kaspar's mystery began to unravel.

Within months the boy could speak, read and write and quickly revealed that his past 12 years had been spent chained within a coffin-like cave in complete darkness. His 'keeper' had supplied food and water but also beaten him if he made any noise and so he literally did not exist, other than in his own mind.

In October 1829, while still in the good professor's care, an unknown assassin attempted Kaspar's murder. This once again unhinged the boy and, for his own safety, he was removed from Professor Daumer, bouncing through a succession of homes and eventually ending up in Ansbach in November 1831. Here, he stayed with the schoolmaster Johann Georg Meyer, with whom he had a rather strained relationship.

At the same time, though, he grew increasingly close to the town's head judge, Anselm von Feuerbach, who got him a job at the courthouse. It was Feuerbach who first publicly advanced the controversial theory that Kaspar was, in fact, none other than the prince of Baden – who reportedly died at birth – and thus the rightful heir to the contested Baden throne. Feuerbach may well have been onto something, for he suddenly dropped dead, quite possibly by poisoning.

On 14 December 1833, Kaspar was lured into a park in Ansbach with the promise that he would be told who his true parents were. There he was stabbed in the chest and died three days later.

The mystery of Kaspar Hauser has continued to live on in more than 3000 books and over 14,000 articles as well as two feature films by Werner Herzog and Peter Sehr. The debate continues, even though, in 1996, the German news weekly *Der Spiegel* published the results of a DNA test that proved that Kaspar had no relation to the House of Baden. The truth of his life and death may never be known.

Kaspar Hauser Sites For background on the mystery and theories about Kaspar Hauser, visit the excellent exhibit at the **Markgrafenmuseum** *(Margravial Museum; ☎ 977 50 56, Kaspar-Hauser-Platz; adult/ concession €2.50/1; open 10am-noon & 2pm-5pm Tues-Sun)*. Displays include the bloodstained undergarments he wore on the day he was stabbed, the letter he carried when first found in Nuremberg and personal effects, including a pocket watch. Some German skills will be of help in understanding the exhibits.

In Platenstrasse, right in the Altstadt, the **Kaspar-Hauser-Denkmal** (1981), shows him both as the scruffy kid he was at his discovery and as the dapper man-about-town at the end of his life. A **Memorial Stone** marks the spot of the attack in the Hofgarten, just east of the Orangery. He's buried in the **Stadtfriedhof**, about 600m south of the Altstadt via Maximilianstrasse, where his tombstone reads: 'Here lies Kaspar Hauser, an enigma of his time, his birth unknown, his death a mystery.'

Gumbertuskirche The main nave of the three-towered Church of St Gumbertus *(Johann-Sebastian-Bach-Platz; crypt open 10am-noon Sun year-round, 3pm-5pm Fri-Sun Apr-Oct)*, right in the Altstadt, exudes the no-nonsense ambience characteristic of Lutheran churches. Behind the altar, though, a door leads to the **Schwanenritterkapelle**, a late Gothic chapel filled with elaborate epitaphs of members of the Order of the Swan. Below here, the **Fürstengruft** holds the sarcophagi of 25 Ansbach margraves. The adjacent Romanesque **crypt** is the oldest section of the church.

Special Events Ansbach's rococo heritage is celebrated each year in late June during the **Ansbacher Rococo Festival**. Other highlights on the cultural calendar include the biannual **International Bach Week**, held in late July, and the **Kaspar Hauser Festival** in September, also every other year.

Places to Stay & Eat Ansbach has a number of good restaurants and hotels.

Hotel-Gasthof Augustiner (☎ 24 32, fax 24 13, Karolinenstrasse 30) Singles/doubles from €35/46. For those putting price and convenience over style and comfort, this place near the train station is a good choice.

Hotel Schwarzer Bock (☎ 42 12 40, Pfarrstrasse 31) Singles €39-60, doubles €75-100. This rococo mansion has nicely furnished, if old-fashioned, rooms and an excellent restaurant serving creative Franconian fare (€6.50-14).

Hotel Der Platengarten (☎ 97 14 20, Promenade 30) Singles/doubles €25/35 (shared bath), €55/70 (private bath). Across from the palace, this hotel has antique-filled rooms and superior cuisine (€9-18) as well as a beer garden.

Getting There & Away Ansbach lies at the juncture of the B13 and the B14, just north of the A6 autobahn. RB trains depart Nuremberg's Hauptbahnhof every half hour (€6.85, 45 minutes). Getting to Rothenburg ob der Tauber requires a change in Steinach (€8.10, 40 minutes).

BAMBERG
☎ 0951 • pop 70,000 • elevation 240m

Bamberg is practically a byword for magnificence. Its main appeal lies in its abundance of fine historic buildings, their richness of styles and the almost complete absence of modern eyesores. Unesco made it a World Heritage Site in 1983.

A bishopric studded with churches, Bamberg was built on seven hills and is therefore also known as the 'Franconian Rome'. Its 'Tiber' is the Regnitz whose canals give the city a relaxed feel. About 8000 students inject a good dose of liveliness into streets, cafes and pubs. Cultural offerings include the world-renowned Bamberg Symphony Orchestra and the ETA-Hoffmann-Theatre; the Calderón Theatre Festival draws thousands every year.

Bamberg is justly famous for its beer. There are nine breweries in town and another 81 in the region, which collectively produce over 200 kinds of beer. A speciality is *Rauchbier*, a dark-red ale with a smooth, smoky flavour and an aftertaste of bacon (sounds gross but is delicious). The hills surrounding the city are dotted with wonderful beer gardens.

History
Bamberg's name derives from the Badenberg dynasty, who built a castle in the 9th century in the spot now occupied by the cathedral. In 1002, Emperor Heinrich II (973–1024) took over the castle, founded a bishopric five years later and thus laid the groundwork for the next 800 years of Bamberg's history as seat of the ruling prince-bishops.

In 1046, its second bishop, a chap named Suidgar, became Pope Clemens II. Outspoken and reform-minded, he died one year later under mysterious circumstances and was buried in the cathedral, along with Heinrich II and his wife Kunigunde.

Over the centuries, Bamberg went through the usual ups-and-downs of wars and plagues, reaching another heyday in the 18th under Prince-Bishop Lothar Franz von Schönborn (1655–1729). He hired some of Europe's finest architects, including Balthasar Neumann and the brothers Georg and Johann Dientzenhofer, to rid the town of its medieval look in favour of the more elegant and 'contemporary' baroque. He ordered many of the buildings torn down and gave tax relief and other incentives to citizens willing to rebuild their homes in this style. Poorer folk simply plastered over the half-timbered facades. Many of these historic

FRANCONIA

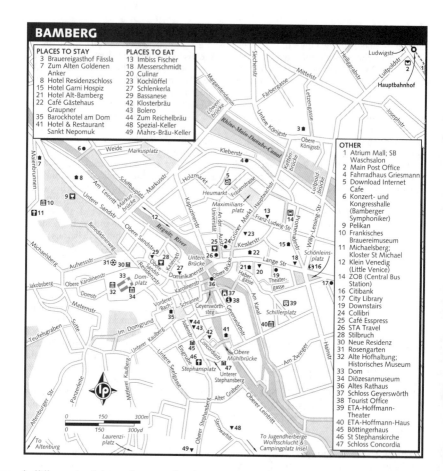

BAMBERG

PLACES TO STAY
3 Brauereigasthof Fässla
7 Zum Alten Goldenen Anker
8 Hotel Residenzschloss
15 Hotel Garni Hospiz
21 Hotel Alt-Bamberg
22 Café Gästehaus Graupner
35 Barockhotel am Dom
41 Hotel & Restaurant Sankt Nepomuk

PLACES TO EAT
13 Imbiss Fischer
18 Messerschmidt
20 Culinar
23 Kochlöffel
27 Schlenkerla
29 Bassanese
42 Klosterbräu
43 Bolero
44 Zum Reichelbräu
48 Spezial-Keller
49 Mahrs-Bräu-Keller

OTHER
1 Atrium Mall; SB Waschsalon
2 Main Post Office
4 Fahrradhaus Griesmann
5 Download Internet Cafe
6 Konzert- und Kongresshalle (Bamberger Symphoniker)
9 Pelikan
10 Frankisches Brauereimuseum
11 Michaelsberg; Kloster St Michael
12 Klein Venedig (Little Venice)
14 ZOB (Central Bus Station)
16 Citibank
17 City Library
19 Downstairs
24 Collibri
25 Café Esspress
26 STA Travel
28 Stilbruch
30 Neue Residenz
31 Rosengarten
32 Alte Hofhaltung; Historisches Museum
33 Dom
34 Diözesanmuseum
36 Altes Rathaus
37 Schloss Geyerswörth
38 Tourist Office
39 ETA-Hoffmann-Theater
40 ETA-Hoffmann-Haus
45 Böttingerhaus
46 St Stephanskirche
47 Schloss Concordia

buildings stand intact because Bamberg emerged from the WWII bombing raids, miraculously, with hardly a scratch.

Orientation

Two waterways traverse Bamberg: the Rhine-Main-Danube-Canal, and, paralleling it further south, the Regnitz, which once separated the secular from the episcopal part of town. It's about a 2km walk from the Hauptbahnhof to Maximilianplatz (known locally as 'Maxplatz'), a good place to start your explorations. Walk south on Luitpoldstrasse, turn right onto Obere Königstrasse

and left over the Kettenbrücke onto Hauptwachstrasse and the square will be on your right.

The city bus hub (ZOB) is on Promenadestrasse, just north of Schönleinsplatz. Several buses, including Nos 1, 2 and 14 connect the train station with the ZOB. Bus No 10 goes from the ZOB to the Domplatz.

Information

The tourist office (☎ 87 11 61, fax 87 19 60, e touristinfo@bamberg.de) is at Geyerswörthstrasse 3 on a little Regnitz island. It's open year-round 9am to 6pm weekdays, to

3pm Saturday (also 10am to 2pm Sunday May to October and December). Staff sells the Bamberg Card (€7.50/14.50 for one/two people), good for 48 hours of admission to city attractions, use of local buses and a walking tour.

The Citibank on Schönleinsplatz is a good spot to change money. The main post office is opposite the Hauptbahnhof at Ludwigstrasse 25. For Web access, go to Download Internet Cafe (☎ 20 14 94), Frauenstrasse 5, which is open till 1am daily and charges €2.50/30 minutes. The Kochlöffel (see Places to Eat) also has a couple of terminals for the same price.

Bamberg's Web site is at **W** www.tour ismus.bamberg.de (also in English).

STA Travel (☎ 924 54 50) has a branch at Austrasse 19, while a few doors down and across the road at No 14, Collibri (☎ 20 85 80) is the city's best bookstore. The city library (☎ 98 11 90) is at Friedrichstrasse 2.

For laundry, try the SB Waschsalon (☎ 20 49 40) next to the Hauptbahnhof in the Atrium mall.

Schloss Geyerswörth

Originally the ancestral home of the patrician Geyer family, Prince-Bishop Ernst von Mengersdorf (ruled 1583–91) took such a liking to its picturesque river setting that he acquired the grounds and mansion and replaced it with Schloss Geyerswörth. It's his coat of arms that graces the portal to the inner courtyard. The palace served as the bishops' primary residence until completion of the Neue Residenz in 1705 (see later in this chapter); it now houses part of the city administration. The **tower** can be climbed for free from 9am to 5pm Monday to Thursday and to 1pm on Friday. Ask for the keys at the adjacent tourist office.

Altes Rathaus

The Geyerswörthsteg, a small footbridge, crosses the Regnitz just outside the Schloss. From here, you'll have the best views of the statuesque Altes Rathaus (Old Town Hall; 1461). It's actually right on the river, perched on a tiny artificial island between two bridges like a ship in dry dock. Gothic at its core, it got a baroque makeover in 1754 and now sports a painted facade. (Note the cherub's leg sticking out from the fresco on the east side, true to the 18th-century fad for trompe l'oeil painting.)

For closer views, turn right at the end of the Geyerswörthsteg, then right again onto Obere Brücke, which will bring you face to facade with the imposing **tower**, a baroque addition by Balthasar Neumann. It provides access to the precious porcelain and faiences – mostly from Strassbourg and Meissen – of the **Sammlung Ludwig Bamberg** (☎ 87 18 71, Obere Brücke 1; adult/concession €3/2; open 9.30am-4.30pm Tues-Sun).

Klein Venedig

The 'Franconian Rome' also has its own Little Venice. A row of diminutive, half-timbered cottages – a former fisher folk colony – hugs the Regnitz's right bank between Markusbrücke and Untere Brücke. The little homes perch on poles set right into the water and are fronted by tiny gardens and terraces. In August, this forms the backdrop for the Sandkerwa festival (see Special Events).

It's worth a stroll, but Klein Venedig actually looks prettier from a distance, especially in summer when red geraniums spill from the flowerboxes. Good vantage points are from the opposite bank along Leinritt and from the Untere Brücke near the Altes Rathaus. This bridge, while modern, sports a lovely medieval statue of a smiling St Kunigunde, Heinrich II's wife.

Böttingerhaus & Schloss Concordia

Two of Bamberg's nicest baroque mansions are on the left bank in the southern Altstadt. Both are the former homes of wealthy privy councillor Ignaz Böttinger. The former is a heavily ornamented grand Italian palazzo (1713) shoehorned into narrow Judenstrasse. Alas, Böttinger was never quite happy here as the place was cold and drafty and soon too small for his family of 14. Three years later, he hired Johann Dietzenhofer to build the even grander Schloss Concordia (Concordiastrasse 28), a moated palace a short walk south of Böttingerhaus. It's now the home of the Künstlerhaus Villa Concordia, a state-sponsored artists' residence, which hosts events and exhibits.

St Stephanskirche

Nearby, the Church of St Stephen was consecrated in 1020 by Pope Benedikt VIII and turned baroque in the 17th century at the hands of Giovanni Bonalino and Antonio Petrini. It's now Bamberg's main Protestant church.

ETA-Hoffmann-Haus

Ernst Theodor Amadeus Hoffmann (1776– 1822) was an 18th-century writer and composer, primarily known for using the fantastical and supernatural to probe the complexity of human experience. Hoffmann came to Bamberg in 1808 as the local theatre's music director, but lost his job after his first performance ended in disaster. He nevertheless stayed in town until 1813, working as a tutor and writer. His former home *(Schillerplatz 26; adult/concession €1/0.50; open 4pm-6pm Tues-Fri, 10am-noon Sat & Sun May-Oct)* is now a small museum.

The Cathedral Quarter

West of the Regnitz sprawls the former quarter of the prince-bishops, moored by the humungous hilltop Dom and dotted with various other religious buildings.

Dom The quartet of spires of Bamberg's cathedral soars above the cityscape. Founded by Heinrich II in 1004, it was consecrated on his birthday in 1012. Its current appearance dates to the early 13th century and is the outcome of a Romanesque-Gothic duel, fought by church architects after the original and its immediate successor burnt down in the 12th century. Politics, rather than passing styles, dictated the final floor plan of this dual choir affair.

The uniformity is remarkable, considering that the plans changed each winter during 20 years of building. The pillars have the original light hues of Franconian sandstone thanks to Ludwig I, who ordered the cathedral cleansed of all post-medieval decoration

in the early 19th century. From May to October, free 30-minute organ concerts take place at noon on Saturday.

The interior is chockfull of superb and often intriguing works of art. In the north aisle, soon after entering, look for the famous **Lächelnde Engel** (Smiling Angel), who smirkingly hands the martyr's crown to the headless St Denis. Nearby is the Dom's star turn, the statue of the chivalric knight-king, the **Bamberger Reiter** (see the boxed text 'Bamberg's Mystery Rider').

In the central nave, near the east choir, is the opulent limestone **tomb of Heinrich II and his wife Kunigunde**, decorated by Tilman Riemenschneider with some pretty odd reliefs. One shows how St Benedict miraculously removes the emperor's gallstones, while another depicts the archangel Michael weighing Heinrich's soul after his death. Also documented is a nifty example of medieval justice: the ordeal suffered by Kunigunde when walking across hot coals to demonstrate her faithfulness to her husband (she survived her injuries, thus 'proving' her innocence).

In the opposite (west) choir is the marble **tomb of Pope Clemens II**, the only papal burial place north of the Alps, decorated with more sensible reliefs of the four virtues (bravery, wisdom, temperance and justice).

Of the several altars, the **Bamberger Altar**, carved by Veit Stoss in 1523, is worth closer inspection. Because its central theme is the birth of Christ, it's also called 'Christmas altar'.

Outside, look for the **Prince's Portal** (1225), which shows Christ in an ornate sculpture of the Last Judgement.

Diözesanmuseum A door in the Dom's south aisle leads to the cloister and the former chapter house built by Balthasar Neumann in 1730 and now home to the Diözesanmuseum *(Cathedral Treasury; ☎ 50 23 25, Domplatz 5; adult/concession €2/1; open 10am-5pm Tues-Sun)*. There's Gothic sculpture and objects from the Dom's former baroque decoration on the ground floor, but the real treasures await upstairs. Besides a bevy of relics, sculpture and liturgical objects, there's a superb collection of 11th-century textiles, including robes once worn by Pope Clemens II and Heinrich II's famous 'star-spangled' cloak with heavy gold embroidery.

Alte Hofhaltung North-west of the Dom, the Renaissance-style Alte Hofhaltung (1570) is a former prince-bishops' palace, built on the site of an 11th-century fortress. Its prettiest section is the inner courtyard surrounded by half-timbered, balconied buildings and reached via the **Schöne Pforte** (Beautiful Gate, 1573). In summer, the Calderón Festival (see Special Events) takes place in the courtyard.

The gabled **Ratsstube** (Council Chamber) is home of the **Historisches Museum** *(Historical Museum;* ☎ *87 11 42, In der Alten Hofhaltung; adult/concession €2/1; open 9am-5pm Tues-Sun May-Oct).* Here you'll find an eclectic mix of art and historical exhibits. Highlights include a model of the pilgrimage church of Basilika Vierzehnheiligen (see Around Coburg later in this chapter) and the 'Bamberger Götzen', which are ancient stone sculptures found in the region. From November to April, it's only open for special exhibitions.

Neue Residenz Across Domplatz, you'll spot the stately New Residence *(*☎ *563 51,* *Domplatz 8; adult/concession €3/2; open 9am-6pm Fri-Wed, 9am-8pm Thur Apr-Sept, 10am-4pm daily Oct-Mar).* It served as the home of Bamberg's prince-bishops from 1703 until secularisation in 1802. In 1697, Lothar Franz von Schönborn entrusted Leonhard Dientzenhofer with the expansion of the palace started by Prince-Bishop Johann Philipp von Gebsattel 100 years earlier.

Inside, you'll be shuffling through about 40 stuccoed rooms stuffed with furniture and tapestries from the 17th and 18th centuries. Showpieces are the dizzying **Kaisersaal** (Imperial Hall) upstairs, whose ceiling is smothered with a complex allegorical fresco by Melchior Seidl.

The edifice also shelters the **Bavarian State Gallery**, whose strengths are in medieval, Renaissance and baroque paintings, with works by Anthonis van Dyck, Hans Baldung Grien and Cranach the Elder. Grien's haunting *Die Sintflut* (The Deluge; 1516) is among those worth a closer look.

After getting your cultural fix, unwind in the residence's small but exquisite baroque **Rosengarten**, from where you can enjoy calming views of the sea of red rooftops in the Altstadt below.

Michaelsberg From Domplatz, Aufsesstrasse leads to Michaelsberg for a rather steep climb up to the top of Michaelsberg with the former Benedictine **Kloster St Michael** (1610), now an old people's home. The monastery church is a must-see for its baroque art and the meticulous depictions of nearly 600 medicinal plants and flowers on the vaulted ceiling. The manicured garden terrace boasts a splendid city panorama.

The historical vaulted cellars of the ex-monastery are an atmospheric backdrop for the **Fränkisches Brauereimuseum** *(Franconian Brewery Museum;* ☎ *530 16, Michaelsberg 10f; adult/concession €1.75/1.25; open 1pm-5pm Wed-Sun Apr-Oct).* Exhibits show plaster(ed) dummies of monks, who began making beer here as early as 1122. There's plenty of historical equipment and a thorough documentation of the process of beer-making from malt production to the final product.

Bamberg's Mystery Rider

The *Bamberger Reiter* is Bamberg's greatest and most enduring mystery. Nobody has a clue as to either the name of the artist or the fetching young king on the steed. The canopy above the statue represents the heavenly Jerusalem, an indication that this person may have been revered as a saint.

One leading theory points towards Konrad III, the Hohenstaufen king buried in the cathedral, another towards St Stephen, the king of Hungary and Heinrich II's brother-in-law. The Nazis seized on the image of the heroic medieval ideal, which became a symbol of Aryan perfection in classrooms during the Third Reich. Göring liked the statue so much, he had a copy made just for himself.

Organised Tours

Guided two-hour walking tours (in German only, €4.50/3) depart from the tourist office at 10.30am and 2pm Monday to Saturday (2pm only November to March) and at 11am on Sunday.

Special Events

Locals and visitors alike let their hair down during the **Sandkerwa**, held throughout the entire Altstadt around the fourth weekend in August. Highlights include the *Fischerstechen*, a kind of boat jousting, and a big fireworks finale.

Besides the **Christmas market** on Maxplatz, another December tradition is the **Bamberger Krippenweg**, which features up to 30 nativity scenes set up in churches and museums all over the city.

German-speakers might also like to check out the popular **Calderón Festspiele**, an open-air theatre festival in the courtyard of the Alte Hofhaltung in late June.

Places to Stay

Campingplatz Insel (☎ 563 20, fax 563 21, Am Campingplatz 1) Bus: No 18 from ZOB to Campingplatz. Site/adult €6/3.50. Camping options are limited to this well-equipped place, in a calm spot right on the river and convenient to public transport.

Jugendherberge Wolfsschlucht (☎ 560 02, fax 552 11, e jh-bamberg@stadt.bamberg .de, Oberer Leinritt 70) Bus: No 18 from ZOB to Rodelbahn. Bed & breakfast €12, including linen. Closed mid-Dec–Jan. Bamberg's hostel is on the west bank of the Regnitz, about 2km from the Altstadt. From the Rodelbahn stop walk north-east to the riverbank, turn left and there it is, past the minigolf range.

Hotel Garni Hospiz (☎ 98 12 60, fax 981 26 66, Promenadestrasse 3) Singles €25-35, doubles €43-53. Good deals on simple but central hotels include this one, just off Schönleinsplatz. Some rooms have balconies.

Café-Gästehaus Graupner (☎ 98 04 00, fax 980 40 40, e hotel-graupner@t-online, Lange Strasse 5) Singles/doubles/triples €27.50/42.50/67.50 (shared bath), €42.50/80/80 (private shower). This is a good central

choice with a popular cafe on the ground floor and comfortable, traditional rooms.

Brauereigasthof Fässla (☎ 265 16, fax 20 19 89, e faessla@t-online.de, Obere Königstrasse 19–21) Singles/doubles €32.50/50. Those interested in serious research of the local beer offerings should consider staying in this guesthouse, whose snug rooms are a mere staircase up from the pub. It's north of the Rhine-Main-Danube-Canal.

Hotel Alt-Bamberg (☎ 98 61 50, fax 20 10 07, Habergasse 11) Singles/doubles €35/60. In a quiet location near the Rathaus, this hotel has good-value rooms with TV and phone (including some set aside for nonsmokers).

Zum Alten Goldenen Anker (☎ 665 05, fax 665 95, Untere Sandstrasse 73) Singles/doubles €45-50. This small, old-world inn north of Michaelsberg has nice, traditionally furnished rooms.

Barockhotel am Dom (☎ 540 31, fax 540 21, Vorderer Bach 4) Singles/doubles/triples €50/80/90. In the Cathedral Quarter, this place has quiet rooms with TV and direct-dial phones. There's a lift and car park, too. Enjoy breakfast in a cross-vaulted Gothic room.

Hotel Sankt Nepomuk (☎ 984 20, fax 984 21 00, e gruener@hotel-nepomuk.de, Obere Mühlbrücke 9) Singles/doubles €70/120. This is a classy establishment in a former mill right on the Regnitz with a superb gourmet restaurant (mains €15-25). Rooms are fully equipped and amenities include bicycle rental.

Hotel Residenzschloss (☎ 609 10, fax 609 17 01, e info@hotel-residenzschloss.de, Untere Sandstrasse 32) Singles/doubles from €120/150. Bamberg's top hotel in a former hospital caters for deep-pocketed travellers but is a tad overpriced. Facilities include a Roman-style steam bath, whirlpool, two restaurants and a lovely house chapel. The breakfast buffet is impressive.

Places to Eat

Specialities include the Fränkischer Sauerbraten (beef, first marinated, then braised), various kinds of sausages and the Bamberger Zwiebel (stuffed onions cooked in beer sauce). The Bamberger Hörnla is the local version of a croissant.

Breweries All of Bamberg's nine breweries have integrated restaurants, which should be the first stop to try local dishes and, of course, what's on tap. Here's a selection:

Mahrs-Bräu-Keller (☎ 534 86, Oberer Stephansberg 36) Dishes €3-10. Closed Mon. Slurp Pilsners in this Art Deco cellar.

Klosterbräu (☎ 522 65, Obere Mühlbrücke 3) Mains €5-10. Closed Wed. This beautiful old half-timbered brewery is Bamberg's oldest. It's usually bristling with a youthful clientele with excellent beers perfect for washing down its solid standard fare.

Schlenkerla (☎ 560 60, Dominikanerstrasse 6) Dishes €2.50-7.50. Closed Tues. This 16th-century restaurant at the foot of the Dom is justly famous for its tasty Franconian specialities and superb Rauchbier served directly from the oak barrel (€1.90 per half litre mug).

Spezial-Keller (☎ 548 87, Sternwartstrasse) Prices €3-9. Closed Mon. Spezial-Keller has its own smoky ale and great views of the Dom and the Altstadt from the beer garden. Every year in November, crowds gather to ring in Bockbier season.

Restaurants If beer is not your thing...

Bassanese (☎ 575 51, Obere Sandstrasse 32) Mains €8-15. This is one of the best Italian restaurants in town with homemade pasta and daily changing specials.

Bolero (☎ 509 02 90, Judenstrasse 7–9) Tapas €2.50 each, mains €8-13. Open dinner only. About 30 tasty tapas are the main draw at this sprawling bodega. Rustic wooden tables, complexion-friendly candlelight and a fun atmosphere transport you straight to southern Spain.

Messerschmidt (☎ 278 66, Lange Strasse 41) Small dishes €5-10, mains €15-22. In the birth house of plane engineer Willy Messerschmidt, who also founded his first company here in 1923, is this stylish restaurant. It oozes old-world tradition with its dark wood, white-linen table settings and formal service. The attached wine tavern has a looser atmosphere but the same prices.

Zum Reichelbräu (☎ 527 98, Judenstrasse 5) Dishes €2.50-9. This bistro has international fare in restored historical surroundings. Pizza, baguette sandwiches, salads and pasta all present great value.

Snacks & Fast Food You'll find fast-food options along Grüner Markt, including a *Kochlöffel* at No 18. A *produce market* is held daily except Sunday on Maxplatz.

Culinar (☎ 299 97 00, Lange Strasse 38/40) Dishes from €2.50. 'Eat, drink & enjoy' is the motto of this modern food temple, which combines a self-service restaurant/bar, butcher, baker, produce vendor, newsstand and tobacco store under its lofty ceiling. The crowd's young and hip and you can get everything from lobster bisque to fried calamari to salads.

Imbiss Fischer (Franz-Ludwig-Strasse 5) Snacks €1.25-2.50. Open until 6pm weekdays, to 1pm Sat. This local snack stand serves decent sausages, chicken drumsticks, liver dumplings and salads sold by weight (€0.60-0.75 per 100g).

Entertainment

Consult the free listings magazines *Franky*, *Treff* or *Fränkische Nacht*, usually in pubs, for the latest 'in' spots and special events.

Theatre & Music Catch a recital or play while in Bamberg.

Bamberger Symphoniker (☎ 964 71 00, Mussstrasse 1) Tickets €18-33. Fans of classical music should try to catch a concert by this famous orchestra, which usually plays in the modern Konzert-und Kongresshalle on the Regnitz north of the Altstadt.

ETA-Hoffmann-Theater (☎ 87 14 31, Schillerplatz 1) This is the best known among Bamberg's theatres. Performances take place at various venues in town.

Cafes & Bars Bamberg cafes serve breakfast, lunch and beer.

Café Esspress (☎ 519 04 31, Austrasse 33) Breakfast €3-12.50. This student-oriented place changes stripes throughout the day, from breakfast cafe to lunch spot to coffeehouse to restaurant and cocktail bar at night. They often have some kind of special meal deal going, such as 'schnitzelfest' or all-you-can-eat pizza and pasta.

Pelikan (☎ 60 34 10, *Untere Sandstrasse 45*) This candlelit pub has occasional live music and an interesting snack and Thai menu (€2.50-8.50). In summer, the beer garden in the inner courtyard is a convivial place to sit.

Stilbruch (☎ 519 00 02, *Obere Sandstrasse 18*) Nearby, this is another fun pub with a friendly crowd and a snack menu in case you get the munchies.

Downstairs (☎ 208 37 86, *Generalsgasse 3*) Open from 10pm daily. An underground vibe reigns at this cool basement bar and dance club where DJs spin an interesting mix of musical styles.

Shopping

Bamberg's main shopping drags are the pedestrianised Grüner Markt, which runs south from Maxplatz, and the parallel Austrasse. You'll find lots of department stores, boutiques and fast-food eateries. Also dotted throughout the Altstadt are around 30 antique stores; the Bamberg Antique Weeks are in August.

Getting There & Away

There are at least hourly RE and RB trains from Nuremberg (€9, 45/60 minutes) and from Würzburg (€14, one hour), as well as ICE trains every two hours to/from Munich (€45, 2¼ hours) and Berlin (€69, 4¼ hours). Bamberg is just south of A70 (Schweinfurt-Kulmbach/Bayreuth) and at the start of the A73 to Nuremberg.

Getting Around

Walking is the best option in town, but you can also rent bicycles from €5/day at Fahrradhaus Griesmann (☎ 229 67), Kleberstrasse 25. The tourist office has a good selection of bicycle-path maps of the vicinity. Cars are a pain in town, so park on the outskirts and walk or take a bus (€1, or €6 for a 'Tourist Ticket' good for 48 hours of unlimited travel). For a taxi, call ☎ 150 15 (flag fall is €2).

AROUND BAMBERG

The rural area to the west and south of Bamberg is known as the **Steigerwald**.

Much of it is a nature park, blanketed by beech and oak forest, and prime hiking and cycling territory. Local rulers took quite a liking to the land as well, giving culture vultures a fine palace and monastery toward which to steer.

Unfortunately, the Steigerwald is not well served by public transportation. If you're not motorised, the bicycle is the best option for getting around.

Pommersfelden

When deciding on a location for a summer residence, Prince-Bishop Lothar Franz von Schönborn picked Pommersfelden, a little village about 20km south of Bamberg just off the B505. Called **Schloss Weissenstein** (☎ 09548-981 80, *Schlossplatz 1; adult/concession 30-min tour €3/2.50, 60-min tour €5/4; tours on the hr 10am-4pm & 4.30pm daily Apr-Oct)*, it is another example of the baroque exuberance so beloved by the bishop.

Johann Dientzenhofer was the lead architect of the horseshoe-shaped three-winged palace. Inside, the dominant feature is a three-storey **double staircase**, canopied by a ceiling fresco by Johann Rudolf Byss showing Apollo as the source of light (and enlightenment) for the four continents.

Upstairs, the highlight is the **Marmorsaal** (Marble Hall), an ostentatious banquet hall used for festivities and concerts. Both staircase and hall are seen on the 30-minute tour. The 60-minute tour also takes in the bishops' private quarters, the mirror room and a gallery of Italian, Dutch and German 17th- and 18th-century paintings. Don't miss a stroll through the fabulous park (€0.50/0.25). The palace, by the way, is still owned by the current count of Schönborn.

Kloster Ebrach

Kloster Ebrach (☎ 09553-922 00; *admission free, tours adult/concession €2.50/1.25; church open 8am-6pm daily Apr-Oct, tours 10.30am & 3pm daily mid-Mar–mid-Nov)*, about 35km west of Bamberg on the B22, probably wins the award for most unusual use of a former monastery: it is now a prison for juvenile offenders.

An outgrowth of Bavaria's first Cistercian abbey, founded in 1127, the current complex dates to the 18th century and is primarily the work of Johann Dientzenhofer. Balthasar Neumann contributed the magnificent **Kaisersaal** (Imperial Hall) and staircase. You can see both on guided tours, usually led by prison guards.

Of greater interest is the attached monastery church, whose oldest section is the Romanesque **Chapel of St Michael**, consecrated in 1134. Construction of the main basilica, which ranks as a fine example of early Gothic architecture, began in 1200, concluding in 1285. It is built in the classic shape of a cross, consisting of a three-nave basilica and a transept. The kaleidoscopic **rose window** in the western facade adds a touch of mysticism. The interior received the usual baroque facelift in the 18th century.

FRÄNKISCHE SCHWEIZ

The Fränkische Schweiz (Franconian Switzerland) is a wedge-shaped rural region between Bayreuth, Nuremberg and Bamberg, characterised by an enchanting landscape that's a bit like a Bavarian 'Brigadoon'. Picture idyllic, narrow valleys carved by sprightly little streams, majestic medieval castles proudly perched on craggy hilltops, pretty half-timbered villages, otherworldly rock formations, over 1000 mysterious caves and about 70 breweries. Artists, especially the late-18th-century Romantic poets, have long been mesmerised by this setting.

The slow pace of hiking and mountain biking best facilitates appreciation of this area, which is also extremely popular with rock climbers who have more than 5000 routes to grapple with. The local tourist offices have maps and can help with finding accommodation, which is generally good value. The region's central information office (☎ 09194-79 77 79, fax 79 77 76) is at Oberes Tor 1 in 91317 Ebermannstadt. The Web site is at Ⓦ www.fraenkische-schweiz.com (some pages in English).

Getting Around

The B470 is the main route through the Fränkische Schweiz, which is best explored under your own steam, although it can be done with public transportation. Coming from Bayreuth or Nuremberg, take the RE train to Pegnitz, then change to bus No 232, which travels west along the B270, stopping in Pottenstein and Gössweinstein. Trips here from Bamberg require multiple change-overs, so pack patience or forget it.

Buttenheim has a train station and is served directly from Nuremberg (€6.60, 50 minutes) and Bamberg (€2.50, 12 minutes); coming from Bayreuth is a bit more time-consuming and requires a change in Nuremberg (€20, 2½ hours).

Pottenstein

☎ 09243 • pop 5500

Pottenstein is a picture-perfect village that is home to Germany's largest stalagmite and stalactite caverns, the **Teufelshöhle** *(Devil's Cavern;* ☎ *208 or 708 41; adult/concession* €3.50/2.50, *9am-4.30pm Apr-Oct, 10am-3pm Tue, Sat & Sun Nov-Mar).* Tours through this glittering underground world cover a distance of 1.5km and last 45 minutes; a highlight is the reconstructed skeleton of a prehistoric bear. In summer, concerts are held in the entrance foyer. The cavern is about 2km outside of Pottenstein, right on the B470. Bus 232 stops here or it's a nice walk from town. Overlooking Pottenstein is the well-preserved 11th-century **Burg Pottenstein** *(*☎ *72 21; adult/concession* €3/2.50; *open 10am-5pm Tues-Sat May-Oct),* which is now a private museum. On tours, you'll see furnished historical rooms, arms and armour, glass, porcelain and ceramics and an art exhibit.

Pottenstein's tourist office (☎ 708 41, fax 708 40), at Forchheimer Strasse 1, is open 9am to 5pm weekdays and 10am to noon Saturday May to September and otherwise 9am to noon and 1pm to 4pm weekdays only.

The nearest train station is in Pegnitz, 14km east of Pottenstein. From here, buses travel west along the 470

Gössweinstein

Gössweinstein is another touristic hub in the region, in large part because of its **Basilika** *(*☎ *09242-264; open 8am-6pm daily*

FRANCONIA

May-Oct). Balthasar Neumann created this honey-coloured vision in stone between 1730 and 1739, with Prince-Bishop Carl von Schönborn footing the bill. Some of the many altars have unusual features, such as the golden globe of the main altar and the tooth extractor wielded by Apollonia, the patron saint of dentists. From May to September, the church is often flooded with pilgrims. Behind the basilica is the 'Grotto of Lourdes', a replica of the famous pilgrimage church in France.

Above looms the tower and stepgabled roofline of **Burg Gössweinstein** *(☎ 09242-456; adult/concession €2/1; open 10am-6pm daily Easter-Oct),* whose history goes back to the 11th century. It got its current neogothic look little more than a hundred years ago under Freiherr von Sohlern, whose descendants still own the place. You'll have panoramic views from up here.

The tourist office (☎ 09242-456, fax 980 40), at Burgstrasse 6, is open 8am to noon and 2pm to 5pm weekdays and 9am to noon Saturday from Easter to October. In winter, it closes at 4pm Monday to Thursday, at noon Friday and all weekend.

Buttenheim

The house in which Löb (alias Levi) Strauss was born is now the newly opened **Levi-Strauss-Museum** *(☎ 09545-44 26 02, Marktstrasse 33; adult/concession €2.60/1.30; open 2pm-6pm Tues & Thur, 11am-5pm Sat, Sun & holidays).* During a fascinating self-guided multimedia tour, visitors can trace the life of the jeans inventor, from his humble beginnings in Buttenheim to his stratospheric success in America. Rooms upstairs focus on the production of the pants, from the fabric to the rivets and labels used. Also here is a collection of vintage Levi's jeans and a short movie about the 'Levi's cult'. It's an entertaining, enlightening and refreshingly un-commercial museum.

BAYREUTH

☎0921 • pop 73,000 • elevation 345m

Since the inaugural Richard Wagner Festival in 1876, 'Wagner' and 'Bayreuth' have been as intimately linked as Tristan and Isolde.

Every year in August, this petit bourgeois town in Upper Franconia awakens from provincial slumber and plays host to an international galaxy of musicians, singers and opera pilgrims. Over 600,000 people vie, by computer drawing, for fewer than 60,000 seats to the festival started by the cantankerous composer himself. As a social event, it's de riguer for prominent figures from politics, academia, industry and the aristocracy.

Bayreuth was first mentioned in 1194 as Baierrute, a name that roughly translates as 'Bavarians' forest clearing'. Owned by the Nuremberg burgraves since 1248, it became the seat of the margraves of Brandenburg-Kulmbach-Ansbach in 1603. The glory days arrived in 1735 in the person of Wilhelmine, favourite sister of King Frederick the Great of Prussia, who was forced into a marriage to Margrave Friedrich. Wilhelmine – herself no artistic slouch – managed to put Bayreuth on the cultural map by inviting the finest artists, poets, composers and architects in Europe to court. Money was somebody else's problem, and by the time she finished, the city was home to some superb rococo and baroque architecture, the Eremitage and the Margravial Operahouse among them.

Wagner arrived on the scene more than 100 years later, in 1872 (also see boxed text 'Richard Wagner'). Once settled in Bayreuth, his presence attracted the philosopher Friedrich Nietzsche as well as composers Franz Liszt and Anton Bruckner.

Sadly, Bayreuth's carefree court life of the 18th century found its dark mirror in the Hitler years. Like Ludwig II before him, Hitler worshipped Wagner and maintained close relations with his daughter-in-law Winifred, at one time even proposing marriage to her. After the war, Bayreuth at first suffered under the weight of this association, but in recent years, the family feuds about the successor of current festival director, Wolfgang Wagner, a grandson of the composer, have dominated the headlines.

Orientation & Information

The Hauptbahnhof is just north of the historic centre. Walk south on Bahnhofstrasse

Levi Strauss: It's All in the 'Jeans'

He was born in Buttenheim on 26 February 1829 and in this bucolic setting, young Löb Strauss (later, 'Levi') began a journey that would spawn an empire, inspire global fashion and span American history from the Gold Rush to today.

Löb's father, a cloth and dry goods dealer, died suddenly of tuberculosis in 1846, plunging his widow and children into serious financial trouble. His mother, Rebecca, saw little choice but to leave Buttenheim and to move her family to New York where two older brothers were already operating a thriving dry goods business.

When word of the tumult and wild riches of the Gold Rush reached the East Coast, Löb, the astute junior partner in the family business, saw a huge opportunity and hurried off for the Wild West to open a West Coast branch. Arriving in San Francisco in 1853, he changed his name to Levi and immediately set up 'Levi Strauss & Co'. It became an immediate success in supplying miners stocking up on their supplies for treks into the fields of gold. The company expanded quickly and had to move several times, eventually settling in Battery Street, still Levi's company headquarters today.

Among Levi's best customers was a tailor named Jacob Davis, based in Reno, Nevada, who regularly bought large bolts of cloth. In a letter written to Levi in 1872, Davis describes how he had found a way to create especially durable pants by enforcing the pockets with rivets. He knew his idea would be a bonanza among miners, but he didn't have the money to obtain a patent. Would Levi be interested in a partnership? Levi was, and in 1873 they received patent #139,121. Levi's jeans were born.

The 'waist overalls' – as they were known in 1890 – quickly became the largest selling workwear item in the American West. The two partners first had their pants sown from a heavy-duty fabric called 'jean' but later switched to a stronger cotton fabric known as 'denim'. The origin of this term is not fully known, but it is widely assumed that it derives from 'serge des Nimes', a fabric invented in Nimes, France.

Levi's jeans were a triumphal success. American GI's took their favourite jeans with them when they shipped off to WWII. And when cowboys swaggered, rode and shot their way across the silver screen in Levi's, something clicked with the world's collective imagination. The humble work pants dreamed up for use in the Gold Rush were no longer a proletarian utility: they'd become a 'fashion statement'.

---

to Luitpoldplatz and on to the pedestrianised Maximilianstrasse, the main drag. The central bus station (ZOB) is also here at Markt. The Eremitage is about 6km east and the Festspielhaus 1.5km north of the town centre.

The tourist office (☎ 885 88, fax 885 55, e info@bayreuth-tourismus.de), at Luitpoldplatz 9, is open from 9am to 6pm weekdays and 9.30am to 1pm Saturday. Staff sell the three-day Bayreuth Card (€8.75), which entitles you to unlimited trips on city buses, entrance to nine museums and a two-hour guided city walk (in German). Also ask about the Verbundkarte (€10/9), good for admission to the Neues Schloss, Eremitage, Margravial Operahouse, Schloss Fantaisie and several other margravial buildings.

Tickets to concerts and other events are also available in the tourist office, which shares space with a full-service travel agency, the Reisebüro Bayreuth (☎ 88 50).

A Commerzbank is opposite the tourist office at Luitpoldplatz 8. There are post office branches across from the Hauptbahnhof and at Kanzleistrasse 3, with a Postbank inside. To send email, visit Café am Sternplatz (☎ 76 16 10), Ludwigstrasse 1, where surfing costs €2.50/30 minutes. The town's Web site (in six languages) is at **w** www .bayreuth.de. One of the biggest bookstores in town is Gondrom (☎ 75 72 60) at Maximilianstrase 18.

FRANCONIA

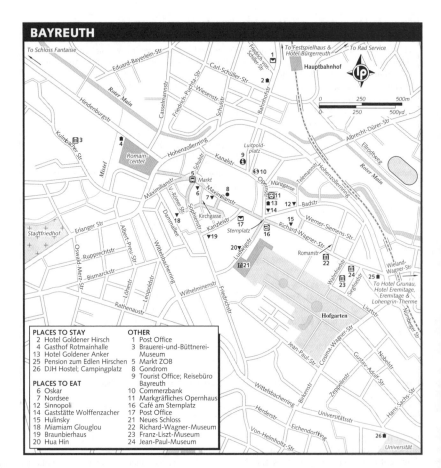

BAYREUTH

PLACES TO STAY
2 Hotel Goldener Hirsch
4 Gasthof Rotmainhalle
13 Hotel Goldener Anker
25 Pension zum Edlen Hirschen
26 DJH Hostel; Campingplatz

PLACES TO EAT
6 Oskar
7 Nordsee
12 Sinnopoli
14 Gaststätte Wolffenzacher
15 Hulinsky
18 Miamiam Glouglou
19 Braunbierhaus
20 Hua Hin

OTHER
1 Post Office
3 Brauerei-und-Büttnerei-Museum
5 Markt ZOB
8 Gondrom
9 Tourist Office; Reisebüro Bayreuth
10 Commerzbank
11 Markgräfliches Opernhaus
16 Café am Sternplatz
17 Post Office
21 Neues Schloss
22 Richard-Wagner-Museum
23 Franz-Liszt-Museum
24 Jean-Paul-Museum

Town Centre

Except during the Wagner Festival in July/August, the streets can be very quiet as Bayreuth slips into a kind of provincial slumber. But this is really the best time to see the sights without queues, and the town's strong musical traditions ensure there are good dramatic and orchestral performances year round.

A favourite musical venue is the **Markgräfliches Opernhaus** *(Margravial Opera House;* ☎ *759 69 22, Opernstrasse 14; adult/concession/under 18 €3.50/2.50/free, combination ticket with Neues Schloss €5/4/free;*

open 9am-6pm Fri-Wed, 9am-8pm Thur Apr-Sept, 10am-4pm daily Oct-Mar, closed during rehearsals and days of performance). Designed from 1744-48 by Giuseppe Galli Bibiena from Bologna, this stunning baroque masterpiece was Germany's largest opera house until 1871. Yet Richard Wagner deemed the place too quaint for his serious work, and conducted here just once. German speakers will especially enjoy the 45-minute 'sound and light' multimedia show, with projected images of the royals and lurid lighting. In May/June the house hosts a festival of opera and ballet, the Fränkische Festwoche.

South of here is Wilhelmine's **Neues Schloss** *(New Palace;* ☎ *75 96 90, Ludwigstrasse 21; adult/concession/under 18 €2.50/2/free, combination ticket with opera house €5/4/free; open 9am-6pm Fri-Wed, 9am-8pm Thur Apr-Sept, 10am-4pm daily Oct-Mar)*, the margravial residence after 1753. On the ground floor is a collection of porcelain made in Bayreuth in the 18th century. The Cedar Room is the site of the annual VIP opening celebrations of the Wagner Festival. Behind the palace sprawls the vast **Hofgarten** *(free, always open)*.

To learn more about the man behind the myth, visit Haus Wahnfried, the composer's former home on the northern edge of Hofgarten, which now contains the **Richard-Wagner-Museum** *(*☎ *757 28 16, Richard-Wagner-Strasse 48; adult/concession €3/1.50, combination ticket with Jean-Paul-Museum & Franz-Liszt-Museum €4/2; open 9am-5pm Fri-Mon & Wed, 9am-8pm Tues & Thur Apr-Oct, 10am-5pm daily Nov-Mar)*. Wagner had this lovely mansion built with cash sent by King Ludwig II. Inside is an undynamic, if comprehensive, chronological exhibit about Wagner's life, with glass cases crammed with documents, photographs, clothing, coins, porcelain and personal effects. Unless you're a Wagner aficionado or at least a German speaker, it's hard to fully appreciate this museum. The composer is buried in the garden, as is his wife, Cosima.

Along with Wagner, the composer and virtuoso Franz Liszt (1811–86) was one of the seminal figures of classical music in 19th-century Europe. Within earshot of Haus Wahnfried is the house where he died, now the **Franz-Liszt-Museum** *(*☎ *516 64 88, Wahnfriedstrasse 9; adult/concession €1.50/0.50; open 10am-noon & 2pm-5pm daily Sept-June, 10am-5pm daily July & Aug)*. Liszt was the father of Wagner's second wife, Cosima. On view are the usual memorabilia, including a sparkling grand piano, his death mask, correspondence and portraits. He's buried in a mausoleum on the Stadtfriedhof, a short walk west of the town centre (or bus No 9).

A few doors north, in the former home of Wagner's daughter, Eva, is the **Jean-Paul-Museum** *(*☎ *507 14 44, Wahnfriedstrasse 1;* *adult/concession €1.50/0.50; open 10am-noon & 2pm-5pm daily Sept-June, 10am-5pm daily July & Aug)*. The 19th-century Romantic poet Jean Paul (his real name was Johann Paul Friedrich Richter) lived in Bayreuth from 1804 until his death in 1825. By all accounts, he was a man who lived large (he had a particular fondness for the local brews) and wrote beautifully, with great imagination and emotional sensitivity.

Outside the Town Centre

North of the Hauptbahnhof, the rather spartan **Festspielhaus** *(1872;* ☎ *787 80, Festspielhügel 1–2; adult/concession €2.50/2; tours 10am, 10.45am, 2.15pm & 3pm; closed Mon, Nov & during rehearsals, during Festival season only morning tours; Bus: No 5 to Am Festspielhaus)* was also constructed with Ludwig's backing. The acoustics of the place are truly amazing as its builders took the body density of a packed house into account.

About 6km east of the centre is the **Eremitage**, a large and lovely park surrounding the **Altes Schloss** *(*☎ *759 69 37, Eremitage; adult/concession/under 18 €2.50/2/free; tours half-hourly 9am-6pm daily, to 8pm Thur Apr–mid-Oct; Bus: No 2 or 3 from Markt)*. It was a gift to Wilhelmine from her husband in 1735 and the couple's summer residence.

The lusciously landscaped park also contains the **Neues Schloss**, anchored by the Sun Temple topped by a gilded Apollo sculpture. Also here are grottoes, whose fountains start gushing on the hour between 10am and 5pm from May to mid-October (10 minutes later in the Lower Grotto). The bus trip out here takes about 20 minutes and costs €1.50.

For a fascinating look at how John Barleycorn is made, head to the enormous Maisel's **Brauerei-und-Büttnerei-Museum** *(*☎ *40 12 34, Kulmbacher Strasse 40; tours €3.50; tours 10am Mon-Sat)*, next door to the brewery north-west of the town centre. A fascinating 90-minute guided tour (in German) takes you into the sweet-smelling bowels of a 19th-century plant, covering all aspects of the business (including barrel-making). The *Guinness Book of World*

Richard Wagner

Richard Wagner (1813–83) was born in Leipzig but spent the last years of his life in Bayreuth. He arrived on 24 April 1872 from Switzerland with his wife, Cosima. With the financial backing of Ludwig II, his biggest patron and protector, Wagner built his spectacular house, Haus Wahnfried.

Wagner's operas, including *Götterdämmerung, Parsifal, Tannhäuser* and *Tristan and Isolde*, are powerful pieces supporting his grandiose belief that listening to opera should be work (his *The Ring of the Nibelungen* is literally four days long), not a social affair, and that music carries messages about life that are too important to ignore.

Wagner designed his own festival hall in Bayreuth. The acoustic architecture in the hall is as bizarre as his works are popular. The orchestra performs beneath the stage, and reflecting boards and surfaces send the sound up and onto the stage, where it bounces from the wall behind the singers and, mixed with the singers' voices, finally makes its way to the house.

Wagner is also well known for his reprehensible personal qualities: he was a notorious womaniser, an infamous anti-Semite and a hard-liner towards 'non-Europeans'. So extreme were these views that even fun-loving Friedrich Nietzsche called Wagner's works 'inherently reactionary, and inhumane'. The Nazis, however, embraced them as a symbol of Aryan might, and even today there is great debate among music lovers about the 'correctness' of supporting Wagnerian music and the Wagner Festival in Bayreuth.

Records lists it as the world's most comprehensive beer museum. Arguably, the best part is the foaming glass of Weissbier served at the end in the bottling room, which is now a private saloon with old-fashioned slot machines. English-language tours can be arranged for groups of 12 or more.

About 5km west of Bayreuth is **Schloss Fantaisie** (*☎ 73 14 00 11, Bamberger Strasse 3; adult/concession €3/2; open 9am-6pm Tues-Sun Apr-Sept)*. In this lovely rococo palace, Duchess Elisabeth Friederike Sophie (1732–80), the daughter of Margravine Wilhelmine, found solace after a failed marriage to Carl Eugen von Württemberg. It's surrounded by lush gardens and houses an exhibit about the art of garden landscaping.

If you need a little pampering after all this sightseeing, head to the new state-of-the art pool, sauna and wellness centre called the **Lohengrin-Therme** (*☎ 79 24 00, Kurpromenade 5; adult/children 3 hrs €8/5.50, all day €11/8.50; open 8am-10pm daily, sauna & wellness 10am-10pm daily)*, near the Eremitage. No-one wears a stitch of clothing in the saunas (Tuesday is women only).

Special Events

The **Wagner Festival** runs for 30 days from late July to August, with each performance attended by an audience of 1900. Tickets cost from €5 to €170, and demand is insane. To apply, send a letter (no phone, fax or email) requesting a ticket order form to the Bayreuther Festspiele, Kartenbüro, Postfach 10 02 62, 95402 Bayreuth, before September of the year before you want to attend and return it to the booking office by 15 October. If you've ordered tickets before, you should automatically receive an order form. During the Festival, returned tickets are sold at the Festivalhalle between 10am and noon on performance days and 90 minutes before curtain. People start lining up at about 6am! For more details, see **w** www.festspiele.de (also in English).

The lucky concertgoers face another endurance test. The opening notes of some operas ring out in the afternoon so people can get home by midnight. Adding to that, the seats are hard wood, ventilation is poor and there's no air-conditioning. But hang in there: on blisteringly hot days, water is sprayed on the roof during the interval!

Places to Stay

DJH hostel (*☎ 76 43 80, fax 51 28 05, e jhbayreuth@djh-bayern.de, Universitätsstrasse 28)* Bus: No 6 to Kreuzsteinbad (€1.40). Bed & breakfast €12.30-13.10, including linen. Closed mid-Dec-Jan. This 150-bed hostel is near the university, about a 15-minute walk south of the centre, and has nicely furnished dorms.

Campingplatz (☎ 51 12 39) Tent/person €1.50/2.50. Open Jul-Aug. In peak season, the city of Bayreuth operates a simple camping ground (with toilets and showers) behind the hostel.

Pension zum Edlen Hirschen (☎ 76 44 30, fax 764 43 28, Richard-Wagner-Strasse 75) Singles €28-43, doubles €46-61. Near the Wagner villa, this is one of the best budget options close to the sights. Most rooms have private bath.

Gasthof Rotmainhalle (☎ 661 77, Hindenburgstrasse 1) Singles/doubles €23/41. Cheap but quite cheerful rooms are available here, steps away from the Rotmaincenter, a major modern shopping mall, and the old centre.

Hotel Grunau (☎ 798 00, fax 798 01 00, Kemnather Strasse 27) Bus: No 7 to Grunau-Park. Singles €45.50-71.50, doubles €64-100. Outside the city centre but near the Eremitage, this modern hotel offers large rooms with all amenities, quiet rooms and a generous breakfast buffet. There's a fitness studio in the building (discounted admission).

Hotel Goldener Hirsch (☎ 230 46, fax 224 83, e goldener.hirsch@bayreuth-online .de, Bahnhofstrasse 13) Singles €46-76, doubles €66-102. This place has public areas with a '70s flair, but rooms are nicely furnished. It's near the train station.

Hotel Bürgerreuth (☎ 784 00, fax 78 40 24, An der Bürgerreuth 20) Singles €46-60, doubles €70-85. On the hill, just north of the Festspielhaus, this is a charming abode with an Italian flair, most evident in the restaurant, considered one of Bayreuth's finest. Rooms are furnished with all modern amenities.

Hotel Goldener Anker (☎ 650 51, fax 655 00, Opernstrasse 6) Singles €56-92, doubles €86-127. The refined elegance of this hotel, owned by the same family since 1753, is hard to beat. It's just a few metres from the opera house.

Hotel Eremitage (☎ 799970, fax 7999711, Eremitage 6) Singles €61-77, doubles €98-118. Right by the Eremitage, this hotel is small (just 11 beds) but choice. Rooms are super-quiet and a bit on the frilly side, but

have views of the park and a good range of comforts. Its gourmet restaurant Cuveé enjoys a loyal following.

Places to Eat

Braunbierhaus (☎ 696 77, Kanzleistrasse 15) Dishes €7-17. Toss back a dark Schinner beer at this pub in the town's oldest surviving building, with decent local dishes. Try their homemade bread.

Hua Hin (☎ 644 97, Ludwigstrasse 30) Lunch €6-7.50, dinner €8-16. Incense and a little fountain lead the way into this temple of tasty Thai food. The menu features all the standards, plus daily specials.

Miamiam Glouglou (☎ 656 66, Von-Römer-Strasse 28) Mains €6-10. Pretend you're in Paris at this delightful restaurant serving classic French bistro cuisine at good-value prices.

Oskar (☎ 516 05 53, Maximilianstrasse 33) Dishes €3-9. This updated version of a Bavarian beer hall bustles from morning to night. Sit in the busy bar, a cosy, hops-decorated room or the wintergarten. The menu includes salads and baked potato dishes, but the speciality is anything involving dumplings.

Sinnopoli (☎ 620 17, Badstrasse 13) Mains €4-8. Eccentric lamps and art form a suitable backdrop for this contempo cafe, which is at its most crowded for the all-you-can-eat weekend breakfast buffet (€10). Otherwise, it has creative pastas, baguettes, casseroles and daily specials.

Gaststätte Wolffenzacher (☎ 645 52, Badstrasse 1) Mains €7.50-12.50. Closed Sun evening. Cluttered but cosy, this traditional restaurant has a daily changing menu.

For value-priced sandwiches and baked goods, stop in at *Hulinsky*, a bakery-deli at Richard-Wagner-Strasse 25. There's a *Nordsee* fish Imbiss at Maximilianstrasse 39.

Getting There & Away

Bayreuth is a stop on the new ICE train line from Dresden to Nuremberg. Regional trains to Nuremberg also depart hourly (€13.50, one hour). Change here for Munich (€51.40, 2½ hours) and Regensburg (ICE train, €31.40, 2¼ hours).

Getting Around

Bus tickets are €1.50 per trip or €4.80 for a day pass. Bus Nos 3, 5 and 9 travel from the Hauptbahnhof right to the Markt in the town centre. For a taxi, call ☎ 660 60. For bike rental, try Rad Service (☎ 85 38 45), Markgrafenallee 5, about 1km east of the Hauptbahnhof.

AROUND BAYREUTH
Kulmbach
☎ 09221 • pop 30,000 • elevation 306m

About 30km north-west of Bayreuth, Kulmbach is a mecca for beer lovers, home of four large and several smaller breweries. If you happen to be in town for the Kulmbacher Bierfest, a large beer festival in late July, you'll be in for a special treat. But any time of year, there's plenty of inviting beer gardens and brewery-pubs, where you can sample the local offerings.

Kulmbach's other claim to fame is a medieval fortress, the **Plassenberg** *(☎ 82 20 11; adult/concession €2.50/2; open 9am-6pm Fri-Wed, 9am-8pm Thur Apr-Sept, 10am-4pm daily Nov-Mar)*. Behind the foreboding bastions awaits a royal residence of considerable charm, especially in the arcaded Renaissance *Schöner Hof* (Beautiful Courtyard), the setting for concerts and other events in summer.

A jail in the 19th century, the fortress now contains several museums as well as the recreated staterooms. Entire armies of tin figurines can be admired at the **Deutsche Zinnfigurenmuseum**, with 300,000 objects the world's largest of its kind. If this doesn't seem terribly gripping, imagine about 170 dioramas re-creating historical or mythological scenes, starting with the dinosaurs and ending with famous battles. Also on the fortress grounds is a museum of historical weapons and armour and a gallery of paintings featuring battle and hunting scenes. A shuttle bus makes the trip up here every half hour.

Kulmbach's tourist office (☎ 958 80, fax 95 88 49) is at Sutte 2. From Bayreuth, a few regional trains make direct trips in 40 minutes (€5.50). Drivers should take the B85.

Kronach & the Frankenwald
☎ 09261 • pop 19,500 • elevation 307m

Another 22km further north is the lovely medieval town of Kronach, sheltered by a fortified wall, embraced by two little rivers and crowned by a fortress. It is poised to celebrate its 1000th birthday in 2003 and is perhaps best known as the birthplace, in 1472, of the eponymous painter Lucas Cranach the Elder. Kronach is also the gateway to the **Naturpark Frankenwald**, a dense forest area with deep valleys carved by rivers and creeks. Popular with hikers and other outdoor fans, it also supplies as many as a million Christmas trees for German homes each year.

Start your explorations in the old town centre, here called the Obere Stadt. Take a spin through the lovely alleys lined with half-timbered houses, eventually swinging by the Gothic **Pfarrkirche St Johannes** for a look at its north portal topped with an emotive stone sculpture of St John the Baptist (1498). Then head up to the **Festung Rosenberg** *(☎ 604 10; adult/concession €2/1; open 9am-6pm Tues-Sun Apr-Oct, 10am-4pm Tues-Sun Nov-Mar)*, one of the largest fortresses in Germany and a never-conquered marvel of military architecture. Enter the complex through an early-baroque gate, built in 1662 by Antonio Petrini. A tour highlight is a subterranean maze of walkways.

Within the fortress is the **Fränkische Galerie** *(☎ 604 10; adult/concession €2/1, combination ticket with Festung €3/2; open 9.30am-5pm daily Apr-Oct, 10am-4pm Nov-Mar)*, where you can admire sculpture and altar paintings by Franconian artists working between the 13th and the 16th century. Highlights include works by Cranach, Tilmann Riemenschneider and the Dürer disciple Hans von Kulmbach.

The Kronach tourist office (☎ 972 36, fax 973 10) at Marktplatz 5 is open from 9am to 6pm Monday to Friday (phones staffed until 9pm) and can help with finding accommodation. The Frankenwald Tourismus Service Center (☎ 01805-36 63 98, fax 01805-32 93 98, same hours) is at Adolf-Kolping-Strasse 1.

Kronach is about 45km north-west of Bayreuth and 33km east of Coburg. Regional trains to/from Bayreuth require a change in Hochstadt (€10.70, 1¾ hours); to/from Coburg, you must change in Lichtenfels (€6.60, one hour). If you're driving, take the B85.

COBURG
☎ 09561 • pop 42,000 • elevation 297m
If marriage is diplomacy by another means, Coburg's rulers were surely masters of the art. Over four centuries, the princes and princesses of the house of Saxe-Coburg intrigued, romanced and ultimately wed into the dynasties of Belgium, Bulgaria, Denmark, Portugal, Russia, Sweden and, most prominently, Great Britain. The crowning achievement came in 1857, when Albert of Saxe-Coburg-Gotha took vows with his first cousin, Queen Victoria, founding the present British royal family (which quietly adopted the name of Windsor during WWI).

Coburg remained an independent duchy until the end of WWI but voted to join Bavaria in 1920. During the Cold War, Coburg languished as a backwater in the shadow of the Iron Curtain but, since reunification, it has undergone a revival of sorts, rekindling visitors' interest in its proud Veste, one of Germany's finest medieval fortresses.

Orientation & Information
Coburg's Bahnhof and central bus station are north-west of the Altstadt. To get to the Markt, head south on Lossaustrasse, then east on Judengasse. The tourist office (☎ 741 80, fax 74 18 29, [e] info@coburg-tourist.de) is just off the Markt at Herrngasse 4, and operates a free room-finding service (from €20 per person). It's open 9am to 6.30pm weekdays (until 5pm from November to March) and to 1pm Saturday. Change money at the Postbank in the post office at Hindenburgstrasse 6.

Veste Coburg
Enthroned above town in a triple ring of fortified walls, the Veste Coburg is a storybook medieval fortress that harbours the amazing **Kunstsammlungen** (☎ 87 90 or 879 79; adult/concession €3/1.50; open 10am-5pm Tues-Sun Apr-Oct, 1pm-4pm Tues-Sun Nov-Mar). Besides works by such star painters as Rembrandt, Dürer and Cranach the Elder, this vast collection also encompasses 350,000 copper etchings, old glass and weapons and lots of fancifully decorated sleighs and carriages.

In 1530, the Protestant reformer Martin Luther, under imperial ban, sought refuge at the fortress for about half a year. His former quarters are a historical highlight.

From April to October, the Veste-Express, a tourist train makes the trip to the fortress every 30 minutes (€1.50/2.50 one way/return). Bus No 8 goes uphill year round from Herrngasse near the Markt (€1.25 each way). The fitness-inclined can also walk up a steepish path for about 30 minutes.

Schloss Ehrenburg
In 1547, Coburg's dukes moved into a new residence, right in town, the Schloss Ehrenburg (☎ 808 80, Schlossplatz; tours in German adult/concession/under 18 €3.50/2/free, combination with Schloss Rosenau €4.50/3.50/free; tours hourly 9am-5pm Tues-Sun Apr-Sept, 10am-3pm Tues-Sun Oct-Mar). This sumptuous tapestry-lined palace is of 16th-century origin and only got its neogothic mantle in the 19th. Albert spent his childhood here and Queen Victoria stayed in a room with Germany's first flushing toilet (1860). The most splendid room is the **Riesensaal** (Hall of Giants), whose baroque ceiling is supported by 28 statues of Atlas.

Markt
A statue of Prince Albert anchors Coburg's central square. Flanking its north side is the ornate **Stadthaus** (Town House), a Renaissance edifice with a trio of stepped gables, red trim and a pretty oriel. Its counterpart is the baroque **Rathaus**, which sports blue-and-gold trim; one of its corners is graced by a two-storey oriel.

Special Events
In mid-July, the streets of this otherwise prim and proper town explode in a feast for

FRANCONIA

the senses during the annual **Samba Festival** which draws around 50 bands and as many as 2000 dancers, not to mention up to 200,000 revellers.

Places to Stay

DJH hostel (☎ 153 30, fax 286 53, Parkstrasse 2) Bus: No 1 from Markt or the Bahnhof (€1.25). Bed & breakfast €13.30, including linen. The spick-and-span youth hostel is in a mock castle 2km from town.

Gasthof Fink (☎ 249 40, fax 272 40, e gasthof-fink.de, Lützelbucher Strasse 24) Bus: No 4. Singles/doubles €25/45. This is a smart modern inn outside town with English-speaking staff and well-equipped rooms. More are available in the nearby Landhaus Fink.

Gasthof Goldenes Kreuz (☎ 904 73, fax 905 02, Herrngasse 1) Singles/doubles €25/50. In town, this old-fashioned guesthouse has a central location on the Markt but the basic rooms could use some sprucing up.

Coburger Tor (☎ 250 74, fax 288 74, Ketschendorfer Strasse 22) Singles €49-78, doubles €60-95. A refined ambience, impeccable service, nicely equipped rooms with thoughtful decor and the attached gourmet restaurant Schaller (mains €18-26) make this place a winner. It's about a 15-minute walk south of the Altstadt.

Places to Eat

The Coburg sausage is a local speciality; pick one up from the rolling kitchens on the Markt (€1.30).

Miles & More (☎ 995 39, Kleine Johannisgasse 6) Dishes €3.50-12.50. No matter the size of your wallet, you'll be able to find something on the menu at this quirky bistro.

Ratskeller (☎ 924 00, Markt 1) Mains €5-15. This rambling place serves good regional dishes from both Thuringia and Franconia.

Café Prinz Albert (☎ 945 20, Ketschengasse 27) Dishes €2.50-5. Closes 6.30pm. This is a good place for breakfast, a snack or coffee and cake.

Getting There and Away

Direct trains travel to/from Bamberg (€8, 40 minutes) and Nuremberg (€16, 1½

hours) every other hour. Travel to/from Bayreuth (€12.40, two hours), Kronach (€6.60, 1¼ hours) and Kulmbach (€8.10, 1¼ hours) requires a change in Lichtenfels.

AROUND COBURG
Rödental

The village of Rödental, about 6km northeast of Coburg, is known for its palace and as the home of the Goebel factory, makers of the world-famous Hummel ceramic figurines.

Schloss Rosenau *(☎ 09563-30 84 13, Rosenau 1; adult/concession/under 18 €2.50/2/free; in combination with Schloss Ehrenhof €4.50/3.50/free; guided tours hourly 9am-5pm Apr-Sept & 10am-3pm Oct-Mar, closed Mon)* is the birthplace of Prince Albert (1819) and a favourite palace of his later wife Queen Victoria. Medieval at its core, Albert's father, Ernst I, had it revamped in neogothic style. A highlight is the ornate **Marmorsaal** (Marble Hall) on the ground floor. The Orangery in the romantic English garden contains the renowned **Museum of Modern Glass** *(☎ 09563-16 06; adult/concession €1.50/1; open 10am-1pm & 1.30pm-5pm Tues-Sun Apr-Oct, 1pm-4pm Tues-Sun Nov-Mar).*

The Goebel family has been manufacturing porcelain figurines since 1871, but they're most famous for the so-called **Hummelfiguren**, cutesy statuettes with names such as 'Apple Tree Boy' or 'Goose Girl' that grace the tchotchke cabinets of millions of collectors worldwide. Each design was created by a nun named Maria Innocentia, who trained at Munich Academy of Fine Arts. At the company-run **Information Centre** *(☎ 09503-920, Coburger Strasse 7; admission free; open 9am-5pm Mon-Fri, 9am-noon Sat)* you get an overview of the art of porcelain making, can observe artists at work and peruse precious collectors' items in the museum.

Bus No 715 makes several trips a day from Coburg's Bahnhof to Rödental. It stops at the Goebel factory; to get to the Schloss, take a taxi from here.

Basilika Vierzehnheiligen

About 25km south of Coburg is a dignified 18th-century pilgrimage church, the Basilika

Vierzehnheiligen (☎ 09571-950 80; Vierzehnheiligen 2; admission free; open 6.30am-7pm daily Apr-Oct, 7.30am-dusk daily Nov-Mar). It stands in the spot where, in 1445, a young shepherd reported having recurring visions of the infant Jesus flanked by the 14 *Nothelfer* (Holy Helpers; hence the name), a group of saints invoked in times of adversity and difficulty since the 14th-century plague epidemic. The shepherd reported the 'little ones' asking for a chapel to be built right here so that they might have a place from which to work their miracles. Lo and behold, miracles did happen and the chapel, consecrated in 1448, quickly became a popular place of pilgrimage for all, from royals to paupers.

When in 1741, the original church was close to collapse, the local abbot commissioned Balthasar Neumann to build a new one. Along with the Würzburg Residenz, Vierzehnheiligen is widely regarded as one of Neumann's crowning achievements. Inside, all attention focuses on the amazing freestanding altar, supposedly placed right in the spot of the initial apparition. The work of stucco artists Johann Michael and Franz Xaver Feichtmayr of Wessobrunn, it is studded with statues of the 14 saints with one of the infant Jesus balancing up on top.

The church is maintained by the attached Franciscan monastery, whose six brothers also provide spiritual counselling to the pilgrims.

Alte Klosterbrauerei (☎ 09571-34 88) Snacks €3-5. Open 10am-8pm. This wonderful brewery is round the back of Vierzehnheiligen, up the hill past the wooden stands peddling kitsch. Grab a table in the sprawling beer garden with stunning views and quaff a half litre of the bracing 'Nothelfertrunk' for €1.75. Snacks include hearty bread-and-sausage platters, but you can also bring your own. Stay long enough and you may glimpse the nun in habit who lugs in cases for refill.

Getting There & Away Vierzehnheiligen is near Staffelstein and Lichtenfels, just off the B173, about a 30- minute drive from Coburg. Regional trains connect Coburg

with Lichtenfels from where there are two buses from at 8.25am and 10.45am weekdays (€1.40, 10 minutes), except for Wednesday, when departures are at 1.45pm and 5.45pm. A taxi is about €5.

Kloster Banz
Across the valley, Kloster Banz (☎ 09573-33 80) is a former 11th-century Benedictine monastery turned conference centre for a conservative political think tank. Today's complex is the work of Leonard and Johann Dietzenhofer (1698–1719), who favoured an Italian baroque look. The church (open 9am-noon & 2pm-4pm daily) features bright ceiling frescoes, altars to the Three Wise Men and the Fourteen Holy Helpers and intricately carved choir stalls. There's a lovely view from the Franz Josef Strauss memorial, which is dedicated to the former party leader of the CSU.

See the Getting There & Away section under Vierzehnheiligen.

WÜRZBURG
☎ 0931 • pop 130,000 • elevation 182m
Charming Würzburg straddles the River Main and is the northern gateway to the Romantic Road and the capital of the Franconian Wine Country (Fränkisches Weinland). Though badly pummelled in WWII (fire bombs destroyed almost 90% of the centre), the city put enormous efforts into restoring its major attractions. The wounds of war are still visible today, but overall recovery has been remarkable indeed.

As you explore the city, you'll repeatedly come across the work of two men who have shaped Würzburg's artistic and architectural legacy: Tilman Riemenschneider and Balthasar Neumann. The latter was the main brain behind the Residenz, an outstanding palace ranked as a Unesco World Heritage Site.

History
Würzburg was a Franconian duchy when, in 686, three roving Irish missionaries – Kilian, Totnan and Kolonat – passed through one day and asked Duke Gosbert if he wouldn't mind converting to Christianity

WÜRZBURG

Weinwanderweg
(Wine Trail)

0   125   250m
0   125   250yd

WÜRZBURG

PLACES TO STAY		OTHER		30	Post Office
10	Pension Spehnkuch	1	Fahrradstation	31	Dom St Kilian
12	Hotel-Gasthof	2	Go Tours;	32	Neumünster;
	Zur Stadt Mainz		Mitfahrzentrale		Lusamgärtlein
13	Hotel Goldenes Fass	3	Central Bus Station	33	Hugendubel
19	Hotel Dortmunder Hof	4	Post Office;	34	Rathaus
20	Hotel Residence		Postbank	37	Würzburger
41	Hotel & Restaurant Rebstock	5	Das Boot		Domschatz
45	DJH Jugendgästehaus	6	Museum im	38	Ärztliche Notfallpraxis;
			Kulturspeicher		Theresienklinik
PLACES TO EAT		7	Tourist Office	39	Residenz;
8	Simsim		Am Congress Centrum		Hofkirche;
11	Kiliansbäck; Erich Zeiss	9	Röntgen Museum		Martin-von-Wagner-Museum
14	Bürgerspital Weinstuben &		Gedächtnisstätte	40	Le Clochard Bistro
	Weingut	15	Omnibus	42	Uni-Café
18	Weinstuben &	16	Sparkasse	43	St Burkhard
	Weingut Juliusspital	17	Deutsche Bank	44	Festung Marienberg;
21	Joe Peña's	22	Haus des Frankenweins;		Fürstenbaumuseum;
25	Brückenbäck		Alter Kranen		Mainfränkisches Museum
26	Zum Stachel	23	Boat Docks	47	H@cm@c Internet Café
29	City Café	24	SB Waschsalon	49	Fahrrad Service
35	Backöfele	27	Marienkapelle		Erthal-Sozialwerk
36	Sternbäck	28	Tourist Office	50	STA Travel
46	Natur-Feinkostladen		Falkenhaus;	51	Main University
48	Café Reu		Stadtbücherei		Building

and – oh, yes – ditching his wife, the duke's brother's widow. Gosbert was said to be mulling it over when his wife, Gailana, had the three bumped off in 689. When the murders were discovered decades later, the three martyrs became saints, Würzburg a pilgrimage city and, in 742, a bishopric.

For the next 1060 years, the city was governed not by a duke or a count but by a 'prince of the church' – a bishop. Würzburg's bishops wielded enormous power, especially after 1168 when Emperor Friedrich Barbarossa promoted them to prince-bishops, thus making them both secular and religious rulers.

The people of Würzburg were less than pleased with this development and repeatedly attempted to regain their independence. The prince-bishops, from the safety of their hilltop fortress of Marienberg, had to quash two bloody uprisings – one in 1400, the other in 1525 during the Peasants' War.

The Reformation brought further instability, but this was quickly brought under control by Julius Echter von Mespelbrunn (1545–1617). One of Würzburg's most

ambitious and powerful prince-bishops, he turned the city into a centre of the counter-Reformation.

Würzburg's 'Golden Age' arrived with the election of three prince-bishops from the house of Schönborn, an artistically inclined bunch who sought greatness in building; the Residenz was built on their shift. Napoleon finally put an end to ecclesiastic rule in 1802; 14 years later, Würzburg became part of Bavaria.

Orientation

The Hauptbahnhof is at the northern end of the Altstadt, which is vaguely shaped like a bishop's hat. (Coincidence? We don't think so.) The central bus station is just west of here. Kaiserstrasse, running south from the station into the Altstadt, is the main shopping street. The Main River forms the western boundary of the Altstadt; the fortress, camp site, coin laundry and hostel are all on the west bank. The 15th-century stone footbridge, Alte Mainbrücke, is the most scenic route across the river. The Residenz is on the Altstadt's eastern edge.

Information

Tourist Offices The main office is in the Falkenhaus (☎ 37 23 98, fax 37 39 52, ⒠ tourismus@wuerzburg.de), a baroque masterpiece on Marktplatz, and is open from 10am to 6pm daily (closed Sunday November to March). Staff here can help find accommodation if you are there in person. For advance reservations, call the toll-free 24-hour hotline at ☎ 0800-194 14 08 (from within Germany only). A smaller tourist office branch (☎ 37 23 35, fax 37 36 52) is at Am Congress Centrum with hours from 8am to 5pm Monday to Thursday and to 1pm Friday.

Money Change money at the Postbank at Bahnhofsplatz 2 or at the Sparkasse on Barbarossaplatz, which has an ATM that changes foreign notes. Deutsche Bank has a branch at Juliuspromenade 66.

Post & Communications The main post office is at Bahnhofsplatz 2, but the one on Paradeplatz has telephone and fax services. The Stadtbücherei (see Bookshops & Libraries) charges €0.75 for 15 minutes of Web access; or look up H@ckm@c (☎ 465 29 67), Sanderstrasse 5, which stays open till 1am and charges €2.50/4 for 30/60 minute sessions.

Internet Resources The town's Web site is Ⓦ www.wuerzburg.de, with sights and hotel listings in English.

Travel Agencies STA Travel (☎ 521 76), Zwinger 6, is the local market leader, but Go Tours (☎ 140 38) on Bahnhofsplatz also has some attractive deals.

Bookshops & Libraries Hugendubel (☎ 35 40 40) has an enormous branch at Schmalzmarkt 12, with a good stock of English-language novels and travel guides. The Stadtbücherei (city library; ☎ 37 32 94) is in Falkenhaus am Markt, the same building as the tourist office. The Universitätsbibliothek (☎ 888 59 06), Am Hubland, is on the eastern outskirts of the city.

University Würzburg's Julius-Maximilian Universität (☎ 310), established in 1582 by Julius Echter von Mespelbrunn, is scattered across town, with the main administrative building at Sanderring 2 in the southern Altstadt. You can study just about everything, but most of the 20,000 or so students are there for medicine or related fields.

Laundry The self-service SB Waschsalon (☎ 41 67 73) is about 800m west of the Main at Frankfurter Strasse 13a. A load costs €3.50, and drying is €0.50 for 10 minutes.

Medical & Emergency Services For a list of doctors or hospitals, ask at your hotel or check the Yellow Pages. For after-hour emergencies (evenings, weekends and Wednesday afternoons) call ☎ 192 22 or visit the Ärztliche Notfallpraxis (☎ 32 28 33), Domerschulstrasse 1 (in the Theresienklinik building).

Residenz

The Residenz *(☎ 35 51 70, Balthasar-Neumann-Promenade; adult/concession €4/3; open 9am-6pm Fri-Wed, 9am-8pm Thur Apr-Oct; 10am-4pm daily Oct-Mar; guided English tours 11am & 3pm Sat, Sun & holidays)* is one of the most important and beautiful baroque palaces in southern Germany. Some sections can only be seen on guided tours.

In 1719, Johann Philipp Franz von Schönborn, unhappy with his old-fashioned digs up in Marienberg Fortress, hired a young architect by the name of Balthasar Neumann to build a new palace in town. Neumann, with a little help from his friends, came up with this enormous horseshoe-shaped complex. It took 24 years to build and another 30 or so to finish the eye-popping interior. In WWII, only the central section escaped unharmed; the rest had to be rebuilt.

Almost immediately upon entering, you'll see Neumann's brilliant **Grand Staircase**, a single central set of steps that splits and zigzags up to the 1st floor. In 1750, the Italian Giovanni Battista Tiepolo – then at the pinnacle of his career – smothered the vast vaulted ceiling with what still is the world's largest fresco. It allegorically depicts the four then-known continents (Europe, Africa, America and Asia) and is essentially a celebration of the arts and a glorification of the prince-bishop as patron *extraordinaire*.

This theme is particularly well reflected in the representation of Europe. The lower half of the composition shows Europa as a queen surrounded by personifications of the various arts – music, painting, sculpting etc. At the bottom of the picture is Neumann himself, dressed in officer's uniform and perched smugly on a cannon. Above the entire scene – somewhere between earth and the heavens – floats the prince-bishop himself.

Allow your eyes and mind to relax a bit in the soothing white stucco of the **Weisser Saal** (White Hall) before facing the next sensory onslaught: the opulent **Kaisersaal** (Imperial Hall). It's canopied by yet another impressive Tiepolo fresco, this one depicting Emperor Barbarossa.

From here, it's off to the meticulously restored staterooms, of which the **Spiegelkabinett** (Mirror Hall) is the most memorable. Gilded stucco drips from its ceiling and walls, which are covered with a unique mirror-like glass painted with figural, floral and animal motifs.

Hofkirche & Hofgarten In the residence's south wing, the **Hofkirche** *(Court Church; admission free; open 9am-6pm daily Apr–mid-Oct, 10am-4pm daily mid-Oct–Mar)* is another Neumann/Tiepolo co-production. It matches the residence in its splendour and brilliant proportions and features side altars by the Italian artist.

Behind the Residenz, the **Hofgarten** *(admission free; open dawn-dusk daily)* stretches out generously. Enter through intricate wrought-iron gates into the lovely French and English-style gardens, partly built on the old baroque bastions. Whimsical sculptures of children, mostly by court sculptor Peter Wagner, are strewn throughout the park, where concerts, festivals and special events take place during the warmer months.

Martin von Wagner Museum Martin Wagner (1777–1858) was a painter, sculptor and art procurer for King Ludwig I. His extensive private collection forms the basis of the Martin-von-Wagner Museum *(☎ 31 22 88, Residenzplatz 2, entrance next to the Hofkirche; admission free)*.

There are three departments: The **Antikensammlung** *(Antiquities Collection; open 2pm-5pm Tues-Sat)* focuses on Greek, Roman and Egyptian ceramics, vases, figurines and marble sculptures from 1500 BC to AD 300. The **Gemäldegalerie** *(Art Gallery; open 9.30am-12.30pm Tues-Sat)* has primarily German, Dutch and Italian paintings from the 15th to the 19th centuries, including works by Tiepolo. Finally, the **Graphische Sammlung** *(Graphics Collection; open 4pm-6pm Tues & Thur)* consists of drawings, copperplate etchings and woodcuts, including some by Albrecht Dürer.

Dom St Kilian

Würzburg's cathedral *(1040–1237; open 10am-5pm Mon-Sat, 1pm-6pm Sun Easter-Oct, 10am-noon & 2pm-5pm Mon-Sat, 12.30pm-1.30pm & 2.30pm-6pm Sun Nov-Easter)* is one of the largest Romanesque cathedrals in Germany, although numerous alterations have added Gothic, Renaissance and baroque elements. The cathedral is famous for its row of elaborate **tombstones** affixed to the pillars; of particular note are those of bishops Rudolf von Scherenberg (died in 1495) and Lorenz von Bibra (died in 1519) on the left, hewn from red marble by Tilman Riemenschneider. Attached to the north transept is the festive **Schönbornkapelle**, the final resting place of the Schönborn bishops, designed by Balthasar Neumann.

Würzburger Domschatz A few steps south of the Dom, a Neumann-designed town house harbours the Cathedral Treasury *(☎ 38 62 90, Marmelsteiner Hof, Plattnerstrasse; adult/concession €2/1; open 2pm-5pm Thur-Sun)*. On display is the usual range of ministerial garments, golden and bejewelled liturgical items and bishop's insignia. Spiritual music and intimate spotlighting of the objects create an almost meditative ambience.

Neumünster

Abutting the Dom, the Neumünster *(☎ 526 91; open 7am-6pm daily)* is a Romanesque church built in the 11th century on the site of the martyrdom of St Kilian, Kolonat and Totnan, who lie buried in its crypt. The Gothic tower and choir stem from the 13th century, while the baroque period brought the addition of the dome and ornamented facade. The north exit leads to the lovely **Lusamgärtlein** with the grave of the celebrated medieval minstrel Walther von der Vogelweide.

Marienkapelle

Next to the tourist office on Markt, the late Gothic Marienkapelle *(1377–1481; ☎ 536 91, Marktplatz; open 8am-6.30pm daily)* is a testimony to the wealth and self-confidence of Würzburg's medieval townspeople. After working his magic for decades, Balthasar Neumann was finally laid to rest in this dignified hall church, next to numerous Franconian knights and burghers. Among them is Konrad von Schaumberg (died in 1499) for whom Riemenschneider designed the tombstone. The prolific sculptor produced the sandstone figures of Adam and Eve above the entrance portal.

Röntgen Gedächtnisstätte

Würzburg's most famous modern scion is Wilhelm Conrad Röntgen, the discoverer of the X-ray in 1895, for which he received the Nobel Prize for Physics in 1901. His laboratory, including the instruments he used, are the heart of the Röntgen Memorial Exhibit *(☎ 351 11 03, Röntgenring 8; admission free; open 9am-4pm Mon-Thur, 9am-3pm Fri)*. To learn more about the man himself and his life as a scientist, visit the other two rooms.

Museum im Kulturspeicher

Würzburg's newest museum is housed in a historic riverside granary that's been cleverly converted into a culture centre. The Museum im Kulturspeicher *(☎ 32 22 50, Veitshöchheimer Strasse 5; adult/concession €3/1.50, combination tickets with Mainfränkisches Museum €4/2; open 11am-6pm Tues-Sun)* is the new home of the **Municipal Gallery** with art from the 19th to the 21st centuries. Regional artists such as Otto Modersohn and Erich Heckel are especially well represented. Under the same roof is the **Sammlung Ruppert**, a collection of post-1945 European concrete art with sculpture, paintings and photographs by such artists as Victor Vasarely and Auguste Herbin.

Besides the two museums, the Kulturspeicher also houses a cafe, a shop and a small stage.

Festung Marienberg

On the Main's left bank, Marienberg fortress smugly overlooks the rooftops from its lofty perch atop the splendid vine-covered hills. In 1201, Würzburg's prince-bishops began construction of a mighty fortress atop castle ruins from the 8th century. From here, they governed – almost without challenge – until 1719. Only Swedish troops in the Thirty Years' War managed to pillage and plunder their possessions after scaling the fortress walls in 1631. This incident prompted subsequent bishops to add the huge bastions.

Besides the museums, the circular **Marienkirche** (706) is a major point of interest. For many centuries, the bishops had their intestines buried here, while their bodies rested in the Dom St Kilian and their hearts at the monastery in Ebrach. The **Maschikuliturm** (1724), a defensive tower, is another Balthasar Neumann creation.

The fortress is a 30-minute walk up the hill from the Alte Mainbrücke via the *Tellsteige* trail, which is part of the 4km-long **Weinwanderweg** (wine hiking trail) through the vineyards around Marienberg. From Easter to October, bus No 9 makes the trip to the castle from the central bus station.

Fürstenbaumuseum The fortress' residential wing now holds the Fürstenbaumuseum *(☎ 438 38; adult/concession €2.50/2, combination ticket with Mainfränkisches Museum €4/3; open 9am-6pm Tues-Sun Apr-Oct, 10am-4pm Tues-Sun Oct-Mar)*. On the 1st floor, the reconstructed apartments of the prince-bishops should give you a good sense of the pompous lifestyle in which these rulers wallowed. A highlight is the so-called **Echtersche Familienteppich**, a huge tapestry showing the entire family of Julius Echter von Mespelbrunn including, oddly, their ages.

Upstairs is an overview of 1200 years of city history. There's plenty to look at but perhaps most memorable are the scale models showing Würzburg in 1525 and after the bombing raids in 1945.

Mainfränkisches Museum The baroque Zeughaus (armoury; 1712) houses the Mainfränkisches Museum *(☎ 430 16, Festung Marienberg; adult/concession €2.50/2, combination ticket with Fürstenbaumuseum €4/3; open 10am-5pm Tues-Sun Apr-Oct, 10am-4pm Tues-Sun Nov-Mar)*. The historic rooms provide a suitable backdrop for the high-quality displays, including a world-famous collection of Tilman **Riemenschneider sculptures**. In another section, porcelain, glass, furniture and other such objects illustrate life during the baroque and rococo era; from the same period are the sketches and drawings by Neumann and Tiepolo. In the **Kelterhalle**, where wine was once produced, is an exhibit about wine making.

St Burkhard & Käppele
On your way up to the fortress, you'll pass **St Burkhard** *(☎ 424 12; open 8am-6pm daily Apr-Oct, 8am-4.30pm daily Nov-Mar)*, a Romanesque basilica with a Gothic extension. Treasures include a Madonna by Riemenschneider and a 14th-century relief depicting the crucifixion.

Further south, in a prime location atop the Nikolausberg, the **Käppele** *(1752; ☎ 726 70; open 8am-7pm daily)* is an onion-domed pilgrimage church by Neumann with an elaborate facade, great ceiling frescos and fanciful stucco. The Stations of the Cross featuring life-size figures by Peter Wagner lead up to the church. Inside, the many votive tablets in the so-called 'Mirakelgang' (miracle aisle) are worth a look. The outside terrace is a great spot for photographs of the Marienberg and the city beyond.

Organised Tours
From May to October the tourist office runs two-hour English-language city walks (€8/6, including admission to the Residenz) daily at 11am from its office at Falkenhaus on Markt. If the idea of walking around in a herd doesn't appeal, you can always rent a cassette player and tape with a recorded tour (also in English) of all the major sights for €5.50 from the tourist office.

Wine Tours & Tasting The fortified Alter Kranen (old crane; 1773) was designed by Balthasar Neumann's son Franz Ignaz Michael to service a dock on the river south of Friedensbrücke. It is now the **Haus des Frankenweins** *(☎ 390 11 11, Kranenkai 1)* where you can sample some of Franconia's finest wines in historic rooms (from €1.50 per glass).

The historic **Weingut Juliusspital** *(☎ 393 14 00, Juliuspromenade 19; tours €4; tours 3pm Fri mid-Apr–Oct)* offers tours (in German) that take in the splendid old wine cellars, rooms and courtyards. The equally atmospheric **Bürgerspital Weingut** *(☎ 350 34 03, Theaterstrasse 19; tours €3.50; tours 2pm Sat Mar-Oct)* does the same. Tours include a glass of the local vintage.

Special Events
The largest European festival of black music, the **Africa-Festival** (information ☎ 150 60), is held in a Woodstock-like venue on the edge of town in late May or early June, complete with tents, food stands and, when it rains, lots of mud. Tickets are available from the tourist office.

Around the same time, thousands flock to the **Würzburger Mozartfest** (information and tickets ☎ 37 23 36) held in the Residenz courtyard and garden. The mood is fantastic, with the golden facade of the palace serving as the ultimate backdrop.

Places to Stay
Camping Kanu-Club *(☎ 725 36, Mergentheimer Strasse 13b)* Tram: No 3 or 5 to Judenbühlweg. Person €2, tent €1.50-3. The nearest camping ground is on the west bank of the Main. The tram stops right out front.

DJH Jugendgästehaus (☎ 425 90, fax 41 68 62, Burkarder Strasse 44) Tram: No 3 or 5 to Ludwigsbrücke. Bed & breakfast €17-19, including linen. This hostel is below the fortress and has room for 254 in three- to eight-bed dorms. You have a five minutes' walk north along river after getting off the tram.

Pension Spehnkuch (☎ 547 52, fax 547 60, Röntgenring 7) Singles/doubles €26/49. This place near the train station has zero frills and little charm but rooms are clean and service is adequate.

Etap Hotel (☎ 270 82 20, fax 270 82 30, Nürnberger Strasse 129), Singles/doubles €32/38. If you have a car, this modern hotel about 6km east of the centre offers great value. It has small, motel-style rooms and charges €4.50 per person for breakfast.

Hotel Dortmunder Hof (☎ 561 63, fax 57 18 25, e info@dortmunder-hof.de, Innerer Graben 22) Singles/doubles/triples from €40/65/90. Come here for cheerful and quiet rooms with shower & WC and cable TV. There's a restaurant on the premises.

Hotel-Gasthof Zur Stadt Mainz (☎ 531 55, fax 585 10, e info@hotel-stadtmainz.de, Semmelstrasse 39) Singles/doubles/triples from €57/87128. Run by the congenial Schwarzmann family, this charming inn dates back some 500 years. Rooms are old-fashioned but sport modern amenities.

Hotel Goldenes Fass (☎ 32 15 60, fax 570 57, e goldenesfass@theaterhotels.de, Semmelstrasse 13) Singles/doubles from €45/53. Rooms come with TV and telephone at this central and good-value place above a pizzeria and near the town theatre.

Hotel Residence (☎ 535 46, fax 125 97, Juliuspromenade 1) Singles €65-85, doubles €70-110. This stylish hotel is near the river and the congress centre and thus a popular choice with business travellers.

Schlosshotel Steinburg (☎ 970 20, fax 971 21, Auf dem Steinberg) Singles/doubles €77/120. Framed by vineyards, this former palace has gorgeous rooms, a pool and sauna and, so they claim anyway, a resident ghost.

Hotel Rebstock (☎ 309 30, fax 309 31 00, e rebstock@rebstock.com, Neubaustrasse 7) Singles/doubles from €96/185. Class,

hospitality and superb comfort distinguish this family-run hotel from the rest of the pack. Rooms in the meticulously restored rococo town house lack no amenities and are decorated with imagination and exquisite furnishings in a style evocative of the south of France. Suites cost a little more. The restaurant (mains €10-20) gets top marks for its superb and inventive international cuisine.

Places to Eat

For a town its size, Würzburg has a great array of enticing pubs, beer gardens, cafes and restaurants, with plenty of student hangouts among them.

Restaurants Würzburg has a great variety of restaurants.

Backöfele (☎ 590 59, Ursulinergasse 2) Mains €6-18. Don't miss this rustic restaurant with romantic atmosphere galore complemented by a delightful menu of traditional and innovative game, steak and fish dishes.

Bürgerspital Weinstuben (☎ 35 28 80, Theaterstrasse 19) Mains €6.50-9. Closed Tues. One of Würzburg's most popular eating and drinking establishments is this huge, labyrinthine place with origins as a medieval hospice. It offers a broad selection of Franconian wines and regional dishes served in cosy dining nooks.

Juliusspital (☎ 540 80, Juliuspromenade 19) Mains €6-15. This is another lovely Weinstube with Franconian delicacies and excellent homegrown wines. The Juliusspital itself was founded as a hospital and poor people's home by Julius Echter von Mespelbrunn in 1576.

Joe Peña's (☎ 57 12 38, Juliuspromenade 1) Mains €9-13. This Tex-Mex joint is popular with student-age revellers and is especially busy during happy hour from 5pm to 8pm and 11pm to midnight. Favourites include fajitas, burritos and enchiladas; the guacamole is prepared tableside.

Schützenhof (☎ 724 22, Mainleitenweg 48) Mains €6-12. Near the Käppele church, this is a wonderful place in summer with superb views, an all-age clientele and good beer, fruit wines and regional food.

Zum Stachel (☎ 527 70, Gressengasse 1) Brotzeit €2-9, mains €7-15, 4-course menu with wine €40. Closed Sun. Housed in a historic 15th-century building, the beautiful but over-touristed Zum Stachel has Franconian fare and an enchanting courtyard.

Cafes Würzburg has an abundance of cafes.
City Café (☎ 145 55, Eichhornstrasse 21) Meals €5-8. Come here for breakfast or tasty snacks named after film stars (it's right below a cinema), including salads, soups, pastas, pancakes and toasted sandwiches.

Sternbäck (☎ 540 56, Sternplatz) Dishes from €2.50, breakfast €2-9.50. This is a busy pub with rustic 1920s decor and 32 baked-potato varieties. Breakfast is served until 5pm. In fine weather, the outside tables are the most coveted.

Brückenbäck (☎ 41 45 45, Zellerstrasse 2) Dishes €3-7. Enjoy great views of the river and the Altstadt (in fine weather from the terrace) at this comfortable west bank cafe. It specialises in exquisite teas but also serves good coffees, light meals and wine.

Snacks & Fast Food On Kaiserstrasse south of Hauptbahnhof is a ***Kiliansbäck*** bakery at No 22, with cheap snack specials and tasty goodies. Next door, the butcher-deli ***Erich Zeiss*** offers sausages, chicken and roast pork sandwiches from €2 to €4.

Simsim (☎ 161 53, Pleichertorstrasse 2) makes outstanding doner and felafel from €3, while ***Natur-Feinkostladen*** (☎ 189 81, Sanderstrasse 2a) sells health-food snacks and grain burgers from €2 and runs a specialist grocery next door.

Entertainment
Trend is the town's monthly listing magazine.

Serious party animals should head to the complex at Gattingerstrasse 17 in eastern Würzburg. Dance temples include ***Airport*** (☎ 237 71), which throbs with a mix of techno, house, blackbeat and disco; and ***Soundpark Ost*** (☎ 230 80), which has two rooms for dancing to a wild mix of musical styles and a third for resting ear drums. Take bus No 26 from the central bus station.

Das Boot (☎ 593 53, Veitshöchheimer Strasse 14) This floating party boat is a Würzburg institution. You can take a trip to Thailand in the restaurant, to England in the bar or to your own fantasy world in the dance club in the machine room.

Omnibus (☎ 561 21, Theaterstrasse 10) This established venue is the best place for live rock, jazz, blues, soul, salsa, folk and other music.

Neubaustrasse and Sanderstrasse are chockfull with student cafe-bars that stay open late and also serve good cheap food.

Le Clochard Bistro (☎ 129 07, Neubaustrasse 20) This place is great for just a drink, but they also serve good sweet and savoury crepes (€3.50-7) and a daily three-course special for €8.50.

Uni-Café (☎ 156 72, Neubaustrasse 2) Hugely popular, with two floors, this cafe has cheap snacks (€3-6) and a fun crowd.

Café Reu (☎ 134 17, Sanderstrasse 21) This gallery-pub-cafe has a young, energetic crowd and good salads and sandwiches (€4-6.50) in a setting of funky mix-and-match furniture.

Getting There & Away
Trains frequently serve Bamberg (€14, one hour), Nuremberg (€14.40, 1¼ hours) and Aschaffenburg (€12.40, one hour).

The Romantic Road Europabus stops at the main bus station next to the Hauptbahnhof. The three-hour trip to Rothenburg ob der Tauber costs €15/21 one way/return, making the train more convenient and cheaper, despite a change in Steinach (€9, 1¼ hour).

The Mitfahrzentrale (☎ 194 48 or 140 85) is on Bahnhofsplatz next to the Go Tours travel agency. A central car rental agency is Europcar (☎ 120 60) at Bahnhofsplatz 5.

Getting Around
Würzburg is best seen on foot. Single bus or tram tickets in town are €1.40, with day passes costing €8.50. Call a taxi at ☎ 194 10 (flag fall €2.50).

Bicycle rental shops include the Fahrradstation (☎ 574 45) at the Hauptbahnhof, with city/mountain bikes for €7/9 (closed Sunday and Monday; use the station side

FRANCONIA

entrance). The nonprofit Fahrrad Service Erthal-Sozialwerk (☎ 359 97 39), in the courtyard at Sanderstrasse 27, rents out two-wheelers for €5 to €7.50 per 24-hour rental.

AROUND WÜRZBURG
Schloss Veitshöchheim

About 8km downstream from Würzburg, the small town of Veitshöchheim is home to Schloss Veitshöchheim (☎ 0931-915 82, Hofgarten 1; tours adult/concession €1.50/1; open 9am-6pm Tues-Sun Apr–mid-Oct) whose exquisite rococo garden is considered one of the most beautiful in Europe.

The Schloss served as a summer residence of the Würzburg prince-bishops from 1680 until 1802 and got the star treatment from none other than Balthasar Neumann. It's closed for restoration throughout 2002, with tours expected to resume in early 2003.

Actually more interesting than the palace itself is the garden (admission free; open 7am-dusk, 8pm at least daily). It's modest in size, measuring only 270m by 475m but, in this case, size definitely does not matter. Dotted throughout are sculptures of animals, humans and gods created by a trio of top sculptors in the 18th century: Johann Wolfgang van der Auvera, Ferdinand Tietz and Johann Peter Wagner. Hedges, pergolas, flowers and fountains provide further eye candy and make this a great spot to relax on a warm day. From April to October, the fountains start spouting on the hour between 1pm and 5pm.

Veitshöchheim is served by train and by local bus No 11 leaving from the Würzburg central bus station. The nicest way to get there, though, is by boat (☎ 556 33). These depart on the hour between 10am and 4pm weekdays (with additional departures on weekends) from the landing docks at Alter Kranen (one way/return €5/7.50; 40 minutes each way).

FRANCONIAN WINE COUNTRY

Würzburg is at the centre of the Fränkisches Weinland, which is roughly hemmed in by three low mountain ranges: the Spessart to the west, the Rhön to the north and the Steigerwald to the east. The Main River snakes through here on its 524km trip from the Fichtelgebirge to the Rhine at Mainz. Along the way, it passes by dozens of picture-perfect villages seemingly lifted straight from a Grimm's fairytale; encircled by ancient walls, dotted with proud steeples and towers, enlivened by ornate facades, many exude an enchanting spell. Time here seems to elapse at a gentler pace and life pretty much revolves around the essentials: church, family, friends, good food and wine – if not necessarily in that order.

For visitors, there are lots of things to do involving the grape, including strolls through the vineyards, wine festivals or sampling the local crop right at a wine estate. Art and architecture aficionados will have reason to rejoice as well, thanks to the active patronage and fat coffers of Würzburg's prince-bishops.

We probably shouldn't encourage you to visit the region by car, but fact is, if you intend to go to several villages, it is the easiest and most convenient way to travel. Public transportation is an option as long as you start in Würzburg, as connections between most villages are limited or nonexistent.

Sommerhausen
☎ 09333 • pop 1500

You just gotta love Sommerhausen's coat of arms, which features a laughing sun and a plump grape cluster. An almost Gallic charm prevails in this tiny romantic wine village, whose cobbled streets lead right into the vineyards. Here a stone bench, there clusters of geraniums spilling out of flowerboxes, or a wrought-iron gate festooned with grape vines. It's no wonder that many artists have fallen in love with this place; you can see their work exhibited in several galleries around town.

The tourist office (☎/fax 82 56), at Hauptstrasse 15, is usually open from 9.30am to 11.30am Monday, Wednesday, Thursday and Friday. Otherwise, Landhaus Kunstgewerbe (☎ 10 61) at Jahnstrasse 11 also has some information. It's open from 4pm to 7pm Tuesday to Friday and 12.30am to 4pm Saturday.

Worthwhile sights include a 15th-century castle, a step-gabled town hall and a church, as well as Germany's smallest theatre, the **Torturmtheater** *(☎ 268, Torturm)* inside a tiny tower with just 50 seats. It was founded in 1946 by Luigi Malipiero, an Italian painter and set designer, and still enjoys a cult following for its cleverly staged and innovative productions. Next door, in a vaulted cellar, is the **Kabarettbühne Bockshorn** *(☎ 14 77, Katharinengasse 3)* where satirical sketches and stand-up comedy are on the program.

Sommerhausen's stock in trade is, of course, its excellent wines. About 10 estates offer tastings, although by prior arrangement only. These include Weingut Alter Steinmann *(☎ 250, Am Plan 4)*, which charges €8.50/11 for five/eight wines accompanied by a hearty Brotzeit. Weinbau Wagner *(☎ 431, Sonnenhof)* charges €7/10 for five/eight wines, or €10/13 with Brotzeit.

A charming overnight option is **Weinhaus Düll** *(☎ 220, fax 82 08, Maingasse 5)*, an olde worlde inn with lovingly decorated rooms with private bath and TV (doubles €50-60). The restaurant speciality is sauerkraut soup (€3.50). Otherwise, it's lots of fresh and seasonal fare, including game, as well as quite a few vegetarian selections (mains €7-14, closed Monday).

Sommerhausen is on the B13, about 18km south of Würzburg and is served by bus No 8066 from that city's central bus station (30 minutes).

Sulzfeld
☎ 09321 • pop 1250

Sulzfeld, with its quiet, cobbled lanes, feels far removed from the hubbub of modern life. Hugging the left bank of the Main, it has not grown much beyond the perimeter of its completely preserved medieval wall, which runs for 900m and is fortified by 18 towers. Access is through three picturesque gates.

Sulzfeld is mostly about just wandering around and soaking up the atmosphere. A good place to start is on Marktplatz, dominated by the three-storey gabled **Rathaus** (1609). Built at the instigation of prince-bishop Julius Echter, its impressive size was a demonstration of the superior wealth of the Würzburg bishopric over its Protestant

rivals, the margraves of Ansbach. The ornate **St Mary's Column** has anchored the square since 1724.

From here, you might start a stroll by heading south on Zehntgasse, which intersects with Kettengasse and then merges with Friesengasse. Many of the houses along here are decorated with ornate **house sculptures**. Various saints and the Madonna with child are popular motifs, and there's an especially neat Trinity where Klostergasse meets Friesengasse.

Perhaps Sulzfeld's main claim to fame is of the culinary kind. The town is famous for its *Meterbratwurst*, which is 100cm of sausage curled up like a pretzel and served with bread and sauerkraut. The Gasthaus zum Goldenen Löwen at the Markt claims to have invented it, but other places in town do just as good a job. The whole thing usually costs €8 to €9; half metres are €4.50 to €5.

If you get stuck, one shelter you might consider is *Gasthaus zum Stern (☎ 56 38, Pointgasse 5)*, a family-run inn in a half-timbered house with snug rooms (singles/doubles €30/50), hearty food and a nice beer garden. The owners make their own wine.

Sulzfeld is about 24km south-east of Würzburg and 3km south of Kitzingen, the wine country's main administrative centre, which is on the B8. Getting to Sulzfeld by public transport requires catching one of the three weekday buses (No 8112) in Kitzingen, which is served by regional trains from Würzburg and Iphofen.

Iphofen
☎ 09323 • pop 4500

A bit east of the Main, Iphofen has preserved a medieval flair largely because of its nearly perfectly intact town wall, punctuated by several towers and gates. Some of the best Franken wines grow nearby, including the famous Julius-Echter-Berg.

Iphofen's train station is south of the Altstadt. Most of the town's 'action' is centred on and around Marktplatz. Just north of here, at Kirchplatz 7, the tourist office (☎ 87 03 06, fax 87 03 08) is open from 10am to 6pm weekdays and to 4pm Saturday.

FRANCONIA

Things to See & Do The tourist office shares a building with the **Vinothek Iphofen** (☎ *87 03 17, Kirchplatz 7; open 1pm-6pm Tues-Thur & Sun, 1pm-9pm Fri & Sat)*, where you can sample and buy superior wines produced by 21 local vintners. Tastes start at €1.50 per 100mL.

A few steps north looms Iphofen's parish church, the **St-Veits-Kirche** whose interior is bathed in yellow and white hues, giving it a dignified and festive ambience. This effect is further enhanced by the luminous stained-glass windows. Art treasures include a Madonna and sculptures of John the Baptist and the apostle John, which are sometimes ascribed to Riemenschneider, though no-one seems to be absolutely sure.

Take a stroll around the church to come face to face with the landmark **Rödelseer Tor** (1456), an almost ridiculously picturesque half-timbered town gate topped by a steep red-tile roof.

Backtrack to Markt where, on the north side, is the recently restored **Rathaus** (town hall), a baroque confection from 1716 with a double staircase typical of this region. South of the square, a 17th-century palais houses the **Knauf-Museum** (☎ *315 28 or 316 25, Am Marktplatz; admission €1.50; open 10am-noon Tues & Thur, 2pm-6pm Tues-Sun Apr-Oct)*. Sponsored by the main local employer, the gypsum factory Knauf, it has 20 rooms filled with replica plaster casts of famous reliefs from such ancient cultures as Egypt, Mesopotamia, Rome and Persia.

Places to Stay & Eat There are a number of accommodation and restaurant options in Iphofen.

Huhn – Das Kleine Hotel (☎ *12 46, fax 10 76,* e *kleines-hotel-huhn@t-online.de, Mainbernheimer Strasse 10)* Singles €30-45, doubles €70. About 300m west of the Altstadt, this place offers modern, romantically furnished rooms with all amenities, and attentive service.

Hotel & Restaurant Zehntkeller (☎ *30 62, fax 15 19,* e *zehntkeller@romantik.de, Bahnhofstrasse 12)* Singles €61-82, doubles €92-143. Iphofen's most historic abode

was once an administrative building for the Würzburg prince-bishops. Today it offers traditional but classy rooms and good meals (mains €13-25).

Cafe Legere (☎ *87 64 13, Marktplatz)* Dishes €2-7. This is a good place for a snack, including baked potatoes, omelettes and soups. The Sunday brunch is €6.

Getting There & Away Iphofen is on the B8, about 30km south-east of Würzburg. Regional trains from Würzburg run hourly (€5.20, 25 minutes). Bikes can be rented at Zweirad-Hermann (☎ *33 31*) at Bahnhofstrasse 36, for €5 per day.

Prichsenstadt
☎ 09383 • pop 3200

Hugging the western edge of the Steigerwald forest, Prichsenstadt is one of the jewels of Old Franconia, as of yet undiscovered by mass tourism and imbued with a dreamy, pristine quality. Nicely decorated half-timbered and baroque houses line its little lanes, where ancient inns beckon you to enjoy a glass of crisp white wine.

Unlike other villages in the Franken Wine Country, Prichsenstadt was part of the territory of the Protestant margraves of Ansbach until 1803. Shortly after the margraves came to power in 1437, Prince-Bishop Johann III of Würzburg attacked and devastated the town. Protected by a town wall, it has seen little strife since, which may account for its peaceful ambience. The nicest way to enter is via the western gate, whose twin towers stand guard like soldiers helmeted with red-tiled pointed turrets.

The tourist office (☎ *975 00*), in the Rathaus at Karlsplatz 5, just past the gate, is open 8am to noon and 4pm to 6pm Monday to Friday.

An oddity in town is Hans Klein's private **Mineral & Fossil Museum** (☎ *70 08, Schulinstrasse 28; admission free; open 9am-6pm daily)*. Displayed in his courtyard is an amazingly quirky array of stuff ranging from geodes to dinosaur teeth. Klein is not always around, but you're welcome to browse and leave money on the honour system if you decide to buy something.

If you get hungry or stuck for the night, options include:

***Alte Schmiede** (☎ 972 20, fax 97 22 49, Karlsplatz 7)* Brotzeit €3.50-6, mains 4.50-10. For sustenance, pop in here for some honest-to-goodness home cooking. Roast duck with dumplings or stuffed cabbage rolls are typical mains. A wooden fish dangling by the door means that fresh carp or trout is on the menu. Rooms with private facilities go for €30/50 singles/doubles.

***Gasthof zum Storch** (☎ 65 87, fax 67 17, Luitpoldstrasse 7)* Singles/doubles from €35/50. In a 300-year-old building, this inn has traditional and slightly frilly rooms with private bath and a restaurant serving the usual hearty fare (mains €8.50-13) as well as wine from your hosts' own estate.

Prichsenstadt is about 40km east of Würzburg and about 50km west of Bamberg, on the B286 just north of the A3. Nondrivers coming from Würzburg should take the regional train to Kitzingen, then change to bus No 8150. Coming from Bamberg by bus requires three changes – in other words, forget it.

ASCHAFFENBURG
☎ 06021 • pop 70,000 • elevation 129m
Aschaffenburg, on the Main River and at the foot of the rolling Spessart hills, is only about a half-hour drive south of Frankfurt. In appearance and mentality, it is probably the least Bavarian of Bavaria's cities. Badly pummelled in WWII, it grew an ugly industrial shell in the '50s and '60s, but retains a charming Altstadt and several memorable sights and parks.

For nearly 800 years, Aschaffenburg was ruled by the archbishops of Mainz before becoming part of Bavaria in 1810. Ludwig I, who took a liking to the place, nicknamed it his 'Bavarian Nice', an allusion to the Mediterranean microclimate here that allows the growth of figs and lemons.

Orientation & Information
The Hauptbahnhof is on Ludwigstrasse on the northern edge of the Altstadt. The tourist office (☎ 39 58 00, fax 39 58 02, ℮ tourist@ info-aschaffenburg.de), at Schlossplatz 1, about 10 minutes' walk south, is open 9am to 5pm weekdays and 10am to 1pm Saturday. On the Internet, look up Ⓦ www.info -aschaffenburg.de.

Schloss Johannisburg
A secondary residence of the Mainz archbishops, the Renaissance-era Schloss Johannisburg sports a striking symmetry: it's an exact square with four 90m-long wings wrapped around a central courtyard, with each corner buttressed by a lantern-shaped tower. Today it houses the **Schlossmuseum** *(☎ 38 67 40, Schlossplatz 4; adult/concession €2.5/2, combination ticket with Pompejanum €4/3; open 9am-6pm Tues-Sun Apr-Sept, 10am-4pm Tues-Sun Nov-Mar)*. You'd need several hours to plough through the entire collection, but absent that luxury you might want to concentrate on the highlights. These include paintings by **Dutch and German Old Masters**, including Rubens, Rembrandt, Cranach the Elder and Hans Baldung Grien. The **Korkmuseum** consists of cork replicas of famous landmarks in antique Rome (Colosseum, Pantheon etc) built to precise scale and with amazing detail by Ludwig I's baker. Also here is the original 18th-century **pharmacy** from Regensburg's St Emmeram monastery.

Since 1969, the palace's east tower has housed a **carillon**, which plays its merry tune daily at 9am, noon and 5pm. One-hour concerts by the city's official carillon-player usually take place at 5pm on Sunday.

Pompejanum
Behind the manicured hedges of the beautiful Schloss garden, above the banks of the Main, perches a replica of a Roman villa, known as the Pompejanum *(☎ 21 80 12; adult/concession €2.50/2, combination ticket with Schloss €4/3; open 9am-6pm Tues-Sun Apr–mid-Oct)*. In 1840, inspired by the excavations in Pompeii (Italy), King Ludwig I commissioned his court architect Friedrich von Gärtner to build this idealised antique-style home. Never intended as a residence, its rooms are decorated with colourful frescoes and intricate mosaic floors. Roman marble sculptures from the

FRANCONIA

Munich Glyptothek provide additional visual accents.

Stiftskirche & Stiftsmuseum

South of the Schloss, Schlossgasse takes you into the heart of the Altstadt with its cobbled lanes and half-timbered houses. On Stiftsplatz you'll come upon the **Stiftskirche** with origins in the 10th century but now an oddly skewed style mix of Romanesque, Gothic and baroque. It's filled with treasures, including a *Resurrection* (1520) from the workshop of Cranach the Elder, several altars and the harrowingly realistic *Lamentation of Christ* (1525) by Matthias Grünewald in the first chapel on the south side.

The attached **Stiftsmuseum** (☎ 33 04 63 or 386 74 14, adult/concession €2.50/1; open 10am-1pm & 2pm-5pm Wed-Mon) has moderately interesting displays of archaeological objects and sacred art. One of the more intriguing items is a medieval chessboard once owned by Cardinal Albrecht of Brandenburg.

Rosso Bianco Collection

Fans of the 'auto-erotic' will delight in the fleet of sports cars, polished to perfection, on view at the Rosso Bianco Collection (☎ 213 58, Obernauer Strasse 125; adult/concession €5/3; open 10am-6pm Tues-Sun Apr-Oct, 10am-6pm Sun Nov-Mar; Bus: Nos 1, 61 or 62 direction Sulzbach to Bischberg). The exhibition halls shelter over 200 two-seaters – from the classic to the unique, the elegant to the outrageous – from around 50 manufacturers, including Ferrari, Maserati, Jaguar and Alfa Romeo. The integrated **Art & Auto-Forum** *(open weekends only)* shows car-themed posters, paintings and sculptures.

Parks & Gardens

Just east of the Altstadt, **Park Schöntal** is a great place for strolls and picnics, with a lake, monastery ruins and a pheasantry.

Three kilometres south-west of the centre, **Park Schönbusch** is a shady 18th-century expanse emulating the carefully designed 'natural' look of English country gardens. It's dotted with ornamental ponds, meadows, creeks, bridges and various follies. Also here is the charming neoclassical **Schlösschen**

(☎ 873 08, Kleine Schönbuschallee 1; tours adult/concession €2.50/ 2; tours in German half-hourly 9am-5pm Tues-Sun Apr-Sept, closed Oct-Mar; Bus: No 4 direction Stockstadt to Schönbusch), once a country retreat of the archbishops. Unless you enjoy period furniture, skip the tour of the 10 rooms.

Organised Tours

Guided 90-minute city walking tours (in German) depart from the main portal of Schloss Johannisburg at 2pm on Sunday, plus 2pm on Saturday in June, July and September (€2.50).

From mid-April to early October Aschaffenburger Personenschifffahrt (☎ 872 88; from €5.50) operates boat tours on the Main from the Flosshafen landing just south of the Willigisbrücke, the city's main bridge.

Places to Stay

DJH hostel (☎ 93 07 63, fax 97 06 94, e jhaschaffenburg@djh-bayern.de, Beckerstrasse 47) Bus: Nos 7 or 41 to Schoberstrasse, plus 10-minute walk. Bed & breakfast €11.25. Closed 20 Dec–20 Jan. This hostel has a nice garden setting and is on the southern edge of town.

Hotel Pape Garni (☎ 226 73, fax 226 22, Würzburger Strasse 16) Singles/doubles €26/48. This simple hotel with basic rooms is not far from Schlossplatz.

Gasthof Goldener Karpfen (☎ 443 69 70, fax 444 96 24, Löherstrasse 20) Singles/doubles from €45/65. This is a cosy place in an old half-timbered house with carp theme decor. It has old-fashioned rooms and a decent restaurant (mains from €6 to €13).

Hotel Wilder Mann (☎ 30 20, fax 30 33 34, e hotelwm@aol.com, Löherstrasse 51) Singles/doubles from €55/75. For a place with centuries of tradition, head to this rustic but elegant inn. The rooms have all modern comforts but are a bit dowdy. The restaurant serves excellent German and regional specialities (mains from €8 to €16).

Places to Eat

Einstein (☎ 277 77, Rossmarkt 36) Snacks €2-7.50. This youthful cafe serves a decent menu of simple but tasty salads, schnitzels and various meatless dishes. The all-you-can-eat Sunday brunch (€10) is popular.

Wirtshaus zum Fegerer *(☎ 156 46, Schlossgasse)* Mains €8-17. At this convivial inn, the kitchen focuses on Franconian and seasonal dishes and makes very good grilled meats. There's a nice vaulted cellar and inner courtyard. The lunch specials are the best deal.

Q-Bar Bodeguita & Cafe *(☎ 36 22 52, Sandgasse 53)* Dishes €6-13. This trendy place with a Hemingway theme has a good appetizer menu and crowd-pleasing mains such as burgers, steaks and grilled salmon. At night, it's a good place for drinks.

Schlossgass' 16 *(☎ 123 13, Schlossgasse 16)* Mains €7.50-12.50. Closed Mon. Locals often cram this living room-sized wine tavern, noted for its delicious Franconian dishes and choice vintages.

Getting There & Away
There is a service at least hourly to/from Würzburg (€12.40, one hour), Frankfurt (RE train; €6.60, 50 minutes) and Munich (ICE train; €62.60, 3¼ hours). The A3 autobahn runs right past town.

Getting Around
Local buses cover all corners of Aschaffenburg and its suburbs. In town, single tickets are €1, day passes €1.75. For bicycle rentals, try Radstation (☎ 37 42 04) in the Hauptbahnhof.

NORTHERN ROMANTIC ROAD
The Northern Romantic Road starts in Würzburg (see earlier in this chapter) and travels south through the Liebliches Taubertal (Tauber Valley), weaving in and out of the neighbouring state of Baden-Württemberg, all the while remaining within the historical boundaries of Franconia. It continues south via Rothenburg ob der Tauber and Dinkelsbühl. See the Allgäu-Bavarian Swabia chapter for the southern section starting in Nördlingen.

LIEBLICHES TAUBERTAL
South of Würzburg, the Romantic Road soon plunges into the Taubertal, an idyllic valley carved by the placid Tauber River. It's a gentle landscape, which, during warmer months, is wonderfully suited for bicycle touring.

Bad Mergentheim
☎ 07931 • pop 22,000 • elevation 210m
Bad Mergentheim's history is inextricably tied to two things: its underground springs and the Order of the Teutonic Knights. Evidence suggests that Stone Age and Celtic tribes enjoyed the local salt springs, which then somehow dropped from the radar screen for nearly two millennia. In 1826, a shepherd rediscovered them quite by accident, and their healing qualities have since turned Bad Mergentheim into one of the most popular and successful spa towns in the country.

This was quite a departure from its earlier incarnation as the seat of the Order of the Teutonic Knights, a Europe-wide military religious order founded during the Third Crusade in 1191. The first knights settled in Mergentheim at the invitation of the local rulers, the count of Hohenlohe, in 1219. After managing to wrangle town rights from Ludwig the Bavarian in 1340, the knights governed the town unchallenged and made important improvements to its infrastructure. In 1525, the order lost its Prussian territories after their leader, Albrecht von Hohenzollern, converted to Protestantism. The remaining Catholics, led by Walter von Cronenberg, established itself in Mergentheim where it remained until dispossessed by Napoleon in 1809. The order continues to exist today in Austria, ostensibly as a charity.

Orientation & Information The Tauber River divides Bad Mergentheim's bustling medieval Altstadt on the south bank from the quiet spa complex. The tourist office (☎ 571 31, fax 573 00) at Marktplatz 3 is open from 9am to 5pm Monday to Friday and 10am to 4pm Saturday from April to October. At other times, hours are 9am to noon and 2.30pm to 5pm weekdays only.

Things to See The town's heart beats on Marktplatz, where the many stately half-timbered and gabled town houses still reflect its medieval heyday. The strapping knight

The Romantische Strasse

The Romantic Road links a series of picturesque Bavarian towns and cities (and a few in Baden-Württemberg). It is by far the most popular among the dozens of Germany's holiday routes designed to get tourists away from the big cities and out into the countryside. Some two million people ply the route every year, which means, of course, lots of signs in English and Japanese, tourist coaches and kitsch galore.

Despite the hordes of visitors, it's worth falling for the sales pitch and taking time to explore this delightful route. You won't be alone, but you certainly won't be disappointed – it travels through some of the most beautiful towns and cities in Germany.

The Romantic Road runs north-south through western Bavaria, from Würzburg in Franconia to Füssen in the Allgäu near the Austrian border. En route, it passes through fabulous countryside and over two dozen cities and towns, including Rothenburg ob der Tauber, Dinkelsbühl and Augsburg. Other highlights include the baroque Wieskirche near Steingaden and the castles of fairy-tale king Ludwig II in Hohenschwangau.

In this book, the northern section of the Romantic Road (Würzburg to Dinkelsbühl) is covered in the Franconia chapter, while the southern section (Nördlingen to Füssen) is presented in the Allgäu-Bavarian Swabia chapter.

The central Romantic Road tourist office (☎ 09851-902 71, fax 902 81, ⒠ tourismus@roman tischestrasse.btl.de) is on Marktplatz in Dinkelsbühl. Staff can help you put together an itinerary and give you accommodation lists and prices. Information on the Internet is available at ⓦ www .romantischestrasse.de. In addition, each town also has its own local tourist office (see Information under each town) whose staff are usually very efficient at finding accommodation in all price ranges.

Travelling the Romantic Road

Train and bus are viable means of transport if you want to explore short segments of the Romantic Road, but you'll find them complicated, tedious and slow for covering the entire route.

balancing atop the octagonal fountain is Teutonic Grand Master Wolfgang Schutzbar, on whose shift the freestanding Renaissance **Rathaus** (1564) on the square's southern end was built. Behind the Rathaus, and just east of Hans-Ehrler-Platz, the Gothic **Marienkirche** has some nifty medieval frescoes and the bronze epitaph to Grand Master Walther von Cronberg by Hans Vischer.

East of the Marktplatz, via Burgstrasse, is the **Deutschordenschloss**, the former residence of the grand masters. The corner towers have impressive Renaissance spiral staircases, especially the so-called *Berwart-treppe* in the lobby of the **Deutschordens-museum** *(☎ 522 12, Schloss 16; adult/concession €3/2; open 10am-5pm Tues-Sun)*. Exhibits here are rather eclectic, ranging from an overview of the Teutonic Order to local history and 19th-century dolls' houses. A tour of the lavish state rooms includes the early neoclassical **Kapitelsaal** (Chapter Hall) with its coffered ceiling. Several grand masters are buried in the baroque **Schlosskirche**, with design contributions by Balthasar Neumann and François Cuvilliés.

Places to Stay & Eat There is a wide range of options in Bad Mergentheim.

Klein'e Pension (☎ 944 40, fax 94 44 44, Wachbacher Strasse 26) Singles/doubles €31/46. This place offers the best value in town, with nice rooms equipped with TV and telephone.

Hotel Deutschmeister (☎ 96 20, fax 96 21 51, Ochsengasse 7) Singles/doubles €42/73. Just off Marktplatz, this is a traditional favourite with a good restaurant and well-equipped rooms.

Hotel Bundschu (☎ 93 30, fax 93 36 33, Cronbergstrasse 15) Singles €55-75, doubles €75-95. Run by a dedicated family, this

The Romantische Strasse

For flexibility and convenience, the ideal way to explore the Romantic Road in depth is, of course, by car (just follow the brown 'Romantische Strasse' signs). If you prefer to let someone else do the driving, take the Europabus. Operated by Deutsche Touring, a subsidiary of Deutsche Bahn, it runs one coach daily in each direction between Frankfurt and Füssen from April to October, with short stops in nearly all towns and villages along the way. Buses leave at 8am daily from the train stations in either town and take about 12 hours to complete the route nonstop.

You can break the journey as often as you'd like, but plan your stops carefully as you'll have to wait a full day for the next bus to come around (reserve a seat before disembarking). Tickets are available either for the entire distance or for shorter segments between any of the stops. In Rothenburg, you can change to buses headed for Munich or to Mannheim via Heidelberg.

Tickets for the entire route cost €74/103 one way/return. Sample fares for other segments include: Würzburg-Rothenburg €17/24, Rothenburg-Füssen €41/57, Rothenburg-München €34/47, Frankfurt-München €67/94. Eurail and German Rail pass holders get a 60% discount; InterRail pass holders, seniors and children aged four to 12 pay half price; students and those under 27 qualify for 10% off. If you want to take your bicycle, you need to make a reservation at least three days before the date of travel by calling ☎ 069-79 03 50. The cost is €6 for journeys up to 12 stops or €12 for longer trips.

Tickets are available from the main booking office (☎ 069-790 30) at Römerhof 17 in Frankfurt-am-Main as well as at many travel agencies, railway stations and EurAide (☎ 089-59 38 89, fax 550 39 65, e euraide@compuserve.com) at the Munich Hauptbahnhof. If you read German, check out the Web site at w www.deutsche-touring.com.

With its gentle gradients and ever-changing scenery, the Romantic Road makes an ideal bike trip. Tourist offices keep lists of 'bicycle-friendly hotels' and have information about public storage facilities. The booklet *Radwandern*, published by the Romantic Road tourist office, contains maps and route suggestions but, alas, it's in German only.

---

is one of Mergentheim's flagship hotels, with romantic ambience, nicely furnished rooms and an excellent restaurant with a local following.

Getting There & Away Regional trains connect Bad Mergentheim with Würzburg (€8.10, 55 minutes) and with Weikersheim (€2.50, 15 minutes) every two hours. The Europabus stops at the car park Altstadt-Mitte.

Weikersheim
☎ 07934 • pop 8200 • elevation 227m

About 13km due east of Bad Mergentheim, Weikersheim is the ancestral home and former residence of the counts and princes of Hohenlohe, a Franconian dynasty that first arrived on the scene in the 12th century. It's a tranquil little town with what action there is centred on the recently restored Marktplatz. Here you'll find the church, the Rathaus, the tourist office (☎ 99 25 75) and several hotels and restaurants. East of here, and announcing its presence with a crest-festooned gate and onion-domed church steeple, is the magnificent **Schloss Weikersheim** (☎ 83 64; adult/concession €4/2; open 9am-6pm Apr-Oct, 10am-noon & 1.30pm-4.30pm Nov-Mar). It is backed by an even more impressive **baroque garden**.

After the last of the local Hohenlohes died childless in the 18th century, the palace was pretty much frozen in time. The furniture, wall coverings and artworks are all original. Highlights of the one-hour tour include the **Chinese Mirror Cabinet** teeming with hundreds of oriental figurines, and the **Rittersaal** (Knights' Hall). This tall banqueting hall pays homage to the family's favourite pastime: the hunt. The coffered ceiling shows hunting scenes, while a menagerie of stucco animals – deer, boar and even a badly proportioned elephant (the artist had never seen one in real life) – inhabits the walls.

From the palace's upper storey windows, you can get a good overview of the gracefully symmetrical gardens whose expansiveness culminates in an arcaded **Orangerie**. About 50 sculptures enliven the park; the whimsical **Zwergengallerie** (Gnome Gallery) near the palace end is quite endearing.

Admission also entitles you to peruse the **Alchemie-Ausstellung** in the former palace kitchen. Palace builder Count Wolfgang II dabbled in the wondrous pseudo-science of alchemy and it's his story, ideas and experiments that are given centre stage here. Alas, all labelling is in German only.

Hotel Laurentius (☎ *910 80, fax 91 08 18,* e *koch-kunst@t-online, Marktplatz 5)* Singles/doubles from €50/66. If you need food or a bed, knock on the door of this charming place run by the energetic Koch family. Koch means 'cook' and, appropriately, their gourmet restaurant with a vaulted ceiling is top notch. Smaller meals are served in the brasserie throughout the day.

Regional trains to/from Bad Mergentheim (€2.50, 15 minutes) come through every two hours. Bus No 7883 runs to Creglingen more or less hourly (15 minutes). The Europabus stops at Marktplatz. Rent bicycles from Velo (☎ 297), Schäftersheimer Strasse 44, for €6 to €10 per day.

Creglingen
☎ 07933 • pop 5000 • elevation 270m

The main reason people stop in Creglingen is to view Tilman Riemenschneider's exquisite Marienaltar in the **Hergottskirche** *(1389; ☎ 74 53, Kirchplatz 2; adult/concession €2/1; open 9.15am-5.30pm daily Apr-Oct, 10am-noon & 1pm-4pm Tues-Sun Nov-Mar).* In 1384, a local ploughman found a 'sacred host' in his field, a 'miracle' that inspired the local rulers, the counts of Hohenlohe, to sponsor a church on the site. More than 100 years later, Riemenschneider created his masterpiece, which is a glorification of the Virgin Mary. Stashed away during the Reformation, the altar was still in mint condition when rediscovered in the 19th century.

The centre shrine shows Mary ascending into heaven accompanied by the apostles. This is orbited by bas-reliefs showing scenes from her life and topped by her coronation. Some of the finest work is in the predella (bottom portion), where Riemenschneider has immortalised himself in the right scene showing Jesus in the temple surrounded by the scribes (he's believed to be the central figure in the group on the right). The church also contains several other altars, which are lengthily described in the leaflet (also in English) you'll get with admission.

The Hergottskirche may be Creglingen's main draw, but the town actually has a couple of other, rather quirky sights. Across the street from the church is the unique **Fingerhutmuseum** *(Thimble Museum; ☎ 370, Kohlesmühle; admission €1.25; open 9am-6pm daily Apr-Oct, 1pm-4pm daily Nov-Mar).* It is run by master thimble maker, Thorvald Greif, whose slight stature and shock of white hair gives him an elf-like appearance. Greif presides over a priceless collection of more than 3000 of these diminutive sewing aids. Some are true pieces of art and highly valuable, especially those made of gold, silver or hand-painted fine porcelain. One of the most precious is 2500 years old and made of bronze.

The church and Thimble Museum are both about 600m south of the village centre where the **Lindleinturm-Museum** *(☎ 72 37, 75 73 or 36 31, Stadtgraben 12; admission free; open 10am-noon Tues & Fri-Sun, 2pm-5pm Sat & Sun Apr-Nov; any other time by prior arrangement)* takes the cake for most bizarre museum. This tower, which was once part of the medieval town fortifications, was the tiny home of Margarete Böttiger, a crotchety woman who bought the place in 1927 and lived here until shortly before her death in 1995 at age 98.

By all accounts, Margarete was quite a character. A maid servant, she remained unmarried, preferring the company of felines, which is why locals called the tower 'Katzenturm' (cat tower), a term she hated. Modern technology, even central heating and hot water, were anathema to her. Bitching about everything to everyone was her favourite pastime. Naturally, her mean-spirited nature didn't exactly sit well with her neighbours, many of whom probably breathed a sigh of relief after her passing. But it was for Margarete to leave a lasting legacy: she decreed that her tower be turned into a museum – sort of a shrine to herself – and to this end bequeathed most of her life savings (about €135,000) to the town for its upkeep. The town dutifully obliged, leaving her place completely intact so you can roam the pintsize rooms for a glimpse into both a disturbed mind and a time long gone.

The staff at Creglingen's tourist office (☎ 631, fax 20 31 61), at Bad Mergentheimer Strasse 14 north-west of the town centre, can help with finding a place to stay.

Creglingen is 13km west of Weikersheim and 20km north-west of Rothenburg ob der Tauber. Bus No 7883 makes the trip out to Weikersheim about hourly (15 minutes), but getting to Rothenburg is a veritable odyssey with multiple changeovers. In other words, forget about it. The Europabus makes a 15-minute stop right at the Hergottskirche.

ROTHENBURG OB DER TAUBER
☎ 09861 • pop 11,800 • elevation 425m

A well-polished gem from the Middle Ages, Rothenburg is the main tourist stop along the northern Romantic Road. With its web of cobbled lanes fringed by higgledy-piggedly houses and enclosed by towered walls, it's almost impossibly quaint, as if perpetually frozen in a distant past. Alas, the taint of over-commercialisation hangs over this popular town and, at times, it can feel a bit like a medieval theme park. From June to October and during the Christmas season especially, Rothenburg gets uncomfortably crowded with gawking day-trippers (an estimated 2.5 million a year), who clog up the narrow streets.

To truly experience the town's considerable magic, visit on a weekday, in winter or spring, or spend the night. Rothenburg is at its most romantic when the yellow lamp-light casts its spell long after the last tour buses have left.

History
Rothenburg's recorded history begins in 970 with the construction of a castle in what is now the suburb of Detwang. In the 12th century, the town came under the control of the Hohenstaufen dynasty, who built another castle in 1142 and obtained town rights in 1172, allowing them to build the fortifications. In 1274, Rothenburg became a Free Imperial City but suffered serious setbacks after an earthquake struck in 1356. During the peasants' war, the town sided with Florian Geyer, the leader of the ultimately unsuccessful uprising. Besieged, attacked and plundered several times during the Thirty Years' War (1618–48), Rothenburg plunged into a deep slumber, which lasted for several centuries. In 1802, it became part of Bavaria. In World War II, the Allies had slated Rothenburg for the same consummate bombing as neighbouring towns, but an American general in love with the town ultimately prevented its complete destruction. Still, about 40% of the Altstadt laid in ruins in 1945.

Orientation
Rothenburg is surrounded by an intact 3.5km-long town wall of which 2.5km are walkable. From the Bahnhof it's a five- to 10-minute walk west along Ansbacher Strasse to the Röderturm, one of the main entrance gates to the Altstadt. From here, Rödergasse, then Hafengasse, lead straight to the Markt, the central square. The main shopping drag is Schmiedgasse, which runs south from Markt to the *Plönlein*, a scenic fork in the road anchored by a half-timbered cottage and fountain that's become Rothenburg's unofficial emblem.

Information
At Marktplatz 2 you'll find the helpful tourist office (☎ 404 92, fax 868 07, ⓔ info@rothenburg.de), which provides numerous services, including room bookings. From May to October, its hours are 9am to 6pm weekdays, with a half-hour break at 12.30pm, and 10am to 3pm weekends. In other months, it closes at 5pm weekdays, at 1pm Saturday and is closed on

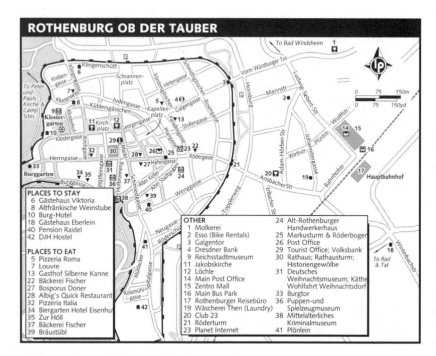

ROTHENBURG OB DER TAUBER

To Bad Windsheim

To Peter-
und-
Pauls-
Kirche &
Camp
Sites

Hauptbahnhof

To Rad
& Tat

PLACES TO STAY
6 Gästehaus Viktoria
8 Altfränkische Weinstube
10 Burg-Hotel
18 Gästehaus Eberlein
40 Pension Raidel
42 DJH Hostel

PLACES TO EAT
5 Pizzeria Roma
7 Louvre
13 Gasthof Silberne Kanne
22 Bäckerei Fischer
27 Bosporus Doner
28 Albig's Quick Restaurant
32 Pizzeria Italia
34 Biergarten Hotel Eisenhut
35 Zur Höll
37 Bäckerei Fischer
39 Bräustübl

OTHER
1 Molkerei
2 Esso (Bike Rentals)
3 Galgentor
4 Dresdner Bank
9 Reichsstadtmuseum
11 Jakobskirche
12 Löchle
14 Main Post Office
15 Zentro Mall
16 Main Bus Park
17 Rothenburger Reisebüro
19 Wäscherei Then (Laundry)
20 Club 23
21 Röderturm
23 Planet Internet

24 Alt-Rothenburger
Handwerkerhaus
25 Markusturm & Röderboger
26 Post Office
29 Tourist Office; Volksbank
30 Rathaus; Rathausturm;
Historiengewölbe
31 Deutsches
Weihnachtsmuseum; Käthe
Wohlfahrt Weihnachtsdorf
33 Burgtor
36 Puppen-und
Spielzeugmuseum
38 Mittelalterliches
Kriminalmuseum
41 Plönlein

Sunday. Some leaflets and an electronic room reservation board are in the foyer, which is always open.

There's a Volksbank with an ATM just to the right of the tourist office on Marktplatz. Dresdner Bank has a branch at Galgengasse 23.

The main post office is in the new Zentro Mall at Bahnhofstrasse 15 opposite the Bahnhof; a small branch is at Milchmarkt 5 in the Altstadt. Planet Internet (☎ 93 44 15), Paradeisgasse 5, offers Web surfing for €3/4.50 per 30/60 minutes from noon to midnight, Friday and Saturday to 1am.

The town's excellent Web site (**W** www .rothenburg.de) is also in English.

In the train station, Rothenburger Reisebüro (☎ 46 11) books Europabus and train transport.

The Wäscherei Then (☎ 27 75), at Johannitergasse 9 near the train station, is both a dry cleaner and a self-service laundry (€3 per load, dryers €1.50 for 25 minutes).

Things to See

Sights mentioned below, while described under their individual headings, can be followed as a walking tour.

Rathaus

The town hall on the Markt was begun in Gothic style in the 14th century and completed during the Renaissance. The 220-step viewing platform of the **Rathausturm** should have reopened after extensive restoration by the time you're reading this (admission is charged). Views over the town and the Tauber Valley are naturally majestic from here. Below the Rathaus is the moderately interesting **Historiengewölbe** *(Historical Vaults; adult/concession €1.75/1.25; open 10am-5pm daily).*

The plastic dummies in re-created scenes of life during the Thirty Years' War are pretty hokey, but the actual subterranean prison and torture room are creepy enough to get under your skin.

Cheese: just one of Bavaria's local products

White Alpine pasqueflower

The food market provides a colourful centrepiece to Freising's bustling central square

Schloss Hohenschwangau

Girls dance for Dinkelsbühl's freedom during the Kinderzeche

ANDREW LUBRAN

Lederhosen rules

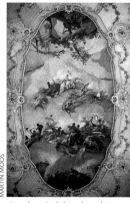
MARTIN MOOS

Augsburg's Schaezlerpalais

ANDREW LUBRAN

Fountain, Schloss Linderhof

ANDREW LUBRAN

The dark blue forest lake of Eibsee – a local beauty spot near Garmisch-Partenkirchen, Upper Bavaria

Jakobskirche

A few steps north of the Markt is the Gothic Church of St Jacob (☎ 700 60, *Klingengasse 1; adult/concession €1.25/0.50; open 9am-5.30pm daily Apr-Oct, 10am-5pm daily Dec, 10am-noon & 2pm-4pm Nov & Jan-Mar daily*). Light filtering in through its glorious 14th-century stained-glass windows gives the church a meditative mood. In the east chancel, the exquisite main altar, the **Altar of the Ten Apostles** (1446), deserves a closer look. The church's undisputed pièce de résistance, however, is the carved **Heilige Blut altar** (sacred blood altar) by Tilman Riemenschneider, on a raised platform at the opposite (western) end of the main nave.

Rothenburg's town council commissioned the work in 1499 to find a suitably grand setting for its treasured reliquary: a capsule made of rock crystal said to contain three drops of Christ's blood. It is integrated within the gilded cross above the main scene, which depicts the Last Supper. In an unusual twist, Riemenschneider chose to place Judas at the centre, receiving bread from Christ to his left. It's worth taking a few minutes to study the amazing emotiveness with which the sculptor managed to imbue these inanimate figures.

Reichsstadtmuseum

A short walk north-west of the Jakobskirche is this former Dominican convent turned Reichsstadtmuseum (*Imperial City Museum; ☎ 93 90 43, Klosterhof 5; adult/concession €2.50/1.50; open 10am-5pm daily Apr-Oct, 1pm-4pm daily Nov-Mar*). The historical beamed rooms where the nuns used to eat, sleep and work now showcase local art, culture and history. Highlights include the superb *Rothenburger Passion* (1494), a cycle of 12 panels by Martinus Schwarz, and a 14th-century kitchen. There's also a huge tankard holding 3¼L, once used to welcome official visitors; it inspired the legend of the Meistertrunk (see boxed text 'Drink and Ye Shall be Free'). Paintings of Rothenburg by the English artist Arthur Wasse (1854-1930), who lived here for many years, show how little the place has changed.

The **Klostergarten** behind the museum (enter from Klosterhof) is a quiet place to shake off the throngs...at least until a bus tour group walks through every now and then.

Burggarten & Burggasse

Strolling south of the museum along the town wall soon gets you to the much livelier Burggarten (Castle Gardens) with stunning views of the Tauber Valley. The park occupies the site of the former Hohenstaufen castle of 1142. After an earthquake levelled the complex, only the **Blasiuskapelle** was rebuilt. Today it's a war memorial.

To get to the park, you'll pass through the **Burgtor** (gate). Wanna-be attackers of the castle were repelled by hot pitch poured through the mouth of the mask affixed to its facade.

For more sweeping vistas, amble east along Burggasse. From this vantage point, you can also see the **Doppelbrücke**, a double-deck bridge that is ideal for watching the fireworks displays during the Reichsstadt-Festtage (see Special Events). Also visible is the head of a trail that leads down the valley and over to the lovely **St-Peter-und-Pauls-Kirche** in Detwang, which contains another stunning Riemenschneider altar. There's a beer garden about halfway along the trail. Continuing east on Burggasse eventually gets you to the...

Mittelalterliches Kriminalmuseum

Spending too much time in the pub could get you locked up in a barrel with only your head sticking out. To encourage you to confess to being a witch, you had to sit on a 'nail chair'. Bad musicians had their fingers and neck clamped into a special 'flute'.

Medieval justice was not for the squeamish, as you'll soon discover during a walk through the fascinating and extensive Medieval Crime Museum (☎ 53 59, *Burggasse 3; adult/concession €3/2; open 9.30am-6pm daily Apr-Oct, 2pm-4pm daily Nov & Jan-Mar, 10am-4pm daily Dec*). Gruesome tools of torture and execution form the core of the exhibit and naturally are the biggest crowd-pleasers. In addition, though, the place documents legal history going back 1000 years, including famous criminal cases, legal proceedings in the Middle Ages, witch trials and so on. Display panels are in English.

Puppen- und Spielzeugmuseum

North of the crime museum, collector extraordinaire, Katharina Engels, has assembled an amazing range of playthings at the Doll & Toy Museum (☎ 73 30, Hofbronnengasse 13; adult/concession €3/2; open 9.30am-6pm daily Mar-Dec, 11am-5pm daily Jan & Feb). On this multi-storey journey into childhood, you'll come across teddy bears and wooden toys, carousels and marionette theatres, tin figurines and dolls, dolls, dolls! – made of porcelain, paper, wood and wax, along with dollhouses, doll tea services, doll stores... It's all traditionally displayed in glass cases and there's a 'dolled-up' shop in front.

Deutsches Weihnachtsmuseum

A few steps north and you're back at Markt. A few more west will bring you to the German Christmas Museum (☎ 40 93 65, Herrngasse 1; adult/concession €2.50/2; open 9am-6pm daily Easter–mid-Jan, 9am-6pm Sat & Sun mid-Jan–Easter). Operated by the Käthe Wohlfahrt emporium (see Shopping later in this section), it depicts German Christmas customs as they developed through the ages. Many of the objects on display, including a great collection of nutcrackers, are donations or loans from private individuals.

East of Markt

Walking east of Markt on Hafengasse leads you past the particularly scenic – and incessantly photographed – ensemble of the **Markusturm** (Marcus Tower) and the Röderbogen (Röder Arch).

Just south of here, down a little alley, is the **Alt-Rothenburger Handwerkerhaus** (Old Rothenburg's Artisans' House; ☎ 942 80, Alter Stadtgraben 26; adult/concession €2/1; open 9am-6pm daily Apr-Oct & Dec). Numerous artisans – including coopers, weavers, cobblers and potters – have had their workshops in this house during its 700-year existence. Because the last person

to inhabit it had an apparent phobia of all things modern, preferring instead to live without running water or electricity, it offers a fairly authentic look at medieval living conditions. Hafengasse turns into Rödergasse, which is punctuated by the **Röderturm** (adult/concession €1.25/0.75; open 9am-4pm daily), which can be climbed for nice city views. At the top is a small photographic exhibit about the air raid on Rothenburg in 1945.

Organised Tours

The tourist office runs 90-minute English-language walking tours at 2pm daily year-round (€3) from outside the Rathaus. A very entertaining walking tour of the Altstadt is conducted every evening by the lantern-toting Nachtwächter (night watchman), dressed in his historical costume. English tours (€3) meet at the Rathaus at 7.55pm, German tours (€2.50) head off at 9.30pm.

Special Events

Check with the tourist office for specific dates for these events.

The **Historisches Festspiel 'Der Meistertrunk'** (see boxed text 'Drink and Ye Shall be Free') takes place around town each year on Whitsuntide (Pentecost), with parades, dances and a medieval market. The highlight, though, is the re-enactment of the mythical Meistertrunk story in the Kaisersaal of the Rathaus. Check with the tourist office on how to obtain tickets in advance.

The play itself is performed three more times, once during the **Reichsstadt-Festtage** in early September, when the entire town's history is being staged in the city streets; and twice during the **Rothenburger Herbst**, a harvest celebration in October.

The **Historischer Schäfertanz** (Historical Shepherds' Dance), featuring colourfully dressed dancing couples, takes places several times between April and October on Marktplatz.

Places to Stay

The tourist office can assist in finding a room, including **private rooms**. The 24-hour room referral hotline is at ☎ 194 12.

Drink and Ye Shall be Free

The year is 1631. The Thirty Years' War – pitching Catholics against Protestants – has been raging for 13 years, finally reaching the gates of Rothenburg ob der Tauber. Catholic General Tilly and 60,000 of his troops have besieged the Protestant market town, demanding its surrender. The town resists at first but eventually cannot stave off the onslaught of marauding soldiers. The mayor and other town dignitaries are captured and sentenced to death.

And that's pretty much where history ends and legend begins.

As the tale goes, in an amazing display of chutzpa, Rothenburg's town council tries to sate Tilly's blood-lust by presenting him with a mug of wine fit for a giant. Tilly, after taking a sip or two, presents the men with an unusual challenge: 'If one of you has the courage to step forward and to down this mug of wine in one gulp, then I shall spare the town and the lives of the councilmen!' Mayor Georg Nusch accepts the challenge and – lo and behold – succeeds! And that's why you can still wander though Rothenburg's wonderful medieval lanes today. Or, so they say...

Of course, it's pretty much accepted that the wine legend is hooey, and that Tilly was placated with hard cash. Nevertheless, local poet Adam Hörber couldn't resist turning the tale into a play which, since 1881, has been performed every Whitsuntide (Pentecost). It's also re-enacted several times daily by the clock figures on the building housing the tourist office.

The camping options are in the suburb of Detwang, on the Tauber River.

Campingplatz Tauber-Idyll (☎ 31 77, fax 928 48, Detwang 28) Tent/person €4.25/3.75. Open Easter-late Oct. This well-equipped and modern camping ground is scenically located in a nature preserve about 1.5km outside the Altstadt.

Campingplatz Tauber-Romantik (☎ 61 91, fax 61 60) Tent/person €4/3.75. Open Easter-late Oct. This is a larger camping ground but with a similarly pleasant location.

DJH hostel (☎ 941 60, fax 94 16 20, e jhrothenburg@djh-bayern.de, Mühlacker

1) Bed & breakfast €14.30-15.10. Rothenburg's heavily booked hostel occupies two enormous renovated old buildings in the south of town. It's extremely well equipped (eg, a film library in the TV room). Reserve ahead or risk being turned away.

Pension Raidel (☎ 31 15, fax 93 52 55, e Gaestehaus-Raidel@t-online.de, Wenggasse 3) Singles/doubles €17.50/35 (shared bath), €35/45 (private bath). In the Altstadt, this inn has traditional decor in the public areas and rooms with unique design features.

Gästehaus Eberlein (☎ 46 72, fax 34 99, e hotel@eberlein.rothenburg.de, Winterbachstrasse 4) Singles/doubles from €32.50/42.50. A familial atmosphere reigns in this charming pension behind the train station. Each of the 21 rooms sports different decor, and guests also have access to sauna, solarium and a fitness room.

Altfränkische Weinstube (☎ 64 04, fax 64 10, Klosterhof 7) Singles/doubles €40/45-55. Tucked away in a quiet side street near the Reichsstadtmuseum, this enchanting inn has atmosphere-laden rooms (with private bath) filled with knick-knacks. At the restaurant (mains €5-12), guests are treated to a riot of flowers, romantic lighting and good-value regional food. A group of German and American locals meets here on Wednesday nights; everyone is welcome.

Gästehaus Viktoria (☎ 876 82, Klingenschütt 4) Rooms €40-50. Guests liking rooms stuffed with lots of neat trinkets will be charmed by this pintsize B&B in a peaceful location adjacent to the northern town wall. All have TV and the sun terrace is perfect for unwinding after a day of sightseeing.

Burg-Hotel (☎ 948 90, fax 94 89 40, e burghotel.rothenburg@t-online.de, Klostergasse 1–3) Singles/doubles from €80/90. This personable, 15-room hotel is built right into the town fortifications. If you're looking for a romantic getaway and price is no object, this is it – the views are phenomenal.

Places to Eat

Bräustübl (☎ 93 10 88, Alter Stadtgraben 2) Dishes €4.50-12.50. This place offers year-round Christmas ambience with twinkle lights and a Santa Claus display. The food is

FRANCONIA

stick-to-the-ribs Franconian, plus a few salads for the artery-conscious.

Pizzeria Italia (☎ *22 25, Herrngasse 8*) Pizza & pasta €4-7, fish & meat €5.50-13.50. This is your better than average pizza joint run by friendly people and with nice sidewalk seating in summer. *Pizzeria Roma* (☎ *45 40, Galgengasse 19*) is similar and usually less crowded.

Louvre (☎ *878 09, Klingengasse 15*) 6–8-course dinners €50-75. At this temple of temptations, 'star' chef Bernard Reiser (as in Michelin star, that is) and his team wow diners with innovative takes on haute cuisine using only exquisite, fresh ingredients. It's classy but not stuffy and has an integrated gallery with monthly changing exhibits. Reservations required, *bien sur*.

Gasthof Silberne Kanne (☎ *56 16, Paradeisgasse 20*) Mains €7-14. It's not much to look at, but to get away from the tourist crowds, this place will do in a pinch. The menu primarily features selections from the animal kingdom with a few token vegie and grain dishes thrown into the mix.

Biergarten Hotel Eisenhut (☎ *70 50, Herrngasse 3–5*) Snacks €3.50-7. In summer, one of the nicest places for a break is this enchanting beer garden behind the Hotel Eisenhut (enter from Burggasse). It's operated by several young people who unfortunately keep erratic hours, so you'll need a bit of luck to find it open.

Snacks & Fast Food

Bosporus Doner (*Hafengasse 2*) Dishes €2.50-6. This place does delicious doner kebabs and other Middle Eastern goodies, including meat-free selections, for eating-in or takeaway.

Albig's Quick Restaurant (*Hafengasse 3*) Dishes €1.25-6.50. Across the street, this is a no-pretensions trough, with half chickens, schnitzels, fries, burgers and other satisfying fare.

Bäckerei Fischer (*branches:* ☎ *94 08 40, Obere Schmiedgasse 10;* ☎ *94 08 30, Rödergasse 13*) Lots of bakeries in town sell the Rothenburg pastry speciality of *Schneeballen* – sweet dough balls dipped in cinnamon or powdered sugar – but Fischer makes the best.

Entertainment

Rothenburg is not exactly a party town but there are a few places to hang out after dark.

Zur Höll (☎ *42 29, Burggasse 8*) This convivial wine tavern is in the town's oldest original building. Wine definitely takes centre stage, although a few snacks and main dishes are available too (€3 to €12.50).

Löchle (☎ *97 04 06, Kirchplatz 8*) The same is true of this charming tavern in the Hotel Reichs-Küchenmeister.

Molkerei (☎ *93 33 10, Schweinsdorfer Strasse 25b*) Closed Mon & Tues. Local youths gather at this fun cafe-bar with occasional live music. Traces of its previous incarnation as a dairy still survive in the decor, although in fine weather the terrace is the preferred place to hang out.

Club 23 (☎ *36 86, Ansbacher Strasse 1*) Open from 10pm Thur & Sat. Near the Bahnhof, this nightclub is a Rothenburg institution and has been throwing dance parties since the disco era. Beers cost €2.50.

Shopping

Note that a city ordinance requires all shop signs to be of the traditional wrought-iron kind (even McDonald's sports a pair of iron 'golden arches').

Käthe Wohlfahrt Weihnachtsdorf (☎ *40 90, Herrngasse 1*) Eternal Christmas reigns at this emporium, with its mind-boggling assortment of decorations, ornaments and souvenirs. While it's easy to dismiss this display as kitsch or overly commercial, the fact remains that many of the items are handcrafted with amazing skill and imagination. Prices are accordingly high.

Getting There & Away

Rothenburg is on a branch line to Steinach, which is served hourly from 5am to 8pm. From here, there's frequent direct train service to/from Würzburg (€8.50, 1¼ hour). Travel to/from Munich may require two or three changes (from €32, three hours).

The Europabus stops at the train station.

Rothenburg has its own exit off the A7 between Würzburg and Ulm.

Getting Around

Rothenburg's entire Altstadt is closed to nonresident vehicles from 11am to 4pm and 7pm to 5am Monday to Friday and all day on weekends; hotel guests are exempt. Galgentor is the only gate that's always open. There are five car parks right outside the walls. Of these, P5 is free, while P4 costs just €2 all day; the others are more expensive. Be sure to memorise the number of the parking lot you used.

Call ☎ 44 05 for taxis (flag fall €2.50).

Some hotels have bicycle rentals, or you can try the Esso petrol station (☎ 67 06), Adam-Hörber-Strasse 38, which charges €8 per day. Farther away and pricier, but with a bigger selection, is Rad & Tat (☎ 879 84), Bensenstrasse 17, with bikes for €12.50 per day.

Horse-drawn carriage rides of 25 to 30 minutes through the city cost about €5 per person, but you can haggle for a better price with some drivers. You'll find them in the Altstadt, usually on Schrannenplatz or Marktplatz.

AROUND ROTHENBURG
Bad Windsheim

If you're motorised, consider making a small detour to this charming little town about 27km north-east of Rothenburg. Here you'll find the delightful **Fränkisches Freilandmuseum** *(☎ 09841-66 80 40, Eisweiherweg 1; adult/concession €4.50/3.50; open 9am-6pm daily Mar-Sept, 10am-5pm daily Oct, 10am-4pm daily Nov–mid-Dec)*, the largest open-air museum in Bavaria.

Reassembled in this 45-hectare park are some 70 homes and farmhouses, most of them original, from different Franconian regions, including the Altmühl Valley and the Steigerwald. Each one is a little mini-museum onto itself, providing insight into the changing social, cultural and religious customs and traditions from the 15th century to today. Pride of place goes to a group of medieval buildings, some partly reconstructed, including a thatched farmhouse from 1367. A lively event schedule, ranging from concerts to cooking sessions, brings in repeat visitors.

From Rothenburg, take the A7 to the B470 east.

FEUCHTWANGEN
☎ 09852 • pop 12,000 • elevation 450m

Travellers often bypass Feuchtwangen en route to Rothenburg or Dinkelsbühl, which is a shame because its historic Altstadt has plenty of sights warranting a stop. You might start a stroll in the Marktplatz, ringed by a harmonious ensemble of half-timbered and step-gabled town houses and anchored by the **Röhrenbrunnen** (1727), a pretty fountain guarded by a statue of Minerva. The tourist office (☎ 904 55) is in the former town hall at Marktplatz 1.

Things to See & Do

From the northern end of the square, steps lead to a **Romanesque cloister**, site of the *Kreuzgangspiele*, a prestigious summer open-air theatre festival. The cloister is actually part of the **Stiftskirche** (13th/14th century), a former monastery church with an eye-catching altar by Michael Wolgemut, a teacher of Albrecht Dürer, and intricately crafted choir stalls. Next door, the **Johanniskirche** (1257) is also worth a look for its choir frescoes and baroque altar.

East of the Markt is the excellent **Frankenmuseum** *(☎ 25 75, Museumstrasse 19; adult/concession €2/1; open 10am-noon & 2pm-5pm Tues-Sun Mar-Dec)*. Period rooms from the baroque to the late 19th century provide glimpses of daily life, while others feature often endearingly naive folk art and a precious collection of faiences.

Those wanting to challenge 'Lady Luck' can do so at the town's newest attraction, the flashy **Casino**, just off the A7 autobahn (exit 111).

Places to Stay & Eat

Gasthof Sindel-Buckel *(☎ 25 94, fax 34 62, Spitalstrasse 28)* Singles/doubles €34/49. This is a solid central inn with cosy rooms equipped with private bath, TV and phone. The restaurant serves Franconian fare, including fresh fish raised in the hotel's own pond (mains €12 to €22).

FRANCONIA

Romantik-Hotel Greifen-Post (☎ 68 00, fax 680 68, Marktplatz 8) Singles/doubles €70/100. At this central charmer, you can pick the period of your room – Renaissance, Biedermeier, English country or 18th-century Romanticism. The gourmet restaurant serves updated versions of German cuisine (mains €15 to €20).

Getting There & Away

Feuchtwangen is on the B25. It's best reached using your own wheels, but regional bus No 805 passes through en route east to Ansbach and south to Dinkelsbühl. The Europabus stops at the Busbahnhof, the main bus station.

DINKELSBÜHL

☎ 09851 • pop 12,000 • elevation 442m

Compared to Rothenburg, Dinkelsbühl has a less contrived feel, as well as fewer tourists and buses. It's a pleasant walk of about an hour around the town's **fortified wall**, its 18 towers and four gates. Don't miss the whimsical Museum of the 3rd Dimension, which is a real trip.

Dinkelsbühl, which lies on the Wörnitz River, traces its roots to a royal residence founded by Carolingian kings in the 8th century. Located at the intersection of two major trade routes, the town rose to prominence in the Middle Ages, primarily as a centre of textile manufacturing. Dinkelsbühl was spared destruction both during the Thirty Years' War and WWII, leaving its lovely medieval Altstadt virtually intact.

Orientation & Information

The Altstadt is five minutes' walk west of the Busbahnhof (central bus station), via Wörnitzer Tor. The tourist office (☎ 902 40, fax 55 26 19, e touristik.service@dinkelsbuehl .de) is on Marktplatz, also known as Weinmarkt, opposite the Münster St Georg. From April to October, hours are 9am to 6pm weekdays, 10am to 4pm Saturday, and 10am to 1pm Sunday. In winter, it closes at 5pm weekdays, 1pm on Saturday and all day Sunday. The central Romantic Road tourist office (☎ 902 71, fax 902 81) is in the same building.

The post office and police station are next to the Busbahnhof.

Altstadt

Start your exploration of Dinkelsbühl on the **Weinmarkt**, the main square, which is lined by a row of picture-perfect Renaissance mansions in mint condition. The corner building is the step-gabled and turreted **Ratsherrntrinkstube**, which once hosted Emperor Karl V and King Gustav Adolf of Sweden and is now home to the tourist office (whose entrance is actually on Segringer Strasse). While here, you might as well duck into the **Hetzelhof**, the picturesque courtyard of a patrician town house, which is entered via a narrow passageway on the opposite side of the street to the tourist office.

Two doors north of the Ratsherrntrinkstube, the **Deutsches Haus** boasts Dinkelsbühl's most marvellous half-timbered facade, while the broad-shouldered **Schranne**, a former granary, rounds off the ensemble. Look for a little box on the latter's north wall; after dark, feeding it the right amount of coins (about €2.50) illuminates the town's most important landmarks for one hour.

Standing sentry over Weinmarkt is the harmoniously proportioned **Münster St Georg**, one of southern Germany's purest late Gothic hall churches. It's filled with treasures of which the **Sebastiansaltar** (1520), donated by the archers' guild, is worth closer inspection. Its triptych graphically depicts the martyrdom of St Sebastian (he was shot full of arrows), while its predella (base) holds the bejewelled bones of St Aurelius, a martyr who was beheaded by Roman emperor Nero in AD 64. A curiosity is the so-called **'Pretzl Window'** donated by the bakers' guild; it forms the upper section of the last window in the right aisle.

If you follow Martin-Luther-Strasse north past the Schranne, you'll soon get to the **Spitalanlage**, founded in 1280 as a hospital and now a seniors' residence and home of the Historisches Museum. Note that the museum may be closed for a thorough overhaul by the time you're reading this. The church was added in 1380, but only some frescoes on the north wall survive from that period. The **Spitalhof** behind the complex is a pretty spot for a break.

Museum of the 3rd Dimension

This museum (☎ 63 36, *Nördlinger Tor; adult/concession* €5.50/4.50; *open 10am-6pm daily Apr-Oct, 11am-4pm Sat & Sun Nov-Mar*) is probably the first dedicated entirely to simulating acid trips. It has three floors of entertainment, with holographic images, stereoscopic mind-blowers and lots of fun for the whole family. Watch a spiral and then see your hand turn concave; see lots of lovely 3D imagery (especially in the nude section on the 3rd floor) and much more. You can easily spend an hour here; ask for the English-language guide (not always available) and follow the numbers. Admission is steep but worth it.

Organised Tours

A night watchman takes visitors on a free tour (in German) at 9pm daily from April to October (Saturday only otherwise). During the same months, hour-long walking tours (€2) depart daily at 2.30pm and 8.30pm (in winter Saturday at 2.30pm only) from the Münster St Georg.

Special Events

In the third week of July, Dinkelsbühl celebrates the 10-day **Kinderzeche** (Children's Festival), commemorating how, in the Thirty Years' War, the town's children persuaded the invading Swedish troops to spare the town from devastation. The festivities include a pageant, re-enactments in the Stadtfestsaal, lots of music and other entertainment. You can order tickets at Ⓦ www.kinderzeche.de.

Jazz fills the streets of Dinkelsbühl's during the **Jazz Festival** in late May, which draws local and international groups and thousands of visitors into the Altstadt. Admission is free on Friday, €10 for either Saturday or Sunday, or €17.50 for the weekend.

Places to Stay

The tourist office can help you find *private rooms* starting at €20/32 for singles/doubles.

DCC-Campingplatz Romantische Strasse (☎ 78 17, *fax* 78 48, *Kobeltsmühle 2*) Tent/person €6/4. Open year-round. This camping ground on a swimming lake is about 300m north-east of Wörnitzer Tor (and well signposted).

DJH hostel (☎ 95 09, *fax* 48 74, *Koppengasse 10*) Bed & breakfast €11.20-12. Closed Nov-Feb. Dinkelsbühl's hostel is in the western Altstadt in a converted 15th-century granary.

Gasthof zum Goldenen Anker (☎ 578 00, *fax* 57 80 80, Ⓔ *goldner.anker@t-online.de, Untere Schmiedgasse 22*) Singles/doubles from €38/69. This congenial inn in a quiet side street comes with traditional but fully equipped rooms and an excellent restaurant (mains €8 to €15). The breakfast buffet is one of the best we've ever seen.

Privat Hotel Dinkelsbühler Kunststuben (☎ 67 50, *fax* 55 35 27, *Segringer Strasse 52*) Rooms €30-60. This snug artist-run B&B has charm and character by the bundle. No room is the same, guests receive personal attention and there's a lovely inner courtyard for relaxing.

Flair Hotel Weisses Ross (☎ 57 98 90, *fax* 67 70, Ⓔ *hotel-weisses-ross@t-online.de*) Singles/doubles from €43.50/61.50. A gathering place for artists for over a century, this delightful hotel has stylish rooms with all the comforts and a gourmet restaurant with *Gemütlichkeit* galore (mains €7 to €15).

Gasthof Goldenes Lamm (☎ 22 67, *fax* 64 41, Ⓔ *goldenes-lamm@t-online.de*) Singles/doubles from €35/56.50. Those in need of relaxation should come to this family-run inn where an ancient wooden staircase leads up to the pleasant rooms. The funky rooftop garden deck with plump sofas is a bonus, as is the attached restaurant with Franconian-Swabian specialities, including some vegetarian choices (mains €5 to €15).

Places to Eat

Also see the hotels listed under Places to Stay for additional eating suggestions.

Weib's Brauhaus (☎ 57 94 90, *Untere Schmiedgasse 13*) Meals €2.25-12. A woman brew master presides over the copper vats at this lively restaurant-pub. Many dishes are made with the house brew, including the popular Weib's Töpfle ('woman's pot').

Cafe Extrablatt *(☎ 22 97, Weinmarkt 10)* Meals €3-10. This trendy bistro bustles morning to night and serves everything from big breakfasts to local fare to healthful salads. Hollywood posters and plenty of knick-knacks form the backdrop.

Deutsches Haus *(☎ 60 58, Weinmarkt 3)* Mains €7.50-17.50. For a splurge, head to this formal restaurant where you'll dine beneath painted ceilings and be surrounded by mahogany panelling.

A good snack place is ***Bäckerei Stadtcafe*** *(Dr-Martin-Luther-Strasse 15)*, which has casseroles, salads and breakfast for €2.50 to €7.50.

Getting There & Around

Dinkelsbühl is not served by trains. Regional buses to/from Rothenburg (€5, one hour) and to Nördlingen (€4, 40 minutes) stop at the Busbahnhof. The Europabus stops right in the Altstadt at Schweinemarkt.

The tourist office rents out bicycles for €5/25 per day/week. From Easter to October, the Altstadt is closed to vehicles from 11am to 5pm Sundays.

NATURPARK ALTMÜHLTAL

The Naturpark Altmühltal (Altmühl Valley Nature Park) covers some of Bavaria's loveliest lands. It sprawls over 2900 sq km roughly west of Regensburg, south of the A6 autobahn, east of Gunzenhausen and north of Ingolstadt. The A9 runs right through it north-south.

The park gets its name from the Altmühl River, a gentle stream that meanders through little valleys before morphing into the mighty Rhein-Main-Donau-Kanal (Rhine-Main-Danube-Canal; see boxed text 'Bavaria's Tower of Babel?') near Beilngries and finally emptying into the Danube at Kelheim.

It's a region largely undiscovered by international travellers, who make up only 5% of all tourists here. The earliest 'visitors' were the Romans, whose empire's northern boundary – the Limes – ran right through today's park.

The main town is Eichstätt, where the park's central information centre is located. Others bigger towns include Gunzenhausen, Treuchtlingen, Weissenburg and Pappenheim west of Eichstätt and Beilngries, Riedenburg and Kelheim east of Eichstätt.

You can explore on your own via extremely well-marked hiking and cycling trails, or canoe for an hour or several days. There's basic camping in designated areas along the river, and camping grounds throughout the region, along with hotels, pensions, guesthouses and hostels.

Planning a Trip

The Informationszentrum Naturpark Altmühltal (☎ 08421-987 60, fax 98 76 54, ℮ tourismus@naturpark-altmuehltal.btl.de, ⓦ www.naturpark-altmuehltal.de), Notre Dame 1, 85072 Eichstätt, is an excellent fount of information. Staff can put together an entire itinerary for free and send you (for face value) maps and charts of the area; information on bike, boat and car rental; and lists of hotels, camp sites and guesthouses throughout the park. However, they won't reserve rooms. Upstairs are exhibits about the park's wildlife and habitats and there's a re-creation of its landscapes in the garden.

Canoeing & Kayaking

Glide past craggy limestone rocks, duck beneath trembling willows swaying above the water or pull up to a pebbled beach for a picnic. Exploring the Altmühltal by canoe or kayak is a great way to sample the park's picturesque charms at a leisurely pace. The slow-moving river meanders for about 150km, with lots of little dams along the way, as well as a few fun little pseudo-rapids about 10km north-west of Dollnstein. Signs warn of impending doom, but tourist officials say that if you heed the warning to stay to the right, these little canoe slides are pretty safe. Just past Solnhofen, you'll be passing the '12 Apostels', a particularly memorable rock formation.

Canoes and kayaks are allowed to travel on the Rhine-Main-Danube-Canal, but it's less relaxing since you'll be sharing the water with excursion boats and freighters and you'd better know basic navigational rules and regulations.

The main season for boat touring is from May to September. During hot summers, the water level in the Altmühl can sometimes sink too low for navigation, so check in advance with the tourist office. Always pack suntan lotion and insect repellent.

Boat touring is hugely popular and it's a good idea to book boats and hotels in advance. Camping is allowed only in designated areas along the river for €3 per tent. Individual travellers do not need reservations.

Tours The two main outfitters are San-Aktiv Tours (☎ 09831-49 36, fax 805 94, W www .san-aktiv-tours.com), Bühringer Strasse 8, 91710 Gunzenhausen, and Natour (☎ 09141-92 29 29, fax 92 29 28, e info@natour.de, W www.natour.de), Gänswirtshaus 34, 91781 Weissenburg. Both have similar trips and prices as well as a fleet of vehicles to shuttle canoes, bicycles and people around the park.

Tours usually run from April to October and last from a half day to three days. You can do it alone or join a group. Prices start at €20 for the half-day trip; one-/two-/three-day trips are around €25/100/150. Packages include the canoe, swim vests, maps, instructions, transfer back to the embarkation point and, for the overnight tours, luggage transfer and accommodation in guesthouses. Longer tours can be arranged as well. Most trips start in Dietfurt near Treuchtlingen.

Rental The tours are a good deal, but there are also plenty of companies renting canoes and kayaks in just about every town along the river. Expect to pay about €12.50/25 per day for one-/two-person boats, more for bigger ones. For an additional fee, staff will haul you and the boats to or from your embarkation point (sample fee: Eichstätt-Dollnstein €22.50 for the first boat, then €2.50 for each additional boat). Besides San-Aktiv-Tours and Natour, companies include Franken-Boot (☎ 09142-46 45) in Treuchtlingen, Lemming Tours (☎ 09145-235) in Solnhofen and Bootsverleih Otto

Rehm (☎ 08422-278) in Dollnstein. In Eichstätt, try Fahrradgarage (☎ 08421-21 10, e info@fahrradgarage), run by friendly, English-speaking Frank Warmuth. You can get a full list of rental outlets from the Informationszentrum Naturpark Altmühltal.

Cycling

With around 800km of trails – most of them away from traffic – the Altmühltal is ideal for leisurely bicycle touring. The weather is most dependable from June to August, but the downside is that trails can get quite crowded, especially on weekends. Advance room reservations are a good idea during this time. More than 100 hotels and pensions in the park have been designated as 'bicycle-friendly', meaning they have special storage facilities, can arrange for luggage transfer or prepare picnic lunches. Look for the green logo.

Trails are clearly labelled with long, rectangular brown signs bearing a bike symbol. The most popular route is the 160km Altmühltal Radweg from Gunzenhausen to Kelheim, much of it paralleling the Altmühl. To get away from the crowds, venture into the idyllic side valleys.

Fahrradgarage in Eichstätt (see Canoeing & Kayaking, Rental) rents out bicycles for €7.50 per day. Staff will bring the bikes to you or bring you with the bikes to anywhere in the park for an extra fee.

You can get a full list of rental outlets from the Informationszentrum Naturpark Altmühltal. Most will also store bicycles; Fahrradgarage charges €0.50 per hour or €1.75 per day.

Hiking

Spring and autumn are the best times for hiking along the park's 3000km of marked trails, including over a dozen long-distance routes. The most scenic one is the Altmühltalweg, which winds for 140km along the river from Treuchtlingen to Kelheim but, unfortunately, sections of it must be shared with bicyclists. Less busy is the Limesweg from Gunzenhausen to Kelheim (110km) along the former border of the Roman Empire. Hiking-trail markers are yellow.

Rock Climbing

The Jurassic limestone mountains in the Altmühltal have long exerted their challenge on rock hounds. You'll find rocks suitable for climbing in the areas of Dollnstein, Konstein/Aicha and Prunn/Essing, with degrees of difficulty ranging from III to X (XI being the toughest).

For rock climbing excursions and courses, contact the Informationszentrum, the Eichstätt chapter of the German Alpine Association (☎ 08421-972 40) at Marktplatz 15, or Sport IN (☎ 0841-472 23) at Jesuitenstrasse 17 in Ingolstadt.

Getting Around

Train Trains run between Eichstätt Bahnhof and Treuchtlingen hourly or better (€3.90, 25 minutes), and between Treuchtlingen and Gunzenhausen at least hourly (€5.40, 15 minutes). RE trains from Munich that travel through Eichstätt Bahnhof also stop in Dollnstein, Solnhofen and Pappenheim. Some require a change in Ingolstadt.

Bus The FreizeitBus Altmühltal-Donautal operates from mid-April to October; buses are equipped to transport bicycles. All-day tickets cost €7.50 for passengers with bicycles, €5 for passengers without, or €17.50 per family with bikes, €12.50 without.

Route FzB1 runs from Regensburg to Kelheim to Riedenburg on weekends and holidays only. Route FzB2 travels between Treuchtlingen, Eichstätt, Beilngries, Dietfurt and Riedenburg with all-day service on weekends and holidays and restricted service on weekdays.

Eichstätt

☎ 08421 • pop 13,800 • elevation 388m

Home to the only Catholic university in Germany (since 1980, 4000 students), Eichstätt's buildings and streets haven't been damaged since Swedes razed the place during the Thirty Years' War (1618–48). It was rebuilt by Italian architects, notably Gabriel de Gabrieli and Maurizio Pedetti, and is thus imbued with a notably Mediterranean flair. Eichstätt makes an excellent base for exploring the Altmühltal park.

Orientation There are two train stations. Mainline trains stop at the Bahnhof, 5km from the centre, from where diesel trains shuttle to the Stadtbahnhof (south of the Altmühl River near the city centre). From the Stadtbahnhof, Willibaldsburg is about 1km south-west up Burgstrasse. For the hostel, take Burgstrasse to Reichenaustrasse and turn right; it's about 300m ahead on the left side of the road.

For the town centre, walk north from the Stadtbahnhof, cross the Altmühl at Spitalbrücke and continue to Domplatz and the tourist office. For the Informationszentrum Naturpark Altmühltal, continue east from Domplatz to Ostenstrasse and then turn left on Kardinal-Preysing-Platz.

Information Eichstätt's helpful tourist office (☎ 988 00, fax 98 80 30, e tourismus@ eichstaett.btl.de), Domplatz 8, is open 9am to 6pm Monday to Saturday and 10am to 1pm Sunday from April to October. Winter hours are 10am to noon and 2pm to 4pm Monday to Thursday, to noon on Friday. The Informationszentrum Naturpark Altmühltal (☎ 987 60), in the Kloster Notre Dame on Kardinal-Preysing-Platz, is open 9am to 5pm (from 10am Sunday) April to October and otherwise 9am to noon and 2pm to 4pm Monday to Thursday, to noon on Friday.

Change money at Dresdner Bank, Westenstrasse 1 at the Markt. The post office is at Domplatz 7.

Buchhandlung Sporer (☎ 15 38), Gabrielistrasse 4, has some books in English. The Universitätsbibliothek (☎ 93 14 14) is in the Ulmer Hof, Pater-Philipp-Jeningen-Platz 6.

In an emergency, you should call the Kreiskrankenhaus (☎ 60 10), the regional hospital, at Ostenstrasse 31.

Willibaldsburg The hilltop castle of Willibaldsburg (1355–1725) houses two museums. The **Jura-Museum** (☎ 47 30, Burgstrasse 19; adult/concession €3/2; open 9am-6pm Tues-Sun Apr-Sept, 10am-4pm Tues-Sun Nov-Mar) is great even if fossils usually don't quicken your pulse. Highlights are a locally found archaeopteryx and the aquariums with living specimens of the same animal species that were fossilised eons ago.

Also in the castle, the 6000-year-old mammoth skeleton is a must-see at the **Museum of Pre-History & Early History** *(☎ 894 50, Burgstrasse 19; adult/concession/under 18 €3/2/free; open 9am-6pm Tues-Sun Apr-Sept, 10am-4pm Tues-Sun Nov-Mar)*. Also on the grounds is a 76.5m-deep well – toss in a coin and listen for about 10 seconds for the ting or the plop. The gardens near the car park afford fantastic views of Eichstätt.

Looking across the valley, you can make out the **limestone quarry** *(open 24 hrs daily; admission free)* where you can dig for fossils. Drive up or take a bus from Eichstätt (€1, 10 minutes). Chisel and hammer may be rented for €1 per day at the **Museum Bergér** *(☎ 46 83, Harthof; adult/child €1.50/0.50; open 1.30pm-5pm Mon-Sat, 10am-noon Sun Apr-Oct, otherwise on request)*. It's at the base of the quarry and displays a lot of geological samples.

Town Centre Eichstätt's centre is dominated by the **Dom**, which is, not surprisingly, rich in riches. Features worth noting include an enormous stained-glass window by Hans Holbein the Elder, and the Pappenheimer Altar (1489–97), carved from sandstone and depicting a pilgrimage from Pappenheim to Jerusalem. The seated statue of St Willibald, the town's first bishop, is also worth a gape.

Behind the Dom is the baroque **Residenz** *(1725–36; Residenzplatz; adult/concession €2.50/1.50; tours 11am Mon-Fri, 3pm Mon-Thur, 10.15am, 11am, 11.45am, 2pm, 2.45pm & 3.30pm Sat-Sun & holidays Apr-Oct)*, a Gabrieli building and former prince-bishops' palace. It has a stunning main staircase and a Spiegelsaal, with its mirrors and fresco of Greek mythology. In the square is a golden statue of Mary atop a 19m-high column.

The **Markt**, a baroque square north of the Dom, is the heart of Eichstätt's commercial district. About 300m north-west of here, on Westenstrasse, is the **Kloster St Walburga**, the burial site of Willibald's sister and a pilgrimage site thanks to a 'mysterious' occurrence: Every year between mid-October and

late February, water oozes from Walburga's relics and drips down into a catchment. The nuns bottle diluted versions of the so-called *Walburgaöl* (Walburga oil) and give it away to the faithful. The walls in the upper chapel are covered with beautiful ex voto tablets as thank yous to the saint.

Organised Tours The tourist office gives 1½-hour walking tours in German (€2.50) from April to October at 1.30pm Saturday (also Wednesday at 1.30pm July and August).

Places to Stay & Eat Eichstätt's restaurant and hotel options include:

Camping Daum *(☎ 54 55, mobile ☎ 0173-2751972, fax 807 63, Westenstrasse 47)* Site €5. Open Apr-Oct. This camping ground is on the northern bank of the Altmühl river, about 1km east of the town centre.

DJH hostel *(☎ 980 40, fax 98 04 15, Reichenaustrasse 15)* Dorm beds €14.30-15.10. Closed Dec & Jan. This is a modern place overlooking the Altstadt, but it's frequently booked up with school groups. Price includes linen & breakfast.

Gasthof Sonne *(☎ 67 91, fax 898 26, [e] info@sonne-eichstaett.de, Buchtal 17)* Singles €31-41, doubles €52-72. This is a perfectly pleasant place with largish rooms – many with balcony – and friendly service. The same family also operates the well-respected restaurant.

Hotel Adler *(☎ 67 67, fax 82 83, Markplatz 22–24)* Singles €38-49, doubles €56-66. If you can afford a bit more, get a room at this hotel in a completely renovated 300-year-old building right on Markt. It offers superb ambience and all the trappings, including bike and boat rental and a generous breakfast buffet.

Café im Paradeis *(☎ 33 13, Markt 9)* Dishes €2.50-12.50. Have a snack or bigger meal inside surrounded by antiques or outside on the terrace with primo people-watching on the Markt. Vegetarians should feel catered for.

There's also fast food on the Markt at *Metzgerei Schneider*, which is open all day, and *markets* are held here on Wednesday and Saturday mornings.

Getting There & Away There's a train service hourly or better between Ingolstadt and Eichstätt (€3.90, 20 minutes). For more connections, see the Getting There & Away entry in the Naturpark Altmühltal section.

Beilngries

☎ 08461 • pop 8500 • elevation 362m

Right near where the Altmühl has been streamlined into the Rhine-Main-Danube-Canal lies little Beilngries. It's been settled since prehistoric times and was under the jurisdiction of the Eichstätt prince-bishops for nearly 800 years until becoming part of Bavaria in 1806. Today, its tangle of narrow lanes often teems with day-trippers, arriving either by bicycle or by boat.

The tourist office (☎ 84 35, fax 96 61, e tourismus@beilngries.de) is at Hauptstrasse 14. From May to mid-October, it's open 9am to noon and 2pm to 7pm Monday to Saturday and 10am to noon Sunday. Otherwise, hours are 9am to noon and 2pm to 4pm weekdays only.

Things to See & Do Much of the medieval wall has crumbled under the passage of time, but nine picturesque guard towers still encircle the central town. As you stroll around, you'll also pass by two churches, the rococo Frauenkirche and the neo-baroque Stadtpfarrkiche (Parish Church), whose colourfully tiled spires are a town landmark. The baroque Rathaus (Town Hall) across the street is a work by Gabriel de Gabrieli, who did his main work in Eichstätt.

Numerous bicycle and hiking trails emanate from Beilngries. Bicycle rental places include the DEA gas station (☎ 392) at Eichstätter Strasse 5a. Rent boats for leisurely trips on the Altmühl at Bootsverleih Beilngries (☎ 89 03) at Obere Weinbergstrasse 22. Staff can also help plan tours.

Places to Stay & Eat Beilngries has a few hotel and restaurant options.

Hotel Die Gams (☎ 08461-61 00, fax 61 01 00, e info@ hotel-gams.de, Hauptstrasse 16) Singles €60-82, doubles €77-113. This is a classy place with large, friendly rooms, some with whirlpool spas in bathrooms that are bigger than most single rooms. The downstairs restaurant has friendly staff and excellent German and international cuisine (mains €10-20).

Hotel Fuchs (☎ 65 20, fax 83 57, e fuchsbraeu@landidyll.de, Hauptstrasse 23) Singles €46-53, doubles €67-77. Cheerful rooms with all the comforts are just the beginning at this charmer, which also counts a fitness centre, with indoor pool, gym and sauna, as well as bicycle rental and an angling pond among its facilities. The restaurant menu includes a few calorie-reduced meals (Brotzeiten €3.50 to €7, mains €7 to €12).

Getting There & Away Bus Nos 9232 connects Beilngries with Eichstätt several times daily in 45 minutes, while bus No 9226 needs about 1½ hours to get to Ingolstadt.

Along the Rhine-Main-Danube-Canal

There's no question that, despite its impact on nature, the Rhine-Main-Danube-Canal between Beilngries and Kelheim still passes through some glorious countryside. The Altmühltal bicycle trail rambles along here, but the nicest way to travel the canal is by boat. From May to early October, several companies run trips from Kelheim to Riedenburg, with stops in Essing and Prunn (€6/9.50 one way/round-trip to Riedenburg, two hours). Some boats continue on to Beilngries and Berching, where you can catch a shuttle bus (operated by the boat companies) back to Kelheim. Note that boats leave from the Altmühl landing docks in Kelheim, not the Danube landing docks.

You can also start your journey in Berching or Beilngries, but there are far fewer departures. Check the schedule with the tourist office in Beilngries.

Riedenburg Riedenburg, is the main town along the canalised Altmühl. It's known as the 'Three-Castle-Town', but two of the three, Tachenstein and Rabenstein, are all but ruins. Only **Burg Rosenburg** (☎ 09442-27 52; open 9am-5pm Tues-Sun Mar-Oct, shows 11am & 3pm Tues-Sun) lords it over

Bavaria's Tower of Babel?

When the Rhine-Main-Danube-Canal opened on 25 September 1992, it created a 3500km long continuous waterway from the North Sea to the Black Sea. It was an amazing feat that many had tried and failed to accomplish, starting with Charlemagne in 793. In the 19th century, King Ludwig I gave it a whack, but more than 100 locks made navigation on his 'Ludwig Kanal' impractical. Only in the 20th century, after 72 years of planning and 32 years of construction, did the willow-draped natural banks of the Altmühl finally yield to an asphalt canal 55m wide and 4m deep. It was a triumph of engineering and a tragedy for nature.

It is estimated that the canalisation of the 171km stretch between Bamberg and Kelheim has caused the loss of about 18 million sq metres of biotopes and pastures. This has destroyed the habitat of dozens of plant and animal species, including several on the endangered list. Experts fear that four out of five resident species will likely disappear, despite the creation of artificial biotopes. The towns along the canal, which once drew their tranquil identity from the gentle river, now seem oddly remote.

Economically, the canal is a flop as well. Built at a cost of more than €3 billion, it continues to operate far below its potential and manages to generate less than 10% of its maintenance costs through shipping fees. Meanwhile, tourist boats flood the villages with mass tourism.

Former Federal Transportation Minister, Volker Hauff, has called the canal 'the most stupid construction project since the Tower of Babel'. Meanwhile, however, Bavaria's state government wants to extend the canalisation even further by straightening and deepening the Danube between Straubing and Vilshofen on the southern edge of the Bavarian Forest. Another environmental disaster in the making? Stay tuned.

the town, originally the dream castle of a medieval minstrel who also happened to be a falconer. Today, a falconer picks up the tradition with a flock of not just falcons,

but also eagles, vultures and other birds of prey.

Burg Prunn It has been incessantly photographed and inspired poets and painters, and for good reason: Burg Prunn (☎ 09442-33 23; adult/concession/under 18 €2.50/2/ free; tours 9am-5pm Tues-Sun Apr-Oct, 10am-3.30pm Tues-Sun Nov-Mar) is what everyone thinks of as the quintessential medieval castle. Framed by velvety woods, its turrets, towers and bulwarks stand sentinel on a rocky bluff high above the canal. It's truly a magnificent sight from below, perhaps even more impressive than from close-up, although the views of the valley from the top are great as well. In 1569, Wiguläus Hundt, a local researcher and humanist, happened upon a hand-written copy of the medieval Nibelungen song, which became known as the 'Prunner Codex' and which is now in the Bavarian State Library in Munich. The epic, of course, inspired Richard Wagner Nibelungen opera cycle.

Befreiungshalle Perching above Kelheim and the Danube is this pale yellow cylinder known as the Hall of Liberation (1863; ☎ 09441-68 20 70, Befreiungshallestrasse 3; adult/concession €2.50/2; open 9am-6pm Fri-Wed, 9am-8pm Thur mid-Mar-Oct, 9am-4pm daily Nov-mid-Mar). It's a monumental piece of architecture commissioned by King Ludwig I to commemorate the victorious battles against Napoleon between 1813-15. Inside, the super-sized winged white marble sculptures of the Roman goddess Victoria are a real trip.

Danube Gorge & Kloster Weltenburg

At Kelheim, the canalised Altmühl meets the Danube, which flows east to Regensburg (see the Eastern Bavaria chapter) and west through the **Danube Gorge**. This is one of the most dramatic stretches of the river as it carves through craggy cliffs and past bizarre rock formations.

The only way to enjoy this natural spectacle is from the water. You can either rent your own kayak or canoe or board one of the tourist boats leaving from the Danube landing docks in Kelheim from mid-March to October (one way/return €4/6.50; bicycles €1.50/3).

At the end of the 40-minute ride, boats dock a few hundred metres from the **Kloster Weltenburg**, an ancient Benedictine abbey, which operates the world's oldest monastic brewery, in business since 1050. Now a state-of-the-art brewery, it makes several varieties, including a Dunkel and a Bock beer, costing from €2.45 to €3.10 per half litre. The Klosterschenke (☎ *09441-36 82, Asamstrasse 32; open 8am-7pm daily mid-Mar–Oct)* with its chestnut-canopied beer garden is one of the nicest in the country, although it can get uncomfortably crowded on warm weekends and on holidays.

For spiritual sustenance, pop into the **Klosterkirche Weltenburg**, a magnificent rococo church by Cosmas Damian Asam and Egid Quirin Asam. Its most eye-popping feature, perhaps, is the high altar which shows St George, triumphant on horseback with the dead dragon and rescued princess at his feet. See if you can spot the stucco sculpture of Cosmas Damian leaning in over the railing from the oval ceiling fresco.

The return boat trip takes only 20 minutes.

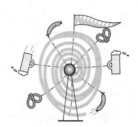

Upper Bavaria

To many visitors, Upper Bavaria (Oberbay-ern) *is* Bavaria. This is the land of thigh-slapping lederhosen lads and women in bosom-accentuating dirndls, of foaming mugs of beer, of giant platters seemingly groaning beneath portions of pork roast with kraut, of snow-capped mountain peaks and lush meadows and quaint villages. Here you'll find confirmation for just about every cliche you've ever heard about Bavaria, and then some. The people of Upper Bavaria have done an extraordinary job of exploiting just these cliches that fuel people's imagi-nations and, in turn, the tourism industry.

Geographically, Upper Bavaria stretches from Ingolstadt in the north to Garmisch-Partenkirchen in the south and Berchtes-gaden in the south-east. In the west, the Lech River separates it from the Allgäu-Bavarian Swabia region. Munich is techni-cally a part of Upper Bavaria but gets its own chapter in this book.

Upper Bavaria is the Bavarian heartland, and many locals are quick to point out that only they are the 'original' Bavarians, unlike the 'newcomer' Franconians and Swabians, who only became Bavarian in the early 19th century.

Almost the entire region is rural, endowed with the kind of scenery that is the stuff of postcards. Nature and architecture blend har-moniously just about everywhere you look. Overall, people here are patriotic, politically conservative, overwhelmingly Roman Cath-olic and proud of their traditions.

Although in many villages time seems to stand still, the tourism infrastructure in Upper Bavaria is state of the art. Every place has a helpful tourist office, there's good public transport and finding accom-modation to suit every budget is almost never a problem.

WERDENFELSER LAND

The Werdenfelser Land is a lovely Alpine and sub-Alpine region in the shadow of the Karwendel and Wetterstein mountain

Highlights

- Take the cogwheel train or pulse-quickening cable car to the 'Top of Germany': the peak of the Zugspitze at 2964m

- Walk, hike, trek or ski through the fabulous mountain scenery of the Alps

- Treat yourself to a gourmet dinner at the triple Michelin-starred Residenz Heinz Winkler in Aschau in the Chiemgau

- Take the hair-raising trip up to Berchtes-gaden's Nazi-built Kehlsteinhaus for superb views, then brush up on Third Reich history at the excellent Dokumen-tation Obersalzberg below

- Visit Ludwig II's most charming palace, the idyllically located Schloss Linderhof

- Drink in the baroque splendour of the Wieskirche, designed by the Zimmer-mann brothers

ranges, which embrace the Zugspitze, Ger-many's highest mountain (2964m). The best-known towns are the skiing resort of Garmisch-Partenkirchen and Oberammer-gau with its famous Passion Play. North of here, Murnau is a nice lakeside resort that

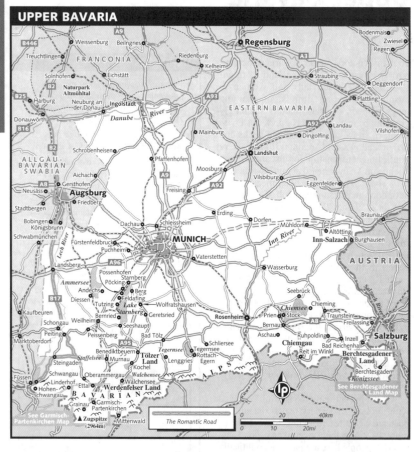

was once the home of an artists' colony led by Wassily Kandinsky and Gabriele Münter.

Throughout the region you will find centuries-old houses with facades decorated in a style called *Lüftlmalerei*, a local version of trompe l'oeil painting, which became popular in the 18th century. The term literally means 'air painting', but is actually derived from the name of the house 'Zum Lüftl', which was owned by Oberammergau's Franz Seraph Zwink (1748–92), who pioneered the practice. Images usually have a religious flavour, but some also show hilarious beer hall scenes or other secular themes. The best examples are in Oberammergau.

Garmisch-Partenkirchen
☎ 08821 • pop 27,500 • elevation 708m

The gateway to the best skiing in Bavaria, Garmisch-Partenkirchen snuggles against the craggy Wetterstein mountain range. It's a year-round resort, drawing hikers, mountaineers and cyclists in summer as much as it does skiers and snowboarders in winter.

In 1935, Garmisch and Partenkirchen were amalgamated to host the 1936 Winter Olympics. To this day, the twin towns host important international skiing events, including world cup races and ski-jumping competitions.

Garmisch (derived from Germareskaue) was first mentioned in 802, while Partenkirchen has origins as a 3rd century Roman settlement called Parthanum. In the Middle Ages, both towns rose to prominence as part of the duchy of Werdenfels, which controlled the northern access to the Scharnitz-Brenner route, an important trade route to Italy. A period of prosperity, which lasted until the Thirty Years' War (1618–48), was followed by a plunge into relative insignificance, which ended in the last century.

Today, each town retains its own distinct flair: Garmisch has the more cosmopolitan and urban flair, while Partenkirchen preserves more of an old-world Alpine village feel.

Garmisch-Partenkirchen makes for a handy base for excursions to Ludwig II's palaces, including Schloss Linderhof, Hohenschwangau and Neuschwanstein near Füssen (see the Allgäu-Bavarian Swabia chapter) and the lesser-known Königshaus am Schachen.

Orientation The railway tracks that divide the two towns culminate at the Hauptbahnhof, with the main bus station right out front and the Bahnhof Zugspitzbahn immediately to the west.

Partenkirchen sprawls out east of the train station; simply follow Bahnhofstrasse straight out, which will eventually take you to Ludwigstrasse, its main artery. To get to the centre of Garmisch, turn left as you exit the station, head north on Bahnhofstrasse, then west on Chamonixstrasse, which culminates at Richard-Strauss-Platz, site of the tourist office. From here, pedestrianised Am Kurpark leads due west to Marienplatz, the other main square.

Information The tourist office (☎ 18 07 00, fax 18 07 55, e tourist-info@garmisch -partenkirchen.de), on Richard-Strauss-Platz, is open from 8am to 6pm Monday to Saturday, and 10am to noon Sunday and holidays. There's an electronic room-reservation board outside, or call the 24-hour automated hotline at ☎ 194 12 for room availability. The Kurtaxe is €1.75 (free for under 16s).

The Sparkasse branches at Bahnhofstrasse 40/42 and Rathausplatz 2 in Garmisch or at Ludwigstrasse 62 in Partenkirchen change money and have ATMs. The post office is opposite the Hauptbahnhof.

For Web access, try GAP Online (☎ 94 50 14) at Ludwigstrasse 13 in Partenkirchen. The town's Web site is at W www .garmisch-partenkirchen.de (also in English). Presse & Buch (☎ 44 00), inside the Hauptbahnhof, sells around 300 international magazines and newspapers as well as books.

The local Klinikum (hospital; ☎ 770) is at Auenstrasse 6 in the south-eastern corner of town near the Eckbauerbahn valley station. The auto association Allgemeiner Deutscher Automobil Club (ADAC; ☎ 01805-10 11 12) has a branch at Hindenburgstrasse 14 in Partenkirchen.

St Martinskirche The St Martinskirche on Kramerstrasse in Garmisch, a short walk north of Marienplatz, was built in the early 18th century by Josef Schmuzer and decorated with stucco-framed frescoes by Matthias Günther telling the story of the life of St Martin. Note the pulpit, which is richly festooned with sculptures of the four evangelists, three virtues and Moses. The enamel nametags in most of the pews indicate the regular seats of parishioners (in other words, don't even think about sitting there during a service).

Ludwigstrasse The heart of Partenkirchen is Ludwigstrasse, lined with houses with facades painted in the traditional Lüftmalerei style. Ludwigstrasse has a long history as a trading route and is still the main commercial strip in this part of town.

Fires in 1811 and 1865 destroyed nearly all of the medieval buildings, except the so-called **Alte Haus** at No 8, and the house at No 47, which today contains the **Werdenfelser Heimatmuseum** (☎ 21 34; adult/concession €1.50/0.50; open 10am-1pm Tues-Sun & 3pm-6pm Tues-Fri). It illustrates the cultural

UPPER BAVARIA

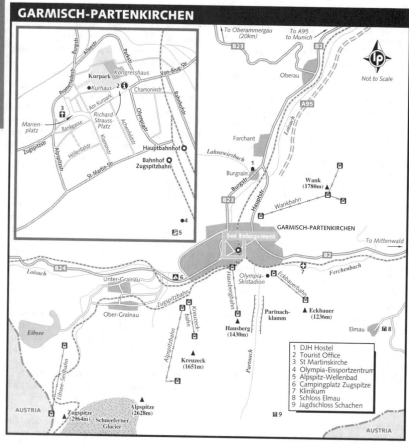

GARMISCH-PARTENKIRCHEN

Not to Scale

1 DJH Hostel
2 Tourist Office
3 St Martinskirche
4 Olympia-Eissportzentrum
5 Alpspitz-Wellenbad
6 Campingplatz Zugspitze
7 Klinikum
8 Schloss Elmau
9 Jagdschloss Schachen

history of the region through exhibits ranging from prehistory to the 20th century. Look for a Madonna sculpture by Ignaz Günther (1725–75), a room full of costumes and masks used in Carnival festivities, Oberammergau woodcarvings and a replica violin-making workshop.

Opposite the museum is the neogothic **Pfarrkirche** (1871) – its most valuable item is a painting by Bartolomeo Letterini showing Mary's ascension to heaven (it's in the left aisle). Nearby, at No 45, is the **Gasthof zum Rassen**, one of the oldest inns in town (see Places to Stay), named for Count Rasso

of Andechs, who once owned large stretches of land around here, as well as a brewery. Inside is the oldest *Bauerntheater* (Peasants' Theatre), which has staged folksy Bavarian plays since 1892.

Zugspitze Skiing in winter and hiking in summer are the main activities on the Zugspitze. Views from the top of Germany are quite literally breathtaking, especially during Föhn weather when you can gaze into four countries. While here, you can also contemplate contemporary art at what may well be the world's highest art gallery, or send an email from the Internet cafe. To get to the top, you can walk (see Hiking), take a cog-wheel railway, a cable car or a combination of all three.

The **Zugspitzbahn** (the cog-wheel railway) leaves from its own station next to the Hauptbahnhof. From here, it chugs along the mountain base westward to the Eibsee, a dark blue forest lake, then winds through a mountain tunnel up to the Schneeferner Glacier (2600m; there's a restaurant here). A cable car makes the final ascent to the summit.

Alternatively, the **Eibsee-Seilbahn**, a steep cable car, sways and swings its way straight up to the summit from the Eibsee lake in about 10 minutes (not for the fainthearted!). Most people go up on the train and take the cable car back down, but it works just as well the other way around. The entire trip costs €32/19.50 adult/child from November to April and €41.50/24.50 from May to October.

Expect big crowds at peak times in winter (especially around holidays) and through much of the summer. Skiers may find it easier, if a little slower, to schlep their gear up on the train, which offers exterior ski-holders.

Jagdschloss Schachen For a glimpse into the fairy-tale world of King Ludwig II without the crowds of Neuschwanstein or Linderhof, you can climb up to his fourth castle, the little-known Jagdschloss Schachen (☎ 920 30; adult/concession €2.50/2; tours 11am & 2pm daily late May/early June–early Oct, depending on the weather). High in the mountains above Garmisch-Partenkirchen, at a lofty 1866m, this Swiss chalet-style palace can only be reached after a gruelling four- to five-hour hike through the Partnachklamm or a three-hour trip from Schloss Elmau.

While the exterior looks fairly innocuous, the inside is a Ludwig extravaganza of the first order, especially in the so-called Moorish Room (also known as the Turkish Room) on the first floor. It's a setting straight out of *Arabian Nights*, complete with fine carpets, peacock feathers, a fountain and brightly pigmented glass windows. Here, the king enjoyed escaping to his fantasy world surrounded by servants dressed in exotic garb and bedecked with turbans, smoking waterpipes, sipping mochas and inhaling incense. The downstairs is more functional, with a dining room, study, bedroom and chapel. At the time of writing, the palace was undergoing gradual renovation, which should be completed by 2003. It's open but not all sections may be accessible; check with the tourist office or call ahead for details.

Berggaststätte Schachenhaus (☎ 29 96 or 43 77) serves food and drink, and has simple sleeping quarters costing €8.20 to €12.80 per person. Call ahead for reservations.

Skiing Garmisch has the country's longest ski season, usually running from November to May (to March at lower elevations). Powder-hounds can take to the slopes on four ski fields: the Zugspitze plateau (2964m); the Classic Ski Area (Alpspitze, 2628m; Hausberg, 1340m; Kreuzeck, 1651m); the Eckbauer (1236m); and the Wank (1780m) (yes, Wank residents do jokingly say '*Ich bin ein Wanker*'). Local buses serve all the valley stations.

Day ski passes for the Classic Ski Area cost €25.50/16.50 adult/child; it's €18.50/12 at Wank only and €15.50/10 at Eckbauer only. Zugspitze passes are €32/19.50. Also available is the Happy Ski Card, which covers all of the above, plus three other ski areas around the Zugspitze, including Mittenwald. A three-day pass (the minimum) costs €75/45.

Cross-country ski trails run along the main valleys, including a long section from Garmisch to Mittenwald. Call ☎ 79 79 79 for a weather or snow report.

Flori Wörndle (☎ 583 00) is a ski school with some of the best rates for ski hire (as well as convenient outlets at the Alpspitze and Hausberg valley stations). Sport Total (☎ 14 25), Marienplatz 18, runs skiing courses and organises numerous outdoor activities such as paragliding, mountain biking, rafting and ballooning. It also rents a wide range of sporting gear.

Hiking Garmisch-Partenkirchen is prime hiking territory and the tourist office has brochures and maps with route suggestions for all levels of expertise. The Zugspitzbahn and all the cable cars are in operation year round, and numerous trails are cleared of snow in winter. The local chapter of the Deutscher Alpenverein (☎ 27 01) can be found at Hindenburgstrasse 38.

Hiking to the **Zugspitze summit** is only possible in the summer months and not recommended for those without mountaineering experience. Bergsteigerschule Zugspitze (☎ 589 99), Dreitorspitzstrasse 13 in Garmisch, is among those offering guided hikes and courses in mountaineering.

The **Partnachklamm** (☎ 31 67; adult/child €2/0.75), a narrow 700m-long gorge with walls rising up to 80m high, is one of the area's main tourist attractions. In winter, you can walk beneath curtains of icicles and frozen waterfalls – a magical sight. Get there by horse-drawn carriage, walking, local bus or your own transportation. It's closed during the spring snow melt.

Other Activities Built for the 1936 Olympics, the **Olympia-Eissportzentrum** (☎ 75 32 91, Am Eisstadion; adult/child €2.50/1.50; open daily year round; check for skating times), just south of the Hauptbahnhof, is one of the largest **ice-skating** complexes in Germany with one large and two smaller rinks. Besides skating, you can also play hockey and curling.

Just south of here, the **Alpspitz-Wellenbad** (☎ 75 33 13, Klammstrasse 47; adult/child per 3 hours €3.75/2.25, all day €5/3; open 9am-9pm Mon-Fri, 9am-7pm Sat & Sun) is a fun pool with waves and a large sauna landscape. Same-day combination tickets good for two hours of skating and three hours of swimming cost €5/2.50.

Special Events Garmisch-Partenkirchen hosts numerous high-profile international skiing and jumping competitions, but on 6 January the focus is on the quirky **Hornschlittenrennen**. About 100 teams of four daredevils each race down a 1200m-long narrow ice track aboard historic wooden sleighs for the title of Bavarian Champion. It's a fun event that each year attracts as many as 10,000 spectators.

The highlight of the cultural calendar is the **Richard-Strauss-Tage** in June, a music festival honouring the composer, who had a villa here from 1908 until his death in 1949. Concerts featuring top international talent take place throughout town; call ☎ 75 25 45 for tickets.

Places to Stay You'll find the full range of accommodation available in Garmisch-Partenkirchen.

Campingplatz Zugspitze (☎ 31 80, fax 94 75 94, Griesener Strasse 4, Grainau) Tent/person/vehicle €2.50/4.75/2.50. The camping ground nearest Garmisch is along the B24 to Grainau. Take the blue-and-white bus outside the Hauptbahnhof in the direction of the Eibsee.

DJH hostel (☎ 29 80, fax 585 36, e jhgarmisch@djh-bayern.de, Jochstrasse 10, Burgrain) Bus: No 3 or 4 from Hauptbahnhof, direction Farchant to Burgrain. Bed & breakfast €12.25, including linen. Closed mid-Nov–Christmas. The hostel is in the suburb of Burgrain, about 3km north of Garmisch. Curfew is 11.30pm.

Haus Weiss (☎ 46 82, fax 91 28 38, Klammstrasse 6, Garmisch) Singles €18, doubles €33-43. Expect no-frills but clean, Bavarian-style rooms (a few with private shower and toilet) at this central property.

Gasthaus Pfeuffer (☎ 22 38 or 75 43 45, fax 46 17, Kreuzstrasse 9, Garmisch) Rooms €43-56. Central and simple, rooms here have cable TV, private bath, and there's a garden as well.

Haus Trenkler (☎ 34 39, fax 15 67, Kreuzstrasse 20, Garmisch) Rooms €45-49. If Pfeuffer is full, you could try this place nearby. Some of its rooms have shared bathroom facilities.

Gasthof zum Rassen (☎ 20 89, fax 39 82, e rassen@t-online.de, Ludwigstrasse 45, Partenkirchen) Singles €33-51, doubles €46-76. Closed Nov. In the same building as the Peasants' Theatre, this historic inn offers atmosphere galore in its public areas, although the rooms are surprisingly plain. All rooms have private bath, and rates depend on size and season. The restaurant here is excellent.

Hotel Schell (☎ 957 50, fax 95 75 40, Partnachauenstrasse 3, Partenkirchen) Singles €25.50-51, doubles €46-92. A five-minute walk from the Hauptbahnhof is this quiet hotel opposite a babbling brook. The more expensive rooms have private facilities.

Hotel Garmischer Hof (☎ 91 10, fax 514 40, e hotel@garmischer-hof.de, Chamonixstrasse 10, Garmisch) Singles €50-70, doubles €81-122. Rooms at this top-notch hotel have balconies, some with views of the Zugspitze. Amenities abound and the downstairs restaurant, while a bit stuffy, is recommended.

Places to Eat Unless noted, restaurants mentioned here are in Garmisch.

Bräustüberl (☎ 23 12, Fürstenstrasse 23) Mains €5.50-14. This place, a bit north of the Loisach River, is quintessential Bavarian, complete with enormous enamel coal-burning stove and dirndl-clad waitresses. The dining room is to the right, the beer hall to the left; main courses (not a vegetable to be seen) average around €10.

Chapeau Claque (☎ 713 00, Mohrenplatz 10) Meals €4.50-10.50. Do stop at this cosy and very French wine bar-bistro with soft lighting and friendly service. Meals include various potato dishes, soups, baguette sandwiches and stir-fries.

Ristorante Colosseo (☎ 528 09, Klammstrasse 7) Mains €6-8. Wood-fired pizza, pasta and salads taste even better when consumed at your window table with front-row mountain views at this upstairs Italian restaurant.

Hofbräustüberl (☎ 717 16, Chamonixstrasse 2) Mains €7-12. Schnitzels and Slavic specialities such as cevapcici (spicy ground-meat rolls) and meat kebabs dominate the menu at this cosy restaurant.

Isi's Goldener Engel (☎ 94 87 57, Bankgasse 5) Lunches €6-11, mains €9-14. This local favourite has wacky decor that blends frescoes, stags' heads and a gilded stucco ceiling. The huge selection of food ranges from simple schnitzel to game dishes. The lunch specials are the best deal.

Konditorei Krönner (☎ 30 07, Achenfeldstrasse 1) Prices €2.25-8.25. Closes at 6pm. At this traditional coffeehouse, you can enjoy mountain views along with pricey cakes on the upstairs terrace. Or pick your sweet poison at the attached bakery for a lot less; Mocca creme and almond Agnes-Bernauer-Torte are specialities.

Renzo (☎ 41 71, Rathausplatz 6) Mains €5-6.50. The menu at this local pizza and pasta emporium in Partenkirchen is as long as the Tower of Pisa is tall.

Gasthaus zur Schrannen (☎ 16 99, Griesstrasse 4) Mains €7.50-12.50. Closed Thur. This atmosphere-laden tavern has Bavarian Brotzeiten such as *Leberkäs* and sausages and well-priced main course specials such as venison ragout for €8.50.

Cafeteria Sirch (☎ 21 09, Griesstrasse 1) Prices €1.50-4.50. Across from the Gasthaus zur Schrannen, this nondescript self-service place offers great value. Half-chickens are €3.20, schnitzels €3.75 and beef goulash with noodles €4.15.

Zirbel (☎ 76 71, Promenadestrasse 2) Meals €3-11. This tunnel-shaped relaxed pub with its warm atmosphere serves snacks and small meals such as chilli con carne and chicken wings.

Nordsee (Klammstrasse 8) serves fish in endless variations, both hot and cold, while the *Schlemmer Eck (Klammstrasse 1)* specialises in meaty sandwiches and soups. Both are open from 8am to 6pm, but are closed on Sunday and holidays. There's an *Aldi* supermarket at the corner of Bahnhofstrasse and Enzianstrasse.

Getting There & Away Garmisch is serviced from Munich by hourly trains (€13.50, 1½ hours). Ask about special packages, which combine the return trip from Munich with a Zugspitze day ski pass. Regionalverkehr Oberbayern (RVO) bus No 1084/9606 travels to Oberstdorf with stops in Oberammergau, the Wieskirche, Neuschwanstein and Hohenschwangau and Füssen.

The A95 from Munich spills into the B2 just north of Garmisch-Partenkirchen. To get to Oberammergau, take the B23. *Vignetten* (motorway permits) for Austria are available from the Aral gas stations at Hauptstrasse 20 and Zugspitzstrasse 42.

Getting Around Bus tickets cost €1 for journeys in town (free with Kurkarte). Bike rental outfits include Fahrrad Ostler (☎ 33 62) at Kreuzstrasse 1 in Garmisch, which rents touring bikes for €10/40 per day/week and mountain bikes for €12.50/60.

Mittenwald

☎ 08823 • pop 8500 • elevation 930m

Mittenwald, 20km south-east of Garmisch-Partenkirchen, is a storybook village crouching at the foot of Mt Karwendel (2384m). It was a famous violin-making centre long before the first tourists arrived. Nowadays it's a favourite Alpine getaway for weary urban types, with a relaxed ambience and snow-capped peaks in winter. A unique microclimate in the Upper Isar Valley keeps the fog – so common in other Alpine resorts – at bay most of the time. The picturesque town centre is studded with statuesque buildings sporting Lüftlmalerei work that rivals that in Oberammergau.

Orientation & Information Mittenwald's centre is compact, so you're unlikely to get lost. The Bahnhof is a short walk south of the Obermarkt, the pedestrianised main commercial drag. To get to the tourist office (☎ 339 81, fax 27 01, e kurverwaltung@ mittenwald.de), head north on Bahnhofstrasse, then right on Karwendelstrasse, which runs into Dammkarstrasse; it'll be on your left at No 3. Hours are 8am to 5pm Monday to Friday and 9am to noon Saturday. From May to September, it's also open from 10am to noon on Sunday. The 24-hour hotel hotline is at ☎ 194 12 (dial the area code when outside of town). The post office is opposite the Bahnhof and there's a Hypovereinsbank at Obermarkt 30. The daily *Kurtaxe* (resort tax) is €1.

Things to See The town centre is dominated by the **Pfarrkirche St Peter und Paul**, which squats at the eastern end of Obermarkt like the dot in an exclamation mark. Another work by the prolific Josef Schmuzer, who designed most churches of note in the Werdenfelser Land, it has a rather jolly steeple with a helmet-shaped copper top and a painted facade. Matthias Günther created the colourful frescoes starring the church's patron saints Peter and Paul.

Outside is a statue of Matthias Klotz (1653–1743), the man credited with turning Mittenwald into one of the European centres of violin-making. His grandson fashioned an instrument used by Mozart and a violin-making school still exists today. To learn more, take a spin around the tiny **Geigenbaumuseum** (☎ 25 11, Ballen-hausgasse 3; adult/concession €1.75/0.50; open 10am-1pm daily & 3pm-6pm Tues-Fri), a short walk behind the church.

West of here, **Obermarkt** is lined by stately houses decorated with Lüftlmalerei. Note especially **Gasthaus Alpenrose** at No 1 by Oberammergau master Franz Zwinck, which uses seemingly secular themes to convey a religious message: at the bottom are the four virtues, in the middle the five senses and on top the Virgin Mary ringed by angels and saints. In other words, observing the virtues and controlling your senses will buy you a ticket to heaven. The **Neunerhaus** at No 24 is another eye-catcher.

Hiking Mittenwald is a year-round outdoor playground, with a wonderful landscape that allows you to pursue a host of activities. There's hiking at all levels of exertion, from short and easy spins around lakes, through gorges and valleys to day-long mountain hikes and multi-day expeditions. The tourist office can make suggestions, and it also sells a good map for €2.

A scenic and easy walk is to Leutasch in Tirol (it's in Austria, so bring a passport, just in case) via the Leutaschklamm gorge. It's 11km return and can be covered in about two to three hours of hiking time. The gorge is usually open 9am to 6pm from mid-May to late October. In June and July, if you start out early, you'll be able to see a pretty rainbow reflected in a waterfall.

Experienced hikers might want to try a ramble on the Mittenwalder Klettersteig. The gondola of the **Karwendelbahn** (☎ 53 96 or 84 80; adult/child one way €11.50/8, return €18/10.50; operates 8.30am-5pm or less, depending on season & weather) takes you to Germany's second-highest mountain station at 2244m. From there, it's a six- to eight-hour hike across eight peaks over 2000m and with wonderful panoramic views.

Skiing Mittenwald has about 22km of downhill slopes (7.6km difficult, 8.4km moderate, 5.6km easy) spread over two main ski areas: Karwendel and Kranzberg. A major adrenalin rush for advanced skiers is the 7km Dammkar run, Germany's first 'free riding' ski area (on unprepared pistes), which is reached via a 400m tunnel from the Karwendelbahn mountain station. Day passes cost €24/16 adult/child.

Beginner and intermediate skiers will probably find the Kranzberg (1400m) more to their liking. The **Kranzbergbahn** (☎ 15 53; day passes adult/child €19/13; operates 9am-4.30pm daily) ferries skiers to the St Anton station at 1220m from where you can either head back down to the valley or take T-bar lifts to other runs.

For equipment hire and ski/snowboard instruction, contact the Erste Skischule Mittenwald (☎ 35 82) at Bahnhofsplatz. A three-hour ski lesson costs €25, with rates lower from the second day.

Places to Stay & Eat There are only a few hotels and restaurants in town.

Camping Am Isarhorn (☎ 52 16, fax 80 91, Isarhorn 4) Bus: No 9608 or 9610. Site/person €6.50/4.50. Closed Nov–mid-Dec. This beautifully situated ground is 3km north of town off the B2 highway.

DJH hostel (☎ 17 01, fax 29 07, e jhmittenwald@djh-bayern.de, Buckelwiesen 7) Bed & breakfast €12.30-13.10, including linen. Closed mid-Nov–late Dec. The local hostel is in an isolated setting in Buckelwiesen, 4km north of Mittenwald. There's no bus service; from the Mittenwald train station take the road to Klais, bear left at the BMW dealer, go up the hill, round the lake and follow the signs – it's about an hour's walk.

Hotel-Gasthof Alpenrose (☎ 927 00, fax 37 20, Obermarkt 1) Singles/doubles from €20/40 (shared bath), €30/60 (private bath). This is a good budget place in an ornate

18th-century building with painted facades. The restaurant offers affordable old-style eating (mains €7 to €13) and live Bavarian music almost nightly.

Gröblalm (☎ 91 10, fax 29 21, e groeblalm@t-online.de, Gröblalm 1–2) Singles €32-50, doubles €60-85. For more peace and quiet, head to Gröblalm where rooms are rustic but filled with amenities, including private baths. The views across the valley are superb.

Restaurant Arnspitze (☎ 24 25, Innsbrucker Strasse 68) Mains €12.50-20. Closed Tues. This is one of the top places in town with gourmet-level local fare.

Gasthof Zum Stern (☎ 83 58, Fritz-Prölss-Platz 2) Mains €5-10. Closed Thur. This place has a spate of local dishes and a beer garden with fantastic views. Upstairs are a few inexpensive rooms.

Sali's Grillshop (☎ 82 26, Hochstrasse 14) Dishes €2-6.50, slightly higher if eating in. Open until 6.30pm. This grill has basic but filling meals such as schnitzel burgers (€2) and great roast chickens (€3.90 for half).

Getting There & Away Mittenwald is served by hourly regional trains from Munich (€16, 1¾ hours), Garmisch-Partenkirchen (€3, 20 minutes) and Innsbruck (€9.50, one hour). RVO bus No 9608 connects Mittenwald with Garmisch-Partenkirchen every 30 or 60 minutes; the trip takes 30 minutes.

Oberammergau

☎ 08822 • pop 5300 • elevation 850m

Oberammergau, about 20km north of Garmisch-Partenkirchen, is a study in genuine piety as well as in religious kitsch and commercialism. The village is known worldwide for its Passion Play, performed every decade by the townspeople (the next one is in 2010; also see the boxed text 'The Passion Play'). It's also a crafts centre, noted especially for woodcarving and glass painting, and a good base for outdoor pursuits.

Two little rivers embrace Oberammergau's centre: the Ammer River and the Grosse Laine River. The Bahnhof is just east of the Ammer, with the compact town centre a few steps east of here. South of the station, on Eugen-Papst-Strasse, is the tourist office (☎ 923 10, fax 92 31 90, **e** info@oberam mergau.de), which shares space with a travel agency at No 9a. Staff can help with finding accommodation from 8.30am to 6pm Monday to Friday and until noon Saturday. The town's Web site is at **W** www.oberammer gau.de, which is also in English.

Things to See & Do Tours of the **Passionstheater** (☎ 923 10, Passionswiese 1; tours €2; tours 9am-6pm daily, less in winter), where the performances take place, include a history of the play and a peek at the costumes and sets.

Oberammergau has some excellent examples of houses decorated with Lüftmalerei. The most beloved are the ones with fairy-tale motifs such as Hansel & Gretl at Ettaler Strasse No 41, and Little Red Riding Hood at Ettaler Strasse 48, which houses an orphanage. The pièce de résistance is the Pilatushaus (see later in this section), which is a Zwink original.

Oberammergau is also famous for its intricate **woodcarvings**, a tradition that harkens back to the Middle Ages. About 120 active artisans chisel away in workshops around town, churning out everything from saints to angels to animals to corkscrews.

If you want to see the artisans at work, head for the aforementioned **Pilatushaus** (☎ 923 10, Ludwig-Thoma-Strasse 10; admission free; open 1pm-6pm Mon-Fri May-Oct), which contains several workshops. Besides carvers, there are also glass painters, potters, creche builders and other artisans. Their work is displayed in the Pilatushaus' gallery and is for sale in its store. Also opening its doors to visitors is Oberammergau's prestigious **Schnitzschule** (Carving School; ☎ 35 42, Ludwig-Lang-Strasse 3; admission free; open 9am-11am Tues & Thur, closed during school holidays & exam periods).

To see some historical examples of local handicrafts, pop into the **Heimatmuseum** (Local History Museum; ☎ 941 36, Dorfstrasse 8; adult/concession €2.25/1; open 2pm-6pm Tues-Sun mid-May–mid-Oct, 2pm-6pm Sat mid-Oct–mid-May). Woodcarvings from the 18th to the 20th centuries, elaborate nativity scenes, wax figurines, toys and glass paintings form the core of this exhibit.

For even more examples of local artistry, head over to **Pfarrkirche St Peter und Paul** (Herkulan-Schwaiger-Gasse 5), which has a graveyard chock-full of elaborate headstones and crosses. The church itself, a light-flooded rococo confection, is another Schmuzer/Günther collaboration (see churches in Garmisch and Mittenwald). Schmuzer's son Franz Xaver did the stucco.

About 1.5km east of the town centre is the valley station of the **Laber-Bergbahn** (☎ 47 70, Ludwig-Lang-Strasse 59; up/down/ return €7.50/6/11; open 9am-4.30pm daily Sept-June, 9am-5.30pm daily July & Aug), a gondola that ferries hikers, skiers and sightseers to the peak of Mt Laber at 1684m. There's a **restaurant** (☎ 42 80) on top and good views of the valley and the Alps. Day ski passes cost €17/12 adult/child.

Oberammergau is also popular for **hiking** and **cycling**. Popular nearby destinations include Linderhof (12km) and Ettal (5km). The tourist office can make suggestions and sells maps.

Places to Stay & Eat If you decide to spend the night in Oberammergau, your options include the following.

DJH hostel (☎ 41 14, fax 16 95, **e** jhoberammergau@djh-bayern.de, Malensteinweg 10) Bed & breakfast €12.30-13.10, including linen. Closed mid-Nov–late Dec. The hostel is about a 15-minute walk south of the Bahnhof on the western bank of the Ammer.

Gasthof zur Rose (☎ 47 06, fax 67 53, Dedlerstrasse 9) Singles/doubles €35/65. This is a beautifully kept traditional inn with 24 rooms furnished in rustic style but with modern amenities, including private bath. The popular restaurant specialises in fish and venison (mains €8 to €16).

Hotel Alte Post (☎ 91 00, fax 91 01 00, Dorfstrasse 19) Singles/doubles €43/71, suites €81. In a cute Lüftlmalerei building right in the village centre, the Alte Post has

The Passion Play

Name the world's longest-running play: is it *The Mousetrap*, the famous 'whodunit' by Agatha Christie? Or Shakespeare's *Midsummer Night's Dream*? The unlikely answer is: the deeply religious *Passionsspiele*, performed in Oberammergau every 10 years (with few exceptions) since 1634.

In 1632, the chaos and famine of the Thirty Years' War created ideal conditions for the Black Plague to rage through Europe. When Oberammergau was struck, 84 people out of a population of 600 quickly succumbed. The survivors vowed to forever stage a play depicting the passion of Christ – if they could be rid of the epidemic. The vow was heard and so, two years later, the premiere took place in the churchyard.

Today, it's a drama of Wagnerian proportions, lasting from 9.30am to 6.15pm with a three-hour break for lunch. The cast consists of 2200 shaggy locals – haircuts are forbidden months ahead of time – with as many as 250 actors on stage at once. The production has changed – slowly – over time. The original text was purged of anti-Semitism, for instance, excising a scene in which Jews were depicted as horned devils. Finally, in 1990, women were allowed on stage; previously, a man had played even Mary's role. And for the first time in 2000, non-Germans and non-Catholics could join in, at least as long as they hailed from Oberammergau. Move over, *Jesus Christ Superstar*.

been a guesthouse since 1612. Full-facility rooms are decked out in modern country style and come in several sizes. The suites sleep up to five people and have a balcony. There's a restaurant too (mains €8.50 to €17).

Gasthaus zum Stern (☎ 867, Dorfstrasse 33) Brotzeit €4.50-8.50, mains €8-12. The menu offers few surprises with its stick-to-the-ribs Bavarian fare, but the dining room is comfortable and uncluttered and there's a beer garden too.

La Montanara (☎ 62 58, Schnitzlergasse 10) Pizza €2.50-7.50, mains €10-20. This upstairs trattoria sports cheerful wine-

themed decor and serves pizzas in two sizes as well as a full menu of meat dishes.

Getting There & Around Hourly trains connect Munich with Oberammergau with a change at Oberau (€14, 1¾ hours). RVO bus No 1084/9606 runs to/from Garmisch-Partenkirchen and Füssen almost hourly. Rent mountain bikes at Ammergauer Radlladen (☎ 14 28), Schnitzlergasse 12, for €12.50 per 24-hour rental.

Around Oberammergau

Ettal About 5km south of Oberammergau and 14km north of Garmisch-Partenkirchen is tiny Ettal, which each year draws tens of thousands of spiritual and cultural pilgrims to its monastery, **Kloster Ettal** *(☎ 740; admission free; open 8am-6pm daily)*. Ludwig der Bayer founded the place in 1330 out of gratitude for having survived a trip to Rome. He brought with him a marble Madonna, now the monastery's most venerated object and part of the high altar in the monastery church. A fire devastated most of the original Gothic structure in 1744, but by 1752 it was all rebuilt in rococo style by Josef Schmuzer.

It's an imposing complex reached via a 100m by 100m courtyard, topped by a vast dome and fronted by a facade festooned with larger-than-life-sized statues of the apostles. You enter through the Gothic portal, one of the few remaining sections from the original edifice. Note the tympanum above the entrance, which shows the crucifixion, with Ludwig the Bayer and his wife looking on.

Inside the nave, you'll inadvertently find your gaze drawn up to the ceiling rather than to the altar, an effect typical of baroque style. The dome fresco, by Johann Jakob Zeiller, is a vivid celebration of the Trinity by St Benedict and his followers with 431 individual figures. The painting blends into the stucco, the work of Johann Baptist Zimmermann of Wieskirche fame.

The monastery is still active, with about 50 to 60 Benedictine monks in residence. They're a rather enterprising bunch, who manage not only a prestigious boarding school but also a publishing business, a hotel with a restaurant, a brewery and a distillery where they fashion the famous Ettaler Klosterlikör.

If you need information or help with finding a place to stay, pop into the Verkehrsamt (☎ 35 34) at Ammergauer Strasse 8, which is open 8am to noon Monday to Friday.

Schloss Linderhof About 4km west of Oberammergau and 24km north-west of Garmisch-Partenkirchen is King Ludwig II's smallest but most enchanting palace, Schloss Linderhof *(1869–78;* ☎ *08822-920 30; adult/concession Apr–mid-Oct €5.50/4.50, mid-Oct–Mar €4/3; open 9am-6pm daily Apr–mid-Oct, 10am-4pm daily mid-Oct–Mar).*

Snuggled against a stark mountain range that wraps around the remote Graswang Valley, Linderhof is an intimate rococo palace and the only one of Ludwig's fantasy constructs finished in his lifetime. It's surrounded by formal French gardens with whimsical fountains, pools and follies. The king actually spent a considerable amount of time here, using it mostly as a retreat and hardly ever receiving visitors.

Like Ludwig's Herrenchiemsee (see later in this chapter), Linderhof was inspired by Versailles and is a tribute to Louis XIV, the 'Sun King'. A bronze statue showing him astride his horse stands in the foyer beneath a ceiling depicting a blazing sun and two cherubs holding aloft the Bourbon family motto.

Linderhof is chock-full of unbelievable treasures that are evidence of both the king's creativity as well as his ostentation. The largest room is his private **bedroom**, anchored by an enormous 108-candle crystal chandelier weighing 500kg. The **dining room** reflects the king's fetish for privacy and new inventions: its central fixture is a dumb-waiter table that rises from the kitchen below, allowing Ludwig to dine without actually ever seeing his servants.

If you're visiting in summer, you'll be treated to gushing fountains and will also be able to see some of the fantastic outbuildings strewn about the gardens. Don't miss the oriental-style **Moorish Kiosk**, which Ludwig picked up at the 1876 World's Fair in Paris. Its centrepiece is a peacock throne featuring three fantastically coloured birds – made of enamelled wrought iron – crouching atop a magnificent silk-covered divan. Just as impressive is the **Venus Grotto**, an artificial stalactite cave used as a stage set for Wagner's *Tannhäuser*. These outbuildings are only open from April to mid-October; the palace itself is open year round.

Bus No 9622 makes the trip out to Linderhof from Oberammergau thrice on weekdays and once on weekends.

Murnau
☎ 08841 • pop 11,000 • elevation 700m
Murnau, about 25km north of either Garmisch or Oberammergau, lost its medieval look to a raging fire in the mid-19th century, but made its mark decades later as a cradle of the modern art movement. It all began in 1909 when the painter Gabriele Münter (1877–1962), a friend of Wassily Kandinsky, bought a simple country house in this town on the Staffelsee, a large lake. Until the outbreak of WWI in 1914, the two spent their summers here together, often joined by fellow artists, including Alex Jawlensky, August Macke, Franz Marc and other avant-gardists. Their gatherings ultimately led to the founding, in 1911, of the artists' group Der Blaue Reiter (The Blue Rider) by Kandinsky and Marc. Marc later moved to the nearby Kochelsee (see the Tölzer Land section later in this chapter).

Münter, herself no slouch in the artistic sphere, stayed in Murnau until her death. During the Nazi era, she fiercely safeguarded a treasure trove of paintings, especially Kandinsky's, considered 'degenerate' by the regime. In 1957, she donated her entire collection to the Städtische Galerie am Lenbachhaus in Munich (see the Munich chapter).

Orientation & Information Murnau's Bahnhof and main bus station is about 700m north-west of the town centre. Take Bahnhofweg to Bahnhofstrasse south, which gets you to Gabriele-Münter-Platz and the tourist office. One block east is Obermarkt, the main artery, with the Schlossmuseum up on a low hill. The Staffelsee is about 1km west of Obermarkt.

Murnau's tourist office (☎ 614 10, fax 34 91, e verkehrsamt@murnau.de), at Kohlgruber Strasse 1, is open 8.30am to noon and 2pm to 6pm Monday to Friday and 8.30am to noon Saturday May to October (no lunch break in August). During the other months, it closes at 5pm Monday to Friday and opens 9am to noon Saturday.

Things to See & Do The **Gabriele-Münter-Haus** *(☎ 62 88 80, Kottmüllerallee 6; adult/child under 18 €2.50/free; open 2pm-5pm Tues-Sun)*, south of the tourist office via Burggraben, was recently restored to the time when Münter lived there with Kandinsky. Highlights include the furniture that the two of them painted, as well as an amazing staircase decorated by Kandinsky. Two rooms focus on the book *The Blue Rider Almanac*, a collection of essays and illustrations which was a ground-breaking manifesto on avant-garde art.

One of Murnau's geographical features that attracted artists was the pleasant **Staffelsee** and its seven islands. Its clear water is among the warmest in the region, making it ideal for swimming. You can also cycle or walk around its 18km circumference or rent row or pedal boats (from €4/6 per hour for two people). From May to October, boats shuttle between the three lake communities (Murnau, Seehausen and Uffing) four times daily. The entire round trip costs €6/3.

Back in town, attractions include the **Schlossmuseum** *(☎ 47 62 07, Schlosshof 4–5; adult/concession €2.50/1.25; open 10am-5pm Tues-Sun Oct-Jun, 10am-6pm Tues-Sun July-Sept)*, with permanent exhibits about the Blue Rider, Münter's later works, the writer Ödon von Horváth, the history of the palace, Murnau landscapes and painted glass. Also worth a look is the **Münter-Brunnen**, a modern fountain on Gabriele-Münter-Platz by the local sculptor Hansi Angerer. It recreates the floor plan of the Münter Haus, with the Kandinsky staircase as its focal point.

Getting There & Away Direct Regional-Bahn (RB) trains go hourly to Garmisch-Partenkirchen (€4, 26 minutes) and Oberammergau (€4, 40 minutes). To get to Kochel, take bus No 9611, with departures almost hourly (40 minutes). Murnau is on the B2.

TÖLZER LAND

The Tölzer Land, some 50km south of Munich, is a fabulous outdoor playground anchored by two beautiful Alpine lakes – the Walchensee and the Kochelsee – and centred on the spa town of Bad Tölz. Its gorgeous landscape has attracted many artists, including Blue Rider member Franz Marc (he of the blue horses fame).

Bad Tölz

☎ 08041 • pop 17,000 • elevation 659m

Bad Tölz is an idyllic and fairly lively spa town, which is a favourite day trip for Munich residents because of the good swimming at Alpamare, the Alpine slide at Blomberg Mountain and the rafting down the Isar River. Bad Tölz is also famous for its Leonhardifahrt, a religious pilgrimage, and for its boys' choir, the Tölzer Knabenchor (see Special Events later in this section). It's also a fiercely proud ice hockey town whose team is a two-time German champion but is currently playing in the second national league.

In the Middle Ages, Bad Tölz achieved prosperity as a waystation in the shipment of goods from Venice to Munich. Goods transported on the land route to Mittenwald were placed on rafts and floated down the Isar.

Orientation & Information The Isar separates the town's spa quarter in the west from the Altstadt in the east. The train station is near the eastern edge of town, about a 20-minute walk from the river.

Bad Tölz's tourist office (☎ 786 70, fax 78 67 56, e info@bad-toelz.de) has two branches. The one at Max-Höfler-Platz 1 is open 9am to noon Monday to Saturday and 2pm to 5.30pm Monday to Friday, with additional weekend hours during high season. The smaller one in the Heimatmuseum at

Marktstrasse 48 is open daily but closes at lunchtime except on weekends. The daily spa tax is €1.80.

For regional information, check the Tölzer Land tourist office (☎ 50 52 06, fax 50 53 75, [e] tourismus@lra-toelz.de) at Professor-Max-Lange-Platz 1.

Altstadt Cobbled and car-free, Bad Tölz' main drag, the **Marktstrasse**, gently slopes through the town centre like a decorative ribbon. Flanked by statuesque town houses with painted facades and overhanging eaves, it is also home to the **Heimatmuseum** *(☎ 50 46 88, Marktstrasse 48; adult/concession €2/1.50; closed Mon).* This sprawling museum in the former town hall touches on practically all aspects of local culture and history. Sprinkled in between interesting collections of painted armoires (the so-called *Tölzer Kisten*), beer steins, musical instruments and folkloric garments are some rather intriguing items. Look for the *Hochzeitsscheiben*, painted circular boards riddled with bullet holes, a local custom still practised during weddings today. Also unusual is the *Nonnengeige* (Nun's Violin), a tall and slender wooden instrument with a single string.

A few steps south of Marktstrasse through Kirchgasse is **Pfarrkirche Maria Himmelfahrt** *(1466; ☎ 76 12 60, Frauenfreithof 2),* a late-Gothic three-nave church with some brilliantly painted glass windows and an expressive floating Madonna. Wandering down Marktstrasse, you'll soon spot the baroque **Franziskanerkirche** *(☎ 769 60, Franziskanergasse 1)* across the Isar. Flanked by lovely gardens, its stark, whitewashed interior is enlivened by several fine altars.

Above the town, on Kavalrienberg, looms Bad Tölz' landmark, the twin-towered **Kavalrienbergkirche** *(☎ 76 12 60, Auf dem Kavalrienberg).* Next to this enormous baroque church, with its large central staircase, is the tiny **Leonhardikapelle** (1718), the destination of the Leonhardi pilgrimage.

Alpamare The *non plus ultra* of German water parks is Alpamare *(☎ 50 99 91, Ludwigstrasse 14; 4-hour adult pass weekday/ weekend €20.50/17.50, child 6-14 weekday/ weekend €15/14; adult day pass weekday/ weekend €29/17.50, child weekday/ weekend €18.50/14; open 9am-9pm Mon-Thur, 9am-10pm Fri-Sun).* This utterly fantastic complex for adults and kids has heated indoor and outdoor pools, a wave and surfing pool, a series of wicked water-slides (including Germany's longest, the 330m-long Alpabob-Wildwasser), saunas, solariums and its own hotel. Public buses stop at Wilhelmstrasse nearby.

Blomberg South-west of Bad Tölz town centre towers the Blomberg (1248m), a family-friendly mountain with a 5.5km natural toboggan track and 7km of ski runs in winter and fairly easy hiking and a really fun Alpine slide in summer.

The **Sommerodelbahn** is a 1286m-long fibreglass track that snakes down the mountain from the middle station. You ride down on little wheeled bobsleds that have a joystick to control braking (push forward to go, and pull back to brake). You can achieve speeds of about 40km/h to 50km/h, but chances are if you do that, you're going to either ram a rider ahead of you or even fly off the track. If you do try for speed, wear a long-sleeved shirt and jeans.

Unless you're walking, getting up the hill involves a chair-lift ride aboard the **Blombergbahn** *(☎ 37 26, in operation 9am-6pm daily Mar-Nov, 9am-4pm daily Dec-Feb, weather permitting).* Stations are located midway up the mountain and at the top. Return tickets to the top are €7/4 adult/child aged up to 14 (or €4/2 one way). Trips to the midway station are €2 each way for either adults or children. Riding up to the middle station and sliding down costs €3.50/3, with discounts for multiple trips.

In winter, day passes good for skiing or the toboggan track are €14/12 on weekends and €13/11 Monday to Friday; sleds rent for €8 per day.

Special Events Each year on 6 November, Bad Tölz celebrates the **Leonhardifahrt**, a famous pilgrimage to the Leonhardi chapel atop Kavalrienberg. It features townfolk dressed in lederhosen and fancy dirndls, marching brass bands and up to 80 flower-festooned horse-drawn carts. St Leonhardi, incidentally, is the patron saint of farm animals.

The **Tölzer Knabenchor** performs once a month at the Kurhaus. Tickets cost €15/7.50 adult/concession; check with the tourist offices for upcoming dates and availability.

Places to Stay The tourist offices can help you find *private rooms* (from €20 per person).

Hotel Landhaus Iris (☎ 783 60, fax 78 36 42, e forster@telda.net, Buchener Strasse 26) Singles/doubles €40/80. The most memorable aspect about this lovely pension is the wonderful hosts who shower each guest with personal attention. A close second are the charming rooms, each furnished with panache and all modern amenities. It's located in the quiet spa quarter.

Marienhof (☎ 76 30, fax 76 31 63, Bergweg 3) Singles €25-37, doubles €50-74. This nearby place is another good bet. Assets include free use of the indoor swimming pool at the clinic next door and free bicycle rental.

Hotel Kolbergarten (☎ 789 20, fax 90 69, e kolbergartenbadtoelz@t-online.de, Fröhlichgasse 5) Singles €46-77, doubles €82-128. This is the town's flagship hotel, with rooms furnished in either traditional Bavarian or elegant English style. It's filled with antiques, and a refined atmosphere prevails.

Places to Eat Bad Tölz offers the full range of eating experiences.

Altes Fährhaus (☎ 60 30, An der Isarlust 1) Mains €15-23. Closed Mon & Tues. This is Bad Tölz' gourmet temple, right on the Isar in a converted ferry house about 2km south of town. Chef-owner Elly Reisser-Kluge prepares a different menu daily, using only the finest ingredients. Anything involving fish is tops. She also has a few double rooms available for €92.

Kolberbräu (☎ 768 80, Marktstrasse 29) Mains €7.50-12.50. This central place oozes Bavarian *Gemütlichkeit* and serves some of the best and most reliable regional food in town.

Salett'l (☎ 79 96 10, Marktstrasse 39) Mains €5-8. Closed Mon. Set back from Marktstrasse, this bistro has woodpanelling and candlelight inside as well as outdoor seating in a snug courtyard. The menu revolves around salads, vegetable dishes, pastas, baguettes and other simple fare. It's one of the few places in town that stays open until after midnight.

Papa's Kesselhaus (☎ 76 62 87, Krankenhausstrasse 37) This is a fun pub, which also serves a good range of snacks, including their famous 'Rennsemmeln', huge and generously filled hot sandwiches. It has cheap lunch specials (around €5) and occasional live music at night.

Gasthof Zantl (☎ 97 94, Salzstrasse 31) Mains €5-15. Closed Fri & Sat. The chef of this traditional inn with its uncluttered dining room adapts the menu to the seasons. In spring, try anything involving *Bärlauch*, a wild herb with a mild garlic taste.

Getting There & Away Bad Tölz is served by the private Bayerische Oberlandbahn (BOB) railway, which connects Munich with the Tölzer Land and the Tegernsee area at hourly intervals. Coming from Munich, be sure to board a train headed to Lenggries. Alternatively, take the S2 from central Munich to Holzkirchen, then change to the BOB. Bad Tölz is at the intersection of the B13 and the B472, just south of the A8 to Munich.

You can rent bicycles at the Haus des Gastes (☎ 78 67 47) on the Kurpromenade.

Kloster Benediktbeuern

About 14km south-west of Bad Tölz, the Kloster Benediktbeuern (☎ 08857-880, Don-Bosco-Strasse 1; adult/concession €2.50/1) is one of the oldest monasteries in Bavaria, founded in AD 739. Destroyed by Hungarian marauders in 955, it was quickly rebuilt and remained a powerful and prestigious institution until its secularisation in 1803. In 1805, an optical laboratory opened on the grounds. Here, famed physicist Joseph von Fraunhofer (1787–1826) developed new types of glass, worked towards greater perfection of the manufacture of optical instruments and discovered the so-called 'Fraunhofer lines', the dark lines in the sun's spectrum. In 1930, the Salesians of Don Bosco, a religious order founded in Italy in 1854, took over the monastery. It operates two universities – one for theology, the other for social work – with 580 students, as well as several other educational centres.

The heavily stuccoed **Basilika St Benedikt** *(open 8am-5pm daily, services at 9am Easter–early Nov)* is an excellent example of early Italian baroque. The ceiling frescoes are by Georg Asam, father of the Asam brothers.

Of greater architectural and artistic importance is the small **Anastasiakapelle** *(1751–53; open 8am-5pm daily)*, a collaboration of some of the finest baroque artists working in Bavaria. The chapel's architect was Johann Michael Fischer, the exceptionally elegant stucco is by Johann Michael Feuchtmayr, Johann Jakob Zeiller painted the ceiling fresco and Ignaz Günther carved the side altars. There's also a small exhibit *(admission free; open 9am-6pm daily Mar-Oct, by appointment otherwise)* in the original workshop rooms detailing the accomplishments of Fraunhofer.

In summer, a series of classical concerts, the **Benediktbeurer Konzerte**, takes place in the basilica or in a baroque festival hall (tickets €15 to €20, student discounts available).

The monastery also runs a ***DJH hostel*** *(☎ 883 50, fax 883 51)*, where bunks in six-bed dorms cost from €14.30 to €15.10 per person. There's also the ***Gästehaus*** *(☎ 881 95, fax 881 39)*, with newly furnished singles/doubles costing from €14.50 to €26.50 per person.

From Munich, regional trains travel hourly to Benediktbeuern (€9, 55 minutes, change in Tutzing). From Bad Tölz, take bus No 9610 or 9612; the trip takes 30 minutes.

Kochel am See
☎ 08851 • pop 4000

The landscape – with its rich palette of colours and motifs – of Kochel, on the lake

---

Carmina Burana

Medieval love poems in a dead language aren't normally the fuel for chart-busting hits. But through the musical genius of composer Carl Orff (1895–1982), the rants of a devoutly hedonistic band of German 'goliards' (or, defrocked monks, minstrels and wastrels in general) have survived to titillate, amuse and become soundtracks for a host of films including *The Omen*, *Excalibur* and *The Doors*.

We are of course talking about *Carmina Burana* (literally, 'Songs of Beuern'), a collection of about 250 raging, erotic and humorous poems contained in a 13th-century manuscript found, by complete accident, in the monastery of Benediktbeuern in 1803.

Early in his career, Orff was principally a music educator whose life was forever changed after he wrote his famous secular cantata, which disregards the musical notation of the Latin originals. The epic premiered in Frankfurt-am-Main in 1937 to immediate acclaim. Orff's choral and instrumental arrangements in treating these celebrations of eroticism, gluttony, drinking and gambling are – by turns – light-hearted, inspirational and downright frightening. Through the driving strains of the *Carmina Burana*, one central fact about the 13th century is made abundantly clear: they sure knew how to party!

---

by the same name, greatly inspired one of the most influential early 20th-century German painters, Franz Marc (1880–1916). Along with Wassily Kandinsky, a sometime resident of nearby Murnau (see the Werdenfelser Land section earlier in this chapter), Marc was a founding member of the artists' group, the Blaue Reiter (Blue Rider; 1911). He is best remembered for his paintings featuring animals, horses in particular.

Marc began visiting the area while still a student at the Munich Academy of Arts, where his father was a professor. He lived here on and off starting in 1908, finally buying a house in 1914. Months later, he volunteered for WWI and was killed in action in 1916. He's buried in the Kochel cemetery.

A lovely villa contains the **Franz Marc Museum** *(☎ 71 14, Herzogstandweg 43, adult/concession €3/2; open 2pm-6pm daily Mar–mid-Jan)*. Aside from about 20 of his paintings, it presents numerous watercolours, sketches and drawings as well as such personal effects as his pipe and his school report card. Works by Kandinsky, Münter, Jawlensky and other friends complement his work.

Kochel has a couple of camping grounds. ***Campingplatz Renken** (☎ 57 76, Mittenwalder Strasse 106)* is open from April to September. It's located right on the lake and counts a restaurant, cooking facilities and children's playground among its amenities. The other is ***Campingplatz Kesselberg** (☎ 464, Altjoch 21/2)*, also on the lake and open from Easter to September. It's slightly smaller.

Bavaria's smallest ***DJH hostel** (☎ 52 96, fax 70 19, Badstrasse 2)* with just 31 beds costing €13.10, and a few hotels and pensions. Contact the tourist office (☎ 338, fax 55 88, **e** info@kochel.de), Kalmbachstrasse 11, if you need a room.

Kochel is about 22km south-west of Bad Tölz and is served several times daily by bus Nos 9610 and 9612 from Bad Tölz via Benediktbeuern (40 minutes). Regional trains from Munich connect with Kochel hourly, with a change in Tutzing (€10.50, one hour).

Walchensee
☎ 08858 • pop 500

Both the Kochelsee and the Walchensee are crystal-clear Alpine lakes, encircled by a spectacular mountainous landscape. Of the two, the latter is considerably larger, more accessible and offers a greater spectrum of water-sports activities. Its pebbled beaches are crowded with swimmers and sun worshippers in the summer months, when water temperatures max out at a tolerable 23°C.

Rumours of Nazi treasure buried in the depth of the lake continue to draw divers, but the lake's real fame is as a hot spot of the windsurfing scene. This is due to a peculiar microclimate, which generates strong breezes during fine-weather days. These start building at about 11am and usually don't die

off until around 4pm or 5pm. It's a phenomenon that occasionally brings in the sports' elite, such as Robbie Naish of Hawaii. Things can get crowded on weekends.

Operators renting gear and offering lessons include Windsurf-Center Walchensee (☎ 261) at Seestrasse 10, and Surfschule Reinhard Post (☎ 745) in Einsiedl.

Walchensee is about 35km south-west of Bad Tölz. It is connected with Kochel via the spectacularly windy Kesselbergstrasse. Bus No 9610 makes the trip out here from Bad Tölz up to six times daily (one hour).

Hiking Numerous hiking trails crisscross the Tölzer Land, from easy spins around the lake to lung-searing mountain climbs. A particularly rewarding day hike with superb views takes you to the peak of the Herzogstand at 1731m, one of King Ludwig II favourite mountains. You can start either near Urfeld on the northern shore of the Walchensee or in Schlehdorf/Raut on the Kochelsee. If you don't feel like climbing to the top but still want to enjoy the views, catch a gondola ride on the **Herzogstandbahn** *(☎ 236; adult/child one way €7/4, return €12/6.50; operates 9am-5.15pm daily Apr-Oct, 9am-4.15pm daily Nov-Mar)*.

A spectacular way to extend this tour is by taking the craggy ridge walk from Mt Herzogstand to Mt Heimgarten (1790m). The route requires cable-use and is not for the vertigo-prone. From here, you could either double back or work your way downhill to the town of Walchensee. All local tourist offices sell hiking maps.

Lenggries
☎ 08045 • pop 8500 • elevation 700m

About 10km south of Bad Tölz, via the B13, Lenggries is the gateway to the **Brauneck ski field**, which offers runs suitable for beginners to advanced skiers. Day passes are €21/13 adult/child aged to 15, and a free ski-bus operates from December to mid-March.

Lenggries is also a popular departure point for white-water canoeing, kayaking and rafting trips on the Isar River. Kajakschule Oberland (☎ 91 69 16, **e** info@ viactiva.de) at Ganghoferstrasse 7 is one of the most experienced outfitters around. Courses start at €100, equipment may be rented for €20 per day. Four-hour rafting tours start at €30, including equipment.

The tourist office (☎ 50 08 20, fax 50 08 40, e info@lenggries.de), Marktstrasse 1, can help you find accommodation. There are a few *guesthouses* with singles/doubles for about €35/70. The oldest hotel in town is *Der Altwirt* (☎ 80 85, fax 53 57, e altwirt -lenggries@t-online.de, Marktstrasse 13), with traditionally decorated rooms starting at €30/60, as well as a nice restaurant.

Lenggries is the final stop on the BOB private railway from Munich (for details see the Bad Tölz section). Bus Nos 9564 and 9553 from Bad Tölz also travel here up to eight times daily (less often on weekends).

TEGERNSEE
☎ 08022 • pop 25,000 • elevation 726m

Backed by the Alps and surrounded by forests, Tegernsee lake is in an ideal setting, a fact that has not gone unnoticed by Germany's money elite – Munich bankers to Berlin politicians – many of whom have their weekend villas here. You'll find few places with a higher concentration of people parading around draped in dead animal skins, their necks and fingers dripping with jewels, and their shiny S-class Mercedes parked nearby.

Tegernsee is punctuated by a quadriga of resort towns: Gmund on the northern shore is the most low-key; Tegernsee on the eastern shore is the most historical, Rottach-Egern in the south the ritziest and Bad Wiessee in the west, with its curative iodine springs, the healthiest. Summer activities include swimming, cycling, hiking, boating and windsurfing. In winter, skiing and snowboarding are options as is, sometimes, ice-skating on the frozen lake.

Tegernsee's tourist office (☎ 18 01 40, fax 37 58) is at Hauptstrasse 2; the office in Rottach-Egern (☎ 67 13 41, fax 67 13 47) is at Nördliche Hauptstrasse 9. In Bad Wiessee, go to Adrian-Stoop-Strasse 20 (☎ 860 30, fax 86 03 30), and in Gmund (☎ 75 05 27, fax 75 05 45) head to Kirchenweg 6.

Tegernsee

The lake's namesake town was once home to one of the oldest and most prominent among the Bavarian monasteries. Founded in 746 by Benedictine monks, it gained fame as a centre for manuscript illumination and had a library that was the envy of other monasteries – and even the Vatican.

After secularisation, the Wittelsbach royal family bought the place and turned it into one of their summer residences. Today the complex contains a brewery owned by Duke Max von Wittelsbach. You can sample his 'product' in the famous **Bräustübl** (see Places to Stay & Eat). The **Church of St Quirin**, with frescoes by Hans Georg Asam, father of the Asam brothers, completes the 'Bavarian Trinity' (palace, brewery, church). The complex also houses a high school.

Fans of biting caricature should check out the **Olaf-Gulbransson-Museum** (☎ 33 38, Im Kurgarten; adult/concession €3/1; open 11am-5pm Tues-Sun) The Norwegian-born Gulbransson (1873–1958) worked for the Munich-based satirical paper *Simplicissimus* and spent much of his adult life in Tegernsee. The museum shows the entire range of his work, from caricatures to oils and drawings.

Rottach-Egern

The double town of Rottach-Egern is the most glamorous of the lakeside communities. Its streets are lined by beautiful old houses with painted shutters and facades; many more, with overhanging eaves and wooden balconies, cling to the slopes of the surrounding hills. For superb views, take the **Wallbergbahn** (☎ 70 53 70, Am Höhenrain 5-7; one way/return €8/13; operates 8.45am-5pm daily Apr-Oct, 8.45am-4.30pm daily Nov-Mar), a cable car to the top of Mt Wallberg at 1772m where there's a restaurant and trailheads. Thanks to good thermal wind conditions, this is also prime terrain for hang-gliding and paragliding.

If you have your own vehicle, a drive up the mountain on the **Wallbergstrasse**, a panoramic toll route to the Moosalm restaurant, is another fun thing to do.

A motorboat winds its way along the clear, emerald water of the Königssee, Berchtesgadener Land

Dip into the Berchtesgaden's Magic Forest

Spire against full moon, Garmisch-Partenkirchen

Rothenburg rooftops

Eiskapelle – a dome reaching 200m above Königssee

Augsburg Dom door knocker

Historische Wurstküche, Nuremberg

Fairytale winter at Neuschwanstein castle, Füssen

Places to Stay & Eat

The tourist offices can help you find accommodation in *hotels* and *private rooms*.

Hotel Garni Reiffenstuel (☎ 92 73 50, fax 927 35 50, Seestrasse 67, Rottach-Egern) Singles €55, doubles €65-90. This is one of the cheaper lakeside hotels, with its own swimming beach and boat rentals. Rooms are comfortable and nicely appointed.

Hotel Bachmair am See (☎ 27 20, fax 27 27 90, Seestrasse 47, Rottach-Egern) Singles €90-175, doubles €145-270. The ritziest resort on the lake is like a little village unto itself. Facilities include a shopping arcade, a panoramic terrace, restaurants and a fancy fitness centre. Rooms are decorated in elegant country style.

Bräustüberl (☎ 41 41, Schlossplatz 1, Tegernsee) Meals €3.50-7. If you're willing to brave the thick smoke, you can join the beer-guzzling tour groups and grizzled locals for sausages, Leberkäs and local cheeses at this historic beer hall.

Getting There & Around

The Tegernsee is about 50km south of Munich. The town of Tegernsee is served by the BOB, a private railway from Munich with a change in Schaftlach (€7.85, one hour).

The BOB also goes to Bad Tölz, again changing in Schaftlach (€3.05, about one hour, depending on connection), or you can take bus No 9557 via Gmund and Bad Wiessee (1¼ hours).

Bus No 9559 connects the lake communities every 30 to 60 minutes.

CHIEMSEE
☎ 08051

Munich residents have a special place in their hearts for this lovely 85-sq-km lake – nicknamed the 'Bavarian Sea' – at the foot of the Chiemgauer Alps. So did King Ludwig II, who built his homage to Versailles – Schloss Herrenchiemsee – on one of its islands.

Most tourists are drawn here only to visit the palace, but the lake's natural beauty and the many possibilities for water sports justify a stay of a night or two.

Orientation & Information

The towns of Prien am Chiemsee and, about 5km south, Bernau am Chiemsee, both on the Munich-Salzburg rail line, are good bases for exploring the lake. Of the two, Prien is the larger and more commercial, while Bernau preserves an idyllic country atmosphere. Other larger lakeside towns are Seebruck on the northern shore and Chieming on the eastern shore.

The brand-new Chiemsee Info-Center (☎ 2280, fax 610 97, W www.mychiemsee .de) is on Rasthausstrasse on the southern lakeshore, just off the autobahn exit Bernau-Felden. It dispenses general and lodging information for the entire lake area from 9am to 8pm Monday to Friday and 10am to 6pm Saturday and Sunday, year round.

Each lake community also has its own tourist office. The one in Prien (☎ 690 50, fax 69 05 40, e info@prien.chiemsee.de) is at Alte Rathausstrasse 11, while Bernau's (☎ 986 80, fax 98 68 50, e tourismus@ bernau-am-chiemsee.de) is at Aschauer Strasse 10.

Schloss Herrenchiemsee

Herreninsel in the Chiemsee is home to another fantastic palace spawned by the fantastical imagination of Ludwig II: Schloss Herrenchiemsee (☎ 688 70; adult/concession €5.50/4.50; tours 9am-5.15pm daily Apr-Sept, 9.40am-4.15pm daily Oct, 9.40am-3.15pm daily Nov-Mar). Begun in 1878 on the site of an Augustinian monastery, it was never intended as a residence but as a homage to absolutist monarchy, as epitomised by Ludwig's hero, French 'Sun King' Louis XIV. Ludwig spent all of 10 days here; when he was in residence, he was a no-show, preferring to read at night and sleeping all day.

The palace is both a copy and an attempted one-up of Versailles, with larger and more richly decorated rooms. Ludwig managed to spend more money on this palace than on Neuschwanstein and Linderhof combined. When cash ran out in 1885, one year before his death, some 50 rooms remained unfinished.

The rooms that were completed each outdo each other in opulence. The vast

Ambassador Staircase, a double staircase leading to a frescoed gallery and topped by a glass roof, is the first visual knockout on the guided tour. Even more extravagant, though, is the positively dazzling **Great Hall of Mirrors**, which runs the length of the garden (98m; 10m longer than that in Versailles!). It sports 44 candelabras and 33 great glass chandeliers with 7000 candles, which took 70 servants half an hour to light. The **Paradeschlafzimmer**, a bedroom, resembles a chapel, with a canopied bed perching altar-like on a pedestal behind a golden balustrade.

The king's private apartment, where he stayed when in residence, is no less lavish. We especially enjoyed his private bedroom, where a big blue glass bubble perches on top of a wildly extravagant golden pedestal, looking much like an eclipsed moon.

Admission to the palace also entitles you to a spin around the **König-Ludwig II-Museum**, where you can see the king's christening and coronation robes, blueprints for even more phantasmagoric architectural projects, and his death mask.

Herreninsel is served by ferry from Prien-Stock (€5.50 return, 15 to 20 minutes) or from Bernau-Felden (€6, 25 minutes, May to October only). The palace is about a 20-minute walk through a lovely park from the boat landing. The palace tour, offered in German or English, takes 30 minutes.

Fraueninsel

This island is home to the **Frauenwörth Abbey**, one of the oldest nunneries in Bavaria founded in the late 8th century. Closed by the secularisation in 1803, it was refounded under Ludwig I in 1837 and is still active today. Worth a visit is the 10th-century abbey church, with a freestanding campanile that sports a distinctive onion-domed top. Opposite the church is the Carolingian **Torhalle** (☎ 08054-72 56 or 903 90, Frauenchiemseestrasse 41; admission €2.05; open 11am-5pm daily mid-May–Sept). Built in 860, it houses medieval objet d'art and sculpture, as well as changing exhibits of regional paintings from the 18th to the 20th centuries.

A return ferry fare, including a stop at Herreninsel, is €6.50 from Prien-Stock and €7 from Bernau-Felden.

Urschalling

Reached via a side road off the highway connecting Prien and Bernau is the tiny Romanesque **Church of St Jakobus**, a hidden gem in the hamlet of Urschalling. Its walls and ceiling are entirely covered in a naively charming fresco cycle of biblical scenes. Painted by an anonymous artist in the 15th century, the images were swathed with white paint a mere 100 years later because they were considered too primitive. In 1923, a cleaning woman accidentally rediscovered them, presumably while trying to rub off a particularly pesky stain. If you find doors locked, get a key from the sexton.

Activities

The most easily accessed **swimming** beaches are at Chieming and Gstadt (both free of charge) on the lake's eastern and northern shores, respectively. For €1.60, you can also use the beach of Panorama Camping Harras (see Places to Stay). Rental **boats**, available at many beaches, range from €4 to €20 per hour, depending on the type. In Prien, Bootsverleih Stöffl (☎ 20 00), Seestrasse 64, has two-seater paddleboats for €4.50 per hour and electric boats for €8 to €18.

The futuristic-looking glass roof by the harbour in Prien-Stock shelters the brand-new **Prienavera** (☎ 60 95 70, Seestrasse 120; adult/concession 3 hours €7/3.50, day pass €10/5; hours seasonal, usually 10am-9pm daily). It's an enormous pool complex with sauna, steam baths, waterslides, Jacuzzi and fitness area. The name is a weak pun on the Italian 'primavera', meaning 'spring'.

Cycling

The tourist office can make suggestions for bicycle and mountain bike routes. A great way to explore the lake is via the 57km **Chiemsee Rundweg**. There are numerous swimming opportunities along the way. Radsport Reischenböck (☎ 46 31), Bahnhofsplatz 6, at the Prien Bahnhof (behind the central bus station), rents city/mountain bikes from €6/10 per day.

Places to Stay

Panorama Camping Harras *(☎ 904 60, fax 90 46 16,* e *info@camping-harras.de, Harrasser Strasse 135)* Person/tent/car €4.90/from €3/1.60 (15% higher for stays under 4 days). This upmarket camping ground is in a dream location on a peninsula with its own private beach. It offers catamaran and surfboard rental, and has a restaurant with a terrace offering lake views. Showers cost an extra €0.80, caravans sleeping three to four people go for €31 to €40, plus €15 for cleaning. It's very popular in summer, so reservations are advised.

Four more camping grounds are located in Chieming, on the eastern lakeshore.

The tourist offices can set up ***private rooms*** in town and in farmhouses from €15 per person.

DJH hostel *(☎ 687 70, fax 68 77 15,* e *jhprien@djh-bayern.de, Carl-Braun-Strasse 66)* Bed & breakfast €14.30-15.10, including linen. Closed Dec & Jan. Prien's hostel is a 20-minute walk from the train station, and can sleep 109 people in several four- to six-bed dorms. The lake is 10 minutes away.

Prices listed here are for rooms with private bath.

Landgasthaus Kartoffel *(☎ 96 70, fax 96 71 67, Aschauer Strasse 22, Bernau)* Singles €23-37, doubles €46-74. Central, yet quiet, this friendly establishment has a progressive flair (Internet access and PC rental), and a lovely restaurant specialising in potato dishes, meats and salads (€5 to €12.50).

Hotel Garni Möwe *(☎ 50 04, fax 648 81, Seestrasse 111, Prien)* Singles €43, doubles €62-82. This lakefront hotel offers excellent value; it has its own bike and boat rental, as well as a sauna and fitness centre.

Hotel Bonnschlössl *(☎ 890 11, fax 891 03, Kirchplatz 9, Bernau)* Singles €43-72, doubles €72-102. For something special yet affordable, head over to this charming hotel in a fully restored palace dating from 1477. The hotel's stylish rooms have lots of amenities.

Hotel Neuer am See *(☎ 60 99 60, fax 609 96 44, Seestrasse 104, Prien)* Singles €40-49, doubles €74-90. This property, opposite Prien harbour, has modern country-style rooms, some with balconies. A popular bakery and a restaurant are on the premises.

Places to Eat

Der Alte Wirt *(☎ 890 11, Kirchplatz 9, Bernau)* Mains €8-12.50. Closed Mon. For great Bavarian cuisine with swift service, drop by this massive half-timbered inn where the Leberkäs is clearly the star of the menu. The waitresses dart round the dining halls as if on rollerblades.

Badehaus *(☎ 97 03 00, Rasthausstrasse 11, Bernau)* Mains €5.50-15. Near the Chiemsee Info-Center, right on the lake, this contemporary beer hall and garden has quirky decor and gourmet fare enjoyed by a mix of locals and visitors. A special attraction is the so-called 'beer bath', a glass tub sometimes filled with a mix of beer and water during particularly raucous parties.

Metzgerei Schmid *(☎ 15 62, Bahnhofstrasse 7, Prien)* Meals €1.50-4. Open till 6pm Mon-Fri, till noon Sat. Come to this butcher-*Imbiss* (snack bar) for sausages, schnitzel, half-chickens, lasagne and other substantial fare.

Westernacher am See *(☎ 47 22, Seestrasse 115, Prien)* Mains €6-11. Great vista, great garden – and the food ain't bad either. Try the trout in garlic butter (€10).

Getting There & Around

Prien and Bernau are served by hourly trains from Munich (€12.40, one hour). Bus No 9505 connects the two lake towns hourly.

Local buses run from Prien Bahnhof to the harbour in Stock. From May to September, you can also take the historic *Chiemseebahn* (1887), the world's oldest narrow-gauge steam train (€1.80/3 one way/return). Combination train/ferry tickets are also available.

Ferries operated by Chiemsee-Schifffahrt (☎ 60 90), Seestrasse 108, ply the lake every hour with stops at Herreninsel, Fraueninsel, Seebruck and Chieming on a schedule that changes seasonally. You can circumnavigate the entire lake and make all these stops (getting off and catching the next ferry that comes your way) for €9. Children aged six to 15 get a 50% discount.

CHIEMGAU

Cradled by the Chiemgauer Alps, the Chiemgau is a perfect year-round outdoor playground. Hiking, mountain biking and bicycle touring are popular activities in summer, while skiing brings in visitors during winter. Like most areas in the Bavarian Alps, the Chiemgau is dotted with *Almen*, rustic mountain restaurants serving local specialities and open mostly from May to September.

Aschau
☎ 08052 • pop 5090

About 5km south of the Chiemsee, tiny and low-key Aschau snuggles into the forested Prien Valley at the foot of the craggy Mt Kampenwand (1669m). It offers an excellent – and cheaper – alternative base to the lakeshore communities and is also home to one of Germany's top restaurants (not cheap). About 10km deeper into the valley is the mountain village **Sachrang** on the Austrian border.

Aschau's tourist office (☎ 90 49 37, fax 90 49 45, ⓔ info@aschau.de) is at Kampenwandstrasse 38, the main drag through town. From May to mid-October, it's open from 8am to 6pm Monday to Friday, 9am to noon Saturday and 10am to noon Sunday. Otherwise, it's closed at lunchtime and on weekends.

Things to See & Do The Gothic parish church is worth a look, but the main sight is the hilltop **Schloss Hohenaschau** *(tours adult/concession €2.50/1.50, includes Prientalmuseum; tours 9.30am, 10.30am & 11.30am Tues-Fri May-Sept, Thur only Apr & Oct)*. It has 12th-century origins but lost much of its medieval look during the Renaissance and baroque periods. Although now a government-owned holiday retreat, large sections – including the chapel, prison, festival halls and interior courtyard – may be visited on guided tours. Also inside is the **Prientalmuseum** *(open during*

castle tours & 1.30pm-5pm Sun Apr-Oct), which chronicles local history. From here, it's about a 15-minute walk up to the castle.

South of the castle is the valley station of the **Kampenwandbahn** *(☎ 44 11 or 906 44 20, An der Bergbahn 8; adult/child aged 5-15 €8.50/5 one way, €14/7.50 return; operates 8.30am-5pm daily May-Oct, 8.30am-5.30pm July & Aug, 9am-4.30pm Dec-Apr)*. It's a nice 15-minute gondola ride to the top, where there's a restaurant and trailheads, including a 1.5km groomed panoramic trail in winter. Skiers have 12km of pistes to play with, including the 5km valley run (all day ski passes cost €20/12.50, less if you start later in the day).

Places to Stay & Eat Aschau can accommodate up to 3200 overnight guests. Prices are very competitive and there are some very classy options.

Prillerhof (☎ 90 63 70, fax 906 37 57, Höhenbergstrasse 1) Singles €25-36, doubles €50-60. Run by an award-winning young hotelier, this is one of the most feel-good and good-value places in the region. Generously sized, the modern rooms have such luxury touches as pantry kitchen, balcony and fluffy bathrobes. A sauna, Jacuzzi and steam room invite you to relax after a day in the mountains or on the lake. There's even a guest laundry.

Gasthof zum Baumbach (☎ 957 90, fax 90 97 69, ⓔ zum-baumbach@t-online.de, Kampenwandstrasse 75) Singles/doubles €46.50/72, extra bed €16. Recently renovated rooms now sport a modern and cheerful look and feature cable TV and telephone; some have a balcony with views of Schloss Hohenaschau. The restaurant serves fresh regional cuisine, including low-fat and meat-free selections and is, along with the beer garden, a popular gathering place.

Residenz Heinz Winkler (☎ 179 90, fax 17 99 66, ⓔ info@residenz-heinz-winkler.de, Kirchplatz 1) Rooms €150-250, 2-storey suites €250-317. Heinz Winkler is one of Germany's top chefs, with three Michelin stars and numerous other awards to his credit. You can sample his supreme creations at the classically elegant Venezianisches Restaurant, part of the historic hotel, which Winkler modernised in 1989. He also runs cooking courses (from €350) throughout the year.

Getting There & Away Regional trains link Prien with Aschau hourly (€1.60, 15 minutes). From Bernau, a shuttle to Aschau and Sachrang began operation in October 2001 (Monday to Saturday only; free to overnight visitors).

Ruhpolding, Inzell & Reit im Winkl

In the eastern Chiemgau are the three classic resorts of Ruhpolding, Inzell (about 13km east), and Reit im Winkl (about 24km south-west). Tourism is the main source of income here and things can get a bit squeezy in July and August and during ski season.

The Ruhpolding Kurverwaltung (resort administration; ☎ 08663-880 60) is at Hauptstrasse 60. Inzell's tourist office (☎ 08665-988 50, fax 98 85 30) is at Rathausplatz 5 and Reit im Winkl's (☎ 08640-800 20, fax 800 29) at Rathausplatz 1.

From Ruhpolding, cables cars go to the top of the **Rauschberg** (1672m) and the **Unternberg** (1450), or you can hike up in two to three hours.

Also in Ruhpolding, the **Vita Alpina** (*☎ 08663-93 88, Brander Strasse 1; admission without/with sauna for 3 hours €9/11.50; open 9am-10pm daily*) is the local wellness complex, with wave pool, steam bath, several saunas, outdoor pool with massage jets and a 76m waterslide.

Ruhpolding's four small **museums** celebrate local heritage with exhibits on everything from bell-making to rural religious art and farming implements. The parish church **St Georg** is an onion-domed baroque affair, which shelters a precious Romanesque Madonna (in the right side altar), a frilly rococo pulpit and a modern jewelled cross.

Activities Fans of two-wheelers can look forward to **cycling** through beautiful scenery on easy to challenging routes. Classic mountain bike routes are the moderate **Chiemgau MTB Marathon**, with a 65km

and a 130km version starting in Ruhpolding; and the 45km **Reit im Winkl-Unken** tour for moderate to advanced riders. Less athletic types might prefer the **Chiemgau Radweg**, which connects the three communities via a 34km route along the valley floor past several small mountain lakes. Bicycles may be rented in all communities.

Nordic skiing is big in the Chiemgau with more than 60km of groomed trails in Ruhpolding, 30km in Inzell and 90km in Reit im Winkl. Ruhpolding, in fact, is home to the national biathlon training centre and has hosted several World Cups, the last in 2002. A nice and easy cross-country terrain is the 'Drei Seen' area between Ruhpolding and Reit im Winkl. The 30km 'Chiemgau-Marathon-Loipe' from Reit im Winkl to Inzell is a good challenge.

There's **downhill skiing** at the Unternberg, but snow levels are not always reliable at these altitudes, although if nature fails, snowmaking machines kick into gear. The Chiemgau's top ski area is the **Winklmoss-Alm/Steinplatte** (1870m) near Reit im Winkl. It's the stomping ground of Rosi Mittermaier, who won two gold medals and one silver medal at the 1976 Winter Olympic Games. Lifts usually operate from late November to mid-April with day passes at €29.50, including the bus from Seegatterl.

All three resorts have ski schools, which also rent skiing equipment, including boots, skis and poles, and also snowboards (about €8 per day).

Places to Stay & Eat There's certainly no shortage of quality private rooms and hotels, with farmhouses being a popular alternative. The Chiemgau, in fact, is the only holiday region in Bavaria that classifies farmhouses into various 'star' categories, as is often done with hotels. The tourist offices can help you to sift through the bewildering choices.

Hotel Europa (☎ 08663-880 40, fax 88 04 49, Obergschwendter Strasse 17, Ruhpolding) Rooms €30-50. Here you'll find newly renovated, modern rooms with all amenities, some with balcony. It also has an indoor pool with sauna.

Gasthof Hirschbichler (☎ *08665-555, fax 60 38, Traunsteiner Strasse 25, Inzell)* Singles/doubles €23/46. Large rooms, a central location and a good-value restaurant with its own butcher shop are the main assets of this friendly place.

Hotel Pension Edelweiss (☎ *08640-988 90, fax 98 89 40, Am Grünbühel 1, Reit im Winkl)* Singles/doubles from €28/45. In a quiet yet central location, this is a family-friendly charmer with Bavarian country-style rooms and a sunny terrace.

Getting There & Around If you're travelling by train from Munich, change in Traunstein (€17.80, two hours). Ruhpolding, Inzell and Reit im Winkl are all connected by regional bus No 9506 with several departures throughout the day. Bus No 9505 travels from Prien am Chiemsee to Reit im Winkl via Bernau. Bus No 9526 goes to Bad Reichenhall from Inzell.

Bad Reichenhall
☎ 08651 • pop 18,100 • elevation 471m
Bad Reichenhall, on the River Saalach, is marooned at the foot of the Berchtesgadener and Chiemgauer Alps. Its history and prosperity has quite literally been built on salt, which has been harvested from the underground mines since Roman times. To this day, Bad Reichenhall is the largest supplier of table salt in Germany as well as a famous spa town thanks to its richly concentrated saline springs. It's equidistant (about 20km) to Berchtesgaden and Salzburg (see later in this chapter), and is a good alternative base for outdoor and cultural explorations.

Orientation & Information Bad Reichenhall's Altstadt is compact but the town itself is quite sprawling. The Hauptbahnhof is a short walk east of the historic centre, with the pedestrianised Ludwigstrasse as the main drag. The tourist office (☎ 60 60, fax 60 61 25), at Wittelsbacher Strasse 15, is open 8am to 5.30pm Monday to Friday (until 5pm November to March) and 9am to noon Saturday (also 9am to noon Sunday, May to September).

There's a Sparkasse at Bahnhofstrasse 17 and a Volksbank at Ludwigstrasse 3. Post office branches are at the Hauptbahnhof and on Rathausplatz. There's even an Internet cafe (☎ 77 00 00) in Getreidegasse 9 (closed Sunday). The town's Web site (W www.bad -reichenhall.de) has sections in English. There's a coin-operated laundry (☎ 39 83) with limited hours at Tiroler Strasse 1.

Walking Tour This tour starts at the Hauptbahnhof and takes in all the main sights in the Altstadt. Turning right on Bahnhofstrasse will soon get you to the tourist office on your right and the **Kurpark** *(open 7am-10pm daily Apr-Oct, 7am-6pm daily Nov-Mar; admission free except during concerts)*, the town's historic spa gardens, on your left.

Enter the gardens, which are anchored by the neobaroque **Kurhaus** on the east (right) side. The bizarre structure on your left is the **Gradierwerk**, an open-air inhalatorium, which benefits people with respiratory problems. The walls of this 170m-long and 14m-high rectangular structure are covered with up to 250,000 blackthorn twigs. These are constantly drizzled with saline spring water, which creates a mist inhaled by people meandering slowly beneath a covered ambulatory. The Gradierwerk has been around since 1912 and is usually in operation from April to October.

Also in the park is the **Wandelhalle**, site of year-round concerts by the 40-head Philharmonisches Orchester *(tickets & information ☎ 86 61; adult/concession €5/2.50, Kurkarte holders free; concerts Tues-Sun)*. In summer, concerts sometimes move to the Kurpark's outdoor pavilion.

Exit the spa gardens onto Salzburger Strasse. Church fans might want to turn left for a detour to the **Church of St Zeno**, about 500m away. It's a three-nave Gothic church, whose Romanesque origins are best in evidence in the fantastic ribbed entrance portal with its vividly sculpted tympanum. Inside, the pulpit, baptismal font and choir stalls, all from around 1520, bear closer inspection.

Otherwise, turn right as you exit the Kurpark and follow Salzburger Strasse to

Ludwigstrasse where you'll soon come upon the famous *Cafe Reber*. Its red awnings and phalanx of flags scream 'tourist trap', but it's actually not a bad place for a coffee and cake break. Or else just sample the local version of the *Mozartkugel*, a chocolate confection with a nougat and pistachio centre (the original hails from Salzburg). In a little square next to the cafe is a cutesy sculpture of Mozart and his wife Constanze.

Continue along Ludwigstrasse to **Alte Saline & Salzmuseum** *(Old Salt Works & Salt Museum; ☎ 700 21 46; adult/concession €4.50/2.50; open 10am-11.30pm & 2pm-4pm daily Apr-Oct, 2pm-6pm Tues & Thur Nov-Mar)*. A fire destroyed the original 16th-century salt works in 1834, but King Ludwig I had it subsequently rebuilt. Guided 45-minute tours (in German) lead you through a network of underground tunnels and bring you face to face with ancient water wheels and pumps. Afterwards, you're free to broaden your knowledge about the 'white gold' (ie, salt) in the museum.

Conclude your tour on Rathausplatz, a few steps south of the Alte Saline and visually dominated by the **Alte Rathaus**. Built in 1849, it's decorated with frescoes depicting Charlemagne, St Rupert, Friedrich Barbarossa and Ludwig I. To get back to the Hauptbahnhof, head west on Poststrasse, which merges with Bahnhofstrasse.

Activities Bad Reichenhall offers the full spectrum of outdoor activities. There are many easy **hiking** trails starting in town, but for a more challenging foray, head up Mt Hochstaufen (1771m) north of the town. The climb to the top takes about three hours from the Padinger Alm, a mountain restaurant (☎ 44 39, closed Mon) at 667m.

South of town, a cable car scales the 1613m **Predigtstuhl** *(☎ 21 27; one way/return €8.70/13.80; operates 9am-5pm at least hourly year round)*. The valley station is on Südtiroler Platz in the southern suburb of Kirchberg (bus No 1). There's a restaurant at the top as well as numerous trailheads.

The local chapter of the Deutscher Alpenverein (☎ 37 31) is based at Sport-Rehrl, Innsbrucker Strasse 16.

Club Aktiv (☎ 672 38), Frühlingstrasse 61, and Sport Müller (☎ 37 76), Spitalgasse 3, are outfitters that can organise various outdoor activities, including mountain biking, canyoning, skiing and mountain climbing.

Places to Stay Prices listed here are for rooms with private bath and include Kurtaxe.

Pension Schwarzenbach (☎ 44 72, fax 665 72, Nonn 91) Singles/doubles from €20/40. Your charming hosts at this lovely pension, with terrific views of the town and the mountains, work hard to make you feel at home. Several hikes start right outside the door.

Hotel Eisenrieth (☎ 96 10, fax 96 11 69, e eisenrieth@hotel-aurora.de, Luitpold-strasse 23) Singles/doubles from €30/40. You can be sure to get a good night's sleep at this quiet and peaceful hotel in the spa district. Many rooms are balconied. The owners speak both English and French.

Hotel Garni Moll (☎ 986 80, fax 98 68 44, e rafting@t-online.de, Frühlingstrasse 61) Singles/doubles €36/66. This place offers comfortable and friendly digs with cable TV and direct-dial phones. It has separate breakfast rooms for smokers and non-smokers as well as an in-house 'wellness area' and bicycle rental. The owners also operate the outdoor outfitter Club Aktiv.

Hotel Neu-Meran (☎ 40 78, fax 785 20, Nonn 94) Singles €45-75, doubles €90-150. This is among Bad Reichenhall's most stylish places, with beautifully furnished sunny rooms, a top-notch chef in the kitchen and a fitness centre with indoor pool, sauna, steam room and small gym.

Places to Eat There is a fair range of restaurants in town.

Bürgerbräu (☎ 60 89, Waaggasse 2) Mains €6-11. Right next to the Rathaus, everything about this traditional Bavarian beer hall is big, including the menu and the portions and, hopefully, your appetite. Each of the rooms has a different ceiling (eg, coffered, vaulted).

Cafe Reber (☎ 600 31 74, Ludwigstrasse 10) Mains €6-10. Open 9am-6pm. This famous coffee-and-cake cafe also serves a few hot dishes at lunchtime.

Piccolino (☎ *98 43 43, Schachtstrasse 2*) Mains €9-16. Open noon-2pm & 6pm-10.30pm, closed Sat lunch & Sun. This pint-sized Tuscan-style bistro is run by a delightful couple (he cooks, she serves) and offers a small menu of freshly prepared, seasonal cuisine.

Schwabenbräu (☎ *969 50, Salzburger Strasse 22*) Brotzeit €2-5, mains €7-10, dinner buffet €7. For a cold snack or casual meal (from salads to roasts), come to this convivial place with a young clientele and a small beer garden.

The local *Nordsee* fish Imbiss is at Ludwigstrasse 16, with a *Kochlöffel* right next door.

Getting There & Around RB trains to/from Berchtesgaden depart hourly (€3.10, 30 minutes). Trains to Salzburg require a change in Freilassing (€4, 40 minutes). Regional buses Nos 9527 and 9528 travel straight to Salzburg's Mirabellplatz several times daily (30 to 45 minutes). Bus No 9526 goes to Inzell in the Chiemgau.

Bad Reichenhall is served by an extensive bus network. Pick up a map at the tourist office.

BERCHTESGADENER LAND
☎ 08652 • pop 8200 • elevation 550

A mere 25km south of Salzburg, Berchtesgadener Land (which turned 900 in 2002) is a self-contained universe of wooded hilltops and valleys framed by six formidable mountain ranges. Germany's second-highest mountain, the Watzmann (2713m), holds court over crystalline lakes, rushing streams, dainty church steeples, and the five communities of the Berchtesgadener Land: Berchtesgaden, Bischofswiesen, Ramsau, Marktschellenberg and Schönau am Königssee.

About half of the terrain is protected within the Nationalpark Berchtesgaden, which offers wonderful hiking and other outdoor opportunities. The park is also home to the pristine Königssee, Germany's highest lake at 603m. In summer, a major draw is the Eagle's Nest, a mountaintop lodge built by the Nazis who had

their southern headquarters at nearby Obersalzberg. This dark chapter of local history is superbly chronicled in the new Dokumentation Obersalzberg exhibit (see later in this section).

History
In word, paintings and song, the great natural beauty of Berchtesgaden has been celebrated for centuries. Such accolades are impressive for a region that actually struck terror into its first settlers. In the early 1100s, a band of Augustinian monks was sent here to establish a monastery. They found a land so wild and inhospitable that they suspected dragons might inhabit it. Their worst fears seemed justified when, one dark winter night, an apocalyptic thunderstorm tore the roofs off their cottages and barraged the valley floor with boulders in violent landslides. Panicked, the brothers fled this godforsaken enclave, seeking shelter in a neighbouring cell. Their archbishop, though, would have none of this dragon business and ordered the wayward monks to return to Berchtesgaden.

A monastery was finally completed in 1122, and the region began to thrive thereafter. Salt and wood soon became the foundation of its wealth and the envy of its neighbours. In fact, well-documented 'salt wars' between Salzburg and Berchtesgaden over mining rights took place during much of the Middle Ages.

In the 16th century, Berchtesgaden became a sovereign state within the Holy Roman Empire, ruled by a prince-abbot until 1810 when it became part of the Kingdom of Bavaria. To its great chagrin today, Berchtesgaden played a pivotal role in the Third Reich. For more information, see the boxed text 'Hitler's Mountain Retreat'.

Orientation & Information
The main community in the Berchtesgadener Land is the town of Berchesgaden, where you'll find the Hauptbahnhof and the central bus station as well as most hotels, restaurants and the main tourist office branch. About 5km south of town is the Königssee community of Schönau, while the Obersalzberg

BERCHTESGADENER LAND

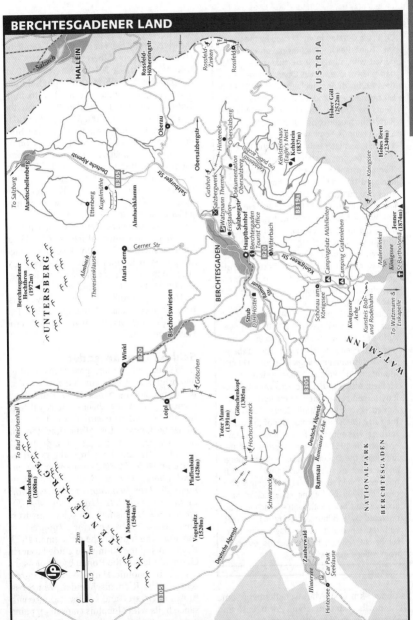

Hitler's Mountain Retreat

Of all the German towns tainted by the pall of the Third Reich, Berchtesgaden has been cursed with a larger share than most. Hitler had fallen in love with its Obersalzberg area in the 1920s during his visits with Dietrich Eckardt, a friend and leading member of the Deutsche Arbeiter Partei (German Workers Party), the precursor of the NSDAP. Hitler kept a small country home here starting in the late 1920s; it was later enlarged into the Berghof.

After becoming chancellor in 1933, the 'Führer' established part-time headquarters here and brought the party brass with him. They bought or confiscated over 32 sq km of land, tore down ancient farmhouses, erected a 2m-high barbed-wire fence, built guardhouses along the three access roads, and eventually turned the Obersalzberg into the fortified, southern headquarters of the NSDAP. It was here where, in 1938, Hitler hosted British prime minister Neville Chamberlain to kick off 'negotiations' that paved the way for the Nazi takeover of Czechoslovakia.

Little is left of Hitler's 'Alpine Fortress' today. In the final days of WWII, the Royal Airforce dropped 1243 bombs in a 90-minute raid that levelled much of the Obersalzberg. The Kehlsteinhaus Eagle's Nest, Hitler's mountaintop eyrie, was left strangely unscathed. After the war, the occupying US military turned part of the mountainside into an Armed Forces Recreation Center (closed in the early 1990s). The remainder of the Obersalzberg was returned to the Bavarian government in 1952. To learn more about the area, visit the Dokumentation Obersalzberg, an excellent exhibit opened in 1999, which has been a wild success, far exceeding visitor projections. Plans for the construction of a luxury resort nearby, though – which is to be operated by a British company – have met with resistance and controversy. Seems that, for Berchtesgaden, there's just no escaping from Hitler's shadow.

The tourist office (☎ 96 70, fax 96 74 00, e info@berchtesgaden.de), is just across the river from the Hauptbahnhof (built by Hitler's architect Albert Speer in 1937) at Königsseer Strasse 2. It's open from 8.30am to 6pm Monday to Friday, till 5pm Saturday and till 3pm Sunday from May to mid-October. During the rest of the year, the hours are 8.30am to 5pm Monday to Friday and till noon on Saturday; it's closed Sunday. The tourist office operates a free booking service and there's also an electronic room reservation board out front. The daily Kurtaxe (resort tax) for overnight guests ranges from €1.25 to €1.75. The region has a decent Web site at W www.berchtesgadener-land.com (also in English).

The Nationalpark Berchtesgaden has an excellent information office (☎ 643 43) at Franziskanerplatz 7 in Berchtesgaden, which is open 9am to 5pm Monday to Saturday. Additional branches are in Schönau, Ramsau and on St Bartholomä peninsula.

To change money, try the Hypovereinsbank at Weihnachtsschützenplatz 2½. The post office and bus station are located at the Hauptbahnhof.

Schloss Berchtesgaden

In the heart of Berchtesgaden, the Schloss has origins as a convent and residence of the prince-abbots. Since 1810, it has been owned by the Wittelsbachs, the royal family of Bavaria, who still throw the occasional bash here. Most of the time, though, the only people traipsing through its hallowed halls are here for the **Schlossmuseum** (☎ 94 79 80, Schlossplatz 2; tours adult/concession €7/3.50; tours 10am-noon & 2pm-4pm Sun-Fri Whitsuntide/Pentecost–mid-Oct, 11am-2pm Mon-Fri otherwise). On display are selections from the treasures of Crown Prince Rupprecht of Bavaria, who founded the museum in 1923. Highlights of the 50-minute guided tour (in German) include the Romanesque cloisters (1180); the Gothic Hall (1400) with great sculpture by Riemenschneider, Veit Stoss, Erasmus Grasser and others; two Renaissance halls with Gobelins (tapestry), paintings and reliefs; and a still functioning

is about 4km east, Marktschellenberg some 9km north, Ramsau about 9km east and Bischofswiesen 5km north-west.

16th-century kitchen. Finish up with a spin around the **Rosengarten** with great views of the Watzmann massif.

Stiftskirche

Adjacent to the Schloss, the Stiftskirche is the former convent church. The interior is largely Gothic, with only the western vestibule and parts of the sidewalls surviving from the Romanesque original. It's filled with riches, notably the marble epitaphs of the prince-abbots, the rococo tabernacle and the Gothic choir stalls.

Salzbergwerk

Berchtesgaden's past as a salt-mining metropolis is recalled during an entertaining tour of the Salzbergwerk *(salt mines; ☎ 60 02 20, Bergwerkstrasse 83; adult/concession/child €11.25/9.75/6.15; tours 9am-5pm daily May–mid-Oct, 12.30pm-3.30pm Mon-Sat mid-Oct–Apr)*. Change into protective miners' gear before boarding a miniature train and rumbling into the chill and blackness of this underground world. Next, you'll be descending further into the depths of the mine by whooshing down a wooden slide. Other highlights of the 90-minute tour include mysteriously glowing salt grottos and the crossing of a 100m-long subterranean salt lake.

Kehlsteinhaus (Eagle's Nest)

Picture this: a hair-raising, 4m-wide road covering an elevation gain of 750m in 6.5km making only one hairpin turn! Carved straight into the mountain, the road rises at a 27% grade before delivering you at a marble-lined, 124m-long tunnel drilled into the solid rock. A brass-clad lift (elevator) then rockets up the same distance vertically, taking you straight to the Kehlsteinhaus, one of the most sinister, yet most exhilarating places in the Berchtesgadener Land.

In 1939, Hitler henchman Martin Bormann engaged 3000 workers to build the road to this mountaintop lodge – in just 13 months – as a gift for the Führer's 50th birthday. Here at 1834m, you'll be presented with one of the world's greatest panoramas.

It's a view that – because of its beauty, thin air, and the audacity of the engineering that made it possible – will quite literally leave you breathless. Ironically, Hitler himself is said to have suffered from vertigo and rarely enjoyed the place. Nowadays, the lodge contains a *restaurant* (☎ 29 69) which donates its profits to charity.

From May to October, the Kehlsteinhaus is open to visitors. Special buses make the 35-minute trip up the mountain from the car park at Hintereck, reached either by private vehicle (parking €2.50) or by public bus No 9549 from the Postamt stop in Berchtesgaden (€3.70 return). Buses from Hintereck to the Kehlsteinhaus operate from 7.40am to 4.25pm daily. The trip, including the elevator ride and admission to the lodge, is €12/7 adult/child aged 4 to 12.

Dokumentation Obersalzberg

Obersalzberg's stint as the southern headquarters of Hitler's Nazi regime is given the full historical treatment at the fascinating Dokumentation Obersalzberg *(☎ 94 79 60, Salzbergstrasse 41; adult/concession €2.50/ free; open 9am-5pm Tues-Sun May-Oct, 10am-3pm Tues-Sun Nov-Apr)*. Don't miss this comprehensive exhibit, which chronicles the forced takeover of the area, the construction of the compound and the daily life of the Nazi elite at Obersalzberg. It goes on to illuminate all facets of the Nazi terror regime, including Hitler's near-mythical appeal, his racial politics, the resistance movement, foreign policy and the death camps. The self-guided tour ends with a visit of a small section of the underground bunker network, where you can watch some gruesome footage underscoring the full extent of the atrocities committed during those 12 years of terror.

To get there, take bus No 9538 to Dokumentation from Berchtesgaden.

Königssee

Framed by steep mountain walls bristling with conifers, the beautiful Königssee (King's Lake) lies like a misplaced fjord 5km south of Berchtesgaden proper in the community of Schönau. Formed by tectonic forces, this pristine lake – 8km long, up to a 1.5km wide and about 200m deep – has clear, emerald water that is actually of drinking quality.

Make a beeline past the bustling tourist village that stretches from car park to lakeshore for a nice and easy 3.5km (return) walk to the secluded **Malerwinkel** (Painter's Corner), a lookout point famed for its picturesque perspective of the lake.

From here you can spy **St Bartholomä**, a romantic onion-domed chapel built on the edge of a peninsula jutting into the lake. It dates back to 1134, but was prettied up with baroque flourishes in the 17th century.

Bayerische Seenschifffahrt (☎ 96 36 18) operates **electric motorboat tours** (€12.50) year round to the peninsula (except when the lake ices over, of course). Boats glide past a statue of St Nepomuk; a cliff where more than 70 pilgrims drowned in 1688; and a waterfall. The much anticipated highlight is the famous **Königssee echo**: The boat stops, a hush falls and the captain hoists his horn and trumpets. And then you hear it – the sevenfold echo rebounding from the cliffs of the Watzmann and the surrounding peaks. It's a reliable performance (except during heavy fog), which apparently has met with failure only once. A few years ago, some yokels hid in the mountain ridges and greatly embarrassed the humourless captain by bleating out a different tune. The incident was such an assault on his dignity that he took the offenders to court!

In the valley, about one hour's hike from the dock at St Bartholomä, is the **Eiskapelle**.

As snow gathers in the corner of the rocks here, a dome emerges that reaches heights of over 200m. In summer as the ice melts, the water digs tunnels and creates a huge opening in the solid ice.

Hiking

You haven't truly experienced the beauty of Berchtesgaden until you've ventured into its nature. The wilds of the 210-sq-km **Nationalpark Berchtesgaden** unquestionably offer some of the best hiking in Germany. A dense network of trails crisscrosses diverse landscapes, from placid lakeshores to craggy peaks, scenic valleys to lush mountain meadows. There are short hikes and multi-day treks, easy rambles and those requiring special equipment, busy trails and others where you'll encounter nary a soul.

We've outlined a couple of hikes below, but for more suggestions start by consulting the brochure *Berg + Tal* (Hill + Dale) published by the Berchtesgaden tourist office. Maps are available here as well as at the Nationalpark information offices, whose knowledgeable staff is really the best source all around.

Another option is the local Alpenverein (☎ 22 07), which has an office at Maximilianstrasse 1, but it's open only from 3pm to 5pm Tuesday and Thursday and until 5.30pm Friday. Outdoor-Club Berchtesgaden (☎ 50 01), at Gmundberg 7, one of the best local outfitters, organises guided hikes from one day to one week, including a climb of Mt Watzmann.

The Magnetism of Mt Watzmann

The placid and serene meadows surrounding St Bartholomä stand in stark contrast to the 1800m of grey massif soaring behind it – the mythical Mt Watzmann. Legend has it that the two big and seven smaller peaks represent a sadistic king, his queen and their children who, after terrorising the land for years, morphed into stone as punishment for their cruelty. 'King' Watzmann, the middle peak, rises to an elevation of almost 2700m and marks the highest point of the park. Its eastern face ranks as one of the most dangerous climbs in the Alpine region. More than 100 people have lost their lives attempting climbs since the peak was first scaled in 1881. Most accidents are caused by rocks, which, dislodged from the unstable limestone, crash down on vulnerable climbers below. This climb should only be attempted by the very experienced and preferably in the company of a skilled mountain guide.

Zauberwald This is an easy 1.5km hike along the shores of the idyllic Hintersee lake, just west of Ramsau, where rowing boats share the water with wild ducks. The trail continues through the 'Magic Forest' where huge boulders are piled in a haphazard fashion along the creek. It starts at the car park Seeklause and should take no more than one to 1½ hours of leisurely walking time. May to July are the nicest months.

Almbachklamm A moderate 8.5km hike takes you through the dramatic Almbach gorge (adult/concession €2/1), which offers terrific views of the rushing stream, pools and waterfalls. It starts at the **Kugelmühle**, Germany's oldest still functioning marble mill (1683), located just west of B305 near Marktschellenberg, and slowly climbs up to the dam at Theresienklause. From here, it spills out into a lovely valley, which leads to the village of Ettenberg with its pilgrimage church. This is a good spot for a picnic or a Brotzeit before heading down a steepish trail back to Marktschellenberg. This hike has an elevation gain of 320m and will take about three hours (walking time only). The best time to do this hike is between May and October.

Skiing

Skiing conditions, especially for downhill, in the Berchtesgadener Land are not as reliable as in Alpine resorts such as Garmisch-Partenkirchen, but snowmaking equipment does its part in stretching the season.

There are five ski areas with about 50km of pistes, plenty of ski schools and outfitters. Five-day ski passes good for all lifts are €100/60 adult/child aged six to 14. There are also about 60km of groomed Nordic tracks. For snow conditions, call ☎ 96 72 97.

The **Götschen** (880m to 1307m) is the training centre of the German women's skiing team as well as popular snowboarding terrain. Local youths especially like the evening skiing when slopes are flooded with lights and music.

Day passes are about €20/15 here and in the **Jenner-Königssee** area (630m to 1800m), which is the biggest of the ski

fields and suitable for more experienced skiers.

Good family playgrounds are **Gutshof** (900m to 1050m) in the Obersalzberg area and **Rossfeld-Zinken** (835m to 1550m) on the border with Austria, which has a separate snowboarding piste with half-pipe. Day passes, which include the trip on the local bus and toll fees, cost €17/11.

Finally, there's the **Hochschwarzeck** (1030m to 1385m), where a tobogganing track is among the attractions.

Other Winter Sports

A big hit with speed freaks is the **Kunsteis Bob- und Rodelbahn** (☎ 96 70 or 17 60) in Schönau. It's a 1.3km-long ice canal with an 11% incline and 18 curves, including a full loop. You can go down in a 'guest' bob or get to speeds of up to 120km/h by co-piloting with a professional racer in a four-person racing bob, although at €77 per person, it's an expensive thrill.

There is **ice skating** available at the **Eisstadion** (☎ 614 05, An der Schiessstätte; adult/concession per session €3/1.25), or you could head out to the Hintersee, which is usually frozen in winter. **Hikers** will find 120km of well-groomed trails.

Watzmann Therme

This is Berchtesgaden's new thermal wellness-and-fun pool complex (☎ 946 40, Bergwerkstrasse 54; tickets 2hrs/4hrs/all day €7.50/10/14; open 10am-10pm daily). It has several indoor and outdoor pools with various hydro-therapeutic treatment stations and fabulous Alpine views, as well as saunas.

Organised Tours

If you want to experience the creepy legacy of the entire Obersalzberg area, including the Kehlsteinhaus, on a guided tour, link up with **Berchtesgaden Mini Bus Tours** (☎ 649 71 or 621 72). Its four-hour English-language tour offers tremendous value at €30 per person. Buses depart from the tourist office at 8.30am and 1.30pm daily between mid-May and October. Tours are limited to eight people, so reservations are advised.

Places to Stay

Berchtesgaden has plenty of *private rooms* from €15 per person. Check with the tourist office about availability.

Camping Of the five camping grounds in the Berchtesgadener Land, the nicest are near the Königssee in Schönau village.

Campingplatz Mühlleiten (☎ 45 84, fax 691 94, e buchung@camping-muehlleiten .de, Königsseer Strasse 70) Bus: No 9541 to Schusterlehen. Site/person €5.10/4.35. Run by a young outdoor enthusiast, this camping ground has new facilities and a central, sunny location. It also offers bed and breakfast in an attached pension at €25 per person.

Camping Grafenlehen (☎ 41 40, fax 69 07 68, e camping-grafenlehen@t-online .de, Königsseer Fussweg 71) Bus: No 9541 to Königssee. Site/person €5.60/4.35. Five minutes from the lake, this camping ground counts a laundry, restaurant and store among its facilities.

Hostels There is only one DJH hostel.

DJH hostel (☎ 943 70, fax 94 37 37, e jhberchtesgaden@djh-bayern.de, Gebirgsjägerstrasse 52) Bus: No 9539 to Jugendherberge. Bed & breakfast €12.25. Closed Nov-late Dec. This 360-bed hostel is in the suburb of Strub and has views of Mt Watzmann. It's a 25-minute walk from the Hauptbahnhof or a short bus ride.

Hotels Hotels in the region include:

Gästehaus Alpina (☎ 25 17, fax 21 10, Ramsauer Strasse 6) Rooms €40-46. Closed Nov–mid-Dec. A five-minute walk from the station, this guesthouse's rooms have Alpine views; pretty basic as far as amenities go.

Hotel Floriani (☎ 660 11, fax 634 53, e hotel_floriani@t-online.de, Königsseer Strasse 37) Rooms €48-77.50. Near the station, this hotel's rooms are furnished in contemporary country style with private bath, cable and minibar; some rooms have balconies.

Hotel-Pension Greti (☎ 946 50, fax 94 65 30, e info@pension-greti.de, Waldhauserstrasse 20) Rooms €40-68. In Schönau, the Greti is a 15-minute walk from the Königssee and has well-appointed rooms, all with bath and balcony.

Pension Haus am Berg (☎ 949 20, fax 94 92 30, e pension.hausamberg@t-online.de, Am Brandholz 9) Rooms €39-58. This pension is only 10 minutes' walk from the station but has great valley views.

Hotel Rosenbichl (☎ 944 00, fax 94 40 40, e hotel.rosenbichl@t-online.de, Rosenhofweg 24) Rooms €60-90. This hotel in the middle of the protected nature zone is exceptional value, and nonsmokers will find solace here. It also has a sauna, whirlpool, solarium and a fitness program.

Hotel Vier Jahreszeiten (☎ 95 20, fax 50 29, e millers-hotel@t-online.de, Maximilianstrasse 20) Singles €40-75, doubles €80-130. Close to the centre, this traditional hotel has panoramic views of the Alps, and a good restaurant (see Places to Eat).

Places to Eat

Between April and October there's a good weekly *market* at Marktplatz on Friday from 8am to 11am, with an incredible array of fresh produce and meats.

Bräustübl (☎ 14 23, Bräuhausstrasse 13) Mains €5-15. This is a huge beer hall that caters to carnivores and puts on a heel-whacking Bavarian stage show every Saturday night.

Express Grill (☎ 23 21, Maximilianstrasse 8) Meals €1.50-3.50. Open 11am-8pm. For a quick bite, this greasy spoon will do in a pinch. Half-chickens go for €3.20, burgers from €1.75 and baked potatoes for €2.

Hubertusstube (☎ 95 20, Maximilianstrasse 20) Brotzeit €5-10, mains €10-17.50. Part of the Hotel Vier Jahreszeiten, this formal restaurant ranks among the town's best. The chef's finest work is with meaty fare, especially venison and sirloin steak. The small vegetarian menu lacks imagination.

Gasthaus Bier-Adam (☎ 23 90, Markt 22) Mains €8-16. Look for the pretty facade with *Lüftlmalerei* (trompe l'oeil) and you've found one of the most popular restaurants in town. The kitchen churns out a good range of traditional fare to suit all budgets, and it has a nice dark beer and cheerful service.

Gasthaus Neuhaus (☎ *21 82, Marktplatz 1)* Mains €4.35-13. Enjoy old-style Bavarian cuisine – sometimes to the sound of folk music – in the cosy dining room, on the nifty terrace or in the beer garden. The best deal is the set three-course dinner for €8.50. Vegetarians have about a dozen dishes from which to choose.

Grassl's Bistro-Cafe (☎ *25 24, Maximilianstrasse 11)* Mains €3-7.50. Open 9am-6pm Mon-Sat. This is an ideal spot for lunch among all those cute porcelain jugs, with tasty soups, sandwiches and daily specials.

Cafe Grassl (☎ *22 80, Maximilianstrasse 15)* Meals €2.50-7.50. Open 8am-6pm Mon-Sat. This affiliated cafe has snacks too but caters mostly to the afternoon coffee-and-cake crowd, which fills tables behind large panorama windows offering mountain views. On sunny days, the action moves to the terrace.

s' Platzl (☎ *69 06 87, Nonntal 8)* Mains €8.50-10. Floral curtains, fresh flowers and rustic furniture create the modern country flair of this gem of a restaurant. The kitchen produces modern cuisine with a Mediterranean touch using only fresh ingredients. There's a long list of wines by the glass to complement the food. Platzl is small, so reservations are advised.

Holzkäfer (☎ *621 07, Buchenhöhe 40)* Meals €3.50-8. Open 5pm-1am Mon-Sat. If you're motorised, check this funky log-cabin restaurant in the Obersalzberg hills. Crammed with antlers, carvings and backwoods oddities, it's great for an evening drink with the locals or a light meal.

Getting There & Away

Coming from Munich requires a change at Freilassing (€24, 2¾ hours). There are direct trains from Salzburg (€6.30, one hour), although the RVO bus No 9540 makes the trip in about 45 minutes and has more departures. Berchtesgaden is south of the Munich-Salzburg A8 autobahn on the B20 and B305.

Getting Around

The various communities of the Berchtesgadener Land are well connected by RVO bus (☎ 94 48 20); pick up a detailed schedule at the tourist offices. Central stops include the Busbahnhof at the train station and the Kurhaus on Bahnhofstrasse. To get to the Königssee, take bus No 9541 or 9542. Bus No 9538 goes to the Obersalzberg, No 9546 to Ramsau and the Hintersee, and Nos 9536 and 9540 to Marktschellenberg.

Look into whether the RVO-Tagesticket (day pass; €6.50) works out cheaper than buying individual tickets. If you're spending an extended period in the area, consider the Berchtesgadener Urlaubsticket (Berchtesgaden Holiday Ticket; €13.50), which is good for unlimited trips on five consecutive days and available from the tourist office.

SALZBURG
☎ 0043-662 (in Germany), 0662 (in Austria, but outside of Salzburg) • pop 144,000

Salzburg, right across the border in Austria, is in a breathtaking setting and brims with magnificent architectural treasures. The baroque spires of the Altstadt, with the Festung Hohensalzburg as a backdrop, are a most memorable sight. The entire old town has been a Unesco World Cultural Heritage Site since 1997.

But aside from pretty buildings, much of Salzburg's magnetism can be explained with the drop of a single name: Mozart. Born here in 1756, the composer did not receive much encouragement from the city in his lifetime, though you wouldn't know it from walking around today.

You'll soon find Mozartplatz with a Mozart statue, the Mozarteum music academy, museums in Mozart's birthplace and later residence, and *Mozartkugeln,* a chocolate confection (sometimes unwittingly translated as 'Mozart's Balls').

Salzburg gets another wave of visitors, mostly from English-speaking countries, for a rather different musical genre: in 1964, the city and nearby hills were alive to the filming of *The Sound of Music.*

We've included Salzburg in this guide because of its close ties to Bavarian history but also because of its proximity to and easy access from major Bavarian cities, especially Munich, the Chiemsee towns and nearby Berchtesgaden and Bad Reichenhall.

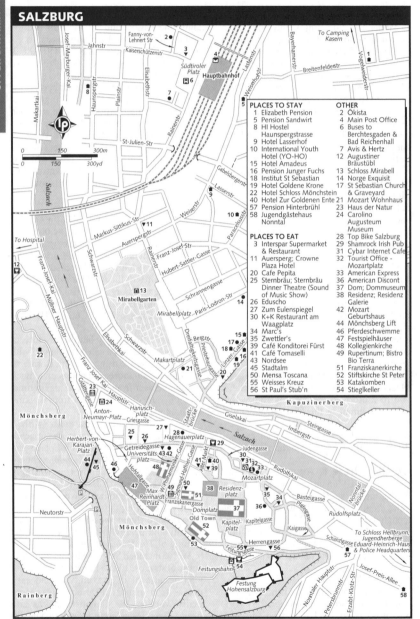

SALZBURG

PLACES TO STAY
1 Elizabeth Pension
5 Pension Sandwirt
8 HI Hostel Haunspergstrasse
9 Hotel Lasserhof
10 International Youth Hotel (YO-HO)
15 Hotel Amadeus
16 Pension Junger Fuchs
18 Institut St Sebastian
19 Hotel Goldene Krone
22 Hotel Schloss Mönchstein
40 Hotel Zur Goldenen Ente
57 Pension Hinterbrühl
58 Jugendgästehaus Nonntal

PLACES TO EAT
3 Interspar Supermarket & Restaurant
11 Auersperg; Crowne Plaza Hotel
20 Café Pepita
25 Sternbräu; Sternbräu Dinner Theatre (Sound of Music Show)
26 Eduscho
27 Zum Eulenspiegel
30 K+K Restaurant am Waagplatz
34 Marc's
35 Zwettler's
39 Café Konditorei Fürst
41 Café Tomaselli
43 Nordsee
45 Stadtalm
50 Mensa Toscana
55 Weisses Kreuz
56 St Paul's Stub'n

OTHER
2 Ökista
4 Main Post Office
6 Buses to Berchtesgaden & Bad Reichenhall
7 Avis & Hertz
12 Augustiner Bräustübl
13 Schloss Mirabell
14 Norge Exquisit
17 St Sebastian Church & Graveyard
21 Mozart Wohnhaus
23 Haus der Natur
24 Carolino Augusteum Museum
28 Top Bike Salzburg
29 Shamrock Irish Pub
31 Cybar Internet Café
32 Tourist Office - Mozartplatz
33 American Express
36 American Discont
37 Dom; Dommuseum
38 Residenz; Residenz Galerie
42 Mozart Geburtshaus
44 Mönchsberg Lift
46 Pferdeschwemme
47 Festspielhäuser
48 Kollegienkirche
49 Rupertinum; Bistro Bio Terra
51 Franziskanerkirche
52 Stiftskirche St Peter
53 Katakomben
54 Stieglkeller

History

Salzburg was the chief town in the region as far back as Roman times. In about 696, St Rupert established a bishopric here. In the 13th century, the local bishops were promoted to prince-archbishops, meaning they had both religious and secular powers over a territory that stretched into Bavaria and as far as Italy. They derived much of their economic strength from mining – of gold, certainly, but even more so of salt, the so-called 'white gold'.

Wolf Dietrich von Raitenau (1587–1612), one of Salzburg's most influential prince-archbishops, initiated Salzburg's makeover into a baroque city. However, an unsuccessful dispute with powerful Bavaria over the salt trade led to his imprisonment, during which he 'conveniently' died.

One of his successors, Paris Lodron (1619–53), managed to keep the principality out of the Thirty Years' War. Salzburg also remained neutral during the War of the Austrian Succession a century later, but by then its power and prosperity was dwindling. During the Napoleonic wars, France and Bavaria briefly controlled Salzburg before it became part of Austria in 1816.

Orientation

The Salzach River bisects Salzburg's centre. The old town (mostly a pedestrian precinct) is on the left (south) bank; it's lorded over by the hilltop fortress – the Festung Hohensalzburg – and home to most of the attractions. The new town and business districts are on the right (northern) bank, along with most of the cheaper hotels. Mirabellplatz, on the right bank, is a hub for public and tour buses. The Hauptbahnhof is about 1km north of Mirabellplatz.

Information

Tourist Offices Salzburg has six tourist office branches, including one at the airport and three on the outskirts near autobahn exits and major highways (open April to October only).

Most useful are the branches at the Hauptbahnhof and in the Altstadt. The former (☎ 88 98 73 40) is a tiny and usually packed office on platform 2a; it's open from 8.45am

to 7.45pm daily year round. The much larger Altstadt branch (☎ 88 98 73 30) is at Mozartplatz 7 with hours from 9am to 6pm (closed Sunday, October to April). In July and August, it's open until 7pm. The regional information office (☎ 84 32 64), in the same building, is open 9am to 5.30pm Monday to Friday and 9.30am to 3.30pm Saturday.

All tourist offices sell a city map for €1, although you could just as easily make do with the free *Hotelplan* (hotel map).

If you would like to request printed information in advance, contact the administrative head office (☎ 88 98 70, fax 889 87 32, e tourist@salzburginfo.at) at Auerspergstrasse 7, 5020 Salzburg, Austria.

Tourist offices and hotels sell the **Salzburg Card**, which provides museum admission, public transport and a bevy of reductions for everything from car rental to concerts. It costs €17/23/30 for 24/48/72 hours. **Salzburg Plus** is a pre-paid card, including meals and accommodation, starting at €94.40 – chances are you'll do just fine without it.

Money Banks in the city centre are usually open from 9am to 6.30pm Monday to Friday and until noon on Saturday. Currency exchange at the train station counters is available daily to at least 8.30pm. American Express (AmEx; see Travel Agencies) also exchanges money.

Post & Communications The main post office at the Hauptbahnhof is open from 6am to 9.30pm Monday to Friday, 8am to 8pm Saturday and 1pm to 6pm Sunday, and has money-exchanging facilities. Cybar (☎ 84 48 22) is an Internet cafe at Mozartplatz 5 next to the tourist office. It's open 10am to 11pm daily and charges €0.15 per minute, with a 10-minute minimum.

Internet Resources Salzburg's Web site, with an English version and a free online accommodation booking function, has two Web addresses: W www.salzburginfo.at and W www.city.salzburg.com.

Travel Agencies American Express (☎ 808 00) is next to the Mozartplatz tourist office. It is open 9am to 5.30pm Monday to Friday, and until noon Saturday. Ökista (☎ 45 87 33), at Fanny-von-Lehner-Strasse 1, near the train station, has the same hours but is closed Saturday.

Bookshops American Discont (☎ 84 56 40) at Kaigasse 6 has new and used English-language titles. By platform 2a in the Hauptbahnhof is Buch + Presseshop, with international newspapers and magazines.

Medical & Emergency Services The Landeskrankenhaus St-Johanns-Spital (☎ 448 20) is at Müllner Hauptstrasse 48, just north of the Mönchsberg. Dial ☎ 141 for an ambulance. The police headquarters (☎ 638 30) are at Alpenstrasse 90.

Laundry Norge Exquisit (☎ 87 63 81), Paris-Lodron-Strasse 16, charges €4.25 per self-service wash and €2 each for dryer and soap. It's open 7.30am to 6pm Monday to Friday and until noon Saturday. Full-service washes and dry-cleaning are also available.

Right (North) Bank

Mozart Wohnhaus Salzburg has not one but two museums dedicated to its most famous son: the Wohnhaus (residence) and the Geburtshaus (birthplace; see Left Bank section later in this section). They're both popular, pricey and feature largely overlapping displays, including musical instruments, sheet music and Mozart memorabilia.

If you've only got time for one, the Wohnhaus *(☎ 87 42 27 40, Makartplatz 8; adult/student/ages 15-18/ages 6-14 €4.75/ 3.60/1.80/1.45; open 9am-6pm daily Sept-June, 9am-7pm daily July & Aug)* is the place to see. This is where Mozart lived from 1773 to 1780 and where his father Leopold died in 1787. Commentary about his family, travels and achievements is accompanied by musical excerpts and delivered via handheld devices activated by infra-red signals.

On the mezzanine level is the **Mozart Ton-und Film-Museum** *(☎ 88 34 54, Makartplatz 8; admission free; open 9am-1pm Mon, Tues & Fri, 1pm-5pm Mon & Thur)*, an archive of celluloid images of the maestro.

Schloss Mirabell This palace was built by the worldly prince-archbishop Wolf Dietrich for his mistress in 1606. Its charming gardens featured in *The Sound of Music* and are a great place to while away the hours. Classical concerts take place year round (tickets ☎ 84 85 86, **e** info@salzburger-schlosskonzerte.at, **w** www.salzburger-schlosskonzerte.at). If

Amadeus, Amadeus

Wolfgang Amadeus Mozart was only 35 years old when he died in 1791, yet he composed 626 works, including 24 operas, 49 symphonies, over 40 concertos, 26 string quartets, seven string quintets and numerous sonatas for piano and violin. Haydn proclaimed him the 'greatest composer' of all-time, and Schubert effused that the 'magic of Mozart's music lights the darkness of our lives'.

Mozart was born in Salzburg and learned how to play the harpsichord at age three. Two years later, his musician father, Leopold, gave a small violin to the child prodigy who, without the benefit of lessons, played well enough, a few days later, to join a professional quartet. Leopold was quick to exploit his son's astounding talent, taking Wolfgang and his sister Nannerl (four years older and also exceptionally gifted) on a successful European concert tour.

At 14, Mozart was appointed director of the archbishop of Salzburg's orchestra. In 1781, he settled in Vienna, where he enjoyed his most productive years. He was also something of a ladies' man: at age 24 he boasted, 'If I had married everyone I jested with, I would have well over 200 wives'. A year later, he married Constanze Weber (despite his obvious affections for her opera-singer sister, Aloysia).

In Vienna, Mozart also suffered his worst bouts of compulsive gambling – losing large sums in billiards, ninepins and cards. He lived too hard and fast for his own good, ate poorly and attended all-night parties probably like those depicted in the Oscar-winning film *Amadeus* (1985). He lies buried in Vienna's St Marx cemetery; the exact location is not known.

Mark Honan

the doors happen to be open, peek inside at the marble staircase draped with baroque sculptures.

St Sebastian Graveyard Behind the 16th-century church of St Sebastian in Linzer Gasse is a small cemetery where some famous corpses have found their final resting place. Dominating the enclosed area is the temple-like mausoleum of prince-archbishop **Wolf Dietrich**.

As you walk towards the mausoleum, also note the **Mozart family** grave, where the composer's father, Leopold, and his wife, Constanze, are interred (it's the third on your left).

There are lots more interesting tombs and epitaphs in the covered walkway next to the church, including a skeleton draped in a robe lying atop a coffin.

Often overlooked, but historically the biggest celebrity to be buried here, is Paracelsus (1493–1541), a pioneering scientist who's considered the father of modern medicine. Look for him on the short flight of stairs leading up to the church at the end of the walkway.

Left (South) Bank

Festung Hohensalzburg One of the largest fortresses in Europe, the Festung Hohensalzburg (☎ *84 24 30 11, Mönchsberg 34; grounds & interior audio-tour adult/concession €3.50/2; open 9.30am-5.30pm daily mid-Sept–mid-June, 9am-6pm daily mid-June–mid-Sept, grounds slightly longer*) is quite literally Salzburg's high point. Begun in 1077, it was enlarged and modified repeatedly by various archbishops, most notably by Leonhard von Keutschach (ruled 1495–1519). His symbol was the turnip, which accounts for the 58 variations of this motif found around the castle.

You can explore the interior on a self-guided tour using an audio-guide with commentary in seven languages. It'll take you through the bishops' lavish staterooms as well as the **Burgmuseum** with exhibits on fortress history, the medieval judicial system, military practices and – incongruously – marionettes. Many people get a kick out

of the grisly torture chamber. Allow about 90 minutes to see it all.

Even if you don't roam around inside, you can still enjoy the sweeping views over the city and south to the Alps, explore the courtyards and visit the terrace cafe.

Getting to the fortress is either a 15-minute wheeze uphill or a ride aboard the **Festungsbahn** (☎ *84 26 82; one way/return with admission to fortress grounds €5.50/6.25, without €2.75/2*). This is Austria's oldest funicular (1892) with rides leaving every 10 minutes from Festungsgasse 4.

Dom The vast Dom on Domplatz was one of the earliest baroque churches north of the Alps at its consecration in 1628. There's been a church in this spot since 774, but the current one was commissioned by Prince-Archbishop Markus Sittikus in 1614 after a devastating fire in 1568 razed the earlier building. Outside the main facade are four large statues symbolising the apostles Peter (with keys) and Paul (with sword), as well as the patron saints Virgil and Rupert (with salt barrel and church model). Also worth a gander are the three bronze doors decorated with allegories of faith, hope and charity (left to right).

Inside, admire the dark-edged stucco, the dome and the Romanesque font where Mozart was baptised. The town's **Dommuseum** (☎ *84 41 89, Domoratorien; adult/concession €4.40/1.45; open 10am-5pm Mon-Sat, 1pm-6pm Sun May-Oct, closed Nov-Apr*) contains ecclesiastical treasures and collectibles.

Residenz The Residenz (☎ *80 42 26 90, Residenzplatz 1; adult/concession/child €7.25/5.50/2.50, including Residenz Galerie; open 10am-5pm daily*) is the town palace used by the archbishops for official entertaining. During a self-guided audio-tour available in seven languages, you'll get a good look at the pompous and extravagant lifestyle to which these men of the cloth treated themselves. Johann Michael Rottmayr created some of the frescoes, which are complemented by rich stucco work and period furniture.

A tour of the Residenz also gives access to the **Residenz Galerie** (☎ *84 04 51; gallery only adult/student/ages 6-16 €4.70/ 3.60/1.80; open 10am-5pm daily Apr-Sept, closed Wed Oct-Mar*) on the 2nd floor. The focus here is on European art from the 16th to the 19th centuries, with good examples of Dutch old masters such as Rembrandt, Rubens and Brueghel, and of Austrian 19th-century artists such as Waldmüller, Makart and Ender.

Franziskanerkirche When you first enter Salzburg's Franciscan church on Franziskanergasse, it might seem dark and unappealing. But continue on and your impression will likely change when you spot the amazing **hall choir** anchored by a freestanding high altar. The choir roof is upheld by a circle of pillars spilling into a net-vaulted canopy, making the whole thing look a bit like a stone forest. The **main altar** is a baroque riot in gold-and-pink marble by Johann Bernard Fischer von Erlach. It integrates an exquisite carved Madonna by Michael Pacher, designer of the original Gothic altar, which was destroyed.

Stiftskirche St Peter The origin of the Stiftskirche St Peter is actually Romanesque (1143), although this is hard to believe given the incredibly ornate baroque cloak it's been wearing since the 18th century. You'll find swirling stuccos, flamboyant frescoes, lots of emotive paintings and 15 side altars. In one of them, off the right aisle, is a memorial tombstone to composer Johann Michael Haydn, who lies buried in the church cemetery, as does Mozart's sister Nannerl, who's honoured with a marble plaque inside.

Accessible from the graveyard are the **Katakomben** (Catacombs, ☎ *844 57 80; adult/concession €0.90/0.60; open 10.30am-5pm Tues-Sun May-Sept & 10.30am-3.30pm Wed-Thur; 10.30am-4pm Fri-Sun Oct-Apr*), which are believed to date back to the early days of Christianity.

Rupertinum The Rupertinum (☎ *80 42 23 36, Wiener-Philharmoniker-Gasse 9, adult/ concession €4.40/2.90; open 10am-5pm Tues-Sun, 10am-9pm Wed, slightly longer in July & Aug*) is a museum of modern and contemporary art – paintings, sculpture, photography, graphics – mostly from Austrian artists. Few are household names among non-aficionados, with the possible exception of expressionist Oskar Kokoschka (1886–1980). The museum is also home to the **Austrian Photography Gallery** dedicated to post-WWII works, including those by Inge Morath, who's well known for her celebrity portraits. In addition, the museum stages up to 20 temporary exhibits per year.

Kollegienkirche Prince-Archbishop Paris von Lodron founded Salzburg's university in 1623, but the Collegiate Church on Universitätsplatz was only consecrated in 1707. It is widely considered architect Johann Bernhard Fischer von Erlach's crowning accomplishment. For a baroque church, its interior is surprisingly austere, with chapels dedicated to the patron saints of the four major university faculties: Thomas Aquinas (theology), Ivo (jurisprudence), Lucas (medicine) and Catherine (philosophy).

From 1800 to 1964, this church was not used for religious purposes. Napoleon, during his occupation of the city in 1800, used it for hay storage, and later it went through stints as a school and a theatre. Only with the re-founding of the university in 1964 was it restored as a place of worship.

Mozart Geburtshaus The smaller of the two Mozart museums is the place where the musical genius was born, the Geburtshaus (☎ *84 43 13, Getreidegasse 9; adult/student/ ages 15-18/ages 6-14 €5.10/4/1.80/ 1.45, combination ticket with Wohnhaus €8/6.20/ 2.90/2.20; open 9am-6pm daily Sept-June, 9am-7pm daily July & Aug*). Mozart lived here for the first 17 years of his life and there's the usual assortment of memorabilia on view.

Pferdeschwemme The Pferdeschwemme (horse trough), on Herbert-von-Karajan-Platz next to the Festival Hall, was a rather elaborate drinking and bathing spot for the prince-archbishops' mounts. Its centrepiece is the marvellous marble 'horse tamer' sculpture by Michael Bernhard Mandl in the basin, which is framed in by a decorative balustrade. This is set against the backdrop of a series of frescoes with rearing equine 'pin-ups' flanking the central image borrowed from Greek mythology: The horse Pegasus is shown kicking off the hero Bellerophon in his hubristic attempt to visit the gods at Mt Olympus.

Haus der Natur Nature nuts could easily spend hours wandering around the enlightening displays in the Haus der Natur (☎ 84 26 53, Museumplatz 5; adult/concession €4.40/2.50; open 9am-5pm daily). Besides the usual flora, fauna and mineral exhibits there are sections on physics and astronomy (pity about the lack of signs in English). The 4th floor is a gory highlight with stomach-churning displays of deformed animals.

Carolino Augusteum Museum This is pretty much Salzburg's local history museum (☎ 841 13 40, Museumsplatz 1; adult/concession €2.90/1.10; open 9am-5pm Fri-Wed, 9am-8pm Thur). The collection is quite interesting and nicely presented, with highlights being Roman mosaics, Gothic statues and paintings by local artists.

Organised Tours

One-hour walking tours (€7.50) of the Altstadt leave from the tourist office at Mozartplatz at 12.15pm daily (not on Sunday from November to March).

The Oscar-winning film was a flop in Austria, but with English-speaking visitors *The Sound of Music* tour is a big hit – and big business for the tour operators. These include Salzburg Sightseeing Tours (☎ 88 16 16, Mirabellplatz 3) and Salzburg Panorama Tours (☎ 87 40 29, cnr Mirabellplatz & St-Andra-Kirche). Tours depart twice daily, last about four hours and cost €30.

The tours take in several film locations, including the church at Mondsee (site of Maria and the Baron's wedding), Schloss Anif (seen at the beginning of the film), the gazebo in Schloss Hellbrunn (scene of Liesl and Rolf's duet *I Am 16 Going On 17*) and Schloss Leopoldskron (the family home). If

you take it lightly, it can be brilliant fun: it's hard to forget manic Julie Andrews impersonators flouncing in the fields, screeching 'the hills are alive' in voices to wake the dead. On the other hand, if you're among an earnest group, the tour can be tedious.

Special Events

The **Salzburger Festspiele** (Salzburg Festival) is the highlight of the city's cultural calendar. It takes place from late July to the end of August, and includes concerts ranging from Mozart (of course!) to contemporary, as well as opera and theatre. Several events take place daily in different locations and prices range from €4 to €340, with reductions for those under 26. Standing-room tickets are only available for performances at the Kleines Festspielhaus (Hofstallgasse 1). Demand for tickets usually far exceeds the supply, so make reservations early. The easiest way to make bookings or to obtain more information is at **W** www.salzburgfestival.at (in German and English).

Other important festivals are at Easter (**Osterfestspiele**) and Whitsunday/Pentecost weekend (**Pfingstkonzerte**). **Mozartwoche** (Mozart Week) is in late January.

Places to Stay

Grab a *Hotelplan* (hotel map) from the tourist office, which gives current prices for hotels, pensions, hostels and camping grounds. Accommodation is at a premium during festivals.

For hotel reservations by phone or fax, contact the tourist office hotline at ☎ 88 98 73-14/5/6/7/8 or fax 889 87 32. The tourist office at Mozartplatz 5 makes in-person room reservations only. The commission is €2.20 for two people, €4.40 for larger parties. The tourist offices also have a list of **private rooms** from €32 per person, but for those you'll have to make your own reservations.

Places to Stay – Budget

Camping Salzburg has four camping grounds, all of them quite good. The following is the most easily reached by public transport.

Camping Kasern (☎/*fax 45 05 76,* **e** *campingkasern@aon.at, Carl-Zuckmayer-Strasse 26)* Person/car/tent €4.50/3/3. Open Apr-Oct. This camping ground is chock-full of modern amenities, including Internet access, guest laundry and TV and video room. It's just north of the A1 Nord exit. From the Hauptbahnhof, take any bus direction 'Centrum' to Mirabellplatz. Then cross the road to the corner of Paris-Lodron-Strasse and take bus No 15 in the direction of Kasern-Bergheim to Jägerwirt.

Hostels Salzburg has a good range of private and independent hostels. Most sell discounted tickets to *The Sound of Music* tour.

International Youth Hotel (YO-HO) (☎ *87 34 60, fax 87 88 10,* **e** *office@yoho.at,* **w** *www.yoho.at, Paracelsusstrasse 9)* Singles/doubles/quads/6–8-bed dorm €29/19/ 16/13 per person, including sheets (deposit €11), discounts for longer stays. This is a great hostel for party animals, with its bar, loud music, cheap beer, and a staff of mostly young native-English speakers. Reservations are accepted online or by phone no earlier than one day before arrival. Showers cost €0.75, Internet access is €0.75 for seven minutes, and breakfast starts at €2.20. One drawback is the 1am curfew, although there's a night porter to let you in.

Jugendgästehaus Nonntal (☎ *842 67 00, fax 84 11 01,* **e** *jgh.salzburg@jgh.at, Josef-Preis-Allee 18)* Doubles/quads/8-bed dorm €21/17/13 per person, including breakfast, slightly lower Dec-Feb; nonmembers €3 extra per night; €2.20 per night surcharge for stays under 3 nights. This is a large, modern and busy HI facility and probably the city's most comfortable and central hostel. To be sure of a bed, make a telephone reservation or just turn up at 11am (reception may be shut otherwise).

HI Hostel Haunspergstrasse (☎ *87 50 30, fax 88 34 77, Haunspergstrasse 27)* Bed & breakfast €14, including linen. Open July–mid-Sept. This hostel, west of Hauptbahnhof, offers dorms with shower and toilet.

Jugendherberge Eduard-Heinrich-Haus (☎ *62 59 76, fax 62 79 80,* **e** *hostel .eduard-heinrich@Salzburg.co.at, Eduard-Heinrich-Strasse 2)* Bus: No 51 or 95 to Polizeidirektion, followed by a 400m walk. Doubles/quads/6-bed dorm €18/16/14, including breakfast & linen. This hostel is south of the centre and has nice rooms, each with shower and toilet.

Institut St Sebastian (☎ *88 26 06, fax 88 26 85, Linzer Gasse 4)* Dorm bed €14, plus for sheets €2.50, singles/doubles €25/42 (shared bath), €30/50 (private bath). This place, next to the St Sebastian Church, has a roof terrace and guest kitchens. Earplugs are useful for the early-morning church bells.

Hotels & Pensions All prices quoted in this section are for the high season.

Pension Sandwirt (☎/*fax 87 43 51, Lastenstrasse 6a)* Singles/doubles €24/37 (shared bath), doubles €45 (private bath). This place is near the rail line but the rooms are reasonably large and quiet.

Elizabeth Pension (☎/*fax 87 16 64,* **e** *info@pension-elisabeth.at, Vogelweiderstrasse 52)* Bus: No 15 to Breitenfelderstrasse. Singles €35-42, doubles €38-63. Rooms here are pretty small but still benefit from a fairly recent overhaul, and the pension's owners are friendly. The pricier rooms have a shower cubicle.

Pension Junger Fuchs (☎ *87 54 96, Linzer Gasse 54)* Singles/doubles €25/32. This place has a good location but is only for those expecting few frills, although the rooms are better than the cramped halls would suggest. All rooms have shared bath.

Pension Hinterbrühl (☎ *84 67 98, fax 84 18 59,* **e** *hinterbruehl@aon.at, Schanzlgasse 12)* Singles/doubles €35/41. This is another basic option and one of the few budget places right in the Altstadt. Rooms have shared bath, and breakfast costs €4 per person (optional). Reception in the downstairs restaurant is open from 8am to nearly midnight.

Places to Stay – Mid-Range & Top End

Unless noted, rooms in these categories have private bath.

Hotel Amadeus (☎ *87 14 01, fax 871 40 17, Linzer Gasse 43-45)* Singles/doubles

€65/130. Amadeus offers adequate rooms with cable TV, including a few cheaper ones with shared facilities. The breakfast room sparkles in dazzling white and blue.

Hotel Goldene Krone (☎ 87 23 00, Linzer Gasse 48) Singles/doubles €36/61 (shared bath), €41/72 (private bath). Just down the road from Amadeus, this is a solid option with some rooms featuring church-like groined ceilings, which add a bit of character.

Hotel Zur Goldenen Ente (☎ 84 56 22, fax 845 62 29, e ente@eunet.at, Goldgasse 10) Singles/doubles €64/101. This charming place in the Altstadt is in a 700-year-old house that retains some original features. Not all rooms are created equal (inspect before you commit), but all have private facilities and TV. There's a good attached restaurant.

Hotel Lasserhof (☎ 87 33 88, fax 873 38 86, e hotellasserhof@magnet.at, Lasserstrasse 47) Singles/doubles from €72/120. Some rooms have a strange mix of modern and rustic fittings. It offers free street parking and bicycle rentals.

Hotel Schloss Mönchstein (☎ 848 55 50, fax 84 85 59, e salzburg@monchstein.at, Mönchsberg Park 26) Rooms from €250. This abode is as palatial as the name suggests. Its pastoral, isolated setting favours those with their own transportation. On the premises is a tiny chapel popular for weddings.

Places to Eat

Salzburg need not be expensive for food. Quick, hot snacks or meals are available from various deli shops located throughout town (see Snacks & Fast Food).

Auersperg (☎ 88 97 80, Rainerstrasse 6–8) Lunch buffet €12.50. Served 11.30am-2pm Mon-Sat. Hotel restaurants are rarely worth the ink on the page, but this one at the Crowne Plaza does an excellent lunch buffet with a range of hot and cold selections. Locals love it.

Bistro Bio Terra (☎ 84 94 14, Wiener-Philharmoniker-Gasse 9) Mains around €12. Inside the Rupertinum, this is a tiny vegetarian restaurant with a cultured clientele and a blackboard menu which changes daily.

Zum Eulenspiegel (☎ 84 31 80, Hagenauerplatz 2) Mains €6.50-13. This multi-story establishment near Mozart Geburtshaus is admittedly a shade touristy, but the food is consistently good and the interior homey. It serves excellent fish specialities, including a superb fish soup provencale (€6.50).

K+K Restaurant am Waagplatz (☎ 84 21 56, Waagplatz 2) Mains €5.50-15, 4-course meal €40. Head straight upstairs to the warren of cosy dining rooms, then choose from light dishes such as soups and salads, or meaty mains such as roast suckling pig with fried potatoes.

Marc's (☎ 84 09 35, Chiemseegasse 5) Mains €5-12.50. Closed Sun. This trendy restaurant manages to combine a cool look with warm ambience in its tunnel-shaped, low-vaulted room. There's a large bar at the front, where you can start the evening with a wine aperitif (400 to choose from). The chef serves Italian cuisine but occasionally pays homage to his Austrian roots as well.

Cafe Pepita (☎ 88 15 76, Linzer Gasse 12) Dishes €7-9. Closed Sun. In fine weather, tables spill into the courtyard and a covered passageway from this tiny bistro near the St Sebastian Church. The menu features stuffed baguettes as well as several salads and other simple fare. It draws a young crowd.

Stadtalm (☎ 84 17 29, Mönchsberg 19c) Mains €4-10. Open until midnight May-Sept, until 7pm Oct-Apr. From its lofty perch atop the Mönchsberg, the Stadtalm offers some of the best views of Salzburg, plus a convivial ambience, good brews and Austrian food. Take the footpath up from near Max-Reinhardt-Platz, or the Mönchsberg lift (€1.45/€2.40 one way/return) from Anton-Neumayr-Platz.

Sternbräu (☎ 84 21 40, Griesgasse 23/Getreidegasse 34) Mains €6-18. In this labyrinth of rooms you can pick from a super-casual to a rather formal ambience, although in summer you may want to opt for the garden where there's a self-service buffet and pizzeria. Otherwise, the food's mostly Austrian. This is the place that presents *The Sound of Music* dinner show (see Entertainment).

St Paul's Stub'n (☎ 84 22 54, Herrengasse 16) Dishes €2.50-8. It's almost as if they're trying to keep this place a secret from tourists. It's upstairs in the yellow house and completely anonymous from the outside. The menu revolves around simple but satisfying dishes such as pasta, salads, pizza and baked potatoes served at long wooden tables until late.

Weisses Kreuz (☎ 84 56 41, Bierjodl-gasse 6) Mains €6-13, 3-course menu €10.50. Tucked away in a quiet side street below the fortress, this restaurant does Balkan and some Viennese dishes. In summer, it has an almost Mediterranean flair, especially on the pergola-covered terrace. The set menu offers the best deal.

Zwettler's (☎ 84 00 44, Kaigasse 3) Mains €3.50-8. Dumplings served in umpteen ways figure big on the menu of this cosy inn, although its delicious desserts are the real diet disasters. Try Salzburger Nockerl'n (a souffle), *Mohr im Hemd* ('shirted moor'; chocolate cake with whipped cream), *Palatschinken* (pancake with jam) or *Kaiserschmarrn* (shredded pancake).

Cafes

Austrians have refined coffeehouse culture. Join them as they chat away an afternoon, sipping their *mélanges* and nibbling on exquisite cakes and pastries.

Café Tomaselli (☎ 84 44 88, Alter Markt 9) This is the city's most famous traditional coffeehouse. It draws a young but intellectual-looking crowd to its spacious but smoke-filled upstairs-downstairs setting with wood panelling, crystal chandeliers, and oil paintings in gilded wood frames.

Café Konditorei Fürst (☎ 84 37 59, Brodgasse 13) On the opposite side of Alter Markt, this is a smaller and stuffier cafe (upstairs is a bit better). Mozartkugeln were invented here and many locals swear that they really are the best. They're certainly the most expensive at €0.75 each.

Snacks & Fast Food

There's a fruit and vegetable market at Mirabellplatz on Thursday morning and another on Universitätsplatz daily except Sunday.

The large *Interspar* supermarket by the Hauptbahnhof has a self-service restaurant; you can fill up for under €5, or half-price after 6pm (open to 7pm Monday to Friday, to 5pm Saturday, closed Sunday). There's a *Nordsee* Imbiss with fish sandwiches from €2 to €3.50 at Getreidegasse 11. *Eduscho* (Getreidegasse 34) is a good place for a quick pick-me-up coffee or hot chocolate (€0.75 per cup).

Good budget deals can also be had in the university *Mensas*. Menus for students (show ISIC card) start at €3; nonstudents pay a bit more. Lunch is from 11.30am to 2pm Monday to Friday only, but don't go too late as some choices may run out. Try *Mensa Toscana* (Sigmund-Haffner-Gasse 11) in the courtyard, which is open from 9am to at least 4pm Monday to Friday, or the *Mensa* at Rudolfskai 42 (closed June to September).

Entertainment

The Sound of Music Show You'd have to be either extremely drunk or a serious *The Sound of Music* junkie to truly appreciate this hokey show, which is popular nonetheless. Besides the famous melodies, you'll also be showered with the kind of Austrian folklore songs the von Trapps used to sing, plus a bit of Mozart and Strauss thrown in for the 'high-brow crowd'. There's even a video interview with Maria von Trapp.

All this can be combined with dinner featuring 'schnitzel with noodles and crisp apple strudels' and other menu items inspired by the musical. Performances run nightly at 8.30pm from May to October at the Sternbräu Dinner Theatre (☎ 82 66 17), at Griesgasse 23. Tickets costs €27 for the show and a drink or €41.50 for the show and dinner; they're available at hotels, the tourist offices and the box office.

Beer Halls & Pubs Beer halls are popular in Salzburg.

Augustiner Bräustübl (☎ 43 12 46, Augustinergasse 4) This atmospheric pub proves that monks can really 'get down' when it comes to making beer. The quaffing clerics have been supplying the lubrication for this huge beer hall for years. You can also buy meat, bread and salads in the deli shops in the foyer (some are pricey), then eat inside or in the large, shady beer garden.

Stieglkeller (☎ 84 26 81, Festungsgasse 10) Open 10am-11pm daily, May-Sept only. At the foot of the fortress, this is a beloved beer garden with excellent views of the Altstadt. Mains cost about €12 to €15, including soup, bread and dessert. The upstairs area sells cheaper self-service beer.

Shamrock Irish Pub (☎ 84 16 10, Rudolfskai 12) Open 3pm-2am Mon-Sat, 2pm-2am Sun. No cover charge. Come here for live music nightly from 9pm – folk, blues, soul, country, you name it.

Getting There & Away

Train There are numerous connections from Bavarian cities to Salzburg. Regional trains depart to/from Munich every 30 to 60 minutes (€21, two hours) with stops in the Chiemsee towns of Prien and Bernau, among others. EuroCity (EC) trains make the trip nonstop in 90 minutes (€24). RB trains travel to/from Bad Reichenhall in just under 30 minutes (€3.90) and to/from Berchtesgaden in 45 minutes (€6.30).

Bus Regional buses depart from right outside the main (west) exit of the Hauptbahnhof and from Mirabellplatz. Bavarian communities served throughout the day include Berchtesgaden (bus No 9450, 45 minutes), and Bad Reichenhall, served about hourly by bus No 9527 (one hour).

Car & Motorcycle The A8 autobahn connects Munich and Salzburg. If you plan to travel beyond Salzburg on autobahns, you'll need to purchase a *Vignette*, a pass available at petrol stations, rest stops and auto-club offices. A 10-day pass costs €4.30 for motorcycles and €7.60 for cars; if you're caught without, you'll have to buy a 24-hour pass costing €65/120 and, since February 2002, are even subject to a fine of up to €2180.

Car-rental agencies in Salzburg include Avis (☎ 87 72 78), at Ferdinand-Porsche-Strasse 7 near the Hauptbahnhof, and Hertz

(☎ 85 20 86), in the same building around the corner.

Getting Around

Bus Salzburg is crisscrossed by 19 bus routes. Single-trip tickets are €1.60, day passes (transferable) €2.90, weekly passes €9. Bus drivers sell only single tickets; all others must be bought from vending machines, *Tabak* (tobacco) shops or the tourist offices.

Car & Motorcycle Driving in the city centre is hard work. Much of the Altstadt is pedestrian-only and parking is limited and expensive. The largest car park near the centre is the Altstadt Garage below the Mönchsberg.

Other Transport Taxis cost €2.50 at flagfall (€3.50 between 10pm and 6am), plus about €1 per kilometre in the centre or €1.75 outside the city. To book a taxi call ☎ 87 44 00.

Top Bike Salzburg (☎ 06272-46 56) rents bicycles for €3/8 for one/four hours and €11 for all day, with additional rates available for longer rentals. It's at Franz-Josef-Kai 1 near the Staatsbrücke and open 10am to 5pm daily April to September (9am to 7pm July and August).

Rates for *Fiaker* (pony-and-trap) for up to four passengers are around €30 for 25 minutes and €60 for 50 minutes, but you can sometimes bargain the drivers down.

INN-SALZACH
Altötting

☎ 08671 • pop 12,000 • elevation 403m

What Lourdes is to France, Altötting is to Bavaria. Each year, more than one million Roman Catholic pilgrims descend upon this innocuous little town to behold a limewood sculpture of Mary, clad in festive robes and blackened from centuries of exposure to candle soot (electric lights are now used). She arrived in Altötting in about 1330, worked a couple of miracles and soon thereafter (starting in 1489) became one of the most popular women in Europe. Kings, dukes and even popes (including

Pope John Paul II) came, along with millions of common folk.

Over the centuries, additional churches had to be built to accommodate the worshippers and today there are six major ones crowding the town centre around Kapellplatz. In the streets, nuns in habits, frocked priests and robed monks mingle with the mostly elderly pilgrims. Countless souvenir shops hawk items that register a perfect 10 on the 'kitsch-ometer' but that are happily snapped up by the faithful. There's definitely something fascinating, almost exotic, about this place, even if religion doesn't do it for you. Note that the town all but shuts down from November to early March.

Orientation &Information Altötting's compact centre is anchored by Kapellplatz, which is a short walk north of the Bahnhof. The tourist and pilgrimage office (☎ 80 69, fax 858 58) is at Kapellplatz 2a and is open from 8am to noon and 2pm to 5pm Monday to Friday and 9am to noon on Saturday between May to October. At other times, it's closed for the weekend starting at noon on Friday. For more information, go to the Web site at **W** www.altoetting-tourisinfo.de.

Things to See Church fans will be in heaven in Altötting. The one not to be missed is the **Gnadenkapelle**, a tiny 8th-century octagonal chapel where you can visit the miraculous Mary perched in her silver and gold altar. She's guarded by the life-sized sculptures of two kneeling men – a prince and a bishop – as well as the hearts of numerous Wittelsbach rulers (including Ludwig II). These are enshrined in silver urns tucked away in niches on the opposite wall.

Inside the chapel and all over the covered outside walkway encircling it, more than 2000 *ex voto* tablets attest to the fact that Mary has continued to be busy in the miracle department. You'll often see the most devout of pilgrims hoping to improve the odds by shouldering heavy crosses and schlepping them around this ambulatory, sometimes crawling on their knees, and reciting the rosary in complete religious ecstasy.

The big twin-towered church south of the chapel, which squats right in the middle of Kapellplatz, is the Gothic **Stiftskirche**. It's the third on the site and the immediate successor of a Romanesque basilica, from which only the western portal survives. Inside, the most interesting sight is a large clock topped by a scythe-wielding silver skeleton, every second signalling someone's death with each swing. Known as the *Tod von Eding*, the macabre fellow was inspired by the black plague, which raged through local lands in 1634.

Proceed to the Gothic cloister, which has some frescoes, ancient tombstones and, incongruously, the photographs of local Wehrmacht members killed during WWII. The double chapel in the south-eastern corner contains the grave of Thirty Years' War general, Count von Tilly.

Attached to the church's northern facade is the **Schatzkammer** *(Treasury;* ☎ *51 66; adult/concession €2/1; open 10am-noon & 2pm-4pm Tues-Sun Apr-Oct)*. The pièce de résistance here is the exquisite *Goldene Rössl* (Golden Horse), a small silver and gold altar smothered with pearls and jewels that was wrought in Paris in 1404. Beneath the tableau is a horse held steady by a servant for his master, French King Charles VI; he's the one depicted in the altar praying to Mary.

East of the Gnadenkapelle, the late-baroque **Kirche St Magdalena** (1697) is drenched in some rather heavy-handed stucco. On the northern side of Kapellplatz is the **Wallfahrts- und Heimatmuseum** *(*☎ *51 66; adult/concession €1.25/0.50; open 2pm-4pm Tues-Fri, 10am-3pm Sat & Sun Apr-Oct)*, where scale models, folk art, prehistoric findings, paintings and other objects tell the history of the town and the role of the pilgrimage.

A short walk east of Kapellplatz, in Kreszentiaheimstrasse, is another of Altötting's more unusual sights, the **Panorama** *(*☎ *69 34; adult/concession €3/2; open 9am-5pm daily Mar-Oct, groups of 10 or more only in winter)*. It's a monumental 360-degree painting of the classical Jerusalem during Jesus' crucifixion and was created by

Gebhard Fugel in 1902/3. A 30-minute surround-sound narration takes you back to the events leading up to this fateful day. If you speak German, it's actually quite impressive.

Across the street, the **Mechanische Krippe** *(Mechanical Creche;* ☎ *66 53, Kreszentia-heimstrasse 18; adult/concession €1.50/1; open 9am-5pm daily Mar-Oct)* features about 130 wooden figurines carved by masters from Oberammergau from 1926–28.

Places to Stay & Eat Altötting has only a limited number of hotels and restaurants.

Hotel Zwölf Apostel (☎ *969 60, fax 843 71,* e *info@hotel-zwoelf-apostel.de, Bruder-Konrad-Platz 3-4)* Singles €40-45, doubles €55-65. This is one of the oldest inns in town, with spruced up, modern rooms with TV (some with direct-dial phones) as well as a good restaurant.

Hotel Zur Post (☎ *50 40, 62 14,* e *hotel .post@t-online.de, Kapellplatz 2)* Singles €50-95, doubles €100-125. Although this is Altötting's flagship hotel, the rooms are surprisingly small and nothing special. The integrated 'Roman' spa and sauna complex, however, with separate sections for men and women, is superb. At the restaurant, the chef gives traditional favourites the creative treatment (lunch mains €6.50 to €12.50, dinner €12.50 to €20).

A good snack place is *Brotzeitstüberl (*☎ *69 04, Kapellplatz 13)* near the Stiftskirche, which serves things like ham and cheese baguettes and schnitzel for €1.50 to €5. It closes at 5pm or 6pm and all day Sunday.

More cafes and cheaper eateries are on the southern side of Kapellplatz, including *La Piazzetta (*☎ *138 54, Kapellplatz 24)*, which does pizza, pasta and salads for €3.50 to €5.50.

Getting There & Away Coming from Munich by train requires a change in Mühldorf (€13.50, 1½ hours). From Landshut, regional trains take about 1¼ hours with a change in Tüssling (€9). Trains to Burghausen leave at least hourly (€3.10, 25 minutes). Altötting is just off the B12, about 93km due east of Munich.

Burghausen
☎ 08677 • pop 18,000 • elevation 350m

About 15km south-east of Altötting, Burghausen was once a flourishing centre of the salt trade and a regional seat of government. Decline set in the 17th century, thus sheltering the town from progress and allowing it to preserve its late medieval appearance. The lovely Altstadt snuggles in a gentle bend of the Salzach River – which separates it from Austria – and is lorded over by Europe's longest castle complex squatting atop a mountain ridge. The modern part of town is north of here, largely spawned by the arrival of the chemical industry in the early 20th century; it still provides jobs for about 10,000 people today.

Burghausen's Bahnhof, in the modern town, is connected to the Stadtplatz, the main Altstadt square, by bus No 1. The main tourist office (☎ 967 69 32, fax 867 69 35, e touristinfo@burghausen.de), at Stadtplatz 112, is open 8.30am to 5pm Monday to Friday and 10am to 1pm Saturday; from July to September also 10am to noon Sunday. There's a second branch at Burg 9, near the northern end of the castle, about 50m south of Curaplatz.

The best views of the castle and the Altstadt are from the Austrian side. Cross the bridge over the Salzach and either drive or walk uphill to the viewpoint.

Burg zu Burghausen Stretched out for 1034m, Burghausen's fortress consists of several building clusters wrapped around six courtyards. The main castle, at the southern end, has a core dating back to 1255 and now houses several museums. Admission to the castle grounds is free.

The **Historisches Stadtmuseum** *(*☎ *651 98; adult/concession €1.50/1; open 9am-6.30pm daily May-Sept, 10am-4.30pm daily mid-Mar–Apr & Oct, closed otherwise)* is the local history museum. It has predictable displays spread out over 30 rooms, including the Gothic *Kemenate*, the wing once inhabited by the duchess and her entourage. The duke and his fellows used to congregate in the *Palas* section, which now houses the **Staatliche Sammlungen**

(☎ 46 59; admission €2.50; open 9am-5pm daily Apr-Oct, 9am-4pm daily Nov-Mar), a collection of late-Gothic paintings by Bavarian artists as well as of furniture from the 15th and 16th centuries.

In the fourth courtyard is the **Folterturm** (☎ 641 90; adult/concession €1.50/0.50; open 9am-6pm daily mid-Mar–Oct, otherwise Sat & Sun only), with a bone-chilling torture chamber, prison cells and dungeons connected via a subterranean walkway to the **Hexenturm** (Witches' Tower). The last person was beheaded in 1831.

In the sixth courtyard, the quite interesting **Haus der Fotografie** (☎ 47 34; admission €1.50; open 10am-6pm Wed-Sun Apr-Oct) chronicles the history of photography and has numerous galleries.

There are several ways to get to the castle. If you're driving, you'll find a car park at its northern end near Curaplatz. Trails leading to the Altstadt are in the second and sixth courtyards while another, via the Georgstor, heads down the other side to the Wöhrsee, a large recreational lake.

From March to October, tours (in German) leave from the tourist office at Burg 9 on weekends and holidays at 11am and 2pm.

Altstadt The castle complex is paralleled by the Altstadt below. The action here centres on the **Stadtplatz**, a long square framed by candy-coloured town houses topped by red tile roofs, giving it a decidedly Italianate flair. Edifices worth closer inspection include the magnificent **Tauffkirchenpalais** at No 97, where Napoleon stayed briefly in 1809; the former **Regierungsgebäude** (government building) at No 108, festooned with elaborate coats of arms and topped by a trio of copper-domed turrets; and the **Rathaus** at No 112, which now houses the main tourist office. The southern end of the square is punctuated by the **Pfarrkirche St Jakob** from where a painted arch leads to the pedestrianised In den Grüben, the former craftsmen's quarter. Many of the Gothic buildings along here house charming boutiques, wine taverns, pubs and restaurants. At No 193 is the **Maut-nerschloss**, the former toll collectors' home, which now houses a jazz venue (☎ 27 41) and

a study centre for contemporary music. Burghausen is famous for its **jazz festivals**, especially the *Jazzwoche* (Jazz Week) in April/May which has brought the creme de la creme of musicians – Ella Fitzgerald to Count Basie – to this little town since 1970.

Places to Stay & Eat The tourist offices can help you find *private rooms* from €15 per person.

DJH hostel (☎ 41 87, fax 91 13 18, ⓔ jhburghaus@aol.com, Kapuzinergasse 235) Bed & breakfast €12.30-13.10. Burghausen's hostel is inside a former monastery at the southern end of the Altstadt.

Pension Salzburger Hof (☎ 91 10 00, fax 91 10 01, In den Grüben 190) Singles/doubles from €35/50. Rooms are nothing to write home about, but the location is great and it has a nice beer garden with views across the river into Austria.

Hotel Post (☎ 96 50, fax 96 56 66, Stadtplatz 39) Singles/doubles from €50/70. This is one of the nicest hotels in town with comfortable rooms, a beer garden sprawling onto Stadtplatz, and a good restaurant serving Bavarian food (mains €10 to €20).

Zum Andechser (☎ 881 82 31, Am Stadtplatz) Mains €3.50-11. Come here for monkish brews and the usual range of Bavarian specialities, consumed either in the woodsy interior or on the big terrace facing Stadtplatz.

Bistro Paparazzi (☎ 39 99, Stadtplatz 111) Mains €5-15. This is a youthful bistro with a good Italian restaurant in the vaulted cellar.

Getting There & Away Trains from Altötting make the trip to Burghausen at least hourly (€3.10, 25 minutes). Burghausen is on the B20.

INGOLSTADT
☎ 0841 • pop 116,000 • elevation 374m
At the far northern end of Upper Bavaria, Ingolstadt is a modern city with a great medieval core, a museum church with the largest flat fresco ever made and an illuminating military museum. From 1472 to 1800, it was home to a famous university, which also figures in Mary Shelley's novel

Frankenstein (see the boxed text 'Franken-stein's Baby' later in this chapter).

Walking around the Altstadt, it's easy to forget that this is actually an industrial city that owes much of its wealth to oil refiner-ies and, above all, to the Audi headquarters and its main factory with 27,000 employees.

Local beer drinkers (read: 'everyone') are especially proud that Germany's Beer Purity Law of 1516 was issued in Ingol-stadt. This demands an investigation, on the part of visitors, as to whether this claim to fame has affected the local brews – Herrn-bräu, Nordbräu and Ingobräu.

Orientation

The Hauptbahnhof is 2.5km south-east of the Altstadt. Bus Nos 10, 11, 15 and 16 make the trip to Rathausplatz, site of the tourist office, every few minutes (€1.50). The Altstadt is roughly in the shape of a baseball diamond bordered by the Danube on its southern edge. Its heart is at Am Stein, where the main north-south drag, Harderstrasse, intersects with Theresien-strasse – which runs west to the Kreuztor and the hostel – and Ludwigstrasse, which runs east to the Neues Schloss. The Audi factory is about 2km north of the Altstadt.

Information

The tourist office (☎ 305 10 98, fax 305 10 99, e touristinformation@ingolstadt.de) is in the Alte Rathaus (Old Town Hall; 1882) at Rathausplatz 2. Hours are 8am to 5pm Monday to Friday and 9am to noon Satur-day. Staff can help you book hotels but not private rooms.

Change money at the post offices next to the Hauptbahnhof or at Am Stein, or one of the banks around Rathausplatz. Web surfing is free at the Stadtbücherei (City Library; ☎ 305 18 31), Hallstrasse 2–4, but it's only open in the daytime. The alternative is Cafe Fronte (☎ 97 51 59), which is inconve-niently located south of the Altstadt at Münchener Strasse 119; it charges €5 per hour and stays open till 1am.

English books, including copies of *Frankenstein*, are sold at Schönhuber (☎ 934 50), Theresienstrasse 6. Menig Presse &

Buch (☎ 97 31 40) at the Hauptbahnhof has international newspapers and magazines.

Things to See

The sights listed in this section are de-scribed in an order that lends itself to a self-guided walking tour of Ingolstadt's Altstadt.

Moritzkirche & Pfeifturm The Moritz-kirche, right behind the tourist office, is In-golstadt's oldest church (1234). The slender tower rising from its southern side served as the town's watchtower for centuries. It can be climbed for wonderful views, usually be-tween 9.30am and 10.30am Saturday; check with staff at the tourist office.

Asamkirche Maria de Victoria Head north on Harderstrasse, then west on Johan-nesstrasse to get to the crown jewel among Ingolstadt's sights, the Asamkirche Maria de Victoria *(1732–36; ☎ 175 18, Neubaustrasse 1½; adult/concession €1.25/0.75; open 9am-noon & 1pm-5pm Tues-Sun Mar-Nov, 10am-noon & 1pm-4pm Tues-Sun Dec-Feb)*. It is one of the most accomplished collabo-rations by the top team of baroque art and ar-chitecture, the brothers Cosmas Damian Asam and Egid Quirin Asam. Originally a prayer and assembly room for a Jesuit-affiliated student congregation, it was turned over to the city in the early 19th century, which has since maintained it as a museum.

Cosmas Damian's trompe l'oeil ceiling (painted in just six weeks in 1735) is the world's largest fresco on a flat surface, and it accomplishes things so trippy you can spend hours staring at it.

To see the thing in proper perspective, walk in six paces from the door, stand on the little circle in the diamond tile and look ahead. The illusions begin when you walk around. From the circle looking east, look over your left shoulder at the archer with the flaming red turban. Wherever you walk in the room his arrow points right at you. Focus on anything – the Horn of Plenty, Moses' staff, the treasure chest – and it will appear to dramatically alter as you move around. Asam took the secret methods he used in the painting to his grave.

A small side room houses the church's most precious possession, the *Lepanto Monstrance* (1708), an amazingly detailed gold and silver depiction of the Battle of Lepanto, which pitted Christians against the Turks in 1571. It's usually locked but you can ask the caretaker, Herr Homm, to let you in for a look.

Diagonally across from the church is the **Tillyhaus** *(Neubaustrasse 2)*, where Count von Tilly, the commander of the Catholic forces in the Thirty Years' War, died in 1632 from battle wounds. He's buried in the Stiftskirche in Altötting.

Fleisserhaus Head south on Konviktstrasse, which is crossed by Kupferstrasse where, at No 18, is the Fleisserhaus *(☎ 305 18 80; admission free; open 11am-6pm Thur-Sun)*. It contains a memorial exhibit about the life and work of Ingolstadt writer and dramatist Marieluise Fleisser (1901–74). A proto-feminist, she drew upon her own struggles to create searing prose dramatising the conflict between the sexes. Oppression, provincialism and isolation prevented Fleisser from attaining recognition until late in life, but her work has undergone a sort of revival – at least in German-speaking countries – since the 1970s.

Liebfrauenmünster Continue south on Konviktstrasse to the city's minster, founded by Duke Ludwig the Bearded in 1425. A vast late-Gothic hall-church, its most distinctive exterior feature is the pair of square towers that – set at a rather steep angle – flanks the main entrance. Inside, a look at the ceilings in the side chapels is especially rewarding. Metaphors, rendered in stone, for the opening up of the heavens to the faithful, these vaults are decorated with sensuously intertwined filigree patterns.

The high altar by Hans Mielich (1560), which celebrates the life of Mary in 90 panels, also deserves a closer look.

Kreuztor & Fortifications South of the minster, Kreuzstrasse leads west to the Gothic Kreuztor (1385), a towered and turreted red-brick confection that looks as if it's been lifted from a Brothers Grimm fairy tale. Until the 19th century, it served as one of the four main gates into the city. The only other gate to survive is the main gate within the Neues Schloss. The former **fortifications**, converted into flats and parkland, still encircle the city.

Stadtmuseum A short walk north of the Kreuztor is the Stadtmuseum *(City Museum; ☎ 305 18 85, Auf der Schanz 45; adult/concession €2/1; open 9am-5pm Tues-Fri, 10am-5pm Sat & Sun)*, with oodles of artefacts housed in a squat fortification. Standouts include a 3000-year-old amber necklace, a stuffed horse that once belonged to Swedish king Gustav Adolf, and a wooden scale model of the medieval city. Also here is the **Spielzeugmuseum** (Toy Museum), with playthings from the 18th to 20th centuries. If you ever wondered how we amused ourselves before TV, this exhibit will have you waxing nostalgic.

Deutsches Medizinhistorisches Museum South of the Kreuztor, Jahnstrasse leads to Anatomiestrasse and the stately Old Anatomy, a former university building, which now houses the Deutsches Medizinhistorisches Museum *(German Museum of the History of Medicine; ☎ 305 18 60, Anatomiestrasse 18/20; adult/concession €2/1, more for special exhibitions; open 10am-noon & 2pm-5pm Tues-Sun)*. Exhibits chronicle the evolution of medical science and the instruments and techniques used through the ages. Birthing chairs, enema syringes and lancets for bloodletting is some of the equipment on view downstairs. Upstairs, the more challenging exhibits are right in the former operating theatre: real human skeletons with preserved musculature and organs, fetuses of Siamese twins, an impregnated uterus and a cyclops. Although presented in a completely scientific, almost clinical, fashion, there's an undeniable ghoulishness to this museum. After your visit, you can recover in the bucolic medicinal plant garden. Bring a picnic, providing you still have an appetite.

Frankenstein's Baby

Mary Shelley's *Frankenstein*, published in 1818, is one of the most enduring monster tales ever written – and not just since Boris Karloff's creepy defining performance in the 1931 movie. The story is legend: the young scientist Viktor Frankenstein travels to Ingolstadt from Geneva to study medicine. Here he becomes madly obsessed with the idea of creating a human being from grisly spare parts robbed from local graves. Alas, when he succeeds, his creature turns out to be a bit of a problem child and promptly sets out to destroy his maker.

So why in the world did Shelley pick Ingolstadt as her novel's setting? For centuries, Ingolstadt, along with Prague and Vienna, was home to one of the most prominent universities in Central Europe. In the 18th century, a cutting-edge, so to speak, laboratory for scientists and medical doctors was housed in a beautiful baroque building, the Alte Anatomie (now the German Museum of the History of Medicine). In the operating theatre on the first floor, professors and students performed experiments on corpses and dead tissue. It was only fitting that Ingolstadt became the imaginary 'birthplace' of Frankenstein's monster.

Shelley originally became aware of Ingolstadt because it was the founding place of a secret society called the 'Illuminati'. Its list of illustrious members included not only Goethe and Herder but also her husband, Percy Bysshe-Shelley.

Ingolstadt has largely refrained from exploiting the Frankenstein myth. You'll find no reference at all to 'the creature' at the History of Medicine Museum (which is interesting nonetheless). German-speakers might consider joining Dr Frankenstein's Murder & Mystery Tour, a spooky nighttime walk led by a character dressed as the good old doctor (adult/concession €6.65/5.10; check with the tourist office for dates and times). The evening concludes around midnight with a visit to 'Frankenstein's Kabinett', a re-created laboratory-cum-Frankenstein-memorabilia-room upstairs at the Gasthaus zum Daniel (see Places to Eat). And may God have mercy on your soul!

Hohe Schule Walk south on Anatomiestrasse, then left on Taschentürmerstrasse and left again on Knopfgasse to Hohe Schule at the corner of Hohe Schulstrasse. Built in 1434 by Ludwig the Bearded, it became the seat of Bavaria's first university in 1472 which was moved to Landshut in 1800. East of here, Hohe Schulstrasse merges with Dollstrasse, Ingolstadt's pedestrianised 'restaurant row', which leads back to the tourist office.

Museum für Konkrete Kunst Just east of the tourist office is a great venue for fans of modern art, the Museum für Konkrete Kunst *(Museum of Concrete Art;* ☎ *305 18 71, Tränktorstrasse 6–8; adult/concession €2/1; open 11am-6pm Tues-Sun).* As aficionados already know, the museum's name has nothing to do with leftover building materials, but features modern abstract paintings and sculpture as well as some neat installations and three-dimensional works.

Neues Schloss & Bayerisches Armee-Museum Unhappy with his lot after returning from wealth-laden France, Ludwig the Bearded ordered the Neues Schloss (New Palace) to be built in 1418. It's a little ostentatious, with its 3m-thick walls, Gothic net vaulting and individually carved doorways, but today it makes a fine setting for the **Bayerisches Armee-Museum** *(Bavarian Military Museum;* ☎ *937 70, Paradeplatz 4; adult/ concession €2.75/2, free on Sun, combined ticket with Reduit Tilly €3.75/ 2.25; open 8.45am-4.30pm Tues-Sun).* This intriguing collection of armaments from the 14th to the 20th centuries includes a collection of 17,000 tin soldiers. It's located at the western edge of the Altstadt, just north of the Danube.

Part Two of the exhibit, which chronicles WWI history, is in the **Reduit Tilly** *(same admission & hours as Bayerisches Armee-Museum),* a fortification on the southern Danube bank and reached via a footbridge.

Museum Mobile North of the Altstadt, this high-tech museum *(*☎ *283 44 44, Ettinger Strasse 40; admission free, tours* *adult/concession €3.50/2.50; open 10am-8pm daily, 1-hour tours operate twice hourly, some in English)* is Ingolstadt's newest attraction. Exhibits on three floors chronicle Audi's history, from humble beginnings in 1899 to the latest successes. Some 50 cars and 30 motorbikes are on view, including 14 prototypes that perpetually glide past visitors on an open lift. To get to the museum, take bus No 11 to the terminus. Also in the museum, you can take two-hour tours of the **Audi factory** *(toll-free ☎ 0800-282 44 44; tours free; tours on production days 9am-2pm.)*

Places to Stay

Azur Campingplatz Auwaldsee (☎ 961 16 16, fax 961 16 17, e *ingolstadt@azur-camping .de)* Tent/site/person €3.50-4.50/5-7.25/4-5.75. This huge camping ground is at Auwaldsee, a lake about 3km south-east of the city centre. Bus services are screamingly inadequate; a taxi from the centre will cost about €8.

DJH hostel (☎ 341 77, fax 91 01 78, Friedhofstrasse 4½, e *jugendherberge .ingolstadt@web.de)* Bed & breakfast €12.25, including linen. Closed mid-Dec–Jan. This seriously nice hostel is in a renovated city fortress (1828). Walk west through the Kreuztor, out of the Altstadt, and the hostel is 150m ahead on the right.

Ingolstadt's hotels, which cater primarily for a business clientele, often drop their prices on weekends (Friday to Sunday) to put the proverbial 'heads on the beds'.

Hotel & Gasthof Zum Anker (☎ 300 05, fax 30 05 80, e *info@hotel-restaurant-anker .de)* Singles/doubles €47/74. Airy, modern rooms with direct-dial phone and cable TV make this central place a good choice. Downstairs is a large restaurant serving typical German cuisine at good prices (mains €6 to €12.50) to a loyal local crowd.

Hotel Bayerischer Hof (☎ 93 40 60, fax 93 40 61 00, Münzbergstrasse 12) Singles/doubles €48.50/76.50. This place has no-nonsense rooms with old-fashioned furniture but modern TV and telephone. It's in a quiet side street near the tourist office and close to sights and restaurants.

Hotel Adler (☎ 351 07, fax 170 98, Theresienstrasse 22) Singles/doubles/triples/quads €60/80/90/95. This is a historic inn right in the pedestrian zone with an atmospheric restaurant and a fitness and spa area. Rooms have benefited from a recent face-lift and now come with a full set of mod-cons.

In Hotel Ammerland (☎ 953450, fax 9534545, Ziegeleistrasse 64) Singles/doubles budget from €55/70, standard from €65/80, comfort from €70.83, suites from €120. If you have wheels, this charming hotel about 4km north of the Altstadt is an excellent choice. A makeover in 2001 resulted in fully equipped rooms, nicely decorated in different hues, from lively reds to sunny yellows to cool blues. All rooms have private bath, cable TV and data ports. Some of the pricier ones have quirky themes such as 'Golfing', 'Africa' or 'Matisse'. Budget-priced family rooms are also available.

Places to Eat

Car-free Dollstrasse is Ingolstadt's 'restaurant row', with at least a dozen restaurants and cafes serving food from around the world.

Antalya (☎ 330 48, Dollstrasse 6) Lunch mains €5-7.50, dinner €9-12.50. Mirrors and paintings contribute to the homey decor at this Turkish restaurant. Try the grilled shish kebab.

Gasthaus Zum Daniel (☎ 352 72, Roseneckstrasse 1) Brotzeit €3-7.50, mains €5-8.50. The oldest pub in town drips with tradition and, according to some locals, serves the town's best pork roast. It also has a small beer garden in the back and a Frankenstein exhibit upstairs.

Restaurant Lemon (☎ 171 00, Tränktorstrasse 2) Mains €12-19. This stylish eatery offers upbeat, contemporary flair and gourmet cuisine inspired by the flavours of the Mediterranean.

Cafe Mohrenkopf (☎ 177 50, Donaustrasse 8) Breakfast €2-8, snacks under €5. This is a meeting place for Ingolstadt's trendoids with a cosy bar and a streetside beer garden in summer. Service can be glacial.

Cafe Reitschule (☎ 931 28 70, Mauthstrasse 8) Meals €3-12.50. Original art and palm trees add splashes of colour to this lively cafe. Anchored by a huge bar, it draws a young and chatty crowd. The food is good value and ranges from tomato soup to rump steak, plus daily specials.

Weissbräuhaus (*☎ 328 90, Dollstrasse 3*) Brotzeit €4.50-8.50, mains €9.50-14. This modern beer hall serves standard Bavarian dishes, including the delicious *Weissbräupfändl* (pork filet with homemade Spätzle noodles). There's a beer garden surrounding a fountain in back.

The university *Mensa* (*☎ 331 91, Konviktstrasse 1*) is open 11am to 2.30pm daily and has an inexpensive salad buffet, plus hot and cold dishes for around €3.50. It's one block south of the Maria de Victoria Church.

In the pedestrian zone, *Condotti* (*☎ 370 77 05, Am Stein 4*) has sandwiches, pizzas, salads and antipasti from €2.50, mostly for takeaway. At night, it's more of a bar.

The Wednesday and Saturday *markets* on Theaterplatz are great places to stock up on fresh produce, baked goods and other goodies.

Getting There & Around

Regional trains chug north to the Eichstätt in the Altmühltal at least hourly (€4, 25 minutes), and there's also an hourly train service to/from Regensburg (€10.70, 1¼ hour) and Munich (€12.40, one hour).

Single journeys on local buses cost €1.50.

AROUND INGOLSTADT
Neuburg an der Donau

☎ 08431 • pop 27,000 • elevation 400m

Neuburg an der Donau scenically hugs the southern Danube bank about 22km west of Ingolstadt and makes for a worthwhile afternoon excursion. Neuburg had already been settled for around 1600 years when its heyday arrived in 1505. That year it became the capital of the principality of Pfalz-Neuburg, the so-called 'Junge Pfalz' (Young Palatinate). Starting with Count Ottheinrich, a succession of rulers built up the town with magnificent Renaissance and baroque edifices. Nearly all of these cluster in the Obere Stadt, atop the Stadtberg, a little hill rising above the Danube west of the Eisenbrücke, the main bridge into town.

The bridge runs into Luitpoldstrasse, which divides the Obere Stadt from the newer commercial centre anchored by Spitalplatz. Beyond, along the Danube, is the sprawling Englischer Garten, a leafy oasis great for walking and cycling. The Bahnhof is about 1km south of the Danube. Bus No 3 loops between the station, the Obere Stadt and Spitalplatz at 30-minute intervals (€0.75 per ride).

Neuburg's tourist office (☎ 552 40, fax 552 42) is at Residenzstrasse A65 in the Obere Stadt and is open 9am to 6pm Monday to Friday and 10am to noon and 2pm to 5pm Saturday and Sunday.

Things to See Concentrate your sightseeing in the movie-set-pretty Obere Stadt, where time seems to move at the speed of drizzling honey. Visible from afar is the **Residenzschloss**, built between 1530 and 1545 by Count Ottheinrich. The palace courtyard is partly flanked by double arcades, which give it a decidedly Italianate look, further aided by the clever sgraffito facade paintings. (Sgraffito is a decorative pattern, usually monochrome, which is scratched or inscribed on plaster.)

The **Schlosskapelle** (1543), the oldest Protestant church in Bavaria, is swathed with ceiling frescoes by Hans Bocksberger. Thanks to their intricacy, the chapel is nicknamed 'Bavarian Sistina', an immodest allusion to the Vatican's Sistine Chapel. In 1665, Elector Philipp Wilhelm had the eastern wing added in baroque style and topped off by the towers that give the palace its distinctive silhouette.

The courtyard also gives access to the **Schlossmuseum** (*☎ 88 97, Residenzstrasse A2; adult/concession €2.50/2; open 9am-6pm Tues-Sun Apr-Sept, 10am-4pm Tues-Sun Oct-Mar*), which has sections on prehistory as well as Neuburg's glory days as a royal residence. Also take time for a spin around the garden with its fantastical **grottoes**, especially the *Blaue Grotte* (Blue Grotto) decorated with white Danube shells.

A short stroll west on Amalienstrasse takes you to the exquisite **Karlsplatz**, the heart of the Obere Stadt. Lined by ancient linden trees and meticulously restored historic houses, it is clearly dominated by the copper cupola of the late Renaissance **Hofkirche** (1607-08). Planned as a Protestant church, it was actually finished by Jesuits. It is decorated in a very subdued baroque style, with creamy white stucco and only hints of gold-leaf flourishes here and there.

The church dwarfs the comparatively modest **Rathaus** (1609) in the square's north-eastern corner, with its double staircase and a gallery on the ground floor. Of the various other ornate buildings around the square, the **Provinzialbibliothek** at the western end stands out for its yellow-and-pink exterior trim. Originally a church, it now houses a historical library and contains a wonderful baroque festival hall upstairs, which can only be seen on guided tours (usually 2.30pm Wednesday, May to October).

Strolling west on Amalienstrasse takes you to the **Peterskirche**, where the altar sculptures by Johann Michael Fischer are noteworthy. Soon you'll pass through the terracotta **Oberes Tor**, a storybook 16th-century town gate flanked by stocky twin towers. East of here is the **Hutzeldörr**, a small park that parallels the town wall and eventually takes you back to the Schloss.

Places to Eat Should hunger strike, you'll find a few options in the Obere Stadt, including *Da Capo* (☎ 427 00, *Residenzstrasse A66*), a modern bistro next to the tourist office; its mains go for €9 to €15.

For more traditional fare, try *Blaue Traube* (☎ 83 92, *Amalienstrasse 49*), the only place right on Karlsplatz. Its mains are €4 to €10, and it also has a few simple rooms at €25 to €50 for doubles.

For your afternoon coffee-and-cake break, try *Altstadtcafe* (☎ 27 86, *Amalienstrasse A44*), which also serves a few hot dishes but closes at 6.30pm.

Getting There & Away Regional trains leave hourly to/from Ingolstadt (€3.10, 15 minutes). The B16 runs right past town and connects with the B13, which leads north to Ingolstadt.

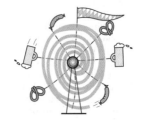

Allgäu-Bavarian Swabia

This double region of Allgäu-Bavarian Swabia (Allgäu-Bayerisch Schwaben) in the south-west of Bavaria has a wonderfully diverse landscape ranging from gently rolling hills to craggy Alpine peaks.

In the north is the Ries Basin, created by a meteorite millions of years ago, with the medieval town of Nördlingen at its centre. Nördlingen is also the region's northernmost town on the Romantic Road, which winds southward to Füssen at the foot of the Allgäu Alps, whose dreamy setting inspired King Ludwig II to build his famous Neuschwanstein castle. In the west the region is bounded by the Iller River as well as Lake Constance, with lovely Lindau holding forth as the only Bavarian town on this giant inland sea. In the east the Lech River forms a natural boundary to Upper Bavaria.

The region's major city is Augsburg, a mere 70km west of Munich and a delightful and stylish metropolis founded by the Romans. It's the capital of Bavarian Swabia, which was once part of the medieval Duchy of Swabia, the larger part of which now lies in the neighbouring state of Baden-Württemberg. The capital of the Allgäu, which more or less begins south of Augsburg, is Memmingen. Some of the country's best cheeses are made in the Allgäu, which also comprises Oberstdorf, a famous skiing resort.

AUGSBURG
☎ 0821 • pop 268,000 • elevation 489m
Augsburg is a city shaped by the Romans, by medieval artisans, bankers and traders and, in more recent times, by industry and technology. Traces of all these phases are evident throughout the city, which is Bavaria's third largest and the administrative centre of Swabia. It's a lively place with a thriving cultural scene and a mellow feel that (in summer, at least) is almost Mediterranean. A main stop on the Romantic Road, it also makes for a suitable alternative base during Oktoberfest if Munich is full.

Highlights

- Arrive early to beat the crowds for tours of King Ludwig II's most famous castle, Neuschwanstein, and his ancestral home, Hohenschwangau

- Explore Augsburg's Fuggerei, the world's oldest welfare community, then take in a show starring the endearing marionettes of the famous Augsburger Puppenkiste

- Climb to the top of the St Georgskirche in Nördlingen for birds-eye views of this perfectly circular town built within a giant meteorite crater

- Ski the slopes of Oberstdorf, the quintessential alpine village

- Wander the streets of lovely Lindau, then rent your own boat or board a ferry for a spin on Lake Constance

History
Augsburg is one of Germany's oldest cities with a pedigree going back about 2000 years. Founded by Drusus and Tiberius, two stepsons of Roman Emperor Augustus, in 15 BC as a military camp called Augusta Vindelicorum, it became the capital of the province of Raetia and

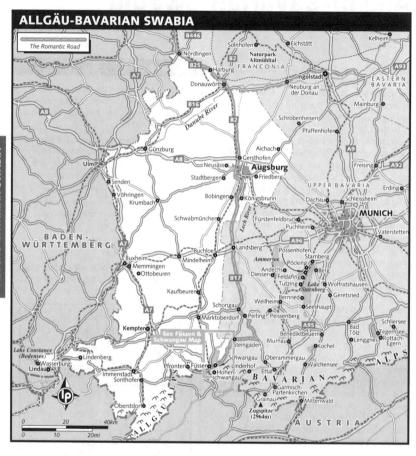

consequently the administrative and economic centre of the Roman Empire north of the Alps.

A bishopric since the 8th century, Augsburg got town rights in 1156 and became a Free Imperial City in 1316, maintaining its independence until coming under control of the Bavarian kingdom in 1805.

It experienced its most glorious times in the Middle Ages, thanks to its dual status as a major trading city (mostly gold, silver, copper) and financial/banking centre. During the Renaissance, two families emerged as the leading figures: the Fuggers (see the boxed text 'Jakob Fugger "The Rich"') and the Welsers.

The latter grew rich by exploiting gold and other natural resources in Venezuela, where they had been granted a concession by the deeply indebted Spanish crown in 1528.

Augsburg also played a significant role in the Reformation. In 1518 Martin Luther was ordered here to appear before the papal legate, Cardinal Kajetan, to disavow his writings.

But Luther, remaining true to his conscience, refused. In 1530 the reformers presented the *Confessio Augustana*, a summary of the Protestant doctrine, to Karl V. The emperor rejected it, but ultimately had to recognise the Lutheran faith as equal to the Catholic in 1555 in what went down in history as the Peace of Augsburg.

Augsburg suffered badly in the Thirty Years' War and more or less languished until industrialisation arrived in the 19th century. In 1897 Rudolf Diesel invented the diesel engine here, and the ME163 built by the Messerschmidt factory was the most advanced fighter plane in WWII.

The presence of this company, so crucial to the German war effort, caused the city to receive a particularly severe drubbing by Allied bombers.

Augsburg is the birthplace of the painter Hans Holbein the Elder (1465–1524); Leopold Mozart (1719–87), father of Wolfgang Amadeus; and the playwright Bertolt Brecht (1898–1956).

Orientation

The Hauptbahnhof is at the western end of Bahnhofstrasse, which intersects with Fuggerstrasse at the Königsplatz, the city's main bus transfer point

Information

Tourist Offices Augsburg's main tourist office is at Bahnhofstrasse 7 (☎ 50 20 70, fax 502 07 45, e tourismus@regio-augsburg .de) and is open 9am to 6pm Monday to Friday. A smaller branch at Rathausplatz (☎ 502 07 24) is open 9am to 5pm Monday to Friday, 10am to 4pm Saturday (to 1pm November to March) and, from April to October only, also from 10am to 1pm Sunday.

Money Change money at the Postbank at the Hauptbahnhof or at any of the banks along Bahnhofstrasse, including Hypovereinsbank at No 11, Citibank at No 2 and Deutsche Bank next door; all have ATMs.

Post & Communications The main post office is adjacent to the Hauptbahnhof. Log on at Surf Inn (☎ 502 22 21 68), inside the Galeria Kaufhof at Bürgermeister-Fischer-Strasse 9, which charges €1.50 per half-hour.

Internet Resources The town's Web site is W www.regio-augsburg.de.

Travel Agencies Fernweh (☎ 15 50 35), Dominikanergasse 10, is a representative

ALLGÄU-BAVARIAN SWABIA

Jakob Fugger 'The Rich'

King maker. Proto venture capitalist. Social benefactor. Jakob Fugger (1459–1525), one of the richest and politically most powerful men in the Holy Roman Empire at the cusp of the 14th to the 15th century, has been called many names. Born into humble circumstances, he was also the quintessential self-made man, embodying a spirit very much valued in today's society.

Originally destined for the priesthood, Jakob Fugger soon realised that his true calling lay in moneymaking and power mongering. Under his stewardship, the family's linen weaving business grew exponentially to the point where their textiles were exported to all corners of Europe.

Next, Fugger turned his interest to financial transactions, such as lending money to a bankrupt Tirolean archduke in return for rights to his copper and silver mines. When Habsburg Emperor Maximilian I needed to finance his battles, Fugger delivered the cash. When Maximilian died in 1519, Fugger made huge 'donations' to the election fund of Karl V to get him the emperor's crown. Such favours, of course, bought enormous influence and power, which in turn further increased the wealth of the Fugger family. Their coffers, apparently, made the Medicis in Florence look like beggars.

Despite such a material orientation, Fugger was in fact a devout man with a social conscience. Between 1514 and 1523 he created the Fuggerei, the world's first welfare colony for poor Catholic seniors (see Fuggerei, later in the Augsburg section). He died, childless, on 30 December 1525, leaving his 'empire' to his nephew Anton. A series of bad loans, though, soon brought the business to the brink of bankruptcy, causing the family to retire from banking and high stakes politics.

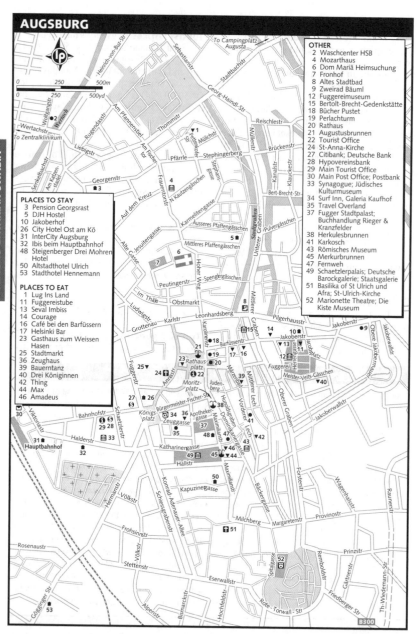

AUGSBURG

PLACES TO STAY
3 Pension Georgsrast
5 DJH Hostel
10 Jakoberhof
26 City Hotel Ost am Kö
31 InterCity Augsburg
32 Ibis beim Hauptbahnhof
48 Steigenberger Drei Mohren Hotel
50 Altstadthotel Ulrich
53 Stadthotel Hennemann

PLACES TO EAT
1 Lug Ins Land
11 Fuggereistube
13 Seval Imbiss
14 Courage
16 Café bei den Barfüssern
17 Helsinki Bar
23 Gasthaus zum Weissen Hasen
25 Stadtmarkt
36 Zeughaus
39 Bauerntanz
40 Drei Königinnen
42 Thing
44 Max
46 Amadeus

OTHER
2 Waschcenter HSB
4 Mozarthaus
6 Dom Mariä Heimsuchung
7 Fronhof
8 Altes Stadtbad
9 Zweirad Bäuml
12 Fuggereimuseum
15 Bertolt-Brecht-Gedenkstätte
18 Bücher Pustet
19 Perlachturm
20 Rathaus
21 Augustusbrunnen
22 Tourist Office
24 St-Anna-Kirche
27 Citibank; Deutsche Bank
28 Hypovereinsbank
29 Main Tourist Office
30 Main Post Office; Postbank
33 Synagogue; Jüdisches Kulturmuseum
34 Surf Inn, Galeria Kaufhof
35 Travel Overland
37 Fugger Stadtpalast; Buchhandlung Rieger & Kranzfelder
38 Herkulesbrunnen
41 Karkosch
43 Römisches Museum
45 Merkurbrunnen
47 Fernweh
49 Schaetzlerpalais; Deutsche Barockgalerie; Staatsgalerie
51 Basilika of St Ulrich und Afra; St-Ulrich-Kirche
52 Marionette Theatre; Die Kiste Museum

ALLGÄU-BAVARIAN SWABIA

office of STA Travel. Travel Overland
(☎ 31 41 57) has an office at Zeuggasse 5.

Bookshops Buchhandlung Rieger &
Kranzfelder (☎ 51 78 80), in the Fugger
Stadtpalast at Maximilianstrasse 36, has
English-language books, as does Bücher
Pustet (☎ 50 22 40) at Karolinenstrasse 12.

Laundry The Waschcenter HSB (☎ 41 94
51), Wolfgangstrasse 1 (take tram No 2), is
open 6am to 11.30pm daily.

Medical Services The most central hospital is the Zentralklinikum (☎ 400 01),
Stenglinstrasse 2. For a doctor or ambulance, call the Rotes Kreuz (Red Cross) on
☎ 192 22.

Rathausplatz

This large, pedestrianised square is the heart
of Augsburg's Altstadt and is anchored by
the **Augustusbrunnen**, a fountain honouring
the Roman emperor. The four figures represent the river Lech and the Wertach, Sin-
gold and Brunnenbach brooks.

Looming over the square are the twin
onion-domed spires of the Renaissance
Rathaus, built by Elias Holl from 1615 to
1620 and crowned by a 4m-tall pine cone,
the city's emblem (also an ancient fertility
symbol). Upstairs is the **Goldener Saal**
(Golden Hall; ☎ 324 91 80, Rathausplatz;
admission €1.50; open 10am-6pm daily), a
large banquet hall with an amazing gilded
and coffered ceiling that is further interspersed with frescoes.

Next to the Rathaus is the **Perlachturm**
(Perlach Tower; ☎ 50 20 70, Rathausplatz;
adult/concession €1/0.50; open 10am-6pm
daily May-Oct & 2pm-7pm Sat & Sun Dec),
a former guard tower. Climb to the top for
panoramic city views.

Dom District

North of Rathausplatz, via Karolinenstrasse
and Hoher Weg, is Augsburg's cathedral, the
Dom Mariä Heimsuchung with origins in
the 10th century but 'Gothicised' and enlarged in the 14th and 15th centuries. Its oldest surviving section is the 10th-century

crypt underneath the west choir. On the
south side are striking bronze doors (1356)
whose 35 relief panels depict Old Testament
scenes. Other treasures include medieval
frescoes, four panel paintings of the Virgin
Mary by Hans Holbein the Elder now affixed to the nave pillars and, above all, the
so-called 'Prophets' Windows'. Depicting
David, Daniel, Jonah, Hosea and Moses,
they are among the oldest figurative stained-
glass windows in Germany (12th century).

The building west of the Dom is the
Fronhof, the former bishop's palace. In the
predecessor of the current 1743 building,
the *Confessio Augustana* was proclaimed
in 1530.

A short walk north of the Dom, the
Mozarthaus (☎ 15 72 28, Frauentorstrasse
30; adult/concession €1.50/0.75; open
10am-5pm Tues-Sun) is where Leopold
Mozart, Wolfgang Amadeus' father, first
laid eyes on the world in 1719. It's now a
memorial museum.

St-Anna-Kirche

A short walk west of the Rathausplatz is the
Church of St Anna (open 10am-12.30pm &
3pm-6pm, closed Sun morning & Mon),
whose rather modest exterior hides a bevy
of treasures. Founded as a Carmelite monastery in 1321, it hosted Martin Luther during his stay in 1518. His rooms have been
turned into the **Lutherstiege**, a small museum about the Reformation. There's a portrait of Luther by Lucas Cranach the Elder
in the eastern choir, while at the opposite
end is the **Fuggerkapelle**, where Jakob Fugger and his brothers are buried. It is considered the first nonsecular Renaissance
structure in Germany. Also pop into the lav-
ishly frescoed **Goldschmiedekapelle** (Gold-
smiths' Chapel; 1420).

Maximilianstrasse

Rathausplatz marks the northern terminus
of the Maximilianstrasse, a grand boulevard lined by proud patrician mansions and
delightful cafes. Also along here are two
more impressive fountains which, together
with the Augustusbrunnen, were created
for Augsburg's 1600th anniversary. The

Merkurbrunnen (1599), at the intersection with Bürgermeister-Fischer-Strasse, is by Dutch artist Adriaen de Vries and features the god Mercury as a symbol of trade. Farther south, near Hallstrasse, is the **Herkulesbrunnen** (1602), also by de Vries, which shows Hercules fighting the seven-headed Hydra while three bathing nymphs look on admiringly. It's supposed to represent Augsburg's commercial importance.

Fugger Stadtpalast In between the two fountains, at No 36–38, is the restored Fugger Stadtpalast (1515), the palatial town house and 'corporate' headquarters of Jakob Fugger. It embraces the **Damenhof** (Ladies' Court), a lovely inner courtyard in arcaded Italian Renaissance style. In 1518 Luther refused to renounce his doctrine in a confrontation with Kajetan outside the palace.

Schaetzlerpalais In 1765 local banker Liebert von Liebenhofen commissioned the charming rococo palace known as the Schaetzlerpalais (☎ 324 41 02, Maximilianstrasse 56; adult/concession €3/1.50; open 10am-5pm Tues-Sun). It was designed by Carl Albert von Lespilliez, a student of François Cuvilliés. The pièce de résistance is the 23m-long ballroom, a riot of carved decorations, stucco and mirrors topped off with a dashing ceiling fresco. It's the perfect setting for occasional concerts.

Today the palais houses two museums. The **Deutsche Barockgalerie** (German Baroque Gallery) offers an exhaustive survey of German 17th- and 18th-century artists, very few of whom are household names. Of note are the paintings by Johann Heinrich Schönfeld, the still lifes by Johann Rudolf Byss, and oil sketches by Matthäus Günther and Johann Baptist Zimmermann.

A deconsecrated church attached to the Schaetzlerpalais now shelters the **Staatsgalerie** (Bavarian State Gallery), which has mostly Augsburg-related works by old masters, including a portrait of Jakob Fugger by Albrecht Dürer.

Ulrichskirchen At the bottom of Maximilianstrasse looms the onion-domed tower of the late-Gothic **Basilika of St Ulrich und Afra**, formerly the abbey church of Augsburg's Benedictine monastery and the burial place of the town patrons. Ulrich, the bishop who helped stop the Hungarians' advance in 955, rests in a splendid baroque tomb. Afra, who died as a martyr in 304 during Diocletian's Christian persecutions, still occupies her original plain Romanesque sarcophagus. Both are in the crypt. Simpert, a 9th-century bishop, is underneath a Gothic baldachin in a chapel off the right aisle.

Adjacent to the basilica, set at a right angle, is the **St-Ulrich-Kirche**, a former preaching hall of the monastery. A Lutheran church since 1524, its peaceful coexistence with its Catholic neighbour has long been a symbol of Augsburg's religious tolerance.

Bertolt-Brecht-Gedenkstätte

East of the Rathausplatz is the Lechviertel, sometimes also known as Jakobviertel, a largely pedestrianised district traversed by rushing little canals of the Lech River. Bertolt Brecht was born here in 1896 and his house has been turned into a memorial museum (☎ 324 27 79, Am Rain 7; adult/concession €1.50/1; open 10am-4pm Wed-Sun). Brecht's work was banned by the Nazis for his communist leanings; he was later shunned by West Germans for the same reason, and it's only recently that the city has honoured one of its most acclaimed sons. For more on Brecht, see the boxed text 'Bertolt Brecht'.

Just north of the Brecht house, the **Altes Stadtbad** (☎ 324 97 79, Leonardsberg 15) is a fanciful Art Nouveau indoor swimming pool with richly ornamented tiles and stained-glass windows. It's worth a look even without taking a plunge. There's a good cafe as well.

Römisches Museum

South of the Brecht house, the Römisches Museum (☎ 324 41 34, Dominikanergasse 15; adult/concession €3/1.50; open 10am-5pm Wed-Sun, 10am-9pm Tues) presents Augsburg's Roman heritage inside a former monastery church (1515). On display is everything from everyday objects like

Bertolt Brecht

Bertolt Brecht was not fond of Augsburg, and Augsburg returned the sentiment.

The famous, if controversial, playwright and poet was born in this city on 10 February 1898. Individualistic and rebellious in spirit, Brecht felt out of place in this tight, bourgeois community, even calling it a 'Scheissstadt' (shit city). Upon graduating from secondary school in 1917, he became a medical student in Munich, where he also began to write. His first play to reach the stage – *Trommeln in der Nacht* (Drums in the Night) – won the coveted Kleist Prize and quickly turned Brecht into a household name in the theatre world.

Soon Berlin, a cultural hotbed throughout the 1920s, exerted its magnetism. Here Brecht developed, over the next decade, his theory of the 'epic theatre'. Unlike 'dramatic theatre', it forces audiences to detach themselves emotionally from the characters and to view the action critically and intellectually. His biggest success was *Die Dreigroschenoper* (The Threepenny Opera; 1928).

MW

A staunch Marxist, Brecht went into exile during the Nazi years, surfaced in Hollywood as a scriptwriter, then left the USA after being called in to explain himself during the communist witch hunts of the McCarthy era. He returned to Germany in 1949, settling in East Berlin where he founded the Berliner Ensemble with his wife, Helene Weigel. Brecht died in Berlin on 14 August 1956. He's buried in the cemetery adjacent to his last home.

Through all these years, Augsburg ignored Brecht as much as he had ignored it. In fact, the first time one of his plays was performed here was in 1982. More recently, though, it seems the city has finally made peace with one of its famous sons. If he had a chance, perhaps Brecht too would feel more at home in this city now, which has since shed some of its stuffiness.

ALLGÄU-BAVARIAN SWABIA

jewellery, glass, ceramics and tools to military items, weapons, sarcophagi, gold coins and tombstones.

Fuggerei

East of the Lechviertel, across Oberer Graben, part of the ring road around the Altstadt, the Fuggerei is the world's earliest welfare settlement. Between 200 and 300 people still live in now modernised 60-sq-metre apartments, the rent having been frozen at 1 Rhenish Gilder (now €0.88) per *year*, plus utilities and three daily prayers. The 52 tidy houses and gardens flank the carfree lanes of this gated community. To make sure that the old folks don't have too much fun, gates are locked from 10pm to 6am (5am in summer). Anyone returning after 10pm is fined €0.25 and double that after midnight!

To see how residents lived before running water and central heating, stop in at the **Fuggereimuseum** (☎ 31 98 81, *Mittlere Gasse 13; adult/concession €0.50/0.25; open 10am-6pm daily Mar-Dec*). Franz Mozart, Wolfgang Amadeus' great-grandfather, once lived next door.

Synagogue

Augsburg's synagogue (1914–17), west of the Altstadt, is a beautiful Art Nouveau temple built by Heinrich Lömpel and Fritz Landauer. Devastated in 1938, it reopened in 1985 and, besides a prayer hall, contains the **Jüdisches Kulturmuseum** (*Museum of Jewish Culture;* ☎ 51 36 58, *Halderstrasse 8; adult/concession €2/1; open 9am-4pm Tues-Fri, 10am-5pm Sun; tours 6pm most Weds*). The permanent exhibit documents Jewish life in the region and explains traditions, rituals and customs using Judaica from the 17th to the 19th centuries.

Marionette Theatre & Die Kiste

In the southern Altstadt, next to the Heilig-Geist-Spital, modern and classic fairytales – *Aladdin* to *Rumpelstilzken* to *The Little Prince* – come to life at the celebrated marionette theatre called **Augsburger Puppenkiste** (☎ *43 44 40, Spitalgasse 15; tickets afternoon €6.40-9, evening €12-16.60; shows 3pm & 7.30pm Wed & Sat, 2pm & 4pm Sun*). The stars on strings are so endearing and the sets and costumes so fantastically elaborate that even non-German speakers will enjoy a show. It's often sold out, so if possible, make advance reservations or else check with the box office or the tourist office for remaining tickets on the day of your visit.

October 2001 also saw the opening of the theatre's long-awaited museum called **Die Kiste** (☎ *450 34 50; admission €4; open 10am-7pm Tues-Sun*). It takes visitors on a journey through the celebrated puppets' 50-year career on stage, TV and film.

Organised Tours

From May to October, the tourist office runs two-hour guided walking tours (in English and German) from the Rathaus at 2pm daily (adult/concession €6/4.50; Saturday only during the other months).

Places to Stay – Budget

Campingplatz Augusta (☎ *70 75 75, fax 70 58 83, Mühlhauser Strasse 54*) Bus: No 23 to terminus, then 2km walk. Tent/car/person €3/3/4. Open year round. This camping ground is on a swimming lake, some 7km from the city centre. Apart from camp sites, it has a few family rooms.

DJH hostel (☎ *339 09, fax 15 11 49, Beim Pfaffenkeller 3*) Tram: No 2 to Mozarthaus. Bed & breakfast including linen €12.30-13.10. This hostel is rather down-at-heel but central. From the tram stop, walk east on Mittleres Pfaffengässchen.

The tourist offices can help you find a private or hotel room (€1.50 fee).

Jakoberhof (☎ *51 00 30, fax 15 08 44, Jakoberstrasse 39-41*) Singles/doubles from €25/32.50. One of the cheapest places is this simple pension near the Fuggerei with free parking and a decent Bavarian restaurant downstairs.

Pension Georgsrast (☎ *50 26 10, fax 502 61 27, Georgenstrasse 31*) Singles/doubles from €32.50/42.50. This place, run by a gaggle of older women, is in the northern city centre and offers few basic frills but full facilities.

Stadthotel Hennemann (☎ *57 80 77, fax 59 26 00, Gögginger Strasse 39*) Singles/doubles from €42.50/60. South of the city centre, near the congress hall, this hotel offers decent, old-fashioned rooms and Bavarian charm.

Places to Stay – Mid-Range & Top End

City Hotel Ost am Kö (☎ *50 20 40, fax 502 04 44, e ulrich@ostamkoe.de, Fuggerstrasse 4-6*) Singles €50-82.50, doubles €65-110. Don't be put off by the 1960s cube architecture. Behind the concrete facade awaits an efficiently run quality hotel with lots of personal touches and a staff that is quick with a smile. Rooms feature updated, yet traditional, decor and the breakfast buffet is out of this world.

Altstadthotel Ulrich (☎ *346 10, fax 346 13 46, e altstadthotel.ulrich@t-online.de, Kapuzinergasse 6*) Singles/doubles from €65/95. This upmarket hotel is in a quiet side street in an old patrician mansion but with modern furniture and amenities. Almost half of the 33 rooms are for nonsmokers.

Ibis beim Hauptbahnhof (☎ *501 60, fax 501 61 50, e h1438@accor-hotels.com, Halderstrasse 25*) Singles/doubles €60/65. This French chain offers the usual comfortable and modern – if fairly characterless and small – rooms. If you need to be close to the train station, this one's a good bet.

InterCity Augsburg (☎ *503 90, fax 503 99 99, e augsburg@intercityhotel.de, Halderstrasse 29*) Singles/doubles from €70/80. Practically next door to the Ibis, the Inter City offers a slightly better standard.

Steigenberger Drei Mohren Hotel (☎ *503 60, fax 15 78 64, e augsburg@ steigenberger.de, Maximilianstrasse 40*)

Singles/doubles from €110/160. This landmark hotel, flanked by the Schaetzlerpalais and the Fugger Stadtpalais, is a stunning place. Elegant touches include marble bathrooms and original art.

Places to Eat

Restaurants & Cafes There are lots of cafes along Maximilianstrasse, including Amadeus at No 67 and Max next door, just in front of the Merkurbrunnen.

Café bei den Barfüssern (☎ 15 93 08, Kanalstrasse 2) Dishes (1.50-2.50. Open till 5.30pm. Affiliated with the Protestant Barfüsserkirche, this is a relaxing place to enjoy the homemade cakes and pastries while sitting next to a little canal.

Helsinki Bar (☎ 372 90, Barfüsserstrasse 4) Dishes €2-5.50. A cafe by day, a bar by night, this place attracts a cool crowd with its Nordic fare and furnishings.

Courage (☎ 349 94 30, Jakoberstrasse 7) Dishes €3-9. Open for dinner only. This cosy restaurant-pub pays homage to Bertolt Brecht. Quotations from his plays decorate the slate ceiling, a life-size Brecht plaster statue overlooks the room and Brecht-themed postcards are for sale.

Drei Königinnen (☎ 15 84 05, Meister-Veits-Gässchen 32) Mains €8.50-12. Lighter cuisine, including interesting salads and pasta, is served here alongside standard regional offerings. Readings and other cultural events take place occasionally, and there's a great beer garden out the back.

Bauerntanz (☎ 15 36 44, Bauerntanzgässchen 1) Mains €6.50-15. A local favourite, this place has big portions of creative Swabian and Bavarian food using choice ingredients. There's outdoor seating in nice weather.

Gasthaus zum Weissen Hasen (☎ 51 85 08, Unter dem Bogen 4) Mains €8.50-16. This historic place has set lunch specials for €5 and a long menu of regional dishes.

Fuggereistube (☎ 308 70, Jakoberstrasse 26) Mains €9-18. Next to the north gate of the Fuggerei, this place has vintage 1970s hunting-lodge decor, but the Bavarian food and service are very good.

Beer Gardens An Augsburg institution, *Thing (☎ 395 05, Vorderer Lech 45)* is among the town's coolest beer gardens.

Lug Ins Land (☎ 15 41 43, Am Lueginsland 5) This is another pleasant one, in the park at the northern tip of the Altstadt at Herwartstrasse.

Zeughaus (☎ 51 16 85, Zeughausplatz 4) Right behind Maximilianstrasse, the Zeughaus was once a 17th-century armoury and is now a trade school, cinema and a superb place for a brew. It also offers tasty vegetarian dishes.

Snacks & Fast Food The local *Stadtmarkt* is a snacker's fantasy and open from 7am to 6pm Monday to Friday and to 2pm Saturday; it's between Fuggerstrasse and Annastrasse. Besides fresh produce, bread and meat, you'll find dozens of stand-up eateries serving everything from Thai to Bavarian to Greek in the Fleischhalle and the Viktualienhalle.

Seval Imbiss (☎ 395 18, Karrengässchen 1) Doners €3. The gleaming Seval Imbiss, near the Fuggerei, has absolutely splendid doners.

Getting There & Away

Air Augsburg has a small regional airport that is the hub of Augsburg Air, a Lufthansa affiliate, with services to Hamburg, Berlin, Düsseldorf, Cologne and Frankfurt. The Munich airport is about 90km due east.

Train & Bus Regional trains connect Augsburg and Munich at least hourly (€9, 45 minutes), with faster and pricier ICE and IC trains passing through as well. RE trains depart every other hour to Füssen (€14.40, two hours) and to Lindau (€24, three hours). The Europabus stops at the Hauptbahnhof.

Car & Motorcycle Augsburg is just south off the A8 north-west of Munich. The northbound B2 and the southbound B17 are part of the Romantic Road.

Getting Around

To/From the Airport The Augsburg Flughafen Express bus connects Augsburg airport with the Hauptbahnhof up to five times Monday to Friday only. Trips take between 20 and 35 minutes, depending on traffic, and cost €4.50, or €7.50 return.

The Lufthansa Airport Bus (☎ 502 25 34) runs between Augsburg's train station and the Munich airport six times daily (one way/return €15/24, 70 minutes).

Public Transport Most rides within town on the bus and tram network cost €0.90; longer trips to the outlying suburbs are €1.80. A 24-hour ticket costs €4.75 and is good for up to three adults.

For bicycle rental, Zweirad Bäuml (☎ 336 21), Jakoberstrasse 70, has a good range of bikes from €5/30 per day/week for a touring bike, €7.50/32.50 for a trekking bike and €15/60 for a tandem.

SOUTHERN ROMANTIC ROAD

In this guide, we have divided the Romantic Road into two sections: the Northern Romantic Road from Würzburg to Dinkelsbühl through Franconia (see that chapter), and the Southern Romantic Road from Nördlingen to Füssen, which goes through Bavarian Swabia and the Allgäu. For details about how to explore this route, see the boxed text in the Franconia chapter.

NÖRDLINGEN

☎ 09081 • pop 21,000 • elevation 433m

Nördlingen, about 70km north-west of Augsburg, lies within the Ries Basin, a huge crater created more than 15 million years ago by a mega-meteorite, which released energy nearly 250,000 times that of the bomb dropped on Hiroshima. The crater – some 25km in diameter – was used by US astronauts to train for the first moon landing.

First mentioned 1100 years ago, Nördlingen is still encircled by 14th-century town walls, broken intermittently by five gates, 16 towers and two bastions. Climb the tower of the St Georgskirche for bird's-eye views.

Orientation

The train station is about a 15-minute walk south-east of the Altstadt. Nördlingen township is almost perfectly circular, with the St Georgskirche on Markt at its centre from where five main roads radiate towards the five town gates. The little Eger River traverses the northern Altstadt, separating the Gerberviertel (tanner's quarter), home to both the Stadtmuseum and the Rieskrater Museum, from the rest of the Altstadt.

Information

The tourist office (☎ 43 80, fax 841 13, e verkehrsamt@noerdlingen.de, w www .noerdlingen.de) is at Marktplatz 2. From Easter to October, it's open 9am to 6pm Monday to Thursday, to 4.30pm Friday and 9.30am to 1pm Saturday. In winter, it closes an hour earlier on weekdays and remains closed Saturday and Sunday. Guided walking tours (in German) depart daily at 2pm from Easter to October (€2, free if under 12).

Gates & Walls

You can circumnavigate the entire town by walking along the sentry walk of the covered town wall (free). Climb up at any of the five gates: **Baldinger Tor**, **Löpsinger Tor**, **Deininger Tor**, **Reimlinger Tor** or **Berger Tor**, located at the end of streets bearing their names.

St Georgskirche

Nearly football field-sized, the late-Gothic Church of St Georg got its baroque mantle in the 18th century. Worth a look are the high altar and the intricate 1499 pulpit.

To truly appreciate Nördlingen's shape and the gentle landscape of the Ries Basin, scramble up the 350 steps of the 90m-tall **Daniel Tower** *(adult/concession €1.50/1; open 9am-8pm daily Apr-Oct, 9am-5.30pm daily Nov-Mar)*. The guard, who actually lives up there, sounds out the watch every half-hour from 10pm to midnight.

Rieskrater Museum

The Ries Crater Museum *(☎ 273 82 20, Eugene-Shoemaker-Platz 1; adult/concession €2.50/1.25; open 10am-noon & 1.30pm-4.30pm Tues-Sun)* is a modern museum in an ancient barn. It explores the formation of meteorites and the effects of such violent collisions on earth. Rocks, including a genuine moon rock (on permanent loan from NASA), fossils and other geological displays shed light on the mystery of meteors. A combination adult/concession ticket with the Stadtmuseum costs €4/2.

Other Museums

The **Stadtmuseum** (☎ 273 82 30, Vordere Gerbergasse 1; adult/concession €2.50/1.25; open 1.30am-4.30pm Tues-Sun Mar-early Nov) has costumes and displays on local history. The **Stadtmauermuseum** (☎ 91 80, Löpsinger Torturm; adult/concession €2.50/1.25; open 10am-4.30pm Apr-Oct) has an exhibition on the history of the town walls and fortification system as well as uniforms and weapons.

Special Events

The 10-day **Nördlinger Pfingstmesse**, held at Whitsuntide/Pentecost (dates vary), is the town's biggest party with beer tents, food stalls and the usual entertainment taking over the Altstadt.

Places to Stay & Eat

Gasthof Drei Mohren (☎ 31 13, fax 287 59, Reimlinger Strasse 18) Singles/doubles €17.50/35. This simple place in a pretty building with white trim and a fancy gable with snail-shaped decoration offers great value. It's attached to a decent restaurant serving meaty mains (€7 to €14) but closed all day Thursday and over lunch on Friday.

Hotel Altreuter (☎ 43 19, fax 97 97, Marktplatz 11) Singles €32.50-45, doubles €49-65. This place has nice, renovated rooms and a popular cafe with cakes and snacks under €5.

Kaiserhof Hotel Sonne (☎ 50 68, fax 239 99, Marktplatz 3) Singles €47.50-55, doubles €75-115. Nördlingen's top abode has hosted an entire parade of emperors and their entourages. Rooms mix modern comforts with traditional charm, while the restaurant serves regional dishes (mains €5 to €12.50)

Cafe Radlos (☎ 50 40, Löpsinger Strasse 8) Snacks €2.50-5, mains €5-10. This hip cafe has it all: art, magazines, a beer garden, global cuisine including vegetarian choices,

readings, an English menu, even Internet access (€1.25 per 30 minutes).

La Fontana (☎ 21 10 21, Bei den Kornschrannen 2) Mains €3.50-11.50. This stylish Italian eatery occupies a vast 1602 blood-red barn. It has a pleasant contemporary flair and fair prices if you stick to pizza, pasta or salad.

Fast-food options include a **Kochlöffel** (Marktplatz 9) for burgers, roast chicken and salads and nearby **Café Ihle** (Rübenmarkt 3) for baked good and sandwiches.

Getting There & Around

Nördlingen is on the B25 which connects with the B26 and B466. There are free parking lots at all five city gates.

Trains leave hourly to Donauwörth via Harburg (€3.90, 33 minutes) with connections to Augsburg and Munich. The Europabus stops at the Rathaus, as does regional bus No 868 to Dinkelsbühl and Feuchtwangen (see the Franconia chapter).

For bicycle rental, try Radsport Böckle (☎ 80 10 40), Reimlinger Strasse 19, or Zweirad Müller (☎ 56 75), Gewerbestrasse 16. Expect to pay about €7.50 per day.

HARBURG

☎ 09080 • pop 6500

Hugging the Wörnitz River, this little town about 15km south-east of Nördlingen has a cute and compact **Altstadt** with plenty of half-timbered and baroque houses. The main reason to stop, though, is the town's namesake castle, the humungous **Harburg** (☎ 968 60; adult/student/child €4/3.50/2.50; tours hourly 10am-5pm Apr-Oct, 10am-4pm Nov, closed Dec-Mar).

Perched paternalistically above the valley, this classic medieval castle – with its covered parapets, towers, turrets, keep and red-tiled roofs – is so well preserved it almost seems like a movie set. You half expect a knight in shining armour to strut across the courtyard, a fair lady at his arm. Construction commenced in 1150 under the Hohenstaufen emperors before passing into the possession of the counts and princes of Oettingen-Wallerstein in 1299, who still own it today.

Tours (in German) last about an hour and take in the church, prison, keep, armoury, festival hall and fortifications. There's a restaurant up here as well. The walk into town takes about 10 minutes, slightly more the other way when you're climbing uphill. For a great panorama of the village and the castle, seek out the Stone Bridge (1702) spanning the Wörnitz. There's a tourist office (☎ 969 90, fax 96 99 30) on Schlossstrasse.

There's hourly train service to/from Nördlingen (€3, 20 minutes) and to/from Donauwörth (€2.40, 13 minutes). Harburg is on the B25.

DONAUWÖRTH

☎ 0906 • pop 18,000 • elevation 403m

About 15km south-east of Harburg, Donauwörth is at the confluence of the Danube and the Wörnitz. From humble beginnings as a fishing village in the 10th century, it reached its zenith as a Free Imperial City in 1301. WWII managed to destroy much of the medieval town, and during rebuilding numerous concessions to modernity were made. Nevertheless, Donauwörth is not without charms, especially along its central artery, the Reichsstrasse, which is about a 10-minute walk north of the train station. The tourist office (☎ 78 91 50, fax 78 99 99) is in the Rathaus at the bottom of Reichsstrasse (open Monday to Friday only).

Things to See

Donauwörth's landmark is the **Rathaus**, begun in 1236 but severely altered through the centuries. The carillon on the ornamented step gable plays (at 11am and 4pm daily) a composition by local boy Werner Egk (1901–83) from his opera *Die Zaubergeige* (The Magic Violin).

From the Rathaus, **Reichsstrasse** heads west, flanked by picture-perfect town homes with steep rooflines and painted in a rainbow of colours. The two oldest are **Cafe Engel** (1297) at No 10 and the 14th-century **Tanzhaus** (Dance House) at No 34, now home to an archaeological exhibit, a restaurant and a concert hall.

Further on, the 15th-century **Liebfrauenkirche** is a Gothic three-nave hall church

decked out with original frescoes; the tabernacle, choir stalls and baptismal font are also worth a peek. Swabia's largest church bell (6550kg) hangs in the belfry.

Continue west to the **Heilig-Kreuz-Kirche** (1717–20), where the pious have flocked for centuries to venerate a chip said to come from the Holy Cross. The church itself is a baroque confection by Josef Schmuzer of Wessobrunn and part of a Benedictine abbey founded in 1125.

In a former Capuchin monastery north of here, via Pflegstrasse, is the delightful **Käthe-Kruse-Puppenmuseum** (☎ 78 91 85, *Pflegstrasse 21a; adult/concession €2/1; open 2pm-5pm Tues-Sun Apr-Oct, 2pm-5pm Sat & Sun Nov-Mar*) with lots of dolls and doll houses by this world-renowned designer (1863–1968). The same building also contains a memorial exhibit to Werner Egk, a student of *Carmina Burana* composer Carl Orff.

South of Reichsstrasse, the **Rieder Tor** – the gateway to picturesque Ried Island – houses the local history museum *(adult/concession €1.50/0.75; open Sat & Sun)*.

Places to Stay & Eat

Kanu Club Donauwörth *(☎ 226 95, An der Westspange)* This riverside camping ground is north-west of the Altstadt.

DJH hostel *(☎ 51 58, fax 24 38 17, Goethestrasse 10)* Bed & breakfast €13.30-14.10. The local hostel was recently renovated and is about a half-hour walk north of the train station.

Pension Graf *(☎ 51 17, Zirgesheimer Strasse 5)* Singles/doubles €22.50/45. Sparse but modern rooms with cable TV await at this little pension right on the Danube and a five-minute walk east of the Rathaus.

Goldener Hirsch *(☎ 31 24, fax 24 31 24, Reichsstrasse 44)* Singles/doubles €25/60. This nice inn near the Liebfrauenkirche has a good restaurant serving Swabian specialities (mains €4.50 to €13, closed Friday).

Cafe Rafaello *(☎ 999 92 66, Fischerplatz 1)*. Mains €4-8. On Ried Island, this is a trendy Italian eatery with a loft-like interior and good pizza and pasta.

Getting There & Away

There's direct hourly service to Nördlingen via Harburg (€3.90, 33 minutes). The Europabus stops at the Liebfrauenkirche. Donauwörth is at the crossroads of the B2, the B16 and the B25.

SOUTH OF AUGSBURG

South of Augsburg, the Romantic Road enters its least scenic stretch, although there are a few worthwhile stops. About 38km south of town is **Landsberg am Lech**, founded by Heinrich der Löwe (Henry the Lion) in 1160. It possesses an especially nice Marktplatz ringed by stately buildings, including the impressive Rathaus. Its awesome facade (1720) is the work of Dominikus Zimmermann, who moonlighted as the town's mayor from 1749 to 1754 while creating the Johanniskirche (1752). Also worth a look is the parish church Maria Himmelfahrt (1458–88), famous for its luminous stained-glass windows.

South of Landsberg, the route enters the **Pfaffenwinkel** (Clerics' Corner), an area with the greatest density of churches and monasteries anywhere in Germany. After the tranquil gateway town of **Hohenfurch**, the Romantic Road travels to **Schongau**, which preserves a largely intact medieval appearance and is the Pfaffenwinkel's touristic hub. The tourist office (☎ 08861-72 16) is at Münzstrasse 5. Sights include the town wall, the Gothic *Ballenhaus*, a festival hall, and the baroque Maria Himmelfahrt church (1753), whose choir stucco bears the distinctive Zimmermann touch.

A worthwhile detour is the **Basilika St Michael** (1220) in Altenstadt, about 2km west of Schongau, which ranks as one of the most important Romanesque churches in Bavaria. It has great frescoes, a delicate baptismal font and a 3.5m-high crucifix from around 1200, which is revered as the 'Great God of Altenstadt'.

The route winds south to **Peiting**, then continues south-east on the B23 to **Rottenbuch** in the romantic Ammertal (Ammer Valley). The town is dominated by an 11th-century Augustinian monastery whose church got its baroque outfit courtesy of Franz Xaver Schmädl and Josef Schmuzer

(stucco) and Matthäus Günther (frescoes). Hiking trails lead from the depth of Ammer Gorge back up to elevations reaching 900m. Check with the tourist office (☎ 08867-14 64) at Klosterhof 36 for maps and directions.

From here, the Romantic Road travels west through **Wildsteig** before rejoining the B17 in **Steingaden**, where one of the route's highlights awaits: the Wieskirche.

Wieskirche

The Wieskirche ('Wies' for short) in Steingaden is the best known among Bavaria's baroque churches and has been a Unesco World Heritage Site since the 1980s. Every year, about a million visitors – art and spiritual pilgrims alike – flock to what rates as the most accomplished work by the brothers Dominikus and Johann Baptist Zimmermann. Dominikus, in fact, became so attached to his life's masterpiece that he moved into a little cottage next to the church where he died in 1766 (it's now a restaurant).

The central object of worship is the rather unassuming **statue of the Scourged Saviour**, now part of the high altar. This figure comes with a rather colourful story. Originally used in a Good Friday procession in 1730, it ended up in the attic of a local innkeeper who revered it greatly. Then, on 14 June 1738, during evening prayers, tears suddenly began oozing from the statue's eyes. A miracle! Over the next few years, so many pilgrims poured into the town that the local abbot commissioned a new church to house the weepy work.

The deluge of visitors hasn't stopped, especially in the warmer months, but not even the hordes can detract from the Wies' splendour. Gleaming white pillars are topped by capital stones that seem like leaping flames against the white, gold and pastel stucco. Above it all, the vaulted ceiling fresco celebrates Christ's resurrection as he is carried on a rainbow, accompanied by cherubim and the 12 apostles. The painting blends wittily with the architecture such as the cherub on the edge of the ceiling fresco whose painted left leg emerges as a three-dimensional stucco leg. The Wies is filled with many other such charming details. If possible, take your time to keep the overwhelm quotient down.

The Europabus makes a 13-minute stop at the Wieskirche, but only on its south-north route (Füssen-Frankfurt). Local bus No 1084 connects the church with Füssen, Schwangau, Oberammergau and Garmisch-Partenkirchen.

FÜSSEN & SCHWANGAU
☎ 08362 • pop 14,000 Füssen, 3700 Schwangau • elevation 800m

Schwangau and Füssen are the two final stops on the Romantic Road. Nestling at the foot of the Alps, they are in fact separate towns about 4km apart but described here jointly because they form two anchors of what is marketed as the **Königswinkel** (Royal Corner). The area gets its name from Ludwig II, the king who built Neuschwanstein, one of Bavaria's biggest tourist attractions. This, as well as his ancestral home, the palace of Hohenschwanstein, are actually in tiny Hohenschwangau, the third 'corner' in this triangle of attractive towns, and still owned by the royal family of Bavaria. It basically just exists to cater for castle visitors.

Never at a loss for tourists (about 1.3 million people come here each year), the local industry was given yet another boost in 2000 with the opening of the melodramatic musical *Ludwig II* in a custom-built theatre on the Forggensee lake.

Ludwig's other castle, Schloss Linderhof, is about 45km north-east of here (see Around Oberammergau in the Upper Bavaria chapter).

Orientation
The only Bahnhof in the Königswinkel is in Füssen, right in the northern Altstadt, steps away from the tourist office and all in-town sights. The Lech River traverses the town and flows into the Forggensee lake reservoir. Schwangau is about 4km east of Füssen via the B17 (the Romantic Road) which, in town, is called Münchener Strasse. Hohenschwangau is more or less in between and south of the two towns, about 5km from Füssen and 3km from Schwangau. Bus No 9713 connects all three.

Information
The slick tourist office – Kurverwaltung Füssen (☎ 938 50, fax 93 85 20, e tourismus@fuessen.de) – is at Kaiser-Maximilian-Platz 1, about three minutes' walk east of the Bahnhof. It's open 8am to noon and 1.30pm to 5pm Monday to Friday and, from May to October also from 10am to 1pm Saturday. There's also an information booth right at the Ludwig II musical theatre. A daily Kurtaxe (resort tax) of €1.50/1.25 in peak/off-peak season is levied for overnight stays.

Tiny Schwangau has its own tourist office (☎ 819 80, fax 81 98 25, e kurverwaltung@schwangau.de, w www.schwangau.de) at Münchener Strasse 2. The Kurtaxe here is €1.15.

Füssen is the bigger town with better infrastructure. There's a Sparkasse at Kaiser-Maximilian-Platz 3, next to the tourist office, with the post office a few steps away at Bahnhofstrasse 10. For Web access, try the Videothek (☎ 383 00) at Luitpoldstrasse 11, south of the tourist office.

Schloss Neuschwanstein
Appearing through the mountaintop mist like a dreamy mirage is the world's most famous castle: Neuschwanstein *(☎ 93 08 30; adult/concession €7/6, combination ticket with Hohenschwangau €13/11; open 9am-6pm Wed-Tues, 9am-8pm Thur Apr-Sept; 10am-4pm daily Oct-Mar).*

Construction on this idealised romantic medieval Schloss began in 1869 and was never completed. The grey-white granite edifice was an anachronism from the start; by the time Ludwig died in 1886, the first high-rises pierced the New York skyline. For all the money spent on it (an estimated €3 million), the king himself was able to enjoy only about 170 days in his dream palace.

A visit to the Wartburg, a medieval knights' castle balanced on a craggy hillside in the Thuringian forest, inspired Ludwig to build his own hill-top fantasy retreat. The king imagined his palace as a giant stage that would allow him to re-create the world of Germanic mythology immortalised in the operas of Richard Wagner, whom he worshipped.

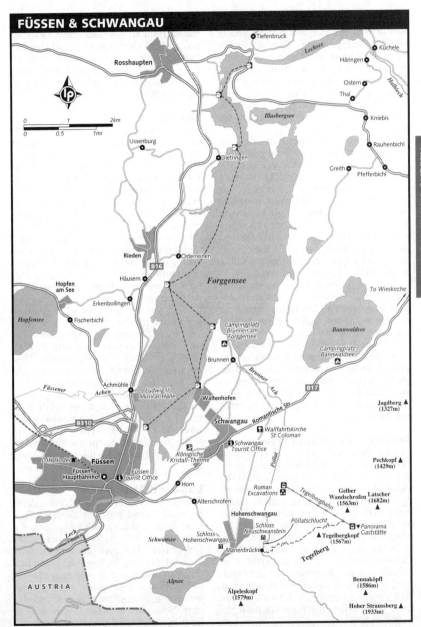

FÜSSEN & SCHWANGAU

Tiefenbruck

Lechsee

Küchele

Rosshaupten

Häringen

Ostern

Thal

Illasbergsee

Kniebis

Rauhenbichl

Ussenburg

Dietringen

Greith

Pfefferbichl

Rieden

Osterreinen

B16

Häusern

Forggensee

To Wieskirche

Hopfen am See

Erkenboilingen

Hopfensee

Fischerbichl

Campingplatz Brunnen am Forggensee

Bannwaldsee

Campingplatz Bannwaldsee

Brunnen

Brunner Ach

Füssener Achen

Achmühle

Ludwig II Musical-Halle

Waltenhofen

B17

Jagdberg (1327m)

Schwangau

Romantische Str.

Wallfahrtskirche St Coloman

Pechkopf (1429m)

DJH Hostel

Füssen

Königliche Kristall-Therme

Schwangau Tourist Office

Füssen Hauptbahnhof

Füssen Tourist Office

Horn

Pöllat

Roman Excavations

Tegelbergbahn

Gelber Wandschrofen (1563m)

Latscher (1682m)

Alterschrofen

Hohenschwangau

Pöllatschlucht

Panorama Gaststätte

Schloss Neuschwanstein

Tegelbergkopf (1567m)

Lech

Schwansee

Schloss Hohenschwangau

Marienbrücke

Tegelberg

AUSTRIA

Alpsee

Älpeleskopf (1579m)

Bennaköpfl (1586m)

Hoher Straussberg (1933m)

0 1 2km
0 0.5 1mi

A theatre designer rather than an architect laid out the initial blueprint, which accounts for its dramatic packaging. Its centrepiece is the lavish **Sängersaal** (Minstrels' Hall) with murals depicting scenes from the opera *Tannhäuser*. Though it wasn't used during Ludwig's time, concerts are now held there every September (tickets €25 to €70; available starting in February through the Schwangau tourist office).

Other completed sections include Ludwig's **bedroom**, a gaudy **artificial grotto** (another allusion to *Tannhäuser*) and the **Thronsaal** (throne room). The sleeping chamber is dominated by a huge bed crowned with intricately carved spires like those of a Gothic cathedral. Built in the style of a Byzantine church, the throne room has a great mosaic floor and a chandelier shaped like a giant crown. Note that there is no throne: Ludwig had ordered it shortly before his death but it was never delivered.

Although Ludwig liked the medieval look, he also enjoyed the latest technologies. A sophisticated hot air heating system kept the rooms cosy and there was running water throughout the castle.

The wooded hills framing Neuschwanstein make for some wonderful walks. For the postcard view of Neuschwanstein and the plains beyond, walk 10 minutes up to Marienbrücke (Mary's Bridge), which spans the spectacular Pöllat Gorge over a waterfall just above the castle.

Schloss Hohenschwangau

Ludwig spent his childhood at sun-yellow Hohenschwangau (☎ 93 08 30; *same hours & prices as Neuschwanstein*), down in the village. Originally built in the 12th century by Schwangau knights, its current visage stems from the 1830s after Ludwig's father, Max II, had the ruin reconstructed in neogothic fashion. It's much less ostentatious and has a distinctly lived-in feeling. Certain chambers are just as surreal as in Neuschwanstein, however. After his father died, for instance, Ludwig had stars painted on his bedroom ceiling, which were illuminated with hidden oil lamps while his highness slumbered.

It was here that Ludwig first met Wagner, and the **Hohenstaufensaal** features a square piano where the composer would entertain Ludwig with excerpts from his latest efforts. Some rooms feature murals from German mythology (including Lohengrin, the Swan Knight).

Tickets

Both castles must be seen on 35-minute guided tours (in German or English). Tickets are available only from the Ticket Centre at Alpseestrasse 12 in Hohenschwangau. In summer, we recommend that you arrive by 8.30am or even earlier to ensure you get a ticket. To avoid disappointment, you can also book your tickets in advance by phone (☎ 93 08 30), by fax (fax 930 83 20) or by Internet (🆆 www.ticket-center-hohenschwangau.de). You'll need a major credit card to guarantee your booking, but you may cancel as late as two hours before your pre-assigned tour time. A nonrefundable booking fee of €1.50 per ticket applies.

When you purchase your ticket, you'll be assigned a tour number and a tour time. Wait by either castle entrance close to the time indicated on your ticket until the digital display shows your tour number. Then put your ticket into the slot next to the turnstiles to meet your tour guide inside.

It is usually possible to visit both castles on the same day. The steep uphill walk from Hohenschwangau to Neuschwanstein takes about 30 to 40 minutes. You can also shell out about €5 per person for a horse-drawn carriage ride, but this is only slightly faster.

Ludwig II Musical

The tragic story of Ludwig II's life unfolds in music, sound and special effects in a hyper-modern theatre built into a protected nature preserve on the western shore of the Forggensee. The musical, sentimentally subtitled 'Longing for Paradise', is part fantasy, part history and all monumental spectacle. Shows take place nightly, plus weekend matinees (no shows on Monday from November to March). It is sung in German with English supertitles.

Tickets (☎ 01805-58 39 44 from within Germany only, ⒠ zentrale@ludwigmusical .com) start at €44 and climb all the way up to a painful €118 for seats in the 'royal' box. Various hotel packages are available (check with any travel agent). Coming from Munich, Panorama Tours (☎ 54 90 75 60, ⒠ panoramatours@autobusoberbayern.de) offers packages which include the ticket to the Ludwig castles and round-trip bus transfer starting at €70/80 on weekdays/ weekends.

ALLGÄU-BAVARIAN SWABIA

The Mystery & Mystique of Ludwig II

Every year on June 13, a stirring ceremony takes place in Berg on the eastern shore of Lake Starnberg. A small boat quietly slices through still waters towards a cross jutting out from the lake, just offshore. A plain wreath is fastened to the cross' front, then the vessel slowly returns. The prolonged notes of a single trumpet cut the reverent silence, its melancholy peal part of this solemn ritual in honour of the most beloved king ever to rule Bavaria: Ludwig II.

The cross marks the spot where, in 1886, Ludwig died under mysterious circumstances. His early death capped the life of a man at odds with the harsh realities of a modern world no longer in need of a romantic and idealistic monarch.

When the 18-year-old Prinz Otto Ludwig Friedrich Wilhelm – aka Ludwig II – ascended the Bavarian throne in 1864, a lonely and joyless childhood lay behind him. His parents, Maximilian II and Marie, took little interest in the romantic epics, architecture and music that fascinated the sensitive youth. In 1867 the king was engaged briefly to Princess Sophie, the sister of Elisabeth (Sisi), the Austrian empress, but as a rule he preferred the company of male hangers-on in the royal court. He also worshipped composer Richard Wagner, who built his Bayreuth opera house with Ludwig's funds.

Bavaria's days as a sovereign state were numbered, and Ludwig became a puppet king after the creation of the German Reich in 1871 (which had its advantages, as Bismarck gave Ludwig a hefty allowance for his support). Although initially an enthusiastic leader, Ludwig now withdrew completely to drink, draw castle blueprints and view concerts and operas in private. His obsession with French culture and the 'Sun King', Louis XIV, inspired the fantastical palaces of Neuschwanstein, Linderhof and Herrenchiemsee – lavish projects that spelt his undoing.

Contrary to popular belief, though, it was only Ludwig's purse – and not the state treasury – that was being bankrupted. But by 1886 his ever-growing mountain of debt and erratic behaviour was perceived as a threat to the natural order of things. The king, it seemed, needed to be … managed.

In January 1886 several ministers and relatives arranged a hasty psychiatric test which diagnosed Ludwig as mentally unfit to rule. That June he was taken, against his will, to Schloss Berg on Lake Starnberg. One evening the dejected bachelor – at 41, he was friendly, throneless and toothless – and his doctor took a lakeside walk. Hours later, both were found drowned in just a few feet of water.

No-one knows with certainty what happened that night. There was no eyewitness nor any proper criminal investigation. The circumstantial evidence was conflicting and incomplete. Reports and documents were tampered with, destroyed or lost, giving rise to countless conspiracy theories.

That summer the authorities opened Neuschwanstein to the public to help pay off Ludwig's huge debts. King Ludwig II was dead, but the myth was just being born.

Altstadt Füssen

Few visitors ever realise that there's more to the Köngswinkel than Ludwig's fancy castles. Füssen's compact historical centre, for instance, contains several pleasant sights. Its tangle of lanes is lorded over by the **Hohe Schloss**, a late-Gothic confection and former summer residence of the bishops of Augsburg. Be sure to see the inner courtyard where you'll do a double-take before realising that the gables, oriels and even windows are merely illusionary architecture, done in 1499. The palace's north wing contains the **Staatsgalerie im Hohen Schloss** *(☎ 90 31 64, Magnusplatz 10; adult/concession €2.50/2, including Städtische Gemäldegalerie; open 11am-4pm Tues-Sun Apr-Oct, 2pm-4pm Tues-Sun Nov-Mar)*. This branch of the Bavarian State Gallery shows primarily late-Gothic and Renaissance (15th- and 16th-century) paintings and sculpture by Swabian and Franconian artists. One floor below is the **Städtische Gemäldegalerie** (Municipal Art Gallery) where the emphasis is on 19th-century artists, mostly from Bavaria. The **Rittersaal**, with its magnificent coffered ceiling, is perhaps the most memorable aspect of the palace.

Below the Hohe Schloss is the former **Benediktinerkloster St Mang** (Benedictine Abbey of St Mang), which traces its history back to an 8th-century missionary by the name of Magnus who founded a monk's cell here. He's allegedly buried in the Romanesque crypt of the abbey's baroque **basilica**, sections of which are adorned with the oldest extant frescoes in Bavaria (AD 980).

Integrated within the complex is the **Museum Füssen** *(☎ 90 31 45, Lechhalde 3; adult/concession/under 14 €2.50/2/free; open 11am-4pm Tues-Sun Apr-Oct, 2pm-4pm Tues-Sun Nov-Mar)*. An exhibit of historical string instruments seeks to support Füssen's claim of being the 16th-century cradle of violinmaking. The museum also provides access to the abbey's festive baroque rooms, including the library and the festival hall, the Romanesque cloister and the **St Anna Kapelle** (830), the oldest section of the abbey but now also cloaked in a baroque mantle. Here, a haunting highlight is the **Füssener Totentanz**, a Dance of Death cycle from 1602, created during the dark days of the black plague.

Tegelbergbahn

Views of the Alps and the Forggensee are truly dazzling from the top of the Tegelberg (1707m), most comfortably reached by cable car *(☎ 983 60; one way/round trip €9/15; operates 8.30am-5pm daily July-Oct, 9am-5pm daily Nov-June, though usually closed for maintenance for 6 weeks in Nov & Dec)*. The last ascent/descent is 20 minutes before closing. After an apple strudel in the Panorama Gaststätte, it's a wonderful hike down to the castles (follow the signs to Königsschlösser) in about two to three hours. For a weather report call ☎ 810 10.

The mountain station is also a prime launch point for hang-gliders and parasailers, while the summer toboggan track right next to the valley station is a winner with kids *(adult/child to age 14 per ride €2.50/2; open 10am-5pm daily, weather permitting)*.

Also here are the ruins of a **Roman bath** *(free; open 9am-5pm daily)* from the 2nd century AD, uncovered during the construction of the Tegelbergbahn in 1966.

The valley station is about 2km southeast of Schwangau and served by bus No 9713 from both the Schwangau village centre and the Füssen train station.

Wallfahrtskirche St Coloman

The little pilgrimage church of St Coloman *(☎ 82 07; usually open 2.30pm-4.30pm mid-May–Sept, check with tourist office)* looks a bit lost in its open meadow next to the main road east of the Schwangau village centre. In 1673, architect and stucco master Johann Schmutzer of Wessobrunn was hired to enlarge what was originally a Gothic structure. It's dedicated to an Irish pilgrim martyred in Vienna in 1012 and sainted in 1245. The church was only Schmutzer's second major commission but already bears his light-hearted stucco imprimatur. A renovation begun in spring 2001 should be completed by the time you're reading this.

Forggensee

The largest lake in the Allgäu, the Forggensee is actually a reservoir created in the 1950s from the bed of the Lech River. Though a controversial move back then, the lake – which is fully filled from mid-June to October – is now a popular water sports centre, including swimming, surfing, sailing and boating. A 32km-long bike trail hugs its shores, the paved sections of which are also popular with inline-skaters. If you don't want to go the whole distance, you can catch a ride on boats operated by Forggensee-Schifffahrt (☎ 92 13 63). Check with the tourist offices about current cruise schedules and where to rent sporting equipment.

Königliche Kristall-Therme

Picture yourself immersed in the warm waters of this brand-new spa complex's outdoor pool at night with a view of the illuminated royal castles and Füssen's Altstadt. It's definitely what sets the Königliche Kristall-Therme (☎ 81 96 30, Am Kurpark, Schwangau; admission 2/4 hr/all day €6.50/9/12; open 10am-10pm Mon-Fri, 9am-10pm Sat & Sun) apart from other such watery oases.

Otherwise, there's the usual assortment of tepid indoor pools, saunas, a jet canal, meditation grotto, hydro-massage nozzles and lots more fun places to unwind. Note that some nights are for nudists only (usually Tuesday and Friday).

Organised Tours

If you're in Munich and would like to see the castles on a tight schedule, consider joining an organised tour. Through Euraide in Munich (see Information in the Munich chapter), you can book the Two Royal Castles day tour to Neuschwanstein and Linderhof with a brief stop in Oberammergau. It operates daily from April to about October and on a more limited schedule in the other months. The cost is €40, plus admission to the palaces. Rail pass and student discounts are available.

Places to Stay & Eat – Füssen

DJH hostel (☎ 77 54, fax 27 70, e *jhfuessen@djh-bayern.de, Mariahilfer-strasse 5)* Bed & breakfast €13.30-14.10 including linen. Closed mid-Nov–Christmas. Füssen's hostel is by the train tracks, a five-to 10-minute walk west of the station. Reservations are strongly recommended.

The tourist offices in Füssen and Schwangau have lists of *private rooms* starting at €11 per person.

Pension Kössler (☎ 73 04 & 40 69, fax 399 52, Kemptener Strasse 42) Singles/doubles from €28/56. Small and with a familial atmosphere, this pension offers outstanding value. Rooms have private bath, balcony, TV and phone.

Hotel Garni Alpenhof (☎ 32 32, Theresienstrasse 8) Doubles €46 (shared bath), €86 (private bath). This central hotel has attractive rooms, a nice terrace and mountain views.

Hotel & Gasthaus zum Hechten (☎ 916 00, fax 91 60 99, e *hotel.hechten@t-online .de, Ritterstrasse 6)* Singles/doubles from €28/56 (shared bath), €44/66 (private bath). Near the main square, this hotel opens up to a quiet inner courtyard and has rooms with TV and phone. Its popular 1st-floor restaurant serves stick-to-the-ribs Bavarian fare in small and large portions (mains €5 to €13). In the same location on the ground floor is a self-service buffet with salads and vegetarian selections for €1 per 100g and hot items for €1.30 per 100g (closes at 6.30pm).

Franziskaner Stüberl (☎ 371 24, Kemptener Strasse 1, cnr Ritterstrasse) Mains €7.50-12.50. Closed Thur. This quaint restaurant specialises in *Schweinshaxe* (pig's trotters) and schnitzel, prepared in infinite varieties. Noncarnivores can indulge in *Kässpätzle* (macaroni and cheese) and other meatless dishes.

Gasthaus Schwanen (☎ 61 74, Brotmarkt 4) Mains €5.50-16. This is one of Füssen's best restaurants in the former home of violinmaker Franz Geissenhof who's depicted in the fountain out front.

Pizzeria Roma Cittá (☎ 54 44, Bahnhofstrasse 6) Mains €4.50-9.50. For a change from Bavarian food, try this dependable pizzeria.

Snack options include fish sandwiches at the local *Nordsee* at Reichenstrasse 40 and

ALLGÄU-BAVARIAN SWABIA

meaty fare at the butcher-deli *Vinzenzmurr* at Reichenstrasse 35.

Places to Stay & Eat – Schwangau

Campingplatz Bannwaldsee (☎ 930 00, fax 93 00 20, e info@camping-bannwaldsee .de, Münchner Strasse 151) Site/person €5.60/6.65. This camping ground with a lovely lakeside location on the Bannwaldsee rents boats and bicycles and has a new solar-heated shower building, two restaurants and a supermarket.

Campingplatz Brunnen am Forggensee (☎ 82 73, fax 86 30, e info@camping -brunnen.de, Seestrasse 81) Site/person €5.60/6.65. Closed 1 Nov-20 Dec. This camping ground at the southern end of the Forggensee has new sanitary facilities, a supermarket, laundry, restaurant with beer garden, and a children's playground. It's a great option if you've got your own wheels.

Feriengasthof Helmer (☎ 98 00, fax 980200, e feriengasthof-helmer@t-online .de, Mitteldorf 10) Singles/doubles from €30/55. Large rooms outfitted in modern country style and with a decent range of amenities are what you'll find at this family-run inn with downstairs restaurant (mains €6 to €13).

Hotel Weinbauer (☎ 98 60, fax 98 61 13, e hotel-weinbauer@t-online.de, Füssener Strasse 3) Singles/doubles from €28/56. Easily recognised by its cheerful *Lüftlmalerei* facade paintings, the Weinbauer is a convivial inn with a good restaurant (mains €5.50 to €12); the wine tavern has a nicely vaulted ceiling.

Pizzeria San Marco (☎ 813 39, Füssener Strasse 6) Mains €5-8.50. This cosy place is a standby for pizza, pasta and salads.

Places to Stay & Eat – Hohenschwangau

Hotel garni Schlossblick (☎ 816 49, fax 812 59, e info@schlossblick-neuschwanstein.de, Schwangauer Strasse 7) Singles/doubles €38/57. This place is a great budget option right below the castles. Most of the 26 newly renovated rooms have a balcony and all have views of one of the castles.

Schlosshotel Lisl & Jägerhaus (☎ 88 70, fax 811 07, e info@lisl.de, Neuschwansteinstrasse 1–3) Singles/doubles from €67/110. This is the village's flagship hotel and the place to stay if you want to be 'king for the day'. It started out as a temporary abode for workers constructing Neuschwanstein, but has been a hotel for over a century. Rooms are stylish and lack no comforts. All have views of at least one of the castles and some in the Jägerhaus building have bathrooms with Jacuzzis and gilded swan taps. The two restaurants serve regional and international food (mains €10 to €22); anything flambéed is a speciality.

Getting There & Away

Train If you're starting out from Munich and want to 'do' the royal castles on a day trip, the best train to catch to beat the crowds is the one that no-one in their right mind would want: the one leaving Munich at 4.57am, getting to Füssen at 7.23am with a change in Buchloe (€18).

The next train departs at 6.51am and arrives in Füssen at 8.57am. Subsequent trains include those at 7.51am, 8.51am and 10.51am; most return trains run at five minutes past the hour until about 11pm. Always check schedules before you go.

Direct regional trains to/from Augsburg via Kaufbeuren depart every two hours (€14.40, two hours).

Bus The most useful bus line in the region is No 1084/9606, which connects the Königswinkel towns with Oberstdorf, the Wieskirche, Oberammergau, Ettal and Garmisch-Partenkirchen several times daily.

The Europabus stops at the tourist office in Schwangau, at the foot of the castles in Hohenschwangau and at Füssen Bahnhof, its southern terminus.

Car & Motorcycle Several roads lead to the Königswinkel: the A7 from Memmingen and Kempten, the B16 from Kaufbeuren and the B17 (Romantic Road) from Augsburg/Munich.

Getting Around

RVA bus No 9713 connects the castles, Füssen, Schwangau and the Tegelbergbahn. Taxis to the castles are about €7.50, or it's about a 5km walk from Füssen and 3km from Schwangau.

With the Alps on one side and the lake-filled plains on the other, the Königswinkel is a cyclist's paradise. The Wieskirche (see earlier in this chapter), about 30km northeast of Füssen, makes for a nice day-trip destination.

In Füssen, you can rent two-wheelers at the Kurhotel Berger (☎ 913 30), Alatseestrasse 26, for around €5 per day. Radsport Zacherl (☎ 32 92), Kemptener Strasse 119, has a much bigger selection from €6/7 in off-peak/peak season. In Schwangau, the AVIA gas station (☎ 89 77) at Münchener Strasse 11 rents a few bikes.

MEMMINGEN

☎ 08331 • pop 41,100 • elevation 600m

Memmingen is the economic and administrative centre of the Northern Allgäu. Founded in 1160 by Duke Welf VI, it reached its heyday after becoming a Free Imperial City in 1268. In 1525, the *Bauernartikel*, the manifesto that lead to the bloody peasants' revolt the same year, was written here. Memmingen is also the birthplace of Bernhard Strigel (1461–1528), a Renaissance artist famous for his altar paintings.

Orientation & Information

The Bahnhof and central bus station are on the eastern edge of the Altstadt, about a five-minute walk from Marktplatz, where the tourist office (☎ 85 01 72, fax 85 01 78, e info@memmingen.de) is at No 3; it's open from 9am to 5pm Monday to Friday and 9.30am to 12.30pm Saturday.

Things to See

Marktplatz is fringed by nicely restored historical buildings. These include the arcaded **Steuerhaus** (1495), a former tax collecting office, which got its gaudy facade in 1906; the Renaissance **Rathaus** (1589) with stucco flourishes from the rococo period

(1765); and the **Grosszunft** (1719), a former patrician gathering and party house.

Just west of Markplatz, the **Stadtmuseum** *(☎ 85 01 34, Zangmeisterstrasse 8; admission €0.50; open 10am-noon & 2pm-4pm Tues-Fri & Sun May-Oct)* has local exhibits. It's in the Hermannsbau, a pretty patrician private residence from 1766.

Further west looms the rather squat octagonal tower of the Gothic **St Martinskirche** *(☎ 856 90; open 2.30pm-5pm daily May-Sept, 2pm-4pm daily Oct, 10am-noon Sat May-Oct)* with superb choir stalls (1501-07). You can climb up the tower at 3pm daily May to October.

A short walk south is the **Antonierhaus** *(☎ 85 02 45, Martin-Luther-Platz 1; adult/concession €1.50/1; open 10am-noon & 2pm-4pm Tues-Sat, 10am-12.30pm & 1.30pm-5pm Sun)*, the former home and hospital run by a religious order called the *Antoniter*. You can learn more about them inside at the **Antoniter-Museum**, but perhaps more interesting is the **Strigel-Museum** in the same building, dedicated to this prominent homegrown artist and his family.

Continue south for a few metres, turn left (east) on Schweizerberg to Rossmarkt, then south along Obere Bachgasse, which follows the little *Stadtbach* creek to Schrannenplatz. A few more steps east, on Gerberplatz, is the **Siebendächerhaus** (1601), so named for its unusual seven overlapping roofs where tanners used to dry their pelts.

A stroll through the largely pedestrianised lanes north of here will take you straight back to the Marktplatz.

Places to Stay & Eat

Memmingen's charms are easily assimilated in half a day, but if you want to spend the night, the tourist office can help you find lodging.

DJH hostel (☎/fax 49 40 87, Kempter Strasse 42) Bed & breakfast €10.50. Closed Dec-Feb. Memmingen's rather simple hostel is just south of the Altstadt, about a 10-minute walk from the Bahnhof.

Parkhotel Memmingen (☎ 93 20, fax 484 39, Ulmer Strasse 7) Singles/doubles from

€65/85. Near the Marktplatz, this modern hotel has fully equipped rooms and an excellent restaurant serving imaginatively updated traditional cuisine (mains €7.50 to €14, weekday lunch special €5.50).

Getting There & Away
Memmingen has direct train connections to/from Munich (€16, 1½ hours), Augsburg (€12.40, 1¼ hours) and Oberstdorf (€10.70, 1¼ hours) via Kempten. It's right at the junction of the A7 and the A96.

AROUND MEMMINGEN
Buxheim
About 4km north-west of Memmingen, Buxheim is home to one of the largest and best-preserved **Carthusian monasteries** in Germany. Founded in 1402 and of Gothic origin, it got its splendid stucco decorations and luminous frescoes in the 18th century courtesy of the brothers Dominikus and Johann Baptist Zimmermann. The dizzyingly ornate **choir stalls** by Ignaz Waibel are from the same period. A **museum** (☎ *618 04 or 719 26; open 10am-noon & 2pm-5pm Mon-Sat, 1pm-5pm Sun Apr-Oct)* gives access to restored monk's cells, the cloisters, the refectory (dining room), library and historical exhibits. The nearby parish church of **St Peter** and the **Chapel of St Anna** also sport the Zimmermann touch. Most of the complex is now a boarding school.

Bus No 964 departs throughout the day (except Sunday) from Memmingen's central bus station by the Bahnhof (€1.80, 12 minutes).

Ottobeuren
The road to heaven may well be a sinuous two-lane blacktop winding through pastures en route to the **Benediktinerabtei Otto-beuren**, a little spa town about 11km southeast of Memmingen. No matter from which angle you approach, you will likely stop momentarily in your tracks, taken aback by the sight of the vast and extraordinary abbey and basilica as it appears like a celestial mirage.

The monastery complex stretches for nearly half a kilometre from the main

church portal to the utility buildings at the back. Inside and out, it's such an exuberant celebration of rococo art and architecture that even an atheist might find religion. Prepare to be seriously overwhelmed.

The abbey was founded in 764 and still has about two dozen active friars today. Scores of top-ranked architects and artists gave their best for nearly two generations to create the extraordinary **basilica** *(1737-66; open 9am-sunset daily, 8.30pm at the latest)*. Side chapels line the nave, which is bisected by a transept, giving the whole thing the shape of a cross. The richness of the decor hits you from all directions: gilded altars, delicate stucco, vivid frescoes, marble pillars, frilly ornamentation, emotive statues and angels, angels, angels.

Of special note is a **Romanesque crucifix** and the **choir stalls**, carved with scenes from the Old Testament and the life of St Benedict. The organs are some of Bavaria's finest and are best appreciated during concerts held at 4pm Saturdays from late February to late November. Half-hour tours run at 2pm on Saturday from April to October. Both concerts and tours are on a donation-basis.

Sections of the former abbot's residence now contain a **museum** *(adult/concession €2/1; open 10am-noon & 2pm-5pm daily Apr-Oct, 2pm-4pm daily & 10am-noon Sat & Sun Nov-Mar)*. Here you can learn a bit more about the history of the abbey, look at sculptures and paintings of various saints and abbots and examine an old pharmacy and a baroque theatre. Be sure to peek into the ballroom-sized **library** with 15,000 volumes and the majestic **Kaisersaal** (Imperial Hall), site of an illustrious concert series held annually from May to September. Tickets sell out early; check with the tourist office (☎ 92 19 50, fax 92 19 92, e touristikamt@ottobeuren .de) at Marktplatz 14, right at the foot of the basilica, for availability.

If hunger strikes, there is a nice cafe in the abbey and several restaurants on Marktplatz along with some reasonably priced hotels. A good choice is *Hotel Engel* (☎ *920 80, fax 92 08 49, Luitpoldstrasse 3)*, which has full-frills modern singles/doubles for €25/50.

Bus No 955 makes the trip out here from Memmingen's central bus station several times daily (€1.80, 15 minutes).

KAUFBEUREN

☎ 08341 • pop 43,000 • elevation 682m

Like many Swabian towns, Kaufbeuren began as a Carolingian royal residence, became a Free Imperial City in the Middle Ages and was absorbed into the Bavarian kingdom in 1802. Behind its largely intact town wall is a web of cobbled lanes and quiet alleys punctuated by churches and proud town houses.

Despite such medieval characteristics, Kaufbeuren has a much more contemporary flair, in large part because of its northern suburb of **Neugablonz**, formed after WWII. It was here where an entire town called Gablonz, originally located in the Sudetenland region in today's Czech Republic, resettled after being expelled. Nearly all townspeople were in the business of making glass and costume jewellery, a trade they still practice today.

In late July, the **Tänzlfest**, during which about 1600 colourfully costumed kids recreate their town's history, draws thousands of locals and visitors.

Orientation & Information

Kaufbeuren's Altstadt is easily explored on foot. The tourist office (☎ 404 05, fax 739 62, e tourist-information-kaufbeuren@online -service.de) is in the Rathaus at the east end of Kaiser-Max-Strasse, the main commercial artery. It's open 9am to 6pm Monday to Friday and to noon on Saturday from May to October; otherwise hours are 9am to 5pm Monday to Friday only. The bus station is a short walk north of here, while the Bahnhof is about 500m south-east, outside of the Altstadt.

Things to See

Start your exploration at the **Rathaus** (1879-81), a neo-Renaissance edifice designed by Georg Hauberrisser. The meeting halls are covered in wall paintings by Wilhelm Lindenschmidt, a friend of King Ludwig II. The wedding room features a painting of Kaiser Wilhelm I, the only portrait of the Prussian emperor in a Bavarian town hall.

Walking west along Kaiser-Max-Strasse will take you straight to the **Fünfknopfturm**, a fortified tower and city landmark. Walk north along the wall and uphill to the **St-Blasius-Kirche** *(open 10am-11am & 2pm-4pm daily)*, built right into the fortifications. Inside, the late-Gothic carved altar (1518) by Jörg Lederer warrants attention, as do the 64 wall panels documenting the lives and deaths of the 12 apostles and other saints. You'll have good views of the town from up here.

Heading back downhill, find your way to Unter dem Berg, where you'll soon come upon the **Crescentia chapel** which holds the remains of a local nun who was sainted in 2001. It stands on the site of the former Carolingian palace.

Turn left (east) on Zitronengasse to arrive at the **St-Martins-Kirche**, a Romanesque-turned-Gothic-turned-baroque-turned-neo gothic church. From here, it's just a few steps south back to Kaiser-Max-Strasse and the Rathaus.

If you're intrigued by the unique community of Neugablonz, take bus No 57 and drop in at the **Gablonzer Haus** *(☎ 669 12, Marktgasse 8; admission €0.25; open 3pm-5pm Tues-Thur & Sat, 10am-noon Sun)*, which tells the story of the people and also displays their jewellery.

Places to Stay & Eat

If you want to spend the night, the tourist office can help find a room. Both hotels mentioned here also have restaurants.

Hotel Goldener Hirsch (☎ 430 30, fax 43 03 75, e *info@goldener-hirsch-kaufbeuren .de, Kaiser-Max-Strasse 39/41)* Singles/doubles from €35/61. This central hotel offers the full range of amenities, including a fitness room and sauna, at a price that won't break the bank.

Hotel Hasen (☎ 96 61 90, fax 966 19 55, Ganghoferstrasse 7/8) Singles/doubles from €31/47. This place is pretty good too. It's near the train station, about a five-minute walk from the Altstadt.

Hirschkeller (☎ 404 04, Innere Buchleuthe 6) Mains €7.50-15. This characterful

ALLGÄU-BAVARIAN SWABIA

restaurant near the Fünfknopfturm serves good-looking regional specialities made from fresh ingredients.

Getting There & Away

Trains to/from Munich depart about every half hour (€12.40, one hour), as do those to/from Augsburg, although this usually requires a change in Buchloe (€9, 50 minutes).

LINDAU

☎ 08382 • pop 24,000 (3500 on the island) • elevation 400m

Lindau occupies the only snippet of Bavarian shore on the Bodensee (Lake Constance), a giant bulge in the otherwise sinewy course of the Rhine River. More than half of its 272km circumference lies in the German state of Baden-Württemberg with the rest in Austria and Switzerland, plus the tiny stretch in Bavaria. The snow-capped Swiss Alps provide a breathtaking backdrop.

Lindau grew from a 9th-century nunnery into a prosperous town thanks primarily to its spot on a major north-south trading route. In the early 13th century it became a Free Imperial City, a status kept until 1802. After secularisation, it briefly became Austrian, then Bavarian in 1805.

Lindau still exudes old-world wealth and romance. The French occupied the place for 10 years after WWII, a period that saw the founding of the casino in 1950 and a, year later, the first annual gathering of Nobel Prize winners in 1951. To this day, every year in late June, scores of scientists descend upon Lindau to exchange ideas and promote research. Rooms are scarce at that time and the rest of summer when holidaymakers invade by the tens of thousands. Make reservations early or head for the hinterland.

Orientation & Information

Lindau's historic Altstadt lies on a pretty little island reached by a causeway. The train and bus stations are in the south-western corner, while the harbour and its lovely promenade are just to the south. The largely carfree historic core extends east of the station; its main artery is Maximilianstrasse.

The tourist office (☎ 26 00 30, fax 26 00 26, ⓔ tourist-information.lindau@t-online.de, ⓦ www.lindau-tourismus.de) is at Ludwigstrasse 68 opposite the Bahnhof. From mid-June to mid-September, it's open from 9am to 6pm Monday to Friday and to 1pm Saturday; hours are slightly shorter in the other months. From November to March, the office is open Monday to Friday only.

Staff sell the *BodenseeErlebniskarte* (adult/children to age 15 €45/25), available April to October, which entitles you to three days travel on boats and mountain cableways on and around Lake Constance, including its Austrian and Swiss shores, as well as entry to around 150 tourist attractions and museums. There are also seven-day (€57.50/35) and 14-day (€85/42.50) versions. There's a Volksbank at the junction of Maximilianstrasse and Zeppelinstrasse. The post office is just north of the train and bus stations on Bahnhofsplatz. Surf the Web at B@mboo (☎ 94 27 67), Zeppelinstrasse 6, for €4.50 per hour between 2pm and 1am (Saturday and Sunday from noon). Clean your dirty laundry at the self-service Wäsche-Center Lindau (☎ 66 98), Holdereggenstrasse 21.

Walking Tour

The train station is only steps away from Lindau's little harbour which is guarded by a lighthouse and a pillar bearing the Bavarian lion. Both date to the middle of the 19th century and thus are historic youngsters compared to the dignified 13th-century **Mangturm**, which once did double duty as a lighthouse and as part of the fortification. The tower, which can be climbed (€1), anchors Lindau's elegant **lakeside promenade** where, in summer at least, you'll find an almost Mediterranean scene, with lots of well-heeled tourists sipping cappuccinos and enjoying lake views beneath cobalt blue skies.

Turn inland just past the Mangturm to get to the Reichsplatz dominated by the **Altes Rathaus** (1422–36), where the Imperial Diet met in 1496. Murals of rather gaudy intensity cover its facade; added in 1975, they're based on 19th-century designs. The current town hall – **Neues Rathaus** – is in the adjacent baroque edifice.

ALLGÄU-BAVARIAN SWABIA

From Reichsplatz, head east on Ludwigstrasse to get to Barfüsserplatz, site of the **city theatre** in a 700-year-old church. Follow Lingstrasse north to Marktplatz, lorded over by two churches and the attractive baroque **Haus zum Cavazzen** with trompe l'oeil murals. Inside is the **Stadtmuseum** (☎ *94 40 73, adult/concession €2.50/2; open 10am-noon & 2pm-5pm Tues-Sun Apr-Oct)* with period furniture, paintings, crafts and some fun historical musical instruments.

Meander west on Cramergasse, then continue via lanes with names like Zitronengasse (Lemon Lane) or Storchengasse (Stork Lane) or by taking the magnificent **Maximilianstrasse** lined with many Gothic and Renaissance town houses. Either way, you'll end up at Schrannenplatz and the **Diebsturm** (Brigand's Tower; 1380), a tiny former jail adjoining the town fortifications. Also here is the **Peterskirche**, Lindau's oldest church (11th century) and now a war memorial. It contains impressive frescoes of the Passion of Christ by Hans Holbein the Elder. A few steps east and south and you're back at the train station.

Places to Stay

Park-Camping Lindau am See (☎ *722 36, fax 97 61 06,* e *info@park-camping.de, Fraunhoferstrasse 20)* Person/tent/car €5.30/3.50/2. Closed Nov. On the lakeshore at the Austrian border, this nice place has a beach, grocery store and restaurant. Take bus Nos 1 or 2 to the ZUP (see Getting Around), then bus No 3 to Leiblachstrasse.

DJH hostel (☎ *967 10, fax 96 71 50,* e *jhlindau@djh-bayern.de, Herbergsweg 11)* Bed & breakfast €16.50, including linen. Singles/doubles €19/38. Lindau's modern hostel is in a beautiful hotel-like complex on the mainland, about 2km from the Bahnhof. Take bus Nos 1 or 2 to the ZUP, then change to bus No 3 direction Zech and get off at Jugendherberge. Reservations are essential, especially for the private rooms.

The tourist office makes room reservations for €2.50, or call ☎ 194 12 for a referral. Private rooms range from €13 to €35 per person. All places listed here are on the island.

Gästehaus Limmer (☎ *58 77, In der Grub 16)* Singles/doubles €20.50/41. This simple pension offers the cheapest stay on the island. It's run by a friendly English-speaking woman and has rooms with TV.

Hotel-Pension Noris (☎ *36 45, fax 10 42, Brettermarkt 13)* Singles/doubles €36/72. This family-run place near the promenade offers pleasantly furnished rooms with TV and comes highly recommended.

Hotel Möve (☎ *94 87 77, fax 64 36,* e *info@hotel-moeve.de, Auf der Mauer 21)* Singles/doubles €48.50/66-76. This good-value place on the island's western end has cheerful rooms with a modern feel, private baths, telephone and TV.

Gasthof Engel (☎ *52 40, fax 56 44, Schafgasse 4)* Singles/doubles €45/80. Rooms at this family-run inn here are quaint but adequate. The restaurant is renowned for its fish dishes.

Hotel Helvetia (☎ *91 30, fax 40 04, Seepromenade 3)* Singles €48.50-92, doubles €45 50-92. Behind a citrus-coloured facade right by the Mangturm awaits this fitness-oriented hotel run by an energetic young couple. Rooms have an artsy touch, and a sauna, solarium, small indoor pool and steam room are on the premises.

Places to Eat

Gasthaus zum Sünfzen (☎ *58 65, Maximilianstrasse 1)* Sausages €4.50-7, mains €11-16. This ancient tavern is an island institution with its own sausage kitchen. The *Lindauer Doppelschröbling* is a local speciality.

Alte Post (☎ *934 60, Fischergasse 3)* Mains €6-13. At this atmospheric restaurant, you'll find good food and a fun beer garden. Every nook and cranny tells a story, and there's a huge regulars' table where members have carved their names.

Cafe-Bistro Wintergarten (☎ *94 61 72, Salzgasse 5)* Mains €4-8. This pleasant glass-roofed and vine-festooned cafe hosts readings and exhibits. There's about a dozen dishes for vegetarians.

Il Mulino (☎ *67 04, In der Grub 30)* Mains €4.50-11. Closed Mon. This is the best place in town for pizza, pasta and salads. The meaty mains are more expensive.

ALLGÄU-BAVARIAN SWABIA

Thai House (☎ *27 53 45, Schafgasse 10*) Mains €7.50-9, lunch special €6. It may not be Bangkok, but the lemongrass and ginger-scented fare here may make for a nice change from Bavarian cuisine.

For snack food, drop in at the butcherdeli ***Vinzenzmurr*** at Maximilianstrasse 27. Schafgasse has several international eateries, including ***Turkiyem*** at No 8, which makes good doners from €2.50.

Organised Tours

Walking tours in English depart from the tourist office at 10am Mondays (€4). Otherwise you can rent a *Stadthörer*, a selfguided audio-tour (in English or German) with commentary about 15 island sites (€5/7.50 half-day/all day).

Weisse Flotte (☎ 94 44 16) runs roundtrip boat tours several times daily from Lindau harbour to Bregenz (Austria) and the mouth of the Rhine (€6.50, one hour). Boats leave from the island's eastern shore, just south of the Casino.

Activities

Lindau is a paradise for **sailing** and **windsurfing**; the tourist office has a list of sports clubs and shops offering equipment rental and instruction.

Lake Constance is also ideal **cycling** territory. Fahrrad Station (☎ 212 61) in the Hauptbahnhof rents them for €7 to €9 per day.

For an easy tootle around the lake, you can rent **row and paddle boats** at Grahneis (☎ 55 14) and Hodrius (☎ 29 77 71), both located on the northern shore, for €5 to €10 per hour.

Lake swimming is possible at several public pools. The nicest is the **Strandbad Lindenhof** (☎ 66 37) in a lovely park in the exclusive western suburb of Bad Schachen (bus No 4).

A good place for **hiking** is the Pfänderberg, a 1064m-high mountain just across the Austrian border, with views of the lake and three countries: Germany, Austria and Switzerland. The **Pfänderbahn** cable car travels up every 30 minutes from 9am to 7pm daily (one way/return Nov-Mar

€4.65/8.05, Apr-Oct €5.50/9.50) from its station near the boat landing in Bregenz.

Getting There & Away

Train Regional trains to/from Memmingen (€12.40, 1½ hours) with onward service to Augsburg (€24, three hours) run several times daily. The trip to/from Oberstdorf requires a change in Immenstadt (€13.50, 1½ hours). Bregenz in Austria is just 10 minutes away (€1.90).

Car & Motorcycle Lindau is on the B31 and also connected to Munich by the A96. It's the western terminus of the scenic Deutsche Alpenstrasse (German Alpine Road) to Berchtesgaden.

Boat Bodensee Schiffsbetriebe (BSB; ☎ 94 44 16) operates year-round scheduled boat service between lake communities. Stops include Wasserburg (€3.60, 20 minutes), Friedrichshafen (€6.80, 1¼), Meersburg (€9.40, 2¾ hours) and Bregenz (€3.20, 22 minutes).

Getting Around

The island is tiny and perfect for walking. For buses to/from the mainland, singles cost €1.40 and a day pass is €3.10. All buses converge at the ZUP (central transfer station) on the mainland. Bus Nos 1 and 2 serve the island.

Island parking is limited, expensive and potentially frustrating since the causeway backs up quickly in the peak months. Leave your car in one of the mainland parking lots instead and either walk or take the free shuttle bus (June to early September).

AROUND LINDAU
Wasserburg
☎ 08382 • pop 2800

About 6km west of Lindau, tiny Wasserburg is charmingly located and a tranquil alternative base for lake explorations. All sites mentioned below are squeezed onto a peninsula, which is also where boats from Lindau and elsewhere dock. The tourist office (☎ 88 74 74) is at Lindenplatz 1, near the train station, a five-minute walk north via Halbinselstrasse.

Schloss Wasserburg, first mentioned in 784 but rebuilt in 1592 by a branch of the Fugger family from Augsburg, is now a posh hotel. Nearby is the church of St Georg where several artists did some fine work, most notably the putti on the altar, the statues of saints and the pietà by Franz Ferdinand Ertinger of Kempten. To learn more about local culture and curiosities, go to the medieval courthouse, which is now the Museum im Mahlhaus *(adult/concession €1.50/0.50; open 10am-noon Tues-Sun & 3pm-5pm Wed & Sat May-Oct)*.

The tourist office can help with finding a room, or try this option:

Hotel Walserhof (☎ 985 60, fax 98 56 10, Nonnenhorner Strasse 15) Singles/doubles from €33/66. This newly renovated hotel is a great place to lay your head down. Rooms come with all the trimmings and there's a sauna and indoor pool for relaxing. The restaurant (mains €8 to €16) serves Swabian specialities and is a favourite with locals.

Wasserburg is on the B31 and connected to Lindau by train and hourly bus.

OBERSTDORF
☎ 08322 • pop 10,000 • elevation 843m
Tucked away in the towering Allgäu Alps, right on the border with Austria, Oberstdorf is Germany's southernmost resort and can get frightfully crowded year round. There are many reasons for its popularity.

The village itself is storybook pretty with a quintessential Alpine character and zero architectural sins. Much of it is pedestrianised, with most traffic kept on the perimeter. The setting is nothing but glorious and the options for outdoor pursuits plentiful.

Alas, Oberstdorf is almost too perfect for its own good, as large crowds can make the place feel claustrophobic. The nicest time to visit is in autumn when you'll find clear skies, multi-hued forests and thinning throngs.

Oberstdorf is a training centre for athletes in the fields of figure skating, downhill and Nordic skiing and often hosts international competitions. It's the first stop on the *Vierschanzen-Tournee*, a prestigious international ski jumping competition.

Orientation & Information
The Bahnhof and central bus station are just north of the carfree centre. The Nebelhorn cable car is on the south-western edge; other lifts are in valleys away from the centre.

The busy tourist office (☎ 70 00, fax 70 02 36, e info@oberstdorf.de), at Marktplatz 7, is open 8.30am to noon and 2pm to 6pm Monday to Friday, and Saturday from 9.30am to noon. The branch office at the Bahnhof (☎ 70 02 17) operates a room-finding service. During peak months, it's open 8.30am to 8pm Monday to Saturday, to 6pm Sunday, with restricted hours at other times.

There's a Sparkasse with money-changing facilities at Bahnhofsplatz 2 and a post office at Bahnhofsplatz 3. Internet access is available at Oberstdorf@Event (☎ 978 50) at Sonthofener Strasse 20, north of the centre for a steep €2.50 per 20 minutes. The town's Web site at W www.oberstdorf .de has sections in English. The main hospital (☎ 70 30) is at Trettachstrasse 16 just east of the Bahnhof.

The Kurtaxe (resort tax) for overnight visitors is €1.50 to €2 per day.

Skiing
In-the-know skiers value Oberstdorf for its accessibility, lower prices and less-crowded pistes. There are about 85km of groomed Nordic tracks, but it's really the downhill terrain that people crave. There are three ski areas – Nebelhorn, Fellhorn and Söllereck – plus the adjacent Kanzelwand area in the Kleinwalsertal on the Austrian side. Thirty lifts ferry skiers up the mountains where they can enjoy 44km of downhill runs of all degrees of difficulty. There's also a competition-quality half pipe and a snowboarding park. The ski season generally runs from mid-December to early April.

Ski passes good for all four areas are €30/57/82 for one/two/three days (children under 15 €17/33/48) during peak season (Christmas to early March) and about 20% lower at other times. Day passes for the Nebelhorn area only are €28/22 for one/two days (children under 15 for one/two days €8/6.25) and for the Fellhorn-Kanzelwand area €29/23 (children €17/13).

ALLGÄU-BAVARIAN SWABIA

Numerous ski and snowboarding schools compete for customers. Check with the tourist office for a complete list. Ski equipment can be rented all over town, with downhill outfits ranging from €8 to €11 per day, including boots.

Hiking

Oberstdorf has nearly 200km of hiking trails, many of which are open year round. The tourist office has maps and can make recommendations. For an exhilarating day walk (six hours of hiking time), ride the Nebelhorn cable car to the upper station, then trek down via the Gaisalpseen, two lovely alpine lakes. Sturdy footwear is a must. On a good day, you'll have sweeping views of some 400 peaks.

An easy and fun trip is a hike through the Breitachklamm (☎ 48 87; admission €2; open 8am-5pm daily Apr-Oct & 9am-4pm daily Nov-Mar, closed during snow melt), a mostly paved trail through a narrow gorge carved by the Breitach creek. In winter, frozen icicles, often forming entire curtains, create a magical setting. It takes about 45 minutes to hike through the gorge to the 'Walserschanze' and 2½ hours to the Gasthaus Waldhaus in the Kleinwalsertal. There's an hourly bus service to the mouth of the gorge from the central bus station.

Other Activities

The vast Eislaufzentrum (☎ 91 51 17, Rossbichlstrasse 2–6), behind the Nebelhorn cable-car station, has three rinks and is the training grounds for top figure skaters.

The Kristallbad (☎ 98 60 10, Promenade 3; 2hrs/4hrs/all day €6.50/9/12; open 10am-10pm daily), with a wave pool and several saunas, is a great place to soothe sore muscles. Note that there's usually nude bathing on Tuesday and Friday nights.

For a culture fix, check out the better-than-average Heimatmuseum (Local History Museum; ☎ 54 70, Oststrasse 13; admission free; open 10am-noon & 2pm-5.30pm Tues-Sun, closed May, Nov & Dec), in a 17th-century town home. Learn how the holes get into the famous Allgäu cheese or how gentian schnapps is distilled and check out the world's largest shoe.

Places to Stay

Campingplatz Oberstdorf (☎ 65 25, fax 80 97 60, Rubinger Strasse 16) Person/tent/car €4.60-5.10/2.60/2.60-4.60. The local camping ground is about 1.5km north of the Bahnhof beside the tracks. Facilities include a coin-op laundry and an Imbiss.

DJH hostel (☎ 22 25, fax 804 46, Kornau 8) Bus: No 1 to Reute, then 7-minute walk. Bed & breakfast €13.30. Closed around Nov/Dec. The hostel in the western suburb of Kornau near the Söllereck chair lift has modern facilities and great views.

Oberstdorf is chockfull of private guesthouses. Note that some owners may be reluctant to rent rooms for just one night, especially during high season. This is usually not a problem in larger hotels or outside the centre.

Till the Cows Come Home

One of the great delights of hiking in the Bavarian Alps is to break for a Brotzeit (snack) at one of the many Almen, simple huts in the mountain pastures where the cattle are brought to graze in the summer. The shepherds who live here in these months often make their own cheese and other products, which they serve, along with drinks, to hungry trekkers.

An important event in the farming year is the Almabtrieb (sort of an Alpine cattle drive) in September, when the animals are brought back down to the valley. Provided none of the cows and shepherds have suffered injuries or sickness, the animals are decorated with magnificent wreaths and garlands. While in Upper Bavaria all cattle are thus adorned, in the Allgäu this is a privilege reserved to the lead cow. Sometimes the animals also wear bells, intended to keep the bad spirits at bay. A successful Almabtrieb is usually an excuse for a big festival and market, which brings together the farmers, locals and visitors. The cattle, meanwhile, head back to their farms where they will spend the winter in the stable before trudging back uphill in late spring.

Pension Christel (☎/fax 52 46, Gerberstrasse 12) Singles/doubles €27/54 (shared bath), €30/60 (private bath). This little pension is north-east of the Bahnhof and offers good value for money.

Zum Paulanerbräu (☎ 967 60, fax 96 76 13, Kirchstrasse 1) Singles/doubles €28/56 (shared bath), €33/66 (private bath). This place is right in the heart of the Altstadt and operates a popular restaurant (mains €5 to €10, closed Tuesdays) with such belly-filling selections as roast leg of pork.

Hotel Hahnenkoepfle (☎ 963 60, 96 36 60, e toni.jost@t-online.de, Finkenstrasse 11) Singles€47-55; doubles €86-106. A few steps east of the centre, this charming pension offers balconied rooms and has a sauna and fitness room on the premises. Dinner (optional) is €8 per person.

Hotel Gerberhof (☎ 70 70, fax 70 71 00, e info@gerberhof.de, Zweistapfenweg 5, 7 & 9) Singles €31-56; doubles €62-112. Environmental awareness is key at this solar-heated hotel near the centre. Rooms are cosy and nicely appointed, and the lavish breakfast is served in a room with panoramic mountain views.

Places to Eat

Beim Dorfwirt (☎ 46 48, Hauptstrasse 6) Mains €8-14. This traditional restaurant at the Hotel zur Traube has a large beer garden. The menu is mostly meaty, but the salad bar provides relief. Service is provided by young women in lederhosen...

Zum Wilde Männle (☎ 48 29, Oststrasse 15) Mains €10-12. This is another traditional restaurant with budget-priced lunch specials (eg, veal goulash for €6.50).

Gasthof Zum Mohren (☎ 91 20, Marktplatz 6) Mains €7-19. Right by the tourist office, this upscale restaurant offers a change from the usual meat-and-potato circuit. Recent offerings included crocodile, lobster, and fondue dinners. The restaurant's dining room is a bit crammed with knick-knacks, an effect multiplied by a mirrored ceiling.

The butcher-deli *Vinzenzmurr*, at Hauptstrasse 1, has sandwiches, sausages and salads for €1.50 to €4.50; there is a bakery as well.

Getting There & Away

Direct trains run to/from Munich (€24, 2½ hours) via Kempten and there are more requiring a change in Immenstadt. RVO bus No 1084/9606 shuttles several times daily between Oberstdorf, Füssen and Garmisch-Partenkirchen.

The B19 runs due south to Oberstdorf from Kempten. Parking in the centre is sparse, expensive and comes with strict time limits. Inexpensive parking lots (free to overnight visitors) are at the village entrance, from where you can either walk or take the electric shuttle.

Getting Around

Electric shuttle buses plough through town at 30-minute intervals from around 7am to 6pm (€0.50 per ride, free with Gästekarte). In winter, a ski bus serves all areas (free with skiing equipment).

ALLGÄU-BAVARIAN SWABIA

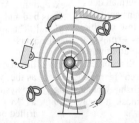

Language

German belongs to the Indo-European language group and is spoken by over 100 million people in countries throughout the world, including Austria and part of Switzerland. There are also ethnic-German communities in neighbouring Eastern European countries such as Poland and the Czech Republic, although expulsion after 1945 reduced their number dramatically.

High German used today comes from a regional Saxon dialect. It developed into an official bureaucratic language and was used by Luther in his translation of the Bible, gradually spreading throughout Germany. The impetus Luther gave to the written language through his translations was followed by the establishment of language societies in the 17th century, and later by the 19th-century work of Jacob Grimm, the founder of modern German philology. With his brother, Karl Wilhelm Grimm, he also began work on the first German dictionary.

Regional dialects still thrive throughout Germany, especially in Cologne, Bavaria, Swabia and parts of Saxony. The Sorb minority in eastern Germany has its own language. In northern Germany it is common to hear Plattdeutsch and Frisian spoken. Both are distant relatives of English, and the fact that many German words survive in the English vocabulary today makes things a lot easier for native English speakers.

That's the good news. The bad news is that, unlike English, German has retained clear polite distinctions in gender and case. Though not as difficult as Russian, for instance, which has more cases, German does have its tricky moments. Germans are used to hearing foreigners – and a few notable indigenous sports personalities – make a hash of their grammar, and any attempt to speak the language is always well received.

All German school children learn a foreign language – usually English – which means that most people can speak it to a certain degree.

Pronunciation

English speakers sometimes hold onto their vowels too long when speaking German, which causes comprehension problems. Nevertheless, there are long vowels, like *pope*, and short ones, like *pop*. Another common mistake is a tendency to pronounce all vowels as if they have umlauts (**ä**, **ö** and **ü**). It's worth practising the difference, as they often change the tense and meaning of a word. In most other respects German pronunciation is fairly straightforward. There are no silent letters, and many foreign words (eg, *Band*, for 'rock band') are pronounced roughly the same as in English.

Vowels

a	short, as the 'u' in 'cut', or long, as in 'father'
au	as the 'ow' in 'vow'
ä	short, as in 'hat', or long, as in 'hare'
äu	as the 'oy' in 'boy'
e	short, as in 'bet', or long, as in 'obey'
ei	as the 'ai' in 'aisle'
eu	as the 'oy' in 'boy'
i	short, as in 'inn', or long, as in 'marine'
ie	as in 'siege'
o	short, as in 'pot', or long, as in 'note'
ö	as the 'er' in 'fern'
u	as in 'pull'
ü	similar to the 'u' in 'pull' but with stretched lips

Consonants

Most consonants and their combinations are roughly similar to English ones, with a few exceptions. At the end of a word, consonants **b**, **d** and **g** sound a little more like 'p', 't' and 'k' respectively. There are no silent consonants.

ch	throaty, as in Scottish *loch*
j	as the 'y' in 'yet'
ng	always one sound, as in 'strong'
qu	as 'kv'
r	trilled or guttural

s	as in 'see' or as the 'z' in 'zoo'
sch	as the 'sh' in 'shore'
st	usually pronounced 'sht'
sp	usually pronounced 'shp'
v	more like an English 'f'
w	as an English 'v'
z	as the 'ts' in 'tsar'

Grammar

German grammar can be a nightmare for English speakers. Nouns come in three genders: masculine, feminine and neutral. The corresponding forms of the definite article ('the' in English) are *der*, *die* and *das*, with the basic plural form, *die*. Nouns and articles will alter according to the case (nominative, accusative, dative and genitive). Note that German nouns always begin with a capital.

Many German verbs have a prefix that is often detached from the stem and placed at the end of the sentence. For example, *fahren* means 'to go' (by mechanical means), *abfahren* means 'to depart'; a simple sentence with the prefixed verb *abfahren* becomes: *Um wieviel Uhr fährt der Zug ab?* (What time does the train leave?).

You should be aware that German uses polite and informal forms for 'you' (*Sie* and *Du* respectively). When addressing people you don't know well you should always use the polite form (though younger people will be less inclined to expect them). In this language guide we use the polite form unless indicated by 'inf' (for 'informal') in brackets.

The following words and phrases should help you through the most common travel situations. Those with the desire to delve further into the language should get a copy of Lonely Planet's *German phrasebook*.

Greetings & Civilities

Hello.	*Hallo.* (*Grüss Gott* in Bavaria)
Good morning.	*Guten Morgen.*
Good day.	*Guten Tag.*
Good evening.	*Guten Abend.*
Goodbye.	*Auf Wiedersehen.*
Bye.	*Tschüss.*
Yes.	*Ja.*
No.	*Nein.*

Where?	*Wo?*
Why?	*Warum?*
How?	*Wie?*
Maybe.	*Vielleicht.*
Please.	*Bitte.*
Thank you (very much).	*Danke (schön).*
You're welcome.	*Bitte or Bitte sehr.*
Excuse me.	*Entschuldigung.*
I'm sorry/Forgive me.	*Entschuldigen Sie, bitte.*
I'm sorry. (to express sympathy)	*Das tut mir leid.*

Language Difficulties

I understand.	*Ich verstehe.*
I don't understand.	*Ich verstehe nicht.*
Do you speak English?	*Sprechen Sie Englisch?/Sprichst du Englisch?* (inf)
Does anyone here speak English?	*Spricht hier jemand Englisch?*
What does ... mean?	*Was bedeutet ...?*
Please write it down.	*Bitte schreiben Sie es auf.*

Paperwork

first name	*Vorname*
surname	*Familienname*
nationality	*Staatsangehörigkeit*
date of birth	*Geburtsdatum*
place of birth	*Geburtsort*
sex (gender)	*Geschlecht*
passport	*Reisepass*
identification	*Ausweis*
visa	*Visum*

Small Talk

What's your name?	*Wie heissen Sie?/Wie heisst du?* (inf)
My name is ...	*Ich heisse ...*
How are you?	*Wie geht es Ihnen?/Wie geht's dir?* (inf)
I'm fine, thanks.	*Es geht mir gut, danke.*
Where are you from?	*Woher kommen Sie/kommst du?* (inf)
I'm from ...	*Ich komme aus ...*

Getting Around

| I want to go to ... | *Ich möchte nach ... fahren.* |

Signs

Eingang/Einfahrt	**Entrance**
Ausgang/	**Exit**
Ausfahrt	
Notausgang	**Emergency Exit**
Auf/Offen/	**Open**
Geöffnet	
Zu/Geschlossen	**Closed**
Rauchen	**No Smoking**
Verboten	
Polizei	**Police**
WC/Toiletten	**Toilets**
Herren	**Men**
Damen	**Women**

What time does	*Um wieviel Uhr fährt*
the ... leave/arrive?	*... ab/kommt ... an?*
boat	*das Boot*
bus	*der Bus*
train	*der Zug*
tram	*die Strassenbahn*

Where is the ...?	*Wo ist ...?*
bus stop	*die Bushaltestelle*
metro station	*die U-Bahnstation*
train station	*der Bahnhof*
main train station	*der Hauptbahnhof*
airport	*der Flughafen*
tram stop	*die Strassenbahn-*
	haltestelle

the next	*der/die/das nächste*
the last	*der/die/das letzte*
ticket office	*Fahrkartenschalter*
one-way ticket	*einfache Fahrkarte*
return ticket	*Rückfahrkarte*
1st/2nd class	*erste/zweite Klasse*
timetable	*Fahrplan*
platform number	*Gleisnummer*
luggage locker	*Gepäckschliessfach*

I'd like to hire ...	*Ich möchte ... mieten.*
a bicycle	*ein Fahrrad*
a motorcycle	*ein Motorrad*
a car	*ein Auto*

Directions

Where is ...?	*Wo ist ...?*
How do I get to ...?	*Wie erreicht man ...?*
Is it far from here?	*Ist es weit von hier?*

Can you show me (on the map)?	*Könnten Sie mir (auf der Karte) zeigen?*

street	*die Strasse*
suburb	*der Vorort*
town	*die Stadt*
behind	*hinter*
in front of	*vor*
opposite	*gegenüber*
straight ahead	*geradeaus*
(to the) left	*(nach) links*
(to the) right	*(nach) rechts*
at the traffic lights	*an der Ampel*
at the next corner	*an der nächsten Ecke*
north	*Nord*
south	*Süd*
east	*Ost*
west	*West*

Around Town

I'm looking for ...	*Ich suche ...*
a bank	*eine Bank/*
	Sparkasse
the church	*die Kirche*
the city centre	*das Stadtzentrum*
the ... embassy	*die ... Botschaft*
my hotel	*mein Hotel*
the market	*den Markt*
the museum	*das Museum*
the post office	*das Postamt*
a public toilet	*eine öffentliche*
	Toilette
a hospital	*ein Krankenhaus*
the police	*die Polizei*
the tourist office	*das Fremden-*
	verkehrsbüro

I want to change some money/ travellers cheques.	*Ich möchte Geld/ Reiseschecks wechseln.*
What time does ... open/close?	*Um wieviel Uhr macht ... auf/zu?*
I'd like to make a phone call.	*Ich möchte telefonieren.*

beach	*der Strand*
bridge	*die Brücke*
castle/palace	*die Burg/das Schloss*
cathedral	*der Dom*
coast	*die Küste*

forest	*der Wald*
island	*die Insel*
lake	*der See*
monastery/convent	*das Kloster*
mountain	*der Berg*
river	*der Fluss*
sea	*das Meer/die See*
tower	*der Turm*

Accommodation

I'm looking for ...	*Ich suche...*
a hotel	*ein Hotel*
a guesthouse	*eine Pension*
a youth hostel	*eine Jugendherberge*
a campground	*einen Campingplatz*
Where is a cheap hotel?	*Wo findet man ein preiswertes Hotel?*
Please write the address.	*Könnten Sie bitte die Adresse aufschreiben?*
Do you have a room available?	*Haben Sie ein Zimmer frei?*
How much is it per night/person?	*Wieviel kostet es pro Nacht/Person?*
May I see it?	*Darf ich es sehen?*
Where is the bathroom?	*Wo ist das Badezimmer?*
It's very noisy/ dirty/expensive.	*Es ist sehr laut/ dreckig/teuer.*
I'd like to book (a) ...	*Ich möchte ... reservieren.*
bed	*ein Bett*
cheap room	*ein preiswertes Zimmer*
single room	*ein Einzelzimmer*
double room	*ein Doppelzimmer*
room with two beds	*ein Zimmer mit zwei Betten*
room with shower and toilet	*ein Zimmer mit Dusche und WC*
dormitory bed	*ein Bett im Schlafsaal*
for one night	*für eine Nacht*
for two nights	*für zwei Nächte*
I'm/We're leaving now.	*Ich reise/Wir reisen jetzt ab.*

Food & Drink

breakfast	*Frühstück*
lunch	*Mittagessen*
dinner	*Abendessen*
menu	*Speisekarte*
restaurant	*Gaststätte/Restaurant*
pub	*Kneipe*
supermarket	*Supermarkt*
snack bar	*Imbiss*
I'm a vegetarian.	*Ich bin Vegetarier(in).*
I'd like something to drink, please.	*Ich möchte etwas zu trinken, bitte.*
It was very tasty.	*Es hat mir sehr geschmeckt.*
The bill, please?	*Die Rechnung, bitte.*
Please keep the change.	*Das stimmt so.* (lit: 'that's OK as is')

Shopping

I'd like to buy ...	*Ich möchte ... kaufen*
How much is that?	*Wieviel kostet das?*
Do you accept credit cards?	*Nehmen Sie Kreditkarten?*
bookshop	*Buchladen*
chemist/pharmacy	*Apotheke* (medicine) *Drogerie* (toiletries)
department store	*Kaufhaus*
laundry	*Wäscherei*
more/less	*mehr/weniger*
bigger/smaller	*grösser/kleiner*

Health

I need a doctor.	*Ich brauche einen Arzt.*
Where is a hospital?	*Wo ist ein Krankenhaus?*
I'm ill.	*Ich bin krank.*
It hurts here.	*Es tut hier weh.*
I'm pregnant.	*Ich bin schwanger.*
I'm ...	*Ich bin ...*
diabetic	*Diabetiker*
epileptic	*Epileptiker*
asthmatic	*Asthmatiker*
I'm allergic to antibiotics/ penicillin.	*Ich bin allergisch auf Antibiotika/ Penizillin.*

LANGUAGE

Emergencies

Help!	*Hilfe!*
Call a doctor!	*Rufen Sie einen Arzt!*
Call the police!	*Rufen Sie die Polizei!*
Leave me alone.	*Lassen Sie mich in Ruhe.*
Get lost!	*Hau ab!* (inf)
I'm lost.	*Ich habe mich verirrt.*
Thief!	*Dieb!*
I've been raped/robbed!	*Ich bin verge-waltigt/bestohlen worden!*

antiseptic	*Antiseptikum*
aspirin	*Aspirin*
condoms	*Kondome*
contraceptive	*Verhütungsmittel*
diarrhoea	*Durchfall*
medicine	*Medikament*
the pill	*die Pille*
sunblock cream	*Sonnencreme*
tampons	*Tampons*

Time & Dates

What time is it?	*Wie spät ist es?*
It's (10) o'clock	*Es ist (zehn) Uhr.*
It's half past nine.	*Es ist halb zehn.*
in the morning	*morgens/vormittags*
in the afternoon	*nachmittags*
in the evening	*abends*
at night	*nachts*
When?	*wann?*
today	*heute*
tomorrow	*morgen*
yesterday	*gestern*

Monday	*Montag*
Tuesday	*Dienstag*
Wednesday	*Mittwoch*
Thursday	*Donnerstag*
Friday	*Freitag*
Saturday	*Samstag/Sonnabend*
Sunday	*Sonntag*

January	*Januar*
February	*Februar*
March	*März*
April	*April*
May	*Mai*
June	*Juni*
July	*Juli*
August	*August*
September	*September*
October	*Oktober*
November	*November*
December	*Dezember*

Numbers

1	*eins*
2	*zwei /zwo*
3	*drei*
4	*vier*
5	*fünf*
6	*sechs*
7	*sieben*
8	*acht*
9	*neun*
10	*zehn*
11	*elf*
12	*zwölf*
13	*dreizehn*
14	*vierzehn*
15	*fünfzehn*
16	*sechzehn*
17	*siebzehn*
18	*achtzehn*
19	*neunzehn*
20	*zwanzig*
21	*einundzwanzig*
22	*zweiundzwanzig*
30	*dreissig*
40	*vierzig*
50	*fünfzig*
60	*sechzig*
70	*siebzig*
80	*achtzig*
90	*neunzig*
100	*einhundert*
1000	*eintausend*
10,000	*zehntausend*
100,000	*hunderttausend*

one million	*eine Million*

Glossary

(pl) indicates plural

Abfahrt – departure (trains)
Abtei – abbey
ADAC – Allgemeiner Deutscher Automobil Club (German Automobile Association)
Allee – avenue
Altstadt – old town
Ankunft – arrival (trains)
Antiquariat – antiquarian bookshop
Apotheke – pharmacy
Arbeitsamt – employment office
Arbeitserlaubnis – work permit
Ärztlicher Notdienst – emergency medical service
Aufenthaltserlaubnis – residency permit
Auflauf, Aufläufe (pl) – casserole
Ausgang, Ausfahrt – exit
Aussiedler – German settlers who have returned from abroad (usually refers to post-WWII expulsions), sometimes called Spätaussiedler
Autobahn – motorway
Autonom – left-wing anarchist
AvD – Automobilclub von Deutschland (Automobile Club of Germany)

Bad – spa, bath
Bahnhof – train station
Bahnsteig – train station platform
Bau – building
Bedienung – service
Berg – mountain
Bergbaumuseum – mining museum
Besenwirtschaft – seasonal wine restaurant indicated by a broom above the doorway
Bezirk – district
Bibliothek – library
Bierkeller – cellar pub
Bierstube – traditional beer pub
Bildungsroman – literally 'novel of education'; literary work in which the personal development of a single individual is central
Bratkartoffeln – fried or roasted potatoes
BRD – Bundesrepublik Deutschland or, in English, FRG (Federal Republic of Germany). The name for Germany today; originally applied to the former West Germany.
Brücke – bridge
Brunnen – fountain or well
Bundesland – federal state
Bundesrat – upper house of German Parliament
Bundestag – lower house of German Parliament
Bundesverfassungsgericht – Federal Constitutional Court
Burg – castle
Busbahnhof – bus station

CDU – Christian Democratic Union
Christkindlmarkt – Christmas market; *see also* Weihnachtsmarkt
CSU – Christian Social Union; Bavarian offshoot of CDU

DB – Deutsche Bahn (German national railway)
DDR – Deutsche Demokratische Republik or, in English, GDR (German Democratic Republic). The name for the former East Germany. *See also* BRD.
Denkmal – memorial
Deutsche Reich – German Empire. Refers to the period 1871-1918.
DJH – Deutsches Jugendherbergswerk (German youth hostels association)
Dirndl – traditional women's dress (Bavaria only)
Dom – cathedral
Dorf – village
DZT – Deutsche Zentrale für Tourismus (German National Tourist Office)

Eingang – entrance
Eintritt – admission
Einwanderungsland – country of immigrants
Eiscafé – ice-cream parlour

Fahrplan – timetable
Fahrrad – bicycle

Fasching – pre-Lenten carnival (in Southern Germany)
FDP – Free Democratic Party
Ferienwohnung, Ferienwohnungen (pl) – holiday flat or apartment
Fest – festival
Flohmarkt – flea market
Flughafen – airport
Föhn – static-charged wind blowing northward from the Alps; most common in autumn.
Forstweg – forestry track
Franken – Germanic people influential in Europe between the 3rd and 8th centuries
Friedhof – cemetery
Freikorps – WWI volunteers
Fremdenverkehrsamt – tourist office
Fremdenzimmer – tourist room
FRG – Federal Republic of Germany; *see also* BRD
Frühstück – breakfast

Garten – garden
Gasse – lane or alley
Gastarbeiter – literally 'guest worker'; labourer from Turkey, Yugoslavia, Italy or Greece after WWII to help rebuild Germany
Gästehaus, Gasthaus – guesthouse
Gaststätte – informal restaurant
GDR – German Democratic Republic (the former East Germany); *see also* BRD, DDR
Gedenkstätte – memorial site
Gemütlichkeit – 'cosiness'
Gepäckaufbewahrung – left-luggage office
Gesamtkunstwerk – literally 'total artwork', integrates painting, sculpture and architecture
Gestapo – Nazi secret police
Glockenspiel – literally 'bell play'; carillon, usually on a cathedral, sounded by mechanised figures often in the form of religious or historical characters
Gründerzeit – literally 'foundation time'; the period of industrial expansion in Germany following the founding of the German Empire in 1871

Hafen – harbour, port
halbtrocken – semi-dry (wine)

Hauptbahnhof – main train station
Das Heilige Römische Reich – the Holy Roman Empire, which lasted from the 8th century to 1806. The German lands compromised the bulk of the Empire's territory.
Herzog – duke
Hitlerjugend – Hitler Youth organisation
Hochdeutsch – literally 'High German'; standard spoken and written German developed from a regional Saxon dialect
Hochkultur – literally 'high culture'; meaning 'advanced civilisation'
Hof, Höfe (pl) – courtyard
Höhle – cave
Hotel Garni – a hotel without a restaurant where you are only served breakfast

Imbiss – stand-up food stall; *also see* Schnellimbiss
Insel – island

Jugendgästehaus – youth guesthouse of a higher standard than a youth hostel
Jugendherberge – youth hostel
Jugendstil – Art Nouveau
Junker – originally a young, noble landowner of the Middle Ages; later used to refer to reactionary Prussian landowners

Kabarett – cabaret
Kaffee und Kuchen – literally 'coffee and cake'; traditional afternoon coffee break in Germany
Kaiser – emperor; derived from 'Caesar'
Kanal – canal
Kantine – cafeteria, canteen
Kapelle – chapel
Karte – ticket
Kartenvorverkauf – ticket booking office
Kino – cinema
Kirche – church
Kloster – monastery, convent
Kneipe – bar
Kommunales Kino – alternative or studio cinema
Konditorei – cake shop
König – king
Konsulat – consulate
Konzentrationslager (KZ) – concentration camp

Kreuzgang – cloister
Kristallnacht – literally 'night of broken glass'; attack on Jewish synagogues, cemeteries and businesses by Nazis and their supporters on the night of 9 November 1938 that marked the beginning of full-scale persecution of Jews in Germany. Also known as *Reichspogromnacht*.
Kunst – art
Kunstlieder – early German 'artistic songs'
Kurfürst – prince elector
Kurhaus – literally 'spa house', but usually a spa town's central building, used for social gatherings and events and often housing the town's casino
Kurort – spa resort
Kurtaxe – resort tax
Kurverwaltung – spa administration
Kurzentrum – spa centre

Land, Länder (pl) – state
Landtag – state parliament
Lederhose – traditional leather trousers with attached braces
Lesbe, Lesben (pl) – lesbian (n)
lesbisch – lesbian (adj)
lieblich – sweet (wine)
Lied – song

Markgraf – margrave; German nobleman ranking above a count
Markgrafschaft – the holding of a Markgraf
Markt – market
Marktplatz (often abbreviated to Markt) – marketplace or square
Mass – one-litre tankard or stein of beer
Meer – sea
Mehrwertsteuer (MwST) – value-added tax
Meistersinger – literally 'master singer'; highest level in the medieval troubadour guilds
Mensa – university cafeteria
Milchcafé – milk coffee, *café au lait*
Mitfahrzentrale – ride-sharing agency
Mitwohnzentrale – an accommodation-finding service (usually long-term)
Münster – minster or large church, cathedral

Münzwäscherei – coin-operated laundrette

Norden – north
Notdienst – emergency service

Ossis – literally 'Easties'; nickname for East Germans
Osten – east
Ostler – old term for an Ossi

Palast – palace, residential quarters of a castle
Pannenhilfe – roadside breakdown assistance
Paradies – architectural term for a church vestibule or ante-room
Parkhaus – car park
Parkschein – parking voucher
Parkscheinautomat – vending machine selling parking vouchers
Passage – shopping arcade
Pfand – deposit for bottles and sometimes glasses (in beer gardens)
Pfarrkirche – parish church
Platz – square
Postamt – post office
Postlagernd – poste restante

Radwandern – bicycle touring
Rathaus – town hall
Ratskeller – town hall restaurant
Reich – empire
Reichspogromnacht – *see* Kristallnacht
Reisezentrum – travel centre in train or bus stations
Reiterhof – riding stable or centre
Ruhetag – literally 'rest day'; closing day at a shop or restaurant
Rundgang – tour, route

Saal, Säle (pl) – hall, room
Sammlung – collection
Säule – column, pillar
Schatzkammer – treasury
Schiff – ship
Schifffahrt – literally 'boat way'; shipping, navigation
Schloss – palace, castle
Schnaps – schnapps
Schnellimbiss – stand-up food stall

Schwul, Schwule (pl) – gay
See – lake
Sekt – sparkling wine
Selbstbedienung (SB) – self-service (restaurants, laundrettes etc)
Skonto – discount
Soziale Marktwirtschaft – literally 'social market economy'; German form of mixed economy with built-in social protection for employees
Spätaussiedler – see Aussiedler
Speisekarte – menu
Sportverein – sport association
SS – Schutzstaffel; organisation within the Nazi party that supplied Hitler's bodyguards, as well as concentration-camp guards and the Waffen-SS troops in WWII
Stadt – city or town
Stadtbad, Stadtbäder (pl) – public pool
Stadtwald – city or town forest
Stau – traffic jam
Staudamm, Staumauer – dam
Stausee – reservoir
Stehcafé – stand-up café
Strasse (often abbreviated to Str) – street
Strausswirtschaft – seasonal wine pub indicated by wreath above the doorway, also known as a Besenwirtschaft
Streifenkarte – public transport ticket
Süden – south
Szene – scene (ie, where the action is)

Tageskarte – daily menu or day ticket on public transport
Tal – valley
Teich – pond
Tor – gate
Trampen – hitchhiking
trocken – dry (wine)
Trödel – junk

Turm – tower

Übergang – transit or transfer point
Ufer – bank

verboten – forbidden
Verkehr – traffic
Viertel – quarter, district
Volkslieder – folk song

Wald – forest
Waldfrüchte – wild berries
Wäscherei – laundry
Wechselstube – currency exchange office
Weg – way, path
Weihnachtsmarkt – Christmas market; see also Christkindlmarkt
Weingut – wine-growing estate
Weinkeller – wine cellar
Weinprobe – wine tasting
Weinstube – traditional wine bar
Wende – 'change' of 1989, ie the fall of communism that led to the collapse of the GDR and German reunification
Wessis – literally 'Westies'; nickname for West Germans
Westen – west
Westler – old term for a Wessi
Wiese – meadow
Wirtschaftswunder – Germany's post-WWII 'economic miracle'
Wurst – sausage

Zahnradbahn – cog-wheel railway
Zeitung – newspaper
Zimmer Frei – room available
Zimmervermittlung – room-finding service; *see also* Mitwohnzentrale
ZOB – Zentraler Omnibusbahnhof (central bus station)
Zuschlag – Surcharge

LONELY PLANET

You already know that Lonely Planet produces more than this one guidebook, but you might not be aware of the other products we have on this region. Here is a selection of titles that you may want to check out as well:

Central Europe
ISBN 1 86450 204 5
US$24.99 • UK£14.99

Central Europe phrasebook
ISBN 1 86450 226 6
US$7.99 • UK£4.50

Munich
ISBN 1 86450 055 7
US$14.95 • UK£8.99

Western Europe
ISBN 1 86450 163 4
US$27.99 • UK£15.99

Europe phrasebook
ISBN 1 86450 224 X
US$8.99 • UK£4.99

Berlin
ISBN 1 74059 073 2
US$16.99 • UK£10.99

Germany
ISBN 1 74059 078 3
US$24.99 • UK£14.99

German phrasebook
ISBN 0 86442 451 5
US$5.95 • UK£3.99

Europe on a shoestring
ISBN 1 86450 150 2
US$24.99 • UK£14.99

Read This First: Europe
ISBN 1 86450 136 7
US$14.99 • UK£8.99

Frankfurt Condensed
ISBN 1 86450 223 1
US$11.99 • UK£6.99

Available wherever books are sold

Index

Text

Bold indicates maps.

Boxed Text

MAP LEGEND

CITY ROUTES

—Freeway— .... Freeway	⊐⊐⊐⊐ ...... Unsealed Road
—Highway— ....Primary Road	—●— .... One Way Street
—Road— .... Secondary Road	▒▒▒▒ .... Pedestrian Street
—Street— .... Street	⊞⊞⊞⊞⊞ ..... Stepped Street
—Lane— .... Lane	⊃= = = ...Tunnel
▒▒▒▒ ....On/Off Ramp	▒▒▒▒▒ .... Footbridge

REGIONAL ROUTES

▓▓▓▓ ....Tollway, Freeway
▓▓▓▓ .... Primary Road
▓▓▓▓ ..... Secondary Road
▓▓▓▓ .... Minor Road

BOUNDARIES

▪ — ▪ ▪ — ▪ ▪ ....International
▪ — ▪ ▪ — ▪ ▪ .... State
— — — — .... Disputed
▪▬▪▬▪ ...... Fortified Wall

HYDROGRAPHY

∿ .... River, Creek	⬭ ⬭ .Dry Lake; Salt Lake
▪—●—●▪ ....Canal	⊙ ↘↗ .... Spring; Rapids
⬭ .... Lake	◉ ↦ ◀ ....Waterfalls

TRANSPORT ROUTES & STATIONS

▬▬●▬ ....Train	⊢—⊢—⊟ Cable Car, Funicular
▬▬Ⓢ▬ .... S-Bahn	- - - - -⊡ .... Ferry
▬▬Ⓤ▬ .... U-Bahn	- - - - - ..... Walking Trail
□□□□□□□, Underground Train	· · · · · · · · ....Walking Tour
▬▬⊟▬▪ ....Tramway	▬▬▬ .... Path

AREA FEATURES

▓▓ .... Building	▓▓▓ .... Market	░░░ .... Beach
⊕ ...... Park, Gardens	▓▓ ...... Sports Ground	T T .... Cemetery

▓▓ ....Campus
⌐ ⌐ .... Plaza

POPULATION SYMBOLS

✪ **CAPITAL** .... National Capital	● **CITY** ....City	● Village ....Village
◉ **CAPITAL** .... State Capital	● **Town** ....Town	▓▓ ....Urban Area

MAP SYMBOLS

▮ ....Place to Stay	▼ ....Place to Eat	● ....Point of Interest

▨ . Archaeological Site	⊞ .... Cinema	▲ .... Mountain	⌁ .... Ski Field
❸ .... Bank	⊡ Embassy, Consulate	🏛 .... Museum	⋒ ...... Stately Home
⊟ ....Bus Stop	⚓ .... Fountain	⊡ ....Parking	⊠ .... Synagogue
⊡ .... Bus Terminal	⊕ .... Hospital	✚ ....Police Station	⊠ ...... Swimming Pool
⌂ .... Camping	⊡ .... Internet Cafe	▣ .... Post Office	⊟ ....Theatre
⊟ ..... Castle, Chateau	⊹ .... Lookout	⊟ .... Pub or Bar	❶ .Tourist Information
▬ ⊟ .. Cathedral, Church	⚲ .... Monument	⊠ .... Shopping Centre	⊡ .... Zoo

Note: not all symbols displayed above appear in this book

LONELY PLANET OFFICES

Australia
Locked Bag 1, Footscray, Victoria 3011
☎ 03 8379 8000 fax 03 8379 8111
email: talk2us@lonelyplanet.com.au

UK
10a Spring Place, London NW5 3BH
☎ 020 7428 4800 fax 020 7428 4828
email: go@lonelyplanet.co.uk

USA
150 Linden St, Oakland, CA 94607
☎ 510 893 8555 TOLL FREE: 800 275 8555
fax 510 893 8572
email: info@lonelyplanet.com

France
1 rue du Dahomey, 75011 Paris
☎ 01 55 25 33 00 fax 01 55 25 33 01
email: bip@lonelyplanet.fr
www.lonelyplanet.fr

World Wide Web: www.lonelyplanet.com *or* AOL keyword: lp
Lonely Planet Images: lpi@lonelyplanet.com.au